Archaeological Findings from the Homeland of Buddha

Archaeological Findings from the Homeland of Buddha

Prem Sagar Chaturvedi

AGAM KALA PRAKASHAN
DELHI-110052

First Published : 2013

ISBN : 978-81-7320-130-1

Published by:
Dr. Agam Prasad, M.A., Ph.D., Diploma in Museology
for **Agam Kala Prakashan**
34, Central Market, Ashok Vihar, Delhi-110052
Ph. : 27212195, 65688806-7
Fax : 91-11-27212195
E-mail : agambooks@gmail.com, agambook@yahoo.com
Website : www.agamkala.com

Laser Typesetting by:
Elegant Printographics
Rohini, Delhi-85.

Printed at:
Chawla Offset
Delhi - 110052

Printed in INDIA

Contents

Preface

Based on the deliberations of a National Seminar on the Archaeological Glory of Eastern Uttar Pradesh, organised by the Department of Ancient History, Archaeology and Culture, D.D.U. Gorakhpur University, Gorakhpur on February 19-20, 2010, the present volume is, in essence, a maiden attempt to delineate an updated archaeological profile of a region which had historically been the homeland of Siddhartha, the Gautama, whom the grateful world reverentially remembers as the Lord Buddha. Exploits of this great apostle of peace and compassion, right from his birth at Lumbini to his last breath at Kushinagar, were confined primarily to that part of land, which falls under the eastern part of present Uttar Pradesh. In the early Buddhist literature, he is found frequenting and propagating his gospels in the land extending from Vaisali in the east to Sravasti in the west and from Kapilavastu in the north to Kausambi in the south. Evidently, except for a portion of northern and western part of the state of Bihar, most of this land falls under the present eastern Uttar Pradesh, comprising twenty-seven districts of Allahabad, Kaushambi, Pratapgarh, Sultanpur, Mirzapur, Sonbhadra, Jaunpur, Chandauli, Varanasi, Ghazipur, Azamgarh, Mau, Ballia, Kushinagar, Deoria, Gorakhpur, Sant Kabir Nagar, Sant Ravidas Nagar, Basti, Gonda, Balrampur, Shravasti, Faizabad, Ambedakar Nagar, Maharajganj, Bahraich and Siddharth Nagar in all. It would, hence, be quite appropriate to call this region as the homeland of Buddha.

Drained by the waters of *Ganga* and *Sarayu*, the two major rivers and a number of tributaries, such as *Son, Belan, Rapti, Rohini, Ami,* etc., the land is well-known for its unique contributions to the history and culture of India. It was in this part of land that the towns of *Prayāga, Ayodhyā* and *Kāśī* , identified respectively with modern Allahabad, Faizabad and Varanasi had been flourishing since the later Vedic times. Kapilavastu, the capital town of the *Śākyas,* Sāranāth, the seat of Buddha's first sermon, and Kushinagar, the place of his demise – all these prominent historical places which keep on drawing the hordes of tourists throughout the year towards them are located in this area.

A number of cultural streams which stand as the identity marks of the land have outflown from this region from time to time. The clan of the *Ikṣhvākus,* who had one of its illustrious scions as Rāma, widely revered by the masses as a deity, had flourished on this region. Lord Buddha who gave his message of peace and non-violence to the world, lived, preached and breathed his last in this part of land. The region gave to the nation its first imperialist dynasty – the *Moriyas* (popularly known as the *Mauryas*), one of whose scions, Aśoka, the great, is known all over the world because of his philanthropic services rendered to his subjects. The Buddhist literature reveals that a major part of the region was under republican governance during the times of Buddha, which stands as one of the earliest evidence of the participatory and inclusive governance in the history of the world. The region is found reverberating with the saintly preachings of Gorakhanath and Kabir who denounced all kinds of externalities and showmanship in religious and social life and stood for its simplicity and purity. It enjoys a unique thread of historical continuity as it has been a major part of almost all the empires which emerged in the northern India from the sixth century BCE to the arrival of the British. A number of epigraphs, coins, art-objects, monuments, etc. attest to its unhampered continuity.

While the rich cultural and historical legacy bestowed to us by this region has been evaluated time and again in different kinds of writings, the archaeological legacy which by its intrinsic nature requires an updated appraisal with the passage of time in the light of fresh evidence procured, has not been given as much focus as it actually deserved. The picture which we have is mostly hazy, fragmented and improperly documented. It exists mostly in parts, as a place-specific, isolated account rather than being a coherent and wholesome archaeological profile. Fresh archaeological data procured from different parts of Buddha's homeland during the last four-five decades have perforce given us an urgent call to re-assess and re-interpret the entire corpus of archaeological material to highlight the great contributions of this area to Indian archaeology. It was because of this urgency that we planned to organise a National Seminar to discuss the entire gamut of this issue, specially with those scholars who have largely been instrumental in archaeological discoveries and their analyses and evaluations in the region.

The deliberations in the Seminar basically centred on two points – historic and prehistoric archaeology. It was observed that from the point of view of historical archaeology, the region is a trend-setter in various aspects. Quite a number of archaeological findings relating to historical period were taken for special discussion and their significance in the stream of national archaeology was re-examined and emphatically reiterated. The two earliest epigraphs – *Piparahwa* and *Sohgaura,* mostly assumed to be pre-Aśokan, are located in this region. Their importance as the first known historical records initiating the palaeographic and epigraphic traditions of the country during the ancient period was given a fresh look. Likewise, several hordes of the punch-marked coins, local coins and not less than fourteen hordes of the Gupta coins, discovered in this region, were thoroughly analysed. It was observed that these conform to an invaluable evidence pertaining to the beginning of coinage in India and also provide an unquestionable affirmation to the economic prosperity and urban character of the region. There are several monuments located at Kaushambi, Sarnath, Shravasti, Kushinagar, Piparahwa(=Kapilavastu), etc. in the form of grand Asokan pillars, Buddhist *stupas* and monasteries, sculptures, etc., built during the Mauryan, Kuṣāṇa and Gupta times which come to us as a rich treasure-trove of this area. The scholars also took note of the fact that, during the Gupta period, Kaushambi and Sarnath emerged as two prominent schools of art, the sculptures of which are found distributed throughout the region. The region is also characterised with the emergence of a unique pottery i.e. Northern Black Polished Ware which is famous for its glass-like lustre and thin fabric. A number of scholarly presentations dealing with all these themes and evidently forming the distinctive features of the historical archaeology of the region were made during this academic meet. Needless to say, most of these are now among the contents of this volume.

While the deliberations on historical archaeology were based on the pre-existing known facts, those on the prehistoric and protohistoric archaeology centred around the newly-found evidence, recovered from a number of sites, such as, Koldihwa, Mahagara, Sohgaura, Imlidih, Narhan, Agiabir, Lahuradeva, Jhusi and several iron-yielding sites recently located in the Sonbhadra and Chandauli districts of the region. For a better understanding of contributions and spatial and cultural inter-connections, the entire region may be divided into three geographical units – the Ganga plain, the Vindhya-Kaimur ranges and the Sarayupar region. The Vindhya-Kaimur ranges are considered to be one of the oldest formations in the world. The Ganga plain came into existence in early Miocene and attained its present form in the late Quaternary.

Sporadic forays for the archaeological explorations in the Vindhya-Kaimur ranges during the pre-independence days notwithstanding, it goes to the credit of late Prof. G. R. Sharma and the members of his team from the Department of Ancient History, Culture and Archaeology, Allahabad University, Allahabad for carrying a systematic exploration of this area since the mid-fifties and exposing its prehistoric character through a continuous work lasting for more than three decades. It came to light that it was in this part of land in eastern Uttar Pradesh that early man lived, hunted and survived for a very long time. Excavations of a number of sites in this area have revealed a continuous sequence of prehistoric cultures right from Lower Palaeolithic to Neolithic which make it the only place in India where a complete sequence of the different cultural stages of early man's development are found preserved.

The Ganga plain of the region came in the prehistoric map of the country only in the 1969 with the chance discovery of the Mesolithic site of Sarai Nahar Rai and consequently, the location of nearly two scores of sites mostly of the same cultural genre on the banks of horseshoe lakes of Ganga by the team of Allahabad University led by Prof. G. R. Sharma. These were scattered within the districts of Allahabad, Pratapgarh, Sultanpur, Jaunpur and Varanasi. The new findings confirmed that the Vindhyan man descended in the Ganga plain in search of food and water at this period of time. That the Mesolithic phase both in the Vindhya-Kaimur range and the Ganga valley gradually transformed itself into Neolithic, is well evident from the excavations of type-sites of Koldihwa and Jhusi respectively. Significantly enough, these have yielded some crucial evidence with regard to the cultivation of rice, domestication of animals and use of ceramics during the sixth-fifth millennia BCE. that has given a new twist not only to the extension of Neolithic horizon but also to the antiquity of rice cultivation in the country.

Till 1974, nothing was known about the prehistoric and protohistoric past of the Sarayupar region, the third geographical division of eastern Uttar Pradesh. Primarily being associated with the life and missionary activities of Lord Buddha, it naturally abounded in Buddhist archaeological remains antedating mostly to Maurya-Kuṣāṇa periods. However, the excavation carried at Sohgaura situated on the confluence of Rapti and Ami in the Gorakhpur district by the Department of Ancient History, Gorakhpur University, Gorakhpur under the supervision of S. N. Chaturvedi in the year 1974, changed the entire spectrum of a region which by that time was considered to be a dark alley for the prehistorians and protohistorians. It yielded the clear-cut evidence of a Neolithic phase characterised with the use of a mat-impressioned, hand-made pottery in which rice husk was used as a degraissant. It opened the door for further possibilities and investigations in the region that led to the excavation of Imlidih on the left bank of Kuwana, a tributary of Sarayu in Gorakhpur district by Purushottam Singh of BHU in 1991-92 and 1995 and of Lahuradeva in Sant Kabir Nagar district by the Department of U. P. State Archaeology, Lucknow under the overall direction of Rakesh Tewari in 1997 and onwards. The latter proved to be a path-breaking archaeological discovery bringing forth the commencement of the Neolithic phase during the seventh-sixth millennia BCE which stands by now to be the earliest evidence of its kind in the entire country. The C^{14} dates procured from the samples of the site have pushed back the antiquity of rice cultivation in the area to the seventh millennium BCE, with a well-evidenced pattern of gradual transformation from the wild varieties in the Mesolithic phase to the cultivated ones during the Neolithic.

Significantly, most of these sites from the Ganga valley ended up as the protohistoric communities with the introduction of copper which was brought from outside the region. These were primarily the self-sufficient farming societies which produced a variety of cereals. We have copious evidence of the use of a plain and painted variety of black-and-red ware and black slipped ware. Beads made of precious and semi-precious stones have often been found. Evidence of a bead manufacturing station has been recovered from the excavated site of Agiabir which suggests that beads made at the site must have been exported to other places besides catering to the local needs. Raw material for this was procured from the Vindhyan sources.

Picture of protohistoric phase in eastern Uttar Pradesh would, however, remain incomplete without indicating to one significant development relating to this phase in the region. Till very recently, it was considered, that iron has a unitary origin. Some eminent scholars were of the view that it was introduced by the Hittites, brought to Gandhara grave area and then gradually diffused eastward along the Gangetic valley. Recent investigations in the Sonbhadra and Chandauli districts by Vibha Tripathi from BHU and Rakesh Tewari from the Department of U. P. State Archaeology, have exploded this myth. Excavations at Raja Nal Ka Tila and Malhar in Karamnasa valley have yielded evidence of iron working complete with iron ore, smelting furnaces, forges along with finished iron objects. The C^{14} dates obtained from the sites have pushed back the antiquity of the use of iron in the region to 1600/1500 BCE, if not earlier. This is undoubtedly one of the earliest time-frame for the use of iron and the practice of iron technology in the entire country.

On the basis of this newly-found evidence, certain points may be adduced with regard to use of iron technology in the region. Firstly, it was not the result of a centrally triggered diffusion and had its local origin. Secondly, Chalcolithic phase in certain parts of eastern Uttar Pradesh either did not evolve independently or was replaced by the iron using communities as early as the first half of the second millennium BCE. Thirdly, role of iron and iron technology in generating surplus agricultural production and promoting the resultant urbanisation should be taken only with a pinch of salt as other factors relating to land use and cropping patterns seem to be more potent contributors than iron. And lastly, with this evidence, the eastern Uttar Pradesh may naturally boast of being a centre of iron technology as early as the first half of the second millennium BCE.

New investigations regarding the prehistoric and protohistoric past of eastern Uttar Pradesh indubitably reflect the importance of this region in the over-all profiling of Indian archaeology. It has certainly added some first-hand contributions to the study of discipline. The Belan valley in the Vindhya-Kaimur ranges presents the continuous sequence of prehistoric and protohistoric cultures, unique in the country, and, hence, is rightly termed as 'the text book of Indian prehistory.' A series of excavations at the sites of Koldihwa, Lahuradeva and Jhusi have successfully brought out that phase of Neolithic culture which had gradually evolved from the pre-existing phases of Epi-Palaeolithic and Mesolithic cultures and is marked with ample evidence of cultivation of rice during the seventh-sixth millennia BCE, a chronological horizon, witnessed nowhere else in the country or even rarely in the entire south Asia. Evidence of the use of iron and iron technology from the Sonbhadra and Chandauli districts of the state has not only changed the whole spectrum of protohistoric technologies but also its impact on the social-economic development of a region known for its first major political consolidation and state formation in the country during the beginning of historical period.

All these new developments, combined with those of historic period, have inspired us to chronicle an updated account of a region largely known to the world by the name of Buddha. It is significant that it is an outcome of the concerted efforts of those scholars who by their painstaking investigations and researches have originally contributed to the making of this archaeological profile of the region. A number of write-ups from their own pens, now forming an integral portion of this volume, naturally enhance its relevance and importance in formulating an authentic account of archaeological contributions of this region. We are hopeful that it would serve the basic objectives for which it has initially been planned and devised and would also immensely help the students and scholars of history and archaeology in understanding the archaeological legacy of eastern Uttar Pradesh, synonymous with Buddha's homeland, in a much better way.

I must express my indebtedness and deep sense of gratitude towards all the scholars who have, very kindly, heeded to my request and shared their investigations and researches by contributing useful write-ups for the sake of this volume which, without their most invaluable cooperation and enthusiastic responses would hardly have seen the light of the day.

I am equally beholden to my colleagues at the Department of Ancient History, Archaeology and Culture, D.D.U. Gorakhpur University, Gorakhpur who extended their unflinching support and help in every possible way right from the organisation of the National Seminar on the theme to the successful publication of this volume.

My special word of thanks are due to Dr. Agam Prasad Ji, proprietor, Agam Kala Prakashan, New Delhi, for accepting my proposal and executing it meticulously and expeditiously to bring out a quality volume.

Gorakhpur
October, 15, 2012

Prem Sagar Chaturvedi

Contributors

RADHA KANT VARMA, an eminent archaeologist, largely credited with exposing the prehistoric cultures of Belan valley in the eastern Uttar Pradesh along with late Professor G.R. Sharma, was Professor and Head, Department of Ancient History, Culture and Archaeology, A. P. S. Rewa University (M. P.). Earlier he had a long stint with the University of Allahabad. He also served as Vice Chancellor, A. P. S. Rewa University (M. P.) and Chairman, Allahabad Museum Society (under Ministry of Culture, Govt. of India). An acknowledged expert in Prehistoric and Protohistoric Archaeology, he has also worked on rock paintings of north Vindhyan region of central India. Apart from a number of research papers and reports in national and international journals, his published works include *Mesolithic Age in Mirzapur and Rock Art of Central India: North Vindhyan Region.*

J. N. Pal is Professor and a leading member of the team of archaeologists in the Department of Ancient History, Culture and Archaeology, University of Allahabad, Allahabad. He also supervised the academic activities of the Department as Head during 2010-12. His research interests include Palaeolithic and Mesolithic archaeology and microware analysis. He has excavated a good number of prehistoric, protohistoric and historic sites in the middle Ganga plain and in the Vindhyan region. He has published a number of books on archaeology and several papers in national and international Journals,

T. P. Verma was formerly Professor in the Department of Ancient Indian History, Culture and Archaeology, Banaras Hindu University, Varanasi. He was also Professor and Head, Department of AIHC and Archaeology, Gurukul Kangri University, Haridvar (Uttarakhand). A renowned epigraphist and numismatist, he has strong grounding in the Sanskrit literature. He has been the editor of *Journal of Numismatic Society of India* for quite a long time. Besides contributing more than 150 papers in research journals, he has authored a number of books including *Gahadavalas and Their Times* (2 Vols.) and *Ayodhya Kā Itihās Evaṁ Purātattva* (in Hindi).

Prem Sagar Chaturvedi was Professor and Head, Department of Ancient History, Archaeology and Culture, D. D. U. Gorakhpur University, Gorakhpur (U. P.). He was also Director, UGC Academic Staff College in the same University. He was one of the team members who conducted the excavation of the prehistoric site of Sohgaura in the Gorakhpur district of eastern Uttar Pradesh. His areas of expertise include Ancient Technologies, Vedic and Buddhist Studies, Art and Architecture. He has published more than fifty research papers in different journals and the book entitled *Technology in Vedic Literature.*

Rakesh Tewari is Director, U. P. State Archaeology Department, Govt. of Uttar Pradesh (India) since1989. He has been directing and conducting explorations and excavations for more than three decades in Uttar Pradesh, Uttarakhand, Bihar, Chhattisgarh, Madhya Pradesh, Maharashtra and in south India. Amongst his recent notable findings, mention may be made of Epi-palaeolithic - Neolithic site of Lahuradeva in the Sant Kabir Nagar district of Uttar Pradesh which has yielded significant evidence about rice cultivation in India as early as the seventh millennium

BCE and the discovery of iron and iron-works in the Chandauli district of the same region which has given a new twist to the origin of iron-working in India. He has also worked on the ancient Deccan routes and archaeological settlements in the Ganga Plain in collaboration with Cambridge researchers. He has to his credit more than 150 publications which include books/monographs and edited books and research papers and reviews in national and international journals. He is the founder editor of *Pragdhārā*, Annual Journal of the U. P. State Archaeology/Department.

Ashok Kumar Singh is Assistant Professor and teaches Archaeology in the Department of Ancient Indian History, Culture and Archaeology, Banaras Hindu University, Varanasi. He has vast experience in the field archaeology of mid-Ganga plain and has directed excavations at Imlidih Khurd (Gorakhpur district), Waina and Bhunadih (both in Ballia district), Agiabir (Mirzapur district) and Hariharpur (Jaunpur district). Recently, he is engaged in excavating the site of Pakkakota in Ballia district. His published works include about thirty papers and three books.

V. D. Misra was Professor and Head, Department of Ancient History, Culture and Archaeology, University of Allahabad, Allahabad. Essentially a renowned archaeologist, he has equal depth in different branches of historical studies. He has published several archaeological reports including that of Mahadaha, in collaboration with his colleagues on the archaeology of Middle Ganga Valley. Along with late Professor G. R. Sharma, he published an important monograph, viz., *Beginnings of Agriculture.* He led the team of archaeologists from the Department that excavated the site of Jhusi in Allahabad district (U. P.) during 1995 – 2003, bringing forth the occupational deposits from the Mesolithic to the early medieval period.

Vibha Tripathi is a senior most Professor in the Department of Ancient Indian History, Culture and Archaeology, Banaras Hindu University, Varanasi which she earlier supervised as Head during 2004 – 2007. An archaeologist of international fame and a versatile scholar, she specializes in the studies of Iron Age in India, covering both its archaeology and technology. Besides, she has also contributed to the studies of geo-morphology, palaeo-environments and settlement systems and even to the study of terracotta arts of the Indus Civilization. She has made extensive studies of the tribal iron technology and has recently concluded a project entitled *Ethno-technological Study of Iron-working around Sonbhadra Region* sanctioned by Indian Science Academy, New Delhi. She has published more than 120 research papers in national and international journals and 08 books which include *Rise of Civilization in the Gangetic Plain : The Context of Painted Grey Ware; Archaeology of Ganga Basin : Shifting Paradigms* (2 Vols.); *History of Iron Technology in India; The Age of Iron in South Asia : Legacy and Tradition; Archaeo-metallurgy in India* (ed.); *The Indus Terracotta* and *Painted Grey Ware – An Iron Age Culture of Northern India.* She is a member of several prestigious academic bodies including National Commission 'Research Council for History of Science, Indian National Science Academy, New Delhi; Central Advisory Board of Archaeology (CABA), Ministry of Culture, Govt. of India, New Delhi and Heritage Study Group, INAE.

Rahman Ali was formerly Professor and Head, School of Studies in Ancient Indian History, Culture and Archaeology, Vikram University, Ujjain (M. P.). He specializes in art, architecture and archaeology and has published a number of papers in national and international journals. His published works include *Temples of Madhya Pradesh : The Paramara Art* and *Art and Architecture of the Kalachuris.* He has also published excavation reports of Sodanga and Mahidpur (both in M. P.).

Neelima Pandey is Assistant Professor and teaches Ancient Indian History and Archaeology at Jai Narain PG College, Lucknow. She specializes in prehistoric studies and has worked on *Mesolithic Age in India.*

Amar Singh is Professor in the Department of Ancient Indian History and Archaeology, University of Lucknow, Lucknow. He has also served the Department of Uttar Pradesh State Archaeology from 1979 to 1987 and has taken part in various projects of exploration and excavation. He specializes in the studies of art, iconography and architecture and also in the study of religion. His published works include scores of papers in several national and international journals and two books in Hindi, viz., *Prāchīna Bhāratiya Durga Sthāpatya* and *Gwalior Durga, Maṁdira Evaṁ Murtiyāṅ.*

Anamika Roy is Associate Professor in the Department of Ancient History, Culture and Archaeology, University of Allahabad, Allahabad. She was a recipient of Commonwealth Fellowship and completed her Ph. D. at Cambridge University. Apart from her specialization in art history, she has equal interests in epigraphy, numismatics and religious studies. She has contributed about fifty papers in national and international journals and has authored four books which include *Amarāvatī Stūpa : A Critical Comparison of Epigraphic, Sculptural and Architectural Evidence; Brāhmī Inscriptions of Northern India* and *Perspectives on Comparative Religion*. Currently, she is working on Gender and Art History.

Prashant Srivastava is Professor in the Department of Ancient Indian History and Archaeology, University of Lucknow, Lucknow. He specializes in Ancient Indian Numismatics and also has a keen interest in ancient mythology. Besides, contributing over fifty research papers to different journals and publications, he has authored a number of books and has given a new dimension to the study of numismatics. His published works include *Encyclopaedia of Indian Coins; The Apracharajas; Art Motifs on Ancient Indian Coins; Aspects of Ancient Indian Numismatics* and *Coins of Ancient India* (the last one in co-authorship with Professor K. K. Thaplyal).

Nirmala Shukla was awarded Ph.D. degree in Ancient Indian History and Archaeology by University of Lucknow, Lucknow. She has special interest in Indian Archaeology and has worked on *Archaeology of Lalitpur District.*

Anil Kumar is Associate Professor in the Department of Ancient Indian History and Archaeology, University of Lucknow, Lucknow. He specializes in prehistoric archaeology, field archaeology and anthropological archaeology. He participated in archaeological explorations and excavations in the states of Uttar Pradesh, Bihar and Orissa and also excavated the site of Mahuadabar in Basti district of Uttar Pradesh. His published works include over seventeen papers in different journals and a book entitled *Origin and Growth of Neolithic Culture.*

R. S. Srivastava is working in the office of Superintending Archaeologist, Archaeological Survey of India, Lucknow (U. P.). He has participated in the excavations of Sringaverapur (U. P.), Sanghal (Punjab) and Lal Kot (Delhi) and in the exploration of Basti, Sant Kabir Nagar and Siddharth Nagar districts of Uttar Pradesh.

Suresh Bala Gogna is Assistant Professor and teaches Anthropology at Pt. Deen Dayal Upadhyay Govt. Girls P. G. College, Rajajipuram, Lucknow. She has special interest in Anthropological Archaeology.

Suniti Pandey is Assistant Professor in the Department of Ancient History, Culture and Archaeology, University of Allahabad, Allahabad. She specializes in Art History and also has interests in Socio-economic History of Ancient India. She has contributed several research papers in national journals.

Maruti Nandan Prasad Tiwari is a senior Professor in the Department of History of Art, Banaras Hindu University, Varanasi. Earlier, he supervised this Department as a Head thrice. He specializes in Ancient Indian Art specially in Jain Art and Iconography. His publications deal extensively with different aspects of Indian art and iconography. These include a number of research papers in national and international journals and books viz., *Jain Art and Aesthetics; Jain Art and Architecture; Elements of Jain Iconography; Ambikā in jain Art and Literature; Jain Pratimā Vijñāna* (in Hindi); *Khajurāho kā Jain Purātattva* (in Hindi)and *Madhyakālīna Bhāratiya Murtikalā* (in Hindi). He has addressed several national and international Seminars and Conferences and has won academic awards and recognitions.

Vipula Dubey is Professor and Head, Department of Ancient History, Archaeology and Culture, D. D. U. Gorakhpur University, Gorakhpur. She specializes in Epigraphic and Palaeographic Studies and also in Numismatics. Besides, her interests include political, social and religious history of ancient India. She has published over fifty papers in national and international journals and has a published book entitled *Gupta Abhilekhon Kā Sāhityika Adhyayana* (in Hindi).

Sarita Kumari is Associate Professor and teaches Ancient History, Archaeology and Culture at Sant Vinoba P.G. College, Deoria (U. P.). She has special interests in prehistoric and protohistoric studies.

Pushpalata Singh is Associate Professor in the Department of Ancient Indian History, Culture and Archaeology, Banaras Hindu University, Varanasi. She specializes in Archaeology and Environmental Archaeology. Her published works include several research papers in different journals and books viz., *Dynamics of Environmental Changes in Prehistoric India; Settlement Pattern in Northern India, Ecology and Archaeology of Kosala Region* and *Vindhya-Madhyagangeya Kshetra Ka Puratattva* (Hindi).

Ravindra Kumar is Associate Professor at Delhi Institute of Heritage Research and Management, New Delhi. He has contributed several research papers on different themes of history and culture in different journals. He has explored over one hundred sites in the middle Gomti basin and north-eastern Uttar Pradesh. He also paid an academic visit to Indonesia.

Sushma Srivastava is Associate Professor in the Department of Ancient History, Culture and Archaeology, Jagat Taran Degree College, Allahabad (U. P.). She specializes in Socio-economic History of Ancient India and has worked on *Maritime Trade in Ancient India.* She has published a number of research papers in national journals. She is also a co-editor of annual research journal *Anveṣhā.*

Piyush Kant Sharma is Assistant Professsor in the Department of Ancient History, Culture and Archaeology, M. D. P. G. College Pratapgarh (U. P.). He has interests in the studies of Ancient Indian Architecture and Sculpture.

Brijbhanu Singh is Associate Professor in the Department of Ancient History, Culture and Archaeology, P. B. P. G. College Pratapgarh (U.P.). He has interests in the studies of Ancient Indian Sculpture and Iconography.

Surendra Kumar Yadav is a Research Fellow at the Department of Ancient Indian History, Culture and Archaeology, Banaras Hindu University, Varanasi. He has worked on the archaeology of the Varanasi region and has published a monograph entitled *Vāruṇeya Kṣhetra Kā Purātāttvika Itihāsa* (in Hindi).

Pragya Mishra is Assistant Professor and teaches History at H. N. Bahuguna P. G. Govt. College, Naini, Allahabad (U. P.). She has interests in pre and protohistoric archaeology of India and specializes in the ceramic industries of the middle Ganga plain. She has published several research articles in the professional journals of archaeology.

Seema Srivastava is a Post Doctoral Fellow at the Department of Ancient History, Archaeology and Culture, D. D. U. Gorakhpur University, Gorakhpur. She specializes in Ancient Indian Sculpture and Iconography. She has a published monograph viz. *Poorvī Uttar Pradesh Men Mūrti Shilpa* (in Hindi) to her credit.

Anupama Srivastava was awarded Ph. D. degree in Ancient Indian History, Culture and Archaeology by Banaras Hindu University, Varanasi. She specializes in Ancient Indian Palaeography and has a published work entitled *Development of Imperial Gupta Brāhmī Script.*

Indu Dhar Mishra is a research scholar in the Department of Ancient History, Archaeology and Culture, D. D. U. Gorakhpur University, Gorakhpur.

Dayamani Kushwaha is a research scholar in the Department of Ancient History, Archaeology and Culture, D. D. U. Gorakhpur University, Gorakhpur.

Sangharsh Rao is a scientist at Remote Sensing Application Centre, Department of Science and Technology, Uttar Pradesh. He has interests in Geology, Geo-archaeology, Remote Sensing and GIS. He has participated in the excavations of Sanchankot (Unnao district, U. P.), Naimiṣaranya (Sitapur district U. P.) and Dwarka (Jamnagar district, Gujrat). He has directed field exploration in the Pratapgarh and Varanasi districts of Uttar Pradesh during the session 2011-12. He has published a number of articles and reports in different publications.

1

Rise and Evolution of Culture in Pūrvāñchal from the Earliest time up to the Beginning of Urbanisation : An Overview

Radha Kant Varma

Eastern Uttar Pradesh or 'Pūrvāñchal' is a geographical expression and includes roughly the eastern end of Uttar Pradesh. It is bounded by Nepal to the north, Bihar state to the east, *Baghelkhand* region of Madhya Pradesh state to the south, the *Awadh* region of Uttar Pradesh to the west and the end of *Doab* (at Allahabad and Kaushambi) in Uttar Pradesh to its southwest. In other words it covers the region known as mid-Ganga valley excluding the region falling in Bihar. My discussions are based on the evidence of the sites located within this area only. The entire region may be divided into three distinct geographical units-The Ganga plain, the *Vindhya-Kaimur* ranges and the *Saryupar* region. The rivers of the three regions mentioned above finally drain themselves into the Ganga. Son and Belan are the main tributaries which form the drainage pattern of the Vindhya-Kaimur region and Sarayu-Rapti are the major rivers of the northern part of the region under discussion. The Vindhya Kaimur ranges are among the oldest formations in the World. The Ganga plain came into existence in Early Miocene and attained its present form in the late Quaternary (Singh, I.B. 2005).

Till a few decades back it was generally believed that the man occupied the Ganga Plain region very late. In the late fifties of the last century Prof. Sharma (I.A-A Review-1956-57) had located a lower Palaeolithic site in *Bariari* on the southern bank of Yamuna river but unfortunately the importance of this discovery was not realized and the it remained unnoticed. We continued to believe that the Ganga plain remained devoid of human population till the recent times. The recent discovery of Middle Palaeolithic assemblage near Kalpi (Singh, I.B., 2005.) in the Yamuna Valley makes it clear that the history of human occupation in the Ganga plain region may be pushed back to late Pleistocene age.

We find this region emerging as a centre of attraction from about the first millennium BCE. onwards when the process of second urbanization starts. A number of cities came into being by 6th century BCE. Some of the cities like Kāśī that came into prominence during that period is still flourishing and has the distinction of being the oldest living city in the world. Kāśī, Ayodhyā and Prayāga which have contributed a lot in the making of overall Indian culture are located in this very region. It was the native land of Lord Buddha and the seventh and 23rd Jain *tīrthaṅkara.* Ādi Shaṅkarachārya and Kabīrdasa, the great reformist *fakir* preached their faiths here. Today, it is one of the most populated areas of the world. History is witness to the fact that up to the present time this region has always been in the lime light and has guided the destiny of India.

Till the mid fifties of the last century almost nothing was known about the prehistory of the region though sporadic discoveries were reported by a few scholars. Systematic archaeological prehistoric explorations were started in the Vindhyan region by the department of Ancient History, Culture and Archaeology under the overall direction of Prof. G.R. Sharma. (*IAR*-1956-57 onwards) The present author made the beginning and explored the then Mirzapur (Varma, R.K. 1964). The result was submitted in the form of a thesis in 1964. From 1963-64 prehistoric exploration of the Vindhyan region from Karvi to Karamnasa was taken up as the departmental project (*IAR* 1963-64 onwards). The explorations added an entirely new chapter which was hitherto unknown. The magnificent river sections of the river Belan that flows in the trough like formation between the Kaimur and the Central Plataeu south of the Ganga in the Meja subdivision of Allahabad and the tributary rivers and rivulets of the Belan river, the Vindhyan hillocks and escarpments, the mid-son valley south of the Kaimurs between Sihawal and Patpara, the Adwa valley that flow between the Son and the Kaimur in a narrow valley were thoroughly explored from 1963 onwards. The geomorphology of both the Belan and the Son Valley is such that no shifting of material was possible. Hence, all the deposits are preserved *in-situ.* The Belan river which is a remnant of an earlier drainage system, its tributaries and *nālās* laid bare the deposits containing the tools and material remains of the Early man. It is the only place in India where a complete sequence of the different cultural stages of man's development was found preserved in the entire valley. This discovery filled up the gaps in the evolutionary cultural sequence of Indian prehistory by providing links in definite stratified deposits (Varma, R.K. 1999). Lower Palaeolithic tools were recovered from the eroding first gravel, lying on the weathered bed rock in the Belan valley and Sihawal formation in the Son valley. Outside the river valleys a very large number of **factory sites** were located. A great homogeneity was observed in the selection of sites in the different cultural stages. Lower Palaeolithic sites were found located on top terraces of the rivers and on hillocks jutting out of the main hills where finer variety of quartzite is available as rubble or can be quarried from the exposed rock mass. Pebble tools were found mixed with the acheulian in the river valley. Special mention may be made of 'Chunk tools' made on flat pieces of stones by removing bold flakes by centrally directed alternate percussion technique. Some tools betray evidence of hafting also. Cleavers that were added later in the tool kit could be used in verieties of ways, by changing the position of hafting. This is evident by a close study of their working edge.

The identification of gravel II with its three sub-divisions, overlying the first silt cleared the picture how gradually the tool technology developed and the set of lower palaeolithic tools were replaced by the tools of blade-flake-scraper tradition. Outside the river valleys Middle Palaeolithic sites were found on the slopes of hills or very low hillocks and on the terraces of the rivers. They consist of the tools of blade-flake-scraper tradition.

The discovery of Gravel III and its blade tool components underlying a deposit (Gravel IV at places) containing narrower, thinner and smaller blades and tools made on narrow blades detached mostly through indirect percussion or pressure technique and on bladelets by retouching-Epipalaeolithic and Mesolithic - settled the **hiatus-problem** of Indian prehistory. It also settled the problem of terminology and development of the Mesolithic tool technology (microlithic industry) raised earlier by Prof Subbarao (*The Personality of India...*; Varma, R.K. 1965) Outside the river valley Upper Palaeolithic sites were found located at the foot of the hills where they meet the low ground, or on top of low outlying hillocks slightly away from the present river bed beyond the flood plain.

A closer study of the tools revealed that the Upper Palaeolithic tools too gradually transformed into the microlithic facie of the Mesolithic (Varma, R.K. and Pal, J.N. 1982). At least three developmental stages represented by three type sites-Amaradan located on the northern side of the medial ridge near the confluence of the Rehi and Son, Patwadh representing the second stage located on the left bank of Son near its confluence with Ghaggar, a small river and the third stage by the Marwa site which is located on the western toe of Chandwa hill on the right bank of Tundiari river in Allahabad district (Varma, R.K. 1999 p. 179). The industries of both the first and second stages are basically chert based while in the tools of the third stage finer material like chalcedony, agate and carnelian etc., have also been used. The main difference in the tools of the different stages lie in their thickness, width, cross section, method of flaking and also secondary retouch. Gradual reduction of length, width and thickness and change over from triangular cross section to rectangular or trapezoidal cross section has been observed.

The discovery of a figurine of mother goddess, made on bone, from Lohanda *nālā* in the Belan valley and the identification of a place of worship, during the excavation at Baghor in Sidhi district, datable to the Upper Palaeolithic period, needs special mention because they throw light on the growing mental faculty of man towards self expression and conceptualization. These are the earliest discoveries of their types in India. It is significant to note that a large number of animal fossils have been found associated with the tool bearing deposits of the middle and upper palaeolithic deposits. In the Belan valley a large number of fossils of *Bos gauras, Bovidae spp., Cervidae sp., Sus, Hippo, Equus sp. Rhino, Elephus etc.,* have been collected from Gravel II. All these fossils have also been found in the lower member of the Baghor formation in the Son valley. It is interesting to observe that beside animal fossils *leaffossils* were recovered from a *tufa* deposit within the Patpara formation near Patpara (Varma, R.K.(ed.) 1994a) This discovery is important from the view point that leaf fossils of such recent date were not reported earlier.

Volcanic ash

Volcanic ash was located for the first time in India on the left bank of Son near Ghoghra on the confluence of the Rehi and Son by Martin Williams and Keith Royce in 1980 (Williams and Royce 1982; Williams and Clarke 1985). This discovery had a worldwide impact. Soon more sites were located in the Son and Narmda Valley (Basu et a1.1987, Acharya and Basu 1993). Research projects were launched to assess the impact of *toba ash* on human cultures, plant and animal life by the university of Cambridge (Pal. J.N 2009). A number of foreign agencies want to collaborate with Allahabad University in working on projects related with *toba ash* (Jones and Pal 2005; Williams et al. 2006). This discovery will be able to fix a datum line for the stone tools preceding and succeeding the *toba ash* deposits in South-east and South Asia particularly.

The Belan and Son valleys have provided OSL dating from Lower to Upper Palaeolithic deposits (Pal, J.N. *A Note on the OSL Ages Obtained from the samples Collected from the Belan and Son Valleys.*) Some C^{14} dates are also available for the Upper Palaeolithic. No sample has so far been dated from Gravel (Unit I). However, sample from the first silt (Unit II) belonging to late Lower Palaeolithic horizon has been dated to 91 k yrs BP. For dating the Middle Palaeolithic, samples were taken from the sandy silty deposit of reddish colour (Unit IV) over lying Gavel II and dated to 55 kyr BP. For dating the Upper Palaeolithic objects samples were taken from Cemented Gravel III (Unit VI). It yielded a date of 20 kyrs. Besides there are four C14 dates also. They are 25430±350; 25790±830 and-390 BP; 26270±660 and 19755±340BP respectively. Gravel IV (Unit 8) belonging to late Upper Palaeolithic period yielding non-geometric microliths. This unit gave a date of 16 kyrs. This horizon has three C14 dates also reading 14140 ± 410 and 390; 11300 : 1 : ±130 BP and 10030±115 BP. (See chart 2, Pal, J.N. *ibid*).

The tool bearing deposits from the Lower to Upper Palaeolithic in the Son valley have been similarly dated. One date has been obtained from the Sihawal silt reading 100 kyrs. This deposit corresponds to the late phase of Lower Palaeolithic culture. The Patpara deposit which overlies the Sihawal silt formation and yields middle palaeolithic tools has been dated to 54±6kyrs. Three dates have been obtained from Baghor formation that yields Upper palaeolithic tools. The dates are36±9 kyrs; 22±3 kyrs and 18 kyrs..(See chart n.3. Pal, J.N. *ibid.,*) The greatest significance of these dates is that they have been obtained from the tool bearing deposits of both the valleys individually and they confirm each other.

The Beginning of Holocene: the Epi-palaeolithic, the Mesolithic and the Neolithic Cultures.

In Europe the Upper Palaeolithic was followed by the Mesolithic and Neolithic with the ushering in of the Holocene. But in India the very existence of the Upper Palaeolithic and Mesolithic was doubtful on account of paucity of stratigraphic evidence. Working on the analogy of the researches made in Europe, Robert Bruce Foote (1916) proposed a theory of *'hiatus'* or a yawning gulf between the Palaeolithic and the Neolithic for India also. The problem in Europe was settled with the excavation at Mas d'Azil in France in 1895 but in India it continued till the discovery of the Belan section was reported in the International Symposium on Carbon 14 and Indian Archaeology in 1971 at TIFR, Bombay. It provided the stratigraphic evidence for both the Upper Palaeolithic and the Mesolithic industries that succeeded the Upper Palaeolithic in the Holocene. It also settled once for all the 'hiatus' problem and the problem of the evolution of Microlithic industries of the Mesolithic and the problem of terminology. Thus the Belan Valley filled all the missing links of the Stone Age Cultures in India. Further, the excavations were conducted in and outside the Rock-shelters on the Kaimur on the Morahana Pahar, Baghahikhor, Lekhahia- Mesolithic sites (Varma, R.K 1964; 1981-83; 1986) and in the Belan Valley at Chopanimando, transitional between the Upper Palaeolithic and Mesolithic (Epi-palaeolithic: Sharma, G.R.et al.) on the one hand and between the food gathering and food producing on the other;(Mesolithic and the Neolithic), Koldihwa, Mahagara (Neolithic sites; Sharma, G.R. et a1.1980) followed by other sites that will be discussed later. The topmost three layers of the Belan section have been correlated with the excavated layers of Chopanimando excavation (Sharma, G.R. 1980). The lowermost deposit or that of period I can be correlated with the third deposit from the top. The middle deposit or that of period II is co relatable with the second layer of the Belan section. The topmost deposit or that of period III of Chopanimando is comparable to the topmost deposit of the Belan section. In the Lekhahia excavation also thick and broad blades were noticed in the bottom most layers (Sharma 1965; Varma 1986). Cockburn (1894) had also noticed them in the bottom most layers in his diggings. Similar tool assemblages were collected and studied from a large number of open air sites throughout the Vindhyan region. Such tools were put under the category of Epi-palaeolithic tools. These are generally made on thick irregular flake or blade and have triangular cross-section on cherty or flinty material. Fluted cores and associated blades make their appearance. The lunates are very broad and their arc is very thick. Most of the tools are made on thick flake blades. Gradually, the epi-palaeolithic tools evolved into microliths with the introduction and evolution of fluted core technique and blunting technique of secondary retouch. All most all the tools were made on blades or bladelets by shaping the tool by blunting parts of the tool as per requirement.

The excavations carried out in and outside the Morahana Pahar and Lekhahia rock shelters revealed a complete evolutionary sequence within the Mesolithic industries. (Varma, R.K. 1964; 1981-83; 1986) At least four phases within the Mesolithic were observed. They are given as under:

I. The earliest phase is represented by non geometric tools made purely of impure cherty or flinty material.

II. In the second phase geometric shapes appear unassociated with pottery. Triangles precede the emergence of trapeze.

III. In the third phase pottery makes its appearance.

IV. In the fourth stage microliths become extremely diminutive and the geometric shapes are made with perfect precision.

The results obtained through above excavations were confirmed by the excavations of Chopanimando (Sharma et al.1980:36-37).We shall revert back to Chopanimando after reviewing what was happening in the Ganga Plain north of the Ganga during this time.

The Ganga Plain in the Holocene

In the year 1969 the chance discovery of the Mesolithic site of Sarai Nahar Rai (25°40' 0" N Long. 81°51' 0") and the location of nearly two scores of sites ranging from the epi-palaeolithic stage to full fledged semi sedentary Mesolithic settlements on the banks of old horseshoe lakes of the Ganga (Sharma *et. al.* 1980: 123-131) within the districts of Allahabad, Pratapgarh, Sultanpur, Jaunpur and Varanasi, by the department of Ancient History Culture and Archaeology, University of Allahabad, added a new chapter in the archaeology of the Ganga Valley. Later Rakesh Tewari et al (2002) located archaeological sites near Kalpi in the Yamuna valley belonging to the Middle Palaeolithic period and datable to 45k yrs with rich faunal remains and a large variety of bone tools. Beside, Mesolithic settlements were also located. There is a continuous record of palynological evidence of grassland for the last about 15k yrs. During the last glacial maxima (LGM), the land form supported a dense network of minor tributaries. These channels were very prominent around 15k yrs. A tectonic event between 8-5 kyrs transformed this landscape of dense river channels into a landscape of ponds and lakes. The dry climatic phase between 5-4k yrs caused shrinkage and siltation of lakes.

The average depth of the alluvial fills is 1300-1400 m.(Singh 1971: 129). With the onset of the Holocene and the growing aridity, the marshy land and water locked Ganga alluvium gradually turned into vegetation friendly land especially near the lakes. A few soil samples collected and examined from the vicinity of Mahadaha (Pant and Pant 1980: 229) and horse shoe lake of Nevari (25°31' 30" E) (Gupta 1976: 109-19) near Sarai Nahar Rai suggested a green land vegetation during the period under consideration.

These lakes/ horseshoe lakes collected enough water to last throughout the year. These lakes with vegetation all round and aquatic fauna could support a good number of both men and animals alike. Such lakes can be seen and located even now on the northern side of the Ganga though a number of them have silted (Fig. No.1).

The growing aridity and comparatively drier climate was a worldwide phenomena. It made the Ganga valley habitable on the one hand but created water scarcity in the Vindhyan region on the other. Water scarcity is a regular phenomenon during the summer months even during the present time. It forces shifting of population to the north into the Ganga Valley.

The man from the Vindhyan region, wandering in search of food, fodder and water descended down the hills near the horse shoe lakes with greenery all around, abounding in vegetal food, aquatic fauna, small game and birds. The man started coming into the Ganga Valley when the old Ganga alluvium *Bhangar* was in the process of formation. The man at this period of time was in the Epi-palaeolithic stage of cultural development. The *Bhangar* formation represents the terminal Pleistocene and the warm and wet early Holocene. They may be correlated with the uppermost three layers of the Belan section. The artifacts collected from the sites are divisible into the following groups:

1. Epi-palaeolithic- transition between Upper Palaeolithic and Mesolithic.
2. Early Mesolithic- characterised by non-geometric microlithic tools.
3. Mesolithic- characterised by geometric microlithic tools.

Sites of the first two categories are represented by a few microlithic tools which are slightly bigger, broader and thicker than the Mesolithic (Fig. 4) and smaller, narrower and thinner than the upper Palaeolithic tools.

The sites of the third category, can further be subdivided into three groups: ABC The sites belonging to group A are represented by a few microliths only and are devoid of any habitation deposit. They may be termed merely as camp sites (Varma, R.K.; 1981-83).

The sites of group B and C have habitation deposit and are represented by burials and hearths. These sites are invariably located on a relatively higher ground beyond the flood plain of the lakes. The sites of group B do not have deposits of more than one or two periods. The sites of group C have thick deposits of more than one or two periods. None of the sites reported so far are associated with pottery. The Microlithic tool assemblage belongs to the geometric stage. The industry may be described as **pre-pottery and geometric in** character. It is comparable with the second phase of the Mesolithic of the Vindhyas (Varma, R.K. 1986) and the IIB phase of Chopani-Mando (Sharma *et.al. 1980)*.

Out of all the sites, three sites namely: Sarai Nahar Rai (25°29' 2" N: 82° 11' 30" E), Mahadaha (25° 29' 2" N: 82° 11' 30" E) and Damdama (26° 1 O'N: 82° 10' 30" E) have been excavated between the years 1970 and 1986. Sarai-Nahar-Rai covered an area of 1,800 sq. m. and revealed an occupation of one period only. The site of Mahadaha covered an area of 8,000 sqm. revealed a habitation deposit of 60 cm. divisible into four period of burial activity. This site was badly disturbed on account of canal building activity. The site of Damdama was the most preserved and extensive site covering an area of 8,750 sqm. The total deposit as revealed by the excavation was 1.5 m. (Varma, et. al. 1985)

The excavations at the three sites have revealed an extremely homogenous material culture of a people whose subsistence economy was primarily based on gathering but hunting too played an important role. These were the first settlers in this part of the Ganga Valley.

Why and how the new comers left their original habitat in the Vindhyan region for an entirely new place with completely different environment and ecological setup, is an important question which needs investigation. The new habitat was completely devoid of the raw material with which the Mesolithic people made their hunting equipments.The new ecological setup demanded a change in the life style also.

At least three factors may be presumed that prompted these people to adopt the new habitat. The first and the foremost reason seems to be environmental change, the second, spurt in population and scarcity of food, fodder and water, the third factor must have been the innate adventurous spirit of man with a longing to see new places and face new challenges.

Regarding the nature of these sites Prof. Sharma was of the opinion that the Ganga Valley sites were campsites "where these people settled for one season. There is no doubt that favourable sites like Sarai Nahar Rai and Mahadaha were visited time and again and thus provided camping grounds to these new immigrants of the Ganga Valley" (Sharma *et. al. 1980:* 28).

The theory of seasonal migration of Prof. Sharma may be taken as only partially correct. In the beginning it might have been a seasonal affair only. But it seems more probable that later (during the Geometric phase of the Mesolithic) the people who came into the Ganga Valley continued to stay on. Out of these excavated sites Damdama has the thickest habitation deposit of 1.5 m. divisible into ten layers and eight phases of burial activity with corresponding floor levels. This hypothesis further finds support from the fact that the microliths gradually become diminutive and their number also decreases in the upper levels. In the uppermost level microliths are almost replaced by bone tools. It means that there was no regular supply of raw material. Had the people been coming seasonally the number of microlithic tools would not have decreased progressively. Moreover, utmost economy was practiced in the manufacture of microliths. The cores are almost nonexistent.

The excavations of the Ganga Valley sites revealed that these people depended heavily for their subsistence on vegetal food. They lived in cluster of houses with their family (?) women, children and old persons.

Round about seventy-one graves were opened that brought to light more than ninety four skeletons. Male and female were almost equally distributed. Among the buried were children as young as 3 years and 60 yrs old men. The average age has been calculated between 18 to 40 yrs.

The excavations of the burials have brought to light a number of interesting facts regarding the pattern of life of the people. We would like to refer to them very briefly here.

It is generally believed that the Mesolithic folk depended basically on hunting and moved from one place to another in search of game animal. But the Ganga Valley people were basically food gatherers. Hunting played only a subsidiary role. We notice that gradually the percentage of microlithic tools is decreasing and the percentage of vegetal food processing equipment such as quern and mullers increasing. It is all the more important when we consider the fact that these heavy objects were not locally available and had to be brought from far off Vindhyan region nearly 100kms away from the site.

These people preferred to make stable bases rather than moving from place to place. The heavy dependence on vegetal food, the heavy food processing tools and easy availability of aquatic fauna in the lakes within the catchment area bound them with the soil. Vegetal resources were abundant and easily available. From these bases they operated unto a distance of safe return within a day because the vegetal food had to be processed at the base station only, on account of food processing equipments being there. In case of hunters it was not necessary for them to come back to the base camp for processing. There is also evidence to suggest that they had now surplus food for the rainy day. A number of pits with plastered walls and unburnt interiors have been brought to light in the excavations at Mahadaha and Damdama. These, in all probability, served as storage pits of grains.

A rough estimate of the population during the last phase at Mahadaha and Damdama has been made using querns and mullers as variables. A family unit normally has only one set of grounding stones and if we use this module for the prehistoric period we can extrapolate a rough population estimate. In the last phase at Mahadaha, 191 querns and at Damdama 110 querns were recovered. If we assume that each unit of 4 to 5 persons used one set the population at Mahadaha would work out to between 700 to 1000 and at Damdama in 550 to 650 persons.

As a corollary to the dependence on vegetal food, the formation of smaller units within a larger group of persons followed. It's a well-known fact that hunting, especially large-scale hunting is a social event but the same may not be true for gathering and processing of vegetal food. A large number of small hearths have been located on each site. The evidence of construction of small hutments at Chopani-mando may be taken as evidence of formation of smaller units in the social setup. Here reference to couple burials which have been marked at the excavated sites of the Ganga Valley are most noteworthy. Couple or multiple couple burials (Varma, R.K.1997: 29-34 in Joshi J.P. (ed.) containing pair/pairs of male female buried together side by side or in two tiers in a set pattern have been excavated on each site. In each grave female was put to the left of the male. There are however three exceptions. In two cases the females were placed to the right of male and in one case both the skeleton are in the opposite directions. There was no time gap between the placement of the first and the second body inside the grave.

Here again some explanations are needed. Did the male and female die together by accident, disease or the man died and the female was killed and buried together? There is no evidence to prove or disprove any of the above options.

On the basis of couple burials it is not improper to postulate the thesis that some sort of family unit of male and female and children had formed in the Mesolithic itself and a new social order was emerging in which the concept of ownership of individual hut, hearth, family and surplus food was being recognized.

In conjunction with the subsistence strategies these people developed important socio-ritual traditions. The meticulous way in which graves were prepared in west-east orientation represents the performance of a ritual belief on a group level. There are a few exceptions only. In case of one couple burial the orientation is north south and south north. These people were not simply concerned with the problem of existence and were thinking about life beyond death and supernatural. They were not simply disposing their dead but were immortalizing them by making elaborate burial in a set pattern within the habitation area. Evidence from Damdama suggests that some sort of fire ritual was performed in the grave itself before burying the dead. The placement of grave goods in the form of microliths, bones, fresh water molluscs, bone and antler ornaments etc. further confirms the above hypothesis. The west east or east west orientation of the graves must have been guided by the position of the sun. The life giving sun must have attracted them. The beginning of sun worship may be traced from these Mesolithic folk.

The success of the socio-economic strategies adopted by these people is further attested to by the fact that now the man was able to indulge in such activities that were not related with food procurement or subsistence only. He was developing an aesthetic sense towards self-beautification by making bone ornaments. Earrings and necklaces have been recovered from these graves at Mahadaha (Sharma *et. al. 1980:* 108-109). Two male individuals (Skl. V and VII) were buried adorned with necklace made from rings, cut out from antlers, the presence of unfinished, partially finished and finished antler ornaments at Mahadaha indicate that the ornaments were manufactured locally. At Damdama in grave VII was found a carved ivory pendant and two bone arrowheads (Varma *et. al. 1985:* 64). The carved pendent had two circles or eyes at either end.

The discovery of these items of adornment raises some important issues. The first and the foremost question is whether these ornaments were indicative of social status or position of authority? At this stage of our knowledge it is difficult to answer.

The skeletal remains of these people had large and robust skulls and they were relatively tall with the stature of males being approximately 173.93 cm to 192.08 cm (Kennedy 1984: 37). Kennedy who had studied the skeletal remains of Sarai Nahar Rai states 'we recognize here an ancient population which was extremely successful in its adaptation to the hunting and gathering way of life carried out in an ecological setting of abundant food resources. Only in this way we may explain the physical responses of this population towards a high realization of their ontogenetic growth potentials and the low incidence of disease related to nutritional stress "(Kennedy *et. al.* 1986 p. 40-41). It is further supported by the fact that here we find people living upto 40 to 60 years of age which is exceptionally high for any Mesolithic society.

How these flourishing pre agricultural settlements were deserted is a question, which needs proper explanation. At none of these sites we find any evidence of settlement after the desertion of the site by the Mesolithic folk. The sites remained unoccupied till the early historical period. The Mesolithic people, though dependent heavily on vegetal food, could not start cultivation. Probably, the stage was not set yet, for the same, but certain points need specific mention such as (i.) both in the Vindhyan region and the Ganga valley sites we start getting semi permanent settlements, thick deposit, evidence of hutments, post holes, pits for storage etc. in the late mesolithic period. In their subsistence economy, wild grains play an important role. It is attested by the findings of rice/grains (wild), quern and mullers. Handmade pottery also appears in which rice husk etc has been used as degraissent. These indicate that the breaking point had reached. It is a well-known phenomenon that cultural development is a cumulative process in which inventions and innovations take place only when the necessary antecedents already exist.

Rock Art

The northern Vindhyan region which includes the sites located in the undivided district of Mirzapur, parts of Varanasi, south Allahabad and Banda in Uttar Pradesh and Baghelkhand etc., a very large number of painted rockshelters have been located. The first painted rockshelter (Lekhahia) was located and reported by Carlleyle (1967 -68) near Rajpur in Sonbhadra district. Subsequently a large number of shelters were reported and studied by a number of scholars (Jagdish Gupta 1967;Varma,R.K 1964; Tewari,R. 1985). The shelters are generally located on the steep side of hillocks, overlooking the deep valley, on one or both the banks of a river, *nālā*, or rivulet flowing on the bed–rock or in deep cavern or a gorge. Besides, they are also found on top and slope of high hillocks overlooking the undulating land slowly merging with the low-lying valley. Only such rock-shelters are painted that are connected with some perennial source of water.

Most of the shelters of northern Vindhyan region were occupied during the Epi-palaeolithic period and were deserted by the end of the Mesolithic. The shelters vary considerably in shape and size.

Within the shelters the paintings are usually executed on the walls and ceilings but at times in difficult locations. No system seems to have been followed in the arrangement of paintings.

In the paintings of the earliest phase, in Baghelkhand and the South Uttar Pradesh region, only single animal figures are found. In the next stage more than one animal figure were painted together forming a group. Here for the first time some effort to compose the figures is seen. It was only in the third stage that hunting or trap scenes appear and the figures revolve round a theme and man first appears. He is depicted as a hunter singly or in group or is shown dancing generally in a group. The paintings are generally executed with hematite (*geru*) or oxides of iron. It is found in a great range of yellows, browns, oranges and reds. They are available in plenty in the Vindhyan formations in the form of nodules or pallets.

Deers Painted realistically

For blacks and very dark browns an oxide of manganese was also used and whites were obtained from kaolina limestone. Some times, white pigment was prepared from mineralized white chalcedony also. Copper compounds were used to obtain a bright shade of green.

The rock art of northern Vindhyas is mostly the product of a people who were primarily hunters and food gatherers. Hence, the subject matter of painting always revolves round animals. Among all the animals, deer seems to be their most favourite animal. Rhinoceros is the second most popular animal. Its depiction is very life like and reflects the ferocity and strength of the animal. Bison was also a popular subject of depiction. Elephant figures have been painted in all its majesty with heavy and strong body generally in flat wash. Wild boar in herd has been realistically painted. *Nilgai* or Blue bull has also been recognized in a number of shelters. In one of the rock-shelters at Ronp, a horse like figure in outline in X Ray style has been identified. In Sivapurva rock shelter a group of animals are identified as donkeys.

Trap scenes are also common. In some cases traps have been symbolised by concentric circles while in others elaborate arrangements have been shown with minute details.

In some of the rock -shelters a number of human figures have been shown dancing. Most of the human figures are simply symbolic. They are generally static, motionless or in other words lifeless. No differentiation has generally been made in a male or female figure.

An evolutionary sequence can be observed in the paintings. It may be summed up as follows:

(1) Naturalistic: These are nearer to their natural figure.

(2) Stylistic: In this stage the body contours vanish and the body form are based on geometrical angles only.

(3) Symbolic: In this stage the rectangle figure is reduced to double or single line and gradually the figures become irregular and distorted sometimes beyond recognition.

(4) Cubist: Finally, the figures become completely cubist and they are represented by dots, loops, dot within a circle etc.

The painted shelters of the northern Vindhyan region, on the basis of the present evidence from excavations were first occupied in the Epi-palaeolithic period – a period of transition from Upper Palaeolithic to Mesolithic. The Mesolithic folk lived in the shelters, made their tools and buried their dead. This makes the position of the rock-shelters of the northern Vindhyan region unique. Since the shelters remained under the occupation of the Mesolithic people only, it is reasonable to suppose that these were the people who were responsible for paintings also.

There are a number of C 14 dates now to arrive at certain conclusions regarding the antiquity of the Mesolithic of the Northern Vindhyan region. By implication that would be the time bracket for the painting activity also. The prehistoric rock-paintings of the northern Vindhyan region can also be assigned the date of the Mesolithic of the region (14,000-13,000 BCE. to 2,0001500 BCE.) because, in my considered opinion, Mesolithic folk were the authors of the prehistoric paintings.

Antiquity of Mesolithic

There are a number of C14 dates now to arrive at certain conclusions regarding the antiquity of the Mesolithic. From the Lekhahia rock-shelter (Bhainsore group), we have four Carbon dates belonging to the Phase III of the Vindhyan Mesolithic. The dates are: TF-417:3560 ± 110 BP (1710±110 BCE) and TF-419: 4240 ± 115 BP (2410 ± 115 BCE).

Two more C 14 dates, determined by Accelerator Mass Spectrometry on human bone apatite were obtained from the same shelter. These dates based upon thorough pre-treatment and sample preparation methods suggest that the skeletons from Lekhahia may have an antiquity two times greater than previously believed: The new dates are:

Geochron 8,370 ± 75 BP (Skl.IV)

Geochron 8,000 ± 75 BP (Skl.XIII, XV)

These are not isolated dates now. There are confirmatory dates from the Belan, the Son and the Ganga Valley sites.

The Upper Palaeolithic horizon (Gravel III) in the Belan valley has given two C14 dates reading 23840 BCE (PRL 86) and 17765 BCE (TF 1245). Another date reading 18000 BP has been obtained from the Upper Palaeolithic horizon (Clark and Williams: 1990 : 13-24).

The Epi-palaeolithic horizon (Gravel IV) in the Belan section has yielded five dates (Varma 1981-83; Possehl and Rissman 1992) reading 13740 ± 400/-380 BP (PRL 603); 11550 ± 180 BP (BS 130); 10980 ± 190 BP (PRL602); 9830 ± 160 BP (BS 131) and 9740 ± 115 BP(SVA 1421).

Baghor II a Mesolithic settlement (Geometric microliths unassociated with pottery in) the Son valley has yielded one C14 date reading 6380 ± 220 BCE (PRL 715) Clark and Williams 1990).

Similar early dates have been obtained from the Mesolithic settlements of the Ganga Valley (Mesolithic Phase II of the Vindhyan region). There is one date from Sarai Nahar Rai TF 1104; 8365 ± 110 BC and one TL date 5000-7000 BCE and two AMS C14 dates reading 6670 ± 65 BCE and 6915 ± 69 BCE.

On the basis of the above discussion the Epipalaeolithic may be placed within a time bracket of 14,000-13,000 BCE to 10,000-9,000 BCE and the Mesolithic between 12,000-11,000 BCE to 2,000-1500 BCE. The dates for the beginning of the Mesolithic are still flexible because we do not have any date from the 1st phase of the Vindhyan Mesolithic. All the dates are from Phase II and III only.

Neolithic Stage : Beginning of Agriculture

Before the middle of the last century except for the reporting of a few stray triangular Neolithic celts and the discovery of a very few small rounded celts nothing much was known about Neolithic culture of the area under consideration. But the explorations conducted by the Universities of Allahabad, Varanasi, Gorakhpur and State department of Archaeology, U.P. brought to light a large number of Neolithic sites on the northern slopes of the Vindhyas, the Saryupar plains of eastern Uttar Pradesh (Singh 1992) and the Ganga plains in Allahabad. Among the important sites mention may be made of Koldihwa, Mahagara, Panchoha, Kukrahata, Deoghat, Koilariha, Futaha, Chauridiha kutia, Bansghat, Daiya and Patehari in the Belan Valley, Jhusi and Hetapatti in the Ganga Plain in Allahabad, Indari, Berauncha, Sinduria Mahalpur, and Tokwa in Adwa Valley in Mirzapur, Bhunadih, and Waina in Ballia district, Lahuradeva in Sant Kabir Nagar, Sohgaura and Imlidih in Gorakhpur district.

The sites on which excavations have been conducted are Koldihwa, Mahagara, Panchoha, Indari, Tokwa (Pal, J.N 2008) Jhusi and Hetapatti (Misra, V.D. *et. al.* 1998; 98-99; 2002=2003 Pal, J.N 2005), Bhunadih (Singh, P and A.K. Singh (1997-98), Waina (Singh, P. and AK Singh 1995-96), Sohgaura (Chaturvedi, S.N .1980) Lahuradeva, and Imlidih (Singh, P. 1992; 2008).

Among all the excavated sites Koldihwa and Mahagara in the Vindhyan region (Sharma, G.R. *op. cit.*) Jhusi in the Ganga plain (Misra, V.D. *op. cit.*), Imlidih, Sohgaura and Lahuradeva in Saryupar region (Singh. P. *op. cit.*) are very important.

Koldihwa and Mahagara

From the advanced Mesolithic settlement of Chopanimando the focus now shifts to Neolithic settlements- Koldihwa and Mahagara, which are at a distance of not more than three kilometers south-west as the crow flies from there.

Excavation at Koldihwa has revealed evidence of three cultural phases: Neolithic, Chalcolithic and Iron Age. The Neolithic deposit at Koldihwa was only .45m but at Mahagara it was 2.60 m. The excavations at Koldihwa and Mahagara present conclusive evidence of the cultivation of rice and its use as the staple food of the people. Palaeobotanical studies recently made by Emma Harvey *et al.* (Harvey Emma *et al.* 2003) the excavated material of Koldihawa and Mahagara have brought to light a range of cereals cultivated by these people. Both wild and cultivated variety of rice *(oryza sativa)* and small millets were used from the beginning. Subsequently, barley, wheat, pulses and sesame were also introduced. Saraswat also came to the same conclusion after studying the Tokwa material (Misra, V.D. p24; 2008). Similar observations have been made on the sites of mid-Ganga valley such as Senuvar. Wild rice and small millets are found in wild form in the Vindhyan region so local origin for the cultivated rice may be postulated. The Vindhyan Neolithic was the culmination of advanced Mesolithic or proto-neolithic of Chopanimando. It supports the hypothesis proposed by Vavilov long back (Vavilov, N.I. 1951). It may also be pointed out that the cultivated rice spread from here to the other Vindhyan and mid Ganga valley sites slightly later. 'It is reasonable to presume that Neolithism marked by cattle breeding and incipient farming migrated to Kaimur region from Belan Valley. The latter had the record of food production from the hunting gathering economy of the Mesolithic times. (Sharma,G.R. *et. al.* 1980). B.P.Singh is also of the view that a good section of Belan valley population moved towards east, and found ecology of the new region akin to the one they were used to.. ..The knowledge of food production and, both the plant and animal species for domestication were brought to the region from the homeland. (Singh, B.P: *The emergence and spread of cropping practices in Middle Ganga Plains.* Paper presented in National Seminar on Middle Ganga Plains Through the Ages). Similarly, the Saryupar region was also influenced by the Vindhyan people.

Besides the evidence of the domestication of rice, we have got evidence of the domestication of cattle, sheep and goat from Mahagara. A cattle pen measuring 12.5×7.5 m. was recognised at the site of Mahagara. It was enclosed by 28 post holes with three openings. Hoof prints of cattle of different age groups were detected in the pen. It clearly shows that domestication of animals had reached to an advance stage. It may be mentioned that the bones of all these animals in their wild form have been found from pre-neolithic levels. 'The evidence thus suggests that these animals were domesticated from their wild prototypes available in the area' (Misra, 1999: 244).

There are three C14 dates from Koldihwa 4530 ± 185 BCE, 5440 ± 240 BCE and 6570 ± 210 BCE. Doubts were raised for such early dates because Mahagara gave very late dates compared to Koldihwa dates. It seems that the samples from Mahagara were contaminated. The recent dates from Lahuradeva reading 5320 ± 90 BP, 6290 ± 160BP(Cal. 5298BCE.) support the date of Koldihwa. A radio carbon date for the Pre-Neolithic Mahagara is 8080 ± 115 B.P. On this basis Neolithic of Koldihwa has been placed into a time bracket of C. 7000-6000 BCE. (Sharma *et. cl.* 1980; Pal 1990). At that time it was supposed to be the earliest date for cultivated rice in the world.

In recent years, however, Japanese and Chinese archaeologists have added much to our knowledge in the field of early agriculture and ceramics. They have pushed back the dates of earliest rice technology to 12000 B.P. and beyond (Agrawal, D.P. 2001). Recent progress in archaeological studies has put the domestication of rice in the middle reaches of the Yangtze River as early as 10,000 years BCE. At the Bashidang archaeological site located, about 20 km north east of the Chengtoushan site, rice husks date back more than 10,000 years. From this evidence the Liyang plain is considered to be one of the earliest places where rice cultivation originated. (Agrawal D.P. 2001. P. 17). We can reasonably hope that the antiquity of cultivated rice will also be pushed back in the *Poorvanchal* when more extensive excavation is done.

Tokwa

The site is located on the confluence of Adwa and Belan rivers in the Lalganj subdivision of Mirzapur. It is nearly 68 kms from Mirzapur and 8 kms east of Baraundha. Excavtion on the site was conducted for several field sessions under the supervision of J.N. Pal (Pal, J.N. 2008) by the Deptt. of Ancient History, Culture and Archaeology, University of Allahabad. As a result cultural deposits of Neolithic, Chalcolithic and Early Iron Age were revealed within a deposit of 4m. There seems to be gap between the Neolithic and the Chalcolithic phases. The lowest deposit of 2.4 7m (Layers 16 to 8) belonged to the Neolithic phase.

The Neolithic deposit comprises of ill-fired cord impressed pottery, rusticated ware and burnished red and black sherds. Among other antiquities mention may be made of bone tools, microliths, beads made on semiprecious stones and terracotta, fragments of quern and mullers. Grains obtained by floatation technique include rice, barley, *til, moong* etc., According to Fuller and Emma Harvey rice was first to be introduced and the rest followed. Animal bones of both wild and domesticated were recovered. Oval or circular plans of hut were observed. Screen walls were made by split bamboo and were plastered by mud.

There is only one C14 date from Tokwa that reads 4797BC, 5976 BC,6407 B.C. After calibrations it would be 6591 BCE (BS2417, 5976BCE) (BS2369), 4797.BCE (BS2464).

Once an effective level of food production had been obtained in the nuclear areas it spread out from there far and wide over the subsequent years and gradually incipient village farming communities were formed, Coinciding with the shift to food production, though not necessarily related to it, is a number of the most important technological and behavioral developments in human history. There was an astronomical increase in the tempo of technical, social and intellectual change in nuclear areas. The village farming stage is typically associated with such basic crafts as *pottery, weaving, stone working by abrasion* (grinding and polishing), with the presence of adequate houses with equipment for new economy, and with stable settlements and religious cults that suggest significant social and ideological orientation. It would not be out of place to mention that the roots of some at least of these developments can be seen prior to food production: stable settlements, houses, stone grinding etc. But there is hardly a doubt that these underwent improvement and intensification with the ushering-in of early farming societies.

Pottery generally is associated with the beginning of farming culture but the beginning of its antiquity in Japan and China predates agriculture and has been dated to 16,000 years B.P. (Yosinori Yasuda: 1999, Vol. 2, No.1, ISSN 0917-1045 p. 1). In Indian context, too, it has been found associated with the mesolithic assemblage at Morahana Pahar, Mirzapur and Chopani Mando in Allahabad. (Varma, R.K. 1965; Sharma, G.R. *et al.*1980). At some places, as we have seen at Mehargarh, it follows domestication. But pottery became common with the advancement of Neolithic economy. The mastery of this craft has been called by Childe the beginning of Science and 'perhaps man's first conscious utilization of a chemical change: It provided a fire proof cooking vessel, a convenient container and water proof storage. In due course of time it became a valuable tool for the archaeologists for tracing cultural relationships and influences.

Jhusi in the Ganga Plain

Nearly a decade back no Neolithic site was known to exist in the Ganga plain north of the river Ganga. But recent excavations (Misra, V.D. *et. al.* 1998; 98-99; 2002-2003; Pal, J.N.

2008) by the University of Allahabad at the site of Samudrakoop in Jhusi have added an entirely new chapter. 16.5 m cultural deposit at the site revealed six cultural phases. They are as follows: 1. Neolithic Period, 2. Pre NBPW Period (Chalcolithic and Early Iron age), 3. NBPW Period, 4. Śunga-Kushāna Period, 5. Gupta Period and 6. Early Medieval Period.

It is significant to note that there is evidence of the presence of Mesolithic culture on the top of geological formation underlying the archaeological deposit of the Neolithic period. Microliths have been found at the nearby site of Nibikalan and Jamunipar near Jhusi. It is clear that this part of the Ganga plain was also occupied when Damdama etc. in the Ganga plain were occupied. But the most significant thing is that while Damdama etc., were deserted the Mesolithic in Jhusi was transformed into Neolithic settlement.

The Neolithic phase at Jhusi, like elsewhere, is characterized by ill fired cord impressed, rusticated burnished pottery. Among other objects recovered mention may be made of bone tools, microliths, quern and mullers and sling balls. Bones of cattle, sheep, goat, boar, *barasingha* etc., have been recovered. The food grains recovered are rice, millet, *moong* and *masoor.* These people made circular huts as is evident from the position of post holes and by the burnt clay lumps with wattle and daub impressions.

The recent excavations at Jhusi have given three dates from the Neolithic horizon. They are 8140 $\pm$ 220BP (Cal. BC to 6,7105,7080), 6760 $\pm$ 190 BP (Cal. BC 5660, 5649, 5642) and 7110 $\pm$ 170BP (cal. BC5990, 5938 and 5932). These dates would place the Neolithic of Jhusi in the latter half of 8th millennium BCE (BSIP, date nos 2524. 2525 and 2526).

Sohgaura, Imlidih and Lahuradeva in Saryupar region

Sohgaura

Sohgaura was excavated under the direction of S.N. Chaturvedi (1980) by the University of Gorakhpur in 1961-62. It was definitely a pioneering effort but it is unfortunate that the work was not enlarged and continued. The excavation revealed that the lowermost deposit belonged to the Neolithic period. It yielded corded ware. Wild rice and rice husk was used as digraissent in the pottery. The overlying deposits 2A and 2B.were those of Chalcolithic period. The Neolithic of Sohgaura was very much akin to that of the Vindhyan Neolithic. The results obtained by Chaturvedi have been confirmed by later explorations and excavation in the Saryupar region.

Imlidih

Imlidih located on the left bank of Kuwana, a tributary of the Saryu, is the most important and representative site of the Saryupar region. The site was excavated by Purushottam Singh of BHU in 1991-92 and 1995. The culture sequence here is divided into three periods, viz. Neolithic, Narhan (Chalcolithic) and Early historical period. The Neolithic deposit is represented by cord-impressed pottery. The Neolithic man lived in wattle- and- daub huts which are evident by the find of reed marks on lumps of earth. Among other structural activities mention may be made of mud-floors, ovens and hearths. Small finds include micro-beads of steatite, beads of terra cotta, agate and faience, bone points and pottery discs. Cattle, sheep,/goat had already been domesticated in Period I. The earliest inhabitants cultivated two crops a year. Cereals like rice (*Oryza sativa*), barley, wheat, *jowar,* millet and *bajra* were cultivated by them. Among pulses and oil seeds mention may be made of lentil, field pea, grass pea, green gram or *mung,* field brassica and seasame or *til* respectively. Jujube, *awla* and grapes were known to them (Singh, P. 2008 pp. 3-19).

Lahuradeva

Lahuradeva is located in Sant Kabir Nagar at a distance of 5kms south to Bhujaini crossing on Basti-Gorakhpur Road. Originally it was surrounded by a lake from three sides. But at present it remains only on the western side. The state department of archaeology Utter Pradesh has been excavating it since 1997 under the overall direction of Rakesh Tewari. The excavations have revealed a fivefold cultural sequence beginning from Neolithic and followed by Chalcolithic (copper age), Early historical period (Iron age), the NBP ware and deposits of early Kushana pd. The Neolithic has been divided into two sub periods-IA and IB.

The abundant aquatic fauna would have attracted the Neolithic man there. The ceramic industry of Pd.IA comprise cord impressed red ware and black-and-red ware. The pots are mostly hand-made. Some of them are wheel turned also. The people lived in wattle-and-daub houses. Cultivated rice and a few wild grasses have been identified by K.S.Saraswat. Recently a number of dates have been obtained from Lahuradeva which read as follows: 5320 $\pm$ 90BP (BS1951) (Cal. BC 4220, 4196, 4161) and 6290 $\pm$ 160 BP (BS1966) (cal BC5298) (Tewari, *et. al.* 2001-2002, 2002-2003).

Pattern of Culture: during the Neolithic period

The above survey of the principal Neolithic sites of the area under study reveals that there is complete homogeneity between the settlement pattern and material culture. It is a pity that none of the sites has been extensively excavated.

All the Neolithic sites are located on the confluence of two rivers or on the banks of some perennial water body. The cultural deposit varies from .45m to 2.5m. They overlie on the geological formation and underlie the chalcolithic deposit with or without gap. At some places like Jhusi it overlies a deposit that yields Mesolithic tools.

There is complete homogeneity in respect of pottery which is mostly hand- made, ill-fired, cord impressed or rusticated in the early levels. Later, sometimes slow wheel turned pottery appears to be used. Pottery types include bowls, vases, vessels, basins, miniature jars etc., Painted sherds have been reported from Imlidih Khurd and Lahuradeva. Sometimes, decorations were also made by luting or incision.

Wild (*Oryza rufiprogan*) and cultivated rice *oryza sativa* and small millets were used in the initial stages. At Lahuradeva both wild (*Oryza rufiprogan*) and cultivated rice *oryza sativa* and wild foxtail grass has also been identified. But later a wide range of cereals came into cultivation. From Imlidih khurd hulled and single row barley, bread and dwarf wheat, Jowar millet and pearl millet beside lentil, green gram, field pea, grass pea brassica, seeds of jujube, *amalaka* and grapes were also cultivated.

Rounded celts of basalt and granite has been reported from Hetapatti and Lahuradeva on the Ganga plain sites of the study area and almost all the sites of Vindhyan region. On most of the sites stone tools like quern and mullers, bone tools and microliths in varying quantities were integral parts of the culture. Bone ornaments like pendants, earrings, bangles, discs, combs have also been reported from some sites, Beads of steatite, agate, fiance and terracotta have been excavated from most of the sites.

Plan of circular or oval huts have been marked on almost all the sites. The available evidence suggests that screen walls of huts were made of split bamboo. Among other structural remains mention may be made of hearths, pits and silo for keeping grains.

Large numbers of animal bones both wild and domesticated have been identified. Domesticated animals include cattle (indicus), buffalo, (*Bubalus bubalis*), sheep, goat and pigs. Dogs and cat were also domesticated. Bones of wild elephants, rhinoceros, stag, deer etc., have been collected from some sites. Aquatic fauna fish, turtle, mollusks etc., were identified on most of the sites.

On the basis of dates obtained from Koldihwa and Tokwa in the Vindhyan region from Lahuradeva in the Saryupar region and Jhusi in the Ganga plain the beginning of the Neolithic culture can be placed between 8th-7th millennium BCE if not earlier. It is presumed that the Vindhyan Neolithic might have had an earlier beginning because here in this region many of the traits of the Neolithic culture evolved during the late phase of the Mesolithic itself independently and spread from there to mid-Ganga valley and Saryupar regions.

The Neolithic culture came to an end by the coming of the copper using people near about 1500 BCE.

Chalcolithic Culture

We have already seen that Neolithic deposits are capped by chalcolithic deposits on all the sites with a break or without break. There are a large number of sites scattered all over the area. Among the important excavated sites mention may be made of Jhusi and Hetapatti in the Ganga Plain in Allahabad and Koldihwa, Mahagara- Kakoria in the Vindhyan region, Agiabir in the Ganga plain and Tokwa in the Vindhyan region, Mirzapur, Rajghat, Sarai-mohana, Kamauli, Aktha in Varanasi, Prahaladpur in Chandauli, Masondih in Ghazipur, Khairadih in Ballia and in the Saryupar region Sohgaura, Narhan and Imlidih in Gorakhpur and Lahuradeva in Sant Kabir Nagar.

The Chalcolithic culture may be divided into two phases on the basis of non-occurrence and occurrence of iron viz., Early and Late Phase. Early phase is devoid of iron implements; in the late phase iron makes its appearance. Thick accumulation on most of the sites indicates that the site remained occupied for fairly long period of time.

There is hardly much difference in the material culture of the Neolithic and Chalcolithic periods, except that in the chalcolithic period copper makes its appearance and a range of new pottery tradition makes its way. The early farming neolithic communities in most part of India ended up as chalcolithic societies with the introduction of copper. Their basic structure was that of village farming society. Each community was basically self sufficient for all practical purposes.

On most of the sites the Neolithic is capped by Chalcolithic deposit. Beside, a large nurnber of new sites appear. They are normally located on the banks of rivers or perennial water bodies. These people also constructed circular or oval wooden- hutments for living. Split- bamboo with mud-plaster on both the sides was used as screen wall. Remains of mud houses have also been found at some places.

The subsistence economy of these people depended on both hunting and farming. They still largely used stone (microliths) and bone tools as they were used during the Neolithic stage. Likewise, polished celts and chisel of basalt, fragments of quern and mullers, hammar-stones, anvil and sling balls made of sandstone or quartzite were used. In the beginning, use of copper was scarce. Occasionally, knife, spearhead, arrowhead and some ornaments of copper were used.

From most of the sites ornaments like beads, pendants, bangles, rings, ear studs made of semi-precious stones were recovered. At Agiabir, a bead manufacturing centre has been identified (Singh, A.K: 2004: *Excavations at Agiabir* (1999-2001) paper read in the workshop *The Archaeology of Middle Ganga Plain*) where raw material came from the Vindhyas. Among miscellaneous objects terracotta beads, gamesmen, disc with or without perforation, balls, dabbers, conical objects, animal heads and figurines may be mentioned.

The excavations have brought to light a variety of charred and uncharred faunal and floral remains. The faunal remains include bones of domesticated animals like humped cattles, buffalo, sheep, goat, dog, pig etc. Among the bones of wild animals mention may be made of deer, antelope, bear and bones of horse. etc. Aquatic fauna like fish and turtle and birds were also found. All these were known to the Neolithic people also.

The Chalcolithic people cultivated rice, hulled and six row barley, three types (club, bread and dwarf) of wheat, field pea, chick-peal green gram, *khesari,* lentil, *kodon* millet. Oil seeds included mustard, linseed, sisamen, sunflower, castor etc. It is clear from the above list that they obtained two crops in a year. They cultivated jack-fruit, mango, grape and date. Nux vomica and *tulsi* plant were known to them.

The ceramic assemblage of the Chalcolithic is varied. Except for Masondih painted pottery has been recovered from all the sites. Black-and red ware painted in white is the most characteristic pottery of the period at Narhan where it accounted for as much as 74 per cent in the lowest levels but reduced to 58 percent in the upper levels (Singh, P. 1999). The other colours used for painting are cream, brownish and red on black surface. Singh has named it as Narhan Culture on the type site Narhan (*ibid*). The Painting motifs consist of linear designs- wavy lines, straight and oblique strokes, dots, semi circle, lattice, concentric arcs, etc., The other associated wares are black slipped ware (different from those found with NBP), red slipped and red wares. Red wares form the majority on all the sites. Sometimes these also are painted with linear designs in white or cream color. Narhan has yielded some red ware sherds with paintings in ochre color. Paintings are executed on interior or exterior surface of the pot. The ordinary red ware has sometimes paintings in black. Sometimes these are decorated with cut, incised, applique, knobbed and corded designs also. The incised designs consist of dots and strokes, simple chevron linear patterns, zig-zag, wavy lines, criss-cross designs, latticed diamonds, thumb nail impressions forming rope on applique rope design. Some pots bear post firing scratch designs also from Sohgaura.

A variety of pots have been found at different sites. They include bowls of different shapes and sizes such as shallow, straight, convex sided, bowl -cum-lid, flat platters, shallow and convex sided dishes and basins, footed and perforated vessels, vases, *handis* with short, concave or carinated necks, *Iota* shaped globular vessels with flared rim and conscripted neck, miniature vases, dish-on-stand, deep troughs and pan with strap handle.

The Chalcolithic culture of the region was not an isolated phenomena. It was related not only with sites of eastern mid- Ganga valley on one hand and those of central India like Malwa on the other which is reflected in the painted motifs.

C14 dates are available for dating the Chalcolithic culture of the area under discussion. They are as follows: There are two dates from Sohgaura:1235 $\pm$ 130BC and 1335 $\pm$ 110BC; one date from Narhan :1123 $\pm$ 110BC; three dates from Khairadih:1120 $\pm$ 90BC; 1030 $\pm$ 160 B C, 945 $\pm$ 150BC : four dates from Jhusi 1340 $\pm$ 90BC ; three dates from Pre-NBP with iron 950 $\pm$ 90BC, 830 $\pm$ 90BC, 780 $\pm$ 90BC.

On the basis of the above dates the chalcolithic of the region under discussion may be placed within a time bracket of 1400/1300BCE and 800B.CE.

There are a few dates that are earlier than the above dates from the eastern part of mid-Ganga-valley. They read as follows: Chirand 720 $\pm$ 105BC, 1050 $\pm$ 85BC, 1540 $\pm$ 90BC, 1585 $\pm$ 100BC, 1655 $\pm$ 100BC; from Senuwar 1770 $\pm$ 120BC, 1660 $\pm$ 120BC, 1500 $\pm$ 110BC, 1400 $\pm$ 110BC.

On the basis of the above C 14 dates the beginning of chalcolithic in eastern part of the mid-Ganga Valley may be placed in 1800/1700BCE.

Pattern of Chalcolithic settlements

The early farming neolithic communities ended up as chalcolithic societies unnoticed in a very smooth manner with the introduction of copper. Their basic structure of village farming society remained the same. Each community was basically self sufficient for all practical purposes except that their isolation had ended and some of them were in close contact with the other regions of western and eastern India. It is evident from the wide variety of cereals they were now cultivating. The three types of wheat that they sowed must have been introduced from different sources (Saraswat, K.S. 1994 pp. 254-346). Likewise, copper too must have had its source from outside the region. The bead manufacturing station recognized in the excavation at Agiabir is suggestive of the fact that the beads made at the site must have been exported to different places besides catering to the needs of the local people. The raw material was brought from the Vindhyan sources. In a nut shell, it presents a picture of 'affluent rural based settlement' (Singh, A.K 2004) .

Iron was making its way in this scenario unnoticed in the cultural milieu of black-and-red ware and black slipped ware using people, gradually in eastern U.P. Among such sites of the region mention may be made of Jhusi, Rajghat, Agiabir, Raja-nal-ka-tila, Khairadih, Narhan, Lahuradeva, Koldihwa, Mahagara, Malhar etc. The earliest iron objects consisted mainly of hunting tools like arrow-heads, spear heads, knives, rods, nails, chisels, clamps, axes. No sickle or ploughshare has been reported on any chalcolithic site of the region. The view of some scholars that the prosperity of the mid Ganga valley was the result of the introduction and use of iron technology needs rethinking. The surplus in grain production had already been achieved on account of double crop system before the use of iron in cultivation. The introduction of iron must have spurred the progress indirectly. The surplus in food production had its own effects. The population increased and with it increased the size of settlements and new avenues for trade and commerce. It prepared the groundwork for the Second Urbanisation..

Vibha Tripathi (Tripathi, Vibha 2008) is of the opinion that iron technology developed in the region independently. Her explorations in the Sonbhadra region and excavations at Raja-nal-ka-tila and Malhar (Rakesh Tewari *et.a1.*1997-98; 1998-99) in Karamnasa valley in Chandauli district yielded evidence of iron working complete with iron ore, smelting furnaces, forges along with finished iron objects (Tripathi, Vibha 2008, pp. 348-381).

On the basis of the C14 dates obtained from the recent most excavations at Nal-ka-tila and Malhar the antiquity of Iron in the region under discussion may be fixed to 1600/1500BCE, if not earlier.

Prelude to Urbanisationon

Even though intensive agriculture is the foundation of almost all early complex cultures yet, it by itself does not provide sufficient drive for all round development. There has to be other factors. A number of scholars like Julian Steward, V.G. Childe and many others have tried to study the problem of cultural complexity of its origins. Their study indicates that early states and empires arose for the most part in arid or semi-arid environments where agricultural production could be easily intensified, either by canals, terracing, building up fields in lake beds, or some other method; and in zones where many different products were available to everyone. "These civilizations were the outcome of the proper mix of population growth, agricultural intensification, trade, and the peculiarities of human mind. The essential component of a growing complex society is the division of a community into functionally interdependent entities of such complexity that no small group of people can maintain all that community's activities.

In some areas the village farming pattern continued for a pretty long duration of time without any significant change or advancement on account of lack of sufficient drive. But in some areas it provided the essentials for higher socio-technical development as a result of factors difficult to comprehend. Even after the early introduction of iron in Eastern Uttar Pradesh, the basic character of the culture did not change till the beginning of the mid-1st millennium BCE. when we notice all round development. The political, socio-economic and the religious scenario under goes a complete change. The old order gives way to new order. Gradually, centripetal tendencies take the upper hand as a result states are formed. With the formation of state and the rise of trade and commerce new social and economic classes emerged. Now we start getting larger settlements, use of bricks and evidence of specialized working groups such as pottery workshop, bead manufacturing workshop, trading centers etc. On the excavated sites we start finding a new type of very fine pottery with extraordinary gloss popularly known as

NBP (Northern Black Polished Ware) with circulation in very wide area succeeding the Black Slipped ware in the study area and PGW in Upper Ganga Valley. On account of the cumulative effect of all these changes Urbanisation followed and a number of cities developed.

References

1. Bruce Foote, R.B. 1916. *The Foote Collection* of *Indian Prehistoric and Protohistoric Antiquities, Notes on their Ages and Distribution,* Government Museum, Madras.
2. Cockburn, J.1894 On Flint Implements from the Kon Ravines of South Mirzapur, *JASB,* p.63.
3. Clark and Williams: 1990 : Prehistoric Ecology etc. *Man and Environment* XV (i);13-24).
4. Gopal, Lallanji and V.C. Srivastava (ed.) 2008, *History of Agriculture in India,* vol. V, part-1. PHISPC.
5. Gupta, H.P 1976. Holocene Palynology from meander lake in the Ganga Valley, district of Pratapgarh, U.P *The Paleobotantist* 2 : 109-119.
6. Kennedy, Kenneth A.R. 1984. Biological Adaptations and Affinities of Mesolithic South Asians. In *The People of South Asia,* edited by JR. Lukacs, pp. 29-57. New York: Plenum Press.
7. Kennedy, Kenneth A.R.1986. *Mesolithic Human Remains from the Gangetic Plain: Sarai Nahar Rai.* South Asia Occasional Papers and Thesis No.10, Cornell University.
8. Misra,V.D., Pal, J.N.and Gupta, M.C, 1998; 98-99; 2002-2003; *Prāgdhārā no.* 9, 10, 13.
9. Misra, V.N. and M.S. Mate, 1965. *Indian Prehistory* 1964.
10. Pal, J.N. and Gupta, M.C., 2005, Excavations at Hetapatti : Some Preliminary Obsevationa, *Journal of Inter-discplinary Studies in History and Archaeology,* vol. 2, Number 1 (summer 2005), pp. 163-168.
11. Pandey, J.N. 1985. *Settlement Pattern and life in Mesolithic period in Uttar* Pradesh. Unpublished Ph.D Thesis Allahabad Univerisity Library.
12. Rakesh Tewari *et al.* Middle Palaeolithic Human Activity and Palaeoclimate at Kalpi in Yamuna Valley 2002 *Man and Environment,* XXVII(2)-2002
13. Singh, R.L. (ed) 1971. *India:* A *Regional Geography.* Varanasi: National Geographic Society of India.
14. Saraswat, K.S. 1994, Plant Economy at Ancient Narhan, in *Excavations at Narhan* 1984-89. P. Singh, Varanasi, pp. 254-346.
15. Sharma, G.R. and Mandal, D., 1980, *Excavations at Mahagara,* Department of Ancient History Culture and Archaeology.
16. Sharma, G.R 1973. Mesolithic lake Cultures in the Ganga Valley, India. *Proceedings cf the Prehistoric Society* 39: 129-146.
17. Sharma, G.R 1975. Seasonal Migrations and Mesolithic Lake Cultures of the Ganga Valley. *In Chattopadhyaya memorial volume* G.R Sharma (ed.).
18. Sharma, G.R, V.D. Misra, D. Mandal, B.B. Misra and Pal, J.N. 1980. *Beginning of Agriculture.* Allahabad : Abinash Prakashan.
19. Singh, A.K., 2004 *Excavation at Agiabir (1999-2001) Some Reflections.* Paper read in Workshop on The Archaeology of Middle Ganga Plain.
20. Singh, I.B.2005: Quaternary Palaeoenvironment of Ganga Plain and Anthropogenic Activity, *Man and Environment* 30 (1) : 1-35.
21. Singh, P.,1993 Archaeological excavation at Imlidih khurd,1992; *Prāgdhārā,* 3.
22. ________, *et. al.* Excavation of Imlidih khurd, *Purātattva,* 22
23. ________, Further Excavation at Imlidih khurd-1993 *Prāgdhārā,* 4

24. __________, Neolithic Chalcolithic Culture of Eastern U.P in Rakesh Tewari (ed.) *Archaeological Perspective of Uttar Pradesh and Future Prospects* State Archaeological Organisation, Lucknow, 1992, pp.67–76.
25. Singh, P., 1999 in The Dawn of Indian Civilisation (Ed.) Pandey, G.C.
26. Singh, P. and A.K. Singh (1997-98), Waina (Singh, P. and A.K. Singh 1995-96).
27. S.N. Chaturvedi (1980) Advance of Vindhyan Neolithic and Chalcolithic Cultures to the Himalayan Terai: Excavation and Exploration in Saryupar region of Uttar Pradesh region: *Man and Environment,* IX, pp. 101-108.
28. Tewari, R, R.K. Srivastava (1996-97) Excavation at Raja-nal-ka-tila, Disrtrict Sonbhadra, U.P Preliminary Observation, Prāgdhārā, 6:77-96 and also Tewari, R, R.K. Srivastava (1997-98) Excavation at Raja-nal-ka-tila, Disrtrict Sonbhadra, *Prāgdhārā,* 7, pp.99-106.
29. Tewari, R, R.K. Srivastava, K.S.Saraswat and I.B.Singh 1999-2000. Excavations at Malhar, District Chandauli (U.P.) 1999: A Preliminary Report, *Prāgdhārā* 10: 69-98.
30. Tewari, R, R. K. Srivastava, K.K. Singh, K.S. Saraswat and I.B. Singh, 2002-2003, Preliminary Report of the Excavation at Lahuradeva, District Sant Kabir Nagar,U.P.-2001-2002: Wider Archaeological Implications, *Prāgdhārā,* 13: 37-68.
31. Tewari, R, R.K. Srivastava (1996-97) Excavation at Raja-nal-ka-tila, Disrtrict Sonbhadra, U.P. Preliminary observation, *Prāgdhārā,* 6:77-96 and also Tewari, R, R.K. Srivastava (1997-98) Excavation at Raja-nal-ka-tila,Disrtrict Sonbhadra, *Prāgdhārā,* 7:pp.99-106.
32. Tewari, R., R.K. Srivastava, K.S.Saraswat and I.B.Singh 1999-2000 Excavations at Malhar, District Chandauli (UP) 1999: A Preliminary Report, *Prāgdhārā,* 10: 69-98.
33. Tewari, R, R.K. Srivastava, K.K.Singh, K.S.Saraswat and I.B.Singh, 20022003,Preliminary Report of the Excavation at Lahuradeva, District Sant Kabir Nagar,U.P.-2001-2002: Wider Archaeological Implications, *Prāgdhārā,* 13: 37-68.
34. Tripathi,Vibha 2008, pp. 348-381 in L. Gopal and V.C. Srivastava, 2008, *History of Agriculture in India.*
35. Varma,R.K. 1964 *Stone Age Cultures* of *Mirzapur,* unpublished thesis, University of Allahabad.
36. Varma, R.K. 1981-83. The Mesolithic Culture of India, *Purātattva* No. 13-14.
37. Varma, R.K. 1985a. *Unique couple burials* of *the Ganga Valley.* Paper read at Gauhati Conference *IAS* and *ISPQUS* and in Facets of Indian Civilization (ed.) by J.P. Joshi: 1997, Varma, RK. p. 29-34.
38. Varma, R K.1985., Misra,V.D., Pal J. N. A Preliminary Report of the Excavation at Damdama (1982-84). *Man and Environment IX.*
39. Varma, R.K. 1986. *The Mesolithic Age in Mirzapur.* Allahabad. Paramjyoti Prakashan.
40. Varma, R.K. 1989. Pre Agricultural Mesolithic Society of the Ganga Valley. p. 55-85 in Old Problems and New Perspectives in the Archaeology of South Asia.
41. Varma, R.K.1994 Holocene Adaptation in the Vindhyan Region and the Ganga Valley in *Art and Archaeology in the Vindhyan Region,* Varma, R.K.(ed)1994)
42. Varma, R.K. 1999 *The Emergence* of *Culture in Vindhya Ganga Region* in Pandey,G.C. (ed.) *The Dawn of Indian Civilisation.*
43. Wadia, D.N. 1966. *Geology* of *India* (3rd ed.) London: Macmillan.
44. Williams, M.A.J. and K.Royce 1982. Quaternary Geology of the Middle Son Valley, North Central India: Implication for Prehistoric Archaeology. *Palaeogeography, Palaeoclimatology, Palaeoecology* 8 : 139-62.
45. Wiliiams, M.A.J. and J.N. Pal, M. Jaiswal, A.K. Singhvi. (ed.) *River Response to Quaternary Climatic Fluctuations: Evidence from the Son and Belan Valleys, North-Central India.*
46. Williams, M.A.J. and Clarke, M.F. 1995 Quaternary Geology and Prehistoric Environments in the Son and Belan Valleys, North Central India, in S. Wadia, R. Korisettar and V.S. Kale (eds) *Quaternary Environments and Geoarchaeology* of *India, pp. 282-308,* Bangalore: Geological Society of India.

2

The Middle Ganga Plain: One of the Early Centres of Agriculture and Domestication

J.N. Pal

Allahabad University has been engaged in archaeological pursuits since 1974 mainly in the Vindhyan plateau and the middle Ganga plain. The other institutions engaged in the recovery of past in the area include Archaeology Department of U.P. State, Banaras Hindu University, Gorakhpur University, Patna University, Department of Archaeology, Bihar, Dr. K.P. Jayaswal Research Institute, Patna and Patna Circle of Archaeological Survey of India. A long cultural sequence from Epipalaeolithic to early medieval period has been brought to light in the area. The area has emerged as one of the early centres of agriculture not only in India but also in the world context. We propose to present in this paper the status of research of early farming and domesticating communities of the middle Ganga plain.

The Ganga Plain has played a major role in the origin and development of the history and archaeology of India. Entire Ganga Plain geographically also has been an important feature in Indian sub-continent. It looks a flat alluvial land, marked by rivers originating from the Himalayas, horse-shoe-lakes and rivulets emerging from these lakes and also rivers originating in the Vindhyan plateau in the south. It has a slope from north west to south east. It is divisible into three main units: (i) Upper Ganga Plain, (ii) Middle Ganga Plain, and (iii) Lower Ganga Plain. In recent years the geologists and geographers in their studies have divided it, on the basis of some distinctive geomorphic features, slightly differently (Singh 2004-2005). From north to south it has been divided into: (i)

Piedmont Plain (sloping area close to Himalayas consisting of Bhabhar belt and *Tarai* belt), (ii) Central alluvial plain (It is the major part of the Ganga plain between the Piedmont plain and the Yamuna Ganga rivers in the south) and (iii) Marginal alluvial plain (north sloping area between Yamuna Ganga rivers and Peninsular craton). From west to east it has been divided into (i) Western Ganga Plain (from Delhi-Aravali ridge to Kanpur), (ii) Median Ganga plain (Between Kanpur to Patna) and (iii) Eastern Ganga plain (Between Patna and Bengal plain or Ganga delta region). However, in the archaeological literature the region between Allahabad and Bihar-Bengal border has been termed as the middle Ganga Plain.

The middle Gangetic Plain measuring about 144, 409 sq km, is bounded by the Himalayan *tarai* in the north, Vindhyan plateau in the south, Ganga-Yamuna confluence in the west and Bihar-Bengal border in the east. It includes modern eastern Uttar Pradesh and plain of Bihar. On the basis of the river system, the middle Ganga plain is sub-divided into the Ganga Plain North and Ganga Plain South. The Ganga Plain North is further sub-divisible into (i) the Ganga-Ghaghara *doab*, (ii) the Ghaghara-Gandak interfluve, (iii) Gandak-Kosi interfluve and (iv) Kosi-Mahananda interfluve and the latter, i.e. the Ganga Plain south into (i) West of Karmanasa, (ii) Karmanasa east interfluve, (iii) Lower Son Valley, and finally (iv) the Magadha-Anga Plain (Singh 1971: 190-92). The Ganga has been the lifeline for the people of area under discussion and it has been the cradle of Indian culture right from the terminal Pleistocene period. Geologists believe that the Ganga plain, a peripheral foreland basin came into existence in Early Miocene, expanded in the Middle Miocene and attained its present form in the Late Quaternary. It has a surface cover of Holocene sediments of variable thickness throughout (Singh 1996a, 1996b, 2004, 2004-2005, 2005). The Ganga plain was initially very rich in wild flora and fauna due to favourable climate, but has now to some extent been changed because of deforestation and excessive hunting and cutting of forest primarily due to pressure of human population.

The middle Ganga Plain was a meeting point of different cultures of north, south, east and west. The area, as per Upanishads, had privilege of hearing philosophical discussion of thinkers of ancient period such as Yājñavalkya and others. The land is associated traditionally with the activities of Rāma of Rāmāyana. Similarly, deductive portions of Māhābhārata are supposed to have got their final shape in this region. It was also a nerve centre of the political, economic and religious upheavals of 6th century BCE and witnessed the second urbanization of the subcontinent.

The middle Ganga Plain is now credited with one of the early centres of origin of agriculture and domestication, which paved the way for development of Chalcolithic cultures and civilization in the early Iron Age in the area. The traditional view (Childe 1951) is still popularly held that the adoption of agriculture resulted in the improvement of human health, improvement in the quality and reliability of human food supply and the overall lessening of labour demand in the food quest. The scholars engaged in the study of modern tribes (Binford 1968, Cohen 1977, Flannery 1969, Meyrs 1971) argue that agriculture should be viewed as an economic strategy necessitated by high population density among hunter-gatherers and/or by declining wild resources (Cohen 1984). Though agriculture and domestication facilitated life cf man but it also brought several problems with it. Adoption of intensified utilization and processing of vegetable food sources by Neolithic and later populations permitted increasing population density but led to lower quality nutrition and an increase in certain pathologies (Kennedy 1984).

The existence of human society, despite a large number of inventions for its betterment, is still based mainly on the plant and animal food supplement. In the Palaeolithic period the man was using wild grains, tubers, fruits and leaves along with wild animals in his food. During the Mesolithic period after keen observation to the plantation, growing and riping of the plants in different seasons due to availability of suitable land, moisture and sunlight he came to the conclusion that the plants get germinated in particular season and after some time, if these are able to survive, get ripened and give eatable grains. Mesolithic period in the early Holocene was much conducive for the growth of plants in comparison to that of the Pleistocene period. In the suitable climatic condition for the natural growth of the plants, some plants, vulnerable and useful were selected for domestication. In the human history, introduction of agriculture and plant domestication played the most crucial role. Several other innovative inventions came in existence along with beginning of agriculture. Domestication of animals, manufacturing of pottery, new advancement in technology especially lithic artifacts, permanent settlements, stable structures and formative stages of family and society and rudimentary trade are some of these features attached with.

The man was hunter/forager and food gatherer for major part of the prehistoric times. The close proximity of varied and productive ecosystem – the river basins, hill foots and mountains – encouraged people to practice what is called broad-spectrum gathering. That is, rather than constantly traveling in search of food, people stayed put and exploited the various seasonal sources of food, fish, wild grains, fruits and game. Around 10,000 BCE many hunter-gatherers living in transitional zones of hills and plains began to develop specialized strategies that led, possibly by accident, to a transformation in human culture. The transition from hunting and food gathering to a food producing economy had a far-reaching impact on the course of human history. The evidence of such transition in India is found in the Mesolithic cultures, which suggests that the agriculture and domestication was a slow developmental process, extending across several millennia but it had a revolutionary effect on human history. The evidence of wild rice, millet, jujube, etc. from excavations of the Mesolithic sites and scenes of plants in the rock paintings in the hilly regions indicate that the plant food was included in the Mesolithic diet. A good number of grinding stones from many of the sites also suggest that the wild grains were pasted for consumption (Misra 2002, 2007-2008).

The natural vegetation has not changed much during the last ten millennia except due to pressure of population and industrialization in the later part of the last century; there was delimitation in vegetation cover. If we accept that the change in climate was not a local phenomenon and see the evidence of Rajasthan, as suggested by G. Singh and his associates, the beginning of Holocene was moist for about 500 years and again another moist phase was between 3000 B.C. and 2000 B.C. (Meher-Homji 1980: 5). The archaeologists generally believe that the climatic amelioration along with technological advancement during the early Holocene resulted in the population increase in early Holocene period (Misra 1989). The climate was becoming adverse when the moist phase was over and man was forced to produce food by farming and domestication.

The changing climatic conditions during early and middle phases of Holocene in the middle Ganga plain played a significant role in the evolution of early farming cultures. The Gangetic Plain was for the first time colonized by the Stone Age Man of the Vindhyas. Continuous cultural sequence from Neolithic/Chalcolithic to medieval period is represented at most of the archaeological sites of the area (**Fig. 1**). Right from the earliest phase, i.e. Epiplaeolithic and Mesolithic, both the regions, Vindhyas and the Ganga Plain, have been in close cultural contacts. Recent excavations have thrown new light on the early farming culture of the area.

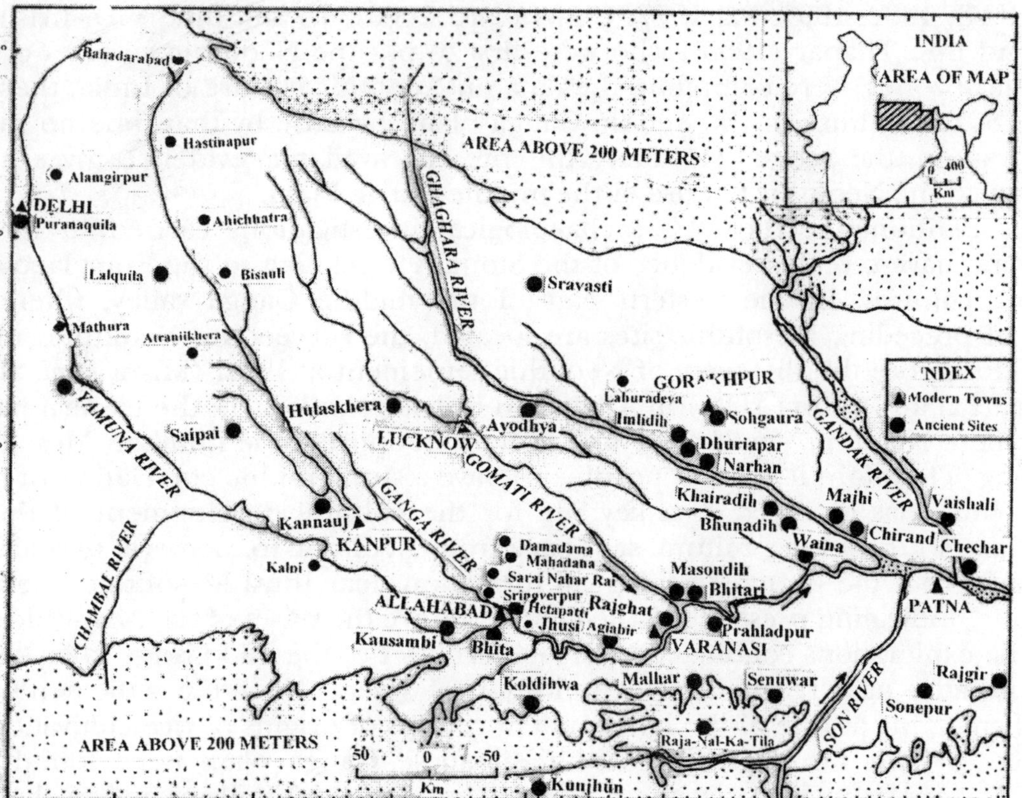

Fig. 1 : Main Archaeological sites in the Ganga Plain and Neighbouring Vindhyas

The hunter gatherers of Epipalaeolithic and Mesolithic period were living close to small rivers and horseshoe lakes and must be using large amount of plant food as it was easily available in plenty. In the Sanai Tal sequence, the evidence of anthropogenic pollens and micro charcoal indicating some kind of intervention in vegetation by the humans since 15 kyrs BP has been obtained (Sharma *et al.* 2001). The change of hunter gatherer economy to agriculture was a result of series of developments in the human behavior, climate change and vegetation change over a long period of time (Singh 2004-2005: 23). Early to mid Holocene climatic optimum (~10,000-5800 C^{14} yr BP) is characterized by a lake environment indicating a sensitive response of the lake ecology to the climatic warming and increased rainfall. Then comes an arid event during 5000-2000 C^{14} yr BP and from ~1700 ^{14}C yr BP there is evidence of climatic amelioration (Sharma *et al.* 2004).

The archaeology of the Gangetic Plain especially the middle Gangetic Plain is getting much attention of scholars. The studies of the bioarchaeology of the Mesolithic culture of the middle Gangetic Plain have been conducted in much detail and national and international seminars/colloquium have been conducted in view of their importance (Misra and Pal 2002; Afanas'ev *et al.* 1996). The study of the Neolithic culture of the Gangetic Plain is also getting its due importance in archaeological literature of India.

The scholars who made concerted efforts to group the Neolithic culture of India in geographical units have put the Neolithic culture of this region in a separate geographic unit (Singh 2002; Thapar 1984; Agrawal and Kharakwal 2002; Allchin and Allchin 1968, 1982, 1997; Pal 1977; Chakrabarti 2006). By the time V.D. Krishnaswami (1965) and B.K. Thapar (1965), who were first to put the Neolithic cultures of India in geographical zones, were compiling the data on Neolithic culture of India, there was no evidence of this culture in the middle Ganga plain, because by that time no site of this culture was on the scene. However, the present available evidence gives a distinct personality to the Neolithic culture of the middle Ganga Plain.

As mentioned earlier the archaeological investigations carried in the middle Ganga Plain have revealed evidence of the Stone Age relating to the Epipalaeolithic and Mesolithic cultures. In the western part of the middle Ganga valley, where a good number of preceding Mesolithic sites are located, the succeeding Neolithic culture was not present before the discovery of Neolithic settlement at Jhusi (Misra *et al.* 2004) and Hetapatti (Pal and Gupta 2005) in Allahabad district; similarly in the eastern part of the region, where Neolithic sites have come to light in appreciable number, Mesolithic sites are missing. Therefore it was not possible to have a stratigraphic correlation of these two cultures. Jhusi has emerged as a key site for the cultural development of the middle Ganga Plain, where a long cultural sequence from Neolithic to medieval period has been unearthed. From the topmost geological formation near Jhusi Mesolithic artefacts have been found, indicating presence of the culture before the onset of the Neolithic culture.

The explorations conducted in the eastern part of the mid Ganga valley during the last five decades have resulted in identification of several Neolithic settlements, and the region is emerging as one of the independent centres of origins of rice cultivation. Earlier the traces of early farming culture in the middle Ganga plain were found in three geographical zones; in Bihar, in the northern slopes of the Vindhyas and in the Saryupar plains of eastern Uttar Pradesh (Singh 1998). Primary context sites pertaining to the Neolithic culture have been reported in eastern Uttar Pradesh and Bihar. The important excavated sites in Uttar Pradesh include Jhusi (Misra *et al.* 2002-2003) and Hetapatti (Pal and Gupta 2005) in Allahabad, Bhunadih (Singh and Singh 1997-98) and Waina (Singh and Singh 1995-96) in Ballia (Singh *et al.* 1994-95), Sohgaura (*IAR 1974-75*: 46-47, Chaturvedi 1985) and Imlidih Khurd (Singh 1992-93, 1993-94) in Gorakhpur, Lahuradewa (Tewari *et al.* 2001-2002, 2002-2003, 2004-2005, 2007-2008) in Sant Kabirnagar district, while Chirand (*IAR 1981-82*: 13-14,Verma 1971, Narain 1970, Varma 1998, Sinha 1994, Roy 1989) in Saran, Chechar Kutubpur (*IAR 1977-78*: 17-18) in Vaisali, Pran (Dr. Bijoy Kumar Chaudhary: personal communication), Taradih (*IAR 1984-85*: 9-10, *IAR 1986-87*: 23-24, *IAR 1987-88*: 9-11) in Gaya, Maner (*IAR 1985-86*: 11-12, *1986-87*: 25-26, *IAR 1987-88*: 11-12, *IAR 1988-89*: 7-8) in Patna and Senuwar (Singh 1990, 1997, 2001, 2004) in Rohtas district in Bihar. Most of these excavated sites are multi-culture sites having yielded archaeological relics ranging from Neolithic to early historical periods (Misra 2007).

Table 2.1 : Neolithic Sites in the Middle Ganga Plain

Name of the Site	*Location*	*Excavated by*	*Thickness*	*Reference*
Jhusi (Lat. 25^0 26' 10"N ;Long. 81^0 54' 30"E)	Allahabad, U.P., on the confluence of the Ganga and Yamuna	University of Allahabad	1.5 m	Misra *et al.* 2002-03
Hetapatti (Lat. 25^0 29' 0" N ;Long. 81^0 55' 31" E)	Allahabad, U.P., on the left bank of the Ganga	University of Allahabad	60 cm	Pal and Gupta 2005
Bhunadih (Lat. 25^0 19' 10"N ;Long. 84^0 5' 11"E)	Ballia, U.P., on the right bank of Bahera nala, a tributary of Ghaghara	Banaras Hindu University	About 50 cm	Singh and Singh 1997-98
Waina (Lat. 25^0 45' 5"N ;Long. 84^0 0' 5"E)	Ballia, U.P. on the left bank of old bed of Chhoti Sarju (Tons), a tributary of the Ganga	Banaras Hindu University	About 40 cm	Singh and Singh 1995-96
Lahuradewa (Lat. 26^0 46'N ;Long. 82^0 57'E)	Sant Kabir Nagar, U.P. on a horseshoe lake	State Archaeology, U.P.	45 cm	Tewari *et al.* 2002-2003
Sohgaura (Lat. 26^0 30' 30"N ;Long. 83^0 15' 25"E)	Gorakhpur, U.P., on the confluence of Ami and Rapti	Gorakhpur University	60 cm	Chaturvedi 1985
Imlidih (Lat. 26^0 30' 30" N ;Long. 83^0 12' 5" E)	Gorakhpur, U.P., on the left bank of the Kuwana river, a tributary of the Ghaghara	Banaras Hindu University	50-60 cm	Singh 1992-93
Chirand (Lat. 25^0 45'N ;Long. 84^0 50'E)	Saran, Bihar, on the confluence of the Ghaghara and Ganga	State Archaeology, Bihar and Patna University	3.5 m	S.R. Roy 1989
Chechar-Kutubpur (Lat. 25^0 30' 10"N ;Long. 85^0 30' 45"E)	Vaishali, Bihar, on the left bank of the Ganga	ASI, Patna Circle		*IAR 1977-78*: 17-18
Taradih (Lat. 24^0 42'N ;Long. 85^0 0'E)	Gaya, Bihar, South-west of Mahabodhi temple	State Archaeology, Bihar	70 cm	*IAR 1984-85*: 9-10, *IAR 1986-87*: 23-24, *IAR 1987-88*: 9-11
Maner (Lat. 25^0 30' 45"N ;Long. 84^0 45' 25"E)	Patna, Bihar, on the bank of the Ganga	Patna University	3.45	*IAR 1985-86*: 11-12, *1986-87*: 25-26, *IAR 1987-88*: 11-12, *IAR 1988-89*: 7-8
Senuwar (Lat. 24^0 56 N';Long. 83^0 56'E)	Rohtas, Bihar, Right bank of Kudra river	Banaras Hindu University	1.50 m	*IAR 1986-87*: 26-28
Pran	Sanmastipur Bihar	Dr. K.P. Jayaswal Research Institute		*Bijoy Kumar Chaudhary: Personal communication*

Excavations conducted at Chirand, Senuwar, Imlidih Khurd, Lahuradewa and Jhusi have thrown welcome light on the corpus of cereals having been cultivated by the Neolithic people of the mid Ganga Plain (Pal 2008, Gupta *et al.* 2008, Pokharia *et al.* 2009).

Regarding the settlement pattern it may be mentioned that all the excavated sites are located on the banks of rivers, generally on the confluence of two rivers, near meander above the flood plain or on horse-shoe lakes as in the case of Lahuradewa. The archaeological deposits are resting on the geological formations. The geological formations at Jhusi and Hetapatti just below the archaeological occupation deposits measure 15 and 10 m respectively. Easy availability of water, cultivable land and also easy availability of food in the form of suitable vegetation, animals and aquatic creatures was the prime consideration for selecting a site for settlement.

The Neolithic horizon at most of the sites lying below a thick deposit of later period could not be excavated on a large scale. However, the limited scale excavations have brought to light evidence of circular or oval huts from almost all excavated sites of the area. Wattle and daub structure is attested by good number of burnt clay lumps with bamboo and reed impression. The hut floors encircled by postholes are marked by potsherds, food processing equipments, microliths, bone tools and other artefacts of daily use. At Chirand, the evidence of pit dwelling has also been reported. Of the other structural remains, mention may be made of hearths, pits and silo probably for storing the grains. A well plastered burnt floor enclosed by two parallel walls at Jhusi was possibly used also for cooking food and firing the pottery.

That the Neolithic people of the Ganga valley as those of the Vindhyas were farming and pastoral communities, is attested by the cultivated variety of rice, barley, wheat, field pea, lentil, green gram, etc. recovered from the excavated sites. However, the botanical evidence obtained from Senuwar and Jhusi in mid Ganga valley read with its counter part of Tokwa in the Vindhyas suggests that in the early phase only rice and some primitive millets were being cultivated (Misra 2007, Harvey *et al.* 2005). With the passage of time, other cereals were also added. The Neolithic deposit at Senuwar (Singh 2001: 109-118) is divided into two subgroups 1A and 1B. From the lowest part of the middle of period IA only grains of cultivated rice, (*Oryza sativa*) were found along with wild plants like jobs tear, fox tail/bandra, wild rice, *jharberi, chaulai* and wild *palaka.* But in the later phase of IA new cereals like barley, wheat, *jowar* millet, lentil, field pea, finger millet (*ragi*) and *khesari* were introduced (Saraswat 2003). The available evidence shows that by the late phase of Neolithic culture in the mid Ganga valley, double crop pattern had become a regular feature. However, it may be mentioned that cereals of the winter and rainy crops including rice (*Oryza sativa*) six-rowed hulled barley (*Hordeum vulgare*), bread wheat (*Triticum aestivum*), dwarf wheat (*Triticum sphaerococcum*), lentil (*Lens culinaris*), field pea (*Pisum arvense*), grass pea (*Lathyrus sativus*), Horse gram (*Macrotyloma uniflorum*), green gram (*Vigna radiata*), (*Sesamum indicum*), linseed (*Linum usitatssimum*), etc. have been reported from the early levels of Jhusi (Pokharia *et al.* 2009).

Domesticated animals include cattle (*Bos indicus*), buffalo (*Bubalus bubalis*), sheep, goat and pigs. Domesticated pig has been found from Senuwar. Domesticated mammals that were not included in food are dog and cat. Besides these, the bones of elephants, rhinoceros, stag, deer, etc. have also been found from some of the sites. Of aquatic fauna whose bones have been found, mention may be made of fish and turtle. Bones of birds have also been found. That the meat was part of their diet, is attested by charred bone fragments and bones with sharp cut mark (Joglekar *et al.* 2008). The available evidence, thus, indicates that besides agriculture and domestication the Neolithic people of the mid Ganga Plain also practiced hunting, catching and fishing.

The Neolithic culture of the Gangetic Plain is marked by a rich and varied ceramic industry. The available evidence indicates that in the early stage of the culture, as indicated at Chirand, Lahuradewa, Jhusi and Hetapatti, people were using hand made pottery but subsequently the slow wheel appears to have been used for the purpose. The ceramic assemblage includes cord impressed ware, ordinary red ware, lustrous red ware, burnished ware (red, black and grey), rusticated ware and crude black-and-red ware and. The clay used for manufacturing the pots is not well levigated. It contains grits, husks and chaff as degraissant. Pots are generally ill fired and have blackish grey core. Pottery types including bowls with varying profile, vases, vessels, basins, miniature jars, *handis*, etc. suggest that these were used for storing, cooking and also as kitchen wares (Figs. 2-5). A large number of vases with rustication and soot mark on outer surface indicate that these were for cooking, possibly for boiling rice. Bowls, basins and vases also have sometimes spouts, suggesting consumption of liquid or semi-liquid food. The cord-impressed pottery is a distinguishing feature. Some times rustication or burnishing is done on the cord impressed surface. A variety of pattern in cording has been found at Jhusi **(Plate I)** and Hetapatti. Some of the pots, generally vases, were made in two parts separately - the body and the rim portion and subsequently these were luted together. Spouts were also luted to the bowls or basins after making them separately. Painted sherds have been reported from Imlidih Khurd, Lahuradewa, Chirand and Senuwar. The post firing paintings in red ochre confined to the rim of pots were found at Chirand and Senuwar. The painting motifs consist of linear designs of criss-cross lines and concentric circles. At Imlidih Khurd painting executed in white red pigment over a bright slip has been reported. Post firing scratch designs, consisting of generally geometric patterns like opposed triangles within concentric circles and floral motifs is another feature of decorating the pots. Scratching is done by sharp instrument. AppliquÈ decorations especially on the shoulder of basins or *handis* also have been found at many sites. On these appliquÈ are executed with chain and rope patterns or incised decorations. Wheel-thrown pots are also reported from the late Neolithic phase of some of the sites like Senuwar.

The rice cultivation and cord impressed pottery are interlinked to each other, having greater antiquity in the Neolithic in a wide area. The cord impressed ware associated with the Neolithic culture (rice cultivation) has been found in south eastern coastal China, in the Yangtze valley, southern China, Japan, Indo China, Gangetic Plain, Vindhyas, eastern and northeastern India and in the Himalayas. It has been suggested that the central position of rice in cultures through out southern and eastern Asia has great antiquity, reflecting both the nutritional value of rice and its long history of cultivation and on the basis of cord impressed ware, early dates for rice cultivation in different regions. Linguistic data and similarity of agricultural rites, rituals and festivals and deep respect for rice all point out remote antiquity in India and strong inter-links among China, Japan and India (Khrakwal *et al.* 2004). There are large number of rituals and festivals associated with rice in these early rice growing regions and several among them are common or analogous (Kharakwal and Yano 2007).

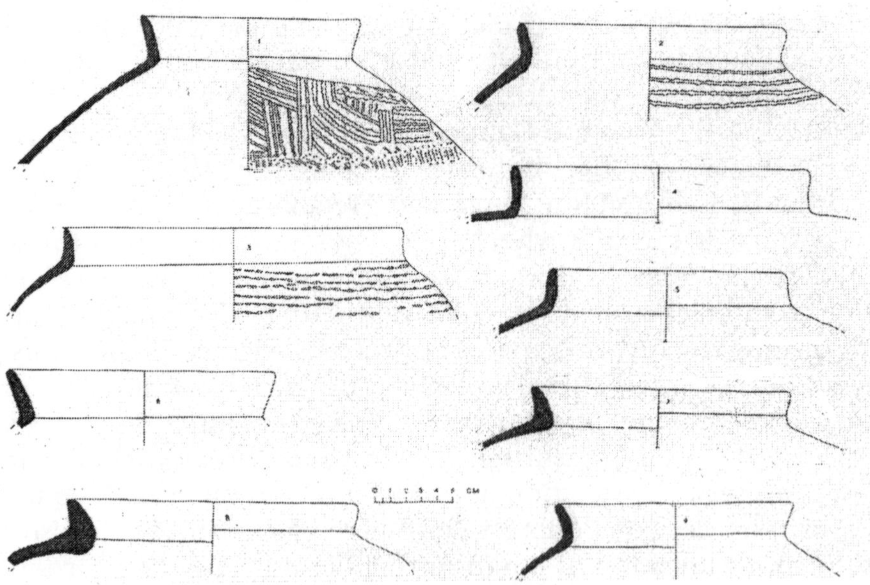

Fig. 2 : Pottery Types, Jars, Jhusi

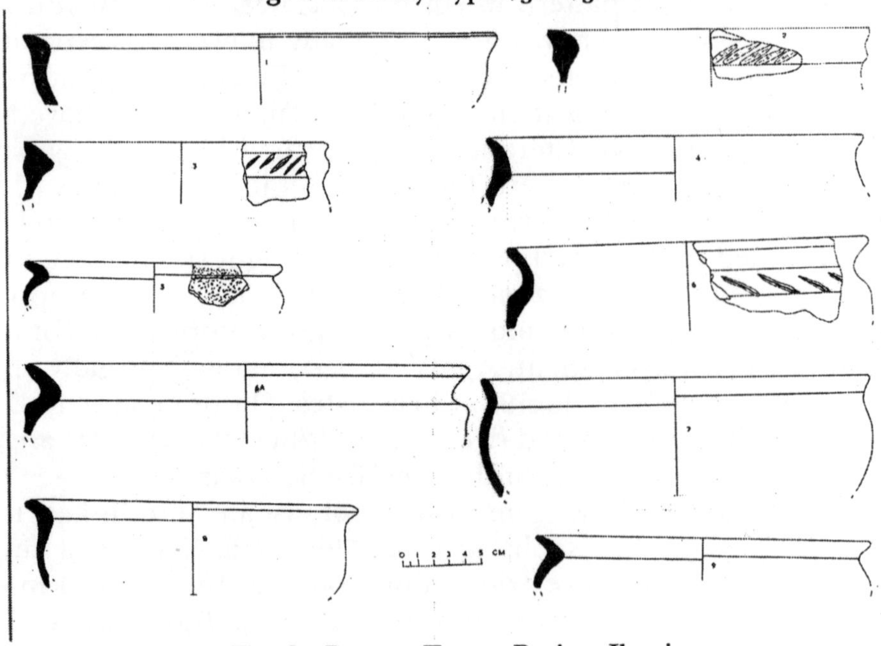

Fig. 3 : Pottery Types, Basins, Jhusi

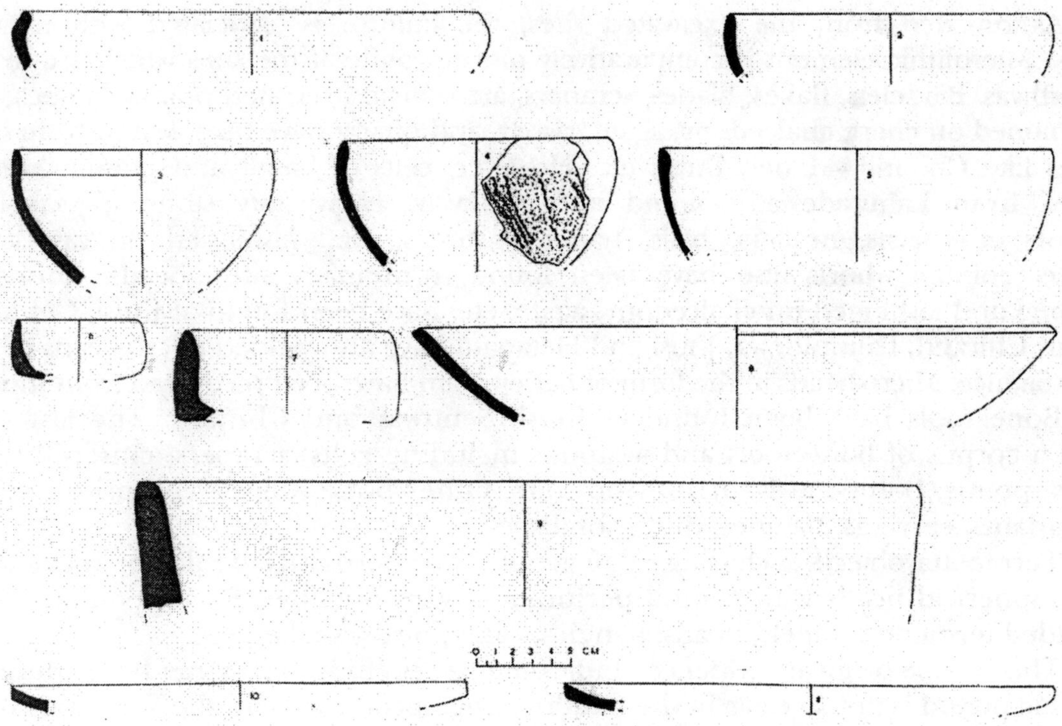

Fig. 4 : Pottery Types, Spouted Basins and Spouts, Jhusi

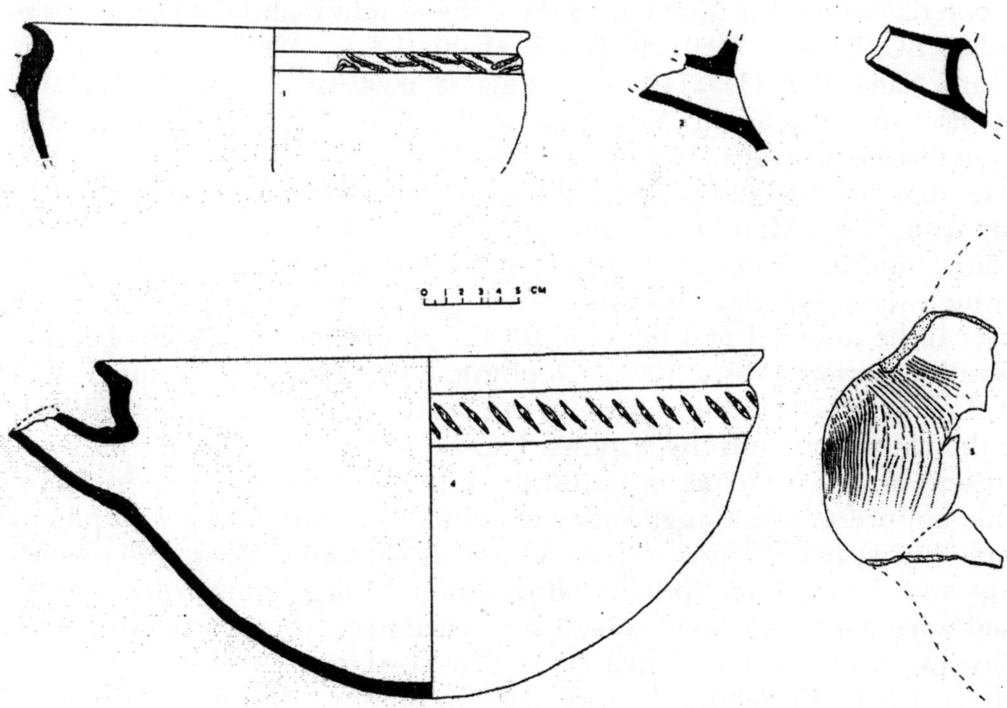

Fig. 5 : Pottery Types, Bowls and Platters, Jhusi

As revealed from the excavated sites, the culture is associated with microlithic industry. Microlithic element is comparatively more prolific at the sites which are nearer to the Vindhyas. Bladelets, flakes, blades, scrapers, arrowheads, serrated points, lunates, borers, etc. fashioned on chert, chalcedony, agate, jasper, and quartz have been found from some of the sites like Chirand, Maner, Jhusi, etc. However, celts of basalt and granite have been obtained from Lahuradewa, Chirand and Senuwar. Heavy-duty stone objects include fragments of querns, mullers, balls, hammer stones, etc., fashioned on sandstone or quartzite. Spindle whorls also have been found from many sites. Beads, finished and unfinished and fashioned on chalcedony, agate, etc. have been found at Jhusi, Chirand and Senuwar. Chirand, Lahuradewa, Jhusi and Hetapatti have also yielded micro-beads of steatite and/or faience. Micro-beads in the form of barley grain have been recovered from Jhusi.

Bone tools have been found at Jhusi, Senuwar and Chirand. The last site has yielded a corpus of bone tools and weapons including celts, scrapers, chisels, hammers, needles, points, borers, awls, arrowheads, etc. Other bone objects comprise ornaments like pendants, earrings, bangles, discs, combs, etc.

Terracotta objects including edge ground potsherds (triangular or rectangular in shape), spherical beads with central perforation were obtained from Senuwar. Chirand has yielded terracotta wheels, beads, bangles, cakes, birds, snakes, etc.

The archaeological evidence indicating a prelude to agriculture during the Mesolithic period is not so clear in the middle Ganga plain as it is in the Vindhyas. With the evidence of hutments, food processing equipments, wild animals and wild grains (rice), microlithic tools, bone and ceramic industries, it can be concluded, that the base for the Neolithic culture was being prepared in the Vindhyas during Mesolithic period. Radiocarbon dates from the Mesolithic sites of the Vindhyas and the Ganga Plain are Baghor II: 6380±220 BC; Paisara: 7420±110 BC; Lekhahia RS I: 6420±75 BC (AMS), 6050±75 BC (AMS); Sarai Nahar Rai: 8395±110 BC; Damdama: 6690±65 BC (AMS), 6915±65 BC (AMS), which confirm that Mesolithic culture was on the scene before the advent of the Neolithic culture, but there is no evidence of stratigraphic contact between the two cultures.

The first farming and pastoral culture of the Vindhyas is the Neolithic culture. As revealed from the Mesolithic culture of the area, hutments, food processing equipments, microliths, bone tools, ceramic industries and wild animals and wild grains, which were domesticated/cultivated and utilized subsequently in the Neolithic period, it can be inferred that the base for the Neolithic culture was being prepared in the Mesolithic period (Misra 2002). Neolithic culture of the Vindhyas is also credited with developing the Neolithic culture in the Gangetic Plain as indicated by comparative study of the culture of both the regions. The excavated sites of the Vindhyas and Ganga Plain present ample evidence of cultural contact of both the regions. The preceding Mesolithic culture of the Ganga valley contains food-processing equipments made on sand stone/quartzite but no pottery, where as in the Vindhyas it is associated with hutments and hand made pottery also. Among the ceramic industries, the cord-impressed ware has much archaeological importance as it denotes the cultural contact of Vindhyas with that of the Ganga Plain. The cord-impressed ware has been found in Neolithic context at Chirand, Chechar Kutubpur, Maner, Taradih, Sohagaura, Lahuradewa, Jhusi and Hetapatti in the middle Gangetic Plain that has techno-typological similarity with that of the Vindhyas. The evidence suggests that the Neolithic pottery of the middle Gangetic Plain has a considerable influence of the Vindhyan Neolithic pottery. It is suggested that the Neolithic culture of the Ganga Plain owes to the Vindhyan Neolithic for its origin.

The problem of the antiquity of the Neolithic culture of the region is still not finally settled but now we have some relevant C^{14} dates from the excavated Neolithic sites of the Vindhyas and Ganga Plain. Considering three of C^{14} dates reading 4530±185 BC (PRL 101), 5440±240 BC (PRL 100) and 6570±210 BC (PRL 224) obtained from Koldihwa as dependable, the culture was dated to the 7th-6th millennium BCE (Sharma *et al.* 1980). But being the only site of such antiquity doubts were raised by several scholars. The C^{14} date belonging to the transitional phase of the Neolithic to Chalcolithic at Koldihwa is 1440±120 BC (PRL 223). The absolute dates obtained from Mahagara also indicated a late date to the culture, though these dates have the possibility of contamination of samples. Two TL dates reading 2265 BC and 1616 BC and four C^{14} dates reading 1440±150 BC (PRL 409), 1330±120 BC (PRL 408), 1440±100 BC (PRL 407) and 1480±110 BC (BSIP) have been obtained from the samples from Mahagara. These dates are not consistent with the stratigraphy possibly due to contamination of samples. In the light of calibrated C^{14} date obtained from Kunjhun, reading 3530-3335, the beginning of the Vindhyan Neolithic culture was proposed to 4th millennium BCE. (Clark and Khanna 1989). Three C^{14} dates have come to light from recent excavations at Lahuradewa in the middle Gangetic Plain, which read as 5320 ̃90 BP (BS 1951) (cal B.C. 4220, 4196, 4161) and 6290±160 BP (BS 1966) (cal BC 5298) (Tewari *et al.* 2001-2002, 2002-2003). Recently three relevant C^{14} dates have been obtained from Tokwa. When calibrated these read 6591 BC (BS - 2417), 5976 BC (BS - 2369), 4797 BC (BS – 2464). An AMS C^{14} date for a carbonized domesticated rice would push the antiquity of the Neolithic culture at Lahuradewa in 7th millennium BCE (Tewari *et.al.* 2004-2005: 40). From the Neolithic horizon of Jhusi three C^{14} dates have been obtained. These dates when calibrated, read 7477 BC (BS – 2526), 5837 BC (BS – 2524) and 6196 BC (BS – 2525). The earliest date obtained from the site would put the beginning of the Neolithic culture of the site in 8th millennium BCE.

Table 2.2 : Early C^{14} Dates from Neolithic Sites

Site	*Calibrated C^{14} dates*	*Remark*
Koldihwa	4530±185 BC = 5432 – 5051 BC, 5440±240 BC = 6190 – 5764 BC, 6570±210 BC = 7505 – 7033 BC (Chakrabarti 2006: 216)	On the Belan in the Vindhyas
Tokwa	4797 BC, 5976 BC, 6407 BC	On the confluence of the Belan and Adwa in the Vindhyas
Kunjhun	1565 BC, 2675 BC, 3530 BC	On the right bank of the Son in the Vindhyas
Lahuradewa	4220 BC, 5298 BC, An AMS date 6442-6376 (mid 7th millennium BC); three more new and early radiocarbon dates from Lahuadewa are: 8317 – 8555 (8436), 8340 – 8696 (8518), 8813 – 9171 (8992)	On the bank of a horseshoe lake in the mid Ganga Plain
Jhusi	7110 BC, 5649 BC, 5938 BC, later half of 8th millennium BCE.	On the confluence of the Ganga and Yamuna

Regarding the span of the Neolithic culture, observations of P. Singh are very significant, 'domestication was a process which took considerable time and domestication of each type of domesticable animal and plant species would have taken place in different ecological niches at different times' (Singh 1991:5, Singh 2002: 128). In the Ganga Plain Neolithic culture and Neolithic way of life lasted for a long time starting from 8th -7th millennium BCE to 3rd -2nd millennium BCE.

The combined testimony of the available C^{14} dates obtained from Koldihwa, and Tokwa in the Vindhyas and Jhusi and Lahuradewa in the middle Ganga Plain would push the antiquity of the Neolithic culture in the northern Vindhyas and the middle Ganga Plain to a hoary past. The antiquity of the early farming culture of the Gangetic Plain on the basis of these dates may be pushed back to the later half of 8th millennium BCE and almost same antiquity may be proposed for the Neolithic culture of the Vindhyas.

To conclude, the discovery as a result of excavations at the Mesolithic sites of Sarai Nahar Rai, Mahadaha and Damdama in the Gangetic Plain by the Department of Ancient History, Culture and Archaeology, University of Allahabad in the sixth, seventh and eighth decades of the last century presented a surprise because Stone Age culture sites of the Mesolithic phase were located in an area totally free of hills - the source of stone supply. Indications of the Mesolithic culture were available from more than 200 sites in the mid-Ganga Plain (Sharma *et al.* 1980) but Neolithic was conspicuous by its absence in this area. It was, therefore, surmised that there was a cultural break after the Mesolithic in this region and settlers of the Chalcolithic phase at Jhusi and other sites probably were not native to this region. But the current excavations at Jhusi have succeeded in discovering below the Chalcolithic phase nearly 1.5 meter thick Neolithic deposit. This excavation is significant because it presents the proof of cultural continuity in an unbroken sequence right from the Mesolithic through the Neolithic to the Chalcolithic which again continued in an unbroken sequence into the historical period down to the time of the Buddha and, further on, up to the early medieval period. In this way, it is an epoch-making discovery, as it has taken the antiquity of the region in an unbroken manner to the Mesolithic times.

The archaeological evidence shows that the Gangetic Plain owed to the Vindhyas not only for its first colonization in the Mesolithic period but, as evident by very close affinity in the ceramic industries, microlithic component, food processing equipments, bone tools, beads and settlement pattern revealed from the excavations at Tokwa and other sites in the Vindhyas and Jhusi and other sites in the middle Gangetic Plain, it can be concluded that both the regions are intimately related to each other for the origin and development of Neolithic culture. The C^{14} dates from recent excavations at Jhusi and Lahuradewa in the middle Ganga Plain and Tokwa in the Vindhyas suggest that this region was one of the early centers of agriculture in the world. The evidence of barley (*Hardeum vulgare*), bread wheat (*Triticum aestivum*) and other winter crops along with summer crop like rice (*Oryza sativa*), etc. from early levels of Neolithic Jhusi (Pokharia and Pal) indicates that the area was in cultural contact with the original home of winter crops right from the early phase of the Neolithic culture. It may be mentioned that in still nearer region, the Himalayan *tarai,* still has some wild barley species. The wild ancestor of the six rowed barley (*Hardeum hexastichum*) is found in eastern Tibet (Randhawa 1980: 104). We can not altogether deny that the the Ganga Plain was not suitable area for the growth of barley and wheat in wild form. There is still possibility that the barley and wheat were present in the area in wild form and were included in the agriculture indigenously.

Recent excavations of the early farming culture sites in the Gangetic Plain have revealed interesting evidence of a center of early origin of agriculture in India. The excavations at Lahuradewa in Sant Kabir Nagar district and at Jhusi in Allahabad district have revealed a Neolithic culture characterized by mostly handmade ceramic industry, bone tools, beads of semi-precious stone, micro disc-beads of steatite, circular hut floors, cultivated and wild cereals and domesticated and wild animal bones. The comparative study of the culture with that of the Vindhyas indicates that its origin lies in the Vindhyan Neolithic culture. The early chronology indicates that it was one of the early centres of origin of agriculture.

The ancient Indian literature has a great deal of reference regarding agriculture and plant domestication (Chopra et al. 1974: 119, Lal 1980). The agricultural process from the preparation of land for sowing to the ripening and reaping of crops followed by the storage of grains are described in detail in literature like Patanjali's *Mahābhāṣhya, Milindpañha,* etc. The *Jātakas* refer to places like Gandhāra, Vārānasī, Śrāvastī and Magadha as rice growing areas. The cereals and pulses like rice, barley, *urad, ragi, sanwa, til,* etc., traditionally used in rituals may be included among the indigenous ancient crops of India possibly having their antiquity to the Neolithic period.

Select Bibliography

Afanas'ev, Gennadii E., Serge Cleuziou, John R. Lukacs, Maurizio Tosi (Eds.) 1996. *Bioarchaeology of Mesolithic India: an Integrated Approach, Colloquium XXXIII, The Prehistory of Asia and Ocenia,* International Union of Prehistoric and Protohistoric Sciences, Forli, Italy.

Agrawal, D.P. and J.S. Kharakwal 2002. *South Aasian Prehistory: A Multidisciplinary Study.* New Delhi: Aryan Books International.

Allchin, B. and R. Allchin 1968. *Birth of Indian Civilization.* Harmondsworth: Penguin Books.

Allchin, B. and R. Allchin 1982. *The Rise of Civilization in India and Pakistan.* Cambridge: University Press.

Allchin, B. and R. Allchin 1997. *Origins of a Civilization: The Prehistory and Early archaeology of South Asia.* New Delhi: Viking Penguin India.

Binford, Lewis 1968. Post-Pleistocene Adaptations. In *New Perspectives in Archaeology.* S.R. Binford and L.R. Binford (Eds.) pp. 313-41. Chicago: Aldine.

Chakrabarti, D.K. 2006. *The Oxford Companion to Indian Archaeology: The Archaeological Foundations of Ancient India.* New Delhi: Oxford University Press.

Chaturvedi, S.N. 1985. Advance of Vindhyan Neolithic and Chalcolithic Cultures to the Himalayan Tarai: Excavation and Explorations in the Sarayupar Region of Uttar Pradesh. *Man and Environment* 9: 101-108.

Child V.G. 1951. *Man Makes Himself.* New York: Mentor.

Chopra, P.N., B.N. Puri, M.N. Das 1974. *A Social and Economic History of India.* Delhi: Macmilan India.

Clark, J. Desmond and Gurucharan S. Khanna, 1989. The Site of Kunjhun II, Middle Son Valley, and its Relevance for the Neolithic of Central India. In *Old Problems and New Perspectives in the Archaeology of South Asia.* Wisconsin Archaeological Reports Vol. 2. J.M. Kenoyer (Ed.), pp. 29-46. Madison: Department of Anthropology, University of Wisconsin.

Cohen M.N. 1977. *The Food Crisis in Prehistory.* New Haven: Yale University Press.

Cohen M.N. 1984. An Introduction to Symposium. In *Palaeopathology at the Origins of Agriculture.* Mark Nathan Cohen and George J. Armelagos (Eds.) pp. 1 ff. Orlando, Florida: Academic Press.

Flannery K.V. 1969. Origins and Ecological Effects of Early Agriculture. In *Domestication and Exploitation of Plants and Animals.* P.J. Ucko and G.W. Dimbleby (Eds.) pp. 73-100. London: Duckworth.

Gupta, M.C., J.N. Pal and V.D. Misra 2008. Beginnings of Agriculture in the Middle Ganga Plain with Special Reference to Recent Excavations at Jhusi. In *History of Science, Philosophy and Culture in Indian Civilization* (General Ed. D.P. Chattopadhyaya) Volume V Part I, *History of Agriculture in India (upto c. 1200 AD).* Lallanji Gopal and V.C. Srivastava (Eds.), pp. 87-99, New Delhi: Concept Publishing Company.

Harvey, E.L., D. Fuller, J.N. Pal and M.C. Gupta 2005. Early Agriculture of the Neolithic Vindhyas (North-Central India). *South Asian Archaeology* 2003 Ute Franke Vógt and Hans-Joachim Weisshaar (Eds.), pp. 329-334. Aachen: Linden Soft Verlog e.k.

Joglekar, P.P., J.N. Pal, V.D. Misra and M.C. Gupta 2008. Faunal Remains Recovered from the Neolithic Phase at Jhusi, District Allahabad, Uttar Pradesh. *Puratattva* 38: 251-259.

Kennedy, K.A.R. 1984. Growth, Nutrition and Pathology in Changing Palaeodemographic Settings in South Asia. In *Palaeopathology at the Origins of Agriculture.* Mark Nathan Cohen, George J. Armelagos (Eds.) pp. 169-192. Orlando , Florida: Academic Press.

Kharakwal, J.S. and A. Yano 2007. Rice Cultivation: Associated Rituals and Festivals with Special Reference to Central Himalayas. In *Traditional Knowledge System and Archaeology with Special Reference to Uttarakhand.* D.P. Agrawal, Manikant Shah Sameer Jamal (Eds.), pp. 83-99. New Delhi: Aryan Books International.

Kharakwal, J.S., A. Yano, Y. Yasuda, V.S. Shinde, and T. Osanda 2004. Cord Impressed Ware and Rice Cultivation in South Asia, China and Japan: Possibilities of Inter-links. *Quaternary International* 123-125: 105-115.

Krishnaswami, V.D. 1965. Neolithic Pattern in India. *Ancient India* 16: 25-64.

Lal, A. 1980. *Prachin Bharat men Krishi (Prarambhik Kal Se 650 Isvi Tak).* Varanasi: Siddhartha Prakashan.

Meher-Homji, V.M. 1980. The Thar Desert: Its Climatic History. *Man and Environment* 4: 1-7.

Meyrs J.T. 1971. The Origins of Agriculture: An Evaluation of Hypothesis. In *Prehistoric Agriculture.* S. Streuver (Ed.) pp. 101-121. Gardencity: Natural History Press.

Misra, V.D. 2002. Origin, Chronology and Transformation of the Mesolithic Culture in India. In *Mesolithic India.* V.D. Misra and J.N. Pal (Eds.) pp. 447-464. Allahabad: Department of Ancient History, Culture and Archaeology, University of Allahabad.

Misra, V.D. 2007. Stone Age Cultures, their Chronology and Beginnings of Agriculture in the North-central India. *Man and Environment* 32(1): 1-14.

Misra, V.D. 2007-2008. Prelude to Agriculture in North-Central India, *Prāgdhārā* 18: 249-261.

Misra, V.D. and J.N. Pal (Eds.) 2002. *Mesolithic India.* Allahabad: Department of Ancient History, Culture and Archaeology, University of Allahabad.

Misra, V.D., J.N. Pal and M.C. Gupta 2002-2003. Further Excavations at Jhusi: Evidence of Neolithic Culture. *Pāragdhārā* 13: 227-229.

Misra, V.D., J.N. Pal and M.C. Gupta 2004. Significance of Recent Excavations at Tokwa in the Vindhya and Jhusi in the Gangetic Plain. *Journal of Interdisciplinary Studies in History and Archaeology* 1(1): pp. 120-127.

Misra, V.D., J.N. Pal, M.C. Gupta and P.P. Joglekar 2010. *Excavations at Jhusi* Archaeological society of India, New Delhi.

Misra, V.N. 1989. Stone Age India: An Ecological Perspective. *Man and Environment* 14(1): 17-64.

Narain, L.A. 1970. The Neolithic Settlement at Chirand. *The Journal of Bihar Research Society* 56: 16-35.

Pal, J.N. 1977. '*Bhārtiya Nava Pāshāṇika Saṅskṛitiyāñ*' (Hindi). In '*Bhārtīya Prāgaitihāsika Saṅskṛitiyāñ* (Hindi). R. K. Varma, pp. 272-282. Allahabad: Paramjyoti Prakashan.

Pal, J.N. 2008. Recent Excavations at Tokwa: Fresh Light on the Early Farming Culture of the Vindhyas. *History of Science, Philosophy and Culture in Indian Civilization* (General Ed. D.P. Chattopadhyaya) Volume V Part I, *History of Agriculture in India (upto c. 1200 AD)*. Lallanji Gopal and V.C. Srivastava (Eds.), pp. 48-69, New Delhi: Concept Publishing Company.

Pal, J.N. and M.C. Gupta 2005. Excavations at Hetapatti (Allahabad District): Some Preliminary Observations. *Journal of Interdisciplinary Studies in History and Archaeology* 2(1) (Summer 2005): 163-168.

Pokharia, A.K., J.N. Pal and Alka Srivastava 2009. Plant macro remains from Neolithic Jhusi in Ganga Plain: evidence for grain-based agriculture. *Current Science*, Vol. 97, No. 4, 25 August 2009, pp. 564-572.

Randhawa, M.S. 1980. *A History of Agriculture in India, Volume I: Beginning to 12th Century*. New Delhi: Indian Council of Agricultural Research.

Roy, S.R. 1989. Chirand. In *Encyclopedia of Indian Archaeology*, Vol. II. A. Ghosh (Ed.) pp.103-105. New Delhi: Munshiram Manoharlal.

Saraswat, K.S. 2003. Plant Economy of Early Farming Communities. In *Early Farming Communities of the Kaimur (Excavations at Senuwar, 1986-87, 89-90)* Volume II. B.P. Singh (Excavator & Editor) pp. 416-535. Jaipur: Publication Scheme.

Sharma S., M. Joachimski, M. Sharma, H.J. Tobschall, I.B. Singh, C. Sharma, M.S. Chauhan and G. Morgenroth 2004. Late Glacial and Holocene Environmental Changes in Ganga Plain, Northern India. *Quaternary Science Reviews* 23(1-2):145-159.

Sharma, C., M.S. Chauhan, S. Sharma, M. Sharma and I.B. Singh 2001. Proxy Records of Holocene Vegetation and Climate Change from Sanai Tal, Central Ganga Plain, Uttar Pradesh. *National Symposium: Role of Earth Sciences Integrated Development and Related Social Issues*. Special Publication No. 65(III): 199-202. New Delhi: Geological Survey of India.

Sharma, G.R., V.D. Misra, D. Mandal, B.B. Misra, and J.N. Pal 1980. *Beginnings of Agriculture*. Allahabad: Abinash Prakashan.

Singh B.P. 2001. Stages of Cultural Development in the Middle Ganga Plain- A Case Study of Senuwar. *Pāragdhārā* 11: 109-118.

Singh, P. 2002. The Neolithic Cultures of Northern and Eastern India. In *Indian Archaeology in Retrospect Volume I: Prehistory (Archaeology of South Asia)*. S. Settar and Ravi Korisettar (Eds.) pp. 127-150. New Delhi: Indian Council of Historical Research and Manohar Publishers.

Singh, B.P. (Ed.) 2004. *Early Farming Communities of the Kaimur (Excavations at Senuwar)*, Vol. I & II. Jaipur: Publication Scheme.

Singh, B.P. 1990. Early Farming Communities of Kaimur Foot Hills. *Purātattva* 19: 6-18.

Singh, B.P. 1997. Neolithic and Chalcolithic Pottery of Middle Ganga Plain: A Case Study of Senuwar. *Ancient Ceramics (Historical Enquiries and Scientific Approaches)*. P.C. Pant and Vidula Jayaswal (Eds.) pp. 3-33. New Delhi: Agam Kala Prakashan.

Singh, I.B. 1996a. Geological Evolution of Ganga Plain- An Overview. *Journal of Palaeontological Society of India* 41: 99-137.

Singh, I.B. 1996b. Late Quaternary Sedimentation of Ganga Plain. *Foreland Basin. Proceeding, Symposium NW Himalay and Fordeep, Feb. 1995*, Geological Survey of India, Special Publication No. 21(1): 161-172. New Delhi: Geological Survey of India.

Singh, I.B. 2004. Late Quaternary History of the Ganga Plain. *Journal of Geological Society of India* 64: 431-454.

Singh, I.B. 2004-2005. Landform Development and Palaeovegetation in Late Quaternary of Ganga Plain: Implications for Anthropegenic Activity. *Pāragdhārā* 15:5-31.

Singh, I.B. 2005. Quaternary Palaeoenvironments of Ganga Plain and Anthropogenic Activity. *Man and Environment* 30(1): 1-35.

Singh, P. 1991. *The Neolithic Origins*. Delhi: Agam Kala Prakashan.

Singh, P. 1992-93. Archaeological Excavations at Imlidih Khurd - 1992. *Pāragdhārā* 3: 21-35.
Singh, P. 1993-94. Further Excavations at Imlidih Khurd - 1993. *Pāragdhārā* 4: 41-48.
Singh, P. 1998. Early farming Cultures of the Middle Ganga Valley, in *Reconstructing History (Essays in Honour of Prof. V.C. Srivastava)* Vol. I (Ed. V.D. Misra). Varanasi: Felicitation Committee.
Singh, P. and A.K. Singh 1995-96. Trial Excavations at Waina, District Ballia (U.P.). *Pāragdhārā* 6: 41-61.
Singh, P. and A.K. Singh 1997-98. Trial Excavations at Bhunadih, District Ballia (U.P.). *Pāragdhārā* 8: 11-29.
Singh, P., A.K. Singh and B. Singh 1994-95. Protohistoric Investigations in Ballia District, Uttar Pradesh. *Pāragdhārā* 6: 21-36.
Singh, P., A.K. Singh and Brahmanand Singh 1994-95. Protohistoric Investigations in Ballia District, Uttar Pradesh. *Pāragdhārā* 5: 21-35.
Sinha, H.P. 1994. *Archaeological and Cultural History of Bihar, (with special reference to Neolithic Chirand).* New Delhi: Ramanand Vidya Bhawan.
Tewari, Rakesh, R.K. Srivastava and K.K. Singh 2001-2002. Excavations at Lahuradewa, District Sant Kabirnagar. *Purātattva* 32: 54-62.
Tewari, Rakesh, R.K. Srivastava, K.K. Singh, K.S. Saraswat and I.B. Singh 2002-2003. Preliminary Report of the Excavations at Lahuradewa, District Sant Kabirnagar, U.P. 2001-2002: Wider Archaeological Implications. *Pāragdhārā* 13: 37-68.
Tewari, Rakesh, R.K. Srivastava, K.K. Singh, Ram Vinay, Rajiv Kumar Trivedi and G.C. Singh 2004-2005. Recently Excavated Sites in the Ganga Plain and North Vindhyas: Some Observations Regarding the Pre-urban Context. *Pāragdhārā* 15: 40-43.
Tewari, Rakesh, R.K. Srivastava, K.S. Saraswat, I.B. Singh, K/K/ Singh 2007-2008. Early Farming at Lahurādewā. *Pāragdhārā* 18: 348-373.
Thapar, B.K. 1965. Neolithic Problem in India, *In Indian Prehistory: 1964.* V.N. Misra and M.S. Mate (Eds.) pp. 87-112. Poona: Deccan College Post-Graduate and Research Institute.
Thapar, B.K. 1965. Neolithic Problem in India. In *Indian Prehistory: 1964.* V.N. Misra and M.S. Mate (Eds.) pp. 87-112. Poona: Deccan College Post-Graduate and Research Institute.
Thapar, B.K. 1984. *Fresh Light on the Neolithic Cultures of India. Purātattva* 13-14: 37-43.
Varma, A.K. 1998. *Neolithic Culture of Eastern India.* New Delhi: Ramanand Vidya Bhawan.
Verma, B.S. 1971. Excavations at Chirand: New Light on Indian Neolithic Complex. *Purātattva* 4: 19-24.

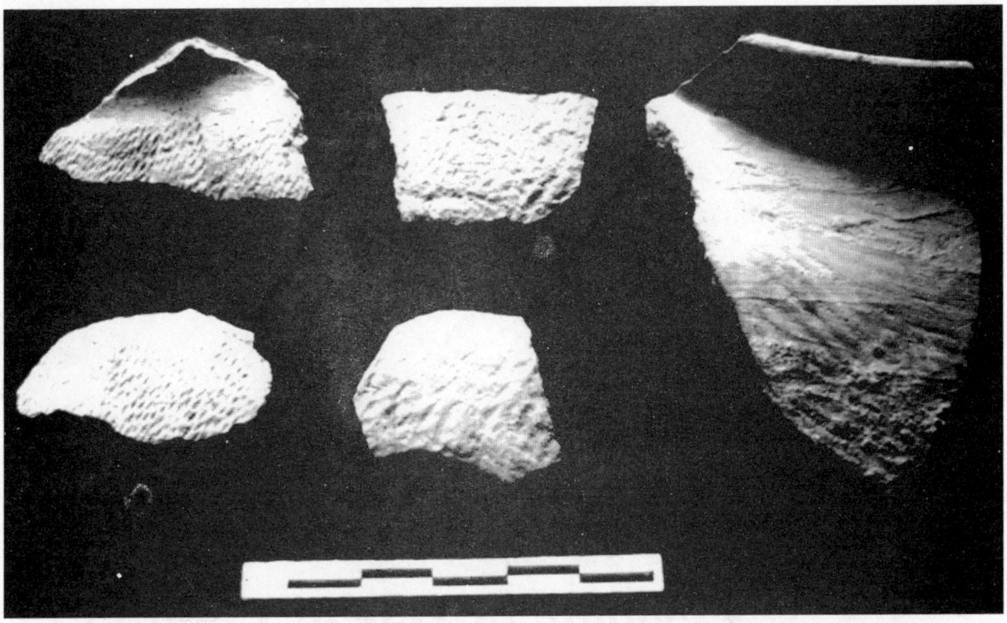

Plate I : Hut floor, Jhusi

Plate II : A burnt plastered floor enclosed by two parallel mud walls, Jhusi

3

Geology of Darad-Gaṇḍakī Deśa : Region of the River Gaṇḍaka

T.P. Verma

Gaṇḍakī Deśa is the name of a kingdom in twelfth century but it has remained unknown to historians as well as to geographers. At least three families, apparently unconnected with each other, of this dynasty ruled over this kingdom and all of them claim to be the scions of king Malayaketu of Sūryavaṁśa. They ruled during the second half of the second millennium of Common Era. At least ten kings of three separate dynasties that successively ruled over the region are known but we know nothing about their mutual relations. They issued six land grants on copperplates. The earliest two copperplates were issued by king Jayāditya II who gives the names of his father and grandfather and his known date is 870 CE. The second family was of Sūryāditya whose known dates are 1020 CE and 1026 CE. He also introduces his father and grandfather. The third family was of king Kīrttipāla Deva whose known date is 1111 CE, a contemporary of king Gaovindachandra of Gāhaḍavāla dynasty. He introduces himself with the name of his father and grandfather. Recently, another copperplate of his son Rāmapāla also was discovered which is dated in 1158 CE. It is interesting to note that Kīrttipāla was subdued by Govindachandra and his son dared to issue his grant when that monarch was dead. Records of these kings reveal that this was the most unfortunate family ever known to history. They used to bear full regal titles like Paramabhaṭṭāraka Mahārājādhirāja Parameśvara but whenever they issued a land grant they were suppressed and sudued by some imperial authority of Kannauj like the Pratihāras or the Gāhaḍavālas.

The find spots of their copperplates point out that the area of their rule extended from Patna in Bihar in the east to Śrāvastī in Gonda circle of the eastern UP in the west. But the most striking feature of these epigraphs is that they designate the country by unusual names. They call it *Daradagaṇḍakī Deśa*; but in some copperplate grants it is also called *Uttara-Samudra* and *Saumya-Sindhu.* The latter two names are of geological interest. No student of history ever knows that this part of the southern Himalayas once upon a time was known as the North Sea or *Saumya-Sindu,* the benign, moderate or mild sea. The word *saumya* also means north. This also reminds us of the geological fact that in the beginning the whole Ganga basin, known to the geologists as Murree Foredeep, was part of ocean; in fact Himalayas emerged out of the ocean that was called Tethys sea. We will see references to this ocean in the Indian literature.

However, the extent of this kingdom of *Daradagaṇḍakī Deśa* remains undefined on account of lack of evidence but it seems that it must have spread from the foot of the Himalayas up to at least northern part of UP, known as *Sarayūpāra* and north Bihar. According Prof. D.C. Sircar "... the district of *Daradagaṇḍakī* was apparently situated on the banks of the Gandaka. This name is, however, applied now to no less than three rivers, viz. (1) the Great Gandaka running through the Gorakhpur, Champaran, Muzffarpur, Saran and Patna districts and joining the Ganges at Patna in lat. $25^0$49'53" and long. $85^0$13'45"; (2) Lesser Gandaka running through the Gorakhpur and Saran districts and falling into the Gogra in lat. $25^0$41' and long. 85^0 14'30"; and (3) Little Gandaka running through the Saran district and Tirhut and joining Bagmati in lat. $25^0$45' and long. $86^0$2'."[1]

Find spots of the copperplates of these kings also point to this region. Out of six copperplates four were recovered from *Sarayūpāraa* region in eastern UP. Two grants came from Champaran district of Bihar. This was the region of ancient Kosala and Mithila. The internal evidence of these grants also points to the same region. The Gorakhpur copperplate grant of Jayāditya II informs that their capital was Vijayapura at the declivity of the northern mountains (*uttaragiri-kaṭake Vijayapuram nāma nṛipādhānī*). Thus it was in the vicinity of the Himalaya Mountain. D.C. Ganguly holds that "The city seems to have situated at the foot of the Himalayas in the northern part of Gorakhpur district."[2] But he does not indicate the exact location. The Gorakhpur grant of Kīrttipāla Deva was issued to a Brāhman of Daviramakula village, which was a Bhaṭṭigrāma, in the Śrāvastī *vishaya* in the *Daradagaṇḍakī Deśa.* This may be taken as an indication that Vijayapura might have situated somewhere near Śrāvastī.

Thus we have a rough idea of the geography of the *Daradagaṇḍakī Deśa.* The terms *Saumya Sindhu* and *Uttara Samudra* occur in the Gorakhpur inscription of Kīrtipāla as well as in the grant of his son Rāmapāla. Kielhorn takes both terms as synonyms.

The word *Darada-Gaṇḍakī* has two words: *darada* means mountain and *Gaṇḍakī* is a famous river emanating from the Himalaya Mountains. We have already discussed the three branches of this river flowing over a wide region and meeting three different rivers in UP and Bihar. Geologists know of a Ganagaka Depression as a part of Indo-Gangetic Depression that was created due to the orogenic activities during the formation of the Himalayas. But this was again a part of the greater orogenic movements in the earth's crust resulting in the origin of mountains of Asia and Europe. To understand the whole process we may briefly discuss the geological formation of these regions because it is a part of our Puranic history.

Geologists are of the opinion that there was a time when the area where the continents of Asia and Europe exit, was a vast expanse of water. This ocean extended from the Atlantic and Mediterranean oceans including the Black Sea, Caspian, Aral Sea and Balkash up to Tien Shan Mountains in the east. The geologists have named this the Tethys Sea. Due to the orogenic activities beneath the crust of the earth, a large chain of mountains came into being in the regions of Asia and Europe. Seismic eruptions also were going on.

The Puranas also mention this event in the form of the eruption of the Meru or Sumeru mountain which is connected with the emergence of humanity in the seventh Manvantara through Manu, the son of Vivasvāna about 120 million years ago. This was the beginning of a new era in the history of the Earth because the sixth round of our galaxy by the Solar System had just completed and the seventh one started. There was a deluge and our present Manu survived it and tied his arc on the top of Meru. Perhaps this was the time when the Indian sub-continent collided with the Eurasian continent. It is also possible that the deluge was caused by this collision and our present Manu, earlier names Śrāddha Deva and Satyavrata, was an inhabitant of this subcontinent. He is also known as *Draviḍeśvara* living on the river *Kṛitamāla.* This story is related in the *Bhāgavatapurāṇa.*[3]

But, however, we are concerned here with the orogenic activities in Asia. Meru is known as *kaseru parvata* (or root-mountains), in contrast with the *kula parvatas* (family mountains) of Southern Peninsula. However, when Manu reached Meru, Himalaya had yet to gain height. This can be inferred by the story of Ilā, the first son/daughter of Manu, who was transformed into a women after reaching the place where Śiva was amusing with his wife Umā. The *Matsyapurāṇa*[4] calls this mountainous place the *Śaravaṇa.* This is also mentioned in the *Rigveda* as *Śaryāṇavata,* where Soma was found;[5] and I have identified it with present Jeravshan or Jerafshan (also Yarkand) River and mountain in Central Asia.[6]

It is not improbable that the arc of Manu was Southern Peninsula which was drifting northwards as is well known to geologists who plead the theory of continental drift. Many such phenomenons are related in the Puranas figuratively. Symbolically, Vishṇu, in the form of a Great Fish, undertook this task of pulling the Arc, i.e. the sub-continent, which in modern geology is called the continental drift, up to the Meru Mountain and tied with it. As a consequence of this collision, the Pamir started gaining height. The top of the Pamir, famous as the 'Roof of the World' was plateau which in Sanskṛit is called *'Pratisṭhāna',* which was the capital of Manu and his progeny Ilā. This was the beginning of a New Era, called Seventh Manvantara that started about 120 million years ago as per Hindu calculation.

At that time Śaravaṇa or Jeravshan seems to have been the abode of Śiva and Umā, the daughter of Daksha from his first wife. This tribe used to live in this area because we know that Pāṇini's mother was a Dākshī (*kanyā*). But when the Himalayas rose to height and gravity of Vedic culture shifted towards south and south-east, his abode also shifted to Kelāsa (i.e. where '*ke*' water '*lāsa*' is galloping or dancing due to abundance; most of the rivers of India emanate from this mountain). Here his second wife, Pārvatī, is the daughter of Himālaya. Thus the period of Ilā and her descendents, chronologically, must antedate the Himālayan period.

It is also said that Himalāya rose as the peninsular plate of a high geological antiquity, is thrusting below it. It formed a great trough to its south; that is to say that the plain of Gaṅgā was a sea for some time until the rivers emanating from the Himālayas from the north and the Vindhyan rivers from south filled it with alluvium brought with them. This was called a 'fore-deep'. A. C. Das quotes D.R. Oldham who says "the depth of alluvium along the outer edge of the Himālaya is great, amounting to about 15,000 to 20,000 feet towards the northern boundary of the alluvial plain." Then he observes "As regards the underground form of the floor of the trough, it has been found that 'it has deepened steadily from south to north at about 130 feet to the mile, and that this slope is continuous for over 100 miles from the southern edge, so that in this way we reach an estimated depth of over 13,000 and probably about 15,000 feet.' This trough ends up on the east where the Assam Range on the Himālaya terminates and on the west as the Salt Range of the Punjab is reached.... It has been described by Mr. Oldham as the 'Gangetic trough' in as much as 'three quarters of its length and more than that proportion of its area lie within the drainage of the Ganges."[7]

On this issue Dr. S. M. Mathur holds "The vast stretch of the Indo-Gangetic alluvium occupies a valley limited on the north and west by lofty Himalayas and on the south by great mass of the peninsular shield. The earliest view about its origin was that it was an ancient sea filled in by deposits brought in by the numerous rivers that flow into and through it. C.S. Middlemiss in 1900 proposed that it was a belt of subsidence where the sinking of the plains went on simultaneously with the rising of the mountains. It was the famous Swiss geologist Eduard Suess who called it a foredeep of the Himalayas. Sir S.G. Burrard later in 1912 advanced the hypothesis, based on geodetic observations, that the Indo-Gangetic trough was a great crustal crack or rift, perhaps as much as 30 km in depth, which developed through a length of over 3,200 km and got filled with alluvium. He further proposed that the rifting was a primary event that caused the compression of the Himalayas to the north. This view was hotly contested by D. R. Oldham in 1917 who analysed and evaluated the existing geodetic and geological data and concluded that the floor sloped upward fairly uniformly from the northern edge of the Peninsula to the maximum depth of 5,000-6,000 m near its own northern limit (15-50 km from the mountains), and it was therefore not a rift or crack."[8]

These scholars are silent about the existence of a sea in the region. However, Mathur speaks about the Tethys or Tibetan Himalaya which means that it was Tethys Sea in which this great mountain rose. Thus the *Uttara Samudra* or *Saumya Sindhu* of the copperplates mentioned above was the Tethys Sea of the geologists.

The trough of the Indo-Gangetic plain was filled up by the silt of Himalayan rivers. D. N. Wadia says "Some experiments by Everest prove that the Ganges conveys annually to the Bay of Bengal, at a conservative estimate, more than 356,000,000 tonnes of sand and clay –an average of over 900,000 tonnes of silt a day." This shows the enormity of the alluvium carried by the Himalayan rivers that filled up this trough known as *Uttara Samudra.*

Dr. Mathur noted four stages of the Himalayan orogenic movements. "The first phase" he notes, "commenced in the Middle Eocene with the close of the Indus-Tsangpo and Indo-Burmese sutures, and collision of the Indian and Eurasian plates. The development of the foredeep (Murree Foredeep) was initiated during this orogeny. The northern part of the foredeep was uplifted during the second phase in the Early Miocene, and the southern boundary of the basin shifted southwards when the Shiwalik sediments were deposited, sourced from the Himalayas (Shiwalik Foredeep). Late Pliocene orogenic movements in the third phase brought about steep rise of the Himalayas and the uplift of the Vindhyan Range along the Son-Narmada Lineament, resulting in sediment supply both from the Himalayas and the Peninsular Shield. The forth and the last phase occurred during early Middle Pleistocene that resulted in the uplift and development of the Shiwalik Range and the Indo-Gangetic Plain."[9]

The third phase gains importance because it can be related to the figurative story of Agastya *ṛishi.* The *Mahābhārata* mentions that once the Himālayas and the Vindhyas both started rising. There seems some natural causes for this phenomenon because when the Peninsular thrust forced the Himalayas from beneath to rise, the speed of the Vindhyas at the same time must have also checked giving rise to the later. This incident is figuratively related in the story of the *ṛishi* Agastya in the *Mahābhārata.*[10] In this narration, it is said that Vindhya Mountain started rising in competition with the Meru (not with Himalayas) and on the request of the gods the *ṛishi* asked the former to wait till he returns from the south; but he did not. Similarly, the drying up of the Indo-Gangetic Ocean is related in the next chapter. It is said that the Devas requested the *ṛishi* to drink the waters of the sea because some demons have made it their hiding place. So he did it. After killing the demons they again requested to release the water but the *ṛishi* told that it has been digested; they will have to do something else if they desire restoration.[11] This was the North Sea known to the epics[12] the memory of which was retained by the peoples of North India at least till the twelfth century CE.

No doubt, the base below the alluvium in the Ganga plain is formed by 'the northern part of the Peninsula'. Mathur speaks about this and says "The Ganga Basin is a negative superorder crustal structure, most probably the northerly extension of the Vindhyan syneclise, and represents a large-scale regional depression on the northern margin of the Indian platform. A syneclise is defined as a negative or depressed structure, of regional order, on the continental platform produced by slow crustal downwrap, which retains its negative character for long period of geological history.

"On the basis of geophysical data the Ganga Basin has been subdivided from east to west, into the undernoted tectonic units.

1. Monghyr-Saharsa Ridge,

2. East Uttar Pradesh Shelf,
3. Gandak Depression,
4. Faizabad Ridge,
5. West Uttar Pradesh Shelf,
6. Sharda Depression, and
7. Delhi-Hardwar Ridge."

Dr. Mathur explains "The ridges are buried structures, which are the northward continuation of features originating on the peninsular area. The Monghyr-Saharsa Ridge constitutes the eastern boundary of the Ganga Basin, while the western margin is formed by the Delhi-Hardwar Ridge.

"The Monghyr-Saharsa Ridge is an extension of the Chota Nagpur Plateau, and is likely to be made up of rock complexes of the Satpura folded belt. Neogene sediments directly lie over the basement and the alluvial thickness above the ridge is not greater than 3,000 m. It is separated from the Faizabad Ridge by almost 300 km of the East Uttar Pradesh Shelf and the Gandak Depression. It is the northwestward projection of the Bundelkhand massif. Neogene sediments also lie directly over it."[13]

Thus the Gandak Depression is not an isolated phenomenon and it is a part of the Ganga Depression which is again a part of Himalayan orogeny. The most important part of this discussion is that the *Daradagaṇḍakī Deśa* is a geological reality, and similarly the *Uttara Samudra* and *Saumya Sindhu* also are not fiction. This again goes to establish that the people of this part of the earth are living here since undeterminable generations the antiquity of which goes to geological times. The other thing is that the Puranic and Epic legends are not myths or fictions; they are figurative accounts of events in the very-very long life of the Vedic people.

References

1. *Ep. Ind.* Volume 35, p. 132.
2. *The Age of Imperial Kanauj*, Bombay, 1964, p. 93.
3. See last chapters of the 8th and 9th Skandhas of *Matsyapurāṇa*.
4. *Matsya.* 12, 1 and 6.
5. *Rv.* IX.65.22; 113. 1 etc.
6. *Manaviki*, No. 1 (July-Dec) 2009, p. 135-45.
7. Das, A.C. *Ṛigvedic India*, Delhi, 1971, p. 18.
8. Mathur, S. M. *Physical Geology of India.*NBT of India, 2004, p. 58.
9. Mathur, p. 20.
10. *Vanaparva*, chapter 104.
11. *Ibid.* chapter 105.
12. Vālmiki's *Rāmāyaṇa*, VII. 34. 29 & 31. There is a mention of *Dakshiṇa Samudra* also that was today's Bay of Bengal. For other mentions of Southern Sea see *ibid.* V.58.8; IV.52.31-32; and IV.60.7.
13. Mathur p. 62-63.

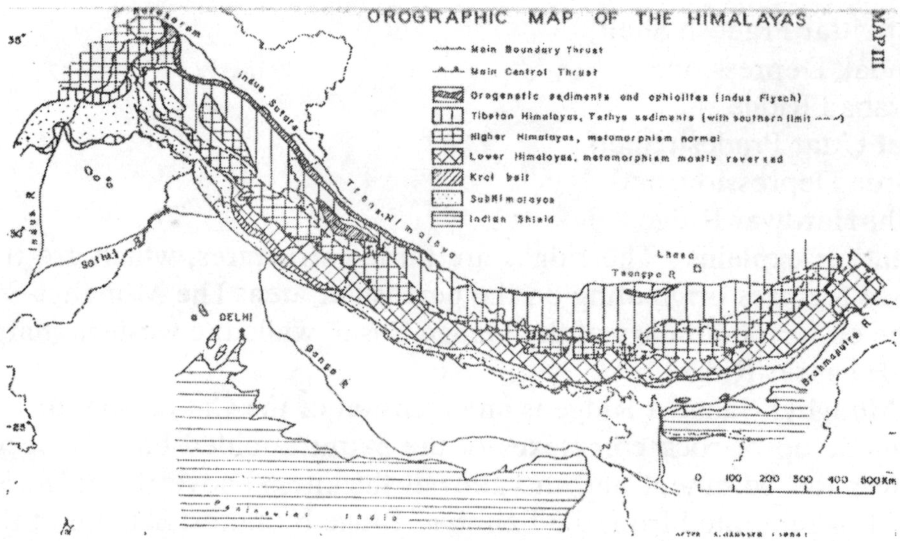

Fig. 1 : The Indus-Ganga-Brahmaputra Basin

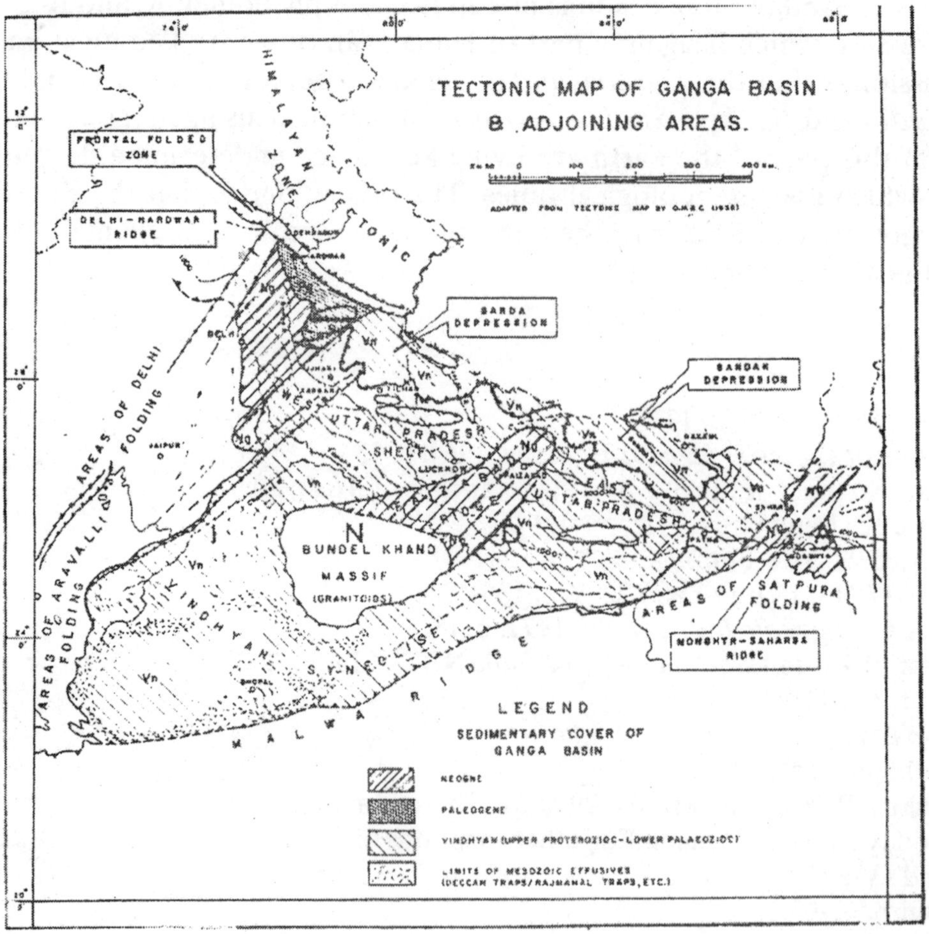

Fig. 2 : Ganga Depression showing three Vindhyan Ridges and Gandaka Depression

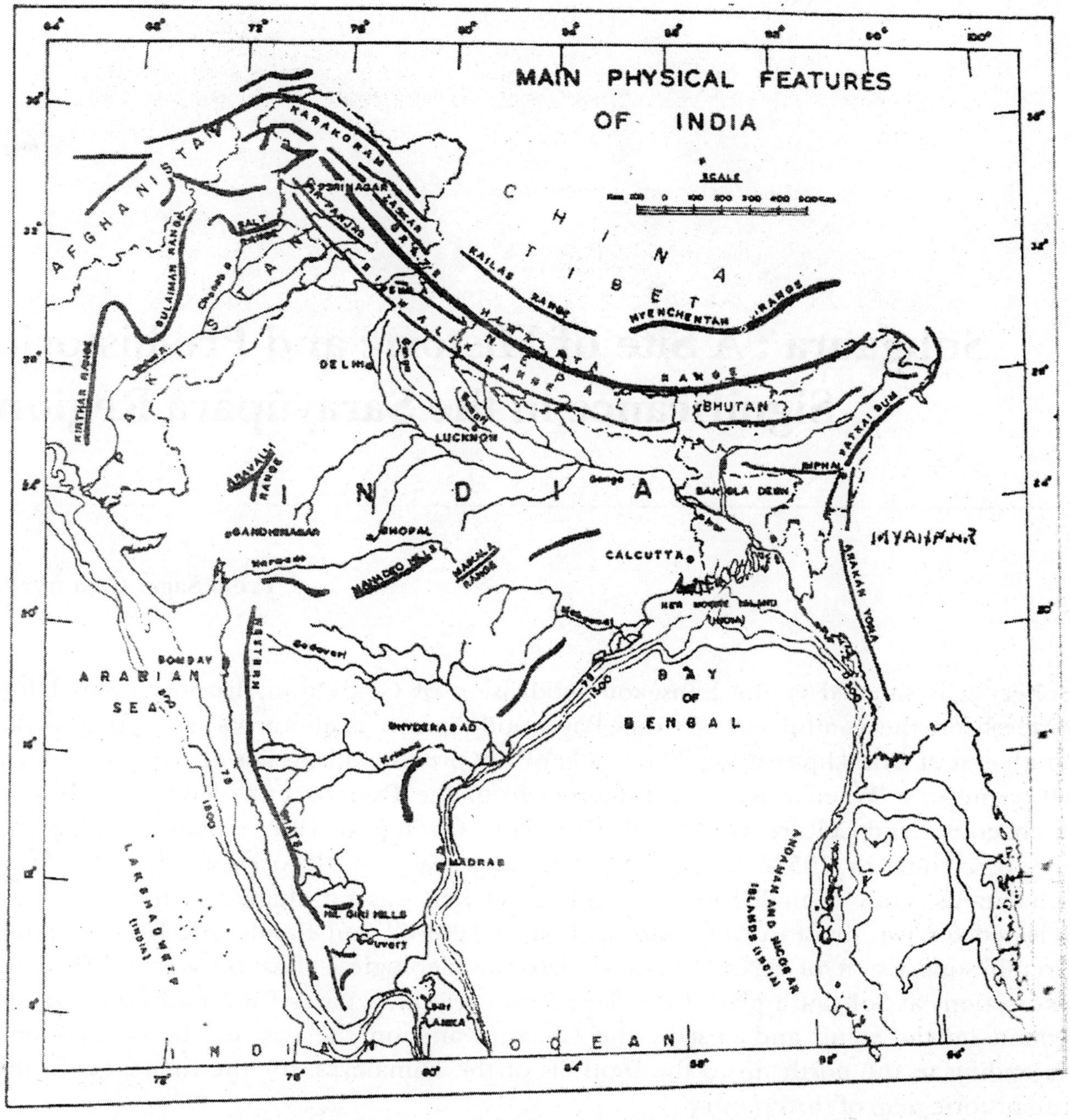

Fig. 3 : Physical map of India: Rivers from Himalaya and Vindhya flow into the Ganga Basin.

4

Sohgaura : A Site of Historic and Pre-historic Significance in the Sarayūpāra Region

Prem Sagar Chaturvedi

Sohgaura is situated in the Bansgaon subdivision of Gorakhpur district in east Uttar Pradesh on the confluence of rivers Rapti and Ami. It is about 30 kilometres to the south-east of Gorakhpur town. The whole of the present village lies on a mound about 60 ha in area. When a team of explorers from the Department of Ancient History, Archaeology and Culture, Gorakhpur University, Gorakhpur (UP) visited the village for the first time in 1958-59, the entire mound was almost occupied by the local inhabitants. Only a small fringe towards the north was uninhabited which was later selected for two phases of excavations first in 1961-62 and finally in 1974 under the overall supervision of S.N.Chaturvedi. The archaeological data recovered from the excavations at Sohgaura placed the Sarayūpāra region, a part of the mid Ganga plain, bound on the south and west by the Ghaghra and on the east by the Gandak and extending to the north up to the foothills of the Himalayas, for the first time, in the pre-historic map of the country.

Prior to the exposition of its prehistoric significance in 1974, the village was known to the indologists since 1894 when V.A.Smith published a copper plate inscription recovered from here. A number of scholars devoted themselves to the study of this inscription, but little interest was taken in the site itself. Dr.W.W.Hoey, the then Collector of Gorakhpur, showed his interest in the site by digging a few trenches but appears to have abandoned his venture as no interesting finds were revealed.

The overall significance of this site to the history, culture and archaeology of the country can be underlined under the following heads:

Sohgaura in Epigraphical Studies

To the epigraphists, Sohgaura is one of the few spots in the country from where inscriptions, usually said to be pre-Asokan or even pre-Mauryan[1] on the palaeographic grounds, have been found. Inscribed in a copper-plate, it was found during digging a foundation of a house by a villager. Later, it was secured by the local Collector who presented it to the Royal Asiatic Society of Bengal in 1893. It came to the public knowledge when it was published by V.A.Smith in 1894[2]and later by Fleet in 1907[3]. The copper-plate is a small rectangular piece measuring 6.4 x 2.9 cm and having a thickness of 1.6 mm. Circular holes are pierced near each corner, which were intended to attach the plate by rivets or nails. It has been cast in a mould and bears a number of superfluous dots. The back of the plate is rough.

The inscription consists of 72 letters, spread over in four lines. Most of the letters bear close resemblances with those of the Aśokan edicts, except a few which do not belong to the standard type. Amongst the latter, mention may be made of letters *ma, ya* and *bha.* The letter *ma* has a conspicuous unusual shape, in which the upper and lower parts are invariably placed apart, - thus . This is an altogether uncommon shape of *ma* in this inscription. We come across the same feature in the letter *ya* in line 1, in which the vertical line is slightly away from the lower crescent - ; and so also in letter *bha,* in line 3, the lower right vertical is left unattached to the upper horizontal line . Some serious changes are also discernible in the medial signs of *i* and *o.* In line 3 the medial sign of *i* is found attached in a reversed manner while inscribing *him* - . This is quite an unusual pattern of putting this sign, may be because of some kind of inadvertence on the part of engraver or more because of the uncertainty in the beginning when its standard placing had not clearly been evolved. The latter seems to be the most plausible answer, because we witness the same type of incorrectness, of course from the standard placements, in the medial sign of vowel *o* which is expressed by putting the upper tick to the right and lower to the left in *ko* - in line 2 and *no* - in line 4. These are obviously not the correct representations of the Aśokan Brāhmī and most plausibly indicate to that pre-Aśokan phase when several parent-forms and placement of the medial signs were not sufficiently evolved to represent the standard types.

It is to be noted that the record does not bear any specific datable material on the basis of which it can be exactly dated. It neither refers to the reign of a king nor bears any particular date. It is solely on the palaeographic grounds, as illustrated above, that most of the scholars have assigned this inscription to the pre-Aśokan times. K.P.Jayaswal was of the view that this belongs to Chandragupta Maurya's time. He took the unusual form of *ma* – as *mo* and thought it to be the first syllable of the word *moriya.* He also tried to define the other symbol - , as an abbreviation of *candagutta* (= Candragupta), by taking the top crescent as *candra,* and the remaining hill-like combination for *gutta* – the upper loop - ∩ for *ga* and the two lower loops - m for *tta* ; and thus altogether *candagutta moriya* or Candragupta Maurya[4]. In order to corroborate his view point, he refers to the Jain tradition of great famine at the end of Chandrgupta Maurya's reign, which according to him, has been mentioned in this record[5]. V.A.Smith thought it to be of the Mauryan period without specifying the reign[6]. Fleet was also of the same view; however, he located it between 320-180 B.C[7]. Expressing almost the same kind of opinion, Buehler asserted that 'the letters of the inscription certainly point to the time of the Mauryas[8].'B.M. Barua took it to be a pre-Mauryan record[9] , but D.C.Sircar is not inclined to place it before the third century B.C[10].

Divergences in the views of dating this record among the scholars notwithstanding, one thing , however, is abundantly clear that most of them are inclined to assign it to a pre-Asokan chronology. This along with the fact that it is one of the few tangible evidences pertaining to the beginning of writing in ancient India, highlights the significance of this record in the history and antiquity of Indian epigraphy which apparently commences from the times of Mauryan king Aśoka. Thus, considered to be pre-Aśokan or pre- Mauryan means that this record transcends the acknowledged limits of the beginning of Indian epigraphy and places it to earlier chronological horizons. Significantly enough, out of four inscriptions usually taken to be pre-Aśokan in the country, two - Sohgaura (Gorakhpur district) and Piprahwa (Siddharth Nagar district) have been found from that part of eastern Uttar Pradesh which fell under the boundaries of ancient Kosala. This provides this region with a unique place in the history of writing in the country which appeared here in a tangible form for the first time and offered a solid base for its development in the subsequent times in other parts of the country.

It is noteworthy that the epigraph at Sohgaura alludes to its content both by the pictographs as well as by syllables. It contains in the upper portion of the engraved inscription two pictographs of the three-storeyed storehouses meant for collecting grains to meet the eventuality of a famine and refers to the same under the text with same number and shape. What does this dual form of representation mean? Can we take it marking to that stage of transition when the pictographs were taken to convey their actual import more candidly and effectively *vis-ë-vis* the syllabic communication about which the concerned engraver was perhaps yet not sure enough? We have discussed it earlier that some of the letters of this record were still in a transitional stage and were yet to attain their standard forms. All these facts, taken together, assign the Sohgaura Copper Plate to a higher antiquity – higher than that of the Aśokan epigraphs - and underline the importance of this record in the history of writing in ancient India. Coincidentally, some of the symbols, such as crescent-on-hill, trees-inside-railings, etc. carved in the upper part of the epigraph, possess close affinities to those found in the punched-marked coins which precede the inscribed coinage in ancient India.

Its Political-Cultural Significance

Though brief in nature, the record contains some useful clues reflecting on the political-cultural life of the pre-Aśokan times. It is quite evident that the area around the Gorakhpur district in east Uttar Pradesh fell under the administrative jurisdiction of Śrāvastī, as the record indicates, and it was to promulgate the order of ministers stationed at this administrative centre (*savatiyāna mahamatana*) to use the grains of the two storehouses during the emergency among the inhabitants of the villages, such as, *Māthura, Cañcu, Modāma, Bhallaka* (which are yet to be identified) that this record was issued. That the region around Gorakhpur district was politically and geographically closely connected with Kosala, having Śrāvastī as its prominent town, since the sixth century BCE, is evident from the Buddhist literature which refers to the ruling clans of the area, the Sakyas and the Koliyas, originally being of the Ikśvāku stock that ruled over Kosala. This continued at least up to the reign of Harsa during the seventh century CE as the Madhuban Copper Plate of his Era 25 i.e. 631CE which records the grant of Somakuṇḍa village under the Śrāvastī *bhukti* to the local Brahmins[11] Bhaṭṭavataswāmī and Bhaṭṭaśivadevaswāmī as *agrahara,* reveals. It has been recovered from the village Madhuban under the Ghosi sub-division of Mau district in east Uttar Pradesh which affirms that the territorial jurisdiction of Śrāvastī *bhukti* extended over the places even beyond the Gorakhpur district in the east and south.

The epigraph of Sohgaura is first of the kind of a *śāsana* inscription in the history of Indian epigraphy which was issued by the ministers to implement a particular measure in their administrative area. This is in complete conformity with the testimony of the *Arthaśāstra* (II.26.10) which provides for the issuance of the written administrative orders by the king or his ministers – the only difference being that whereas the orders issued by the former were to contain the description of the king's opulence, the name of the country, his dynastic and personal names, the latter had just to refer to the name of the country and the ministers[12]. Evidently, the Sohgaura Copper Plate contains the name of the country and makes reference to the ministers who issued it and, therefore, falls under the latter category. The administrative measures, taken by the ministers and mentioned in this epigraph also correspond well with those alluded to in the Rock Edict III of the Mauryan king Aśoka who instructs his officials – *Yukta, Rājuka* and *Prādeśika* – to go for the tours of their administrative areas every five years and implement his orders[13]. It is noteworthy that the *śāsana* of Sohgaura was issued from a camp at *Manavasiti* (?) which suggests that the ministers took a tour of this part of land, encamped here and, looking at the condition of the villages, issued the order to use the grains of the two granaries among the residents of the villages listed in the epigraph.

Construction and existence of the granaries are known to us at least since the Harappan period. Material evidences of several of these storage devices for grains have come to us from a number of places including Harappa and Mohen-jo-daro. It is generally presumed that these were meant for storing the agricultural tax which was levied and collected by the state in kind. No where do we find that those were also meant for any emergency arising because of a flood or a famine. The inscription from Sohagaura is significant in the sense that it is the first inscribed archaeological document which records the construction of two granaries to meet out the requirements of the inhabitants of the listed villages only during an emergency arising out of a flood or famine. As the entire Bansgaon sub-division of the Gorakhpur district from where this inscription has been recovered still falls under a flood-prone zone during the Monsoon season, there is a greater possibility, that the people of the area had to face recurrent floods in the past which made the life difficult and miserable as the people had to face starvation and death and, therefore, in order to redress this eventuality, concrete steps were taken by the state by storing a buffer stock of grains. That these kinds of measures were often taken by the state, is also evident from the Stone Plaque Inscription of Mahasthan[14]found from the Bogra district of present Bangladesh which refers to the storage of supplies for famine relief. Like that of Sohgaura, it is also taken to be pre-Aśokan and almost contemporary by some of the epigraphists[15], primarily on the palaeographic grounds. As the common content of both these inscriptions is comparable with that of the *Arthaśāstra* which directs the state to distribute grains during famine[16], Bhandarkar has assigned them to the pre-Aśokan times[17]. The measures taken for the public welfare as sketched in these inscriptions indubitably suggest that the Mauryan state had evolved as a welfare state, conceptual framework for which is found broadly outlined in the *Arthaśāstra.* This is expressly evident from the Girnar inscription of Mahakṣatrapa Rudradāman of Śaka Era 72 i.e. 150 century CE which refers to the construction of the Sudarśana reservoir in the Kathiawad region by the first Mauryan ruler under the supervision of the provincial administrator Vaiśya Puṣyagupta[18]. It also provides that Aśoka not only maintained it but also decorated it with conduits (*praṇālibhiralaṁkṛitam*) which definitely facilitated distribution of water to nearby arable areas. That the public welfare measures obtained a new dimension under the third Mauryan ruler Aśoka, is amply demonstrated from his different inscriptions which are replete with the concerns of the king for the material and sipiritual well being of his subjects. The inscription from Sohgaura is just one example of the same stock, expressing the public concerns of the Mauryan rulers.

We may point out to yet another cultural dimension revealed by this epigraph. On its upper portion, we find engraved the pictographs of two architectural forms, bearing close resemblances to each other. As discussed earlier, these appear to be the pictographs of the two three-storeyed storehouses, referred to in the content, dedicating which to the public welfare is the primary concern of the epigraph. The pictographs reveal that both storehouses are raised on the four upright pillars and have been built by the gradually decreasing three tiers having coverings of thatched roofs. Though these may not be representing the actual shapes and sizes, one thing is nevertheless obvious that these were erected on pillars, most plausibly, wooden which come to us as the most significant part of the building since the Vedic period. We come across in the Vedic literature references to *sthūṇa, skambha* and *stambha* and also to such large buildings which were erected on thousands[19] (*sahasra*) of pillars. Building of the Vedic houses (*śālās*) is elaborately sketched in the two *suktas* of the *Atharvaveda* (III. 12; IX. 3) which provide that these were created mostly by wood. We have ample evidence to suggest that wood continued to be principal building material up to the Mauryan period. The archaeological evidence, recovered from Kumarhar, Bulandibagh and Gosai Khand around the present city of Patna in Bihar which is usually identified with Pātaliputra, the capital town of the Mauryas, have yielded a large quantity of wooden pillars and planks mostly employed for raising rampart around the capital town of the Mauryas. Reference may also be made here to lithic architecture which evolved in the form of structural *stūpas* and rock-cut *caityas* and *vihāras* during the Maurya-Śuṅga-Sātavāhana times. This has widely been acknowledged by the art historians that many of these existing architectural forms are the reproductions of their wooden prototypes. In view of these facts and also on the basis of the shapes of the two three-storeyed pictographs engraved at the upper part of this epigraph, there is every possibility that these storehouses were essentially the products of the wood-work. These also testify that the architects of the age possessed the required expertise and ingenuity to erect the multi-storeyed buildings.

Prehistoric Significance of Sohgaura

Before the final excavation[20] of Sohgaura in 1974, no one ever imagined that the *Sarayūpāra* region of the mid- Ganga plain has any thing to do with the prehistoric archaeology. It was largely considered as the land of the Lord Buddha which abounded in Buddhist and historical archaeology. Recovery of a large number of epigraphs, coins, pottery, seals and sealings, sculptures, monuments, etc. further confirmed its historical archaeological profile. The myth was, however, exploded after the successful completion of the excavation of Sohgaura in 1974 which revealed a continuous sequence of cultures from the Neolithic period to the present time. The findings at Sohgaura opened the possibilities for similar other findings in subsequent times which prominently brought the *Sarayūpāra* region of east Uttar Pradesh in the prehistoric map of India, extending its prehistoric horizons to Mesolithic-Neolithic times.

The excavation at Sohgaura, though limited in nature[21], brought out the six-fold cultural sequence, ranging from the Neolithic (Period I) to the medieval (Period VI).

The remains of Period I, revealed from the lowest most deposit belonging to the Neolithic phase, included small pieces of ill-fired, hand made pottery with a course or medium fabric, most of the sherds either rusticated or cord-impressed. Wild rice and rice husk were used as degraissants in the making of this pottery. The Neolithic of Sohgaura bears close affinities with that of the Vindhyan region.

The overlying 2A and 2B deposits were identified as belonging to Chalcolithic period. This heralds a new era with the occurrence of the various shades of plain and painted black-and-red, black-slipped, grey and red wares. However, hand-made pottery was also found continuing with them. Black-and-red ware, painted in white, is the most characteristic pottery of this period. The painted black-and-red ware has vertical and horizontal bands, oblique and radiating lines and concentric semi-circles. Most of the designs are found on the black-slipped ware also in addition to criss-cross. The common shapes are bowls and dishes. Few sherds of Painted Grey Ware were also discovered from these levels. They are, however, no match in fabric and design to the typical sherds of this ware. The presence of this ware at this site is not strange as it occurs as far east as Vaiśālī. Nevertheless, it is noteworthy that here it has been found in association with painted variety of black-and-red ware.

The next period is distinguished by the appearance of the N. B. P. Ware. However, the predominant pottery assemblage is red in colour. The notable shapes include lipped bowls, vase with elongated body and chamfered rim and various types of bowls, jars and *gharas* usually associated with N. B. P. Ware elsewhere. The tradition of painted pottery continues in this period also. Other finds include terracotta and carnelian beads, cast and punched-marked coins. A burnt brick open drain and several ringwells also belong to this period. A large number of clay sealings have also been discovered. These are either inscribed with proper names in the Brāhmī characters of the third – second centuries BCE or with designs.

In the period which follows the N. B. P. Ware, we find the presence of various other pottery- types, stamped pots, terracotta figurines, beads and coins. The dominant pottery is a kind of plain red ware represented by various kinds of lids, bowls and jars. A number of coins belonging to Ayodhyā and Pāñchāla and also to the Kusana rulers have been recovered from this phase. Among the several terracotta figurines of this phase, two deserve special mention. One of them is a mould-made figure of Lakṣhmī holding lotus with long stalk in both hands and wearing an elaborate head-dress and ornaments. The other is the head of a male figure with foreign ethnic features having deep holes for eye-balls and nostrils. The fan-like head-gear is tilted backwards.

The Period VI of Sohgaura belongs to medieval antiquities. No regular structure of this period has been found except an open elliptical oven with rubbles all round. Quite a large number of pot-sherds were recovered with ash and sand from this oven. Such types of ovens have also been noticed on the surface in the unexcavated area. The pottery of this period includes various kinds of *ghaḍas,* carinated *hāṇḍīs* and spouted vessels. Some of them are decorated with stamped or decorated designs. Sherds of glazed ware were also found in the assemblage.

One notable feature of this phase is a very large number of glass bangles indicating a flourishing glass industry. These are mostly in double colours but few of them are also in polychrome. Stratified glass has also been used in manufacturing the bangles. It has been observed that in many cases tiny studs have been placed around the outer edge. Other antiquities from this phase include a good number of beads of glass and semi precious stones, coins of Akbar and Sharki Sultans of Jaunpur.

Thus, the excavation carried at Sohgaura has brought to light an unhampered, continuous sequence of cultures[22], having their origins sometimes during Neolithic and flourishing up to present day. We have got two C^{14} dates - 1235 +130BC and 1335 +110BC - from the Chalcolithic phase (2B)[23]of this site which places it at least to the middle of the second millennium BCE. With this chronological horizon for Chalcolithic, the beginning of Neolithic phase at Sohgaura may not be assigned later than the start of the second millennium BCE.

Rarely do we find in the country any other instance of a site with complete rural settings similar to that of Sohgaura, enjoying such a hoary antiquity and sustaining its existence uninterrupted up to present day. Located on the highlands at the confluence of Rapti and Ami on a vast flood prone riverine belt, it provided a favourable conduit to transit men and materials through waterways to reach out the hinterland villages that remained inundated and marooned many of the months of the Monsoon season[24]. It is not just a coincidence that the epigraph recovered from the site brings forth the creation of storage facilities for grains to be distributed during emergency, which in all probability were located at Sohgaura and not in *Vasagame*[25] i.e. Bansgaon as is usually being assumed. A continuous flow of cultures from the Neolithic period as revealed by the excavation of this site, added with the discovery of a Copper Plate, not only highlights its great prehistoric and historic character, but also signifies its vintage position as a great rural settlement which, because of its topography, continued to play a vital role as a local administrative centre, catering to the needs of the hinterland. The discovery of Neolithic at Sohgaura in 1974 was first of its kind in the entire *Sarayūpāra* region which not only transformed our archaeological perspective for this area but also paved the way for several other potential findings[26] in the years to come.

References

1. Jayaswal, K.P., *Epigraphia Indica* (*E.I.*) , vol. xxii, p.3; Barua, B.M., *Annals of Bhandarkar Oriental Research Institute* (*ABORI*), vol. xi, p. 32; *Indian Historical Quarterly*(*I.H.Q.*) vol. x, p.54.
2. *Journal of Asiatic Society of Bengal* (*JASB*, Proceedings), 1894, p. 84.
3. *Journal of Royal Asiatic Society* (*JRAS*), 1907 p. 509ff.
4. *E.I.* vol. XXII, P.3
5. *Ibid.*
6. *JASB,* 1894,(Proceedings), p.86.
7. *JRAS,* 1907, p. 509.
8. *Indian Antiquary* (*I.A.*), vol. xxv, 1896, p. 266.
9. *ABORI,* vol xi, p. 32; *I.H.Q.* vol. x, p.54.
10. *Select Inscriptions Bearing on Indian History and Civilization,* vol.1, Calcutta, 1965, p.58 (Foot-note no.1)
11. *E.I.* Vol. I, P. 71-74.
12. *Deśaiśvaryavaṁśanāmadheyopacāramiśvarasya, deśanāmadheyopacāramaniśvarasya, Arthaśāstra,* II.26.10.

13. *Pañcasu pañcasu vasesu anusaṁyāna niyatu etāyeva ayaya imāya dhammānusasṭhīya yathā ajāya kammāya,* Girnar Rock Edict.
14. *E.I.* Vol. XXI, p. 83-84.
15. Barua, B. M., *I.H.Q.* Vol. X, p. 57 ; Pandey,R. B., *E.I.* Vol. XXI, p. 54.
16. *Durbhikṣe rājā bījabhaktopagraham kritvā'nugraham kuryāt, Arthaśāstra* IV.78.3.
17. *E.I.* Vol. XXI, P. 85.
18. *Mauryasya rājñasya candraguptasya rāṣṭiyena vaiśyen puṣyagupten kāritam, aśokasya mauryasya yavanarājenntusaṣpenadhiṣṭhāya praṇālibhiralaṁkṛita kṛitā, Select Inscriptions,* I, Calcutta, 1965, p. 175-80. The interest of the Mauryan rulers in providing irrigational facilities to farmers is also affirmed by Megasthenese who speaks of the government officials *agronomoi,* who looked after, among other things, sluice gates on rivers in order to ensure distribution of irrigational water to tillers. See, Strabo, *Geographikon, Book* XV. I. Sec. 50.
19. *rājanavanabhidruhā dhruve sadasyutyame/ sahasrasthūṇa āsāte// RV.* II.41.15;
*rājanā kṣatramahriyamānā sahasrasthūṇam vibhrithaḥ saha dvau / ibid.*V.62.6.
20. The excavation at Sohagaura was carried out in two phases by S. N. Chaturvedi under the auspices of Department of Ancient History, Archaeology and Culture, Gorakhpur University, Gorakhpur. At first, it was taken in 1961-62 but, unfortunately, it could not be completed. It was, however, in the year 1974 that the actual nature of the site could be successfully exposed. In the first phase Chaturvedi was assisted by D. N. Tripathi and in the second by the present author and Krishna Nand Tripathi.
21. Unfortunately, because of the limited resources, it could not be extended in a large area. Only two trenches, measuring 5x5 metres were dug out of which only one could be dug up to natural soil. Significantly enough, it revealed a continuous sequence of cultures from the Neolithic period to the present day.
22. Description of prehistoric findings of Sohagaura is based on a brief report published in *Man and Environment,* IX, 1985, pp. 101-108, by S. N. Chaturvedi, personal knowledge of the author and the antiquities kept in the museum of Department of Ancient History, Archaeology and Culture, D. D. U. Gorakhpur University, Gorakhpur.
23. Chaturvedi, S. N. *Man and Environment, op.cit*
24. This is the usual phenomenon even today.
25. The reading of the term is highly disputed. See for details, Roy, S. N. *Bhāratīya Purālipi Evaṁ Abhilekha* (in Hindi), Allahabad, 1994, p.141. Moreover, Bansgaon is about 20 kilometres to the south of Sohgaura, obviously far away from the find spot of this Copper Plate and has not yielded any archaeological clue till date to suggest anything about its antiquarian character.
26. In the subsequent years, Purushottam Singh of Banaras Hindu University excavated the site of Imlidih in Gorakhpur district in 1991-92 and 1995 and Rakesh Tewari of state archaeology department, Uttar Pradesh excavated the site of Lahuradeva in Sant Kabir Nagar district 1997 onwards which have brought to light flourishing phases of Neolithic cultures that have undoubtedly established the prehistoric character of the *Sarayūpāra* region extending in antiquity at least to seven millennium BCE.

5

Lahuradeva Investigations and Sarayūpāra

Rakesh Tewari

Abstract

Multidisciplinary investigations, carried out at Lahuradewa in District Sant Kabir Nagar, have been a turning point in the archaeology the Sarayupar area in particular and Middle Ganga Plain in general, which have provided evidences for the antiquity of human activity going back to early Holocene, beginning of rice cultivation in *c.* 7th millennium BCE, interactions between western India and this part of the country during the third millennium BCE, and appearance of iron in second millennium BCE.

Trans-Sarayu area, popularly known as Sarayūpāra, is bounded by the Sarayu River in the west and south and the Gandak or Sādanīrā River in the east while the Himalayan foothills and Nepalese *tarai* mark its northern limits. This area forms a distinct north-western geo-unit of the Middle Ganga Plain (Fig. 1) and is graced by the aura of Lord Rāma and Buddha. On the basis of genealogical tables elaborated in the ancient Indian literature it has been supposed that this area would have been under the Ikṣhāvaku rulers since c. 3200 BCE (Pusalkar 1965; Pathak 1963; 1992). Further it was also suggested that the future archaeology may reveal evidence comparable to Harappan chronology from this area (Pathak 1992). On the other hand most of the archaeologists believed for a long time that the archaeological evidence of this area hardly goes a little earlier than Buddha; say some where around 800-700 BCE.

Subsequently, excavations at the ancient site of Sohgaura (situated at the confluence of the Rapti and Ami rivers in District Gorakhpur) conducted during the sixties and seventies by the University of Gorakhpur revealed a much earlier cultural deposit (Chaturvedi 1985). A good number of ancient sites considered to be containing contemporary cultural material were also brought to light during the course of exploration projects formulated by the Universities of Gorakhpur and Banaras Hindu University. Excavators of Sohgaura surmised an antiquity of third millennium BCE for the first settlers of this site on the basis of stratigraphic considerations. However, even this breakthrough could not change the general perception regarding the archaeology of this area. Subsequent excavations at Narhan (Singh 1994), Dhuriapar (Singh 1992a) and Imlidih Khurd (Singh 1993, 1994) located in the same district also revealed pre-Buddhist cultural remains comparable with that of Sohgaura and accelerated the archaeological activities in this area. Consequently, more and more pre-Buddhist sites listed along the Kuwana and the Ami rivers and from other areas during the extensive surveys undertaken by various scholars (Singh *et al.* 1990, 1991, 1992; Tewari & Srivastava 1994; Tewari & Mani 1996; Mani 1998) attested that the Sarayūpāra area was inhabited much before the advent of Buddha. Though a TL date from the pre-Narhan (chalcolithic) deposit could be obtained at Imlidih Khurd as *c.* 1700 BC (Pant 1995/96) in want of more scientific dates the antiquity of first settlers of the region remained unsolved. We took the baton from this point and focused on the selection of a suitable site for further investigations to address this issue.

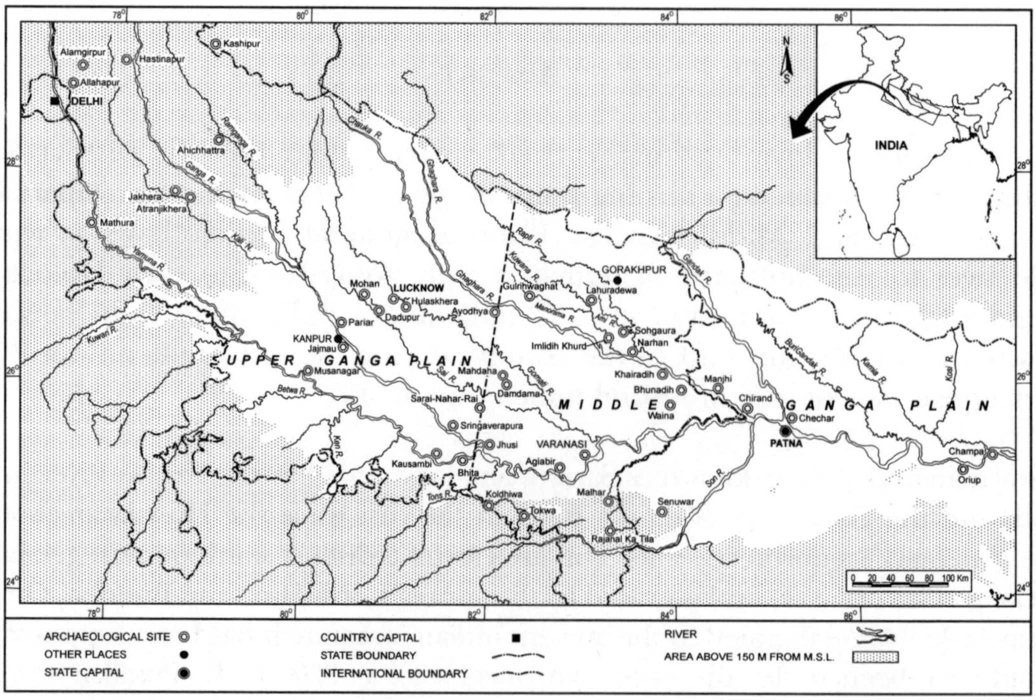

Fig. 1 : Map showing important Early Farming sites located in Upper and Middle Ganga Plain (U.P. & Bihar)

The required clue came from the ancient site of Lahuradewa noticed by Krishna Nand Tripathi a resident of this village, explored and published by Chaturvedi (1980) and further assessed by a number of scholars (Singh *et al.* 1990; Singh 1990; Tewari & Mani 1996). This site is located in Kuwana-Ami Doab (on Lat. 26^0 46' N; Long. 82^0 57' E; Fig.1) in district Sant Kabir Nagar. It is about 5 km south to the Bhujaini-crossing situated on the Basti-Goarkhpur Highway No. 28. A large lake surrounds the site from three sides. Two-fold investigation involving archaeological excavations at the ancient mound and palynological study of the sediments of the adjoining lake were initiated in the session 2000-2001 which continued up to 2005-06 with a gap in 2004-05. The outcome of these works have been submitted in a number of preliminary reports and research papers (Tewari *et al.* 2002, 2003, 2006, 2008; Saraswat 2005; Saraswat & Pokharia 2004, 2006; Chauhan *et al.* 2005; Singh and Saxena 2004; Saxena *et al.* 2006; Prasad *et al.* 2004; Sharma *et al.* 2004; Tewari, *et al.* 2008).

Outcome of the investigations at Lahuradewa

The archaeological excavation revealed about 4.00 m thick habitation deposit representing the five-fold cultural sequence. Their representative finds and conventional and radiocarbon dates available so far are briefed in Table-1. Period I (*c.* 9th - 2nd millennia BC), represented by about 1.20 m thick cultural deposit and designated as Early Farming Culture, is divided into two sub-periods (IA and IB) on the basis of the nature of deposits, cultural material and radiocarbon dates. About 45-50 cm thick sediments of **sub-period IA** was composed of clayey sand and *kankar* nodules. Radiocarbon dates for the carbonized remains collected from the deposits of this sub-period range between *c.* 9th to the beginning of *c.* 3rd millennia BCE.

The presence of charcoal and a series of three radiocarbon dates on them show that the antiquity of human activity at this site begins from about 9th millennium BCE. However, we are not clear that whether the structures represented by the posthole traced on lowest layers are of the same period. It may be surmised in this regard on the basis of an available AMS date of *c.* cal. BC 6442–6376 for the domestication of rice that the sedentary activities would have begun at least by this time and the process of exploitation and cultivation of wild rice would have been underway before that. Apart from the postholes, the remains of rammed clay-floors, burnt clay chunks bearing reed like impressions, provide evidence to surmise that the earliest settlers were constructing circular or oval huts, based on wooden posts, having clay plastered reed-screens. An irregular channel (drain) is a notable subsequent structure of this sub-period. It was traced for a length of about 12 m. It has been found connecting two large and deep depressions (ditches) during the subsequent excavations. The channel (*nālī*) is dug through the lowest layer and natural soil. Originally it was only 30-50 cm broad at upper level and about 50-60 cm deep. Subsequently, it became broader due to silt depositions and overflows. Finally, the channel was filled up and became defunct towards the upper level. The post-holes found on the surface of the sealing level of the channel clearly show that once it became flat, wooden structures were constructed over that.

Table 5.1 : Radiocarbon dates from Lahuradewa, district Sant Kabir Nagar (U.P.)

Cultural Period	*Representative finds*	C^{14} *dates BC/ BP*
Period IA	Marked by the presence of domesticated and wild rice along with foxtail grass and jobs tear, and a few wild taxa, red and black-and-red wares often bearing corded patterns.	BS-2145: cal. BC 3090 (2916) 2879, charcoal; BS-2148: cal. BC 3363 (3328, 3323, 3174, 3159, 3119, 3106, 3105) 3020, charcoal; BS-2151: cal. BC 3654 (3635, 3553, 3542) 3382, charcoal; BS-1951: cal. BC 4220, 4196, 4161, charcoal; BS-1967: cal. BC 5298, charcoal; ERL-6442: cal. BC 6442–6376 (AMS), rice husk; PRL-3030: cal BC 8317 – 8555 (8436), charcoal; PRL-3031: cal BC 8340 – 8696 (8518), charcoal; PRL-3032: cal BC 8813 -9171 (8992), charcoal;
Period IB	Introduction of copper artefacts and barley, wheat and lentil. Continuation of red and black-and-red wares often bearing corded patterns; a few paintings and incised designs; slipped pottery. Inclusion of pedestal bowl and dish or bowl-on-stand. Steatite beads and domesticated /wild *rice* continued.	BS-1950: cal. BC 2135 (2078) 2056, charcoal; BS-2274: cal. BC 2919 (2700) 2570, charcoal; ERL-6903: cal. BC 2345 (2273) 2200 (AMS), barley grain
Period II	Marked by the appearance of earthen bins, enhanced quantity of painted and plain black slipped and black-and-red wares, BRW, steatite beads, dish-on-stand, bowl-on-stand, pedestal bowl.	BS-1938: cal. BC 1519 (1435) 1399, charcoal; BS-2150: cal. BC 2012 (1884) 1750, charcoal;
Period III	Continuity of earlier cultural assemblage and introduction of IRON	BS-1939: cal. BC 1205 (1205) 1188, charcoal
Period IV	Painted/Plain Northern Black Polished ware etc.	
Period V	Red ware, brick structures	

The characteristic **pottery** of sub-period IA is represented by mostly hand made coarse variety of red and black-and-red wares of coarse variety often comprising cord impressions on their exterior surface (Figs. 2-4). A few sherds also show decoration by incised patterns and fine red slip. Two potsherds from the upper most levels of the deposits of this sub-period bearing cording, red slip and incised and painted decoration on their exterior surface (Fig.5) are noteworthy. Water vessels, pedestal and knobbed bowls, some of which decorated with applied rope-pattern, were the important shapes, in the ceramic assemblage.

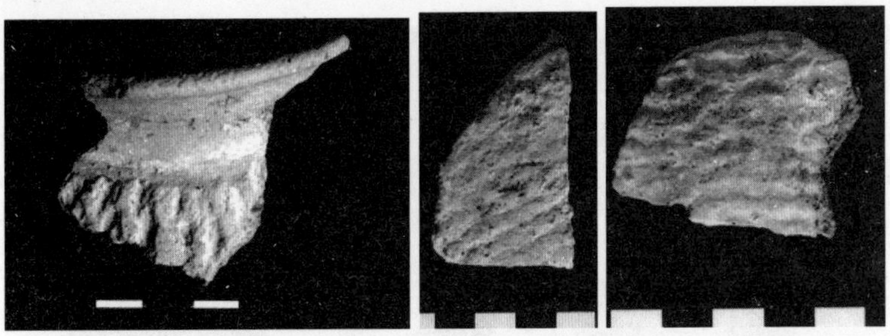

Figs. 2, 3, 4 : Corded pottery from the lower layers

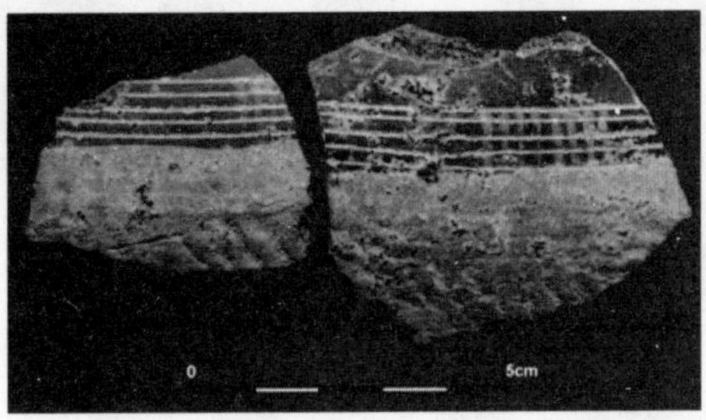

Fig. 5 : Decorated potsherds, upper level, Lahuradewa Period IA

According to Kripa Shankar Saraswat the carbonised **floral remains** of this sub-period comprise wild and domesticated rice (*Oryza rufipogon* and *Oryza sativa*) have been found as simple carbonised grains, carbonised rice husk-pieces, carbonised grains in the core of the pottery and rice husk/impressions in the matrix and core of the pottery (Figs. 6, 7). An AMS radiocarbon determination on a grain of domesticated rice husk-clot from the lowest deposits has given a date of 6409 BC (ER-6442: Cal. BP 8359 yr). Other than that, remains of wild and weedy rice (*Oryza* cf. *rufipogon*), foxtail-millet (*Sataria* cf. *glauca*), goose-foot / *bathua* (*Chenopodium album*), job's tear (*Coix lachrymal-jobi*), Artemis (*Artemisia* sp.), flat sedge (*Cyperus* sp.) and catchfly (*Silene conoidea*) have also been recovered from Period IA. The seasonality for their fruiting, tentative usage and cultivation covers almost all-the-year-round, which indicates the sedentary nature of the Lahuradewa settlers. The details regarding the morphological features of the floral remains are discussed in detail elsewhere (Tewari *et al.* 2006, 2008). The study of wood charcoal pieces have resulted in 12 and 24 taxa respectively in the remains collected from the deposits of sub-periods IA and IB (Table-2). The information indicates the immediate surrounding vegetation of Lahuradewa settlement.

Mostly charred **faunal remains** from Period IA, studied by Pramod Prabhakar Joglekar, except a few, comprise small and very small fragments. They provide evidence of only wild mammals and a few non-mammalian animals. Wild mammals utilized for food were the gaur (*Bos gaurus*), sambar (*Cervus unicolor*), spotted deer (*Axis axis*), wild pig (*Sus scrofa cristatus*), porcupine (*Hystrix indica*), mongoose (*Herpestes edwardsi*), hare (*Lepus nigricollis*) and common squirrel (*Funambulus pennanti*). One species each of small- and medium-sized bird was present in the assemblage that could not be identified. Bulk of the faunal material contained remains of at least four species of freshwater fishes – *Rita rita, Wallago atta, Laubuca laubuca* and *Labeo rohita.* It is clear from the evidence that freshwater mussel (Lamellidens sp.) were also part the diet of period IA.

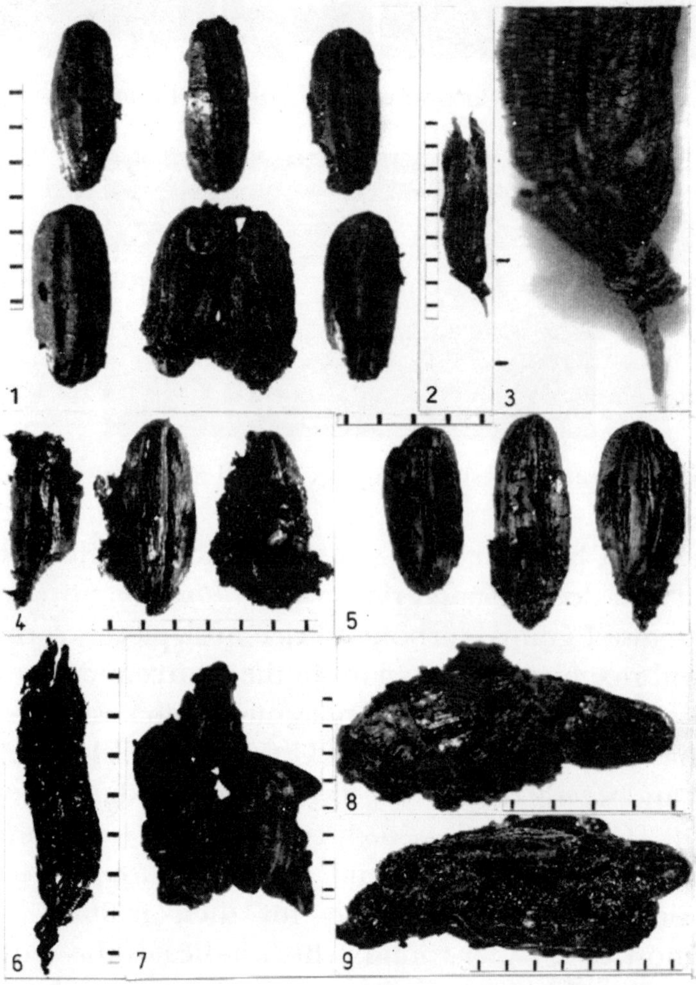

Fig. 6 : Rice grains, Lahuradewa, Period IA (after K.S. Saraswat)

Fig. 7 : Rice husk inclusion in a potsherd from Period IA, Lahuradewa

Table 5.2 : Wood charcoal remains identified from Lahuradewa excavations Period I

S. No.	Taxa	Period IA *c* 7000-3000 BC	Period IB *c* 3000-2000 BC
1.	*Acacia catechu / nilotica* (Khair, Babul)		*
2.	*Adhatada vesica* (Adusa)	*	*
3.	*Adina cordifolia* (Haldu)	*	*
4.	*Aegle marmelos* (Bel)	*	*
5.	*Alangium salvifolium* (Akol)		*
6.	*Albizia* cf. *procera* (Siris)		*
7.	*Anthocephalus cadamba* (Kadamba)		*
8.	*Artocarpus* cf. *lakoocha* (Badahal)		*
9.	*Bambusa* sp. (Bamboo)		*
10.	*Bombax ceiba* (Semal)		*
11.	*Butea monosperma* (Palash)		*
12.	*Dalbergia cf. sissoo* (Sheesham)		*
13.	*Drypetes roxburghii* (Putranjeeva)		*
14.	*Emblica officinalis* (Anwala)	*	*
15.	*Erythrina* cf. *subarosa* (Panjira)		*
16.	*Ficus glomerata* (Gular)		*
17.	*Holoptelea integrifolia* (Chilbil)	*	*

18.	*Logerstroemia parviflora* (Dhaura)	*	
19.	*Madhuca indica* (Mahua)		*
20.	*Mitragyana parviflora* (Keim)	*	*
21.	*Murraya koenigii* (Meetha-Neem)		*
22.	*Pongamia pinnata* (Karanj)		*
23.	*Pterospermum acerifolium* (Machakunda)	*	*
24.	*Srerculia villosa / urens* (Udal / Karrai)	*	
25.	*Syzygium cumini* (Jamun, Jambolana)	*	*
26.	*Terminalia arjuna* (Arjuna)	*	*

(After K.S. Saraswat)

The important **associated cultural components** of sub-period IA include a few lithic artefacts, beads, charred and un-charred floral and faunal remains, etc. One of the lithic-components, a sand stone piece, seems to be from the Himalayan foot-hills, while another one a small flake appears to be of Vindhyan origin. The *beads* include a good number of micro-to-medium-sized beads made of white or cream coloured steatite (comparable in size, shape and manufacturing technique with those of Harappan tradition) (Fig. 8), besides an example each of faience and carnelian. These beads have been found from the lowest to upper levels of this sub-period but considering their size and other probabilities they have been associated with the upper levels of IA and sub-period IB.

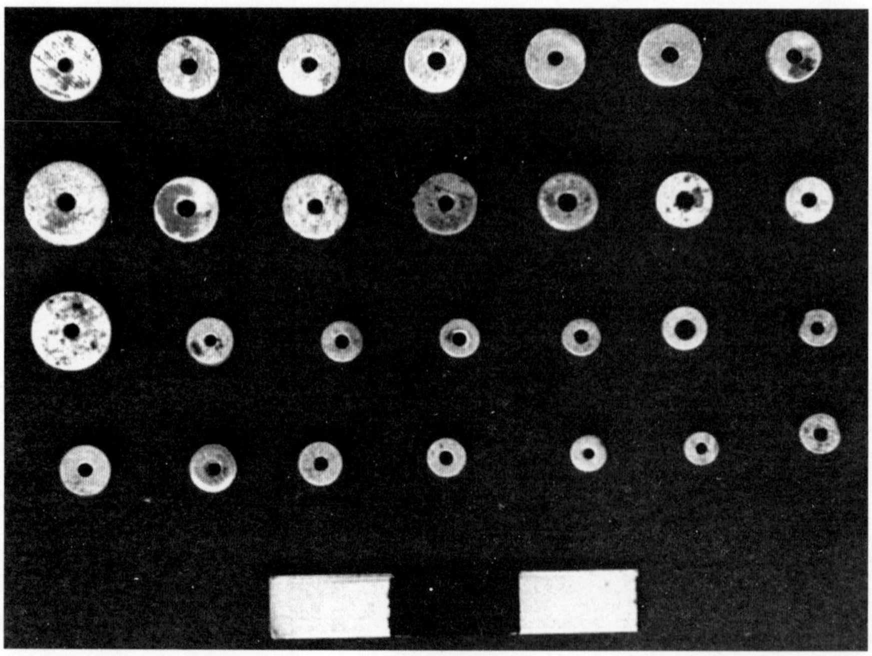

Fig. 8 : Steatite beads 1A/1B

Sub-period IB, represented by 50-60 cm thick cultural deposit, is datable between *c.* 3000-2000 BCE on the basis of radiocarbon dates. The beginning of sub-period IB is marked on the basis of the appearance of bowl or dish-on-stand (Fig. 9). New shapes in pottery such as beaker, perforated vessel, spouted vessel and dish or bowl-on-stand in this sub-period are also notable. Black-and-red ware of this phase shows an improved variety, sometimes comprising black or red slip and burnishing on one or both sides. Some of the potsherds bear painted decorations.

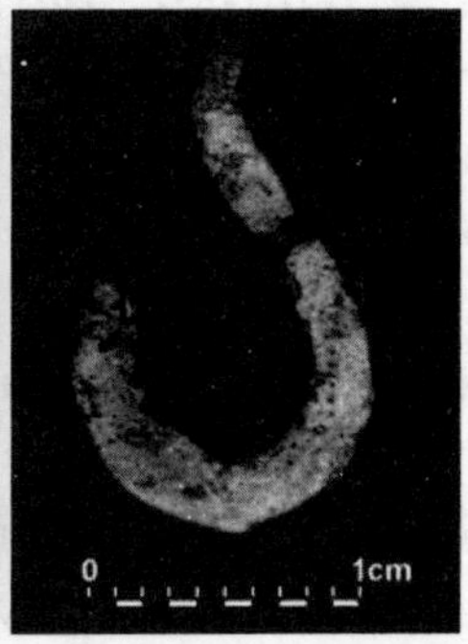

Fig. 9 : Dish-on-stand; **Fig. 10 :** Copper arrowhead; **Fig. 11 :** Copper fishing hook: Period IB

The most notable find of sub-period IB is the appearance of **copper artefacts** comprising a copper arrowhead (Fig. 10), a fishing hook (Fig. 11) and a clamp from its lower deposits. The arrowhead is made on copper sheet measuring 3.00 cm in length and 1.4 cm in breadth. Fishing hook is 1.5 cm long and 1.00 cm broad, and appears to be made of copper wire. Considering the radiocarbon dates and stratigraphic context these finds may be placed in early 3rd millennium BCE. Since the oldest copper finds from the middle Ganga Plain have not been dated earlier than *c.* 2000 BCE, the copper artefacts of Lahuradewa are so far the earliest known representatives of this metal in this region.

Small **associated finds** of sub-period IB, include beads made of terracotta, steatite (micro-to-medium sized), carnelian, faience and semiprecious stones, charred and un-charred bones (often bearing cut-marks), a finely made small bone-awl, a broken antler-bangle, medium sized broken stone pieces, a small stone scraper. Representative remains of structural activities such as post-holes and burnt mud-clots with reed-marks show that the tradition of wattle-and-daub dwellings of sub-period IA continued in sub-period IB.

Floral remains of sub-period IB includes domesticated rice (*Oryza sativa*), wild or weedy rice (*Oryza* cf. *rufipogon* and *Oryza officinalis*), barley (*Hordeum vulgarae*), *dwarf-wheat (Triticum sphaerococcum),* bread-wheat *(Triticum aestivum), lentil (Lens culinaris),* job's tear (*Coix lachrymal-jobi*), foxtail-millet (*Sataria* cf. *glauca*), goose-foot/*bathua* (*Chenopodium album*), job's tear (*Coix lachrymal-jobi*), Artemis/Mugwort (*Artemisia*sp.), flatsedge (*Cyperus* sp.), Kodon-millet (*Paspalum scrobiculatum*) and catchfly (*Silene conoidea*). Appearance of barley is important in association of a dish-on-stand in a level dated by conventional radiocarbon determination of associated charcoal content to 4170 $\pm$ 180 yr BP: Cal. BC

2700 Yr (BS – 2274). AMS date of barley at this level, however, turned up to 2345 (2273) 2200 yr BC (ERL – 6903).

The faunal remains of Period IB represent wild mammals such as the *gaur, sambar,* spotted deer, and wild pig. Except porcupine small wild mammals like mongoose, hare and common squirrel continued to be hunted or trapped for food. Appearance of domestic goats (*Capra hircus*) on the scene is an important feature of this sub-period. Buffalo is represented by only one fragment, but it is unclear weather it was domestic or wild. Presence of a panther, perhaps consumed after an encounter during hunting activity, is another notable find. IB has a clear evidence of bandicoot rat, a species that survives along humans if enough food is available throughout the year. Non-mammals such as birds, reptiles and fishes continued to be used as a major food resource like the previous phase.

Period II exhibit an enhanced agricultural production as evidenced by a good number of earthen storage bins (Fig. 12), almost in every part of the excavated settlement and a larger concentration of carbonized grain and seed remains. Appearance of tiles, terracotta *chaukis,* along with the painted black slipped ware (thin variety) and other painted potteries (Fig. 13, 14) from the very beginning of this period were noticeable finds. Period III is characterized by the appearance of highly corroded iron artefacts (Fig. 15).

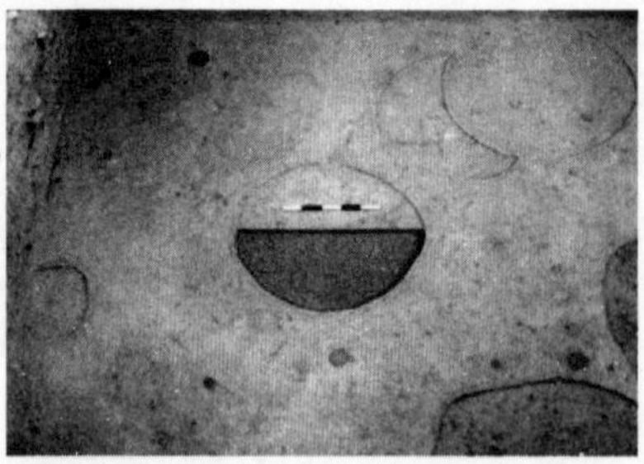

Fig. 12 : Earthen bins, Period II

Fig. 13 : Painted potsherds, Period II

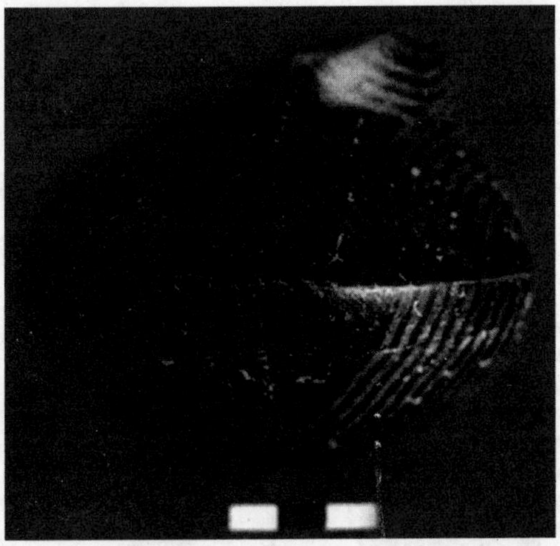

Fig. 14 : Painted potsherds, Period II

Fig. 15 : Iron artefacts, Period III

Investigation of lake-deposit

A small trench measuring 1.00 x 1.00 m was excavated to a depth of about 2.80 m on the dried up lakebed of the Lahuradewa-lake, at a distance of about 75 m from the archaeological site. Twenty-eight soil samples were collected from the sediments at an interval of 20 cm. The 2.80 m thick lake-deposit (Fig. 16) showed a succession of about 80 cm thick peat deposit followed by 2 m thick muddy sediments. Six radiocarbon dates of the successive sediments represent a time span of last 10,000 years (Holocene).

Indra Bir Singh and others (Singh & Saxena 2004; Saxena *et al.* 2006) have observed that the **Lithological Succession** of the lake profile shows about 80 cm thick peat deposit at the base representing a time span of 10000 to 5800 yr BP with rate of deposition of 1mm/100yr. The peat was formed under very humid condition in a lake with prominent swampy areas similar to present-day *Bils* (*Beels*) in Ganga delta region. During 5800 – 2188 yr BP, lake accumulated sediments at a rate of 1.7mm/100 yr. Rate of sedimentation increased to 4 – 7 mm/100yr in the last about 2 000 yr. Stable carbon isotope studies indicate that initially lake and surrounding area supported C-4 type grasses. Later C-3 type vegetation became prominent.

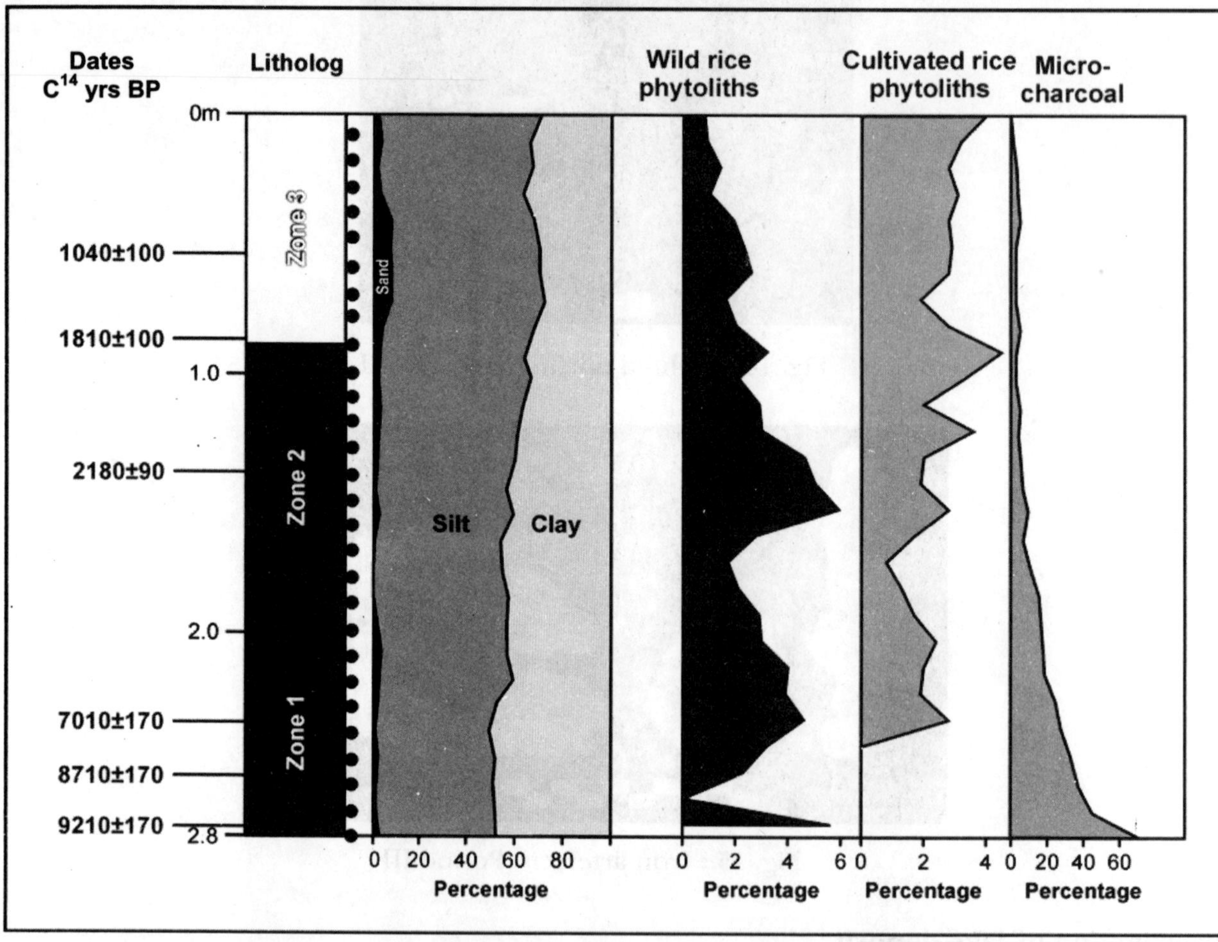

Fig. 16 : Lahuradewa lake profile showing distribution of grain size, wild rice phytoliths, cultivated rice phytoliths and microcharcoal. The Lake Profile represents approximately 10 kyrs history (After I.B. Singh).

According to Mohan Singh Chauhan *et al.* (2005) the **Pollen Analysis** of the Lahuradewa-lake-sediments (Fig.17) show grasses dominated in the open vegetation between *c.* 9500 and 8700 yr BP, together with meagre trees, under cool and dry climate. The invasion of the open vegetation by a few more trees envisages an amelioration of the climate between *c.* 8700 and 5700 yr BP. Expansion of lake due to increase of monsoon rainfall is also suggested during this period. Appearance of cerealia pollen from *c.* 7500 years BP has been suggested as an indication of the anthropogenic pursuits. On the basis of considerable enhancement of *Bambax,* advent of *Madhuca indica* as well as better representation of shrubby and certain other vegetation, open vegetation with patchy occurrence of forests and further increase in monsoon rainfall during *c.* 5700 to 2600 yr BP is suggested. Alternatively, increase in tree population *c.* 5700 yr can be related to change in landform due to reduced rainfall. The time of 5000-4000 yrs is considered a period of reduced southwest monsoon. The consistent presence of cerealia pollen along with other cultural pollen taxa from *c.* 5000 yr BP is considered to be suggesting the expansion of agricultural practices in the area. Presence of *Cannabis sativa* has also consistently been noticed at this time. The presence of *Trapa* (*singhara*) pollen in good numbers suggests that it would have formed a major part of the subsistence, for the local inhabitants.

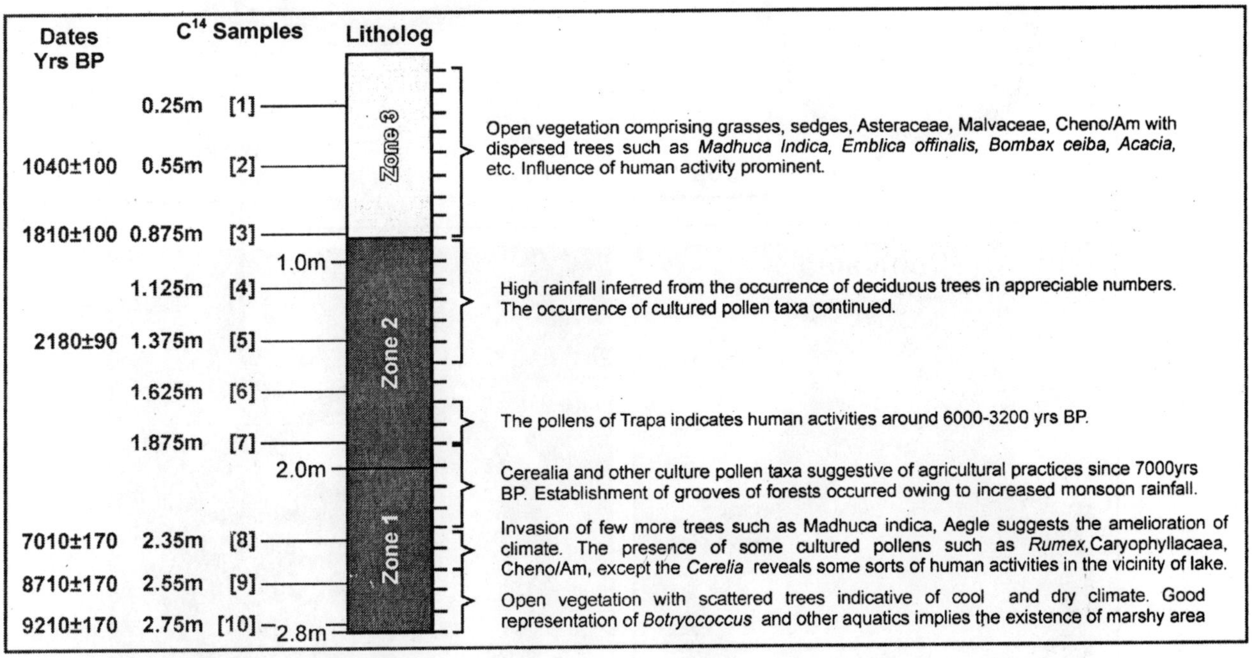

Fig. 17 : Pollen profile, Lahuardewa lake (after M.S. Chauhan)

The study on **Phytoliths** by Anju Saxena *et al.* (2006) in Lahuradewa lake sediments throughout the lake-bed profile revealed pronounced variations in shape and size of phytoliths (Fig. 18). Dominance of grass phytoliths is marked over non-grass phytoliths. Changes in grass phytoliths through time has been considered as related to the changing palaeovegetation, in response to the climatic shifts, especially the rainfall. Differentiation is established between the leaf-phytoliths of wild and domesticated forms of rice. In wild form of rice, number of scales on the edge of fan-shaped phytoliths is eight while in those of domesticated form it is nine and more. The presence of wild-rice phytoliths are observed since *c.* 10000 yr BP, while cultivated rice phytoliths appear in the deposits from *c.* 8300 yr BP and onwards.

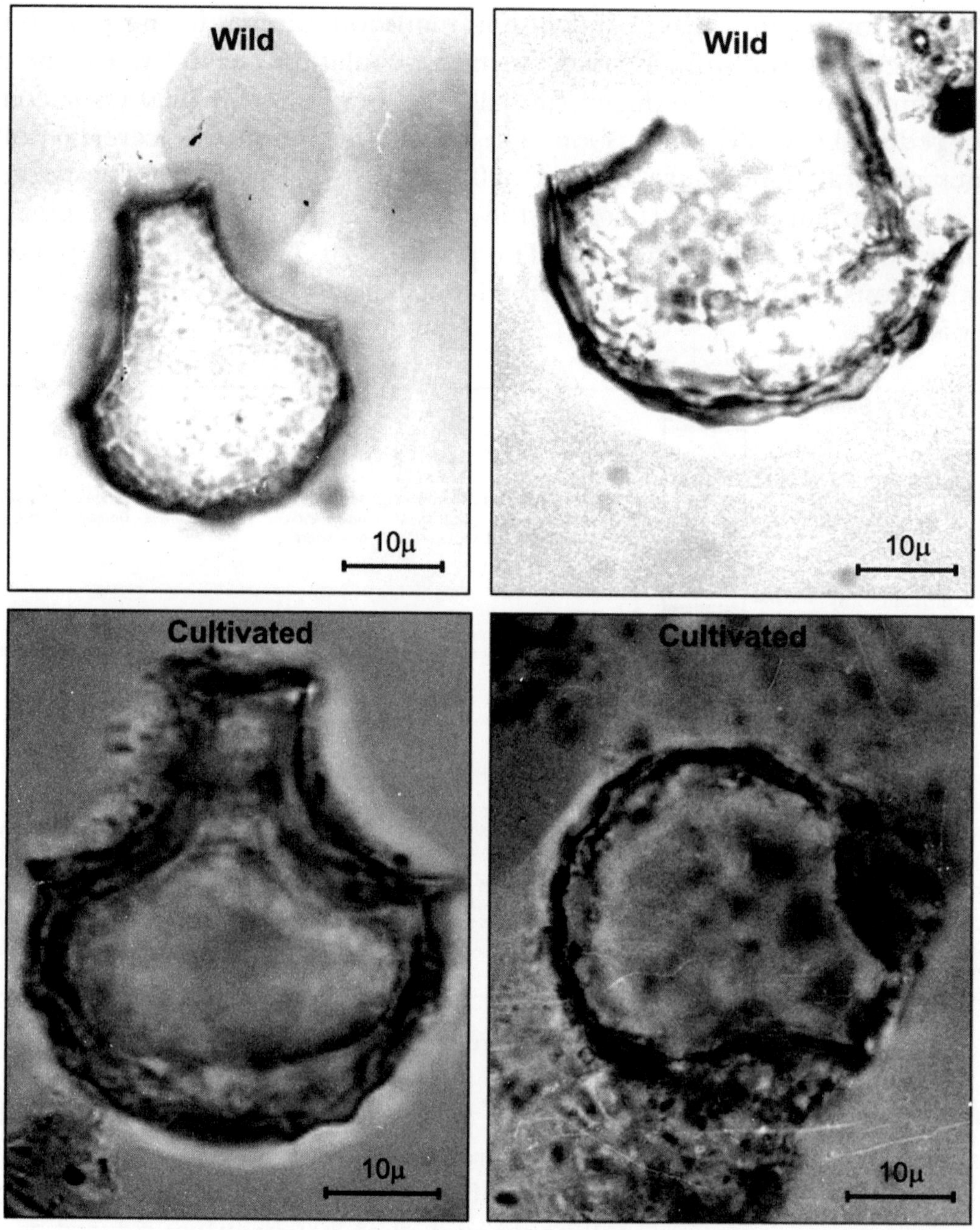

Fig. 18 : Wild and cultivated phytoliths of rice

The presence of **micro-charcoal** has been observed (Sharma *et al.* 2004) in all the 28 sediment samples of the Lahuradewa Lake, which indicate regular fire-events caused by human activity in the catchment area of the lake since last 10,000 yr BP (Fig. 16). The charcoal fragments in the bottom peat sediments of the succession occur in large proportion and almost all of them belong to grasses indicating thereby that open grass vegetation was well developed in region during *c.* 10,000 – 7822 yr BP.

The study on **fossil diatom** assemblage from Lahuradewa Lake sediments (Prasad *et al.* 2004) records rich and diverse forms in almost all the samples. The enhancing presence of various euterrestrial diatom species present in the upper horizon of peat and mud sediments is considered indicators as of rice paddy fields in the vicinity of the lake since *c.* cal. 9720 BP. Benthic and tychoplanktomic diatoms of paddy fields bloom in summer with good amount of water and can survive dry period by forming resting spores.

Conclusion

On the strength of the evidence revealed in the excavations at Lahuradewa it is suggested that this area of Sarayupar comprised largely grassland and there were a few thickets of trees at least since beginning of Holocene. The proportion of trees and grasses, however, varied slightly with the increase and decrease in rainfall during the fluctuating climate phases. As indicated by the consistent presence of tiny charcoal pieces in the lake sediments human activity is going on in Lahuradewa area since *c.* 9th millennium BCE.

The closeness and exploitation of wild flora by the early inhabitants of Lahuradewa would have culminated in plantation of certain plants including rice. At least by the mid 7th-millennium BCE they domesticated rice (*Oryza sativa*). However, gathering of wild flora, fishing and hunting remained their major food resources. They used coarse variety of red and black-and-red wares decorated with cord marks and constructed wattle and daub dwellings. Seasonality documentation of plant species recovered indicates their round the year sedentary settlement.

The appearance of domesticated barley (*Hordeum vulgare*) and domesticated grains of other cereals (including wheat, lentil and millets etc.) after about 5000 yrs BP corroborates an impetus in farming activity. Apart from the continuation of earlier hunting and gathering practices domestication of animals was also prevalent.

The presence of micro to medium sized steatite beads in the beginning of *c.* 3rd-millennium BCE and subsequent presence of barley, wheat and pulses along with dish-on-stand, copper arrowhead and fishing hook and domesticated goats (*Capra hircus*) (well known cultural components of the western and north-western South Asia culture complex) show interaction between the Middle Ganga Plain settlements and western part of the Indo-Pak sub-continent (well known as Harappan Zone).

Taken together the evidence from Lahuradewa and other sites of Sarayupar (such as Sohgaura and Imlidih Khurd) as well as other parts of the Middle Ganga Plain (e.g. Khairadih, Senuwar, Chirand) (Tewari 2009; 2010) the earlier perception that Harappans did not interact with this part of the country and that during the Harappan Culture this area was not inhabited by human settlements needs revision.

Since the iron has been found in an early context at various sites of the Ganga plain and other areas (Tewari 2003, 2004, 2010b; Singh 2002) the presence of highly corroded iron artefacts in the deposits of Period III datable to *c.* 12th century BCE at Lahuradewa is also notable. In view of these finds more careful observation is required in the future excavations in the region regarding the presence of this metal in the contemporary deposits.

Select Bibliography

Chaturvedi, S.N. 1980. 'Excavations at Sathiaon-Fajilnagar, District Deoria and Explorations in the Districts of Gorakhpur and Basti of Uttar Pradesh', *History and Archaeology*, I: 333-340.

Chaturvedi, S.N. 1985. 'Advance of Vindhyan Neolithic and Chalcolithic Cultures to the Himalayan Tarai: Excavation and Explorations in Sarayupara Region of Uttar Pradesh', *Man and Environment* IX: 101-108.

Chauhan, M.S., A.K. Pokharia and I.B. Singh 2005. 'Preliminary Pollen Analytical Investigation of Early Holocene Sediments from Lahuradewa Lake District Basti (Sant Kabir Nagar), U.P.', *Prāgdhārā* 15: 33-38.

Mani, B.R. 1998. 'Two Seasons of Archaeological Investigations in Trans Ghaghara Plains (District Basti and Siddharthanagar, U.P.) 1995-97,' *Prāgdhārā* 8: 107-36.

—— 2004. 'Excavation at Siswania (District Basti, U.P.): 1995-1997,' *Purātattva* 34: 100-115.

Pant, P.C. 1996. 'Archaeology and history: some problems of historical reconstruction', in K.M. Srimali (ed.) *Indian Archaeology Since Independence*, pp. 5-15. Delhi: ASHA.

Pathak, V.N. 1963. *History of Kosala*. Delhi, Varanasi, Patna, Motilal Banarasidas.

—— 1992. 'Bhartiya Itihas mein Rāma', in B.P. Singh and T.P. Verma *Śrī Rāma Viśvakoṣa*' (Hindi), pp. 112-13, Varanasi, Siddharth Prakashan.

Prasad, V., M. Sharma, A. Saxena, I.B. Singh 2004. 'Archaeology of Lahuradewa Area, Ganga Plain 7: Fossil Diatom assemblage from Lahuradewa lacustrine sediments as clues for Human activity', *Abstract: Joint Annual Conference (IAS, ISPQS, IHCS) and National Seminar on the Archaeology of the Ganga Plain (28-31 December 2004)*, p. 45, Lucknow: Directorate of U.P. State Archaeology.

Pusalkar, A.D. 1965. 'Traditional History from the Earliest Times to the Accession of Parikshit', in R.C. Majumdar (ed.) *The Vedic Age*, pp. 271-322, Bombay, Bhartiya Vidya Bhawan.

Saraswat, K.S. 2005. 'Agricultural Background of the Early Farming Communities in the Middle Ganga Plain,' *Prāgdhārā* 15: 145-177.

Saraswat, K.S. and A.K. Pokharia 2004. 'Archaeology of Lahuradewa Area, Ganga Plain 2: Plant Economy at Lahuradewa – A Preliminary Contemplation,' *Abstract: Joint Annual Conference (IAS, ISPQS, IHCS) and National Seminar on the Archaeology of the Ganga Plain (28-31 December 2004)*, p. 46. Lucknow: Directorate of U.P. State Archaeology.

Saraswat, K.S. and A.K. Pokharia 2006. 'The Emerging trends of Early Agricultural Economy in Middle Ganga Plain, with special reference to Lahuradewa in South Asian Context', *Abstracts: International Seminar on First Farmers in Global Perspective*: 17-18. Lucknow: Directorate of Archaeology.

Saxena, A., V. Prasad, I.B. Singh, M.S. Chauhan and R. Hasan 2006. 'On the Holocene record of phytoliths of wild and cultivated rice from Ganga Plain: evidence for rice-based agriculture', *Current Science* 90 (11): 1547-1551.

Sharma, M., V. Prasad, A. Saxena, I.B. Singh 2004. 'Archaeology of Lahuradewa Area, Ganga Plain 8: Microscopic charcoal in lacustrine sediments of Lahuradewa, as evidence of Human Activity', *Abstract: Joint Annual Conference (IAS, ISPQS, IHCS) and National Seminar on the Archaeology of the Ganga Plain (28-31 December 2004)*, pp. 48-49. Lucknow: Directorate of U.P. State Archaeology.

Singh, B.P. 1985-86. 'Excavations at Khairadih', Journal of Bihar Puravid Parishad, IX and X: 78-86.

—— 1990. 'Early Farming communities of Kaimur Foot-Hills', *Purātattva* 19: 6-18.

—— 2004. *Early Farming Communities of the Kaimur* I & II. Jaipur: Publication Scheme.

Singh, I.B. 2002. 'Late Quaternary evolution of Ganga Plain and proxy records of climate change and anthropogenic activity', *Prāgdhārā* 12: 1-25.

Singh, I.B. and A. Saxena 2004. 'Archaeology of Lahuradewa Area, Ganga Plain 4: Geomorphology and Stratigraphy of Lahuradewa Lake', *Abstract: Joint Annual Conference (IAS, ISPQS, IHCS) and National Seminar on the Archaeology of the Ganga Plain (28-31 December 2004)*: p. 45. Lucknow: Directorate of U.P. State Archaeology.

Singh, P. 1992. 'Neolithic-Chalcolithic cultures of Eastern Uttar Pradesh', in Tewari, R. *Archaeological Perspective of Uttar Pradesh and Future Prospects*, pp. 67-76. Lucknow: U.P. State Archaeological Organisation.

—— 1993. 'Archaeological Excavations at Imlidih Khurd –1992', *Prāgdhārā* 3: 21-35.

—— 1994a. 'Further Excavations at Imlidih Khurd – 1993', *Prāgdhārā* 4: 41-48.

—— 1994b. *Excavations at Narhan (1984-89)*. Delhi & Varanasi: BHU & B.R. Corporation.

—— 1996. *Prelude to urbanization in the Sarayupar Plain.* Chennai: Indian History Congress (fifty seventh session) Presidential Address (Section V).

—— 2003. 'Archaeology of the Middle Ganga Plain,' *Man and Environment* XXVIII (1): 1-6.

Singh, P., A.K. Singh and I. Singh 1991. 'Exploration along the Kuwana River in District Gorakhpur and Basti', *Prāgdhārā* 1: 69-82.

Singh, P., A.K. Singh, I. Singh 1992. 'Trial digging at Dhuriapar', *Prāgdhārā* 2: 55-60.

Singh, P., A.K. Singh and I. Singh 1992. 'On the Trails of Narhan Culture', *Prāgdhārā* 2: 33-34.

Singh, P., A.K. Singh and B. Singh 1995. 'Archaeological Investigations in Ballia (U.P.)', *Prāgdhārā* 5: 41-61.

Singh, P. and A.K. Singh 1996. 'Excavations at Waina, District Ballia, (U.P.)', *Prāgdhārā* 6: 41-61.

—— 1998. 'Excavations at Bhuna Dih, District Ballia (U.P.)', *Prāgdhārā* 8: 11-29.

—— 2000. 'Excavations at Agiabir, District Mirzapur (Uttar Pradesh)', *Prāgdhārā* 10: 31-55.

Singh, P. A.K. Singh and R.N. Singh 1997. 'Explorations along the Choti Sarayu (Tons) River', *Prāgdhārā* 7: 33-50.

Tewari, R. 2003. 'The origins of iron-working in India: new evidence from the Central Ganga Plain and the eastern Vindhyas,' *Antiquity*, Vol. 77 (297): 536-544. http://antiquity.ac.uk/ant/077/Ant0770536.htm

Tewari Rakesh 2004. 'The Myth of Dense Forests and Human Occupation in the Ganga Plain,' *Man and Environment,* Vol 2: 102-116.

Tewari, R. 2009. 'Perspectives in Archaeology of the Ganga Plain,' *Prāgdhārā* 19: 1-15.

Tewari, R. 2010. 'Changing Dimensions of Pre-Iron Age Cultures of the Middle Ganga Plain', in V. Tripathi and P. Upadhyay (eds.) *Archaeology of the Ganga Basin: Paradigm Shif.*: pp. 277-304. Delhi: Sharada Publishing House.

Tewari, R. 2010b, 'Updates on the antiquity of iron in South Asia,' *Man and Environment,* Vol. XXXV (2): 81-97.

Tewari, R. & B. R. Mani 1996. 'Further Archaeological Investigation in Sarayupar area', *Prāgdhārā* 6: 149-168.

Tewari, R. & R.K. Sriwastawa 1994. 'Exploration along the Ami River and its nearby areas in districts.

Tewari, R., R.K. Srivastava and K. K. Singh 2002. 'Excavation at Lahuradewa, District Sant Kabir Nagar, Uttar Pradesh,' *Purātattva* 32: 54-62.

Tewari, R., R.K. Srivastava, K.K. Singh, K.S. Saraswat, I.B. Singh 2003. 'Preliminary report of the excavation at Lahuradewa, district Sant Kabirnagar, U.P.- 2001-2002', *Prāgdhārā* 13: 37-68.

Tewari, R., R.K. Srivastava, K.K. Singh, K.S. Saraswat, I.B. Singh, M.S. Chauhan, A.K. Pokharia, A. Saxena, V. Prasad, M. Sharma 'Second preliminary Report of the excavations at Lahuradewa, District Sant Kabir Nagar, U.P.: 2002-2003-2004 & 2005-06,' *Prāgdhārā* 16: 35-68.

Tewari, R., R.K. Srivastava, K.S. Saraswat, I.B. Singh, K.K. Singh 2008. 'Eraly Farming at Lahuradewa,' *Prāgdhārā* 18: 347-373.

6

Agiabir : An Important Pre-historic Settlement of Eastern Uttar Pradesh

Ashok Kumar Singh

The protohistoric settlement of Agiabir (Latitude 25° 13′ 52″ N ; longitude 82° 38′ 41″ E) was discovered by the author in 1998-99 (Singh, 1998-99) and the archaeological excavations were carried out at the site for five field seasons (1999-2001 and 2005-2007) by the Banaras Hindu University. During the first three seasons excavation was conducted under the direction of Prof. P. Singh and the present author and in last two seasons excavation was conducted by Prof. V. Tripathi. This settlement is located on the left bank of Ganga, near Katka railway station on the Varanasi – Allahabad section of Northern Railway in District Mirzapur. There are three mounds extending in more than 40 acres. The main mound alone measures about 500 m x 500 m. Excavations were carried out at the western part of this settlement (Mound-1) and also in the eastern and central part of the main mound (Mound-2) and on the Mound 3, which have revealed uninterrupted sequence of cultures from second half of the second millennium BCE to the post-Gupta period (Singh & Singh, 1999, 2000, 2001 & 2003).

These excavations resulted into the documentation of the following culture - sequence:

Period I	:	Narhan culture (1300 B.C. - 900 B.C.)
Period II	:	Pre NBP with Iron ((900 B.C. - 600 B.C.)
Period III	:	NBPW culture (600B.C. - 200 B.C.)
Period IV	:	Śuṅga - Kuṣhāṇa Period (200 B.C. - 300 A.D.)
Period V	:	Gupta and post Gupta deposits (300 A.D-700 A.D.)

In the second and third seasons excavation was conducted in a 20 m x 20 m area on the southern part of the main mound which resulted into the discovery of a large house - complex of burnt bricks and datable to Period IV. It comprised 11 rooms of various sizes having altogether 5 building levels (Singh & Singh, 2001 : 157 - 159).

Remains of Period I (Narhan culture) were documented in the lowermost 60 cm cultural deposit. The inhabitants of this period lived in wattle-and-daub houses. Fragments of burnt clay with reed marks and patches of floors, ovens and post-holes have been recorded. Two silos, obviously used for storage of grains, were recorded from this period. The main ceramic industries of this period comprised Black-and-red ware (mostly medium and coarse fabrics), black slipped ware (in a limited quantity but in fine fabric) and red ware. A few sherds of Black-and-red ware and black slipped ware bear linear paintings in white as in the case of Narhan. The main types in Black-and-red ware are bowls, storage jars, lipped basins and dish-on-stand . Some sherds of Black- and- red ware bear cord impressions on the exterior. In black slipped ware the important shapes are deep bowls, *Loṭā* shaped vessels and pedestal bowls. In rẹd ware no kitchen ware vessels are reported except for legged perforated bowls with several perforations at the base .Vases and storage jars, some bearing applique designs on the exterior, are the other types in this ware.

A bead manufacturing workshop is an important discovery of this period. Twenty - four stone beads (16 finished and 08 unfinished), one bead each of bone and shell together with waste stone chips were recovered. Among the beads made of semi - precious stones, agate was the most favored material and the presence of unfinished beads of this stone right in earliest period demonstrates that it was manufactured locally. This tradition of bead making was continued in the subsequent two periods as well. It would thus be logical to conclude that bead manufacturing was an important industry and obviously it was exported to other contemporary settlements, besides catering to the aesthetic requirements of the local inhabitants. Faience was another interesting material and its presence in sizeable numbers, particularly in Period III is an important discovery, indicating its local manufacture and trade (Singh & Singh, 2000 : 141 - 149). The inhabitants of Period I at Agiabir made the best use of the neighboring Vindhyan hills. The easy accessibility of siliceous stones in the hills opposite this site led to the manufacture of beads and microliths locally.

Among the other noteworthy finds of this period are the microliths including blades, cores, bladelets, retouchers and flakes. This industry comprises chips, flakes, bladelets, cores and retouchers. Besides, some stone nodules were also found. The stone lumps used here are banded agate, chert, jasper, quartz and chalcedony.

Other antiquities comprise terracotta beads, gamesmen, bone points and pottery discs. An incense burner or lamp of baked clay is a noteworthy find of this period. Only one fish hook of copper was recovered. No iron object was found. The inhabitants of Agiabir were not entirely vegetarians. Food was supplemented by meat as indicated by the discovery of a large numbers of animal bones with cut marks. Fire places alongwith charred bones provide adequate evidence for the roasting of meat.

Period II belonged to pre - NBP deposit which was marked by the introduction of iron artefacts. The inhabitants of this period continued to live in wattle - and - daub houses, as in the preceding period. Traces of burnt floors and reed marks have been recorded. The main ceramic industries of this period are black slipped ware and Red ware but this period witnessed the total absence of Black - and - red ware. The antiquity comprises bone points, beads of terracotta and semi - precious stones and a few copper and iron objects.

Period **III** was marked by the occurrence of the NBP ware with a 4 m thick deposit on the main mound. The other ceramic assemblage of this period comprised of black slipped ware, grey ware and red ware. Straight sided and flanged bowls, dishes with incurved rim are the principal types in black slipped ware, grey ware and NBPW. Bowls, lipped basins and vases are the main types in red ware. Some painted sherds of NBP were also recovered which is well comparable with the NBPW potteries of Rajghat period **IB** (Narain, & Roy, 1977). The inhabitants of this period continued to live in wattle - and - daub houses as in the preceding period. Remains of rammed floor, ovens were recorded in this period. Burnt brick structures were not recovered from this period presumably due to the limited nature of excavation. The small finds comprise beads of agate, carnelian, jasper, steatite and terracotta, bone points, skin rubbers and discs of terracotta and copper and iron objects.

During the 2000 - 2001 excavation, the most important discovery of the NBP period was a cache of copper and iron objects found in a room. This cache was buried in layer (12) and was resting on the top of layer (13). The copper vessels were kept upside down. The copper objects *in situ* include three vases (*Haṅḍas*) with flaring rim and body diameters of 41, 37.6 and 35 cm respectively, two carinated *hāṅdīs* with featureless rims and body diameters of 31 and 31.8 cm respectively, one lid -like object, one *Loṭā* shaped vessel with the diameter of the mouth of 27.6 cm, one bowl with incurved rim and diameter at the mouth of 15.1 cm, one miniature bowl with featureless rim and diameter at the mouth of 11 cm and a mirror. All these objects except the *Loṭā* were placed upside down at the depth of 6.60 m below the datum. The iron objects include two swords with lengths 69.5 and 64.5 cm respectively and a lamp stand of 1.07 m long. The upper portion of this lamp stand was decorated with a bowl with four raised dots at the rim and a circular plate is fitted just below (Singh & Singh, 2002 : 109 -115). P.K. Chattopadhyay did the chemical study of some of these objects. It shows that these objects were made of high tin bronze (Singh & Chattopadhyay, 2002: 101-106).

Similar cocking vessels of hammered copper have been recovered from the Śaka - Pārthian city of Sirkap of first century CE (Marshall, 1951 : 258, PI. 174, Nos. 257 - 258). A copper vessel of the similar type was reported earlier from Chandraketugarh (District - 24 Paraganas, West Bengal) from surface (Gosh, 1989: 95 - 96) and another vessel was found from Mahasthangarh (Bangladesh) from Kuṣhāṇa levels.

Mirror in the shape of circular metal discs, originally polished on its one side and plain or with a design or decoration on the other, has been found in a limited number at many sites. Two copper mirrors with long tang are reported from Harappa (Vats, 1940: 391). The diameter of these mirrors is 16 cm to 17.5 cm. The finest example of mirrors (nineteen in number) are from Taxila, where they are found only in Śaka - Pārthian city of Sirkap datable to 1st century BCE - CE (Marshall, 1951 : 215, 584 - 85, PI. 182, Nos. 208 - 211). They are circular in size and varying between 5.55 and 16.5 cm in diameter. Three mirrors have been found in the Kundanagar Hoard in Brahmpuri (District Kolhapur, Maharashtra) placed in a large metal pot buried in a room of the Sātavāhana period (first - third centuries CE) (Khandalavala, 1960 : 27 - 95) and two copper mirrors are reported from Mason Dih (district Ghazipur, UP), one in NBP levels and the other in the Gupta levels (*IAR*, 1964 - 65: 42 - 43; Ghosh, 1989, I : 348). Two handled circular bronze mirrors with recessed face have been reported from Rairh (Puri, 1998 : 43; PI. XXI, No, 14). Similar knobbed vessels were recovered from Wari-Bateswar region of district Narshingdi (Bangladesh) (Pathan, 1989; Basa *et al.*, 1998) and Bon Don Ta Phet (Thailand) (Rajpitak, 1979 : 26-31).

As regards the swords, identical iron swords found at Taxila vary from 52 to 85 cm in length and belong to first century CE. Strabo and Arrian state that the Indian soldiers carried broad swords three cubits in length in the fourth century BCE. (Marshall, 1951 II: 542 - 43, PL. 164). Iron lamp stand of this size are not reported from any other site in India. The two lamp stands *(candelabra)* recovered from Taxila have been dated to the first century CE. (Marshall, 1951 II: 542). These consist of a plain vertical rod with a tripod base and leaf like terminal or ring at the top. The height of these lamps varies from 52 cm to one meter (Marshall, 1951 : 542, PI. 163, Nos. 33 - 35). From the above description, it is clear that cooking vessels, swords and lamp stands occurring at other sites belong to a much later date than those from Agiabir.

Two silos were also exposed in the vicinity of this cache in the northern and southeastern sides of the house. A uniform burning of 20 cm at the base of layer (13) was noticed throughout the excavated area of 5.15 x 2.50 m. As the excavation was confined to a small area, it is difficult to determine whether this burning is deliberate or accidental. A similar burning activity of the same period was noticed in the corresponding levels at Narhan (Singh, 1994 :14) and Jhusi (personal information).

The new carbon dates of NBPW period at Agiabir demonstrates that this period commenced around 1000 BCE. The two radio carbon dates of middle phase of NBPW at Agiabir read as 889˜63 and 830 BCE respectively (Tripathi & Upadhyay, 2009 : 55-56). The above dates indicate that the human activities of Period III (NBPW Period) at Agiabir may be placed in first millennium BCE.

Period IV belongs to the Śuṅga - Kuṣhāṇa period. It was represented by red ware and red slipped ware with bowls with incurved rim, large storage jars, sprinklers and bottle, necked jars, button - knobbed and inkpot lids, basins and miniature vessels as the main types. The houses of the period were made of burnt bricks. The structural activity shows three phases. In the upper phase structures were largely built of re - used material and followed more or less the earlier plan. As stated earlier, a house complex of 11 rooms with a courtyard and a boundary wall was noticed .The plinth area of this complex is 18 m 50 cm (east - west) and 12 m 80 cm (north - south). There were two entrances to this structure, one from the southeast corner and other from northern side.

Rooms 1 and 4 are rectangular in size and measure 6.20×2.50 and 5.15×2.40 metre respectively. The bricks used in these rooms and in the boundary wall are of

44× 29×5 cm, 39×28×5 cm and 42×28×5 cm In size. Three ovens made of burnt bricks were noticed in rooms No.2, 8 and 9. Floors made of burnt bricks were exposed in room No. 1 and in the courtyard. This courtyard was used in two phases. In the first constructional phase, the house contained as many as 11 rooms, all around the central courtyard which is rammed. In the subsequent phase the area of the courtyard was increased by demolishing Room Nos. 3 and 4 and encompassing this area into it. The courtyard, which had a rammed base earlier, was now provided with a pavement of burnt bricks.

Small finds of this period comprised terracotta human and animal figurines, beads of semi precious stones and terracotta, bone points and an almost complete votive tank. Thirty-six copper coins were recovered from these rooms in different layers of which 16 coins were recovered from Room No. 4 alone.

The habitational remains of Period V belonged to the Gupta and post-Gupta times. Some walls of the preceding period were used in this period and two walls of 12 m 70 cm (north-south) each were constructed by reused bricks. An almost square structure of 1.35×1.40 m size was constructed in this period for religious purpose. The structural activity and other finds of this period show that this area was used as a religious complex during this period. Mention may be made of few long ovens (size 4.18 ,3.70, and 3.10 m), presumably used as community kitchens on festive/religious occasions. Extensive damage has been done to the structures of this period by brick robbing in recent years. The ceramic industry comprises essentially of red ware with some sherds of red polished ware. Other small finds comprise of terracotta human and animal figurines, terracotta beads and discs, antimony rods of copper and iron objects.

One seal of ivory and five sealings of baked clay are the important discovery. The seal recovered from Agiabir belongs to a special category. This seal was recovered from inside a room near the suspected main entrance on the eastern side of Mound - 2. It bears five letters engraved in Brāhmī characters of early fourth century CE having legend *'Skandnāga'*. Another sealing bearing the legend *'Hariṣeṇasya'* in pre - Gupta Brāhmī characters was recovered from trench YE -6 - II. The palaeography of this sealing belongs to the late third or early fourth century CE. About 400 sealings bearing the legend *'Hariṣeṇasya'* were discovered from Rajghat (Varanasi) (Narain & Roy, 1977). The other sealing having legend *'Rudrapalasya'* in Gupta Brāhmī characters was discovered from the trench YE 6 - I at the main mound. Two sealings bear symbols only.

The mound continued to be inhabited during the Gupta period as also in the post - Gupta times. However, the remains of these periods could not be documented in the limited excavations. Fragments of stone jambs of temples with Krishṇa - līlā scenes carved on them and broken sculptures of Ambikā, Gaṇesha, Sūrya and *Ek Mukh* Śivalinga datable to tenth - twelfth centuries CE are lying on the present - day temple of *Lutabir* located south- west of present Agiabir village. (Singh, 2001 : 201- 205).

Besides, two test pits measuring 2 m x 2 m in size were excavated on Mound - 3 located 1/2 km east from main mound. Remains of the mid phase of NBP were noticed in the lower level of these trenches. These continued to be inhabited till the Gupta Period.

The first settlers occupied the western part of Mound-I and subsequent settlements gradually shifted to the eastern sides along the Ganga. Incidentally the remains of Period I were found located in the peripheral area of the main mound, which appear to be a flourishing Urban Centre. The maximum expansion of the township is seen during the mid phase of the NBP period (*circa* 400 B.C.) when the population expanded upto Mound-3 (half km. east of the main mound) also. I therefore incline to summarize that stone bead production was one of the important factors in Period I which gave impetus to the growth of the settlement by providing prosperity in general and cultural interaction through long distance trade in particular. I firmly believe that a horizontal excavation at Agiabir which is still awaiting, will provide stage-by-stage evolution of urbanization in the Middle Ganga plains, on one hand and contribution of art, craft and traded items on the other.

References

Basa, K.K. and S.S. M. Rahman, 1998. 'Bronze Knobbed Bowls from Wari, Banglaesh :Implication for trade', *Journal of Bengal Art*, 3 : 291 - 98.

Ghosh, A *(Ed.)*, 1989. *An Encyclopaedia of Indian Archaeology*. New Delhi: Munshiram Manoharlal.

Khadalavala, Karl 1960. 'Brahmapuri - A consideration of the metal objects found in the Kundangar Hoard', *Lalit Kala* 7: 27 - 95.

Khadalavala, Karl, 1960. 'Brahmapuri - A Consideration of the Metal Objects found in the Kundangar Hoard', *Lalit Kala*, No. 7, New Delhi, Lalit Kala Academy, pp. 27 – 95.

Marshall, John. 1951 (reprinted 1975). *Taxila*, Vol. I- III . Delhi , Motilal Banarasidas.

Narain, A.K. & T.N. Roy, 1977. *Excavations at Rajghat*, Part II, Varanasi, Banaras Hindu University.

Singh Ashok Kumar, 1999. 'Explorations at Agiabir, District – Mirzapur (UP)', *Prāgdhārā*, No. 9 (1998 – 99), Lucknow, Journal of the UP State Archaeological Department pp. 51 –56.

Singh, P. 1994. *Excavations at Narhan (1984 – 89)*. New Delhi & Varanasi, B.R. Publishing Corporation & Banaras Hindu University.

Singh P. & A. K. Singh, 1999. 'Agiabir – 1999 : A Preliminary Report', *Purātattva*, No. 29, 1998 – 99, New Delhi , Bulletin of the Indian Archaeological Society, pp. 117-119.

Singh P. & A.K. Singh, 2000. 'Excavations at Agiabir, District – Mirzapur (UP)', *Prāgdhārā*, No. 10 (1999 – 2000). Lucknow, Journal of the UP State Archaeological Department pp. 31 – 55.

Singh P. & A.K. Singh, 2001. 'A Rare Discovery of Metal Objects from Agiabir, District Mirzapur, Uttar Pradesh', *Man & Environment*, XXVI (2), Pune, Journal of the Indian Society for Prehistoric & Quaternary Studies, Pune, pp. 109–115.

Singh P. & A.K. Singh, 2004. *Archeology of Middle Ganga Plain – New Perspectives (Excavations at Agiabir)*, Shimla & New Delhi, Indian Institute of Advanced Study & Aryan Books International.

Tripathi, V. & P. upadhyay, 2009. *Excavations at Agiabir (2006-07)*, *Purātattva*, No. 39, pp. 50-57.

Vats, Madho Sarup, 1940 (reprinted 1997). *Excavation at Harappa*, Vol. I & II. New Delhi, Munshiram Manoharlal.

7

The Neolithic Culture in Allahabad District

V.D. Misra

The Neolithic culture constitutes a distinct chapter in the history of man. In the initial stage of its study, it was presumed that this phase (Neolithic) was characterized by sedentary settlement, domestication, cultivation, use of polished celts and pottery[1]. But subsequent researches about the culture established that the use of polished celts and pottery was not an essential ingredient of the culture in the beginning. From Greece[2], Turkey[3], Western Asia[4], Iran[5], Afghanistan[6] and North-western India[7] Neolithic sites without pottery were brought to light. It was also noticed that the polished celts did not constitute an essential feature at all of the Neolithic sites. In the context of India, in the light of ecological-geographical factors, Neolithic cultures often with varying profiles have been noticed. Piecing together the available evidence, the Neolithic culture in Indian sub-continent is divided into seven fold divisions[8]:

- (i) North- Western India
- (ii) Northern India (Kashmir valley)
- (iii) North-Central India (Vindhyan region)
- (iv) The Mid-Ganga plain covering eastern Uttar Pradesh and Western, Southern and Northern Bihar
- (v) South-East India covering parts of Bihar and Orissa
- (vi) North-Eastern India covering Assam and other sub-Himalayan region
- (vii) Southern India covering peninsular India comprising Tamilnadu, Andhra Pradesh and Karnataka.

In the following pages, an attempt has been made to bring out the salient features of the Neolithic culture of Allahabad district. The area under discussion comprises parts of north-central India and parts of the mid Ganga plain. The district of Allahabad is marked by two different types of geographical zones. The southern part of the district comprising parts of Meja, Karchhana, Bara and Koraon sub-divisions is hilly while the other part particularly the area lying to the north of the Ganga is plain.

The Neolithic Culture of the Vindhyas in Allahabad District

In the Belan valley, the Neolithic sites located so far, include Koldihwa, Mahagara, Panchoh, Kukurahata, Deoghat, Koilariha, Futuha, Chauridih - Kotia, Bansghat, Doria, and Patehri, all falling in Koraon sub-division while in the plain to the north of the Ganga, the important sites being Jhusi and Hetapatti. Of these Koldihwa[9], Mahagara[10] and Panchoh[11] in the Vindhyan area and Jhusi[12] and Hetapatti[13] in the Ganga plain have been excavated. In the following pages, a brief report is being placed about these excavated sites:

Koldihwa : The archaeological site of Koldihwa (Lat. 24° 54' 30" N., Long. 82° E.) is situated on the left bank of the Belan at a distance of about 85 km to the south-east of Allahabad city in the Koraon sub-division of Allahabad district. The site, roughly rectangular in outline and flat in elevation, is fairly extensive (500 m×200 m), the longer axis being west-east. The mound is eroded partly by the river and nullah and partly by bad land topography as a result of which it is broken into a number of small mounds of which two are situated along the river and the other one lying at the south-east corner. The site was excavated by the Department of Ancient history, Culture and Archaeology, University of Allahabad during 1972-73, 1973-74, 1974-75 and 1975-76. A three fold cultural sequence - Neolithic, Chalcolithic and Early Iron Age was exposed. The Neolithic deposit (0.45 m) rests on compact natural soil. The salient feature of the Neolithic culture included hand made pottery, rounded celts fashioned on basalt, blades and miroliths along with querns, mullers and ring-stones fashioned on sand stone.

Mahagara : (Lat. 24° 54' 50'' N., Long. 82° 3' 20'' E.) is situated on the right bank of the Belan to the west of confluence of the old and new channels of the river, just opposite Koldihwa. The mound, irregular oval in form, is bounded on the south-east by the old channel and on the south-west by the new channel of the Belan. It measures about 800 sq. m. The site was excavated by the Department of Ancient History, Culture and Archaeology, University of Allahabad for three seasons, 1975-76, 1976-77 and finally 1977-78. It is a single culture site. The index trench brought to light 2.60 m thick occupational deposit. The excavations at the sight exposed as many as 18 hutments, circular or oval on plan. These were found littered with potsherds, animal bones, fragments of querns, mullers, hammer stones, microliths, rounded polished celts, etc. On the periphery of floors of these hutments, post-holes were detected.

A cattle-pen measuring 12.5×7.5 m surrounded by eight floors (four house units) was exposed at the site. The pen, irregular rectangular on plan was enclosed by 28 post-holes with three openings. According to the excavator, absence of any post-hole inside the cattle-pen indicated that it would have been open to the sky. Hoof prints of cattle of different age groups were detected in the pen.

Panchoha : The Neolithic site of Panchoha (Lat. 24° 55' 45" N., Long. 82° 30" E.) is located at the distance of 2.5 km north-west of Koldihwa on the right bank of the Belan. The site was found disturbed on account of ant and cultivation. A small trench laid out in 1975-76 brought to light 0.60 m thick deposit. Traces of circular or oval floors were detected at the site. Archaeological objects identical to those of Neolithic Koldihwa were obtained.

The Neolithic culture of the Vindhyan region in Allahabad district is characterized by sedentary settlement, handmade pottery comprising corded, rusticated, burnished red, burnished black and occasionally crude black and red ware, ground stone celts of rounded variety with rectangular or oval cross section. Food processing equipments like quern, muller, hammer stone, microliths and domestication of animals and cultivation of plants, single tanged bone arrowheads, earthen discs with central perforation generally made of broken pottery, spherical terracotta beads, shell pendants are some other objects found at these sites. Of the animal bones found from these sites, mention may be made of bones of cattle, sheep, goat, deer, antelope, etc. Remains of aquatic creatures like turtle, fish, etc. were also recorded along with the bones of birds. Cattle, sheep and goat appear to have been domesticated.

Both burnt rice and rice husk along with rice chaffs have been found embedded in the potery. It appears that rice husk was used as degraissant. Palaeobotanical studies have revealed that the people were using both wild as well as cultivated rice *(Oriza sativa)*. Recent studies of Emma Harvey and Dorian Fuller[14] of the botanical material of Koldihwa and Mahagara have thrown welcome light on the range of cereals cultivated by the Neolithic people of Koldihwa and Mahagara. The crops identified include rice, barley, wheat, pulses, sesame and small millets. The available evidence from both Koldihwa and Mahagara indicates that wild and cultivated varieties of rice and small millets were used from the beginning of the Neolithic settlement. Barley, wheat, pulses and sesame were introduced at these sites subsequently. At Tokwa (Mirzapur district) Dr. Saraswat[15] tentatively has come to a similar conclusion. He has identified rice, wheat, barley, green gram, lentil and small millets. According to his preliminary observation, the Neolithic people were cultivating rice and small millets in the beginning. Subsequently, they also started cultivating barley, wheat, green gram, lentil, etc. Supportive evidence has also been obtained from Senuwar[16] in Rohtas district of Bihar. At this site, the Neolithic period is divided into two sub-groups: IA and IB. from the lowest part to the middle of sub period I A only grains of cultivated rice were obtained. But they were also using wild plants like job's tear, fox *tail/kodon,* wild *rice,jharberi, chaulai andjangali palak.* But in later phase of I A, there was a major shift in cultivation. New cereals like barley, wheat, jwar millet, field pea, finger *millet/ragi* and *khesari* were also introduced. The introduction of double crop pattern, clearly indicates that agriculture had started playing a major role by the later phase of the Neolithic culture at the site.

The range of cereals cultivated during the Neolithic phase at Koldihwa and Mahagara raises some interesting issues. While rice, small millets, green gram, etc. constituted *kharif* crops to be raised during the rainy season, barley, wheat and lintel etc. the winter crops, were raised during the winter season. The cultivated cereals whether *kharif* or winter crops were initially wild grasses. Stone Age man started gathering seeds of these grasses for consumption. This would indicate that the first cultivation of any cereal would have taken place only in that area where its proto types were available. Viewed against this background the distribution of wild rice is found over a wide area covering eastern India, south East Asia and south western China. The distribution of wild barley, wheat, lentil, etc. on the other hand is recorded from the border of Pakistan, Afghanistan to Iran, Levant, Turkey, etc. This would suggest that rice and possibly small millets were available in wild form in the Vindhyan area before these were cultivated. But wheat, barley, etc. would have been introduced in this area i.e. in the Vindhyan area only when the people of the Vindhyan area came in contact with the people of north and north-western India. The cultivation of rice in the north and north-west and those of barley and wheat in the Vindhyan region could have been possible only through north-south dialogue. Ideas and information could have exchanged hands in dim distant past.

The origins of the Neolithic culture of the Vindhyan region in Allahabad raise interesting point. Had they come from out side with readymade ingredients of a Neolithic culture or had their moorings in the pre-Neolithic culture of the Vindhyas? In the present state of our knowledge the Neolithic culture of the Vindhyan region of Allahabad district represents its independent personality. For understanding the origins of this Neolithic culture, the excavations at Chopani Mando[17] on the Old Belan in Koraon sub-division of Allahabad deserve our attention. The site is situated at a distance of only 3 km from Koldihwa and Mahagara. A total habitational deposit measuring 1.55 m was exposed at the site. This deposit has been divided into three cultural phases. Phase I Epipalaeolithic, phase II Mesolithic and phase III Advance Mesolithic or proto Neolithic. The last phase i.e proto-Neolithic is characterized by handmade pottery and some new tool types like isosceles triangle and tranchet. The plans of hutments, hearths, food processing equipments like querns, mullers along with anvils, hammer stones, ring stones were the other characteristic features. Burnt clay lumps with reed impression suggested wattle and daub structure. The presence of wild rice, however, when viewed in the context of the presence of food processing equipments and traits of semi sedentary settlement, would suggest the collection of wild rice during this phase. The appearance of hand made pottery in the proto-Neolithic phase of Chopani Mando on the one hand

and its presence at all the Vindhyan Neolithic sites excavated so far is another linkage between the two. The occurrence of the tranchets during the proto-Neolithic phase at Choapani Mando on the one hand and its occurrence at Koldihwa, Mahagara and Panchoh on the other would suggest continuity between the two i.e. Proto-Neolithic and Neolithic. This would indicate transition from the gathering of the wild rice to that of its cultivation. In this connection, it may be pointed out, that presence of wild sheep, goat and cattle is recorded from gravel III and IV and from Chopani Mando in the Proto-Neolithic context. At Mahagara, these animals are found domesticated. This would suggest that these animals were domesticated from their wild proto types available in the area during the earlier period and were not introduced in the area as readymade breeds from outside. The microlithic component of the Vindhyan Neolithic culture also constitutes a running theme from Mesolithic to the Neolithic without any break. The evolution of the Vindhyan Neolithic from the underlying Mesolithic is thus clearly indicated. The available evidence indicates that the Neolithic people of the Vindhyas, besides cereals, were also consuming flesh of animals, aquatic creatures and birds also. Hunting and catching went on along with agriculture and domestication of animals. For computing the chronology of the Neolithic culture of the Vindhyas both archaeological data and C^{14} dates are available. Even then one has to admit that the question is still in melting pot. On this point the following points deserve attention:

(i) In the Vindhyan area transition from the proto Neolithic to Neolithic is documented. We start getting evidence of quasi-sedentary settlement during the late Mesolithic period. It is demonstrated by the presence of hutments, food processing equipments like querns, mullers and hand made pottery. Collection of wild rice is indicated.

(ii) There is a linkage between the late Mesolithic and Neolithic in the construction of hutments, use of food processing equipments, hand made pottery and microliths.

(iii) As per available evidence, in the late Mesolithic phase people had started collecting wild rice but in the Neolithic period rice was being cultivated even though the old practice of collecting wild rice was still in vogue.

(iv) All the available Vindhyan Neolithic sites are characterized by hand made pottery. These sites are devoid of metal. Bone tools are very limited. This would indicate that people depended heavily on stone tools whether microliths or heavy duty tools. A primitive character of this Neolithic culture is indicated.

C^{14} dates have been obtained from Koldihwa[18] and Mahagara[19]. From Koldihwa three dates reading 4530 ± 185 B.C., 5440 ± 240 B.C. and 6570 ± 21 0 B.C. have been obtained. Mahagara has yielded six dates of which two are thermoluminiscenct (T.L.) dates and the rest C^{14} dates. The two T.L. dates read 2265 B.C. and 1616 B.C. The four C^{14} dates read 1400 ± 150 B.C., 133O ± 120 B.C., 1440 ± 100 B.C. and 1480 ± 110 B.C.

From two more Neolithic sites of the Vindhyan region of Allahabad district, C^{14} dates are also available. Three calibrated C^{14} dates from Kunjhun[20] River-face (Sidhi, Madhya Pradesh) read 1565-1265 B.C, 2665-2675-2515 and 3530-3535 B.C. In the light of these dates Possehl and Rissman have proposed a time bracket of 4000 B.C. to 1200 B.C. for the Neolithic culture of north-central India. Recently three C^{14} dates have been obtained from Tokwa (Mirzapur, Uttar Pradesh) when calibrated these read 6591 B.C. (B.S. 2417), 5676 B.C (B.S. 2669) and 4797 B.C. (B.S. 2464). In the light of the available dates from Koldihwa and Tokwa the antiquity of the Neolithic culture of Allahabad (Plateau region) may be pushed to 7th millennium BCE.

The Neolithic Culture of the Ganga Plain in Allahabad District

From the recent excavations at Jhusi on the confluence of the Ganga and Yamuna and Hetapatti at a distance of 9 km to the north of Jhusi on the left bank of the Ganga remnants of the Neolithic culture have been found.

Jhusi : (Lat. 25° 26' 10" N., Long. 81° 54' 30'' E.), the ancient Pratiṣhṭhānpur is located on the left bank of the Ganga within a marked meander very close to the Ganga-Yamuna confluence at a distance of 7 km to the east of Allahabad city. The Department of Ancient History, Culture and Archaeology, University of Allahabad conducted excavations at Samudrakup mound of Jhusi for five seasons 1995-96, 1998-99, 1999-2000, 2002-03 and 2003-04, exposing a number of trenches in different areas of the mound. The total thickness of cultural deposit at the site is about 16.5 m. The occupational deposit is divisible into seven cultures: (1) Neolithic, (2) Chalcolithic, (3) Pre NBPW with iron, (4) NBPW period, (5) Śuṇga-Kuṣhāṇa period, (6) Gupta period and (7) the early medieval period. There is continuous settlement from Chalcolithic to Gupta period. However, after the Neolithic period on the one hand and the Gupta period on the other, the localities excavated appear to have been deserted for some centuries. The site was reoccupied in the early medieval period.

The Neolithic occupational deposit at Jhusi measures 1.5 m. This deposit has yielded hand made pottery comprising cord impressed ware, rusticated ware, the burnished red ware, burnished black ware and crude black-and-red ware, microliths, pieces of grinding stones and animal bones. The evidence of rice husk in the pottery used as degraissant is also detected. It appears that the habitation during the Neolithic period was in a limited area as this evidence has come only from the southern fringe of Samudrakup mound of Jhusi. The overlying layer 44, the sealing layer of Neolithic deposit marked by gritty and sandy material, evidently result of erosional activity yielded rolled pieces of potsherds and animal bones. Its bottom line is zigzag, indicating a time gap between the end of the Neolithic and the beginning of the Chalcolithic suggesting thereby that the area was unoccupied for a considerable time after the Neolithic period.

From the Neolithic horizon has come the evidence of circular huts, walls of which appear to have been constituted by bamboo and reeds smeared with mud plaster as is evident by the burnt clay lumps with wattle and daub impression. Evidence of hut floors, hearth and oven has also been obtained from this phase. Hand made potsherds, charred and semi-charred animal bones and charred grains have also been found from the hut floors. A sand stone quern fragment and a potsherd having rubbed ends, a trapeze fashioned on chalcedony and steatite beads were also recorded from one floor.

The ceramic industries characterizing the Neolithic phase at Jhusi are thick to medium fabric and ill-fired. The core of the pots is blackish, greyish and occasionally reddish. Clay used for the manufacture of these pots is not levigated. Tempering material like rice husk, millet husk and chaffs have been found in the pottery. The pottery, on the basis of surface treatment, is divisible into five wares: (i) cord impressed ware, (ii) rusticated ware, (iii) burnished red ware, (iv) burnished black ware and (v) crude black-and-red ware. Of the available shapes mention may be made of jars, basins, spouted vessels, bowls and platters. Some of the basins are spouted. Applique decoration has also been recorded.

The Neolithic phase of Jhusi has also brought to light a number of beads made of paste material like steatite. Unperforated and unfinished specimens indicate the local manufacture of the beads. Micro disc beads of steatite, small cylindrical beads of banded agate and flat truncated beads of banded chalcedony have also been reported from this horizon. The stone beads are characterized with hourglass perforation. Microliths comprise retouched/utilized blades, backed blades, truncated and retouched blades, scrapers, triangles, trapeze, points, drills and lunates. This lithic industry is based on chert, chalcedony, carnelian and quartz.

Of the bone tools mention may be made of simple arrowheads, side scrapers and end scrapers. The archaeo-botanical studies indicate the presence of rice, wheat, barley, lentil, pea, grass pea, horse gram, sesame, etc. Charred remain of grape, *āṅwlā* and *bēr* are also met with.

The faunal assemblage contained mainly the remains of domestic mammals-cattle, buffalo, sheep and goat. Among the bones of wild animals mention may be made of *chausingha, sambar,* spotted deer, mongoose, jungle cat and a species of small mammal. Among the non-mammalian remain mention may be made of fish, falem and egret, etc.

The available evidence would indicate that the Neolithic people at Jhusi besides agriculture and domestication also resorted to hunting, catching and fishing as well.

Hetapatti : (Lat. 25.49386° N., Long. 81.91686° E.) is located on the left bank of the Ganga at a distance of about 9 km to the north of Jhusi. It is at a distance of about 20 km from Allahabad in north-east direction, just opposite to Salori, Chilla and Chandpur localities of Allahabad city. The site is quite extensive with 1500 m length (north-south) and 700 m width (east-west). The archaeological site is disturbed by recent *nālās* and rain gullies. It is divided into three mounds, HPT I, HPT II and HPT III. HPT II is about 10 m high from the surrounding area and it contains archaeological deposit upto early medieval period. The other two mounds, HPT I and HPT III with a height of 6 m contain archaeological deposit upto NBPW and Kushāṇa periods respectively. There is extensive exposure of geological formation measuring about 7 m in thickness on which the archaeological deposit is resting. The site was brought to notice of archaeological world by the department of Ancient history, Culture and Archaeology, University of Allahabad as early as 1998 and an extensive exploration at the site resulted in the discovery of a good number of the chunks of semi-precious stones like chert, jasper, chalcedony, etc along with flakes, flake fragments, blades, blade fragments and finished tools. In the light of the available evidence it appears that the Mesolithic people were the first to visit the area. In the light of the occurrence of microliths at Jhusi, Nibikalan, Jamunipur, etc., this supposition appears validated. The exploration besides microliths, also resulted in the discovery of Neolithic hand made corded and rusticated wares, the Chalcolithic black-and-red ware, black slipped ware and ordinary red ware, the NBP ware and typical Kushāṇa ware.

The excavations at the site have been conducted for the three seasons. A 70 cm thick Neolithic deposit was encountered at the site. From the Neolithic horizon have been obtained hand made corded, rusticated, burnished black and burnished red ware along with microliths and animal bones. Traces of round or oblong hut floors have also been detected. The pottery types include shallow and deep bowls, basins often with luted spoutes, jars, etc. From the Neolithic horizon have been obtained a good number of animal bones. Burnt clay lumps with bamboo and reed impressions have also been found in good number. Wattle and daub structure is strongly suggested. Fragments of querns and mullers of sand stone and quartzite are other noteworthy objects recovered from Neolithic horizon. Animal bones and soil samples collected from the Neolithic level are under study. It is hoped that when analysis is complete a welcome light would be thrown on the range of animals encountered and vegetal world of the Neolithic people. It is not unlikely that the picture would be alike that of Jhusi.

For computing the chronology of the Neolithic culture of the Ganga plain of Allahabad district, the following points deserve attention:

(i) The Neolithic culture, as revealed from the excavations at Jhusi and Hetapatti compare well with its counterpart of the north-central Vindhyas. It is characterized by hand made pottery comprising corded, rusticated and ordinary red ware. The shapes in the ceramic assemblage are very limited. Clay used in the manufacture of the pottery is not levigated. Pots are not well fired. Animal bones are found from the horizon. Round and oblong floors have also come to light. Microliths are found in appreciable number. No metal object has been found from the Neolithic phase. Viewed against this background, the Neolithic culture as exposed at Jhusi and Hetapatti present a primitive character.

(ii) Three C^{14} dates obtained from the Neolithic phase of Jhusi when calibrated read 7477 B.C. (B.S. 2526), 5837 B.C. (B.S. 2524) and 6196 B.C. (B.S. 2525). Comparable dates have been obtained from Lahuradeva[21], another Neolithic site of the mid-Ganga plain. The relevant dates read 5320±90 B.P. (Cal. B.C. 4220,4196 and 4161) and 6290±160 B.P. (Cal B.C. 5298). An AMS C^{14} date for carbonized domesticated rice would put the antiquity of the Neolithic culture at the site to 7th millennium BCE. The C^{14} dates obtained from Koldihwa and Tokwa in the north-central India as indicated earlier also support the high antiquity of the Neolithic culture of the Ganga plain in Allahabad district.

The aforesaid discussion would indicate that the Neolithic culture was flourishing both in the plateau region as well as in the plain area of Allahabad district. In the light of available evidence the plateau Neolithic culture had its root in the Mesolithic culture of the area as is evident from the excavations of Chopani Mando. However, the roots of the Neolithic culture of the plain may be traced to the Neolithic culture of the plateau area. In this connection it may be pointed out that the Neolithic culture of both the areas share almost identical characteristic features with the exception of polished celts. In the plateau area, the archaeological objects going back to the Lower Palaeolithic period have been obtained where as in the plain, the descent of Stone Age man can be traced back to only late Upper Palaeolithic period. As the Gangetic plain was devoid of stone, authors of the stone using culture of the late Upper Palaeolithic and Mesolithic cultures of the plain could have come from an area where stones for making tools were available. The available C^{14} date of the Neolithic culture of the plateau region, on the one hand, and that of the plain region, on the other, almost coincide indicating thereby the flourishing of the Neolithic culture in both the areas i.e. the plateau zone and the plain zone almost simultaneously.

References

1. George, A. Christoponlos (ed.) 1974, *Prehistory and Protohistory,* Theocharis, D.R. *History of the Hellenic World,* pp. 56-57.
2. *Ibid.*
3. Singh, P. 1997. *The Neolithic Origins.* Agam Kala Prakashan, New Delhi, pp. 39-58.
4. *Ibid,* pp. 59-92.
5. *Ibid,* pp. 93-118.
6. *Ibid,* p. 121; see also Srivastava, V.C. 1982. *The Prehistoric Afghanistan. A Source Book* (Allahabad), pp. 45-46 and pp. 212-216.
7. Ashthana, Shashi, 1985. *Pre Harappan Cultures of India and the Borderland,* pp. 110-120; see also V.D. Misra 1999. 'Agriculture, Domestication of Animals and Ceramic and other Industries in Prehistoric India: Mesolithic and Neolithic', pp. 240-41. *The Dawn of Indian Civilization,* Vol. 1, Part I (Ed. G.C. Pande); also Agrawal, D.P. and I.S. Kharakwal, 2002. *South Asian Prehistory,* Aryan book International, New Delhi, pp. 166-87.

8. Thapar, B.K. 1984. 'Fresh Light on the Neolithic Cultures of India, Archaeological. Perspective of India, *Purātattva* no. 13-14, p. 37; Misra, V.D. 1999 *op. cit.*, pp. 239-240; D.P. Agrawal and J.S. Kharakwal 2002, *op. cit.*, pp. 157-224.
9. Misra, V.D. 1977. 'Excavations at Koldihwa: Some Preliminary Observations', in *Some Aspects of Indian Archaeology*, Prabhat Prakashan, Allahabad, pp. 107-119; Misra, B.B. 2006. 'Koldihwa - A Key Site for the Neolithic and Chalcolithic Cultures of the Vindhyas', in *Art, Archaeology and Cultural History of India* (U.N. Roy Felicitation Volume, Part I) ed. C.P. Sinha, B.R. Publishing Corporation, Delhi, pp. 143-181.
10. Sharma, G.R. and D. Mandal 1980. *Excavations at Mahagara,* Department of Ancient History, Culture and Archaeology, University of Allahabad.
11. *Indian Archaeology: A Review,* 1975-76, p. 47.
12. Misra, V.D., J.N. Pal, M.C. Gupta and P.P. Joglekar 2009. *Excavations at Jhusi (Pratishthanpur): A Fresh Light on the Archaeological Profile of the Middle Ganga Plain,* Indian Archaeological Society, New Delhi, pp. 20-28.
13. Pal, J.N. and M.C. Gupta 2005. 'Excavations at Hetapatti (Allahabad District): Some preliminary Observations'. *Journal of Interdisciplinary Studies in History and Archaeology,* Vol. 2, No.2 (Winter 2005), pp. 325-330.
14. Harvey, E.L., D. Fuller, J.N. Pal and M.C. Gupta 2005. 'Early Agriculture of the Neolithic Vindhyas (North-Central India)', in *South Asian Archaeology* 2003 (Eds. Ute Franke vogt and Hans-Joachim Weisshaar), Aachen Linden: SoftVerlog e.k. pp. 329-334.
15. Saraswat, K.S. (personal communication).
16. Singh, B.P. 2001. 'Stages of Cultural Development in the Middle Ganga Plain- A Case Study of Senuwar', *Prāgdhārā* 11, pp. 109-118.
17. Sharma, G.R., V.D. Misra, D. Mandal, B.B. Misra and J.N. Pal 1980. *Beginnings of Agriculture,* Department of Ancient History, Culture and archaeology, University of Allahabad, pp. 37-76.
18. Possehl, G.L. and Paul C. Rissman 1992. *Chronologies in Old World Archaeology,* Vol. I, p. 461.
19. *Ibid.*
20. *Ibid.* see pp. 473-74 for Kunjhun, p. 474 for Mahagara and p. 474 for Koldihwa.
21. Tewari, et al. 2001-2002. 'Excavations at Lahuradeva, District Sant Kabimagar', *Purātattva* 32, pp. 54-62; Tewari, et al. 2002-2003, 'Preliminary Report on the Excavations at Lahuradeva, Sant Kabimagar'; D.P. 2001-2002, 'Wider Archaeological Implications', *Prāgdhārā* 13, pp. 37-68.

8

Technological Innovations and Cultural Development in Proto-Historic – Early Historic Vindhya – Ganga Plain

Vibha Tripathi

The spirit of innovation is an integral part of human nature. Man has also been called *Homo-Faber* and *Homo-technicus* as tools and implements are almost essential for human survival. The technological innovations are nearly fundamental to human temper and civilizational growth. It is because of the evolving nature of resource utilization by human kind that a three stage theory was proposed by C.J. Thomson as early as 1836. We view the growth of human civilization in three Ages, viz. Stone Age, Copper-Bronze Age and Iron Age. The Age of Iron was the most evolved one of the three stages of technological growth.

We propose to take a close look here at the growth of technology and the associated culture in the most fertile land of India that is the Ganga Plain, especially in the Central parts of the Plain. The alluvium is devoid of most of the mineral deposits which are needed in day-to-day life such as stones for tools, implements or semi-precious and precious material recognized as status symbol by society from time immemorial. The raw materials like ores for metals are hardly available for exploitation in these plains. It stands to reason to assume that a symbiotic relationship existed between the two zones of this region that is the adjacent hills and the alluvial plains. It must have been only at a later stage when there was a free flow of ideas and people that-there developed a truly evolved centre of cultural growth that gave rise to urbanized centres in the region. It will be worthwhile examining the process of development spanning over the millennia to get into the foundations of such cultural changes. Since iron represents the most evolved technological stage and also the one that had the potential to influence the material production capable of exerting an impact on material prosperity, the discussion will focus largely on growth of iron technology and its impact on life of the cultures of the Middle Ganga Plain during the proto-historic and early historic periods. However, before we deal with iron technology, its status and impact on the culture, a brief outline of the cultures in the region is called for.

1. Culture in the Ganga Plain

The adjacent hilly terrains of the Vindhya-Kaimur ranges are dotted with various stages of Palaeolithic cultures. The alluvial plain of Ganga and its tributaries is occupied first by Early farming community followed by the Chalcolithic settlers. With beginning of agriculture during the Neolithic age, migrations may have started towards the plains in search of more suitable pastures. Since then, we come across veritably an uninterrupted occupation of a major part of the plain almost till the early medieval period. The geo-ecological environment of the Gangetic Plain was conducive to human occupation and sustenance of culture. The alluvial soil, congenial climatic condition with a good rainfall, perennial rivers, forests and thick vegetal cover supporting rich flora and fauna-all were haven for humankind. The plains were bordered by hills of the Vindhya-Kaimur ranges that provided minerals and other essential commodities meant for fulfilling the requirements of the emerging cultures. Such a congenial environment sustained people and cultures that eventually attained great heights in the cradle of the alluvial plain (Fig.1)

A stretch of thousands of kilometers of alluvium, this has been divided into three parts, because of the nature and characteristic features of the land, i.e. the Upper, Middle and Lower Ganga Plain. The Upper Ganga Plain (from Hardwar in Uttarakhand to the site of Kausambi near Allahabad) was first occupied by the Ochre Coloured Pottery (OCP). It was followed by a culture dominated by an independent cultural horizon of Black-and-Red Ware (BRW) at a few sites in Rajasthan (Jodhpur and Noh) and Western part of Uttar Pradesh (Atranjikhera, Jakhera, Abhaipur, Dadupur, etc.). The Painted Grey Ware culture (PGW) succeeds it. At most of the other sites the Black-and-Red-Ware (BRW) and PGW co-existed at the same time.

In the Middle and lower parts of the plain, that has higher rainfall, more wet condition and more clayey soil in larger parts of this stretch there are thick arteries of drainage system irrigating the land. It has emerged as one of the earliest regions to have started crop cultivation and early use of iron. The sites in the Vindhays such as Koldihwa are known for high antiquity of rice cultivation with dates going back to 7th millennium

BCE. More recently Lahuradeva in Sant Kabir Nagar has catapulted the Middle Ganga Plain for early dates of 8th -7th millennium BCE from its Neolithic cultural horizon. The cord impressed pottery of Lahuradeva is akin to Koldihwa and other sites in the hills showing close relationship between the hills and the plains. The evidence of early farming is also evidenced at sites like Chirand, Senuar and smaller settlements like Imlidih, Bhumadih, etc. The early farming cultures of this region have the distinction of largely using bone tools perhaps due to scarcity of stone in the region. Variety of crops like rice in both its wild and domesticated varieties, wheat, barley and several varieties of millets were cultivated by these communities.

It is followed by Chalcolithic culture, a period that introduces metals. The dominant ceramic tradition of this period is BRW accompanied by Black Slipped Ware (BSW) of both painted and plain varieties, Red Ware and a Grey Ware. The important Chalcolithic sites are Kausambi, Ayodhya (Dist. Faizabad), Rajghat (Varanasi), Prahladpur (Chandauli), Masondih, (Ghazipur), Nal Ka Tila (Sonbhadra) Malhar (Chandauli), Tilaurakot, Khairadih (Ballia), Sonpur, Vaisali, Rajgir, Champa, Taradih (Gaya), extending up to the Lower Ganga Plain, seen at sites like Pandu Rajar Dhibi (dist. Burdwan), Mangalkot (Dist. Burdwan), Hathikhera, Mahishdal (Dist. Bankura). Noteworthy is a group of sites like Sohgaura, Narhan, etc. in Saryupar plain wherein stone has sparingly been in use. Such sites have been labeled as Narhan culture by Singh (1994), after the site in Gorakhpur district excavated by him. At most of these sites, the earliest ceramic culture is Black and Red Ware. Copper objects in a small numbers are generally present at these sites. Animal husbandry, substantiated by food gathering and hunting, was the primary mode of livelihood, though agriculture was being commonly practiced. A large number of bones – either charred or with cut marks – suggest a heavy reliance of cattle rearing and hunting. River shell and snails were also eaten. Bones of elephant, rhino, buffalo, ox, stag and deer have been found from sites like Chirand (*IAR* 1963-64:60; 1964-65: 46).

Besides the early evidence of crop cultivation, metallurgy appears to be another prominent feature of archaeology of Middle Ganga Plain. Iron has been introduced in the Ganga Plain in Chalcolithic cultural milieu. The cultural scenario hardly undergoes change initially, at least at the early strata of Iron Age cultures, i.e. early stages of PGW in the upper Ganga Plain and BRW using cultures in the middle and lower parts of the Plain. Recent evidence of introduction of iron in the Vindhya-Ganga region has pushed back the antiquity of iron to as early as 1600-1500 BCE, if not earlier, (Tripathi, 2001; Tewari, 2003, 2010). This technological development aided and accelerated the pace of growth and prosperity leading to rise of cities in this region in subsequent centuries.

The PGW in the Upper Ganga Plain and the BRW bearing culture in the middle and lower Ganga Plain were succeeded by the Northern Black Polished Ware culture (NBPW). The beautiful ceramic exhibits great sophistication and technological acumen of its manufacturers. The NBPW culture has a wide distribution found almost throughout the subcontinent. NBPW exhibited a great mastery in ceramic art that has intrigued the experts of the field till date.

The NBPW culture has been dated between 8th -7th BCE to 3rd-2nd century BCE on the basis of C^{14} dates reported from several sites of the Middle Ganga Plain. This is the area of Janapadas dotting the Ganga Plain. Historically the Mahājanapadas were taking shape during this period that culminates to the rise of Magadhan imperialism. It will be interesting to delve deep into the process of growth of culture, especially in the Middle Ganga Plain and identify the key factors that brought about changes of far reaching consequence in this region.

There could be several factors responsible for bringing about material prosperity in the Middle Ganga Plain. Special mention may be made of congenial ecological setting, conducive environment, social, political and economic- that led to high culture in the region. But for over all cultural development, basic sustainable material prosperity is a pre- requisite. In this, the role of technology is vital. We propose to take a close look at this aspect of material culture at this juncture.

Among the early technologies developed and harnessed by humankind are stone followed by copper-bronze and then iron. The growth of culture was excruciatingly slow during the Stone Age. Bronze Age cities rose in the valleys of Tigris, Euphrates and Indus. But after the decline of these cities the iron technology emerged as a savior of human civilization. Iron being a commonly occurring mineral on earth's crust was more easily accessible. We still live in the Age of Iron and steel. However, the origin and development of iron technology has still engaged the attention of scholars. It is not aimed to go into the depth of the subject here. Suffice it to state that iron technology in the region of enquiry here has assumed great significance because of the recent excavations in the Vindhya-Ganga Plain that have yielded C^{14} dates going back to the first half of the second millennium BCE. It is aimed to confine the issue of occurrence of iron to the region of the Middle Ganga Plain.

2. Emergence of Iron and Its Significance

"Iron as an innovation represented a new line of development, a recombination of previously existing knowledge which resulted in an entirely new technological configuration"(Wallace 1971:467-476). This statement makes it amply clear that iron started a new technological configuration that represent a spirit of innovation by a class of specialists in the field of technology. It also facilitated production that in turn improved the quality of life of its time.

Much has been written about the role of iron in economic growth and the process of urbanization. It is not opportune to open the issue afresh at this juncture. However, it may be noted that the metallurgy of iron being a complex one took a long time to attain a level of expertise to contribute to the productive mechanism. At the initial stage, the new technological know-how was harnessed largely for war and hunting. Besides the hunting tools, we come across only nails, chisels, rods, clamps, etc. the latter must have been used to carpentry, perhaps for manufacturing carts, chariots, etc. these were integral parts of war machinery of the ancient days. It must have provided an edge to the army equipped with iron weapons and chariots in the wars that were being waged almost incessantly for consolidation of power. We may return to such issues a little later. Suffice it to say here that a new era was heralded in the Gangetic Plain with advent of iron. A true age of iron dawned upon the region, albeit gradually. The technological advancement had a long term impact on the make up of culture of the region. It will be worthwhile taking a close look here at the advent and growth of iron technology in the Middle Ganga Plain and its impact on the human culture.

2.1 The Beginning of Iron in the Vindhya-Ganga Plain

The Vindhya-Ganga Plain has emerged as a key region in the Indian subcontinent to have started the use of iron as early as the first half of the 2nd millennium BCE. Radio-carbon dates from Eastern Vindhyas from sites like Malhar and Raja-Nal-Ka-Tila have placed the region as an iron production centre. In the neighbourhood, there are several sites like Kausambi, Dadupur, Jakhera, Jhusi, Aktha that have yielded early C^{14} dates from iron bearing levels. Some of these C^{14} dates are as early as 18/1700 BCE (see table 1). We come across only a limited number of iron objects at Early Iron Age.

Koldihwa (*IAR*, 1973-74:27), a Chalcolithic site in the Vindhyan plateau had yielded an iron axe, arrowheads, crucibles and pieces of slag. It may be noted that iron is found along with microliths in the Vindhyas (in District Mirzapur-Sonbhadra), such as at Morahana Pahar, Baghair Khor, near Bhaisaur and several other microlithic sites. This may indicate either a continuation of Microliths till late or an early beginning of iron in this belt. Recently, this region has yielded the earliest evidence of iron so far from the site of Malhar. The evidence is also corroborated by excavations at Raja-Nal-Ka-Tila, nearby (Table 1). There are consistent radiocarbon dates ranging from 1600-1500 BCE to 1100-1000 BCE from these sites from BRW using culture (Tewari, 1998, 2003, 2010). These sites yielded iron along with BRW of an early variety. In the considered opinion of the excavator, the dates of beginning of iron at Malhar should go back to pre-1500-1400 BCE (see Table 1). The dates of Raja-Nal-ka-Tila from middle of iron bearing strata are: 1200 ± 90 BCE, 1200 ± 100 BCE, 1423-1307 cal. B.C. (Birbal Sahni Institute of Palaeobotany and 1030 ± 90 (PRL), the calibrated date is for the mid phase of iron bearing level. Therefore, the dates of beginning of iron at the site should be much earlier. How much the newly acquired technological know-how influenced the cultural make-up may be examined briefly in the following discussion.

In general at the earliest stage, as seen above, the number and types of iron objects is very limited. The scarcity of iron objects and the elementary types of hunting – fishing tools are suggestive of the fact that iron at this level is a product of solid-state reduction. Most of the analysed specimens show slag inclusion due to low temperature

(1100°C to 1300°C) and inefficient metallurgical skill. The archaeo-metallurgical studies have revealed that the metallurgical skill was not sufficiently developed at this stage. The wrought iron had plenty of slag inclusions in the matrix of ferrite indicating a solid state reduction.

In the succeeding century, Northern Black Polished Ware culture takes over the major part of North India. At certain sites it was contemporaneous with the late phase of Painted Grey Ware culture on the one hand and the Megalithic cultures on the other. The span of this culture is extensive, spreading over more than half a millennium. Several changes take place during this period. For instance, permanent structures of baked bricks, fortification, writing, coinage, beautiful terracotta figurines with stamped decorations, etc. are introduced in course of the NBPW cultural period. The metallurgy of iron undergoes innovations, discernible in evidence of steeling and case hardening or carburization. A relative increase is recorded both in the number and types of iron object (see Tripathi, 2001 see Table2). There is a common principle that is applicable here, that is the economic out-put is directly proportional to the technology in-put. There is thus a qualitative and quantitative improvement in iron objects. Better quality objects with weapons like javelins, lances, swords, daggers, blades, elephant goads appears along with the earlier types. Agricultural implements, which were rarely reported earlier at the previous stage, and were found only from a few sites (Jakhera yielded sickle and ploughshare, and Atranjikhera an axe), become relatively frequent now.

Bloomery iron having solid-state reduction technique remains the norm but, as noted above, improvisation in technological skill was clearly evident. Carburization was known. Quenching has been well attested by literary evidence (Pāli *Sutta Nipāta* part I.168; *Khuddaka Nikāya,* Pt I p. 282 *Phalo divasai samtattar udake pakkhipatto chitachittayati sadhūpayati*). Whether the cases of carburization noted in certain specimens are examples of deliberate effort or were accidental may be a subject of dispute. It is likely that the artisans were employing these techniques judiciously according to the requirement and function of tools.

The pace of technological advance received new impetus with stable socio-political life during the Śuṅga-Kuṣāṇa and Gupta periods. The urban phase of Indian history exposed at sites of the middle Ganga Plain like Kausambi, Bhita, Sravasti, Rajghat, Ramnagar, Bhitari, Agiabir, Khairadhih, and further east at Chirand, Vaisali, Rajgir, Sonpur, etc. attest a frequent use of metals, especially iron during the period of second century BCE to fourth-fifth century CE. Analytical work undertaken show a better understanding of metallurgical processes as well as nature and type of ore deposits being tapped. Special mention may be made of study of iron objects from sites like Khairadih in Ballia district (U.P.) on river Ghaghra. The study of iron objects of the site shows a rich repertoire of iron tool types, especially at Śuṅga-Kuṣāṇa levels. Some of the objects were analysed at Banaras Hindu University. Most of them indicate pure wrought iron with some slag inclusion. A spearhead, however, shows pearlite and ferrite phase though slag inclusion is detectable. The microstructure also suggests quenching and tempering; both are rare features. The other samples have banded structure of ferrite and pearlite with elongated slag inclusions. Bhanu Prakash (personal communication) feels that the microstructure of an axe indicates carbon content in iron due to forge-welding of a number of sheets of iron objects. The skill of iron technology at Khairadih is detectable in manufacture of this axe with shaft hole. The radiograph confirms use of good lamination technique in its manufacturing. No joints or seams could be detected even in the radiograph. This may be termed a masterpiece, so far as the metallurgical expertise is concerned. A similar specimen has been noted at Sringverpur (Hari Narain, *et al.* 1998).

The metallurgical skills developed further to the highest degree of sophistication under the state patronage in the Gupta period. The art of smithy had attained its culmination during the Gupta imperial rule (3rd-4th to 5th-6th centuries CE.), which is said to be the golden period of Indian history. The iron metallurgy culminates with production of massive structures like Mehrauli Iron Pillar at Delhi during 5th century CE. Taxila has yielded a rich repertoire including some armour grade weapons in the opening centuries of Christian era. Sisupalgarh (a Gupta period site) yielded a caltrop, a weapon to be used in the battlefield to curb elephants. A rich variety of objects are reported from the sites of the Gupta period. With the availability of samples, some objects of this period have been analysed. Hari Narain at NRLC, Lucknow analysed five objects from Sringverpur (Hari Narain *et. al.* 1998:44-53, Fig. 23A). It has been observed that different techniques were applied on separate categories of objects; for example, a spoon had a lower hardness than that of an axe. The carbon content varied from 0.1% to 0.6%. There was also evidence of rapid cooling and widmanstatten structure with ferrite and pearlite. Edges were found to be carburized further, giving them greater hardness and strength. This high carbon zone is restricted to deeper areas and had low slag inclusion too. Most of Sringverpur objects belong to a category of mild steel with clear evidence of cementite in the matrix. Lamination technique was prevalent especially for knife blades, axes, etc. for greater efficacy (Hari Narain *op. cit.*).

The most remarkable object is the Delhi Iron pillar dated to 4th-5th century CE. Scholars have expressed differing views on the technique of production, corrosion resistance and many other technical aspects of this iron pillar at Delhi (Bardget 1963:3-10, Ghose, 1963:31-35 and Lahiri *et al.*, 1963:46-54. For details see Balasubramaniam, 2001). It is an excellent quality wrought iron product about 7375 mm in diameter at the bottom and 304 mm at the top. It is estimated to weigh more than 6096 kg. It was built by forge-welding large pieces of wrought iron. The quality of iron is so good that it still maintains its anticorrosive property. A number of hypotheses have been put forward and many corrosion studies are being carried out by scientists and metallurgists.

The study of these objects shows that ironsmiths were well adept in cementing and forge-welding small rods of iron and strongly forging them to shape such large objects. It also indicates that the ancient craftsman had mastered the operation and technological control of the ancient iron making furnaces to produce iron of uniform composition on such a large scale.

Suffice it to say that the ancient Indian smiths had a thorough knowledge of the importance of carbon alloying and also probably hardening and tempering. These technical skills must have been acquired over a long period before the craftsmen could have ventured to take up such a challenging job. This expertise in constructing such colossal structure has surprised even modern metallurgists.

The recent excavations that have forced us to take a fresh look at advent of iron are Raja-Nal- Ka-Tila and Malhar in Karamnasa valley in the district of Chandauli and Sonbhadra, respectively. They have yielded evidence of iron working complete with iron ore, smelting furnaces, forges along with finished iron objects. There are rich iron ore deposits. The areas called Lohsan, Geruwatva Pahar, etc. are hillocks littered with nodules of haematite that could easily be picked up for smelting without any mining. Our own survey of the Sonbhadra region has brought forth an extensive iron working area along with evidence of traditional iron smelting that was prevalent in the region till a couple of decades back. These sites situated in close proximity of ore deposits on one side and prosperous ancient centres like Kausambi, Bhita, Jhusi, Rajghat, Ramnagar, Agiabir, etc. on the other, assume a special significance. The rivers flowing through the Vindhyas join the Ganga either directly or through some smaller tributary must have been an invaluable source of communication between the two zones. Sharma, decades back had assigned 1100/1000 B.C. dates to iron bearing deposits of Koldihwa and Kausambi. The recent C^{14} dates ranging between 1100/1200 BCE. to 1600-1500 BCE from the Iron Age deposits of Malhar and Raja-Nal-Ka-Tila are significant indeed. As stated earlier, they assume much greater significance for introduction of iron because of their land-locked geographical location in the heart of India. Once iron technology came of age, its impact was perceptible in various sectors of socio-economic life as will be clear from the discussion below.

3. Economy, Trade and Technology

"Technology provided the surplus that allowed the society to support the arts and gave the population the leisure to experience and enjoy the artistic achievements" says Thomas R. De Gregory (1989:69). We will like to examine as to how this statement is applicable to the cultural growth of the Ganga Plain.

3.1 Growth of Agriculture

"Agriculture and animal husbandry have certainly been the most important of all human inventions to date" reiterated Toynbee (1978:187).

Christaller (1933) who had shed light on significant features of settlement pattern has placed a good agricultural land with a network of rivers at the hub of his centre place theory. The first order centres have rich fertile extensive alluvial plains around which there are satellite settlements engaged in cultivation of variety of crops and commodities.

The third order centres are located farther away which provide resource like minerals for commodities. In the present context all these criteria are fulfilled by the Ganga Plains. We come across evidence of beginning of agriculture right at pre-Neolithic period.

Not only there is a consistent growth of agriculture, a quick spread of cultivation of variety of crops is also evidenced in the Ganga Plains. Growth of agriculture is closely related with migrations and an interaction between different cultural zones, at early stages. Although the Neolithic-Chalcolithic settlers residing closer to streams and rivulets in the Vindhya-Kaimur belt had taken a lead in cultivation of crops like rice *Oryza sativa* (Sharma, 1980:36) as evidenced at Mahagarha and Koldihwa dated by C^{14} to 5440±40, 4530±185. Even the Mesolithic site at Chopnimando yielded wild variety of rice that came to be cultivated in the next period. But true development of agriculture must have taken place only in the fertile Gangetic alluvium as evidenced at Lahuradeva in district Sant Kabir Nagar having a date as early as 8th–7th millennia BCE for cultivation of crops. Nearby, Narhan (Distt. Gorakhpur, U.P.) and Senuwar IA & B (Distt. Rohtas, Bihar) at the foothills of the Kaimur hills yielded a rich variety of cereals as noted earlier (Singh, 1994).

Senuwar IA yields rice (*Oryza Sativa*) along with wild rice, job's tear, foxtail/bandra, *chaulai* and *palaka* of wild variety. But towards its later phase (of I A itself) cereals like barley, wheat, Jowar millet, lentil, field pea, finger millet (*Ragi*) and *khesari* were introduced, (Saraswat 2003). The evidence coming forth from Jhusi is rich in cereals. The crops reported from earlier levels of Jhusi are rice (*oryza Sativa)* six-rowed hulled barley (*Horendum vulgare*), bread wheat (*Triticum aestivus*), dwarf wheat (*Triticum sphaerococcum*) lentil (*lens culinaris*), field pea (*pisum arvense*), grass pea (*Lathyrus sativus*), horse gram (*macrolyloma uniflorum*), green gram (*vigna radial*), sesame (*sesamum indicum*), linseed (*linum usitatssimum*) etc. (Pokharia and Pal 2009). The cultural phase is dominated by a cord impressed pottery found from the Vindhyas to the Middle Ganga Plains.

A good evidence of cereals is recovered from Narhan (Saraswat *et al.* 1994:255-342). Mention may be made of (*Triticum*) kodon millet (*psaspalum scrobiclatim*), pearl millet (*bajra- pennisetum typhoides*) and pulses like chick pea or gram (*cicer arietinum* L.), field pea (*pisum sativum*), green gram (mung) (*vigna radiate*), horse gram or kulthi (*dolichos biflorus*) grass pear, khesari (*lathyrus sativus*), lentil (*lens culinaris*), moth bean, and aconite bean (*vigna acoritifilia*). Oil seeds like sarson (*brassica juncea*), sesame (*sesame indicum*), linseed or flax (*linum usitatissium*) are also found. Noteworthy is the evidence of the pips of grapes, dates, and jackfruits as also of watermelons.

Mention may be made of rice at the Neolithic levels at sites like Chirand. At the Chalcolithic levels rice has been found at Ahar (Udaipur, Rajasthan) Pandu Rajar Dhibi, Mahishdal and Mangalkot in Bengal. More recently very early dates of rice cultivation (C. 5000 B.C.) have been reported from the Saryu Par Plains (Neolithic Lahuradeva, Distt. Sant Kabir Nagar). The radiocarbon determinations are 5320±90 and 6290±160 BP (5298 cal. BC). Such early evidence of agriculture clearly establishes that the middle Ganga plain was not only occupied in 6th-5th millennium BCE but a settled life with a fairly stable economic life was a norm as is clearly evidenced by the archaeological records.

It may be pointed out however, that despite the knowledge and use of a rich variety of cereals, the reliance on animal diet was no less significant as evidence of animal bones in excavations testifies. Agricultural implements are few and far between. Even after the advent of iron, this new medium was hardly employed in agricultural sector. It is only at the later phase of PGW or early phase of NBPW period that agricultural implements of iron show up. Most of the iron objects fall in the category of hunting and war weapons or are implements like chisels, axes or building material like nails, clamps, rods, etc. It shows the social priority of technology application. The first iron ploughshare appears in the 7th century BCE. context at Ganawaria or a little earlier at Jakhera. Otherwise, iron sickles were the only agricultural implements found till NBPW period. At the initial level, thus economic activities seem to have taken a back seat.

The priority of society seems to be more on consolidation of power through wars, feuds or friendly alliances and migrations. Expansion of territory was possible through colonization of maiden lands and/or deforestation. This process must have continued well up to the PGW or even early NBPW periods. We come across a large number of new sites of various categories during the NBPW period. The older settlements show expansion in size and richness in material remains. This phenomenon very well coincides with the rise of *Mahajanapadas*, as pointed earlier.

One may deduct from this brief discussion that though agriculture was being practiced for several centuries, even double cropping was known as early as Chalcolithic period. However, large-scale production generating surplus became possible only with use of better tools and implements. This could start only in the middle of the first millennium BCE with application of iron technology in this sector. The rising demographic chart during the period might have been a consequence of frequent immigrations to important territories that were expanding in every direction including the political significance of such places.

3.2 Inter-regional Contacts and Trade

Right from the Mesolithic times, seasonal migrations had opened new avenues and passages of interactions. It must have intensified further with time and rising needs for larger varieties of minerals including, ores of copper, iron and later still of silver (for coins) and other metals used for alloying. Precious and semi-precious stones had attracted the society right from the Neolithic times. It is as well testified by rich variety of beads and other ornamental artefacts and decorative items.

The foundation for trade was laid down right at that state. Interactions between two independent cultural zones represented by PGW and BRW in Upper and Middle Ganga Plains may be witnessed at sites like Kausambi. A few iron objects were also found at BRW level at Kausambi. Interestingly, even Koldihwa in the ore-rich Vindhyas yields an early evidence of iron. Significantly, the recent evidence of the early dates of iron (1500-1400 BCE) at Malhar and Raja-Nal-ka-Tila are not far from Koldihwa. This region may have emerged as supply zone of iron (in the plains nearby). Such intra-regional contacts must have developed because of inter-regional relations during the succeeding NBPW period. The NBPW itself, with its sophisticated nature was a commodity of trade.

The Buddhist literature coinciding with the NBPW cultural phase has made frequent references to traders undertaking voyages to distant islands as well as through difficult overland terrains. The merchants of the early historic times were powerful enough to establish their own centres for commerce, raise their own army for protection on distant voyages, issue their own coinage. Such a merchant class of the early Historic period, states Ghosh (*op. cit.*: 22) was 'the direct outcome of the economic system.' Anāthapiṇḍaka, an eminent merchant of Buddha's time had paid Ajātashatru in gold coins by covering the entire surface area of the mangrove as its price (*Chullavagga* VI.4.1). Thus the economic prosperity of the merchant class of 6th-5th century BCE is almost legendary. Whether it was the consequence of the growing political power or it was the economic affluence that supported and provided the background for the latter, may be a debatable issue.

Coinage comes to be used during this period with introduction of silver Punch marked coins and copper coins. The importance of coinage as a signifier of growing economic activity cannot be over emphasized. A definite use of coinage in India starts during the early phase of NBPW culture. Coins have occurred throughout the region mentioned above, including at Sri Lanka in a well dated context of 5th century BCE. Such a dispersal of coinage not only testifies a growing trade and commerce through out this region but also a political authority of high stature.

Writing has also been known during this period. Buhler (1962: 38-39), quoted by Allchin 1995) had advocated that script was first introduced in South Asia by merchants in c. 800 BCE, 'in the form of borrowing of a nucleus of letters from a North Semitic alphabet, which sometime later was adapted by Brāhmaṇ scholars and transformed into a script well suited to represent the phonetic structure of both Saṅskṛit and Prākṛit. This transformation may, he hazarded, have been completed by c. 500 BC." (Allchin, *op. cit.*: 210). He suggests that writing was initially used in a mercantile context for secular functions possibly at a much earlier date than hitherto believed. Religious activities continued in the usual oral tradition. This is testified by literary evidence, observes Allchin. Thus there appears to be a strong evidence of presence of script in pre-Mauryan times. This must have facilitated in accounting and maintenance of records, especially to traders. Recent evidence of NBPW at Sri Lanka substantiates economic relations with the island.

The earlier contention that writing came to be practiced during the Mauryan times, especially with Aśokan edicts has to be modified with occurrence of Brāhmī characters inscribed on potsherds found at Anuradhapur in Sri Lanka in 5th century BCE. It must have started even earlier in the Middle Ganga Plain to have reached Sri Lanka in

5th century BCE. Thus the early interactions between India and Sri Lanka have been primarily cultural and economic in nature. With rise of political power and state patronage the relations among the territories of South Asia must have intensified further, during the later periods.

3.3 Art-craft and Technology

Efficacy of commerce and trade is highly dependent on merchandise and efficient trade organization. The production capability and quality of the commodities produced is directly inter-linked with the tools and implements available to the artisan class. With availability of good quality metal tools for craft production, the quality as well as quantity of production must have understandably improved. We know that in India copper and bronze was a rare commodity outside the zone of the Harappan civilization. Simple copper tools are low in efficiency as cutting/drilling tools. Throughout the Gangetic plain with a few exceptions, the Chalcolithic workers depended largely on stone and bone implements with minimal use of metals as functional implements in craft production. It was in such a milieu that iron was introduced in the Ganga Plain in the 2nd millennium BCE as a technological innovation. As stated above, at the initial stage of its introduction, iron was used largely for war and hunting or at the most in carpentry as chariots or carts were integral parts of war machinery of the Vedic and even post Vedic age. Iron being a rare commodity at the early stage, only the privileged few of the society could have had access to the newly acquired commodity. It is fully borne out by the small number and limited typology of iron objects at BRW and PGW levels. For example there are135 iron objects at PGW at Atranjikhera and 346 at NBPW period. The megalithic culture of southern India is fairly rich in iron objects but iron is used there almost exclusively for war and hunting purposes. It is only during the second stage of Iron Age that there is a typological diversification and the number of iron objects shows an increase. The metallurgical skill also improves with age. Steely iron with greater amount of malleability and ductility could be produced with knowledge of carburization, quenching and tempering, (see Tripathi 2001).

It is at this stage that around 7th-6th century BCE iron comes to be utilized for the first time in production mechanism. Agricultural implements are used as indicated by ploughshare, sickle, hoe, *khurpi*, celts thus helping a better yield of crops. The artisans' tools also show an improvement with growing numbers of chisels used by carpenters, and masons. Other tools of artisans are plumb bob, tongs, rods, pipes and variety of blades of knives. Iron objects come to be used in household and as building material too during the NBPW period (Fig 1).

Such application of technological know-how in production of better quality goods and in larger numbers must have provided an incentive to trade and commerce and also raised the standard of living of people in general. Literature provides a long list of crafts and professions that flourished during the early historic times. Arthaśāstra frequently refers to such craft villages (*Shilpa grāma or the Kammārgāma* mentioned in the Pāli Texts) involved in economic activities and management of economic affairs.

Social changes follow the specialization of craft production. Full time craftsmen, artisans, masons, bead makers, weavers came into existence with rising demand of commodities for trade. The socio-political systems channeled its resources towards production. The technological skill was directed towards this end. A comparative study of material remains of Early Iron Age and Middle to Late Iron Age fully corroborates this fact (fig. 2). Thus technological innovations contributed towards economic prosperity and growth of specialized centres of craft production. Villages of carpenters, weavers, smiths, potters, etc. find frequent mention both in Pāli and Saṅskṛit literature. The term '*nigama*' stands for a merchant town as a merchant is called *naigama* (*Amarkośha* II, 9.78). *Pattana* is a port-town that must have evolved for maritime trade activities. The *Periplus of Erythrian Sea* (Schoff 1912) dateable to the early centuries of the Common Era (CE) describes the export of Indian iron to the Abyssinian Port. We come across detailed description of technique of sword making in 5th-6th CE by Varāhamihira. Thus iron technology in India had attained great heights by this period and had a demand for it in the ancient world. One hears of the *śrenis* or merchant organizations which became powerful enough in due course of time some where in the early centuries of the Common Era to manage their own affairs without interventions, including by the state. The commercial activities leading to specialized groups may have eventually led to a new kind of social structure. Complex society must have been born out of it that is reflected in class-based society and also in social stratification that became a landmark of Indian social system.

The foregoing discussion on technological development, especially with iron metallurgy at its centre, provides us an insight into the life and culture of India, especially of the Vindhya-Ganga plain in the mid Ganga valley. The region has not only emerged as one of the key areas where iron was learnt independently at a very early age, but gradually brought about positive changes in the socio-economic milieu. The evolution of metallurgy took several centuries to be effective in a true sense. The social adaptation of the newly emerging technological innovation was indeed slow as fully corroborated by the comparative assessment of the material remains brought forth by excavations. The changes nevertheless were slow but persistent eventually leading to the rise of a strong political organization culminating In the emergence of sixteen *Mahājanapadas* which evolved out of the innumerable *janapadas* located across the entire Gangetic Plain.

References

Allchin, R.F., 1995, *The Archaeology of Early Historic South Asia: The Emergence of Cities and States.* University Press, Cambridge U.K.

Balasubramaniam, R. 2001, *Delhi Iron Pillar: New Insights.* New Delhi: IIAS Shimla and Aryan Books International.

Bardget, W.E. and J.F. Stanner. 1963. 'The Delhi iron pillar: a study of corrosion aspects'. *Journal of the Iron and Steel Institute*. 210:310.

De Gregori, T.R. 1989. *Theory of technology-continuity and change in Human Development* – Affiliated East – West Press Pvt. Ltd., New Delhi.

Ghose, M.K. 1963. 'The Delhi iron pillar and its iron'. *National Metallurgical Laboratory Technical Journal* 5 (1): 31-35.

Hari Narain, Jai Prakash, O.P. Agrawal and M.V. Nair. 1998. 'Metallographic Studies of Iron Artefacts of Domestic use Tools and Weapons from Sringverpur (250 BC-600 AD). Uttar Pradesh'. In *Archaeometallurgy in India* (Ed.) Vibha Tripathi. Delhi: Sharada Publishing House. Pp. 44-53.

Lahiri, A.K. 1963. 'Some observations on corrosion resistance of ancient Delhi iron pillar and present time Adivasi iron made by primitive method.' *NML Technical Journal* 3(1): 46-54.

Schoff, W.H. 1912 *The Periplus of the Erythrian Sea,* (translation) New York, London, Longmans Green and Co.

Singh, P. 1994. *Excavations at Narhan (1984-89)*. Varanasi: Banaras Hindu University.

Tewari, R. 1998. 'In quest of early Iron Age sites in Karmanasa valley'. *Prāgdhārā* 8: 57-61. Journal of UP State Archaeology Department, Lucknow.

Tewari, R. 2003. 'The Origin of Iron Working in India: new evidence from the central Ganga plain and the Eastern Vindhyas.' *Antiquity* 77: 536-544.

Tomlin, E.W.F. 1978. Arnold Toynbee: A selection from his works, Oxford University Press.

Tripathi, V. 2001. *The Age of Iron in South Asia: Legacy and Tradition.* New Delhi: Aryan Books International.

Wallace A.F.C. 1972 'Paradigmatic Process in Culture change', *American Anthropologist.* 74 (3): 467-76.

Table 1 : Radiocarbon Dates from Iron Age level

Sl. No.	*Sites*	*Radiocarbon dates in BP/BC on the basis of half life 5730 ± 40 years*	*Calibrated*
Raja Nal- Ka –Tila			
1.	BS-1378 1996-97 Trench No. U - 19 (6) 1.95-2.00#m With iron	2626±110 BP 676±110 BC	822 (773) 486 BC
2.	PRL - 2047 1996-97 Trench No. U-20 (6) 2.08-2.10#m With iron	2980±90 BP 1030±90 BC	1196 BC- 1188 BC -1164 BC-1143 BC -1132 BC-976 BC -970 BC-930 BC
3.	BS – 1299 1995-96 Trench No. A-I Pit sealed by layer No. (6) With iron	2914±100 BP 960± 100 BC	1118 (963) 859 BC
4.	BS – 1300 1995-96 Trench No. A-I (6) 2.00#m With iron	3150±110 BP 1200± 110 BC	1423 (1307) 1144 BC
5.	PRL-2049 1996-97 Trench No. T-19 (6) 2.00#m With iron	3150±90 BP 1200± 90 BC	1406 BC -1198 BC 1186 BC-1164 BC 1143 BC-1132 BC
Malhar			
6.	BS - 1623, MLR II Trench No. XAl, Layer No. (3) Depth 0.55 cm	3550 ± 90	1886, 1664 1649, 1643 BC
7.	BS - 1593, MLR II Trench No. Al, Layer No. (3) Depth 90-100cm	3650 ± 90	2010 ,2001, 1977, 1750 BC
8.	BS-1590 MLR II Layer No. (4) 80 cm	3850 ± 80	2283, 2248, 2233, 2030 BC
Dadupur			
9.	BS-1822 Trench No. DDR-3, A -1	3368± 80 B.P. 1420± 80 B.C	1679 (1522) 1422 BC
10.	BS-1759 Trench No. DDR-3, A-1	3480 ± 160 BP 1530 ± 160 BC	1882 (1685) 1465 BC
11.	BS-1825 (Pit sealed by (12)	3532 ± 90 BP 1580 ± 90 BC	1739, 1706, 1695 BC
Lhuradewa			
12.	BS-1939	2940 ± 100 B.P.	1205, 1205, 1188
Jhusi			
13.	AU/JHS/ 9 2075C-15 (46) 1210	2730±90	897 (806) 789 BC
14.	AU/JHS/ 12 2077C-15 (49) 1240	2900±90	1107 (973, 956, 941) 844 BC

Sl. No.	*Sites*	*Radiocarbon dates in BP/BC on the basis of half life 5730 ± 40 years*	*Calibrated*
15.	AU/JHS/ 16 2081C-15 (53) 1325	2780±90	966 (830) 799 BC
16.	AU/JHS/ 18 2083C-15 (62) 1520	3290±90	1597 (1490, 480, 1450) 1400 BC
Aktha			
17.	S-3580	3350±160 1660 ± 218	Un calibrated
18.	S-3849	3460±180 1771 ± 248	Un calibrated
Komaranhalli, Karnataka			
19.	PRL-46 (TL)	1320 ± 400	---
20.	PRL-47 (TL)	1380 ± 300	---
21.	PRL-47 (TL)	1200 ± 280	---
22.	PRL-49 (TL)	1130 ± 500	---
23.	PRL-50 (TL)	1440 ± 290	---
Hallur, Karnataka			---
24.	TF-570 (C^{14})	2970 + 105 BP 1385-1050 BC	---
25.	TF-573 (C^{14})	2820 + 100 BP 1125-825 BC	---
Veerapuram, Andhra Pradesh			
26.	PRL-729 (C^{14})	----	1374 (1186,1183,1128) 921
27.	PRL-729 (C^{14})	----	1293 (1047) 899
28.	PRL-730 (C^{14})		1679 (1493, 1476, 1458) 1319
Vidarbha, Maharashtra			
29.	PRL-1361 (C^{14})	2940±160	1393 (1205, 1205, 1188, 1181, 1149, 1144, 1129) 917
30.	PRL-1452 (C^{14})	3080±120	1490 (1381, 1334, 1321) 1131
31.	PRL-1456 (C^{14})	2820±100	1185 (973, 956, 941) 834
Gufkaral, Jammu & Kashmir			
32.	----	----	1888-1674
33.	----	----	2195-1900
Charsadda, Pakistan			
34.	----	----	1200-900

Table 2 : Iron Objects at different cultural stages

Tool Type	*Name of Tool*	*Early Stage*	*Middile Stage*	*Late Stage*
Hunting Tool	Spear heads	*	*	*
	Arrow heads	*	*	*
	Points	*	o	o
	Socketed tangs	*	o	o
	Blades	*	*	o
	Spear lances	o	*	o
	Dagger	o	*	*
	Sword	o	*	*
	Elephant goad	o	*	*
	Lances	×	×	*
	Armour	×	×	*
	Helmet	×	×	*
	Horse bits	×	×	*
	Caltrop	o	o	*
Agricultural Tools	Axes	*	*	*
	Sickles	*	*	*
	Spade	×	*	o
	Ploughshare	×	*	o
	Hoe	×	*	*
	Pick	o	o	*
Household objects	Knives	*	*	*
	Tongs	*	o	o
	Discs	×	*	o
	Rings	×	*	o
	Spoons	×	*	*
	Sieve	×	×	*
	Cauldron	×	×	*
	Bowls	×	×	*
	Dishes	×	×	*
Structural and craft tools	Rods	*	o	o
	Pins	*	o	o
	Nails	*	*	*
	Clamps	*	*	*
	Chisel	×	*	*
	Pipes	×	*	o
	Sockets	×	*	o
	Plump bob	×	*	o
	Chains	×	*	*
	Door hooks	×	*	*
	Door handle	×	×	*
	Hinges	×	×	*
	Spikes	×	×	*
	Tweezers	×	×	*
	Anvils	×	×	*
	Hammers	×	×	*
	Scissors	×	×	*
	Saw	×	×	*

Definite existence *	Confirmed data not available o	Non-existence ×

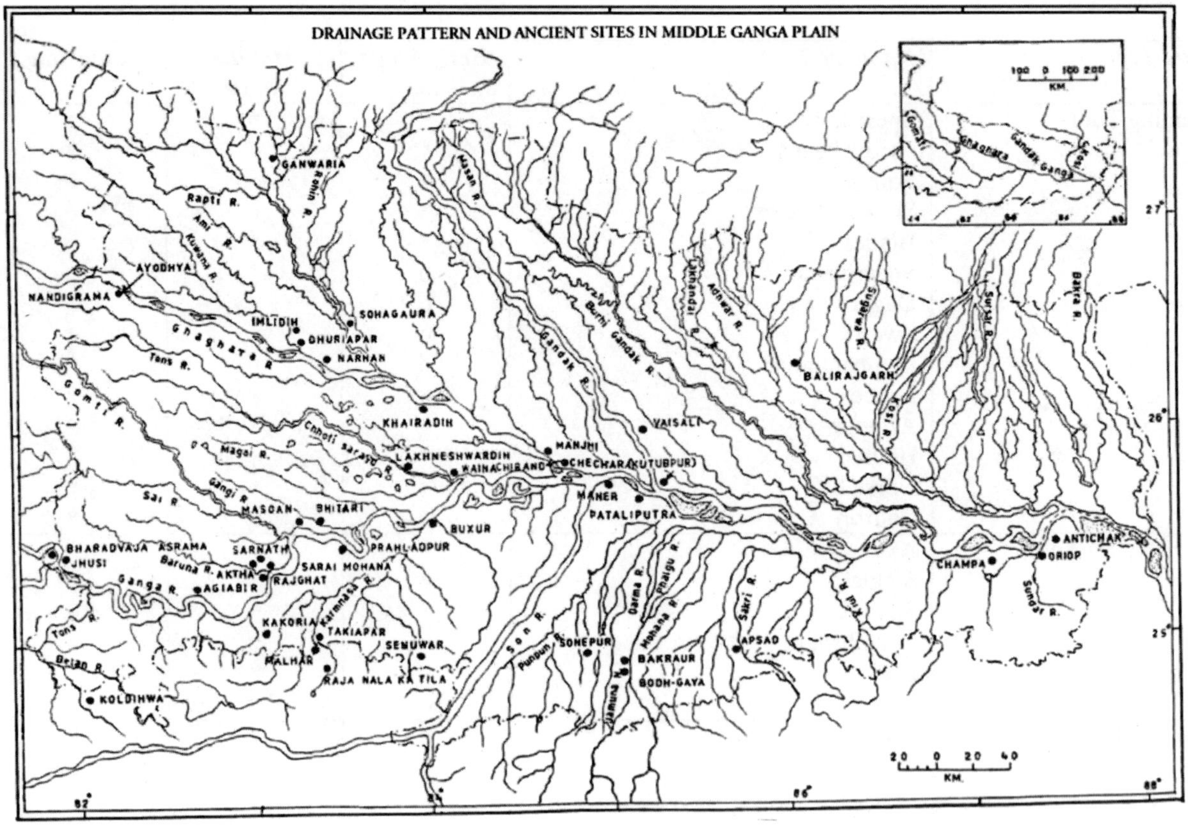

M ap 1 : Drainage pattern and Archaeological sites of the Middle Ganga Plain

Fig 1 : Iron objects (Śuṅga-Kuṣhāṇa period, Khairadih, Ballia, (UP)

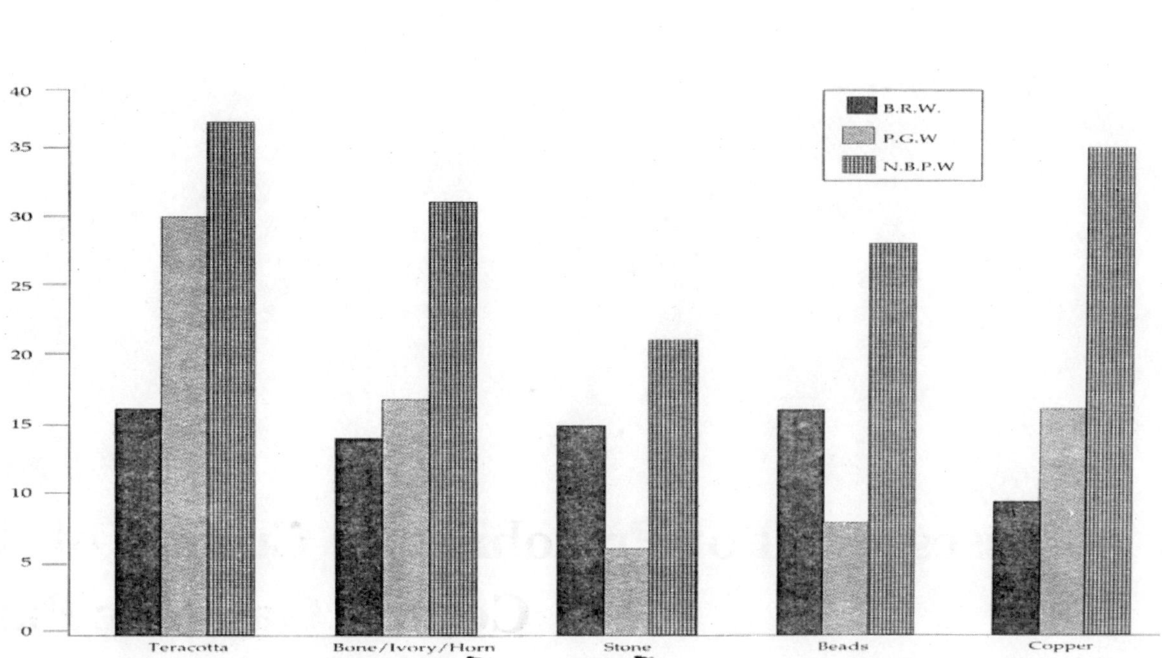

Fig 2 : A relative graph of material remains from various cultural periods

9

An Assessment of Protohistoric Culture of the Central Gangetic Plain

(With Special Reference to Sarayūpāra Region)

Rahman Ali

Geographically, the Central Gangetic plain is located between 24°.30' - 27°.51' North and 81°.04'-84°.51' East - roughly covering an area of 144, 409 square Kilometers.[1] The entire land is covered by the administrative units of districts of Allahabad, Pratapgarh, Sultanpur, Jaunpur, Varanasi, Banda, Mirzapur, Sonbhadra, hilly parts of Chandauli in Uttar Pradesh and northern Bihar along the western margins of the Raj Mahal hills.

The physical geography indicates us to divide roughly the whole land into two sub-groups, i.e., the northern and the southern; the former is the plain part of this zone comprising of the northern parts of districts of Allahabad, Pratapgarh, Sultanpur, Jaunpur, Varanasi (U.P.) and the northern Bihar whereas the later spans over the southern parts of districts of Banda, Mirzapur, Sonabhadra and the hilly parts of Chandauli district in eastern Uttar Pradesh.[2] The northern sub-division is larger and drained by a number of tributary of Ganga, i.e., the Gandaka, Budhi- Gandaka, Bagmati, Koshi, Mahananda, and several small streams, devoid of hills but dotted with a series of ox-bow lakes, *Jhīls* and natural *tālas* etc.

The Sarayupar region is an integral part of the vast Gangetic plain. It is flat land sloping from the northern - west to south east and hence forms a distinct geographical and cultural entity. The land is divided into three broad divisions - (1) *Tarai* (2) Bhāṅgar on the upland, (3) *Kachhāra* on the flood prone low-land. The tract running parallel to the foot hills of Himalayas is known as *Tarai*, characterised by many streams, swamps, forests and heavy annual rain falls. The upland *Bhāṅgar* extends over a large arca while the expansive *kachhāra* of Rapti river cuts diagonally across and reduces its area. The southern edge of the upland in Gorakhpur district is skirted by river Ghaghra, whereas in the Basti district, it is sharply distinguished from the *Khādara* through a series of higher ground locally called *Dhūsa*, marking the former bank of Ghaghra. At present, the major administrative unit of the valley comprises of the area of district of Gorakhpur, Deoria, two tehsils of district Gonda and district Saran of north western Bihar. The region is drained by several rivers including Ghaghra, Manwar, Kuwana, Rapti, Ami and Chhoti Gandaka. Of these Ghaghra and Rapti emanate from the Himalayas. The river Ghaghra is mighty one and flows over a wide and sandy bed (1180 Kms. in length) and covers 1,27000 square kilometers area. Thus the distinct geographical situation of this area, enriched with all the essential facilities and natural resources, attracted the proto-historic man to cease his savage life. The recent discoveries of Neolithic / Chaleolithic sites and archaeological excavations, have opened the new vistas of the early human societies. The evidences yielded by these excavations have shed ample light on the cultural activities of the proto-historic man of Central Gangetic valley as well as on the condition of the people of Sarayupar region. We may, however, discuss the problem under some of the major diagnostic traits or features to reconstruct the coherent picture of proto –historic society of the region.

Neolithic-Chalcolithic Culture : It was in about 6000 BCE when the "Neolithic Revolution" was taking place in the northern slopes of Vindhyan out-crops and by-and-large the Gangetic plain, with all its floral and faunal resources, was exploited only sporadically. The scholars like D.P. Sharma have discovered the stray triangular Neolithic Celts from the Khaga sub-division of district Fatehpur (U.P.) from eight sites.[3] Likewise, Chirand (District - Saran, Bihar) was already noticed though Prof. H.D. Sankalia had doubts about the true - Neolithic settlement at Chirand. Nevertheless, the outer fringe to the south, characterised by the hilly tracts, continued to be inhabited by the Neolithic folk in Uttar Pradesh, Madhya Pradesh, Bihar, Orissa and West Bengal. Interestingly, the excavations at Koldihwa[4] and Mahagara[5] have indicated towards the transitional phase and these have been dated to a period ranging between 7000 BCE to 4500 BCE. It indicates towards the sedentary life, domestication and the cultivation of rice, domestication of cattle, sheep and goats and also the use of hand-made pottery with the cord-impressions. It is to be noted that the evidence at Mahagara exhibit the most advanced form of Neolithic phase in the upper-most strata. Here 18 circular/oval floors, littered with artifacts and a large cattle-pen with hoof marks in clusters have been noticed. Further, the standardised ceramics and food processing equipments like the querns, mullers of medium and portable size as well as the specialised tools like the celts, adzes and chisels have been found. The scholars have visualised even the defined family units in the light of findings.

Thus, the Neolithic people emerged as one of the earliest (circa-6560 BCE.) independent farming communities in the southern fringes of the Gangetic plain. The flood-plain available close to their settlement was most suitable for the cultivation of rice, which could be raised without the aid of any man-made irrigation device. It also did not require manuring. In other words, we may, however, assume that the cattle was not used in agricultural activities as further substantiated by the observations of hook-joints in cattle-bones.

Copper Age

The breakthrough in proto- history of Gangetic plain comes with the copper during this phase when the chalcolithic / proto historic culture was characterised by the presence of the Ochre Coloured Pottery and Copper Hoard implements. A large number of village settlements came into existence. In fact,Ochre- Coloured Pottery (OCP,) was, for the first time, recognised by B.B. Lal in 1946 during the excavations of Copper Hoard sites of Bisauli and Rajapur Parasu (U.P.). Subsequently, in 1952 similar pottery was found in the lowest levels of Hastinapur (1954-55) and Bahadarabad excavation by Y.D. Sharma and also by H.D. Sankalia at Nasik (1955). Now, more than 100 sites have been explored and excavated in upper Gangetic *doab.* Geographically, it has wide distribution from Haridwara to Sringverapur (Allahabad). At Koldihawa, in Phase-II, and Kaushambi Pd. I, and Chirand-Period- I (Bihar) its presence has equally been noticed.

Thus, its expansion in the Sarayūpāra region is indicated and confirmed. The T.L. analysis of the sherds has widely confirmed its chronology, ranging from 2600 BCE to 1300 BCE. Most-probably, this culture, originated in pre-Harappan times as co-eval but different, might have gone through a long process of evolution, i.e., the earliest bearing incised designs evolved from cord impressed and hand-made pottery.[6] The single C^{14} date from Takiapar (Varanasi, district) stands as 2780 BCE[7] which may, however, be actually an earlier date for ochre colourd Pottery horizon.

The cultural material and advanced equipments of the Ochre Coloured Pottery people indicate to a fairly advanced stage of technologico-economic and cultural life over a primitive agricultural community. They had, most probably, relations with Malwa region if fortified settlements with bastions are index of urbanisation; several centres were coming into existence in Malwa culture.

Simultaneously, the chalcolithic people from the nuclear zone in the Vindhyan outcrop appear to have intruded into the entire central and lower Gangetic plain up to West Bengal as evidenced by Chirand, Sonpur, Pandu Rajar Dhibi and Mahisadal sites. These people had a long span of life in this region and gradually entered into the Iron Age.

To reconstruct the co-herent picture of Neolithic/Chalcolithic cultures of Sarayūpāra region, we may, however, evaluate ceramic assemblages yielded by the archaeological excavations conducted by the archaeological departments as well as educational institutions recently.

Among the ceramic assemblages, the cord impressed, handmade pottery related with the Neolithic culture is considered to be the earliest. In Sarayūpāra region, it has been picked up from Sohgaura (Gorakhpur) and Chirand (Saran, Bihar) from first layer of earliest period which has been ascribed to the Neolithic Age. The same pottery has been found in the excavations at Koldihwa, Mahagara and other Neolithic sites of Vindhyan range. The upper levels are of the chalcolithic culture. This ceramic of Koldihwa is cord impressed, hand-made (ill-fired) and constitutes 69.27% of the total items of pottery, while the plain red-ware and the crude black-and-Red ware accounted for 28.15% etc.

Some pots of Red ware were produced on the slow wheel turntable and washed with red-ochre on both the surfaces[8]. Later on, several other sites have been brought to notice which yielded this type of ceramics.

Painted Grey Ware (P.G.W.)

Painted Grey Ware occupies a very crucial position in the proto-historic and historical archaeology. It was first noticed at Ahichhatra (Dist. Bareilly)[9] from the lowest levels but its full significance was not then realised. Later on, it turned up in the excavations at Hastinapur,[10] Rupar,[11] then in central India from Malwa-in the core of rampart at Ujjain,[12] Kayatha, and Besnagar etc. fixing the southern limit of the ware and in the east at Vaisali in north Bihar etc.[13] This pottery has been noticed through out in a large area at Sohgaura (Distt. Gorakhpur, U.P.). The P.G.W. co-exists with the plain Black-and-Red ware, plain and painted Black-and-red ware, Grey ware and also with painted black slipped ware. Period-II at the site was characterised by the appearance of the Northern Black-Polished ware while the other wares of the preceding period also continued. The overall evidence of upper Gangetic Valley do indicate that P.G.W. might have its genesis in the Central Indian Chalcolithic. The Malwa Chalcolithic ended roughly about 1400 BCE and the P.G.W. settlement entered into the Gangetic region during the period ranging from 1400 BCE to 1300 BCE.

Black and Red Ware

This group of pottery had been attracting the attention of both Indian and foreign scholars. The pottery is so called because it has a characteristically black interior and black-and-red or black-and grey exterior with the black confined to the upper part of the vessel. Amongst the factors responsible for its growing recognition, the wide distribution, both in space and time, is most important. The ceramic occurs at many sites in India from Rupar (Distt. Ambala) in the north to Adichannalur (Distt. Tirunnaveli, Tamilnadu) in the south and from Amra and Lakhabawal (Distt. Jamnagar) in the west to Pandu Rajar Dhibi (Distt. Burdwan - West Bengal) in the East. The span of time, however, is also equally wide and ranges between 2400 BCE to the early centuries of the Current Era.[14] Thus the distribution of the black-and-red ware, both in time and space, has given the rise to three pertinent questions-

I. Whether the Black and Red ware has similarity in technique throughout without any cultural or chronological implications,

II. Whether Black-and-Red ware is a cultural trait of group of people moving from one region to another,

III. Whether Black-and-Red ware is a combination of both the above mentioned issues.

There had been a long debate on these issues among scholars like Subba Rao, H.D. Sankalia, S.P. Gupta etc.[15] However, the Black-and-Red ware has invariably been found in the Ghaghra Valley during the excavations at Imlidih (Distt. Gorakhpur,U.P.), Khairadih (Distt. Ballia, U.P.) Lahuradeva (Distt. Sant Kabir Nagar, U.P.), Sravasti (Distt. Bahraich, U.P.) etc. All these sites are situated in Ghaghra Valley: Besides these, more than 60 sites have been discovered by S.K. Bhatt in Basti district alone. These sites are waiting for horizontal excavations to shed more light on the specific culture of the area.

Northern Black Polished Ware (N.B.P.)

The Northern Black Polished ware (N.B.P.) is a well known ceramic ascribed to circa 600 BCE. It has been associated with the period of second urbanisation in India though the archaeological evidence for urban elements are missing at all related centres reported so for. This distinct pottery, most probably, originated in the cradle of eastern India. Now, it has been noticed in different shades from different centres of Madhya Pradesh - Eran, Ujjain, Besnagar, Sodanga (Ujjain) far away from Taxila, Rupar and Sanghol etc.

In Ghaghra Valley, the excavations at Imlidih Khurd and Khairadih have attested its occurrence while at Narhan it has been picked from Pd. III by the excavator who has ascribed it to circa 600 BCE.[16] It is interesting to note that the ceramic had appeared in different shades like the orange, golden, silver, red, pink, steel-blue and brown-black etc. Till now, more than 416 sites of N.B.P. have been listed, and its area of distribution covers a distance of 2121 kilometers from north to south and about 1790 kilometers from east to west. The scholars like B.B. Lal, B.P. Sinha, Sanaullah and T.N. Roy have studied about its manufacturing, features and chronology etc. in different contexts. However, its tradition in its original place in Ghaghra Valley is significant.

Lustrous Red Ware

The Lustrous Red Ware is a unique ceramic which has been picked up during the excavations at Imlidih Khurd. The limited number of sherds of the tubular spouts prove its presence at the site. Though these are less in number yet significant for the pottery has been found at Maheshwar Navdatoli and Sodanga (Distt. Ujjain). Scholars presume that the pottery was used for ritualistic purposes but different varieties of spouted sprinklers at the site confirm its local production at Ujjayini and the contacts with the Roman traders even with people of Gangetic Valley and beyond.[17]

The recent archaeological explorations/excavations in central Gangetic doab-Ghaghra Valley have yielded the assemblage of ceramics-Red ware, Black-slipped ware, Grey-ware and Black-slipped ware, bearing different varieties of paintings. These evidence need our attention to study them more scientifically in the region.

Food and Economy

The recent researches have indicated that the food production was started and controlled by man in about 18000 B.P. (Fredwendorf - 1981) in the Valley of river Nile in southern Egypt. The assemblage consists of the food remains and artefacts suggesting strongly the food producing culture. The Egyptian discoveries raised questions, creating thorough debate among scholars about the date of Neolithic culture and its diagnostic traits.

Coming to Indian scene, the first chronological evidence about the sedentary life and pottery manufacturing comes from Chopani-Mando (Sharma, 1980, 100) which has been dated between 12190 ± 390 B.C. (PRL 603) and 8080 ± 115 B.C. (SUA). This was the first evidence of open air sedentary life started in phase - I (Epi-Palaeolithic) and represented by the post - holes of huts.

The most significant evidence is the finding of the rice-husk of wild variety. It was for the first time when the hand made pottery and the kits for storage purposes appeared. The over-all picture of habitation and the objects prove that the people were gatherers of wild rice and were on the threshold of effective food production.[18] The proto-Neolithic period at Chopani-Mando has been ascribed to circa 9th - 8th millennia BCE. Almost similar situation has been noticed during the excavations at Mahadaha, a Mesolithic site in Gangetic doab. According to Sharma (1980)- Koldihwa, Mahagara might have been primary villages of farming communities. The excavations at Koldihwa revealed a three fold sequence of cultures covering the Neolithic, Chalcolithic and Iron-age deposits. Palaeobotanical analysis of the rice-husks used in the paste of pottery showed that the rice belonged to the domesticated variety. The C^{14} date obtained from its Neolithic deposits is 7th-5th millennia BCE. It provides the earliest evidence for rice cultivation in South Asia. However, the settlement of early farming community in central Gangetic plain has been further substantiated by the excavations at Lahuradeva giving the C^{14} dates of two samples to circa 6th-5th millennia BCE. It is marked by the presence of grains of rice corresponding to *oryza-sativa*-cultivated grains, which affirm that some sort of agriculture was being carried in Lahuradeva region. Some grains of wild form of rice comparable to *oryza-rufipogon* have also been found.

Further, a few grains of fox tail grass (*seteria cf. glauca*), ocurring in wild state through out in the region of Lahuradeva were also picked up. These are still gathered and cultivated by the tribes. Thus the evidence of Lahuradeva almost supports the dates of production of rice at Koldihwa in Belan Valley.[19] The other evidences of charred grains, rice-husk from Chirand besides the wheat and moong as well as carbonised grams, club-wheat, dwarf-wheat, green-grams and rice etc. from Narhan have further substantiated to the production of food grains in central Gangetic doab and Sarayupar regions[20].

The Chalcolithic man of central Gangetic doab had substituted his diet with meats of animals invariably. The excavations at Narhan and other sites have yielded the charred and semi-charred bones of animals like antlers, bones with cut chopped marks. The study of collected bones confirm that the animals like deer, buffalo, cow, sheep and goat etc.

were hunted and fishing was also done by the man. The chopping marks confirm skinning and butchery practices etc. in society.

Settlement Pattern

The structural remains at Lahuradeva in Pd. I and Pd. II correspond to the Neolithic and Chaleolithic phases respectively. The evidence of some post-holes and the chunks of burnt clay with reed-like impressions do indicate the type of houses built by the man.[21] Almost similar evidence have been noticed at Narhan excavations for a large floor was exposed which was mode of clay-mixed with pot-sherds. The evidence of beaten earth floor was also noticed in period-I at Narhan. However, the complete house-plan could not be reconstructed at Narhan. [22] Similar is the case at Lahuradeva where the post-holes were sealed by layer 12 and cut into 13 which did not help much to draw any alignment.[23]

However, an important feature of the settlement at Lahuradeva attracts our attention. It ia an irregular channel running through all the three quadrants layed at the site. It was traced for a length of 12 meters. The channel is about 23-53 cms. broad. The post holes were found super-imposing the channel which indicates that the hut to which they belong was erected after the channel was silted up to its top.[24] Thus, we may, however, assume that the house was built twice or more times. Perhaps, at Narhan and Lahuradeva, the heavy rain fall / floods etc. destroyed the small villages more than once, and lastly the sites were left barren. However, the plans of the huts, size of floors, post holes, pits and hearths and ovens inside the house etc. indicate to the sizes of the villages and families of proto-historic Gangetic doab specially of the Sarayupar region.

Apart from the above mentioned major traits, the recent excavations have yielded other objects like the beads of semi-precious stones, terracotta beads, eye-laces of bone/horns, copper eye-laces; and the weapons of the copper and iron etc. The evidence confirm the luxurious life of the contemporary man. Besides these obijects, a good number of different varieties of the associated ceramics have also been picked up which require more scientific research in the light of new discoveries in future.

The above discussions are based on the available materials which, undoubtedly confirm the fast advancement of the proto-historic man/cultures of gangetic plains. These evidences further substantiate to the fact that Saryūpāra region might have played significant role in the fast progress of proto-historic cultures and had been one of the impotant zones for difusion of many of the cultural traits to other parts of our country.

References

1. Singh R.L., *India : A Regional Geography, National Geographical Society of India,* Varanasi, 1971, pp. 183.
2. Singh, P. & Singh, A.K., *The Archaeology of Middle Ganga Plain : New Perspectives,* (Excavations at Agiabir), M/s. Aryans Books International, New Delhi, 2004, pp. 4-6.
3. Sharma, D.P., "Some New Finds from Fatehpur District", *Purātattva,* no. 11, 1979-80, p. 65.

4. Shahi, M.D.M., *Aspects of Indian Archaeology*, M/s. Publication Scheme, Jaipur, 1994, pp. 67-68.
5. *Ibid.*
6. The pottery from Lal Qila, Alamgirpur, and Ambakher has Harappan affiliation. The third stage is represented by Ataranjikhera and Saipai with thick bands of paintings.
7. I.A.R. 1973-74.
8. *Op. cit.*, pp. 69-70.
9. Ghosh, A. and Panigrahi, K.C., *Ancient India* No. 1, 1946, p. 58.
10. Lal, B.B., Excavation at Hastinapur, *Ancient India,* No. 10, 11, 1954-55.
11. *Indian Arcaheology, A Review,* New Delhi, 1953-54, p. 6.
12. *Indian Archaeology, A Review,* New Delhi, 1956-57.
13. *Indian Archaeology, A Review,* 1958-59, p. 12.
14. Now, the date of Black-and Red ware has been pushed back to 4500 BCE at Koldihwa (Allahabad, U.P.) and circa 2100 BCE at Mahidpur (Distt. Ujjain, M.P.) while at Narhan the C^{14} date has come to 1335.
15. For details - see Shrivastava, K.M., *Community Movements in Proto-historic India,* Agam Kala Prakashan, New Delhi, 1979, Pp. 40-41.
16. Purushottam Singh, *Excavation at Narhan* (1984-89), PP. 22-23
17. For details, see, Ali, Rahman & Trivedi, A. (et. all) *Buddhist Remains of Ujjain Region* (*Excavations at Sodanga*), M/S Sharda Publications, Delhi, 2004, P. 10.
18. Thapar, B.K., 1984, "Fresh Light on the Neolithic Culture of India," *Purātattva,* No. 13,14, (1981-83), New Delhi, 1984, P. 39.
19. Tewari, Rakesh, Saraswat, K.K. et. al. "Preliminary Report of the Excavation at Lahuradewa, Distt. Sant Kabir Nagar : 2001-2, *Prāgdhārā,* Govt. of U.P, Lucknow, 2003.
20. The discovery of sun flower seed (*Carthmous -tinctorious*) from Narhan is significant in north India. Similar is the case of mustard.
21. Tewari, Rakesh, et. al, *op. cit.*
22. Singh, Purusottam, *op. cit.*
23. Tewari, Rakesh, et. al. *Ibid.*
24. *Ibid.*

10

Beliefs and Rituals : Earliest Settled Communities in Eastern Uttar Pradesh

Neelima Pandey

Abstract

This paper focuses on the burial practices of Mesolithic people, being the earliest settled communities of Eastern Uttar Pradesh. Burials from sites of Eastern Uttar Pradesh help us to reconstruct the beliefs, rituals, and supernatural aspects of Mesolithic man and his society. The paper is based on secondary sources.

Religion is primarily concerned with belief of man in supernatural aspects. It finds its expression in the cognitive tradition on one hand and rites associated with such beliefs on the other. As such very little is known about the religion of pre-literate societies. This is not because of the fact that they did not attain such cognitive abilities to develop a system of beliefs and practices; but it is because they have left very little evidence in this regard for us to reconstruct the world of their ideas and beliefs.

However, archaeology has become capable enough to afford some evidence of this nature. In Indian context the remains of the earliest stages of prehistoric period are too shadowy as yet to yield any information, but with Mesolithic period the first archaeological information in this respect is available. Most significant evidences available to us are of burials and paintings, which provide us with a deep insight into the beliefs and rituals of Mesolithic people. Among the primitive people, attitude towards the dead is of much significance as it invited both awe and curiosity. In this context disposal of dead and rites associated with it provide much evidence. The disposal of dead in a community with special care and attention and a consistent set of rites associated with it is in itself a proof of the fact that community had developed some sort of imagination regarding life after death.

Similarly, aesthetic expressions of Mesolithic people in the form of cave and rock paintings could be related to religious rituals or magical aspect of their life. Ethnographic evidence provided by the recorded practices of hunting communities in the isolated pockets sometimes help to interpret such archaeological evidences.

In Indian prehistoric context, the evidence of burials have been found from Mesolithic and succeeding horizons. It cannot be said however that the earlier man belonging to Palaeolithic Cultures had no practices associated with the dead. But in the lack of evidence, the study of burials, the rites associated with dead and beliefs regarding life after death can only be postulated in Mesolithic context and that of succeeding cultures. It is in this context that burials acquire greater significance in studying Mesolithic cultural practices.

The paper focuses on the burial practices of Mesolithic people, who happen to be the earliest settled communities of eastern Uttar Pradesh. With the help of the prehistoric archaeological evidences an effort has been made to reconstruct beliefs and rituals of Mesolithic people or society in broader context. Three major sites of Ganga basin - Sarai Nahar Rai, Mahadaha and Damdama are burial-cum-habitation sites; burials from these sites help us to reconstruct the beliefs, rituals, and supernatural aspects of Mesolithic man and his society.

Before we deal with burials of Ganga basin in eastern Uttar Pradesh, taking an overview of burial practices in world context will be helpful. We have evidences of burial from very early periods of human evolution. The earliest evidence in this regard comes from the Middle Palaeolithic times. The Neanderthal man is regarded to be first among the human ancestors showing evidence of pre-occupation with life after death. Neanderthals buried their dead with food and tools laid along with the body. At Shanidar cave in Iraq, a thirty year old man has been found buried with flowers covering his body. The pollens of the flowers have been found as evidence, and their possibility of have-blown inside the cave is eliminated by careful comparison. Several other Neanderthal burials are known with evidences of religious cult connected with the cave bears.[1] From Upper Palaeolithic cultures, we have similar evidences. Gravettian (Later Perigordian) hunters buried their dead ceremonially dressed in their finery and scattered over the red ochre.[2] Some sort of continuity of such practices may be traced even in contemporary societies.

Large cemeteries belonging to Mesolithic have also been discovered in Northern Europe. At Vedback in North-Eastern Zealand, a Mesolithic cemetery was uncovered in 1975 during the construction of a school. This cemetery is dated to approximately 4000

BCE and contains the graves of at least twenty-two individuals of both sexes of various ages. A variety of grave goods and burial practices have been noticed here. In many graves powdered red ochre was used to adorn individuals.[3] Excavations at Skateholm in Southern Sweden have uncovered three cemeteries from the Late Mesolithic.[4] Here, from first cemetery eight dog graves have also been found along with fifty seven graves with sixty-two individuals. Almost every imaginable type of burial has been found here including cremations and inhumations, the latter showing individuals in positions such as supine, sitting, extended, flexed and one individual even buried on his stomach. It has been suggested that both positions in grave and the type of grave-goods vary with the age and sex of individual.[5] During later years Mesolithic burials and cemeteries have been reported from many places including the under water sites in the Baltic, Nedrest in Jutland and Stroby Egede in Zealand.

The Mesolithic burials from the sites discussed above in the world context and those obtained from Indian sites are significant in many ways in studying the life of people at that cultural stage. The study of skeletons helps in distinguishing racial features of population. This may provide valuable insight about the evolution of human race, racial admixtures that might have taken place and migration of people from one region to other through generations. Langhnaj, a Mesolithic site from Gujrat reveals that the Mesolithic inhabitants there inherited a mixture of Mediterranean and Veddit traits.[6] Similarly, the age of the person represented by the skeletal remains, can be ascertained at the time of the death. Studies of a large number of skeletons may give some idea of life expectancy and in some cases the cause of death, disease, nutritional status etc. For instance from the studies of cemeteries at Vedback, Den Mark and at Stakeholm in the Southern Sweden it has been noticed that skeletons are generally robust with little indication of disease or malnutrition.

Along with these racial, demographic and medico-pathological aspects a wide variety of information on the socio-cultural aspect of Mesolithic peoples is also provided by the burials. In some cases, the violent causes of death provide evidence for interpersonal and inter-group conflict and warfare. The simultaneous burial of three individuals in a single grave at Vedback - an adult male with a lethal bone point through his throat, an adult female and a child - suggests violent death.[7]

In the cases of mass burials some kind of social relationship among the individuals may be inferred. Taking again an example from Vedback in North Eastern Zealand, a new born infant was found buried next to an adult female which obviously leads to believe that they were mother and son.

Burials associated with grave-goods seem to have some cultural meaning. Grave goods which usually consist of the valuables of the Mesolithic man such as tools, ornaments, and food remains are at the most general level indicative of emergence of belief in life after death.

Again, the way in which burials had been made and the skeletons had been placed, suggest the activity of burying the dead had taken the form of ritual being performed by social group. This might be the beginning of primitive religion. From the more specialized and in-depth studies of the burials and from revelation of more sites with burials many more aspects of human life during Mesolithic period may be illuminated.

In Indian context, evidence of burial have been found from several Mesolithic settlements. These include Langhnaj and Dhansura in Gujrat, Bagor in Rajasthan, Bhimbetka, Adamgarh, Dorothydeep and Jambudeep rock shelters in Madhya Pradesh; Baghaikhor and Lekhahia rock shelters, Chopani Mando, Sarai Nahar Rai, Mahadaha, Damdama, Harahi-Bhituli (Dhansari lake, Pratapgarh), Kurha (Allahabad) in Uttar Pradesh.

Further, an attempt has been made to draw some conclusions regarding beliefs and rituals of earliest settled communities i.e., Mesolithic Communities of eastern Uttar Pradesh. This attempt is based on the study of three major sites of Ganga basin viz. Sarai Nahar Rai, Mahadaha and Damdama located in Pratapgarh district of Uttar Pradesh and excavated by Allahabad University.[8]

Site of Sarai Nahar Rai yielded fourteen burials situated within habitation. General orientation of the burials was in West-East direction in extended and supine position. Specific feature of the graves was placement of 3 to 4 cm thick soft cushion of soil below the skull. Skeletons had their one hand lying along the side of the body and the other placed across the abdomen. Noteworthy fact was that male skeletons had their right hand on abdomen where as female skeletons had their left hands on the abdomen. Microlithic tools, animal flesh seem to be kept as grave- goods as animal bones have been found from the graves.

The presence of grave-goods indicates that these people performed some rituals with their burial practices and had belief in life after death.

Grave No. VII of this site is important as four corpses were buried in it at the same time. Two skeletons are of male and the other two identified as females. It seems that a pair of male-female was placed first in the grave then another pair was kept above them and buried. A remarkable feature of this grave is positioning of the males and females where females were placed to left of males.

In Hindu mythology direction matters. We have many examples from mythology in this regard. Most popular one is of *Ardhanārīshwara.* It has been interpreted in Hindu mythology that, left side denotes closeness to heart, or is the direction of dependent whereas the right direction denotes dominant position.[9] Can this concept of dependent or *vāmāngī* and dominant be imposed on prehistoric burial placement is a question in itself, but single graves having female skeleton with left hands placed on their abdomen and double burials having females placed on the left side of male skeleton couldn't be devoid of ritualistic meaning.

Other important interpretations that have been made are demographic and pathological ones. On the basis of fossilization of bones, dissolution of joints of skulls and molars etc. age of skeletons at the time of death has been estimated between 16-35 years. The average age has been determined to be 17-31 years in the case of males and 16-32.5 years in females.[10] Some pathological observations have been made by Kennedy *et. al.*

and Sharma[11] of skeleton in Grave No. X concluding that the person was left hander and engaged in an occupation requiring constant use of both hands, may be wood cutting, cutting of heavy massive animals for flesh etc.

Mahadaha too is a cemetery-cum-habitation site. Twenty-eight graves containing thirty-two skeletons came into light from this site.[12] Mostly, skeletons (twenty-one) had West-East orientation, with heads pointed towards West like the general trend of orientation represented at other Mesolithic sites of Ganga basin and Northern Vindhyas. Five skeletons were placed in East-West and four in SE-NW orientation. This might be due to prevalence of more than single set of beliefs and rituals. The stature of individuals and the causes of their death viz. natural or unnatural also might have some bearing over the practices.

Generally the dead were buried in an extended - supine form with an exception of Grave No. XXIV to be flexed type. Hands were laid alongside the body with three exceptions. In one case, one hand was placed on abdomen and the other along side the body, in another, left arm was placed on chest while the right lying along the body. In one burial, both the hands had been placed on the chest.

The graves were filled with burnt clay lumps and fragments of charred animal bones. Similar material was obtained from the pit-hearth present at the site. Similarity in material indicates that hearth material was used in filling the graves. It is quite possible that some rites were associated with the burial in which hearths and fire had significant role. Grave No. I and Grave No. V yielded double burial in which one of the skeletons belong to male sex and the other to female. These graves attain maximum width at Mahadaha indicating that they were intended to receive two individuals.

It is clear that double burials containing one male and one female skeleton cannot be devoid of meaning. It may be stated that probably the two individuals died simultaneously. Moreover, the choice of single grave for the two indicates that some relationship had existed between the two. As the two double burials show different modes of placement of individuals[13], it may be inferred that the couples in either graves had different kind of relationships between them. The different mode may also be related to the different statuses, different recognitions attached to their relationships by the community or different causes of their death. It may be further inferred on the basis of similar age groups (17-18 years) to which both the sexes of the couples belonged that the couples had some sort of mating relationships. It is obvious to suggest that the couples formed a very basic unit from which the primary family had evolved.

Maximum number of graves have been revealed from the site of Damdama. A total of forty-one graves (forty-nine skeleton) came into light. The graves are shallow in all the cases without any exception. They are oblong on plan with tapering ends. Generally the dead were placed in an extended and supine position with West-East orientation, the head facing towards West.[14]

With single burials, double (four)[15] and multiple (one)[16] burials have also been found. Grave No. VI is of interest; being a double burial both the skeletons in this grave have two different orientation, South-North (female) & North-South (Male) respectively.

The width of the graves and placing of human bones clearly indicates that the graves were prepared for two individuals. It is also interesting that one of the double burials (Grave No. XVI) bears two male skeletons. Grave No. XX has female skeleton placed right of the male skeleton. Only one example (Grave No. XVIII) of multiple burial has been reported from the site. Two male and one female skeletons are buried collectively having West-East orientation. All these graves are in same locality.

Evidences of burials goods too have been reported from Damdama. Burial goods constituted of arrow-heads, animal bones, ornaments etc. In Grave No. VII two arrow heads and one perforated pendant made of bone were obtained. These objects were found near the left tibia. It is not unlikely that the grave in question contained remains of a significant member of the community.[17] A cluster of unused, un-rubbed, bright red coloured hematite pieces have been reported from Grave No. XI placed near the foot of skeleton.[18] It is also noticeable that in most cases a hearth is situated next to a burial indicating some ritualistic purpose.

At Damdama nine cultural phases have been revealed. Remarkably during initial six phases all the skeletons were oriented in West-East direction with just a single exception (Grave No. XVII, E-W). It seems that people who occupied the site initially were very particular about orientation of their dead while burying them. During later phases exceptions to W-E orientation increases and in the last phase i.e., phase no. IX no particular orientation can be said to be dominant one. Out of thirteen graves excavated from phase IX, only five were oriented in W-E direction. Besides, four skeletons had NE-SW orientation, three SE-NW and one E-W orientation.

There may be two factors behind such a change taking place over the phases. Either the people during the later phases lost their belief associated with the selection of orientation or they had evolved a set of more differentiated belief patterns and rites associated with them. In this process they must have chosen differing orientations with respect to varying statuses of their dead and different causes of their death.

References

1. Bhattacharya, D.K.; *An Outline of Indian Prehistory*, Delhi, 1996.
2. Clark, G.; *The Stone Age Hunters*; Thames and Hudson, London; 1967:57.
3. Albrethsen and Brinch Petersen; *Excavation of a Mesolithic Cemetery at Vedback*, Denmark; 1977.
4. Larsson, L.; Late Mesolithic Settlement and Cemeteries of Sķateholm, Southern Sweden, in *'The Mesolithic in Europe'* (Papers presented at the third international symposium, Edinburgh; 1985) C. Bonsall Ed., 1989 : 367-378.
5. Price, Douglas T.; 'The Mesolithic and Hunter Gatherers : myths and meanings' in *Man and Environment*, Deccan College, Poona; 1991:101-107.
6. Ehrhardt, S. and Kemeth A.R. Kennedy; *Excavations at Langhnaj* : 1944-63, Part III, Poona; 1965.
7. See reference no. 3

8. Sharma, G.R., V.D. Mishra, D. Mandal, B.B. Misra and J.N. Pal, *Beginnings of Agriculture,* Allahabad; 1980.
9. In Hindu Mythology direction matters. Few examples in this regard from mythology are :
   (i) The world-rejecting (*Aalaukika*) Shiva raises his left foot when he poses as Naṭrāja while the world-affirming (*Laukika*) Krishna bents his right leg when he plays the flute.
   (ii) The sacred thread (*Yagyopawvīta*) hangs on the left shoulder while offering sacrifices to deties where as it hangs from the right shoulder while offering sacrifices to ancestors.
   (iii) Wives sit to the left of the husband often on the left lap in case of Devīs (*Parvatī*). In indifference to these rules governing direction the female half of the *Ardhnārīshwara* occupies the left side. Even when Vishṇu (or Krishṇa) takes a half-women form his consort Laxmi (or Radha) is on left. Together, or apart, the goddess remain *'Vāmāṅgī'* - the left-sided one.

   Left is side occupied by the heart. It is the side for the one who rules the heart - a man's wife, a mothers' child. With the one who is dear on the left, the right hand is free to wield the sword or hold the scriptures.
10. Pal, J.N., 'Mesolithic Human Burials in the Ganga Plain, North India', in *Man & Environment,* No. XVII (2), 1992 : 35-44.
11. Kennedy, K.A.R., *Recent Developments in Physical Anthropology of Prehistoric Man in India in Indian Prehistory* : 1980; V.D. Misra, J.N. Pal (Eds); Allahabad, 1997 : 196-202.
12. See reference no. 8
13. Two double burials have been revealed from the site of Mahadaha. Grave No. I from phase I yielded a double burial. In this burial female was placed left to the male. Similarly, Grave No. V also yielded a double burial but the remarkable difference is that female was placed above the male.
14. Exceptions to W-E orientation at Damdama:

(i)	Grave XVII,	Phase III	E-W
(ii)	Grave XXVIII	Phase VII	NW-SE
(iii)	Grave XXXII	Phase VIII	SW-WE
(iv)	Grave XXXIX	Phase VIII	WE-SW
(v)	Grave I	Phase VIII	E-W

15. Double burial Graves are four in number -

(i)	Grave No. XVI	(Two male)
(ii)	Grave No. XX	(Male-female)
(iii)	Grave No. XXX	(Male-female)
(iv)	Grave No. XXXVI	(Male-female)

16. Multiple burial grave is Grave No. XVIII. Its and unique example. No other site in Ganga basin has yielded multiple burial.
17. *I.A.R.**, 1983-84 : 90-91.
18. *I.A.R.*, 1986-87 : 83-84.

---

* Indian Archaeological Review, Bulletin of Archaeological Survey of India, New Delhi.

11

Buddhist Architecture in Eastern Uttar Pradesh

Amar Singh

The history of Buddhist architecture starts from the life time of Buddha himself during the sixth century BCE. According to tradition, once Buddha, while he was staying at Rājgir, accepted the offer of sixty *Vihāras* in Rājagṛiha provided by a local merchant for the use of Saṅgha community.[1] When king Bimbisāra visited Buddha at Gṛidhakūṭa Mountain he gifted the Veluvana (Veṇuvana) to Buddha in order to felicitate his devotees to visit him. Bimbisāra also built a royal residence here for the Buddha where he stayed for some time.[2] The other *vihāras* built at Rājgriha during the life time of Buddha were Jīvakāmravana and Maddhakuchchhi-migadāya.[3] At Śrāvastī, a rich merchant Anāthapiṇḍika built a *vihāra* for Buddha and his Saṅgha, which was popularly known as Jetavana vihāra.[4] The other important monasteries which came into existence during the life time of Buddha were, the Pūrvārāma Vihāra erected by Viśākhā and Rājakārāma in the neighbourhood of Śrāvastī,[5] the Ghoṣhitārāma and Kukkuṭārāma at Kauśāmbī,[6] the Kālakārāma donated by the banker Kālaka at Sāketa,[7] and Kūṭāgāraśālā Vihāra was built by the Lichchhavīs for Shākyamuni at Vaiśālī.[8] King Śuddhodana also gave a palace situated on the north of the Kapilavastu to build a monastery for the Saṅgha.[9]

At Rājgṛiha, District Nalanda in Bihar, no traces of archaeological remains of sixty *viharas* donated by a local merchant are found. The site of the Veṇuvana Vihāra and its *Prāsāda* (royal residence) provided by Bimbisara to Buddha and his Saṅgha is identified located between the New Rajagriha and the Satdhara at the foot of the Vaibhara hill but nothing of architectural importance was found during excavation of the mound by

Archaeological Survey of India in 1905-06, except the foundation of a room and the bases of nine brick *stūpas* surrounded by concrete floor.[10] The foundation of the room might have been the remains of that *prāsāda* which was provided by Bimbisāra to Buddha and *Stūpas* might have been built on the relics of the monks who resided here in the Vihāra made of some perishable material. According to Pāli texts the site of the mango garden of Jīvaka was situated somewhere between the eastern gate and the Gṛidhrakūṭa on the foot of the Chhaṭha-giri and the Mardakukṣhi monastery was situated close to the foot of the Gṛidhrakūṭa.[11] Jīvaka was a royal physician of Bimbisāra and Ajātaśatru and a great devotee of Lord Buddha. He presented his mango groove to Buddha and constructed a monastery consisting of night quarters and day quarters, cells, huts, pavilions and a Mūlagandha-kuṭī for the Lord Buddha and surrounded the mango groove with a copper coloured wall eighteen cubits high.[12] The site, identified as Jīvakāmravana Vihāra, was excavated by the Archaeological Survey of India (mid-eastern circle) from 1953-54 to 1958-59 and four oblong structures with large elliptical walls and subsidiary rooms were revealed.[13] Two elliptical halls were parallel to each other, one larger elliptical hall, 228 ft x 38 ft, with walls, 3 ft 6 inches wide, built of rubble in mud mortar on the northern side and other comparatively smaller elliptical structure on the western side, attached with subsidiary rooms, surrounded by a compound-wall were excavated.[14] Three of the halls have openings, most probably for the gateways in the larger sides as in some of the caves (Karṇa Chopar and Sudāmā) at Barābara Hill. At present all the building structures are reduced to the foundation. It appears that the elliptical halls were probably meant for communal living.

The Buddhist monasteries which are exposed during the excavations at Sarnath are seven in number which are situated in three different places. First row of Monasteries known as II, III and IV, made of Kuṣhāṇa and Gupta bricks are covered under the extensive area of the Dharmachakra-Jina-vihāra, Monastery I which was a gift of Kumārdevī, the Buddhist queen of Govindachandra Gāhaḍavāla, King of Kannauja (1114-1154). Monastery VI is located on the west of the Dhamekh *stūpa*, belongs to eight or ninth century and was built over an earlier structure of Gupta period. Other monasteries V and VII are situated side by side on the south of the Dharmarājikā *stūpa*. Monastery V was built during the Gupta period and Monastery VII is a smaller structure of medieval period raised on the old ruins of early date.[15]

Except Kumāradevī Vihāra almost all the monasteries of Kuṣhāṇa and Gupta Periods are similar on plan with living-cells flanking the centre courtyard, entered by a doorway in front of which was an entrance-chamber (*pratyupasthānaśālā*). The open courtyard was surrounded by a running *verandah* supported on pillars. Each monastery was also attached with a refectory, kitchen, store-room, guard-room and well etc. To take out water from the courtyard, covered drains were provided under the *verandah* (observation is mainly based on the description of monastery V, fig.1).[16]

According to V. S. Agrawala the Kumāradevī Vihāra has an open paved courtyard on west with row of cells on the other three sides and two gateways facing east. The basement of the monastery is built of carved and moulded bricks decorated on both the faces.[17]

The Buddha also visited Kauśāmbī, the capital city of Vatsa Janapada and delivered several discourses and spent his ninth rainy season here.[18] At that time, three great monasteries namely Ghoṣiṭārāma, Kukkutarama and Pāvārika Ambavana were built here.[19] Of these only remains of Ghoṣitārāma Monastery were found during the excavation conducted by the University of Allahabad from 1951 to 1956.[20] The monastery was identified by the finding of an inscription of first century CE on the site in the year 1951, which states that a monk named Phagol donated a stone slab to be used for the worship of all the Buddhas by the monks residing in the Ghoṣitārāma monastery, the abode of the Buddha.[21] An inscription of the famous nun Budhamitrā of the 3rd year of Kaniṣhka's reign provides information that she has donated three statues of the Bodhisattva to this monastery.[22] Generally, the Buddhist remains of almost all the important monasteries are found slightly away from the towns and cities as it is said in the Vinaya that the Lord's stay would be neither too far from a village (or town) nor too near,[23] but remarkably, the Ghoṣitārāma monastery is situated right against inside of the defense wall, just near the eastern gate.[24] The finding of the Northern Black Polished Ware from the site indicated that its initial construction started in c. sixth century BCE. Other available evidence shows that it was continuously occupied up to sixth century CE through sixteen successive phases of structural activity and it had been extensively re-built many times (thrice) using bricks.[25] The monastery facing north-west consisted of a square courtyard surrounded by cells of monks, of which 29 are still traceable, with a *verandah* on inner side enclosing the main *Stūpa* and several other subsidiary *stūpas* and the whole establishment enclosed by a boundary wall.[26] According to excavator, the Main *Stūpa* was initially built in fifth century BCE[27] but it is remarkable that Huien Tsang saw a 51 m high *stūpa* credited to Ashoka in the Ghoṣitārāma. When Fa-hien visited Kaushāmbī (early 5th century), he found monks residing in the Ghoṣitārāma but by the time of Huien Tsang (seventh century) it had become a deserted ruin.[28]

The ruins of Śrāvstī are scatterd in and around modern Saheth-Maheth, overing an extensive area of about 5 Km. Saheth sector is mainly religious with remains of Buddhist shrines, *stūpas* and monasteries including famous Jetavana-Vihāra and Maheta sector is fortified residential city area with remains of Buddhist, Jain and Brahmanical monuments. The beautiful Jetavana Vihāra was presented to the Buddha by Anāthapiṇḍika, a rich merchant. It was a big area purchased from prince Jeta for as many gold coins as would cover the whole ground. There he created Gandha-Kuṭī vihāra for Buddha in the centre and around it, according to set plan, constructed residence for eighty great disciples and the whole compound was gifted to the Saṅgha. The Buddha liked this place so much that he stayed here for 24 rainy seasons.[29] The remains of Jetavana Vihāra are lying near the main road leading to Balarampur-Baharaich. The ruins covering roughly an area about 500 x 150 m consist mainly of plinth and foundations of monasteries, *stūpas* and temples.[30] There are remains of 4 monasteries, 8 temples and 14 *stūpas* found in the excavation at the site.[31] The ruins so far brought to light belong to from Mauryan period to 12th century CE.[32] The Buddha resided in the Gandha-kuṭī. At present the remains of a Gupta structure consisting of a rectangular terrace with stairs facing east, a pavilion and a small shrine is identified with Gandh-kuṭī which most probably was originally a wooden structure in the beginning.[33] Another important residence of the Buddha at Jetavana, the Kosambakutī, was also probably a small wooden hut. At present there is a small brick structure measuring 5.75 x 5.45 m. An inscribed image of Buddha belonging to Kushāṇa period was found here which was set up by Bhikkhu Bala. Hiuen Tsang in the seventh century saw this image within a small brick temple.[34] A relief from the Bharhut Stūpa, depicting the purchase of Jetavana, shows both the Kosamba-kutī and the Gandha- kutī from where we can have an idea of their structures which appear as wooden huts.[35] The architectural composition of all the four monasteries found in the Jetavana Vihāra compound is almost similar to each other. One of them, monastery no.19 is the largest building containing a temple just on the front of the gate-way, a well in the courtyard, twenty-four cells for the use of monks and a portico. The monastery appears to have been re- built three times on the same foundations, first built in the Gupta period, then in the early medieval period and in the last during Gāhaḍawāla period.[36]

Kūṭāgāraśālā Vihāra was built by the Lichchhavis at Vaishālī for the Śākyamuni. The site is situated 3 km. away from the main town. The excavation has revealed the extensive remains of a monastery with an open courtyard, a *verandah* and cells.[37]

According to Buddhist tradition, king Suddhodana of Kapilavastu gave the Saṅgha the summer palace of Prince Siddhārtha, situated in the north of the capital city, to build a monastery. Sāriputra, one of the main disciples of Buddha, organized a large number of monks to set up monastic living there.[38] The remains of Kapilavastu monastery and Stūpa are found at Piprahwa and Ganwaria in the Siddharthnagar district of U.P. The site of monastery was excavated by K. M. Srivastava of A.S.I. The seals found in one of the monastery at Piprahwa bear an inscription which mentions, *"Om devaputra vihāre Kapilavastu bhikhu saṅghasa"* indicating that the Kuṣhāṇa king Kaniṣhka, entitled as Devaputra (1st Cent. A. D.), built a Vihāra at Piprahwa.[39] In all 4 monasteries were excavated here and 3 monasteries at Ganwaria, a village situated near the main site, each consisting a courtyard, *verandah* and cells for the monks as usual.[40]

The archaeological remains revealed by the excavations of above mentioned sites are not earlier than the Mauryan and the Śuṅga - Kuṣhāṇa periods. It appears that, in the beginning, monasteries were made up of some perishable materials like woods, bamboo, mud and mud bricks, which vanished in due course of time and some of them have been renovated to such an extent with new material, that, they have lost their identity and originality and now it is not possible to identify their real shape and form. As no architectural remains of early monasteries are found during excavations, we can have an idea of architecture of early Buddhist monasteries from the unearthed examples raised in the later periods. These brick–built monasteries were usually quadrilateral on plan with living-rooms flanking the centre courtyard, entered by a doorway in front of which was *verandah* or porch. The open courtyard had sometimes a central *maṇḍapa* resting on pillars around it and a running *verandah* with pillars resting on a raised plinth on all the four sides. The central courtyard was surrounded on two or three sides by square cells, each serving as the abode of a monk. One of the cells, after facing the doorway in front, was the shrine containing a *stūpa*, in earlier monastery and an image of Buddha in later monastery of Mahāyāna period for worshiping. Beside the assembly hall, each monastery was attached with a refectory, kitchen, storeroom, washing place etc. To take out water from the courtyard, covered drains were provided under the *verandah*. Thus, the excavated remains at Rājgṛiha, Sāranātha, Śrāvastī, Kapilvastu and Kauśāmbī provide us sufficient material to reconstruct the architecture of early Buddhist monasteries in the eastern Uttar Pradesh.

The earliest form of Buddhist shrines or temples in eastern Uttar Predesh are noticed at Sarnath. An open platform sometimes surrounded with a railing on which an object of worship, such as, a *stūpa*, was placed. The type is represented by a *stūpa*-sanctuary or circular *chaitya-gṛiha*, which was exposed in 1914-15 by H. Hargreaves in the north of the Main shrine.[41] The structure first came into existence during the Mauryan period in the form of a square platform which evidently formed the base of a brick-built ring shaped miniature *stūpa* in the centre. Perhaps a stone railing was also raised around the *stūpa* in the Śuṅga period as indicated by the inner circle above the square platform and the coping-stone depicting a scene of *stūpa*-worship and solitary cross-bar discovered from this area. Stylistically, the coping stone and the cross-bar may be assigned to the second century BCE. Later on, during the Kuṣhāṇa period a small portico facing south and a brick-built circumambulatory wall was added, which is represented by the foundations of the outer circle. After the *chaitya-gṛiha* had collapsed in the Gupta period, it was re-built with the same material in the shape of a square temple attached with a small porch facing east. The size of the bricks, a damaged image of the Buddha in Gupta style, terracotta sealing datable to sixth century CE, recovered from the excavated site, would suggest the date of the temple in the late Gupta period.[42]

Another example of an apsidal structure which was most probably a *chaitya*-hall was excavated on the west of the main shrine near Aśokan pillar. The brick-built structure was 25 m in length and 11.58 m in width with a semi-circular shape at the back. The antiquities found at the site are dated ranging from the Mauryan to Gupta period. However, the date of this apsidal *chaitya* hall may be assigned to the Kuṣhāṇa period.[43]

A terraced temple of Eduka-type (mentioned in the *Viṣhṇudharmottara-Purāṇa*)[44] or *trimedhi*-type Buddhist shrine was revealed by the archaeological excavations at Sarnath. It was a lofty brick structure of Gupta period surmounted by an octagonal tower locally known as the Chaukhaṇḍi. Originally, the monument was built in three terraces above a rectangular ground terrace. The facades of the terraces were decorated with *tulāpīṭha*, pilasters and niches. An image of Buddha in *Dharmachakrapravartana*-pose assignable to the fifth century CE was found from the site which was probably kept on the top of the

Buddhist shrine. The site has also yielded images of Bodhisattva Maitreya, Padmapāṇi and Vyālas in the classical Gupta style of late 5th century. The other surviving remains of the terraced brick temples of the Gupta period are located at Ahichhatra and Pawaya near Gwalior which suggest that the *garbhagṛiha* of these shrines was placed on the top.[45]

A brick built small structure of only a square *jagatī* with projections on the corners represents an example of *Pañchāyatana* type. It is located between Dharmarājikā and Dhamekh *stūpas* on the southern side of the court-yard of the Main Shrine. The *jagatī* is decorated with *patravallī, padma, grāsmukhas,* ornamental lattices, pilasters and mouldings showing characteristic features of Gupta period.[46] The purpose of the shrine and its mode of worship are not known as there is no any cult object or symbol present at the site. The *jagatī* or *adhiṣṭhāna* is not approachable from any side as stairs are not attached to it. It appears that five votive *stūpas,* four on the corner projections and one in the centre of the *jagatī* might have been installed. The remains of *Pañchāyatana* type temples at Deogarh and Nalanda give the idea that the *Pañchāyatana-pūjā* was in vogue during the Gupta period. As mentioned in the *Purāṇas,* there wre two main traditions of *Pañchāyatana* -worship: (i) five gods representing their cults, giving central place to any one favourite deity, were worshipped and (ii) the cult deity was installed in the centre and the four subsidiary shrines were represented by various aspects of the same god.[47]

On the north of Dharmarājikā *stūpa,* the Main Shrine or the Mūlagandhakutī, resembling a *sarvatobhadra* temple, was originally a Mauryan structure attributed to Ashoka. It was rebuilt in the Gupta and post Gupta periods. Its present remains appear to be of late seventh and early eighth centuries, made of bricks by re-using stone door frames and architectural pieces of the fifth and sixth centuries. It is square on plan 18.29 m. on each side with prominent *bhadra* projections on three sides each containing a small shrine with doorway and a stepped entrance on the east attached with a closed rectangular court and an open courtyard in the front. The *Vedībandha* of the temple is ornamented with tall *kumbha, tulāpītha, kapota-pali* and *kalaśa* mouldings. The *jaṅghā* is decorated with pilasters topped by *chandrasālās* and *chaitya*-window motifs. The massive walls of the building suggest that its superstructure was very lofty. According to Hiuen Tsang, it was 61 m high.[48]

Numerous stone architectural fragments including doorframes, *āmalakas, bhūmiāmalākas, karṇa-kūṭas,* pieces of *madhya-latā* of *nāgara śikhara,* pillars and pilasters and various other parts of the seventh-eighth centuries temples are found scattered in and around Sarnath and Varanasi. Some of these are preserved in the Sarnath Museum and Bhārata Kalā Bhawana (B.H.U.). The available fragments of the doorways from Sarnath and Varanasi belonging to the Gupta and the post Gupta periods have T- shaped format of lintel, basically the copy of wooden version in the stone. The doorframe shows generally three *śākhās* composed of *patravallī* or *padmapatra-śākhā, srīvṛkṣ-śākhā, rūpa-śākhā* carved with standing male and female figures, pot bellied *yakṣas* and *gaṇas* in different poses and *maṇibandha-sākhā* with diamonds alternating with rosettes. Lower portion of the doorjambs bear a male figure (*pratihārī* or *dvārapālas*) standing with a staff or flower in his hand on both sides and the river goddesses Gaṅgā and Yamunā standing on their mounts also appear at the base. A doorjamb from Sarnath has three panels, the central carved with a *kīrttimukha* and shows *maṇibandha* and *patra-śākhās*.[49] Another doorjamb from Varanasi in the Bhārata Kalā Bhavan has four *śākhās* decorated with *patravallī, maṇibandha, stambha-śākhā* with *ghaṭapallava* base and *srīvṛikṣa-śākhā* with a *pratihāra* figure at the base.[50] The fragments of pillars collected from various sites mostly show their typical characteristics of the Gupta period. These pillars are mainly two types, one is *vṛittākāra* (circular) with *ghaṭa* base ornamented with *kīrttimukhas* on the shafts at different intervals and an inverted *ghaṭa* on the top while the other is four sided (*chaturāsra*) below, eight sided (*aṣṭāsra*) in the middle and sixteen sided (*soḍasāsra*) above toped by *ghaṭa-pallava* capital. Both the types are present at Sarnath and the second type is also reported from Rajghat, Varanasi.

The *stūpa,* literally a mound, was a funeral monument made of mud, bricks or stones over the body of relics of a celebrated personality, usually a king or a saint and in the Buddhist context, it symbolized the *mahāparinirvāṇa* (the death) of the Buddha. When Buddha died at Kusinagar, his relics were divided among eight ruling families and in all ten stupas were raised at Rajgṛiha, Vaishālī, Kapilavastu, Rāmagrāma, Pāvā, Kusinārā and some other places to commemorate Buddha.

The earliest archaeological remains of a Buddhist *stūpa* is found at Piprahwa identified as Kapilavastu in Siddharth Nagar District. It contained an inscribed stone casket with relics of the Buddha. The *stūpa* survived to a height of 6.71 m with a diameter at the ground level of 2.074 m and according to excavator appears to have been enlarged thrice. The first and the earliest *stūpa* was made of baked bricks and consisted of a simple dome with chambers on the top and ground level containing relic-caskets. As the inscriptional evidence shows and *Mahāparinirvāṇa Sutta* testifies, the Shākyas of Kapilavastu had raised a *stūpa* over their share of relics immediately after the *nirvāṇa* and cremation of the Buddha, the date of this first phase *stūpa* may be assigned to 5th century BCE. [51]

By the time of Aśoka, the original commemorative character of *stūpa* graduallly developed as a dedicatory and votive and Buddhist started worshipping them. According to Buddhist tradition, he opened up seven out of eight original *stūpas* containing relics of the Buddha, divided them into several parts and raised numerous *stūpas* at all important places. It appears that when Aśoka visited Sarnath some of the holy spots related to main events of Buddha's life were identified and *stūpas* were set up to commemorate these events.

A *stūpa* called as Dharmarājikā was built by Aśoka to represent one leading event. It was about 30.4 m high and originally crowned at its top by a monolithic polished railing made of Chunar sand stone. The *stūpa* was brick-built and had a diameter of about 14 m, which underwent six enlargements, the first in the Kuṣhāṇa period, the second during the 5th or 6th century CE with addition of circumambulatory (*pradakṣhiṇāpatha*) around the *stūpa* comprising a stone wall attached with four gates, one on each direction, the third in the seventh century when *pradakṣhiṇāpatha* was filled up and access to the *stūpa* was provided by placing four monolithic staircases; the fourth and fifth enlargements were made in the ninth-eleventh centuries and the latest in the twelfth century when the monastery of Kumārdevī was built. The famous colossal red sand stone Bodhisattva image installed in the third year of Kanishka and the image of the Buddha seated in *dharmachakrapravartana-mudrā* was found at this site.[52]

Dhamekha *stūpa* with probably Mauryan nucleus is considered one of the most sacred places at Sarnath. The solid cylindrical brick structure 28.50 m in diameter at the base and about 42 m in height consists of a circular drum to a height of 11.2 m. resting on the ground without the usual basement or *jagatī*. It has stone casing and shows eight faces, each having a *rathikā* or niche for an image of the Buddha. Below the niches is a band of carving depicting scrolls of lotus leaves and buds, geometrical and floral patterns that are stylistically assignable to the late sixth century.[53]

Thus, from the above observations, it appears that architectural activities in eastern Uttar Pradesh started right from the life time of the Buddha but we do not find any archaeological evidence before Mauryan period. When Aśoka visited Sarnath, some *stūpas* like Dharı .arājikā and Dhamekha were built using Mauryan bricks. A polished stone railing was also provided on the top of a *stūpa* and a stone pillar with lion capital was erected in front of a *stūpa*. The architecture of the monasteries was almost unchanged from early to medieval periods. Many brick shrines and votive *stūpas* were also raised from Mauryan to medieval periods. These were built in various forms such as circular, apsidal, square and rectangular on plan where as *panchāyatana*, terraced and *sarvatobhadra* type buildings are also remarkable. We cannot have a firm idea about their superstructure as most of them are ruined. During the Gupta period we find more elaborate development of *jagatī*, *vedibandha*, *jaṅghā*, doorframe and pillar etc. The *jagatī* was an optional member. The *vedibandha* was comprised of a tall *kumbha*, *kalaśa*, plain *antarapaṭṭa* and *kapota* mouldings. Stone doorframes were ornamented with *tri-śākhās* generally using *patra*, *maṇibandha*, *stambha* and *rūpa-śākhās*. In some buildings carved and moulded bricks were used and stone made doorjambs, pillars, architraves and ceilings were also applied to provide strength.

References

1. *Chullavagga*, 239, 19 (ed. Bhikkhu Jagadisha Kassapa, Nava-Nalanda Mahavihara, 1956).
2. Singh, R. P. B., 2003. *Where the Buddha Walked*. Varanasi. p. 196.
3. Ghosh, A., 1987. *Rajgir*. New Delhi. pp. 30-31.
4. Venkataramayya, M. 1981. *Śrāvastī*. New Delhi. p. 12-23.

5. Cunnningham, A., 1854. *Budhist Monuments of Central India.* London. pp. 309-350, Mitra, D., 1950. *Buddhist Monuments.* Calcutta, p.32, Venkataramayya, M., 1981. *Śrāvastī.* A. S. I., New Delhi, p. 4.
6. *Ibid.*
7. *Ibid.*
8. *Ibid.*
9. *Ibid.* Singh, R.P.B., op. cit., pp. 65-72.
10. Ghosh, A., 1987. *Rajgir.* A. S. I., New Delhi. pp. 12-14; *Annual Report* (1905-06) Archaeological Survey of India , p. 94.
11. *Ibid.*
12. Singh, R.P.B., *op. cit.*, p. 201.
13. *Indian Archaeology – A Review* (1953-54, p. 9; 1954-55, p. 16; 1957-58, p. 16; 1958-59, p. 13).
14. *Ibid.*
15. Agrawala, V. S.; *Sarnath,* Archaeological Survey of India, New Delhi, 1984, pp. 14-25.
16. *Ibid.*, p. 16.
17. *Ibid.*, pp. 21-22.
18. Bapat, P.V. 1956. *2500 Years of Buddhism.* New Delhi. (Reprint 1987), p. 190.
19. Singh, R.P.B., *op. cit.*, p. 176.
20. *Indian Archaeology – A Review* (1953-54, p. 9; 1955-56, p. 20).
21. Singh, R.P.B., *op. cit.*, p. 179.
22. *Indian Archaeology – A Review* (1953-54, p. 9).
23. *Ibid.* (1953-54, p. 9; 1955-56, p. 20).
24. Singh, R.P.B., *op. cit.*, p. 179.
25. *Indian Archaeology – A Review* (1953-54,p.9; 1955-56, p. 20).
26. Singh, R.P.B., *op. cit.*, pp. 179-181.
27. *Indian Archaeology – A Review* (1953-54,p.9; 1955-56, p. 20).
28. Singh, R.P.B., *op. cit.*, pp. 179-181; Indian Archaeology – A Review (1955-56, p. 20).
29. Law, B.C., 1854. *Śrāvasti in Indian Literature.* London. p. 24.
30. Venkataramayya, M., *op. cit.*, p. 2.
31. *Ibid.* pp. 12-24.
32. *Ibid.*
33. *Ibid.*, p 19; Singh, R.P.B., *op. cit.*, pp. 171-172.
34. *Ibid.*
35. Cunningham, A., 1962. *The Stūpa of Bharhut.* Varanasi. pp. 85-86.
36. Venkataramayya, M., *op. cit.*, pp. 13-15.
37. Singh, R.P.B., *op. cit.*, p. 227.
38. *Ibid.* p. 64.
39. *Ibid.* pp. 65-72.
40. *Ibid.*
41. Hargreaves, H., 'Excavations at Sarnath', Archaeological Survey of India, Annual Report 1914-15, Calcutta, 1920, p 106-108.
42. Kumar, Krishna, 'A circular Caitya-Gṛha at Sarnath', Journal of the Indian Society of Oriental Art (New Series), vol. XI (1980-81), pp. 63-70.
43. Agrawala, V. S., *op.cit.*, p. 20.

44. *Vishnudharmottara-Purāṇa,* III, 84, 1-15 (ed. By Priyabala Shah, Oriental Institute, Baroda, 1958).
45. Deva, Krishna, *Encyclopeadia of Temple Architecture,* vol. II, Part I, Delhi, 1988, pp 24-26.
46. *Ibid.*, p. 54.
47. Singh, Amar, 'Tradition of Panchāyatana Pūjā', *Purāvṛitta,* Journal of the Department of A. I. History & Archaeology, No. 1, Lucknow University, 2000-2001, p. 110.
48. Deva, Krishna, *op.cit.*, pp. 121-122; Agrawala, V. S., op.cit., p. 18.
49. Deva, Krishna, *op.cit.*, p. 122.
50. *Ibid.*
51. Srivastava, K.M., *Discovery of Kapilavastu,* New Delhi, 1986.
52. Agrawala, V. S., *op.cit.*, p. 17-18.
53. *Ibid,* pp. 23-24.

12

In Defence of Kauśāmbī School of Art

Anamika Roy

Before analyzing the influence of Kauśāmbī school, it is necessary to consider the spread of 'Kauśāmbī style' and its antiquity. The question that has been haunting the intellect of the scholars was there really an influence that came from Mathura? Or Mathurā being a cosmopolitan centre overshadowed other centers. The art historians have often questioned whether there was a Kauśāmbī school of art? They are not very vocal and rather hesitant in accepting Kauśāmbī as a school. There are several humble voices, though not as vibrant as Mathurā, that Kauśāmbī flourished as an independent centre from the Gupta period. It is undeniable that Kauśāmbī was a centre of independent images from the Gupta period onwards. What happened before that? An art tradition does not grow in isolation. There are other forces /factors that contribute for its growth. Kauśāmbī had been a flourishing trade centre and a Mecca for Buddhist monks and nuns.

The allegation that Kauśāmbī employed the second class craftsmen is not justified. It is true that there was no royal road to Kauśāmbī art and it did not enjoy the open royal patronage. After Kaniṣka I Kauśāmbī came under the rule of a local dynasty, Maghas. One must remember that art tradition does not follow the dynastic rule, but when the royalty encourages the art tradition, it changes the course of its development.

How and when Kauśāmbī developed its own style, is again a debatable question. Usually, it is asserted that it was only with the advent of the Guptas that Kauśāmbī developed its own style. The power was transferred from the Kuṣāṇas to the Maghas in the 2nd century CE. Could it bring out any change? It was a period of several important changes in the field of art and palaeogarphy. In the famous Śiva-Pārvatī image, standing Śiva was carved during the period of Bhadramagha. The Buddha image (pl.2) that aroused an interesting art historical debate also mention the name of Bhadramagha. Did this local dynasty encouraged such activity the direct evidence of which are still awaited.

There are several sacred and secular images which worked as a model and Kauśāmbī took a lead in carving these sculptures for the first time. Kauśāmbī has been stamped as a centre of Buddhism. The image of the Buddha (pl.11) may have been a matter of debate whether it was carved under the impact of any style or it betrays a fancy towards archaism.

The *Mahāvaṁśa* (480.34) narrates that five hundred Buddhists monks from Kauśāmbī went to Sri Lanka. It may apppear far fetched, but some of them must have taken art tradition with them.

Digressing from the Buddha images for a while, there are Buddhist artifacts where Kauśāmbī paved the way. The *Āyāgapaṭṭa* (pl.1) from Kauśāmbī, which is termed in the inscriptions as '*pūjāye śilā*' is significant. Dedication of such a slab was prevalent among the Jainas. Following their tradition, this slab is also known as Buddhist *Āyāgapaṭṭa.*

Another interesting fact is that this inscription says that the Buddha used to reside here in the *Ghoṣhitārāma* monastery, which automatically connects it with the Buddhist activity - the art not lagging behind.

Kauśāmbī gets the credit of carving the nativity scene for the first time in the Northern India. Mathurā may boast of carving abundance of *śālbhañjikā* and Aśoka *dohada.* Sanchi and Bharhut may have chiselled the dream scene of Māyā, but a detailed scene is for the first time carved at Kauśāmbī (Pl.16) in the 2nd century BCE. This portrayal becomes popular and more extensive in the art of Amarāvatī and Gandhāra. In the panel under discussion, Māyā is depicted standing under a Śāla tree in a *tribhaṅga* (cross-legged) posture holding the branch of the tree. Three male deities (the first two are identified with Indra and Brahmā) are receiving the infant Siddhārtha, whose presence is depicted through foot prints and there are two female slaves at the left side.

The other panel is of a charming lady on a pillar, decorated with a broad girdle which is partially covering her diaphanous body. She is holding the branch of a tree. These scenes are very popular. The inscription on it says, '*pusasa thabho*'. The palaeography is of the 2nd century BCE. Obviously, Kauśāmbī has its own tradition of carving '*stambha yoshita*' and nativity scenes.

Here the question is not whether Kauśāmbī looked for inspiration or Kauśāmbī provided an inspiration. The fact is Kauśāmbī had its own independent tradition and credit may go to strong hold of Buddhism and artists- native and foreigner.

There are two important inscriptions, which establish that there were donors and scribes of scythian origin. There was a Liyaka, who has been considered same as Nayasa and Layaka of Mathurā and Ahicchatra inscriptions and the other one was Phāgul of *Āyāgapaṭṭa* inscription (Negi, 1966,46). The double humped bull (pl.7) from Bactria signify the fact that the artists from this region were residing at Kauśāmbī and were keen to leave their thumb prints.

There are lions (pl.8) in different postures from Manhai (a place 4 Km. away from Kauśāmbī). The lions postulating from the podium of the image of the Buddha (pl.11) show a Persian influence. In fact, the term *'siṁhāsana'* is based upon *'sarvamanishyakuleega'*. Dharayavatsu is depicted hunting the animal, counting the teeth of lion and crushing two lions in two chambers. (Tripathi, H.S. 2005,5)

Obviously, the artists of Persian origin were living here and they helped in building the unique style of Kauśāmbī and were bound to leave the stamp of their native land.

Kauśāmbī has been recognized as a centre of 'Bhāgavata religion.' The oldest recognized reference to Bhāgavata religion is found in the Besanagar pillar inscription from Vidishā. Mathurā may have been the cradle land of Vāsudeva Kṛiṣṇa, never the less, the symbolic presence of Bhāgavatism has been traced at Kauśāmbī. Makardhvaja and Tāladhvaja (Pls. 9&10) have been taken as the presence of Saṅkarṣhaṇa and Prdyumna (Misra, R.N. 1978, 312). On another pillar, Pradyumna (pls. 12& 13) with arrows and his wife has been recognized. (Misra, R.N. 1978, 302). Mathurā mentions the religion of Pañcavīra, but from Kauśāmbī such an evidence is still missing. But, there are other significant evidence that testify that Kauśāmbī has its own tradition of Vaiṣṇava images. We may begin with the instance of Sheshshāyī Viṣhṇu from Shivapur Hathigaha (Allahabad, National Highway Phaphamau). It is five ft.tall and two and a half feet wide, four armed Viṣhṇu image resting on Sheshnāga. In this image of Shivapur (Shukla, V.C., 1997, 19), the Āyudha Puruṣha is not in a gesture of bravery, but in a perplexing mood. The couple depicted is also interesting as they are also depicted in a perplexing gesture and arguing. This depiction is unique in several ways. Usually, Āyudha Puruṣhas are shown in an aggressive and attacking posture. This posture appears before the killing of Madhu Kaiṭabha, when Viṣṇu was still in his *yoganidrā* and the *devas* were praying to awaken him from his sleep (Shukla, V.C.1997, 19-20). In this way, this image is different from Deogarh and Bhitaragaon, and this is the distinct feature of Kauśāmbī. At Bhitaragaon, Deogarha and Udaigiri the scene is more elaborate.

There is also a spiritual indication of this form. Sheṣha is the Universe. Suvira Jaiswal has pointed out about the influence and assimilation of Nāga cult in Vaiṣhṇavism. (1967, 52). We will see further that Kauśāmbī had been a centre of Nāga cult also.

Scholars have so far paid attention to Śiva Pārvatī image of the period of Bhadramagha (year 139). Usually accepted date for the reckoning of the Maghas is the Śaka Era i.e. 78 year of the Current Era (CE). Thus this image should be of 78+139= 217 year of the Current Era. There is yet another image in the Los Angeles city Museum. It shows standing Śiva. The head dress of Pārvatī is known for its archaism, which is a distinct attribute of Kauśāmbī school. These images are much discussed and are considered not only the specimens of Kauśāmbī school but also the evidence of Śaivism. But Kauśāmbī had a much earlier tradition. The region has the credit of constructing the

Ekamukhaliṅga Śivaliṅga. It is found from Allahabad. It is three ft. above the ground and has a thickness of about seventy five cm. It shows both eyes half closed and *Jaṭā* in hair style. Reh, a place not far from Allahabad reports a Śiva liṅga (? Jaya Stambha) of the period of Menander. Bhita has reported one *śivaliṅga* (Marshall, Excavations at Bhita, Annual Report Archaeological Survey of India, 1911-12, p. 39-44) The most important is *śivaliṅga* in Allahabad Museum from Kauśāmbī. Chandra has dated it around the 2nd century BCE. (1971, .63). Thus the scholars are seeking in vain the uniqueness of Kauśāmbī in Śiva Pārvatī image. Kauśāmbī initiated the carving of *śivaliṅgas* also.

Whenever the question of an independent school of Kauśāmbī has been raised, the scholars have quoted the Yaksa cult and emphasised that it has an earlier tradition than Mathurā (Misra, R.N. 1978). Not only the Yakṣa cult, it has a fascinating tradition of Nāga cult also. A five hooded Nāga image of the 2nd century CE is installed in Allahabad Museum. It was a period when the Nāga images in human forms were being carved. Two such Nāga images have been found from Kauśāmbī. They may not throw much light on Nāga cult, but they do delineate the significance of carving the Nāga image. Both the images (Pls. 3 & 4) are in the G.R. Sharma Memorial Museum. The Nāga is five hooded, holding pine-apple in its right hand and creeper in left. There is a *dharmacakra* at the top. The other image is also five hooded, holding pine-apple in right and flower with stem in the left hand. The Nāgas holding the fruit is a distinct feature of Kauśāmbī as it is not prescribed in any of the text (Shukla, V.C. 1997). There is no doubt that in the later period, the place was associated with the Nāgas. But there is a very early epigraphic reference to it also. It shows the association of the region with the Nāgas at a very early stage.

The reference occurs (Roy, S.N. 1988, 79-83) in a short inscription at Ajagara village of Pratapgarh district, Uttar Pradesh of the 2nd century BCE.

The inscription is significant as it shows how myth and cult of the Nāgas were popular here. The epigraph says:"*This tank called Nahuṣha, the presiding deity of which is Kubera Yakṣa, and capable of removing curse and illusion and is the gateway of religious merit, was dug on the occasion of Yakṣa-fair in the honour of Yakṣinī Sudarśanā.*

References of *Nahuṣha* and *Saptamatṛkas* are important here. It is possible that the tank itself was called *Nahuṣha ḥrada.* Here the epigraphic line probably contains an echo of the well known Paurāṇic story as how King *Nahuṣha* was turned into a snake owing to curse of sage Agastya. It further says that king *Nahuṣha* could discard the curse at the edge of a tank.

The three Kauśāmbī inscribed Buddha images (Pl. 2), which mention year 83 of Bhadramagha are quite interesting. As the reckoning is considered to be in the Śaka Era, the dates for these inscriptions stand to be 83+78=161 CE. The Brāhmī employed in thsese inscriptions is also significant. The forms of *ma, sa* , *sha* and *ha* may be regarded as the precursors of the Gupta Brāhmī. For the script of this period Dani (1986, 90) says that a regional style developed from this period and it should be treated as 'Kashambi Style" of writing. Coming to the style of the sculptures, we are struck by the contrast.

Plate 1 : Āyāgapaṭṭa

Plate 2 : Headless Buddha Image of the period of Bhadramagha

Plate 3 : Nāgadevatā holding pine fruit

Plate 4 : Details of the scene

Plate 5 : From Manhai

Plate 6 : Lion and Śrī Vatsa

Plate 7 : Double Humped Bull
(some times identified with Menander)

Plate 8 : Lions in different postures

Plate 9 : Tāla Dhvaja (Manhai)

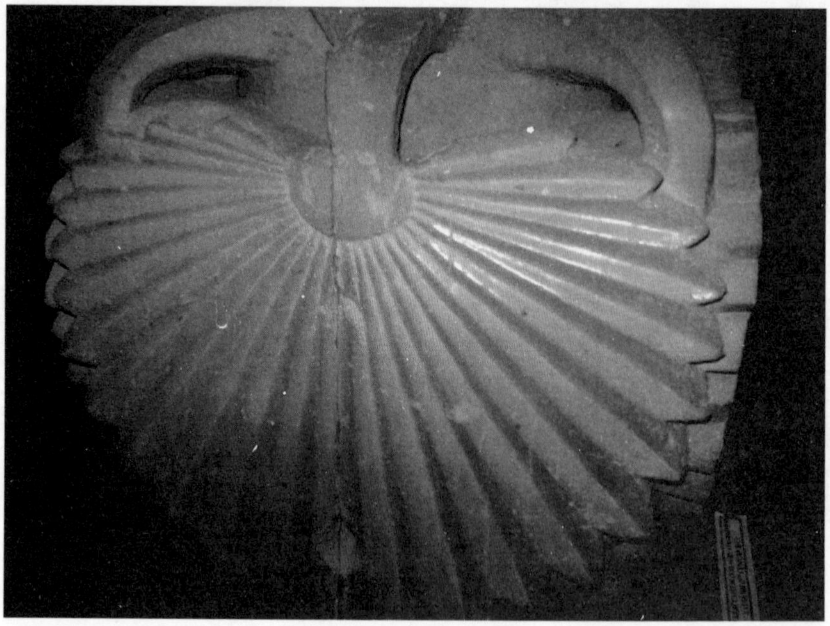

Plate 10 : Details

Plate 11 : Buddha Image showing archaism

Plate 12 : Rati and Kāmadeva

Plate 13 : Pañca Shara of Kāmādeva

Plate 14 : Kauśāmbī Pillar (fragment) in Shaṅkha script

Plate 15 : Shaṅkha script pillar from Kauśāmbī

Plate 16 : Nativity scenes from Kauśāmbī

Plate 17 : Deatails Māyā as Śālabhañjikā

Plate 18 : Hārīti

Plate 19 : Lotus Lamp inscription of the 6th century CE.

Harle (1974, 19) thinks that these images are but a variant of Mathurā Kuṣāṇa style. R.C. Sharma (1984, 210-12) has shown that stylistically the sculptures antedate the inscriptions. So far as the archaism of these sculptures is concerned, Sharma is right. But his suggestions that the sculptures were used 50-60 years after the construction is hypothetical. These images are supposed to be carved under the 'Anyor style' of Mathurā. They may be taken as the artist's fancy towards archaism, which was a hall mark of Kauśāmbī. Even the Buddha image from Mankunwar of the period of Kumāragupta dedicated by Buddhist nun Buddhamitrā, shows the same pattern of archaism.

Kauśāmbī had the tradition of local artists and artisans from an early time. Usually, it is asserted that Kauśāmbī as a school could emerge quite late, but an early evidence of settlement of the artists shows that Kauśāmbī as a school developed much earlier; in fact, the depictions like nativity scene, *stambha yoṣhita* etc. show that the seeds were sprouting in the 2nd century BCE.

One question is also posed with regard to the art of Kauśāmbī - from where did It get the stones? The answer is that it was brought from Pabhosā, a popular place only 4 km. away from Kauśāmbī and surrounded by hills. It is also a possibility that some of the images were carved at Pabhosā itself and supplied to Kauśāmbī. As a matter of fact, Kauśāmbī had an earlier tradition and Pabhosā worked as a supplier. Pabhosā had a tradition of the *sūtradhāras* also who worked from Pabhosā to Kauśāmbī (Shukla, V.C. 1997, 29). There are epigraphical evidence to this effect. One inscription mentions Podhaki son of Prayāgdhara, yet another mentions Sarvadatta and Shaṅkkhadeva. The name Shaṅkhadeva also occurs in an inscription of Kauśāmbī. The inscription is composed in late Gupta Brāhmī (Roy, S.N. 2003, 46) and the last line says *Shankkhdevasyakṛitiriyam.* Two inscriptions in Shaṅkha script are housed in the G.R. Sharma Memorial Museum (Pls. 15&16). There is a symbol of conch in both the inscriptions . It could be the mark of their family.

Coming back to the moot question, what do we mean by school of art? Some may be very famous and some may not be as famous. The art of Mathurā has eclipsed other centres and mesmerized the art historians.

Kauśāmbī had been the trade centre for a very long period. It was also a place where all important religious sects flourished. It took a lead in carving images concerned primarily with Buddhism, Śaivism and Bhāgavatism. Even local cults like Yakṣa and Nāga had an early beginning here. It was a working place of not only the local artists but also of the foreign artists. Different generations of Scythians, perhaps patronised by Maghas used to work here.

It is usually accepted that Kauśāmbī emerged as a school of art from the times of the Guptas. It can hardly be denied that, like other centres, Kauśāmbī too contributed a lot in the development of Gupta art. However, there are certain evidence which provide clear-cut antecedent stages of its development from the second century BCE. During the first century CE, it seems to have started its own script and style. So it cannot be said that many alien artists present here were working on a borrowed art style. The presence of scythians at Kauśāmbī during the 2nd-3rd century CE had the royal patronage. Hence, the debate regarding the influence of Mathurā or the *Anyor* style is baseless.

In short, we can say that just like Mathurā, Sārnātha, Gandhāra, and Amarāvatī, Kauśāmbī also registers itself as a distinct style, more precisely, as a school of art.

References

Chandra Pramod, *"Stone Sculptures in the Allahabad Museum"*, 1971, Bombay.

Dani, A.H., *"Indian Palaeography"*,1986, New Delhi.

Harle, J.C. *"GuptaSculptures"*, 1975, Oxford

Jaiswal Suveera, *"Orgin & Development Of Vaishnavism"* , 1967, Delhi.

Misra, R.N. *"Bhārtīya Mūrtikalā"*,1978, Delhi.

Negi, J.S. *"Some Indological Studies"*, 1966, Allahabad

The *Mahāvaṁsa*, ed. W. Geiger, P.T.S., London, 1958, London.

Roy Anamika "The dated Image Inscriptions of the period of Maghas: And the Discrepancy in Art & Script", *Citi -Vīthikā*, Vol. II Nos. 1-2, Allahabad, 1996-97.

Roy, S.N., 'An Early Epigraphical Reference to the Yakṣa Cult' in *"Rural Life & Folk Culture in Ancient India"*, 1988, Allahabad.

'Kauśāmbī Ke Abhilekhon kā Sāṅskṛitik Pariprekṣhya' (in Hindi) in *"Cultural Heritage of Allahabad Region"* 2004, Allahabad.

"Bhārtīya Purālipi Evaṁ Abhlekha" (in Hindi) 2008 Allahabad.

Sharma, R.C. , *"Mathura Sculptures"* Delhi, 1984.

Sharma, G.R. *"Excavations at Kauśāmbī"* 1957, Allahabad.

Shukla, V.C., "Bhārtīya Kalā ke Vividh Āyām", (in Hindi), Allahabad, 1997.

Tripathi Aruna, *"The Buddhist Art of Kauśāmbī"*, 2003, Delhi.

13

Early Coinage of Eastern Uttar Pradesh

Prashant Srivastava

In this short essay, an attempt has been made to present an overview of the early coinage of eastern Uttar Pradesh. The scope of the essay precludes delving in the matter in any detail. However, all the major series of early Indian coins, up to *circa* 650 CE, known from eastern Uttar Pradesh, have been taken up for a brief discussion. References have been given at the end of each of the eight sections, and a Select Bibliography, at the end of the essay.

Punch Marked Coins

The name, punch marked coins, first used by James Prinsep in 1835, is merely a descriptive appellation derived from the system of manufacture peculiar to these coins, the coins being made by the punching technique. With the advent of these coins, believed by a vast majority of scholars to be the earliest available coins of India, 'we see money in the very infancy of the numismatic art'. Some scholars believe that the punch marked coins are of foreign origin, but their indigenous origin has been conclusively proved by Cunningham and others. According to a vast majority of scholars, the earliest punch marked coins were issued by the silversmiths or bankers, but later on, the state took over the responsibility for issuing coins, and made it its prerogative. Punch marked coins are available in silver and copper, the silver ones being more numerous than the copper ones; a few lead punch marked coins have recently been reported from the Vidarbha region, and may be compared with the *sīsakahāpaṇa* mentioned in jātaka literature. A few gold punch marked coins have been reported, but some scholars have doubts as to whether they are genuine or not. The silver punch marked coins were called *dharaṇa*, and the standard silver coin weighed 32 *rattīs*, that is about 56 grains. Kauṭilya speaks of silver *dharaṇa* of almost

80 *rattīs*, but no such actual specimen is known so far. The copper punch marked coins were denoted by the term *kārshāpaṇa*, and the standard copper coin weighed 80 *rattīs* or about 144 grains. In practice, there were some other additional denominations also. Cunningham had, in his collection, punch marked coins varying in weight from 250 grains to 9 grains, that is from 1¾ *kārshāpaṇa* to 1/16 *kārshāpaṇa* or a *māshaka*.

Punch marked coins can be, and have been, classified variously, but Smith's classification, based on the metal (silver or copper), shape (ingots, bent bars, rectangular, square, oval, or circular), and the number of symbols on the reverse (none, one, two, three, or more), proposed for the punch marked coins in the collection of the Indian Museum, Calcutta, seems to be by far the most scientific. On the basis of their area of circulation, the punch marked coins have been divided into two classes—(i) those confined to some area, that is the punch marked coins of the local series, and (ii) those that circulated almost throughout the country, that is the universal or imperial series. According to P L Gupta, the punch marked coins of the local series were issued variously by the Śūrasena (Mathurā region), Uttara Pañchāla (Rohilkhand), Dakshiṇa Pañchāla (doab region), Vatsa (capital at Kauśāmbī), Kuṇāla (Gonda-Bahraich districts), Kosala (Avadh), Kāśī (Varanasi region), Malla (area around Deoria), Magadha (south Bihar), Vaṅga (Bengal), Kaliṅga (Orissa), Andhra (Godavari-Krishna region), Aśmaka (area south of Godavari), Mūlaka (area west of Hyderabad), Saurāshṭra (Kathiawar), and Gandhāra (Takshaśilā-Pushkalāvatī region). The coins from these regions differ from one another in fabric, weight, quality of metal, and devices. The coins of Śūrasena, Uttara Pañchāla, Dakshiṇa Pañchāla, and Saurāshṭra use the same symbols, but there is difference in form and execution. Bent bar coins are peculiar to the Gandhāra region. The coins from Bengal bear three symbols, while some *janapadas* issued coins with four symbols. The coins of Kāśī, Magadha, Vatsa, and Saurāshṭra have thin fabric, while those of Malla, thick. Some Kāśī (?) coins are cup-shaped. The universal series has five symbols, the sun and *ṣhaḍarachakra* being constant, and three others, variable. In almost all hoards of the punch marked coins of the local series, coins of the universal series are absent, and *vice versa*; in very rare cases are the two series of punch marked coins found together. From this, it is inferred that when Magadha became a pan-Indian empire, the local type of punch marked coins of the kingdom of Magadha became the universal series. While Pāṇini in the fifth century BCE refers to *nishka, śatamāna, viṁśatika, triṁśatika*, etc, besides *paṇa*, Kauṭilya in the fourth century BCE refers only to *paṇa* with its fractions. This has been taken to show that by the time of the *Arthaśāstra*, *paṇa* currency had superseded other types of currencies. Michael Mitchiner, too, classifies the punch marked coins into the local series and the universal series (which he calls the 'Magadha-Maurya' series), but he further classifies these coins into four sub-classes : (i) heavy weight-standard with multiple-punch type, in middle Ganga valley west of Varanasi, that is the Kosala region; (ii) heavy weight-standard with single-punch type, in Gandhāra; (iii) light weight-standard with single-punch type, in Avanti and Konkan; and (iv) light weight-standard with multiple-punch type—the Magadha-Maurya series, which had a wide area of circulation.

The symbols on the punch marked coins were impressed by separate punches at various points on the surface of the coin. They often overlap, and on certain coins, where the symbols are numerous, this overlapping results in 'a confused jumble'. Some scholars are of the view that the different symbols were impressed at different times; others are of the opinion that all the symbols were impressed at the same time, but using different punches, when the blank was hot. The symbols on the obverse are larger in size, and usually different, from the symbols on the reverse. Coins of the universal series bear, on the obverse, five symbols on an average; the reverse is either blank, or occupied by two symbols on an average. Rarely are both the surfaces of the coin equally crowded with symbols, whose number on one side is known to go up to even 10 or 12. It has been noticed that often a symbol is confined to the coins of one area, or a particular type or variety, or a particular period. These symbols are regarded as the official guarantee of the validity of the coin, and are considered, variously, as of religious or mythological in nature, or as official marks or symbols of the ruling dynasty or king, or as marks of bankers. Theobald's classification of the symbols on the punch marked coins, proposed nearly a century ago when only about 400 of them were known, is no longer acceptable. A new classification has been proposed, in which these symbols are divided into five classes : (i) natural symbols, including quadrupeds, birds, aquatic creatures, reptiles, insects, human figures, trees and plants, and heavenly bodies; (ii) geographical symbols, of which the hill and the river are the most common; (iii) geometrical symbols, like the straight line, curved line, circle, dotted circle, square, divided square, rectangle, etc; (iv) weapons and structures, like bow-and-arrow, spear, trident, *stūpa* (?), *chaitya* (?), etc; and (v) miscellaneous symbols, like the *nandipada*, triskeles, *svastika*, taurine symbol, etc. The human figure, sometimes armed, on punch marked coins, is usually shown singly or in groups of three. Quite interesting is the appearance of an ithyphallic man on a punch marked coin reported from the collection of Jan Lingen of the Netherlands. This might very well be the first representation of this kind in ancient Indian coinage.

According to Cunningham, punch marked coins were in circulation in India as early as 1000 BCE. But the antiquity of coinage in India cannot be taken much before the sixth century BCE. Loventhal says that in southern India, punch marked coins circulated up to 300 CE, while in northern India, they went out of circulation three or four centuries before their use was discontinued in the south. But in certain archaeological excavations, punch marked coins were found in levels datable from the sixth century BCE to the early centuries of the Current Era (CE). Three punch marked coins were unearthed by Cunningham from under the foot of the *vajrāsana* of the Buddha at the Mahabodhi temple at Bodhgaya, the deposit being made in the time of the Kushāṇa ruler, Huvishka (second century CE). The *purāṇas* in a Mathurā inscription of Huviṣhka may refer to silver punch marked coins. At Sisupalgarh, moulds for manufacturing punch marked coins were found in the stratum datable to *circa* 300 CE. Buddhaghoṣha, in the Gupta period, refers to the prevalence of the old *nīla-kārshāpaṇa* side by side with the silver coins of the Śakas. The view of S R Goyal, however, that the find of punch marked coins along with those of King Hoshangshah of Malwa, who ruled in the first half of the fifteenth century CE, shows that they continued in circulation as late as that period, does not seem to be convincing.

The series of punch marked coins, imperial as well as local, available from eastern Uttar Pradesh, may be dealt with in some detail.

Imperial Series of Punch Marked Coins

The Magadha series of punch marked coins are divided into a number of types by various scholars. For instance, P L Gupta and Terry Hardaker divide them into six types. Doubts have been expressed regarding the authenticity of the coins placed by them in Type I. Their Types II to IV represent the early local issues of the Magadha *janapada.* These coins are heavier than the coins of the later series, have a big and thin flan, and bear the six-armed symbol almost at the centre of the flan, and the solar symbol; there might be some other symbols, too, but the main types had not yet become fixed. Type V is a transitional series. The weight of the coin was gradually reduced from 'nearly half *śatamāna*' to *kārshāpaṇa,* which weight is adhered to in Type VI; the coins of Type VI, having a small and thick flan, are later issues and ultimately evolved into the imperial series, when Magadha became a pan-Indian empire. As noted above, this imperial series has five symbols, the sun and *ṣhaḍarachakra* being constant, and three others, variable. Coins of this series have been found practically all over India, including eastern Uttar Pradesh.

Kāśī Series of Punch Marked Coins

The punch marked coins of the Kāśī *janapada,* all in silver, are believed to form one of the earliest series of ancient Indian coins, being dated between *circa* 600 BCE and 465 BCE. The coins have been divided into two broad classes—those issued by the *janapada* before its annexation by Kaṁsa of Kosala, an event known from Jātaka literature, and those issued after the said annexation. The independent coins of the Kāśī *janapada* have been dated between *circa* 600 BCE and 525 BCE. These coins are large and thick, and conform to the standard of 5 *śāṇa,* 2½ *śāṇa,* 1½ *śāṇa,* and ½ *śāṇa.* There are also some scyphate of cup-shaped coins, which conform to the *viṁśatika* standard; half units of the *viṁśatika* standard are also known. The 5 *śāṇa* and *viṁśatika* pieces bear four symbols, a pair of identical and small sized one, and two other large sized ones. However, the 2½ *śāṇa,* 1½ *śāṇa,* ½ *śāṇa,* and ½ *viṁśatika* pieces bear only one symbol, and the *śāṇa* pieces bear two symbols. The coins issued after the annexation of Kāśī by Kosala have been dated between *circa* 525 BCE and 465 BCE. They have been issued on the *viṁśatika* standard, but are smaller and thicker than the scyphate *viṁśatika* coins mentioned above. They bear four symbols, either two pairs of two symbols, or one pair of identical symbols and two other symbols. Later on, these *viṁśatika* coins were replaced by the *kārshāpaṇa* coins, usually bearing four symbols, and, rarely, five. There is also a suggestion that the second class of coins was issued conjointly by the Kāśī and Kosala *janapadas.*

Kosala Series of Punch Marked Coins

Coins of the Kosala *janapada* are all in silver, and issued on two different standards—*viṁśatika* and *kārshāpaṇa*; half units of *viṁśatika* standard, and half and quarter units of *kārshāpaṇa* standard, are also known. Most of the coins of the *viṁśatika* standard, and some coins of the *kārshāpaṇa* standard, are 'small and dumpy'. The coins of the Kosala *janapada* generally bear three symbols, of which one is repeated. The weight of the coins tends to decrease with the passage of time. The Kosala series has been dated between *circa* 525 BCE and 465 BCE (P L Gupta and Hardaker 1985; Hirano 1999-2000; Rajgor 2001).

Malla Series of Punch Marked Coins

Coins of the Malla *janapada* have been found from the region around Gorakhpur. They are archaic in appearance, and bear a single large symbol in the centre. The symbol might have been punched while the blank was still hot, which might account for the scyphate shape of the coins. The weight standard adopted by the Mallas for their coinage is not known for sure, although there is a suggestion that various coins might conform to half and quarter units of the *śatamāna*, and five *śāṇa* and 1½ *śāṇa*. The Malla series has been dated between *circa* 550 BCE and 320 BCE.

Ayodhyā Series of Punch Marked Coins

These silver coins, slightly scyphate, have been found from a hoard discovered in a village near Ayodhyā. These coins seem to follow two weight standards—five *śāṇa*, and the half unit of *śatamāna*. All the coins of the former standard, and some coins of the latter standard, bear a single symbol, shaped like a star with five points. The remaining coins of the latter standard bear two different symbols, one occupying the centre of the coin, and the other relegated to a corner of the flan. The Ayodhyā series has been dated between *circa* 600 BCE and 400 BCE.

Besides the scyphate or cup-shaped coins from the areas around Varanasi and Ayodhyā, and from the Malla *janapada*, there are also some scyphate coins from the Kuntala region. These usually bear two symbols—a two-armed pulley-like symbol as the principal one, and a smaller, auxiliary one. It has recently been suggested that some cup-shaped coins might also have come from the Gandhāra region. All these are more or less oval in shape. Some are of relatively pure silver, while others, heavier and of thicker fabric, are of highly alloyed silver. They are made by flattening round globules of silver, which gave them the peculiar cup or saucer shape. Terry Hardaker reports some cup-shaped coins, which he feels come from the Gandhāra region, bearing no punch marks, and having only bankers' marks. These pieces have been struck in the centre 'with the edge of a large blunt punch containing no visible design', perhaps to give the cup shape to the blank. Under normal circumstances, such blanks would then have been marked with symbols. That these pieces bearing no punch marks were in actual circulation seems to be suggested by the 'moderate wear' they show. A N Lahiri thinks that the common 32 *rattī* coins evolved from the 48 *rattī* local Kāśī-Kosala coins of the cup-shaped type made out of metal globules. But the 32 *rattī kārshāpaṇa* was rarely made by this method of flattening metal globules, and mostly by sheet-cutting method. The number of symbols punched on these common punch marked coins was increased from four (of the cup-shaped coins) to five (Allan 1936; Pratipal Bhatia 1989; Cribb 1985; Cribb 2005; S R Goyal 1995b; Gupta 2004; Gupta and Hardaker 1985; Handa 2009; Hardaker 2005-2006; Hirano 1999-2000; Hirano 2009; Kosambi 1992; A N Lahiri 1971; Mitchiner 1973; Murphy 2003-2004; Rajgor 2001; Upadhyaya and Chaturvedi 1972).

Ayodhyā Coins

The Ayodhyā series of punch marked coins has been dealt with above. The coins of the kings of Ayodhyā have been divided into two distinct series: (i) square cast coins, and (ii) round die-struck coins. The former generally bear the figure of a bull, rarely an elephant, before a symbol on the obverse, and a group of symbols in different combinations on the reverse. The rulers known from the coins of Series I are (alphabetically), Dhanadeva, Jyeșhțhadatta, Mūladeva, Naradatta, Poțhadeva (Praușhțhadeva), Śivadatta, Vāyudeva, and Viśākhadeva, although some scholars would place Naradatta and Śivadatta of Ayodhyā coins among the rulers of Mathurā. Dhanadeva may be identical with the homonym of Ayodhyā stone inscription, who has been referred to therein as sixth in descent from Pușhyamitra. Coins of Dhanadeva, Vāyudeva, and Viśākhadeva have similarity of device—Gajalakșhmī, standing, while Śivadatta's coins show Gajalakșhmī, sitting. Praușhțhadeva and Mūladeva, known from bull type of coins alone, are to be placed earlier than Dhanadeva. Bela Lahiri proposes the following chronological order—Praușhțhadeva, Mūladeva, Vāyudeva, Dhanadeva, Viśākhadeva, Śivadatta, Naradatta, and Jyeșhțhadatta. The rule of the kings who issued square cast coins could be dated from the middle of the first century BCE to the second half of the first century CE. Their rule seems to have terminated with the conquest of this region by Kanișhka I.

The series of round die-struck coins seems to have been issued when the Kușhāņa rule over the region slackened after Kanișhka. These coins bear a bull on the obverse, and a cock or a *nandipada* on the reverse. The kings known are (alphabetically), Ajavarman, Āyumitra, Devamitra, Kumudasena, Mādhavavarman, Saṅghamitra, Satyamitra, and Vijayamitra. According to Bela Lahiri, of these rulers, Kumudasena, Ajavarman, and Mādhavavarman seem to be earlier as is indicated by the presence on their coins of a square incuse, which is characteristic of the earliest die-struck coins of India. Curiously, of the Ayodhyā kings, Kumudasena alone has the title of *rājan* on his coins. On the basis of the forms of the letter *ma* on the coins, Bela Lahiri suggests the following order of succession of the other rulers—Saṅghamitra, Vijayamitra, Devamitra, Satyamitra, and Āyumitra. The coins of this series may be placed between *circa* 150 CE and the end of the third century CE, the latter date marking the beginning of the Imperial Gupta period. It seems that the rule of the local dynasty of Ayodhyā was brought to an end by one of early Imperial Gupta rulers, for the Purāņic evidence shows that Chandragupta I exercised authority over Sāketa. The bull, common to both the series, is a characteristic local device. From some seals discovered at Rajghat are known Dhavasena, his son Vișhņumitra, and the latter's son Saṅghamitra, and also one Vijayamitra and his son Śivamitra. Saṅghamitra and Vijayamitra of these seals may be identical with the homonyms of coins (Allan 1936; Bopearachchi and Pieper 1998; Bela Lahiri 1974; Mitchiner 1975-1976; Smith 1972).

Kauśāmbī Coins

Kauśāmbī, the ancient capital of the Vatsa *janapada*, has been identified with modern Kosam, near Allahabad. The early coins from this site are of four classes, namely uninscribed and inscribed cast coins, die-struck coins of early kings, Dhanadeva's coins and their degenerate copies, and Magha coins. The cast coins form the earliest coinage of Kauśāmbī. Barring the city coins of Kauśāmbī, and the coins of kings Sudeva (?) and Bahasatimita [I] which resemble the uninscribed cast coins, all the coins are uninscribed. Some of these early coins from Kauśāmbī are *ḍamaru*- or drum-shaped. Coins of this shape are so far known only from Kauśāmbī. The second class of coins of Kauśāmbī belongs to the period from the second century BCE till the region was conquered by Kanishka I, whose coins and a seal have been found at Kosam. Coins provide evidence for more than two dozen kings who ruled for about two centuries. Since it gives an average reign of less than eight years, some of these kings would have ruled contemporaneously in different parts of the *janapada*. The kings known from these coins are (alphabetically) Agrarāja, Agnimitra, Aśvaghoṣha, Bahasatimita (Bṛihaspatimitra II), Īśvaramitra, Jyeṣhṭhabhūti, Jyeshṭhamitra, Parvata, Prajāpatimitra, Praushṭhamitra, Priyamitra, Rāḍhamitra, Rājamitra, Rajanīmitra, Rāmamitra, Sarpamitra, Satyamitra, Suramitra, Varuṇamitra, and Vavaghoṣha. It has been suggested that the Kauśāmbī rulers, particularly kings with *mitra*-ending names, had blood relationship with the Śuṅgas. If the indigenous coins with names of kings were being manufactured in the first half of the second century BCE, then it is difficult to understand as to why Pushyamitra and others of the early Śuṅga rulers did not issue coins in their names. In view of the lack of any other evidence for the chronology of kings, one has to fall back on typology and palaeography of the coin legends. Coins of Vavaghoṣha, Prauṣhṭhamitra, and Jyeṣhṭhamitra show, besides tree-in-railing (which is common on Kauśāmbī coins), the Ujjain and taurine symbols, while *svastika* occurs on those of Vavaghoṣha and Jyeshṭhamitra. Only the coins of Jyeṣhṭhamitra and Jyeshṭhabhūti bear the device of standing male figure. Some coins of Prauṣhṭhamitra, Jyeṣhṭhamitra, Agnimitra, and Bṛihaspatimitra II have been countermarked with *nandipada*. Amongst the rulers of Kauśāmbī, Īśvaramitra alone used the title of *rājan* on his coins. Bull and tree-in-railing is the most common device on the local Kauśāmbī coins. Other devices include, variously, the horse (on the coins of Bṛihaspatimitra I), lion (on the coins of Aśvaghoṣha), male figure (on the coins of Jyeṣhṭhamitra and Jyeṣhṭhabhūti). Ujjain symbol, too, is quite common. Other symbols met with are *nandipada*, *jayadhvaja*, wavy line, etc. There seems to be a break in the issue of the local coins of Kauśāmbī during Kaniṣhka's rule. Shortly thereafter, 'Bull : Tree-in-railing' type of coins of Dhanadeva, and their imitations, were struck. Then follow the coins of Nava, and those of the Magha kings; the latter have been dealt with separately. The coins of Nava are similar to the Magha coins. Altekar places him later than the Maghas, in the third or fourth century CE, but Bela Lahiri takes him to be earlier than the Maghas, as, in her opinion, the peculiar tree on his coins is similar to that on the coins of Dhanadeva of Kauśāmbī, rather than that on the coins of the Magha kings. This view is supported by the stratigraphic context of the coins from the Kosam excavations. His copper coins bear the bull to the right, sometimes with a wheel above, on the obverse; the reverse has a tree-in-railing, spear, and *chāmara*, and the legend *...navasa*.

Some city coins of Kauśāmbī are also known. They are of three main types. Type 1 bears, on the obverse, an elephant on pedestal, triangular-headed symbol, six-arched hill, wavy line, Ujjain symbol, and the legend *K[o]sa[ṁ]bi* above. On the reverse are tree-in-railing, Ujjain symbol, hill, tank with fishes, and *nandipada*. A variety of this type bears the legend *Kosaṁbi*, with Ujjain symbol on the obverse; the reverse is blurred. Type 2 is rectangular, and shows the figure of bull facing a standard on the obverse, and a circle in the middle with surrounding legend *Kosaṁbiya* on the reverse. Type 3, round in shape, bears the legend *Kasabikanaṁ* on the obverse, and a circle with dots surmounted by a crescent on the reverse. The legend seems to refer to the people of Kauśāmbī.

Some coins from Kauśāmbī appear to be guild issues. Some such coins bear the legend *negama* and *Gadhikana*, respectively. Three *negama* coins are known. They all show the lower portion of a railing, and a three-peaked hill, and the legend *negama* below, on the obverse. On the reverse, the first coin, which is rectangular, shows a *svastika*; the second, a round one, shows a seven-spoked wheel inside a circle of dots; and the third, a square one, a *triratna* (or *nandipada*). A round coin bears the legend *Gandhikanaṁ*, in the characters of *circa* second century BCE, on the obverse, and a square with four compartments on the reverse, and is taken as a coin of the *gandhikas*, 'dealers in perfume', who formed a guild. The dealers in perfume find reference in epigraphs from Bharhut, Mathurā, Karle, Pitalkhora, and Amaravati (Allan 1936; Altekar 1942a; Altekar 1942b; Altekar 1953; K D Bajpai 1960; Bopearachchi and Pieper 1998; Kothari 1991; Bela Lahiri 1974; Bela Lahiri 1976; Mitchiner 1975-1976; J P Singh 1971; Thaplyal 1996)

Magha Coins

The Maghas, known from coins, seals, and inscriptions ranging from years 51 to 139 (= 128 to 217 CE), are identified by some scholars with the Meghas known from the purāṇas as rulers in Kosala. There is a view that the dynasty should be taken as Māgha, named after its founder, and the name-endings of the kings of this dynasty should also be read as *māgha*. The Magha kings known from coins are King Magha, Vāsiṣhṭhīputra Bhīmasena (also known from inscriptions of year 51 and 52), Poṭhasiri (also known from epigraphs of years 87 and 88), Bhadramagha (also known from inscriptions of years 83, 87, and 88), Śivamagha (also known from a seal and an epigraph), Vaiśravaṇa (also known from inscriptions, one being dated 107), and Bhīmavarman (also known from inscriptions dated years 130 and 139). Kings Satyamagha and Vijayamagha are known from coins alone. There are coins, on which the legends have been tentatively read as *Puramagha* (?), *Yajñamagha* (?), *Śaṅkhamagha* (?), and *Jayamagha* (?). The succession of kings from Bhīmasena to Bhīmavarman can be determined by the dated inscriptions; the other rulers seem to be later than Bhīmavarman. The Maghas appear to have ceased as a political power before *circa* 300 CE. The epigraphs of the Maghas have been ascribed to the Gupta era by Cunningham, Fleet, and Sohoni, the Kalachuri era by K P Jayaswal, and the Śaka era by Marshall, Sten Konow, and Motichandra. Of these, the Gupta era is ruled out on the grounds that the Guptas could not have allowed members of a feudatory family to issue coins in their own name, and also that the Maghas should have mentioned the Guptas as their overlords in their epigraphs, which is not the case. These inscriptions appear to be dated in the Śaka era. The Magha coins, generally struck in base metal, bear the tree device, and most of them also show the bull device. Other symbols like the three-arched hill, a ladder-like symbol, a *nandipada*, etc, may also be seen on some of these coins. The name of the issuer is given in the obverse legend in bold Brāhmī characters. A M Shastri has published a hoard of 2,942 Magha coins from Kauśāmbī (Handa 2003-2004; Bopearachchi and Pieper 1998; A M Shastri 1979).

Kushāṇa Coins

According to traditional scholarship, about 165 BCE, there was much political upheaval in Central Asia, as a result of which the Hiung-nu (Hūṇa) tribe was displaced from its original homeland. This tribe, in its turn, forced the Yueh-chih tribe out of its original habitat in

Tocharistan in Central Asia. While one branch, Little Yueh-chih, moved towards Tibet and settled there, the other one, the Greater Yueh-chih, reached northwestern India by way of Seistan and Bactria. Chinese sources inform that in Bactria, the Yueh-chihs had five small principalities, four of which were subjugated by K'ieou-t'sieou-k'io (Kujula Kadphises), the chief of the fifth one. However, according to some recent writers, the Kushāṇas were a branch of the K'ang-chü race, which was of Scythian descent and originally belonged to the lower Jaxartes region. This branch allied itself with the Yüeh-chih, and settled in Ferghana. The capital of Ferghana was called Erh-shih around 101 BCE, but by 36 BCE, it was called Kouei-chouan, perhaps after its founder who belonged to Kouei-chouang branch of the K'ang-chü. Kujula Kadphises is known to have ruled up to the age of past eighty, and was succeeded by his son, who was earlier identified as V'ima Kadphises, but there is epigraphic evidence to show that V'ima Takshuma was the son and successor of Kujula Kadphises, and that V'ima Kadphises was the son and successor of V'ima Takshuma. The establishment of Kuṣhāṇa power over some territories of India proper took place some time during the reign of V'ima Kadphises, or, perhaps, even in the time of V'ima Takshuma. After him came the Kaniṣhka group of kings. Kaniṣhka I ruled over an extensive dominion extending at least up to Vārāṇasī in the east and Kashghar, Yarqand, and Khotan in the north, and was succeeded by Vāsiṣhka, Huviṣhka, Kaniṣhka II, Vāsudeva I, etc. The Kuṣhāṇa empire started disintegrating after Vāsudeva I. Numismatic evidence shows that among his successors, Kanishka III ruled over both the eastern as well as the western provinces of the Kushāṇa empire, but Vāsudeva II could retain only the western provinces. The Kushāṇas continued as a political power at least up to *circa* 350 CE, when the Allahabad pillar inscription of Samudragupta mentions a *Daivaputraṣhāhi-ṣhāhānuṣhāhi* as submitting to that Imperial Gupta ruler.

Kuṣhāṇa coins are reported from as remote regions as Ethiopia and Iraq. The Kuṣhāṇas were the first power in India to issue profuse gold coinage. Besides, they also struck abundant copper coins, and rare silver ones. The gold coins of the Kuṣhāṇas were based on the weight standard of the Roman *aurei*, and weighed around 123 grains. The copper coins are available in three weights—260 grains, 130 grains, and 65 grains. The silver coins are so few that nothing definite can be said about their weight standard. 'The line of descent of the new (Kuṣhāṇa gold) issue must be traced...through the Roman *aurei* which were first issued in abundance by Augustus and which at the beginning of the Christian era made their way into India....' The Kuṣhāṇa coins are manufactured by the die-striking method, and are invariably round in shape. The obverse of the coins of Kujula Kadphises bears the bust of the Indo-Greek ruler, Hermaios, or his own helmeted head; one type even has the figure of a bull on the obverse. But from the time of V'ima Kadphises onwards, the device of king sacrificing at an altar becomes common, Huviṣhka being the only ruler not using it on his coins. Other Kuṣhāṇa obverse devices include king seated on a throne, or on cushions, or on clouds, or reclining on a couch, or riding an elephant. The bust of the king, sometimes enclosed in a frame, may also be seen on some coins. The reverse of the coins of Kujula Kadphises bears, variously, "Macedonian soldier' or camel; V'ima Kadphises depicted Śiva, anthropomorphically or symbolically.

The reverse of the coins of Kaniṣhka I and Huvishka are interesting for the great variety of deities appearing on them. These deities belong to a varied pantheon—Indian, Central Asian, West Asian, Zoroastrian, Graeco-Roman. The Zoroastrian deities form the most represented creed on Kuṣhāṇa coins, and we have depictions of *Ardochsho, Athsho, Mao, Miiro, Lrooaspo, Oado, Orlagno, Oanindo, Pharro,* etc. The Graeco-Roman pantheon was the least represented, with deities like *Elios* (Helios), *Selene, Uron, Ephaistos* (Hephaistos), *Erakilo* (Herakles), *Riom,* etc occasionally making their appearance, although usually in Iranian garb. Indian deities include Śiva, Umā, Kārttikeya as Skanda-Kumāra, Viśākha, and Mahāsena, and the Buddha. *Nana-Nanaia-Nanashao* is a very frequently depicted goddess. Such representations, no doubt, reflect the spirit of eclecticism with which the Kuṣhāṇa kings seem to be imbued. The deities depicted on coins also seem to emphasize the 'right and might of the Kuṣhāṇa rule'. The obverse legend on the coins of the Kadphises group of kings is in Greek, while the reverse legend is in Prakrit language and Kharoṣhṭhī script. These legends give the name and titles of the issuing king. But the rulers of the Kaniṣhka group used only Greek language, written in Graeco-Kuṣhāṇa script. The obverse legend gives the name and titles of the issuing king, while the reverse legend gives the name of the deity represented. This label inscription on the reverse is very interesting, and helps us in identifying the deity represented when the depiction is indifferent. Some Kuṣhāṇa coins are reported from eastern Uttar Pradesh also, like Śṛiṅgaverapura in the Allahabad district (Cunningham 1971; Gardner 1971; Lal 1993; R C Majumdar 1988; von Mitterwallner 1986; B N Mukherjee 1978; Rosenfield 1967; Senior 2001; Sircar 1980; Whitehead 1914).

Imperial Gupta Coins

The Imperial Guptas began ruling towards the close of the third century CE, somewhere in eastern Uttar Pradesh and Bihar, or in Bengal. The first two rulers, Gupta and Ghaṭotkacha, are styled *mahārāja*, perhaps denoting their feudatory status. Chandragupta I, the son and successor of Ghaṭotkacha, is the first *mahārājādhirāja*, that is sovereign ruler, the first king of his dynasty to issue the coins, and, perhaps, also the founder of the Gupta era. His rise to prominence seems to be linked to his marriage with the Lichchhavi princess, Kumāradevī. This marriage led to the amalgamation of the Gupta and the Lichchhavi states, which was later inherited by Samudragupta. He brought almost the whole of northern India under his rule, and even made a bid for supremacy in the south. After the shameful Rāmagupta interregnum, we find Chandragupta II on the throne. He defeated the Kārddamaka Kṣhatrapas of Kathiawar, and is also believed to have led military expeditions to Bengal and Bactria. His son and successor, Kumāragupta I, proved himself to be an able administrator, and he kept intact the vast empire he inherited from his ancestors. But towards the close of his reign, he had to face internal troubles, as well as the onslaught of the Hūṇas. However, the Hūṇa invasion was repulsed by his son, Skandagupta, perhaps while he was still a prince. After Skandagupta, a number of Imperial Gupta rulers, like Purugupta, Kumāragupta II, Budhagupta, Vainyagupta, Bhānugupta, Narasiṁhagupta, Kumāragupta III, and Chandragupta III, are known from various sources—epigraphic, numismatic, and sigillographic. But their order of succession is not known for sure. Vishṇugupta, who reigned around the middle of the sixth century CE, is the last known Imperial Gupta king.

The Imperial Guptas were the first Indian rulers of indigenous origin to issue gold coins, and their significant monetary issues are mostly in that metal. Initially, they seem to have followed the standard of the Roman *dinarius aureus* of 122.9 grains, and the coins of

Chandragupta I and Samudragupta weigh, on an average, 120 grains. But the weight goes on increasing during the successive reigns, till it approximated the traditional weight of the Indian *suvarṇa* of 80 *rattīs* (about 144 grains). If the silver coins of the King-and-Queen type of Chandragupta I and Kumāradevī are taken as fake, Chandragupta II was the first Imperial Gupta ruler to issue silver coins after his conquest of Kathiawar. These silver coins follow the weight standard of the Kārddamaka Kṣhatrapa coins of 36 grains. Rāmagupta seems to be the first ruler of his family to issue coins in copper, although, on the basis of a copper coin from Sanghol, reportedly bearing the legend *Lichchhavayaḥ* on the obverse, and *Chandragupta* on the reverse, it has been suggested that Chandragupta I might have been the first Imperial Gupta ruler to issue coins in copper. As the weights of the copper coins range from 18 to 89 grains, it is extremely difficult to determine the standard they followed. Certain brass and lead coins have also been ascribed to the Imperial Guptas. The Imperial Gupta coins are die-struck pieces; only the *Garuḍa*-with-outstretched-wings type, ascribed by some scholars to Kumāragupta I and Skandagupta, were manufactured by the *repoussĕ* technique. They are all round in shape.

The obverse of the gold coins is occupied by the figure of the king in various postures; only on the *Aśvamedha* type, the obverse has the scene of the horse sacrifice in place of the royal figure. The king is usually shown standing, holding a standard, or some weapon, alone, or in the company of his queen or some deity or a parasol-bearer. Sometimes, he may be riding a horse or an elephant. On some coins, he is shown indulging in his favourite hobby, like playing on the lyre or hunting wild beasts. Thus, we have *Apratigha*, Archer, *Aśvamedha*, Battle-axe, *Chakravikrama*, *Chhatra*, Couch, Elephant-rider, Elephant-rider-lion-slayer, Horseman, Horse-rider-lion-slayer, Kārttikeya, King-and-Queen, Lion-slayer, Lyrist, Rhinoceros-slayer, Standard, Swordsman, and Tiger-slayer types of gold coins. The reverse is usually occupied by the figure of some deity—Lakṣhmī, *Siṁhavāhinī Devī*, Gaṅgā, or Kārttikeya. But the *Aśvamedha* type has the figure of the chief queen on the reverse, instead of the figure of some deity. Chandragupta I is believed to have issued the King-and-Queen type of coins only. Samudragupta issued six types of gold coins—Standard, Archer, Battle-axe, *Aśvamedha*, Lyrist, and Tiger-slayer, of which, coins of the first five types are available from eastern Uttar Pradesh. The gold coins of Kācha have also been found in that region. Chandragupta II issued eight types of gold coins—Archer, Lion-slayer, Horseman, *Chhatra*, Couch, King-and-Queen-on-Couch, Chakravikrama, and Standard, of which, the first six types are definitely known from eastern Uttar Pradesh. In fact, the only available specimen of the King-and-Queen-on-Couch type comes from the village of Badauli near Ayodhyā. The Chakravikrama type is definitely known from only one specimen, that from the Bayana hoard. But there are reports of another specimen with a goldsmith of Shahganj, near Jaunpur. Of the 15 types of gold coins of Kumāragupta I—Archer, Horseman, Lion-slayer, Tiger-slayer, Kārttikeya, Swordsman, Elephant-rider, Elephant-rider-lion-slayer, Rhinoceros-slayer, *Aśvamedha*, *Chhatra*, *Apratigha*, Lyrist, King-and-Queen, and *Garuḍa*-with-outstretched-wings, only the first five types are definitely known from eastern Uttar Pradesh. Skandagupta is believed to have issued four types of gold coins—Archer, King-and-Female, *Chhatra*, and Horseman, of which only the first type is definitely known from eastern Uttar Pradesh. Of the coinage of the successors of Skandagupta, only the Horseman-lion-slayer type of Bhānugupta Prakāśāditya is definitely known from eastern Uttar Pradesh.

The silver coins of the Imperial Guptas are of two types, namely the Western India type showing the royal bust on the obverse and *garuḍa* on the reverse, and the *Madhyadeśa* type with the royal bust on the obverse and fan-tailed peacock on the reverse. Chandragupta II is the first Imperial Gupta ruler, who is definitely known to have struck silver coins. But all his silver coins are of the Western Indian type, issued for circulation in the erstwhile Kārddamaka territories in western India. His son, Kumāragupta I, issued silver coins for circulation in the Ganga plains or *Madhyadeśa* as well, and these are called the *Madhyadeśa* type of Imperial Gupta silver coins. As seen above, these are markedly different from the Western Indian type of silver coins. Although the head of the king on the obverse is retained, it does not resemble the Kshatrapa head; the Greek letters are absent; the date of issue is given in front (and not at the back) of the royal head; the *garuḍa* on the reverse is replaced by a fan-tailed peacock; and the prose legend is replaced by a metrical one, reading *Vijitāvaniravanipatiḥ Kumāragupto divaṁ jayati.* On some *Madhyadeśa* type of silver coins of Skandagupta, the circular legend is *Vijitāvaniravanipatir-jayati divaṁ Skandaguptoyam*, and on some other coins of this type, it is *Vijitāvaniravanipatis-Srī-Skandagupto divaṁ jayati.* Budhagupta was the last Imperial Gupta ruler to issue *Madhyadeśa* type of silver coins. These coins bear the legend *Vijitāvaniravanipatiḥ Śrī-Budhagupto divaṁ jayati.* It is the *Madhyadeśa* type of silver coins of the Imperial Guptas, which are known from eastern Uttar Pradesh. This type of silver coins, with an average weight of around 36 grains, became very popular, and was imitated by the Hūṇas, Maukharis, Puṣhyabhūtis, and others.

The devices of the gold and silver types are often copied on the copper coins, and we have Altar or *Garuḍa*, Archer, Bust, *Chakra*, *Chhatra*, Crescent-and-*Garuḍa*, Crowned head, *Garuḍa*-with-*ku*, *Jitaṁ Bhagavatā-Padmanābhena*, *Kalaśa*, King's head, Lakshmī, Peacock, Standing king, and Vase type of copper coins.

Initially, under the Kuṣhāṇa influence, the Imperial Gupta kings are shown wearing central Asian dress—long coat, trousers, and long boots. But gradually, this dress was replaced by the Indian *dhotī.* The male deities always wear *dhotī.* Goddesses and queens are shown wearing *sārī*, *cholī*, and an upper garment. Both male and female figures wear necklace, ear rings, armlets, rings, etc; the females wear, in addition to these, also bangles, girdle, and anklets. Among the animals represented on Imperial Gupta coins, the horse and the elephant are seen as the mount of the king; horse also occurs independently on the *Aśvamedha* type. Tiger, lion, and rhinoceros are shown as the prey of the royal hunter. The *Siṁhavāhinī Devī* has the lion as her mount. The birds represented on these coins include *garuḍa*, the royal insignia of the Imperial Guptas, and the peacock.

The legend on both the obverse and the reverse is in Sanskrit, written in the Brāhmī script. The obverse has a circular legend, usually metrical; sometimes, the personal name of the king is written vertically under his left arm on the obverse, which is reminiscent of the Chinese style of writing. The reverse legend is shorter, and usually gives the title(s) and/or name of the issuing king.

The gold coins of the Imperial Guptas bear on the reverse, 'a small geometric type of drawing…consisting of a circle or parallelogram, usually hanging down from a line with a number of prongs or dots above it'. Similar symbols are also seen on Kushāṇa coins, but there, they represent monograms of individual kings, while they do not seem to have the same significance on the Imperial Gupta coins, and Altekar seems to be right when he concludes that probably 'early Gupta mint-masters regarded these symbols on their prototype as merely decorative elements which they were free to diversify in any artistic way they liked'. Initially, the Imperial Gupta coins show considerable Kushāṇa influence—their weight is based on the Kushāṇa gold coins; the king wears the Kushāṇa type of dress; the deity bearing the *cornucopiae* on the reverse seems to be modelled after *Ardochsho*. But the Gupta mint masters gradually Indianized the coinage, and, in course of time, traces of foreign influence almost vanished from the coins (Ashvini Agrawal 1989; Allan 1914; Altekar 1954; Altekar 1957; R D Banerji 1933; R G Chandra 1960; C D Chatterji 1957; Fleet 1888; S R Goyal 1995a; S R Goyal 2005; C S Gupta 1983; P L Gupta 1998; Manmohan Kumar 1978; Prashant Srivastava 1996; Thaplyal, forthcoming).

Pushyabhūti Coins

The silver coins of the Pushyabhūtis and the Maukharis are known from the Bhitaura hoard. This hoard of 531 coins was found in an earthen pot in the village of Bhitaura near Faizabad (Uttar Pradesh). Of these 531 coins, one is a gold piece of the Later Indo-Scythian type, 522 silver coins, and eight copper coins. The copper coins all belong to Pratāpāditya II of Kashmir. Three of the 522 silver coins are *Ādivarāha drammas*, while one is of uncertain type. The remaining 518 silver coins are all of the *Madhyadeśa* type of Imperial Gupta silver coins, that is bearing the royal head to the right and the date of issue on the obverse, and a fan-tailed peacock and the Brāhmī legend, *Vijitāvaniravanipati-śrī*-[name of issuer-]*divaṁ jayati* on the reverse. The names, and in many cases also the date, on 192 of these coins are lost; 284 coins bear the name Śrī Śīlāditya (generally identified with Harsha); nine bear the name Śrī Pratāpaśīla (generally identified with Prabhākaravardhana); 32 are Maukhari coins; and one belongs to a king named Harśa (not Harsha).

The Pushyabhūtis, who played an important role in the political history of northern India in the sixth-seventh centuries CE, are believed to be of *vaiśya* origin. In the *Harshacharita*, Bāṇa refers to Pushyabhūti as the first ruler of this dynasty, but the genealogy, found in the epigraphs, is Naravardhana, Rājyavardhana [I], Ādityavardhana, Prabhākaravardhana, and his two sons, Rājyavardhana II and Harsha. While the first three are called *mahārāja*, denoting their feudatory status, the last three are called *mahārājādhirāja*, showing that they were sovereign rulers. The predecessors of Harsha are generally placed in the period *circa* 500-606 CE. The rule of the Pushabhūtis came to an end with Harsha in 647 CE.

Two kings of this dynasty, namely Prabhākaravardhana and Harsha, are known from the Bhitaura hoard to have issued coins; Rājyavardhana had an exceptionally short reign and could not strike his money. Nine silver coins of the *Madhyadeśa* type of the Imperial Guptas, found in the Bhitaura hoard, bear the bust of the king to the right and the date of issue (year 11) on the obverse. The reverse has a fan-tailed peacock, and the Brāhmī legend *Vijitāvaniravanipati Śrī-Pratāpaśīla divaṁ jayati.* Hoernle would ascribe them to Pratāpaśīla Śīlāditya of Kashmir. However, as Pratāpaśīla is mentioned in the *Harshacharita* as another name of Prabhākaravardhana, Richard Burn and D Devahuti regard these coins as issued by this Pushyabhūti ruler. Hoernle ascribed all the 284 silver coins of the *Madhyadeśa* type of the

Imperial Guptas, issued in the name of *Śrī-Śīlāditya*, too, to King Pratāpaśīla Śīlāditya of Kashmir. But Richard Burn and D Devahuti suggest that the *Śrī-Śīlāditya* coins should be ascribed to Harsha, who is styled Śīlāditya, not only in the *Harshacharita*, but also by Hiuen-tsang. These coins bear the bust of the king to the right, and the date of issue on the obverse, and a fan-tailed peacock with the Brāhmī legend *Vijitāvaniravanipati Śrī-Śīlāditya divaṁ jayati* on the reverse. The dates range from year 1 to 33. Besides, a single gold coin of Harṣha is also available, but from the Farrukhabad district. It bears a five line Brāhmī legend mentioning Harṣha on the obverse, and Śiva and Pārvatī on Nandin on the reverse. The Puṣhyabhūti silver coins have an average weight of around 36 grains. The lone gold coin weighs 113.5 grains. All these coins are die-struck and round in shape (K D Bajpai 1976; Richard Burn 1906; Devahuti 1964; D Devahuti 2001; Pires 1934; Thaplyal 1985).

Maukhari Coins

A number of Maukhari families are known to have ruled in the Gaya region, in Rajasthan, and even in Karnataka in southern India. But the Maukharis of Kannauj played a significant role in the political history of northern India in the sixth-seventh centuries CE. The early kings of this dynasty include Harivarman, Ādityavarman, and Īśvaravarman; all three seem to be subordinate to the Imperial Guptas. Īśvaravarman's son, Īśānavarman, was the first independent ruler of the family. He made extensive conquests, assumed the title of *mahārājādhirāja*, implying sovereign status, and issued coins. He was followed by Śarvavarman, Avantivarman, and Grahavarman, respectively. A Nalanda seal mentions King Su... as the son of Avantivarman; he might have ruled for a short period after the death of Grahavarman at the hands of Śaśāṅka and Devagupta, before Harṣha took control of Kannauj, or he ascended the throne of Kannauj after Harṣha (and probably after Aruṇāśva also).

Three Maukhari rulers, Īśānavarman, Śarvavarman, and Avantivarman, are known to have issued coins. Thirty-two such coins, all in silver and with an average weight of 36 grains, are known from the Bhitaura hoard. They are of the *Madhyadeśa* type of Imperial Gupta silver coins, with the royal head to the right and the date of issue on the obverse, and a fan-tailed peacock with the Brāhmī legend reading *Vijitāvaniravanipati Śrī*-[name of the issuer-]*divaṁ jayati* on the reverse. The reading of the dates on these coins is extremely doubtful, so much so, that N G Majumdar, who examined the coins, reported that the dates have generally totally disappeared and it is not possible to read them. The era used on these coins is also not certain. As some of the dates seem to have two, and some, three digits, the possibility of the use of at least two different eras cannot altogether be ruled out (Richard Burn 1906; D Devahuti 1964; D Devahuti 2001; Pires 1934; Thaplyal 1985).

Select Bibliography

Agrawal, Ashvini 1989. *Rise and Fall of the Imperial Guptas.* Delhi.

Allan, John 1914. *Catalogue of the Coins of the Gupta Dynasties, and of Śāśāṅka, King of Gauḍa, in the British Museum, London.* London.

Allan, John 1936. *Catalogue of the Coins of Ancient India, in the British Museum, London.* London.

Altekar, A S 1942a. New Kings and Interesting Coin Types from Kauśāmbī. *Journal of the Numismatic Society of India* 4, pp. 1-16.

Altekar, A S 1942b. Further New Coins from Kauśāmbī. *Journal of the Numismatic Society of India* 4, pp. 133-145.

Altekar, A S 1953. Origin and Early History of Coinage in Ancient India. *Journal of the Numismatic Society of India* 15(1), pp. 1-26.

Altekar, A S 1954. *Catalogue of the Gupta Gold Coins in the Bayana Hoard.* Bombay.

Altekar, A S 1957. *The Coinage of the Gupta Empire.* Corpus of Indian Coins, IV. Varanasi.

Bajpai, K D 1960. New Copper Coins from Kauśāmbī and Vidiśā. *Journal of the Numismatic Society of India* 22, pp. 131-133.

Bajpai, K D 1976. *Indian Numismatic Studies.* New Delhi.

Banerji, R D 1933. *The Age of the Imperial Guptas.* Manindra Chandra Nandi Lectures, 1924, revised by the author in 1929-1930. Varanasi.

Bhatia, Pratipal 1989. Coins. A Ghosh (ed), *An Encyclopaedia of Indian Archaeology* 1 (New Delhi, 1989), pp. 10-14.

Bopearachchi, Osmund, and Wilfried Pieper 1998. *Ancient Indian Coins.* Brepols, Turnhout.

Burn, Richard 1906. Some Coins of the Maukharis and of the Thanesar Line. *Journal of the Royal Asiatic Society of Great Britain and Ireland,* 1906, pp. 843-850.

Chandra, R G 1960. A New *Chakravikrama* of Chandragupta II. *Journal of the Numismatic Society of India* 22, pp. 261-263.

Chatterjee, C D 1957. Some Unique Gold and Brass Coins of the Imperial Guptas. *Bulletin of the U P Historical Society* 2. Lucknow.

Cribb, Joe 1985. Indian's Earliest Coins ? *Coins Haords* 7, pp. 278-281.

Cribb, Joe 2005. *The Indian Coinage Tradition : Origins, Continuity and Change.* Nashik.

Cunningham, Alexander 1971. *Coins of the Indo-Scythians, Sakas, Kushans.* Reprinted from *Numismatic Chronicle* 1888-1892. Indian reprint, Varanasi.

Devahuti, D 1964. The Coins of Harsha Śīlāditya—A Reappraisal. *Journal of the Numismatic Society of India* 26(1), pp. 40-46.

Devahuti, D 2001. *Harṣha—A Political Study.* New Delhi.

Fleet, J F 1888. *Corpus Inscriptionum Indicarum* 3. Inscriptions of the Early Gupta Kings and their Successors. Calcutta.

Gardner, Percy 1971. *Catalogue of the Coins of the Greek and Scythic Kings of Bactria and India, in the British Museum, London.* Indian Reprint, New Delhi.

Goyal, S R 1995a. *The Dynastic Coins of Ancient India.* Jodhpur.

Goyal, S R 1995b. *The Coinage of Ancient India.* Jodhpur.

Goyal, S R 2005. *The Imperial Guptas.* Jodhpur.

Gupta, C S 1983. Gupta Lead Coins. *Numismatic Digest* 7, pp. 56-59.

Gupta, P L 1998. *The Imperial Guptas* 1. Varanasi.

Gupta, P L 2004. *Coins.* Reprint, NBT, New Delhi.

Gupta, P L, and Terry Hardaker 1985. *Ancient Indian Silver Punch-marked Coins of the Magadha-Maurya Kārshāpaṇa Series.* Nasik.

Handa, Devendra 2003-2004. Coins of King Magha. *Numismatic Digest* 27-28, pp. 39-42.

Handa, Devendra 2009. Early Indian Lead Coins. *Studies in Indian Numismatics* (Special Centenary Volume of the Numismatic Society of India, Varanasi), pp. 109-135.

Hardaker, Terry 2005-2006. "Punchmarked" Coins with no Punchmarks ? A Puzzling New Find. *Numismatic Digest* 29-30, pp. 1-6.

Hirano, Shinji 1999-2000. Novel Types of Local Punch-marked Coins. *Numismatic Digest* 23-24, pp. 1-6.

Hirano, Shinji 2009. Ayodhyā Hoard-type Punch-marked Coins in the Middle Ganges Area. *Studies in Indian Numismatics* (Special Centenary Volume of the Numismatic Society of India, Varanasi), pp. 136-144.

Kosambi, D D 1992. *Indian Numismatics.* Reprint, New Delhi.

Kothari, Narendra 1991. New Kauśāmbī Coins. *Numismatic Digest* 15, pp. 10-17.

Kumar, Manmohan 1978. A Unique Gupta Copper Coin from Sanghol. *Prāchya Pratibhā* 6(1), pp. 67-70.

Lahiri, A N 1971. Early Indigenous Coins of Northern India. D C Sircar (ed), *Early Indian Indigenous Coins,* (Calcutta, 1971), pp. 48-77.

Lahiri, Bela 1974. *Indigenous States of Northern India (*circa *200 BC to 320 AD).* Calcutta.

Lahiri, Bela 1976. India's Earliest Inscribed Coins : The City Issues. *Journal of the Numismatic Society of India* 38(2), pp. 35-54.

Lal, B B 1993. *Excavations at Śṛiṅgaverapura (1977-86)* 1. Memoirs of the Archaeological Survey of India 88. New Delhi.

Majumdar, R C 1988. The Disintegration of the Empire. Chapter V, in R C Majmudar, A D Pusalker, and A K Majumdar (ed), *The Classical Age.* The History and Culture of the Indian People 3, (Bombay, 1988), pp. 33-41.

Mitchiner, Michael 1973. *The Origins of Indian Coinage.* London.

Mitchiner, Michael 1975-1976. *Indo-Greek and Indo-Scythian Coinage,* 9 vols. London.

von Mitterwallner, Gritli 1986. *Kuṣāṇa Coins and Kuṣāṇa Sculptures from Mathurā.* Mathura.

Mukherjee, B N 1978. A Note on Reverse Devices on Coins of Kanishka I and His Successors. *Numismatic Digest* 2(2), pp. 34-43.

Murphy, Paul 2003-2004. A New Punchmarked Hoard from the Mathura Region. *Numismatic Digest* 27-28, pp. 19-29.

Pires, E A 1934. *The Maukharis.* Madras.

Rajgor, Dilip 2001. *Punch-marked Coins of Early Historic India.* San Jose (California), USA.

Rosenfield, J M 1967. *The Dynastic Arts of the Kushāṇas.* University of California Press.

Senior, R C 2001. *Indo-Scythian Coins and History,* 3 vols. Lancaster, Pennsylvania, London.

Shastri, A M 1979. *Kaushambi Hoard of Magha Coins.* Nagpur.

Singh, J P 1971. Negama and City Coins. D C Sircar (ed), *Early Indian Indigenous Coins,* (Calcutta, 1971), pp. 101-110.

Sircar, D C 1980. The Kushāṇas. Chapter IX, in R C Majumdar, A D Pusalker, and A K Majumdar (ed), *The Age of Imperial Unity.* The History and Culture of the Indian People 2, (Bombay, 1980), pp. 136-153.

Smith, V A 1972. *Coins of Ancient India—Catalogue of the Coins in the Indian Museum, Calcutta, including the Cabinet of the Asiatic Society of Bengal* 1. Reprint, Varanasi.

Srivastava, Prashant 1996. *Aspects of Ancient Indian Numismatics.* Delhi.

Thaplyal, K K 1985. *Inscriptions of the Maukharīs, Later Guptas, Puṣpabhūtis, and Yaśovarman of Kanauj.* Delhi.

Thaplyal, K K 1996. *Guilds in Ancient India.* New Delhi.

Thaplyal, K K forthcoming. [*Imperial Guptas : A Political History*].

Upadhyaya, D, and S N Chaturvedi 1972. Two Gold Punch-marked Coins. *Journal of the Numismatic Society of India* 34, pp. 153-156.

Whitehead, R B 1914. *Catalogue of the Coins in the Punjab Museum, Lahore* 1. The Indo-Greek Coins. Oxford.

14

Archaeological Glory of Kushinagar

Nirmala Shukla

The ruins of Kushinagara are situated near the town of Kasia (lat. 26° 44' N.; long. 83° 55' E.; District Kushinagar, Uttar Pradesh). The state of Bihar starts after about 20 km east of Kushinagar. It is bounded on the east by Bihar state, on the south - west by Deoria District, on the west by Gorakhpur District, and on the north - west by Maharajganj District. It is part of Gorakhpur Division and Is located near the *Hiraṇyavatī* River.[1] (Photo No. 1,2,3). It is an important *Buddhist* pilgrimage site, where Gautama Buddha died.

In ancient times, it was known as *Kushāvatiī* (Jātakas). It finds mention in epic *Rāmāyana* as the city of *Kusha* the son of *Rāma,* the famous king of *Ayodhyā.* It was known as *Kasia,* a celebrated center of the *Mallas* kingdom of ancient India. Later, it came to be known as **Kushīnārā**[2], one of the four most important holy sites for Buddhists.

E. Buchanan, an officer of East India Company, arrived here in the course of his survey-work. H. H. Wilson, in 1854, made the suggestion about the identity of *Kushinagar* with Kasia, which was established by the archaeological explorations and excavations first by Alexander Cunningham in 1861-62 and then by A.C.L. Carlleyle in 1874. Consequently, a number of *stūpa* and *vihāra* structures which adorned this site were explosed.[3]

The monuments of Kusinagara are situated in three distinct groups, the Main comprising the Main Stūpa and Nirvāṇa Temple with the other surrounding monuments, the shrine called Matha-kuar to its south-west and the Cremation Stūpa a little less than a kilometre to the east of the latter.

The first group is the most important and extensive of all the three, with the Main Stupa and Nirvana Temple at the centre, both standing on a raised plinth, and ruins of numerous monasteries, smaller *stūpas* and shrines surrounding them[4]. (Photo No.1)

The Main Stūpa - The Stūpa was excavated and completely exposed by Carlleyle in 1876. It was then a huge mass of brickwork in a tottering condition, representing the core of what must once have been a grand structure, which, inclusive of its pinnacle, might once have reached the height of nearly 45.72 m. The plinth on which the Stūpa and the temple were erected was 2.74 m higher than the ground-level. Above it, stood the cylindrical neck of the Stūpa to a height of 5.49 m fringed along its top with the remnants of a row of decorative and miniature pilasters. Further, projecting beyond the faces of the plinth along its eastern and southern sides, are seen half-concealed smaller *stūpas,* forming the usual accompaniments of the earlier structure. (Photo No.4)

An inscribed copper plate was recovered from the *Stūpa.* The inscription on the copper-plate contained the text of the *Nidāna-sūtra.* The vessel was found to contain, among other minor objects, some silver coins of Kumāragupta, a Gupta emperor of the fifth century CE. The trench was driven further to a depth of about 10.36 m almost in level with the natural soil, leading to the discovery of the circular plinth of a 'perfect little *stūpa,*' 2.82 m high, with a small niche on its western exterior enshrining a terracotta figure of Buddha sitting cross-legged in meditation. The *stūpa* was in a well-preserved condition and thus should not have been much earlier than the main Stūpa encasing it[5]. The digging was carried to a further depth of 0·84 m, where a piece of rotten wood was found and the water-table reached.

The Nirvāṇa Temple - The temple stands on the same plinth as the Stūpa behind it. As mentioned above, the ruins of this temple and the reclining Nirvāṇa statue inside were discovered by Carlleyle in 1876. The statue measures 6.1 m in length and is executed out of one block of sandstone of mixed reddish colour probably from Chunar. It represents the Dying Buddha reclining on his right side with his face turned towards the west. It is placed on a large brick pedestal with stone posts at the corners and once faced with stone slabs on all the sides. The western side of the pedestal facing the entrance, however, bears sculptures representing three human figures, each carved in a shallow niche cut into a solid block of stone. The figure to the extreme left represents a female in mourning with dishevelled long hair and crouching forward in grief with her hands resting on the ground. The figure to the extreme right is indistinct but may represent a male or female, also in grief, as indicated by the head resting on the right hand[6]. The central figure represents a man sitting cross-legged with the back turned towards the spectator. Right below him is an inscription datable to the fifth century CE. (Photo no. 5a, 5b)

The Western Group - Ranged around the Stupa and the Nirvāṇa temple are to be seen a number of brick structures which were raised from time to time as complements to the nucleus formed by the most sacred monument. Close to the entrance of the temple, to the north-west, one sees some structural ruins at a level much lower than that of the long array of buildings to the west. A seal depicting the coffin of Buddha in between two *śāla* trees and the legend *mahāparinirvāṇa* and *bhikṣhu-saṅgha* in two lines, two other seals with a similar legend and a clay tablet with the figure of standing Maitreya and the well-known Buddhist formula have been recovered. All the legends were in a script assignable to the fourth century CE.

The Southern Group - The monuments in this group represent mostly small-sized *stūpas* before one reaches to the holy monuments. The carved brickwork and ornamental pilasters and cornices of their basements, which resemble closely the earlier plinth of the Main Stūpa, are some of the distinctive features of these monuments.

The Eastern Group - The most important and interesting of the ruins in the eastern group is the large platform-like brick structure, the main monument at the north-western end. The second or upper terrace is smaller, thus leaving a margin of about 3·66 m for a brick-paved procession-path all around it.

Since there is no mention of any such structure by Hiuen Tsang, it may be assigned to a date later than the seventh century CE.

Against the north-western corner of this terraced building was discovered a small structure built of large-sized bricks, the largest to be found at the place (48.26×25.4×762 cm and 46.20×25.4×6·99 cm) resembling bricks commonly assigned to the Mauryan age. The walls exist only in three courses of bricks with a thickness of 48·26 cm. The structure represents a small chamber, 2.54×2.92 m, and its eastern wall appears to go further northwards. In the corner formed by this projecting wall, copper coins, eight of Kaniṣhka and four of Kadphises II, were found mixed with charred substance, indicating that this building had been destroyed in the Kuṣhāna period. To the eastern side of the plinth of the main monument are also to be seen a few small-sized *stūpas* partly concealed in the plinth.

The Northern Group - In the area further west, some of the walls contain bricks of very large sizes usually ascribed to the Mauryan age. Similar large bricks were found in the same area in the course of deep digging, though the structures to which they belonged had already disappeared. The digging further yielded an interesting terracotta female figurine of perhaps the first century CE and a fragmentary stone inscription of the fifth century CE.

The western monasteries ranged in front of the Nirvāṇa temple.

The Cremation Stūpa (Ramabhar)

Nearly 1.61 Km. to the east of the Matha-kuar shrine is a colossal *stūpa* (about 50 ft.

high), locally known as Ramabhar-stūpa and believed to represent the spot of the cremation of Buddha. Surrounded by shrines and votive *stūpas,* its plinth is 155 ft. in diameter at the base and is built in two or more terraces, over which rises the drum, 112 ft. in diameter[7].

It stands on a mound facing the road from Kasia to Deoria. There is a sheet of water, called Ramabhar Jhil or pond, close to it, which dries up in summer. Cunningham tried to dig it but left the attempt[8]. In 1910, another attempt was made by Hirananda Shastri, who, by sinking a shaft at its centre, went down to 1.52 m below the water-level and found brick flooring and corners of walls. He then exposed part of the eastern face of the mound and discovered that it represented an unusually large *stūpa* with a huge circular drum, 34.14 m in diameter, resting on a circular plinth, consisting of two or more terraces, and 47.24 m in diameter at the base. From the point of dimension the *stūpa* appears to have been double the size of the Main Stūpa of the Main Site[9]. Hundreds of clay seals, with the usual Buddhist formulae inscribed on them in medieval characters, were found in the excavation. (Photo No.6)

The archaeological evidence recovered from the site of Kushinagar points to its glorious existence between the Mauryan period and the tenth century CE.

References

1. Debala Mitra, *Buddhist Monuments* , (Calcutta 1971) Pg. 66.
2. राजकीय बौद्ध संग्रहालय कुशीनगर, 2003.
3. धर्मरक्षित, कुशीनगर का इतिहास, पृ. 120.
4. A.S.R. For 1905-06 pg. 63.
5. A.S.R. For 1906-07 pg. 98.
6. A.S.R. For 1910-11 pg. 68.
7. A.S.R. For 1911-12 pg. 190.
8. Debala Mitra, *Buddhist Monuments* , (Calcutta 1971) Pg. 67.
9. Gorkhpur District Gazeteer, Pg. 261.

Plate 1 : View of river

Plate 2 : Staelite image of Kusinagar

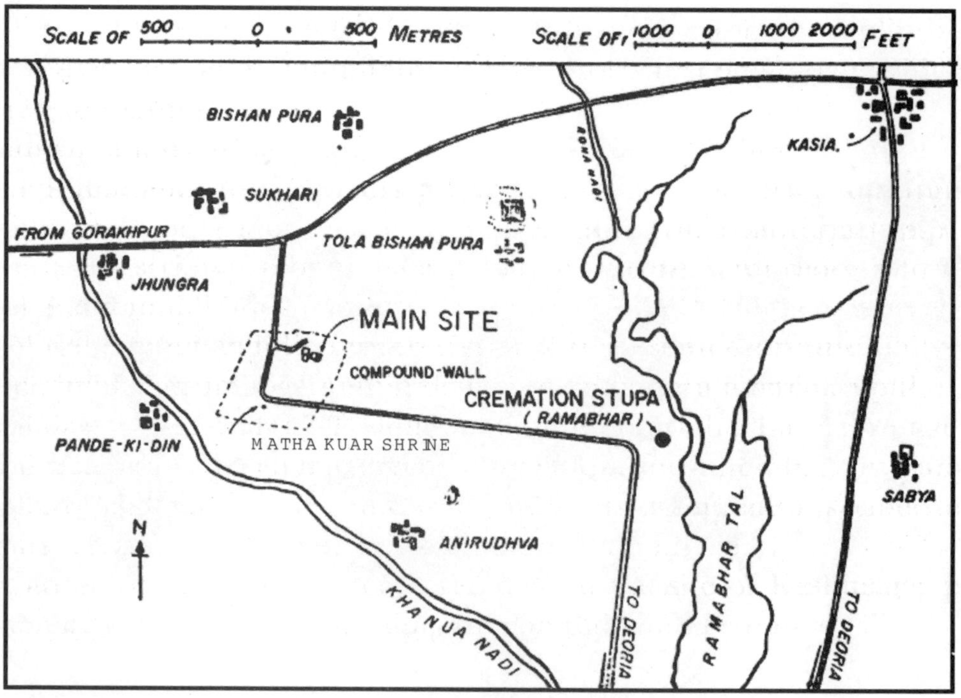

Plate 3 : Location map of stūpa

Plate 4 : Main stūpa

Plate 5 : Nirvāṇa stūpa

Plate 5 a : Nirvāṇa stūpa

Plate 5 b : General view of the main stūpa and nirvāṇa temple (Photo No.5b)

Plate 6 : Rambhar stūpa

15

Śrāvastī: A city of Socio-cultural Amalgmation in between Gangetic Plains and Northern India

Anil Kumar

The ancient city Śrāvastī or Sahet-Mahet (Lat. 27°31' N, Long. 82°' E), situated in district Śrāvastī, Uttar Pradesh, was one of the ancient cities of Kosala kingdom during the lifetime of Buddha. A well known story of the donation of Jetavana by Anāthapiṇḍika, a wealthy merchant of the city to Buddha, testifies its economic prosperity which was maintained by a growth in trade and commerce.

For the first time, Śrāvastī was noticed by Cunningham.[1] He visited Śrāvastī in the early part of 1863 and located the twin mounds of Sahet and Mahet which he identified as the Jetavana monastery and the ancient city of Śrāvastī respectively of the Buddhist literature. Cunningham resumed work in 1876 in the monastic area and was able to expose stūpas and smaller shrines of a comparatively late date.[2] He was followed by Hoey who excavated areas both in Sahet and Mahet.[3]

Vogel's excavation in 1908 also settled the identification of Sahet-Mahet with Sravasti.[4] Marshall and Sahni resumed work in 1910-1911 and exposed a few more buildings in the Sahet[5], with the objective to determine the antiquity and culture-sequence of the ancient site including the massive fortification. A small scale excavation was conducted by Prof. K. K. Sinha, Department of Ancient Indian History, Culture and Archaeology, Banaras Hindu University, Varanasi in 1959.[6] A team of archaeologists of Kansai University, Osaka, Japan conducted excavation at Jetavana (Sahet) during 1986-89 and further in 1991 onwards.[7]

From the evidences procured by these archaeologists and scholars time to time, we can draw a picture of cultural development at Śrāvastī. These provide us a peep as how a culture originated, continuously evolved to reach at its peak in the form of an urban unit and was subsequently deserted by people due to unfavourable economic conditions.

The excavations conducted by Kansai University revealed six cultural periods which are as follows:

Period I : Black and Red Ware and Black slipped Ware (8th century to 7th century BCE)
Period II : Early Northern Black Polished Ware (6th century to 4th century BCE)
Period III : Late Northern Black Polished Ware (3rd century to 1 st century BCE)
Period IV : Kuṣhāna phase (1st century CE to 3rd century CE)
Period V : Gupta phase (4th century CE to 6th century CE)
Period VI : Post Gupta phase (7th century CE to 1st century CE)

Period I is represented by Black and Red Ware (BRW) and Black slipped ware ceramics only in a limited area which is the lowest level, whereas the cultural contents of Period II are observed all over the site. Early Northern Black Polished ware is major ceramics of Period II. Period III is also constantly found through all the excavated areas which are represented mostly by the presence of late Northern Black Polished Ware (NBPW). Remains of Kuṣhāṇa phase *i.e.* Period IV are more plentiful in the southern half of the site. In other parts of the site this phase is quite limited. Gupta phase represented by Period V is only concentrated in the southern half of the site just after Kuṣhāṇa phase. Period VI, seems to be an occupation after the decline of the urban city. It is interesting that the occupation of Period VI is represented not by habitational structures but by temple complexes.

From Period I to Period VI several floor levels of different natures have been found. Period I is represented by only one floor-level indicating that the occupation in this period was for a short time. There is no gap between Period I and Period II. Period II has several floor levels in which Northern Black Polished ware became a dominant pottery. Each level is marked with many pits containing pottery, ash, charcoal and animal bones. Remains indicate to the existence of working places for the manufacturing of iron tools, glass beads, semi-precious stone beads and bone tools which were major working activities of Period III. Finding of several floor levels from this phase indicate that it existed for a considerable period of time. Significantly, this period has yielded the evidence for the existence of a rampart which must have been an important element for erecting a defence-architecture around the city. In Period IV, the habitation activity decreased in its size. Evidences indicate that densely settled area was shifted towards the southern half of the city during this period. Period V witnessed a total desertion of habitation which happened, at first, in the southern half but by the end of this period total habitation seems to have been deserted. In Period VI, it was again rehabited to some extent, but it lost its urban character which we witness during the early period. A brick-built Hindu temple was constructed in the area during the last period.

It is interesting to note that the rampart constructed in Period III was maintained until the end of Period IV. In Period V, there is no evidence of the use of rampart.

On the basis of archaeological evidences, we can make certain observations regarding the importance of this site :

1. At Sravasti, first occupation came around 8th or 7th century BCE, which has been confirmed from the cultural contents at the lowest level, *i.e.,* Period I. The deposit of Period II begins just over the floor of Period I, which was on the natural soil.
2. The human occupation in the middle Gangetic plains now goes back to the Neolithic stage as early as the seventh millennium BCE with a continuous cultural development resulting into Chalcolithic and iron using phases. It shows that above technological progress was able to develop its own cultural complex in middle Gangetic plains. From Neolithic stage at Chirand fragmentary potsherds of Black and Red ware have been found which is the most characteristic cultural trait of the region during the protohistoric period.[8] In all the parts of middle Gangetic plains Black slipped Ware appeared mostly along with Black and Red Ware, which indicates to its linear development from the former Chalcolithic phase.
3. Although some scholars argue that Black and Red Ware in the eastern half of the Gangetic plains came from Banas culture in the southern part of Rajasthan[9], but its spread in this region from lower or middle Gangetic plains is more reasonable to accept rather than speculating its origin from the Banas region[10].
4. The spread of Black and Red ware people seems to have introduced iron in this part of the Gagentic plain sometimes during the beginning of the first millennium BCE. This helped people in cleaning the thick forests and vegetation which mostly covered the Gangetic valley. It was perhaps during this time that the settlement at Śrāvastī came into existence.
5. It is also noteworthy that this expansion of people resulted into the formation of a network, which connected different parts in and around Gangetic valley. This is evident from the material milieu of the Black and Red ware sites which have vast cultural uniformity.
6. Archaeological evidence provides that Painted Grey Ware (PGW) appeared sometimes during the later half of the 2nd millennium BCE in the eastern Punjab[11]. The excavation at Bhagwanpura indicates that the Painted Grey Ware people lived here side by side with the late Harappan people, though both had different cultural traditions.
7. Śrāvastī was perhaps the place outside of Ganga valley where Black and Red Ware, and Painted Grey Ware NBPW cultures came in contact, may be because of growing trade. The urbanisation that set in here perhaps began with the amalgamation of these cultures, consequently leading to the constant socio-cultural contacts.
8. Śrāvastī was situated at a strategic point, which connected the Gangetic plain with the foothills of the Himalayas. It was also located on the main east-west route.
9. Period III is the phase of advance urbanisation at Śrāvastī. Several features such as use of NBPW, erection of rampart for fortification, variety of metallic implements for domestic and other uses etc., located in the archaeological material, provide clear testmony to this effect. Goods were produced in a

large scale and were traded with the people of north and north-west India. This led to the framing of socio-cultural contacts and integration with other parts of the country including the foot-hills of Himalayas in north. Thus, Śrāvastī assimilated the cultural atmosphere of the northern region as well as that of the Gangetic plains.

On the basis of above analysis, it can be said that the constant cultural interaction with north India and north-west India was one of the most influential factors to the development of the city of Śrāvastī. It is supported by the availability of NBPW in abundance at this site. It is also interesting to note that not only Black and Red ware and NBPW cultures interacted with each other at this site but it also witnessed a cultural amalgamation between Painted Grey ware distribution region and NBPW distribution region.

Śrāvastī was located on *Uttarāpatha* which connected the Gangetic plains and north India. It was actually a trading post on the route of Gangetic plains and Himalayan region in India. The availability of NBPW in abundance indicates that Śrāvastī not only introduced the techniques of production of NBPW but also evolved as a regional centre for the production and circulation of NBPW in Gangetic plains. Similarly, evidence of PGW shows that it was imported into this site from the north-west region where it appeared in later half of the 2nd millennium BCE. In fact, we find that during the early half of the 1st millennium BCE, Gangetic plains were divided roughly into two cultural regions — Black and Red ware and NBPW and PGW - both of them finding their covergence at Śrāvastī which led to its socio-economic transformation and rise as a city. Development of trade on large scale with other parts of India and outside fuelled the process of urbanisation which reached to its climax due to socio-cultural amalgamation of different cultures.

References

1. A. Cunningham, Archaeological Survey of India Report, Vol. I, p. 330-48.
2. A. Cunningham, Archaeological Survey of India Report, Vol. XI, p. 78.
3. Hoey, *Journal of the Royal Asiatic Society of Bengal,* LI. 1892.
4. J. Ph. Vogel, "Excavation at Sahet-Mahet", Annual Report of Archaeological Survey of India, 1907-1908, p. 81.
5. Annual Report of Archaeological Survey of India, 1910-1911.
6. K.K. Sinha, *Excavations at Śrāvastī*-1959, Varanasi. 1967.
7. Aboshi, Y. And K. Sonoda *ed,* 1997. *Excavation at Jetvana (Saheth)- A Buddhist site in Uttar Pradesh,* Kansai University.
8. Sinha, B.P., 1979. 'Neolithic culture of the Gangetic valley' *Archaeology and Art of India,* p. 34-52.
9. Gaur, R. C., 1969. 'Nature of Pottery complex of Black and Red Ware phase at A tranjikhera' in *Potteries in Ancient India,* (ed.) B. P. Sinha, p.112-117.
10. Dikshit, K.N., 1969. 'A note in the problem of the plain Black and Red Ware in Northern India' in *Potteries in Ancient India,* (ed.) B. P. Sinha.
11. Joshi, J. P., 1993. 'Excavations at Bhagwanpura 1975-76 and other explorations and excavations 1975-81 in Haryana, Jammu & Kashmir and Punjab, ASI, New Delhi.

16

A Unique Early Historical Tank at Śṛiṅgaverpura

R.S. Srivastava & Suresh Bala Gogna

The ancient site Śṛiṅgaverpura is also known as Surya Bhita and the excavated site is located on the left bank of the river Ganga in Tehsil Saraon, District Allahabad, Uttar Pradesh (Lat. 25° 35' 14.06" N; Long 81 ° 38' 30.27" E). It is about 36 kilometers west-north-west of Allahabad. The site is located between river Ganga and Yamuna near their confluence; one has to cross the river Ganga at Phaphamau at a distance of 5 km. After one leaves the Allahabad-Faizabad road and turns left on the road which goes to Lucknow via Rae-Bareli, there is a place called Mansurabad. About 3 km. from it towards Lalgopalganj, there is a sprawling road side called Bhagwatipur. Here a narrow though metalled road forks off southwards, taking to Śṛiṅgaverapur at a further distance of about 3.5 km. from the highway.

The site is associated with the story of Rāmāyaṇa which avers that Lord Rāma spent one night over here along with Sita and Lakṣhmaṇa when he was on the way to Prayāga during his exile for fourteen years.

It was one of the ancient sites taken up for the excavation under a project. "Archaeology of the Rāmāyaṇa sites" under the Joint Directorship of B.B. Lal, K.V. Sunder Rajan and K.N. Dikshit from 1977 to 1985.

Archaeologically, the site is spred over on a large mound. It stretches along the river Ganga for a distance of about 1 km. The ancient site sprawls roughly north-south along the left bank of the river Ganga. Seven different parts of this mound namely, SVP-1 to SVP-7 were selected for excavation.

The Sequence of Cultures

The excavation at this site revealed seven cultural periods starting from about the end of the second millennium BCE up to the late medieval periods. In brief the culture contents of the various periods are as given below:

Period-I	:	O.C.P. (1050-1000 BCE)
Period-II	:	Painted Grey Ware (950-700 BCE)
Period-III	:	Northern Black Polished Ware (700-200 BCE)
Period-IV	:	Śuṅga-Kuṣhāṇa Period (200 BCE to 200 CE)
Period-V	:	Gupta and Late Gupta (300 CE to 600 CE)
Period VI	:	Early Medieval Period (1000 CE to 1300 CE) and
Period VII	:	Late Medieval Period (1700 CE to 1800 CE)

Period-I

The earliest settlement at Śṛiṅgaverpura is represented by Red Ware Industry, with its two sub-varieties. In one case, the pots were made of well levigated clay and, were well fired, while in the other the fabric was coarse and the firing somewhat indifferent. There is, however, evidences of an occasional slip in both the cases. A few sherds with raised horizontal bands and shallow incised designs, such as wavy, comb like pattern, parallel lines, and appliqué designs were found. There are also traces of painting in a few cases. The shapes include jars with prominently outturn rims, vases with disc-base and platters, bowls with featureless or inverted rims, shallow basins with horizontally splayed-out rims. Some of the fragments are suggestive of types like the dish-on-stand (?) and bowl or basin with tubular or short channel. There are also a few specimens of lid, with either a central depression made by fingers or a curved knob. While it remains to be seen as how far this ware compares with the Ochre Coloured Ware, the excavator's view is that it represents an east-ward extension of the O.C.P. The occurrence of pieces of mud plaster with reed impression suggests that the houses were made of wattle and daub hutments. Not many antiquities were recovered from this period. There are pottery discs, with or without a central perforation, and a small fragment of a flake with carination.

Period-II

After a short break, the site was reoccupied by a different set of people who used the Black-Slipped, Black and Red Ware, Burnished Grey Ware and associated Red Wares. It is further sub-divided into periods, IIA and IIB. The former is characterized by the occurrence of coarse Black and Red Ware and Burnished Grey Ware which tend to peter out in IIB. Painted Grey Ware has also been found in it which suggests a stage of contact between PGW culture and the Black Slipped Ware culture in this area early in the eight century BCE. Amongst the antiquities of this period as a whole, mention may be made of points and a barbed arrow-head of bone, a bone pendant and beads made variously of terracotta, jasper and one of gold as well. The presence of clay lumps with reed-impression indicates that houses were made of wattle and daub during this period also.

Period-III

Having an average thickness of 2.80 m, the period started without any break of occupation from the previous one. It is characterized by the use of the Northern Black Polished Ware (NBPW). It was during this period that the settlement, which was hitherto rather small, began to expand along the right angle of the river. This period also witnessed tremendous growth in a number of ways. As the time passed, system of coinage and weights came into being and houses began to be constructed of kiln fired bricks. The period is divided into three sub-periods, A, B and C. In sub-period IIIA, the NBPW occurred in abundance and in a variety of shades, golden, silvery, indigo, steel-grey and of course black. The Black Slipped Ware also continued in this sub-period. A few sherds of the Painted Grey Ware were also found. Specific mention may be made of a sherd which had a fine Grey Ware fabric. It was painted on the interior with black lines and had the typical NBPW finish on the exterior over which a row of sigmas was further painted in black pigment. Such a sherd clearly shows the close relationship between the Painted Grey Ware and the Northern Black Polished Ware.

In sub-period IIIB, the miniature bowl, Ahichchhatra type 10A and carinated *handi* made their appearance, whereas in sub-period III-C the quality of the NBPW was on the wane and coarse Grey Ware became preponderant. No burnt brick structures were met within sub-period IIIB. However, burnt brick structures were noticed in sub-period IIIC. It Is also marked with the use of writing. The period came to an end around 200 BCE. A burnt layer running all around the section indicates to its destruction by fire.

The important antiquities of this period as a whole include, three copper vessels (one of them spouted), long-handled ladle, dishes and bowls, terracotta female figurine, balls, beads of semi-precious stones, terracotta and gold, cylindrical weights of agate and chalcedony, bone points, copper and iron objects, spherical punch marked coins of silver as well as of copper.

Period-IV

The succeeding period having an occupational thickness of about 2.754 m has no trace of NBPW nor even of the Grey Ware. This period is divisible into two sub periods IVA and IVB. The notable feature of the former is the Red Ware Pottery, bowl with incurred rim and dishes with flat base and vertical rim. In sub-period IVB bowls with vertically sharpened rim, sprinklers, vases with long vertical neck, ink-pot type lids dominate the scene. Burnt brick structures ascrible to different phases were also noticed. In this context, a structural complex, which consisted of several rooms with successive brick-floorings, a drain and a soakage pit, is a notable finding.

Amongst the antiquities of Sub-period IVA particular mention may be made of a coin of the Lanky Bull and also those of Ayodhyā, besides the Śuṅga terracottas. The antiquities of Sub-period IVB comprise seals and sealings in characters of the first century BCE – CE Brāhmī, one of them reading Dhankasa and another Gosalakas, and a couple of coins of Wima Kadphises (50-78 CE).

In Sub-period IVB, the most important discovery of the site was a unique and significant hydraulic system of Kushāṇa period in the form of massive burnt-brick Tank-Complex.

The site of Śṛiṅgaverpura is a fairly big mound. It stretches along the river Ganga for a distance of about one kilometer. Every year during the rainy season, the river Ganga plays great havoc with the mound. The Tank, consisting of two units with an elaborate Inlet and Interconnecting system, was dug in the natural soil in low-lying area SVP-4 to the north of SVP-1. The sides of the Tank were retained in a terraced fashion by three successive burnt-brick walls with battered back against the natural soil. Besides being the largest brick Tank ever revealed through an excavation in the country, it is unique in a number of ways.

The brick Tank at Śṛiṅgaverpura cut the bank of Nullah at an appropriate point and diverted the excess water into a specially dug channel which brought it to the area where the Tank was planned. Cut into the natural soil, this channel (called Feeding Channel) (figure no. 1) was approximately measured 16.30m in width at the top, but with its slanting sides, narrowed down to about 2.70 m at the bottom. It has a depth of 5.40m from the top. There is a stepped ledge infront of the Inlet Channel through which the water passed from the Silting Chamber to Tank A. (pl. no. 1). The water from the Inlet Channel did not fall directly on the floor of the Tank A. Instead, it cascaded over a series of steps.

From the Feeding Channel, specially dug for another purpose, the Ganga water first went into two successive Silting Chambers. From here, through another channel, water entered into the tank, which is paved with usually large bricks. The water dashed against the mouth of the Tank. From the Feeding Channel, near the middle part of the arc, the water entered into the Tank proper through a two metre wide channel lined with backed bricks. The water gushing into the Tank did not erode the base and the side walls as the bricks at the base of the Inlet Channel were arranged in a stepped fashion. A part of the floor of the Tank near the inner mouth of the Channel was found to have been paved with usually large bricks, measuring 64×48×12 cm. and laid in two courses. But the average size of the bricks used in the construction of the Tank was 41.5 to 44.275 to 28.5 and 6 to 7 cm. Further, the bottom of the Silting Chamber was about 1.35 m higher than that of the feeding Channel. This rise in the bottom level withheld a considerable part of the silt and mud from entering the Silting Chamber, which was not in a straight line with the former but to its side with the result that the water lost a part of its force before entering the Chamber.

From the Silting Chamber, the water entered Into the brick Tank of which the various parts have been marked as A, B and C on the plan (figure no. 1). There is a stepped ledge in front of the Inlet Channel through which the water passed from the Silting Chamber to Tank A. This stepped ledge helped considerably to the inrushing water. The bottom of the Inlet Channel was about 2.32 m. higher than that of the Silting Chamber. This arrangement was of help in two ways. First, it did not allow the silt in the lower part of the water-column in the Silting Chamber to get into Tank A. Secondly, since only the water from the upper part of the Silting Chamber entered the Inlet Channel, the water-thrust was also reduced correspondingly.

Tank A

There is stepped ledge in front of the Inlet Channel through which the water passed from the Silting Chamber to Tank A (Pl. no. I). The water from the Inlet Channel did not flow directly on the floor of the Tank A. Instead, it cascaded over a series of steps.

The Tank A is not in a perfect rectangular form. In stead, it widens out a bit evidently to let the incoming water spread out horizontally.

It has two Retaining Walls, one behind the other (pl. no. I). These walls were placed in the terraced fashion and each one leaned backward against the natural soil. This type of arrangement is technically known as vertical warping and is adopted even now-a-days in the construction of water tanks.

There is a yet another feature of this Tank. Its bottom slopes down the southern side i.e., opposite to the Inlet Channel. As a result, silt, whatsoever, still left in the water, was carried down to the southern side and allowed to settle there. In the south-east corner, a staircase (pl. no. I) was provided to take this silt out time to time.

The inner part of the Tank A starts with the turning outwards of the Lowest Retaining Walls from this point to the other side of the channels. There is another platform with 17 courses intact. The inner (south-western) part of the Tank was not only bigger in width than the outer (north-eastern) one but was also relatively deeper. The Lowest Retaining Wall went down to a depth of 47 courses, at one place coming down from the top of the platform of the Second Retaining Wall.

Tank B

The Tank B was the main source of water supply. Staircases were provided to it along the sides at frequent intervals to enable the people to come-down to the level of the water to fetch it. The first lot of steps was provided on the platform which separated Tank B from Tank A. From this platform, two sets of steps went up, one each at the top of the Second Retaining Wall (pl. no. II). The same arrangement was made further to the south. Over two sets of staircases descended down to the level corresponding to the top terrace of the Lowest Retaining Wall. From that level a brick-on-edge ramp ran downwards to be joined on the bed of the tank.

From Interconnecting Channel I the water did not fall directly on the floor of Tank B, but cascaded, as in the case of Tank A, over the series of steps, the final fall being only about half metre. The Channel (Interconnecting Channel I) that carried the water from Tank A to Tank B was located at a height of 1.20 m above the bed of Tank A. This ensured that only clean water from the upper level of Tank A entered into Tank B. The bed of the Channel had a minor slope towards Tank B, 10 cm in a length of 5.30 m. Thereafter, there was a gradual fall of water which cascaded over a flight of ten steps, each step consisting of a single course of bricks (pl. no. II). With this final fall of about 55 cm, the water touched the bed of Tank B. At northern end, Interconnecting Channel-I measured .28 m in the width which expanded to 1.37m at the end of its flow towards Tank B. At its southern most extremity, the width of the Channel is 1.40 m.

Rising from the eastern end of the eastern platform, there was a staircase comprising six steps and leading to the top level of the Second Retaining Wall. In the northern part, Tank B had Three Retaining Walls. Of these the lowest had the maximum height i.e., 3.34 m. consisting of 49 courses of bricks. It sloped back at an angle of about 10° to the vertical. The Second Retaining Wall, placed at a distance of 2.19 m behind the top edge of the Lowest Retaining Wall, stood to a height of 2.09 m and consisted of 32 courses of bricks. The angle of repose of this wall was also about 10° to the vertical. Its width of 43cm was obtained by placing a single brick lengthwise. The Third Retaining Wall was placed 2.14 m behind the Second. It stood to a height of 1.72 m and had 26 courses. Like the Second Retaining Wall, it too was 43 cm. in width. Its angle of slope was about 13° to the vertical. All the retaining walls were interlocked with the natural soil behind by means of short walls placed at suitable intervals. The total height of the Three Retaining Walls was 7.15m from the bed-level. (figure No. :1)

There were four wells unearthed in Tank B. Wells 3 and 4 lay respectively at a distance of about 15m and 20m, south of Wells 1 and 2. While well 3 was nearer to the Lowest Retaining Wall on the western side (figure no. II), well 4 was nearer the corresponding retaining wall on eastern side. Both the wells were found to be circular on plan.

In the southern half of Tank B, at the southeast corner, four retaining walls were noticed. At the southwest corner of Tank B, there was a channel (marked as Interconnecting Channel 2) on the plan (figure no. 1) which carried the water further to the south Inlet Channel. There was a significant rise from the bottom-level of the Silting Chamber. In the Interconnecting Channel I there was, again, a significant rise from the bed of Tank A. In the case of Interconnecting Channel 2, there was no such significant rise from the bed of Tank B.

The width of the opening in the south-west corner of Tank B was 2.20 m at the bottom. The width of this gap at the level of the topmost course of the Lowest Retaining

Wall was 4.37 m. The Interconnecting Channel 2 had no absolute symmetry between its two sides. The Lowest Retaining Wall on its western side measured 20.60 m in length at its base, that on the eastern side, it had a length of 21.60 m. at the corresponding level. At the point of the junction between Interconnecting Channel 2 and Tank C, the width of the channel measured 3.93 m at the lowest points of two opposite corners of the Lowest Retaining Wall.

Tank C

Tank C stands out by itself. It was more or less circular on plan, a feature which, incidentally, breaks the angularity – dominated monotony of the entire complex. This Tank C had three Retaining Walls. At the top-level of the Lowest Retaining Wall, the measurement across, i.e. from one point to another on the opposite side varied from 9.75m to 10.20 m. This variation was due to the fact that the Tank was not in a perfect circular shape. The water that entered the Tank B was clean enough, but which reached Tank C was the cleanest. The diameter of the Tank C kept on increasing with each succeeding Retaining Wall placed behind the one below it. (Plate No. III)

The steps that led from the ground-level on the eastern side of Tank C down to its lower-levels were very winding. The structural components of Tank C are — the Lowest Retaining Wall which is fully intact all around, the Second Retaining Wall and the Third Retaining Wall that does not exist with staircase. The staircase from the top-level of the Second Retaining Wall goes downward; from this level four steps are running in an east-west direction landing mid way within the body of the Second Retaining Wall. From this landing, four steps, running north-south, led down to a single course footing on the top-level of the Lowest Retaining Wall. From here, six steps, also running in the aforesaid direction came down to a landing within the body of the Lowest Revetment. The steps below this landing numbering four, again changed their direction, which this time was east-west. These steps did not reach the bed of Tank C but stopped 13 courses above the bottom of the Lowest Retaining Wall.

The Interconnecting Channel II between Tank B and Tank C and the Lowest two Retaining Walls lying on the western side were extending towards north at a distance of 12.75m from the corner of Tank B. The staircase was important as it was on the right hand side i.e. western side whereas the other staircase of Tank B was found on the eastern-side.

Finally, the storage Tank C which has an outlet for excess water, flowed in the downstream, the river Ganga.

Important antiquities which were recovered from the brick Tank are terracotta head of three-eyed Śiva, head of three eyed-Pārvatī, figure of Kubera, and figure of Hārīti/Shaṣhṭhī, each holding a child, and figure of Naigameṣa etc.

The ancient site of Śṛiṅgaverapura is one of the most important excavated sites of the middle Ganga basin with rich cultural traditions and archaeological remains dating from the end of the second millennium BCE to late medieval period. The site can be compared with similar archaeological sites at Kaushāmbī, Śrāvastī, Rajghat, and Bhita etc., in route from Kaushāmbī to Kapilavastu so far as the material culture and antiquity is concerned.

Period-V (300-600 CE)

The pottery used during this period was a bright Red-Slipped. So far as the shapes are concerned, variants of the ink-pot type lids and sprinklers continued, but bowls with footed base and jars with dropping rim were introduced as the new forms. Moulded pots also appeared. Amongst the antiquities, special mention may be made of terracotta figurines stylistically ascrible to the Gupta times.

Period-VI (600-1300 CE)

This period is marked by the presence of the post Gupta period, from about the sixth-seventh century CE. A noteworthy find of this period was that of silver coins of the Gahadavāla king Chandra, which lay in a small pot along with some jewellery, including a gold ring.

Period-VII (1700-1800 CE)

This is the last period of occupation, found in the excavation. It belonged to larger house complexes; the house walls had been robbed but the plaster was still standing.

The major contribution of the excavation at Śriṅgaverapura is the finding of an historical brick Tank which is unique in the entire Middle Ganga Plain. It was designed in a unique manner. It was fed through a channel which was cut into the natural soil and received water from the up-stream of the Ganga when the river was in spate. Through this Feeding Channel the Ganga water, first got into two successive Silting Chambers; from here, through burnt brick channel, water entered into the Tank A which is paved with usually large bricks. Then water went to Tank B and finally, to the storage tank called Tank C which had a outlet for the excess water in down stream of river Ganga.

Acknowledgements

We are extremely grateful to Professor B.B. Lal former (Director General, Archaeological Survey of India), Shri I.D. Dwivedi, Superintending Archaeological of India, Agra Circle, Agra and Director General, Archaeological Survey of India, New Delhi to reproduce the photographs and drawings. Special thanks to Shri Vishnu Kant Kulshratra, Assistant Superintending Archaeological of India, Excavation Branch, Purana Qila, New Delhi for providing valuable information and suggestions.

References

Lal B.B., (1993) : Excavation at Śriṅgaverapura 1977-86 (Vol. I) *Memoirs of the Archaeological Survey of India* No. 88.

Lal B.B. and Dikshit K.N. : Śriṅgaverapura : A key-site for the Protohistory and Early History of the Central Ganga Valley, Purātattva No. : 10 (1978-79) pp. 1-7.

Lal B.B. : Planned Co-operation between Arcaheologists, Scholars of Ancient Literature – A Crying Need pp. 5-21 : *Man and Environment,* Vol. XVI No. : (January-June 1991)

Indian Archaeology – A Review-1977-78 pp. 54-56.

Indian Archaeology – A Review-1978-79 pp. 57-59.

Indian Archaeology – A Review-1979-80 pp. 73-74.

Indian Archaeology – A Review-1980-81 pp. 67-68.

Indian Archaeology – A Review-1981-82 pp. 66-67.

Indian Archaeology – A Review-1982-83 pp. 91-92.

Indian Archaeology – A Review-1983-84 pp. 84-85.

Indian Archaeology – A Review-1984-85 pp. 85-86.

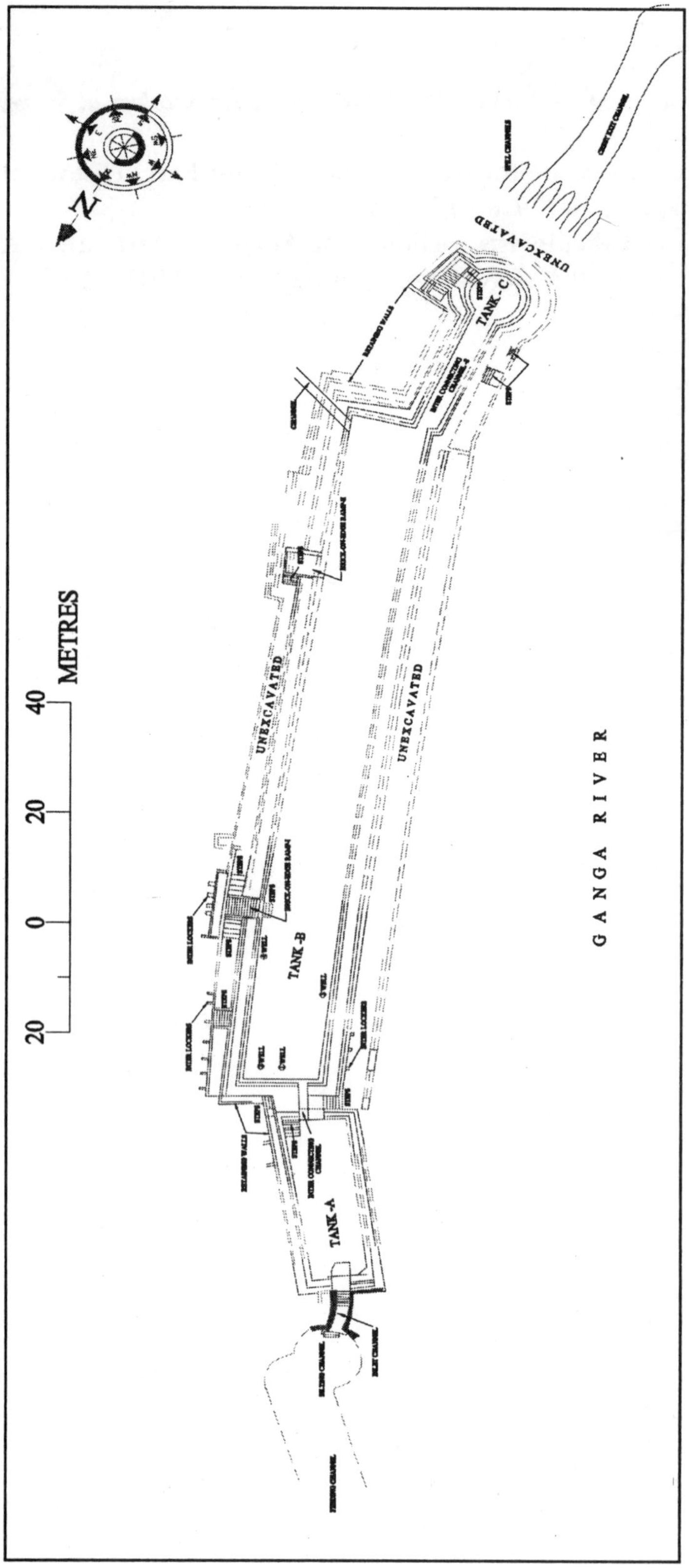

Site Plan of Brick Tank, Śṛiṅgaverapura District - Allahabad

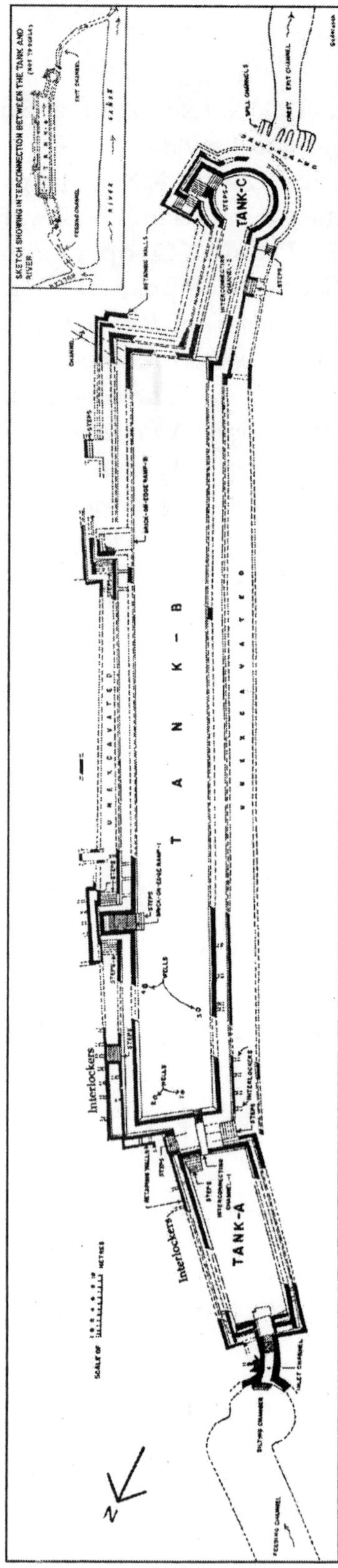

Fig. - 1 : Key plan of Brick Tank

Plate : A view of Silting chamber, Inlet channel and Tank A (after B.B. Lal)

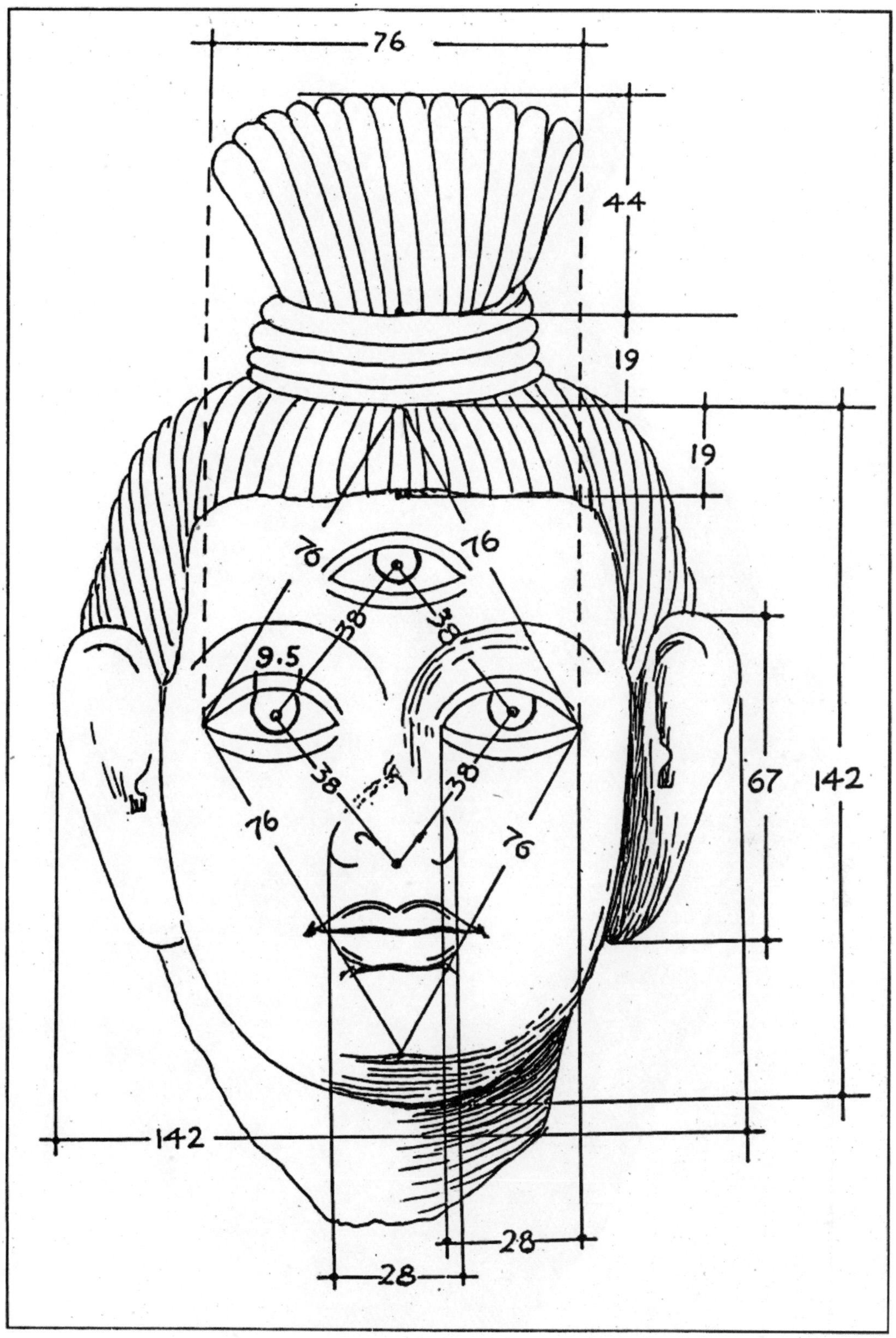

A Terracotta head of three-eyed Shiva (After B.B. Lal)

A Terracotta head of three-eyed Shiva (After B.B. Lal)

A Terracotta head of three-eyed Shiva (After B.B. Lal)

A Terracotta head of three-eyed Shiva (After B.B. Lal)

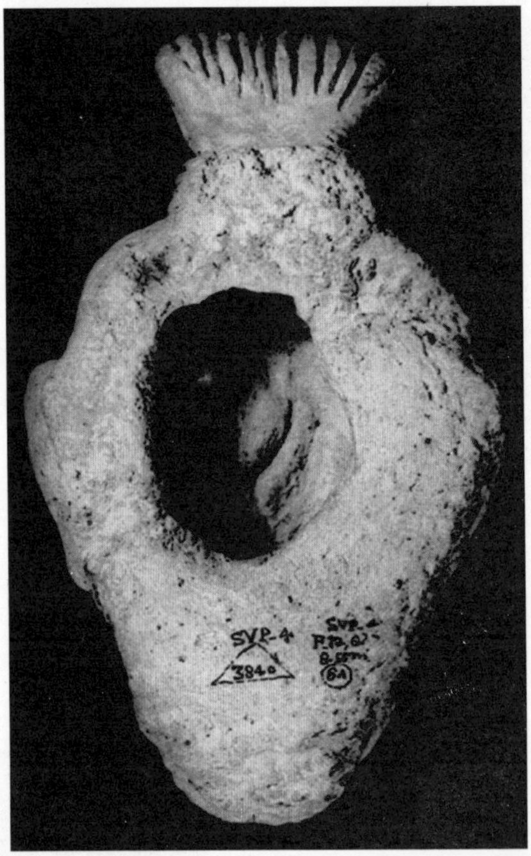

A Terracotta head of three-eyed Shiva (back view) (After B.B. Lal)

A Gold coin of Vasu (After B.B. Lal)

A Terracotta head of Kuber
(After B.B. Lal)

A Terracotta head of Kuber (side view)
(After B.B. Lal)

A Terracotta head (After B.B. Lal)

A Terracotta head of three-eyed Parvati (After B.B. Lal)

17

Some Unique Sculptures of Kaushāmbī

Suniti Pandey

Kaushāmbī (25° 20' 30" N, 81° 23' 12" E) is situated to the left side of river Yamunā about 51.2 Kms. south west of Allahabad. Kaushāmbī, the kingdom of Vatsa Janapada was one of the important city of middle Ganga Valley. Kaushāmbī was epicenter of both political and cultural activities. Archaeological excavations of Kaushāmbī between 1949-66 by the department of Ancient History, Culture and Archaeology, University of Allahabad under the direction of Prof. G. R. Sharma had brought to light many art objects. Various types of stone and clay sculptures, unearthed from Kaushāmbī, are a document of great significance in the history of Indian art.

Motifs in art have always worked as a valuable vehicle to carry important messages not only within the confines of a particular country, but also to distant lands when interaction started during the times of earliest civilization in the world. Transportation of ideas was never restricted to the cultural traits of various societies. Carrying of ideas with the help of motifs had no special bias either for land route or a maritime one. Few winged animals, human beings, anthropomorphic figurines, double humped camels and some unique art motifs of Kaushāmbī reflect the interesting examples of Indian art.

Double humped Camel

On the abacus of the capital of a pillar, a seated double humped camel is depicted surrounded by four lions. These animal figures have been shown in naturalistic form and represent a very significant trend of realism in ancient Indian art. In this motif of Manhai (Kaushāmbī)[1] (Photo 1) belonging to second-first century B.C.E. the central position has been assigned to the gracefully seated double humped camel. The depiction of double humped camel reflect the Bactrian influence on art. On a monumental bas. relief of a procession of tributaries on the north staircase of the Apadana[2] (Persepolis) double humped camel is depicted. Among the tribute-bearers from twenty three countries, that were subject to the empire of King Darius of Persia, were Bactrians with double humped camel (Photo 2). The artistic depiction of the camel in circa 5th century B.C.E. in Persian art influenced the art of India. Copper Coins of Menander also portrays double humped Bactrian camel.

Winged Lions : (Photo 3, Hamdan)

Winged lion motifs have lion figurines with wings on the upper parts of the body. Some terracotta plaques of winged lions (Allahabad Museum, No. 5328, 5418) have been found from Kaushāmbī (Photo 4). On the left side of a plaque is the head of an elephant with a raised trunk and lifted forelegs. Behind the animal's head is a man holding a sword in his right hand, his left extended hand grasps the neck of a charging winged lion standing on its hind legs. The man is wearing a gown with a decorated waist band. On another terracotta plaque (Allahabad Museum, No. 4697) a furious winged lion pouncing upon elephant from the above on the right. The forelegs of the elephant are bent and lifted. He is excreting dung due to fear. A man standing on the left is holding a sword in his right hand probably for attacking the lion. In similar type of terracotta plaque from Kaushāmbī (G. R. Sharma Museum, Allahabad University) a winged lion is pouncing on the elephant and a man is also shown wearing transparent coat without sleeves and grasping lion's neck with his left hand.

The subject of all these examples is similar to the story of Gilgamesh; a hero who is mentioned in clay tablets found at Nippur in Mesopotamia.[3] A hero fighting with winged lion on both sides have been found from Persepolis.[4] The alien motif of winged lion fighting with a man is found on a pillar relief of Mathurā also.[5]The earliest example of this type is found on a seal from Mohenjodaro[6] where a man is grasping neck of a Tiger standing on his lifted forelegs. On the coins of Euthydemus, Demetrius, Kujula Kadaphises - Heracles is shown with skin of lion on his shoulders.[7] Some lion figurines with beautiful leaf shaped curved wings are depicted on the pillars of Kaushāmbī[8] (Photo5). Their whole body has animal character except wings. In the art of Kaushāmbī, belonging to 2nd Century B.C.E. to 1st Century C.E. the winged lion motifs became popular in stone and clay sculpture. Winged animals were popular in foreign art specially in Mesopotamia. Barua[9] mentions that the leonine figures with human or lion faces are represented to relieve the sense of monotony and to improve the tone of rhythm in art. Winged lions are also depicted on the northern gate of Sanchī and Bharhut.[10]

Anthropomorphic Lion

These animals are composite figures having body parts belonging to human being and various animals (Photo 6,7). In some examples belonging to 1st century B.C.E. to 1st Century C.E. face is of human while body neck and ears are of animals. Gradually by 2nd century C.E. the face, skull, hairs, ears, hands and breasts are entirely human. The plain round abacus of a pillar of Kaushāmbī[11] is surmounted by two sets of winged animals with human faces, seated side by side and facing opposite directions. Female faces are round with open eyes and smiling lips and the hair depicted by ridges is plaited in two braids, falling on either side of the head and held by forelegs which are shaped like human hands. The ears are adorned with big disc shaped earrings decorated by spiral lines. The wings have a curled pointed tip and the feathers are indicated first by lozenges and then by lines. The heads and forelegs protrude from the abacus. The lower half of the wing is marked by lozenges while the upper end curves like a leaf (Photo 8). These winged lion motifs have been found from Mathurā, Sānchī, Bharhut, Amrāvatī etc.[12] In these motifs male faced winged lions are wearing turban type headdress on their head. These human faced anthropomorphic lions are depicted in stone sculptures only from Kaushāmbī. Their representation in terracotta art is not visible.

Winged Human figure : (Photo 9)

One of the new and interesting subjects of 2nd -1st century B.C.E. of the art of Kaushāmbī is winged human figures. Though this type of figurines have been found from various sites but the largest number is from Kaushāmbī. On a terracotta plaque a male figurine is wearing turban like headdress on his head. The figurine is decked with earrings, torque, necklace and keyur. A curved wing is shown on his left shoulder (E/61 G.R. Sharma Museum, Allahabad University). In similar type of another example (Allahabad Museum No. 2545) (Photo 10) the man is holding a lotus in his right hand. On a terracotta plaque the male is wearing a turban. His whole body is decorated with ornaments. His left hand is akimbo and in his right hand he is probably holding *Vīnā*. This type of figurines are housed in G.R. Sharma Museum, Allahabad University and Allahabad Museum. In another example (Allahabad Museum, No. 5394) the male is wearing a high headdress, a round earring stumped with rosettes, a thick torque, a necklace with inverted *triratna* pendant and armlets. Below the necklace a peacock head is visible and the decorated wings coming out of shoulders are curved towards the head at the end. In another example (Allahabad Museum, No. 5398) (Photo 11) a man is shown seated on a peacock. He wears a necklace with a round pendant. A semi-circular wing is on his right shoulder; the empty space of the plaque is decorated with rosettes and tiny pin tops.

According to iconographic features and presence of peacock as a vehicle of the deity, it may be a represatation of Kārtikeya though the wings on the shoulders are a strange feature. In stone sculpture this deity is generally seen seated on the back of a peacock but the wings are absent. In the contemporary literary text *Mahābhāṣya*, Patañjali (2nd Century B.C.E.) mentions Skanda but its representation in art is not known. Skanda became popular by the name of Kārtikeya in later period. These winged male figurines are identified with Kāmadeva by V.S. Agrawal.[13] According to him, Kāmadeva is son of Lakshmī. In Pauranic Kośha Kāmadeva is described as born from Lakshmī. Winged male figurine with bow from Mathurā has been identified with Kāmadeva by P. L. Gupta.[14].

The winged figurine with *Vīnā* is termed as Yaksha by G. R. Sharma but the presence of musical instrument – *Vīnā* and wings identify them with Gandharva (*Bhāgvata Purāṇa* 12.08.24).

Besides these winged male terracotta figurines, some winged female terracotta figurines have been found from Basārh (Patna Museum No. 1773, Vaiśālī). Spooner and Zimmer have mentioned that the figure has Mesopotamian influence. The figure is holding lotus stalk in both the hands with wings on the shoulders [15].

Coomarswamy [16] has termed that the deity as winged goddess standing on lotus has West Asiatic influence. According to iconographic features this deity was termed as winged Lakshmī holding lotus flower. The stone sculptures of winged figurines from Bharhut, Sānchī, Amrāvatī, Bodhgayā[17] has interesting features. The upper human part has wings while lower part of the body is like a bird.

Though the references of winged and fabulous animals have been found in Vedic texts but their depiction in the art of early period is conspicuous by their absence. The term lion is used as a simile to denote the strength and vigour of Gods like Indra, Marut and Agni. Winged lion *(Siṁhaḥ Pakṣhagamaḥ, Rāmāyaṇa, Kiṣhkindhā Kāṇḍa, 42.16)* were residing on the Somagiri mountain on the junction of India with the sea. Fabulous animals with different forms were called *Ihā-mṛiga* animals. In Rgveda the mythical forms of animals are called *Yatu*.

The wings applied to animal and human forms are symbolic of divine strength and swiftness. These winged figurines had some decorative value or divinity in Oriental art. They were borrowed from Mesopotamian art to Greek art. In early Greek art the winged male figure or Eros and winged female figure or Nike are constantly occurring in art. Death (Thanatos) often appears as a winged figure in art and his brother Sleep also have similar wings growing from their shoulders. Winged lions are symbolic of royalty, strength, power and divinity.[18]

Yakṣha with Double Flute

Some interesting *yakṣha* figurines from Kaushāmbī have been portrayed holding double flute in clay and stone sculptures. The blowing of double flute was not common in India. Terracotta *yakṣha* figurine (Allahabad Museum, No.543) (Photo 12) with wrinkled face and short legs is depicted blowing double flute from his both hands. The flowing striped skirt held up at the waist indicate the foreign influence on the dress. Another *Yakṣha* terracotta figurine (Allahabad Museum, No 3362) is also blowing double flute. Other terracotta examples of above type have been also found from Mathurā and Bhitā.[19] Another example of stone sculpture from northern gateway of the Sānchī Stūpa[20] a man wearing a peaked cap and short skirt and blowing a double flute. In Buddhist art of Gāndhāra[21] relief a man is depicted blowing double flute. These types of sculptures were popular in foreign countries[22] in 6th-5th century B.C.E. and later periods. This double flute is popular in modern times also and is termed as *Algojā*.

The art of Kaushāmbī portrays an art idiom which borrowed motifs, forms and techniques from other countries (West Asiatic). Ancient Indian art had embraced some decorative motifs influenced by foreign art which exist as signatures of foreign culture and artistic activities. These fabulous animals and winged figurines indicate terrifying aspect of nature while sphinxes – the body of a lion with a human head, projects the combined excellence of mind and body of the king. These motifs portray natural phenomena and animals as living manifestations of the gods. Lion symbolizes the king power and royalty while wings show divinity.

Kaushāmbī was a commercial city situated at a strategic point for trade and commerce therefore the population of the city must have comprised people of different nationalities, creeds and vocations. Some of the foreigners stayed back in India and were assimilated in the Indian culture. As a result, the artist who was receptive to new trends and tendencies had adopted alien features, symbols and motifs in their artistic activities. These new motifs have been portrayed in art from Post-Mauryan period due to free environment for the development of art. Infiltration of alien themes and artifacts were natural sequence of foreign contacts. Thus the art of Kaushāmbī provides some unique, rare and interesting sculptures which have important place in the field of ancient Indian art.

References

1. Sharma, G.R (Ed.) *History to Prehistory*, Allahabad University, 1980 p.31.
2. Huot, Jean Louis, *Persia* Vol .1, from its origins to the Achaemenids, Nagel Publishers Geneva, 1965, photo No 16.
3. *Iraq*, Vol. XXXVIII, pt. I, p.23.
4. Schemidt, *Persopolis* II, pl. V.12
5. Agrwal, V.S, *Indian Art*, Prithvi Prakashan, Varanasi, 2003, fig 383.
6. Mackay, E.J.H., *Further excavation at Mohan-jodaro*, Munshiram Manohar Lal Publisher Pvt. Ltd. New Delhi 1998, Vol. II, pl. LXXXIV, Fig 75. Whitehead.
7. R.B.,Catalogue of coins in the Panjab Museum, Lahore, Indic Academy Varanasi, 1971, Vol. I- *Indo-Greek Coins*, pl.1.8, 18, 19; pl.XVII.8.
8. Sharma G.R, *Op. cit.*, p.50.
9. Barua, B.M., *Barhut Stone as a story Teller*, Indological Book Corporation, 1979 pt.I, p.58.
10. Barua, *Op.cit.*, Section III pl. XXXII-25 Marshall and Foucher, *The Monuments of Sanchī*, Vol. III, pl. LXXXIX 7 a-b, pl. XCVIII.
11. Sharma, R., *op.cit.*, p.50 (Housed in G.R Sharma Museum, Allahabad University)
12. Agrawal, V.S., *Op.cit.*, fig 60-63 p.252.
13. Agrawal,V.S , *Op.cit.*, p.324.
14. Mathurā museum, No.2849 Gupta, P.L., *Gangetic Valley Terracotta Art*, Prithvi Prakashan Varanasi 1972, p.91.
15. Zimmer, H., *Myths and Symbols in Indian Art*, Pantheon Books, Newyork, 1946 p.93, Archaeological Survey of India 1913-14.
16. Coomarswamy A., *History of Indian and Indonesian Art*, Dover Publication, New York, p.12.
17. Barua, *Op.cit.*, pt. II, pl. LII ,LIII ,XXI; Marshall and Foucher, *Op.cit.*, Vol III, Pl. XCVIII , XVIII; Sivarammurti , Amrāvatī ,pl. XVI , fig 2.
18. *Encyclopedia of Religion and Ethics*, Ed. By James Hastings, Edinburg T & T Clark, New York 1974, Vol. 12, pt12, p. 740-41.
19. Mathurā, Pl. XII, 40, *Journal of U.P. Historical Society* IX., pl. 12-407; Indian Museum, Calcutta No.12670, Bhitā.
20. Zimmer H., *The Art of Indian Asia*, McClelland & Stewart, Ltd. Toranto, 1955, Vol. 2, pl. 10.
21. Marshall, John, *The Buddhist Art of Gāndhāra,* University Press, Cambridge 1960, Fig 82.
22. *Encyclopedia of World Art*, Vol .I, New York, Toronto, London, 1959 p.360 Archaeology Vol XXI, No2, 1969, p. 130, *Encyclopaedia of theAmerican Academy in Rome*, Vol. II , Pl. 21, Fig. 5.
Higgins, *A Catalogue of Terracottas in the Department of Greek and Roman Antiquties*, British Museum, London, 1954, Vol. I, Fig 1179.

Photo - 1

Photo - 2

Photo - 3

Photo - 4

Photo - 5

Photo - 6

Photo – 7

Photo - 8

Photo - 9

Photo – 10

Photo - 11

Photo - 12

18

काशी-सारनाथ की गुप्तकालीन कला शैली

मारुति नन्दन तिवारी

काशी, परंपरा और इतिहास, दोनों ही दृष्टियों से विश्व की प्राचीनतम नगरियों में एक है, जिसका महत्त्व धर्म और संस्कृति के समन्वयमूलक अजस्त्र प्रवाह के कारण विश्व की अन्य किसी भी प्राचीन नगरी की तुलना में कहीं अधिक है। पुण्यतोया गंगा काशी की आत्मा और पहचान हैं, जो भारतीय परंपरा की संवाहिनी और ब्राह्मण देवत्रयी (ब्रह्मा-विष्णु-शिव) से सम्बद्ध हैं, जो गगा की विलक्षणता है।

कला और संस्कृति की चर्चा करते समय पता नहीं किन कारणों से सारनाथ और उसके प्रारंभिक एवम् परवर्ती, कलावशेषों की प्रस्तुति कुछ इस रूप में हुई है मानों सारनाथ की काशी से अलग स्वतंत्र सत्ता थी? वास्तव में सारनाथ काशी के व्यापक भौगोलिक, सांस्कृतिक परिसीमन का ही भाग रहा है। अत: काशी की संस्कृति एवं कला की चर्चा के प्रसंग में एक समग्र दृष्टि के अंतर्गत सारनाथ और काशी-वाराणसी के विभिन्न भागों का समवेत रूप में अध्ययन किया जाना चाहिए, तभी सही मायने में संस्कृति एवं कला की दृष्टि के संदर्भ में उसके योगदान का मूल्यांकन किया जा सकता है। प्रस्तुत लेख में गुप्तकालीन कला की पृष्ठभूमि में हम काशी-सारनाथ शीर्षक के अंतर्गत वस्तुत: यही प्रयास करेंगे।

यदि पुरातात्त्विक साक्ष्यों को देखें तो पांचवी शती ई. में जिस समय सारनाथ में श्रेष्ठतम् बौद्ध मूर्तियाँ (चित्र सं. 2-3) बन रही थी, उसी समय काशी के विभिन्न क्षेत्रों में भी गुप्त कला शैली की जीवंत मूर्तियों का निर्माण हो रहा था। राजघाट (मृण एवं प्रस्तर मूर्तियाँ, सुंदर केश सज्जा वाली नारी एवं अर्द्धनारीश्वर मूर्तियों के खंडित शीर्ष भाग, नेमिनाथ की प्रस्तर मूर्ति), बकरियाकुण्ड (गोवर्धन धारी कृष्ण की महाप्रमाण मूर्ति-सम्प्रति भारत कला भवन, वाराणसी में संगृहीत, चित्र सं.5), कन्दवा (12वीं शती के कर्दमेश्वर मंदिर के दक्षिण अधिष्ठान में बाद में संलग्न की गई गुप्तकालीन शिव गण आकृति, भेलूपुर (तिलाभाण्डेश्वर मन्दिर की शिवलिंग एवं दक्षिणामूर्ति शिव की मनोहारी मूर्ति), गायघाट (मयूर पंखों के सुंदर फैलाव से निर्मित प्रभामंडल वाली शूलधारी कार्त्तिकेय की भव्य मूर्ति,

चि. सं. 6), चौक (ध्यानस्थ महावीर की आध्यात्मिक चिन्तन में डूबी मनोज्ञ मूर्ति, चित्र सं. 8) गुप्तकालीन कलाकृतियाँ (भैरव तालाब का एक मुखी शिवलिंग) काशी में गुप्तकला की व्यापकता की दृष्टि से उल्लेखनीय हैं।

सारनाथ में मौर्य शासक अशोक के समय (तीसरी शती ई.पू.) कला की गतिविधियाँ प्रारंभ हुईं। स्तूप (धर्मराजिका स्तूप) एवं सिंह शीर्ष स्तंभ (चित्र सं. 01) सारनाथ में मौर्यकला के श्रेष्ठतम उदाहरण हैं। कुषाण काल में सारनाथ की कलात्मक गतिविधियों में एक ठहराव की स्थिति थी, तभी मथुरा से भिक्षु बल द्वारा निर्मित बोधिसत्व की विशाल प्रतिमा सारनाथ आयी जो कुषाण कला का एक मुख्य उदाहरण है। गुप्तकाल में (चौथी शती ई. के अंत से छठी शती ई. के मध्य) स्वतंत्र कला शैली एवं बौद्ध विषयक मूर्त स्वरूपों, दोनों ही स्तरों पर सारनाथ की कला-श्रेष्ठता पुनः स्थापित हुई।

सारनाथ की गुप्तकालीन मूर्तियाँ निःसंदेह भारतीय कला की सर्वश्रेष्ठ कृतियां हैं, जिनमें शैली का परिष्कार और ओज स्पष्ट है। ध्यानमुद्रा, धर्मचक्र प्रवर्त्तन मुद्रा, भूमि स्पर्श मुद्रा में बैठी और अभय एवं वरदमुद्रा में खड़ी बुद्ध की भावपूर्ण मूर्तियों में आध्यात्मिक चिन्तन की अभिव्यक्ति श्रेष्ठतम स्तर पर हुई है। इन मूर्तियों में हल्के और इकहरे बदनवाली बुद्ध आकृतियों का आवयविक अनुपात, शारीरिक सौष्ठव और ओज प्रशंसनीय है। पारदर्शक वस्त्र तथा आकृतियों में लता-वल्लरियों का लयात्मक प्रवाह, उनकी ऊर्जा और स्वरूप-सौंदर्य दोनों को व्यक्त करते हैं। बुद्ध के आध्यात्मिक चिन्तन और अन्तर्दृष्टि के भाव की सहज अभिव्यक्ति इन कृतियों की भावभूमि को एक दूसरे ही स्तर पर ले जाती है, जो काशी-सारनाथ की गुप्त कालीन मूर्तियों का निजस्व रहा है।

सारनाथ संग्रहालय में सुरक्षित धर्मचक्रप्रवर्तन मुद्रा वाली बुद्ध की पद्मासीन मूर्ति गुप्त कला ही नहीं वरन् संपूर्ण भारतीय कला की एक अद्वितीय रचना है। प्रस्तुत मूर्ति में बाह्य (कायिक) और अभ्यंतर (आध्यात्मिक) मान्यताओं को पूर्ण संतुलित रूप में संयोजित और अभिव्यक्त किया गया है। भारतीय मान्यताओं और स्वरूपात्मक लक्षणों का संतुलन तथा आध्यात्मिक चिन्तन का भाव बुद्ध के लोककल्याणकारी स्वरूप को अभिव्यक्त करता है। बुद्ध के मुख पर आध्यात्मिक शान्ति और करुणा का भाव है। आसन पर मध्य में स्थित धर्मचक्र के दोनों पार्श्वों में दानदाताओं की एवं अन्य आकृतियाँ बनी हैं जो मानो बुद्ध के धर्मोपदेश का लाभ उठा रही हैं। पारदर्शी वस्त्र बुद्ध के शारीरिक सौष्ठव की अभिव्यक्ति में पूर्णतया समर्थ है। इस मूर्ति में गंधर्वद्वय से वेष्ठित अलंकृत प्रभामंडल अलौकिक है, जिसके अलंकरण में काशी की पाषाण उकेरन की दक्षता और भव्यता दोनों प्रतिबिम्बित हैं। पीठिका पर धर्मचक्र के दोनों ओर दो मृग आकृतियों का अंकन बुद्ध के उपदेशों की अभीष्ट परिणति शांति का प्रतीकात्मक प्रस्तुति है।

धर्मचक्र प्रवर्तन मुद्रा वाली मूर्ति के अतिरिक्त सारनाथ से बुद्ध की भूमिस्पर्श मुद्रा में भी कई मूर्तियाँ प्राप्त हुई हैं। साथ ही, बुद्ध की कई मानवाकार स्थानक मूर्तियां भी मिली हैं, जिनमें उन्हें अभयमुद्रा में अभय प्रदान करते रूपायित किया गया है। उपरोक्त सभी मूर्तियाँ सारनाथ संग्रहालय में सुरक्षित हैं। ये मूर्तियाँ गुप्तशैली के ओज और जीवन्तता की उदाहरण हैं।

सारनाथ में गुप्तकाल में ही बौद्ध देववाद का अतिशय विस्तार हुआ, जिसमें काशी के शिल्पियों का भी महत्त्वपूर्ण योगदान था। इसी समय बुद्धचरित और उनसे संबंधित महत्त्वपूर्ण घटनाओं (जन्म, महाभिनिष्क्रमण, संबोधि और परिनिर्वाण) को साथ-साथ एक ही फलक पर उत्कीर्ण करने की परंपरा लोकप्रिय हुई। कथात्मक विषयों की सूक्ष्मता के साथ उत्कीर्णन, इन मूर्तियों की दुर्लभ विशेषताएँ हैं। ऐसे कुछ फलकों पर केवल चार दृश्य-जन्म, संबांधि, धर्मचक्रप्रवर्तन और निर्वाण ही प्रदर्शित हैं, जबकि कुछ में बुद्ध जीवन से संबंधित आठ घटनाओं का अंकन किया गया है। सारनाथ संग्रहालय में प्रदर्शित एक फलक पर क्रमशः बुद्ध के जन्म, मारघर्षण और साथ में संबोधि तथा निर्वाण की घटनाएँ उकेरी हैं। ऊपर बुद्ध के भिक्षादान तथा नलगिरि गज को शांत करने जैसे आख्यान उकेरे हैं। इसी फलक पर तीसरे खंड में स्वर्ग से बुद्ध के अवतरण और इसके पार्श्व में श्रावस्ती के चमत्कार का दृश्यांकन है, जिसमें बुद्ध अनेक बुद्ध के रूप में प्रदर्शित हैं। सबसे ऊपरी खंड में धर्म चक्र-प्रवर्तन और उसके पार्श्वों में निर्वाण दृश्य हैं।

मथुरा से कौशाम्बी होते हुए काशी-सारनाथ की कला शैली पूरी तरह परिष्कृत रूप में और श्रेष्ठतम् स्तर पर सारनाथ सहित काशी में सर्वत्र अभिव्यक्त हुई जिसमें उसका सहज और प्रकृति-नैकट्य रूप प्रकट हुआ। गुप्तोत्तर काल में छठी शती के उत्तरार्द्ध से एक कला-केन्द्र के रूप में काशी-सारनाथ के महत्त्व का विस्तार होता है, जिसे पूर्वी भारत की पाल शैली की बिहार-बंगाल की मूर्तियों में प्रमाण के रूप में स्पष्टतः देखा जा सकता है। यह प्रभाव विस्तार निश्चित तौर पर काशी-सारनाथ की पूर्वांचल की गुप्तकला शैली के सहज-स्वाभाविक कलात्मक सौंदर्य और प्रकृति-साहचर्य (लताओं और पुष्प अलंकरण वाला प्रभामंडल) एवं मानवाकृतियों की शारीरिक रचना में कालिदास की रचना के अनुरूप प्रकृति के तत्वों के समागम के कारण ही अन्य क्षेत्रों में स्वीकार्य हुआ।

काशी की संस्कृति और इतिहास पर विचार करने से प्रतीत होता है कि पुरातात्विक दृष्टि से राजघाट और साहित्यिक दृष्टि से कम से कम महाभारत काल यानी 1000 से 800 ई.पू. के मध्य काशी का सांस्कृतिक-राजनीतिक महत्त्व स्थापित हो चुका था। यह विद्या और ज्ञान की नगरी थी, इसीलिए बोधगया में ज्ञान प्राप्ति के बाद बुद्ध ने काशी की ओर प्रस्थान किया और काशी में शान्त और प्राकृतिक-आध्यात्मिक ऊर्जा सम्पन्न उस स्थल को धर्म चक्र प्रवर्तन (उपदेश) के लिए चुना जो छठी शती ई. पू. में सारनाथ के नाम से ज्ञात नहीं था। सारनाथ का स्वतंत्र उल्लेख बुद्ध के काशी आने के काफी बाद से मिलता है। वस्तुतः ऐतिहासिक-सांस्कृतिक अध्ययन में काशी के व्यापक संदर्भ में सारनाथ का उल्लेख काशी-सारनाथ के रूप में करना ही उचित होगा और पूर्वांचल की गुप्तकला शैली को काशी-सारनाथ शैली कहना अधिक समीचीन होगा।

गुप्तकाल में सारनाथ में जहाँ केवल बौद्ध मूर्तियाँ बनी, वहीं काशी के अन्य भागों में ब्राह्मण धर्म से संबंधित शिव (शिवलिंग, दक्षिणामूर्ति, शिवगण), विष्णु की गोवर्धनधारी कृष्ण, कार्त्तिकेय (दो मूर्तियाँ) और जैन तीर्थंकर (महावीर एवं नेमिनाथ) तथा बुद्ध की भी कुछ मूर्तियाँ बनीं। भारत कला भवन में वाराणसी से मिली अधिकांश मूर्तियाँ सुरक्षित हैं।

काशी के विभिन्न क्षेत्रों की गुप्तकालीन मूर्तियों में सहज, स्वाभाविक शरीर रचना एवं भाव तथा नैसर्गिक एवं निश्च्छल सौंदर्य समान रूप से द्रष्टव्य हैं। सारनाथ की भूमि स्पर्श-मुद्रा में या धर्मचक्र प्रवर्तन मुद्रा में बुद्ध की मूर्ति हो या फिर राजघाट, चौखम्भा, चौक, गायघाट, भेलूपुर (तिलभाण्डेश्वर मन्दिर) एवं बकरियाकुण्ड क्षेत्रों से प्राप्त कार्त्तिकेय (दो मूर्तियाँ), गोवर्धनधारी कृष्ण, अर्द्धनारीश्वर, दक्षिणामूर्ति शिव एवं एकमुखी शिवलिंग या महावीर की मूर्तियाँ हों या शिवगण की आकृति (कर्दमेश्वर मंदिर, कन्दवा) हों - सभी उदाहरणों में ऊर्जा, जीवन्तता एवं अन्य गुप्त कलाशैली की विशेषताएँ समान रूप से व्यक्त हैं। इनमें समान रूप से अलंकरण तथा रूप-सज्जा किंचित् भी कृत्रिम न होकर मनभावन और सहज हैं। शारीरिक चेष्टाएँ और मुखाकृतियों के भाव विषयानुरूप और मनग्राही हैं। यदि सारनाथ की धर्मचक्र प्रवर्तन मुद्रा वाली श्रेष्ठतम् मूर्ति में बुद्ध के मुख पर करुणा और गहन चिंतन का भाव व्यक्त हुआ है तो भेलूपुर के समीप तिलभाण्डेश्वर मन्दिर की दक्षिणामूर्ति में भी वही ओजपूर्ण भाव है। दोनों ही मूर्तियों की भाव-भूमि एक है, केवल अभिव्यक्ति का कलेवर एक दूसरे से अलग दिखता है, ठीक वैसे ही जैसे व्यक्ति-व्यक्ति में बाह्य दृष्टि से भेद होता है। जहाँ तक मुखमण्डल का प्रश्न है, मूर्ति चाहे सारनाथ की बुद्ध मूर्ति हो या काशी के अन्य क्षेत्रों से प्राप्त कार्त्तिकेय, गोवर्धनधारी कृष्ण या तीर्थंकर की मूर्ति हों, आकृतियाँ पूरी तरह तरुण रूप में ऊर्जायुक्त एवं सहज दिखायी गयी हैं।

संदर्भ

वी.एस. अग्रवाल, ''गुप्त आर्ट'', *जर्नल ऑफ दि यूनाइटेड प्रोविन्स हिस्टॉरिकल सोसाइटी*, खण्ड 18, अंक 1-2, जुलाई-दिसम्बर, 1945, पृ. 101-34।; ''सारनाथ'', डिपार्टमेण्ट ऑफ आर्कियोलॉजी, दिल्ली, 1965।; *गुप्त आर्ट*, वाराणसी, 1977

एस.के. सरस्वती, *ए सर्वे ऑफ इण्डियन स्कल्पचर*, कोलकाता, 1957

एस.पी. गुप्ता, *रूट्स ऑफ इण्डियन आर्ट*, दिल्ली, 1980
जे.सी. हार्ल, *गुप्त स्कल्पचर्स*, आक्सफोर्ड, 1974
जोहाना जी. विलियम, *दि आर्ट ऑफ गुप्त इंडिया-इम्पायर ऐण्ड प्रॉविन्स*, नई दिल्ली, 1983
रमानाथ मिश्र, *भारतीय मूर्तिकला का इतिहास*, दिल्ली, 1978
स्टेला क्रमरिश, *इण्डियन स्कल्पचर्स*, कोलकाता, 1933
एम.एन.पी. तिवारी, ''जैन आर्ट ऑफ गुप्त पीरियड'', *मार्ग* (दि गोल्डेन एज-स्पेशल वाल्यूम), (सम्पा.), कार्ल खण्डेलवाला
उषा रानी तिवारी, *स्कल्पचर्स ऑफ मथुरा एण्ड सारनाथ - ए कम्परेटिव स्टडी*, नई दिल्ली, 1998
एस.एल. हन्टीगटन, *दि आर्ट ऑफ एशियण्ट इण्डिया*, न्यूयार्क, टोक्यो, 1985
पी.के. अग्रवाल, ''गुप्त टेम्पल आर्किटेक्चर'', *प्रज्ञा* (काशी हिन्दू विश्वविद्यालय), खण्ड 8(1), 1967, पृ. 51-65

छायाचित्र 1 : अशोककालीन सिंह-शीर्ष, सारनाथ

छायाचित्र 2 : सारनाथ की गुप्त-कालीन बुद्ध मूर्ति (धर्मचक्र प्रवर्तन)

छायाचित्र 3 : बुद्धा-प्रीचिंग (दो हिरण) सारनाथ, 5वीं शताब्दी ई., नेशनल म्यूज़ियम, दिल्ली

छायाचित्र 4 : बुद्ध, मथुरा, 5वीं शताब्दी ई., राजकीय म्यूज़ियम, मथुरा

छायाचित्र 5 : गोवर्धनधारी कृष्ण, वाराणसी (उत्तर प्रदेश), चौथी शताब्दी ई. भारत कला भवन (ए. नं. 147)

छायाचित्र 6 : कार्तिकेय, वाराणसी (उत्तर प्रदेश), पांचवी शताब्दी ई. भारत कला भवन (ए. नं. 156)

छायाचित्र 7 : गुप्तकालीन गण, कर्दमेश्वर मंदिर, वाराणसी

छायाचित्र 8 : गुप्तकालीन महावीर मूर्ति, वाराणसी (भारत कला भवन)

19

अभिलेखों में पूर्वी उत्तर प्रदेश

विपुला दुबे

सत्ताईस जिलों से निर्मित पूर्वी उत्तर प्रदेश अपनी भौगोलिक संरचना (चित्र सं० 1), समशीतोष्ण जलवायु, वनस्पतियों की बहुलता एवं जल की प्रचुरता के कारण आदिकाल से ही मानव के आकर्षण का केन्द्र रहा है, जिसका प्रमाण यहाँ के नव पाषाणकालीन पुरास्थल (कोल्डीहवा, महगड़ा, सोहगौरा, लहुरादेवा इत्यादि) एवं पुराभिलेख हैं। उल्लेख्य है कि इस अंचल से प्राप्त अभिलेखों में भी इस क्षेत्र की प्राकृतिक संरचना की अभिव्यक्ति 'सौम्य सिन्धु', 'उत्तर समुद्र', 'दरद गण्डकी', 'सरूवार' जैसे अभिधानों में हुई है।[1]

इतिहास संरचना के वस्तुनिष्ठ साक्ष्य अभिलेखों के उत्कीर्णन की अविकल परम्परा मौर्य सम्राट अशोक के काल से आरम्भ हुई लेकिन पाँच ऐसे अभिलेख प्राप्त हैं[2] जो अपनी लिपिगत विशेषता, विषय–वस्तु, एवं लेखन शैली के आधार पर प्राङ् मौर्य युगीन माने जाते हैं। यह मात्र संयोग है या इस पूर्वी अंचल का वैशिष्ट्य कि भारत के इन प्राचीनतम अभिलेखों में से दो अभिलेख : पिपरहवा बौद्धकलश लेख[3] एवं सोहगौरा ताम्रपत्र अभिलेख[4] इसी क्षेत्र से सम्बद्ध हैं। ध्यानाहर्य है कि पूर्वी उत्तर प्रदेश से बहुसंख्यक अभिलेख (द्र0. अभिलेखों की सूची सं0 2), मुहरें, एवं मृण्मुद्राएँ मिली हैं,[5] जो इस क्षेत्र के इतिहास की मुखर साक्षी हैं।

प्रस्तुत आलेख में पुराभिलेखों में उपन्यस्त पूर्वी उत्तर प्रदेश के इतिहास के विविध पक्षों का एक सर्वेक्षण तथा अभिलेखों का संक्षिप्त इतिवृत्त प्रस्तुत है।

पूर्वी उत्तर प्रदेश के सिद्धार्थनगर जनपद के पिपरहवा नामक स्थान से प्राप्त बौद्ध कलश लेख भारत का प्राचीनतम अभिलेख है। इस बौद्धकलश लेख की प्राप्ति डब्लू0सी0 पेप्पे महोदय को 1898 ई0 में उस समय हुई थी जब वे पिपरहवा के टीले का उत्खनन करवा रहे थे। स्तूप के भीतरी भाग से अन्य अवशेषों के साथ एक अभिलिखित कलश भी मिला, जिसकी गर्दन (शीर्ष) पर दो पंक्तियों में लेख खचित है। इसका उद्वाचन सर्वप्रथम ब्यूलर महोदय ने किया तथा लेख का प्रकाशन भी उसी वर्ष *जर्नल ऑव द रोयल एशियाटिक सोसाइटी* (1898,

पृ0 387) में किया गया। प्राक् मौर्य ब्राह्मी में निबद्ध इस लेख की विषय–वस्तु से ज्ञात है कि शाक्य मुनि बुद्ध के 'देहावशेष' को पवित्र स्मृति के रूप में कलश (मंजूषा) में स्थापित किया गया था। इस पुनीत कार्य को तथागत के शाक्य वंशीय बन्धुओं ने ही सम्पन्न किया। लेख में कहा गया है कि सुकीर्ति ने अपने भाईयों, बहनों, पुत्रों, दाराओं (पत्नियों) के साथ मिलकर शाक्य भगवान् बुद्ध के शरीरावशेष को स्थापित किया। सिंहली परम्परा से भगवान बुद्ध के महापरिनिर्वाण की तिथि 483 ई. पू. ज्ञात है। इस लेख की लिपि भी पाँचवी शताब्दी ई. पू. के उत्तरार्द्ध की प्रतीत होती है क्योंकि इसमें दीर्घ स्वरों एवं ऊष्म वर्णों (श, ष, ह) का अभाव है। अस्तु महापरिनिर्वाण के पश्चात् ही किसी समय बुद्ध के शरीरावशेष को निधि के रूप में संरक्षित किया गया तथा उसके ऊपर स्तूप बनाया गया। यह अभिलेख *महापरिनिब्बान सुत्त* के उस उद्धरण को पुष्ट आधार प्रदान करता है जिसमें तथागत के शरीरावशेष से कपिलवस्तु के शाक्यों द्वारा हिस्सा मांगने का दावा करने तथा कुशीनारा के मल्लों द्वारा उसे आठ भागों में विभाजित करने का उल्लेख है।[6]

पूर्वी वर्ग की प्राकृत भाषा एवं दो पंक्तियों में निबद्ध यह लेख गेय है। यद्यपि इसका छन्द स्पष्ट नहीं है तथापि कतिपय अभिलेख शास्त्रियों ने इसे आर्या, उपगीति अथवा उद्गीति छन्द में निबद्ध बताया है।[7] यह अभिलेख तथागत के देहावशेष को निधि के रूप में स्थापित करने का प्रथम साक्ष्य है। ध्यातव्य है कि छन्दोबद्ध अभिलेख लिखने की परम्परा गुप्त काल से आरम्भ हुई, इस दृष्टि से भी इसका महत्त्व बढ़ जाता है। यह अभिलेख सिद्ध करता है कि संघ में महिलाओं के प्रवेश ने बुद्ध से जुडे श्रमण भक्तों की दृष्टि को उदार बनाया क्योंकि ब्राह्मण परम्परा में 'शरीरावशेष' को पवित्र नदी में प्रवाहित करने अथवा अन्तिम संस्कार में भाग लेने का अधिकार महिलाओं को नहीं था जबकि यह लेख तथागत के शरीरावशेष को कलश में स्थापित करने के पुनीत कार्य में महिलाओं (भगिनि, दाराओं) की सहभागिता की लिखित सूचना प्रदान करता है।

इस क्षेत्र के पुराभिलेखों में सोहगौरा ताम्रपत्र का अपना अलग ही वैशिष्ट्य है। संयोगात् भारत के प्राचीनतम पुराभिलेखों में परिगणित सोहगौरा ताम्र लेख[8] गोरखपुर जनपद के बाँसगाँव तहसील के सोहगौरा नामक स्थान से प्राप्त है। आमी एवं अचिरावती के संगम पर बसा सोहगौरा जहाँ आदि जन सन्निवेश का प्राचीनतम स्थल है, वहीं यहाँ से प्राप्त 'ताम्रलेख' 'सुशासन' का प्राचीनतम लिखित दस्तावेज भी है।

इस ताम्रलेख का आन्तरिक एवं बाह्य साक्ष्य, विषयवस्तु एवं ताम्रपत्र के शीर्ष भाग पर अंकित तीन मंजिले दो अन्नागार (कोष्ठागार), कमल कलिकायुक्त नाल, प्राकार में वृक्ष, अर्द्धचन्द्र, प्रतीकात्मक महत्व रखते हैं। ये चिन्ह आहत मुद्राओं पर प्राप्त होते हैं, तथा चित्रलिपि से अक्षरलिपि तक आने का इतिहास प्रस्तुत करते हैं। ये चिन्ह सोहगौरा ताम्र–लेख की विषय वस्तु की मूक व्याख्या करते प्रतीत होते हैं, (चित्र सं0 2) जिसकी विवेचना आगे की गयी है।

सोहगौरा ताम्र लेख कई दृष्टियों से महत्वपूर्ण है। प्रथम तो यह कि उच्चपदस्थ राजकर्मचारियों (श्रावस्ती के महामात्रों) की ओर से निर्गत 'शासन' का यह पहला लिखित प्रमाण है। इस लेख में दो कोष्ठागारों में राज्य की ओर से संगृहीत 'अन्न' के सम्बन्ध में स्पष्ट आदेश है कि इसे आपातकाल में ही उपयोग में लाया जाय सामान्य स्थिति में इसके अन्न को कोई ग्रहण न करें, (निश्चय ही यह राजाज्ञा एवं अन्न का संग्रह राज–शासन की सतर्कता का अद्भुत उदाहरण है)। इस लेख की लिपिगत विशेषता, ताम्रपत्र के शीर्ष भाग पर अंकित चिह्नों के आधार पर अधिकांश अभिलेखशास्त्री इसे प्राङ्–मौर्य युगीन मानते हैं। स्पष्ट है कि अति प्राचीन काल से इस क्षेत्र की जनता को कभी नदियों की बाढ़ की विभीषिका से, तो कभी अनावृष्टि जैसी प्राकृतिक आपदाओं के कारण संकट का सामना करना पड़ता था, जिसके प्रति श्रावस्ती के महामात्रों के कार्यक्षेत्र में आने वाली बांसगांव तहसील के उन गाँवों के निवासियों के प्रति राज शासन इतना सचेत था जो इस प्रकार की आपदा से सर्वाधिक प्रभावित होते थे। ध्यातव्य है कि 'शासन' (Charters) की उत्पत्ति ही सत्य संरक्षण, दुर्व्यवस्था के दूरीकरण एवं

जनकल्याण की स्थापना के लिए हुई, न कि राजाओं के शौर्य वर्णन के लिए । विषय–वस्तु के आधार पर अभिलेख दो वर्गों में विभक्त है – प्रतिष्ठा शासन एवं दानशासन या ताम्र शासन। सोहगौरा ताम्रपत्र की विषय–वस्तु प्रच्छन्न रीति से 'कोष्ठागार' का निर्माण एवं उनमें संगृहीत अन्न के सम्बन्ध में आदेश है, इसलिए यह लेख प्रतिष्ठा शासन के अन्तर्गत ही परिगणित होना चाहिए। लेख में 'वसगमे' (बाँसगाँव) के पूर्व आये 'सिलिमाते' पद की व्याख्या आदेश पत्र की प्रकृति को ध्यान में रखकर नहीं की गयी है। कुछ अभिलेख शास्त्री इसे बांसगांव का विशेषण मानकर इसका अर्थ 'श्रीमान' करते हैं,[9] जो कोष्ठागार के सन्दर्भ में उचित नहीं प्रतीत होता। यहाँ 'सिलिमाते' कोष्ठागार की संरक्षिका देवी का सूचक प्रतीत होता है। ध्यातव्य है कि ऋग्वेदीय[10] युग में चान्द्रदेवी 'सिनीवाली' अन्नदेवी, पशुधन की देवी के रूप में प्रतिष्ठित थीं। यास्क ने निरुक्त[11] में सिनीवाली की व्याख्या अन्न (*'सिनं अन्नं भवति'*) किया है। यह चान्द्र (**First moon day**) शक्ति, उर्वरता, आह्लाद, गर्भसंरक्षण की देवी के रूप में जानी जाती थी। यही देवी अथर्ववेद[12] में विष्णु पत्नी के रूप में वर्णित है तथा इस देवी तथा सरस्वती को 'वाजिनीवती' विशेषण से सम्बोधित किया गया है जिसका अर्थ होता है 'अन्न शक्ति'। रामायण में सीता को 'धान्यमालिनी' कहा गया है जो इन देवियों के अन्नवती होने की सूचना प्रदान करता है। इसलिये यहाँ इसकी सम्भावना प्रबल दिखायी देती है कि 'सिलिमाते' 'श्रीमाता सिनीवाली (लक्ष्मी) है, जिसकी पुष्टि प्रतीक चिह्नों से भी हो जाती है। त्रिचैत्य पर बना अर्धचन्द्र, ताम्रपत्र के शीर्ष पर अंकित 'नालयुक्त कमल कलिका, प्राकार में वृक्ष, ये सभी लक्ष्मी के प्रतीक हैं। गुप्त मुद्राओं पर भारतीयकरण की प्रक्रिया में देवी लक्ष्मी के दाहिने हाथ में कार्नुकोपिया के स्थान पर उत्तरोत्तर नालयुक्त कमलकलिका ही प्रदर्शित की गयी है। चूँकि प्रतिष्ठा प्रकार के अभिलेखों में धार्मिक कृत्य से सम्बद्ध देवी–देवताओं के वन्दन–आराधन की परम्परा थी, इसलिए यहाँ भी 'कोष्ठागार की देवी' का स्मरण बड़ा स्वाभाविक था। चूँकि अभिलेख अत्यन्त लघु है, इसलिये विषय का प्रवर्तन भी प्रतीकात्मक ही किया गया है। यह लेख शासन पत्रों के लिए विकसित होने वाले विशिष्ट आभिलेख–तत्व देव–वन्दना का सूत्रपातक भी कहा जा सकता है।

मौर्य सम्राट अशोक के छः अभिलेख पूर्वी उत्तर प्रदेश एवं उसके सीमावर्ती क्षेत्र (नेपाल) से प्राप्त हैं।[13] इनमें पाँच लघुस्तम्भ लेख तथा एक (अहरौरा) लघु शिला अभिलेख है।[14] रानी के प्रयाग स्तम्भ लेख को छोड़कर सम्राट के सभी प्रज्ञापनों का सम्बन्ध बौद्ध धर्म से है। अहरौरा उत्तर प्रदेश से प्राप्त पहला लघुशिला लेख है जिसमें बुद्ध के देहावशेष को मंचारूढ़ करने (स्तूप में स्थापित करने) का उल्लेख है। उल्लेखनीय है कि सम्राट अशोक अपने प्रवासों (पड़ावों) की गणना तथागत के शरीरावशेष को स्तूप में स्थापित करने की तिथि से करता है, यथा, वह कहता है कि यह श्रावण प्रवास बुद्ध के अवशेषों के मंचारूढ़ के किये जाने के दो सौ छप्पन रातों (अर्थात् दिनों) के बाद किया गया *(एस सावने विवुथेन दु वे सपंना – लाति सति अं मं चे बुधस सलीले आलोढेति)*। यह संदर्भ अशोक के द्वारा 84,000 स्तूपों के निर्माण की परम्परा का समर्थन करता दिखाई देता है। इस अभिलेख को प्रकाश में लाने का श्रेय प्रयाग विश्वविद्यालय के प्राचीन इतिहास विभाग के पूर्व अध्यक्ष प्रो0 जी0आर0 शर्मा एवं उनके अन्वेषक दल को है।[15]

लघु स्तम्भ लेखों में दो (सारनाथ एवं प्रयाग संस्करण) महामात्रों को सम्बोधित हैं तथा इन्हें 'शासन' (*हे वं इयं ससने*) कहा गया है। ये लेख अशोक के प्रत्यक्ष शासन के अन्तर्गत परिगणित हैं, जिनमें वह आदेश देता है कि कोई भिक्षु अथवा भिक्षुणी संघ में फूट डालने में शक्य न हो सके। ऐसा दुस्साहस करने वाले भिक्षु अथवा भिक्षुणी को श्वेत वस्त्र पहनाकर 'अनावास' (अयोग्य स्थान) में रखा जायेगा।[16] सम्राट अशोक इसी की एक प्रतिलिपि – चौपाल में रखने का भी आदेश देता है, जो बौद्ध संघ से जुड़े सभी के लिए था। इन संघ भेद अभिलेखों से स्पष्ट है कि अशोक के काल तक आते – आते बौद्धसंघ के अनुशासन में शिथिलता आ गयी थी, जिसे रोकने का राजकीय प्रयास सम्राट ने किया। तृतीय संगीति का आयोजन भी इसी की परिणति था। रानी

का प्रयाग लघु स्तम्भ लेख[17] एक मात्र ऐसा लेख है जिसमें सम्राट् अशोक की पत्नी 'कारूवाकी' का उल्लेख है। कारूवाकी को सम्राट की द्वितीय (देवी) रानी तथा तीवर की माँ कहा गया है। इस स्तम्भ लेख में महामात्रों को आदेश दिया गया है कि आम्र वाटिका, विश्रामगृह, दानगृह अथवा अन्य सभी दान देवी कारूवाकी के नाम से गिने जाने चाहिए। यह अभिलेख सिद्ध करता है कि कारूवाकी सम्राट अशोक की प्रिय पत्नी थी लेकिन कारूवाकी की कोई व्यक्तिगत पहचान नहीं बन पायी थी क्योंकि कारूवाकी का परिचय प्रियदर्शी की द्वितीय देवी एवं तीवर की माता के रूप में दिया गया है जो मनु के *'पितारक्षति कौमारे भर्त्तारक्षति यौवने'* का स्मरण दिलाता है।

सम्राट अशोक के अन्य दो लघु स्तम्भ लेख रूम्मिनदेई[18] एवं निगालीसागर[19] का सम्बन्ध भी बुद्ध एवं कनक मुनि बुद्ध से है।

रुम्मिनदेई स्तम्भ लेख से ज्ञात है कि बीस वर्षों से अभिषिक्त देवानां प्रिय प्रियदर्शी (अशोक) राजा ने लुम्बिनी की तीर्थ यात्रा की क्योंकि शाक्य मुनि यहाँ उत्पन्न हुए थे। अस्तु, इस स्थल को गौरव प्रदान करते हुए सम्राट अशोक ने इस ग्राम को *बलि* नामक कर से मुक्त कर दिया तथा इसे *षष्ठ भागिक (षड़ भाग भृतो राजा रक्षेत् प्रजाम्)* के स्थान पर *अठभागिक* घोषित किया। इतना ही नहीं, उसने बुद्ध के पवित्र जन्म स्थल को भी पत्थर की सुदृढ़ दीवार से आवेष्टित करवा दिया। पूजा स्थलों के उपादान के रूप में दीवारों की स्थापना का यह प्राचीनतम साक्ष्य है। अपने इस पुनीत कृत्य को चिर स्थायित्व प्रदान करने के लिए शिला स्तम्भ (*शिला थमे च उसपापिते*) बनवाया जिस पर यह लेख उत्कीर्ण है। निगालीसागर लघु स्तम्भ लेख में चौदह वर्ष से अभिषिक्त प्रियदर्शी द्वारा कनकमुनि बुद्ध के स्तूप को दुबारा बढ़ाने अथवा दोगुना विस्तीर्ण करने एवं बीस वर्ष से अभिषिक्त राजा के द्वारा इस स्थल को स्वयं आकर गौरवान्वित करने एवं शिला स्तम्भ खड़ा करने का वर्णन है।[20]

पूर्वी उत्तर प्रदेश पर मौर्यों के पश्चात शासन करने वाले शुंग शासकों में से धनदेव का एक शिलालेख[21] अयोध्या से प्राप्त है। यह अभिलेख अयोध्या से लगभग एक मील दूर स्थित राणो पली नामक भवन में बनी बाबा संगत बख्श की समाधि के पूर्वी द्वार से प्राप्त हुआ था। दो पंक्तियों में निबद्ध यह लेख गद्यबद्ध है। भाषा प्राकृत् से प्रभावित संस्कृत है। लिपिगत आधार पर जगन्नाथ अग्रवाल एवं साधुराम ने इसका काल प्रथम शताब्दी ई. पू. का उत्तरार्द्ध तो कुछ ने इसे प्रथम शती ई0 में उत्कीर्ण माना है।[22] इस अभिलेख से शुंग काल में वैदिक याज्ञिक अनुष्ठान के पुनर्वर्तन का ठोस प्रमाण प्राप्त होता है। पुष्यमित्र शुंग को इस अभिलेख में कोसल का अधिपति, सेनापति एवं दो अश्वमेघ यज्ञों का यजनकर्त्ता बताया गया है। पुष्यमित्र के लिए 'सेनापति' उपाधि का प्रयोग *मालविकाग्निमित्र* में भी हुआ है। अभिलेख के उत्कीर्णन का लक्ष्य पुष्यमित्र से छठी पीढ़ी में उत्पन्न कौशिकी पुत्र धर्मराज धन (देव) द्वारा अपने पिता फल्गु की स्मृति में 'केतन' निर्माण का उल्लेख करना था। 'केतन' का अर्थ 'भवन' एवं 'ध्वज' दोनों होता है। यहाँ इसकी प्रबल सम्भावना दिखायी देती है कि धनदेव ने एक ऐसे भवन (मन्दिर = देवकुल) का निर्माण करवाया जिसमें फल्गुदेव की प्रतिमा स्थापित की गयी होगी अथवा इसका आशय उस ध्वज स्तम्भ से है जो फल्गुदेव की समाधि पर स्थापित किया गया होगा। कवि भास के *प्रतिमानाटक* में इक्ष्वाकु राजाओं की प्रतिमाओं को देवकुल में स्थापित करने का उल्लेख मिलता है। परवर्ती काल में कनिष्क की मथुरा से प्राप्त विशाल प्रतिमा एवं कुषाणों की उपाधियाँ *(सर्वलोग ईश्वरस महीश्वरस)* राजाओं में देवत्व की अवधारणा को पुष्ट करती हैं।

कुषाण शासक कनिष्क के चार अभिलेख पूर्वी उत्तर प्रदेश के कौशाम्बी[23] (01), सारनाथ[24] (01) एवं श्रावस्ती[25] (02) से प्राप्त हैं। ये सभी अभिलेख बौद्ध धर्म से सम्बन्धित हैं तथा बोधिसत्व की प्रतिमा एवं छत्र–यष्टि निर्माण के प्रसंग में प्रतिमाओं पर उत्कीर्ण हैं। सारनाथ लेख, बोधिसत्व प्रतिमा एवं एक अष्ट पार्श्वीय पाषाण यष्टि के तीन पार्श्वों पर अंकित है। ये अभिलेख एफ0ओ0 ओरटेल द्वारा सारनाथ की खुदाई में 1904–05 ई0 में प्रकाश में आये। बौद्ध धर्म में तथागत की मूर्ति निर्माण के ये प्राचीनतम अभिलिखित एवं भौतिक साक्ष्य हैं। कनिष्क के

द्वारा प्रवर्तित ब्रोड् प्रकार की सुवर्ण मुद्रा पर भी बुद्ध का अंकन स्थानक शैली में प्राप्त है, तथा यूनानी लिपि में **Boddo** (बोड्डो) लेख है। सुविदित है कि महायान के प्रभाव में बुद्ध की प्रतिमाओं का निर्माण आरम्भ हुआ यद्यपि *अंगुत्तर निकाय* में बुद्ध ने अपनी प्रतिमा निर्माण का निषेध यह कहते हुए किया था कि निर्वाण के पश्चात 'धर्मकाय' ही शेष रहता है, जिसका स्थूल अंकन नहीं किया जा सकता। कनिष्क के अभिलेखों से विदित है कि प्रारम्भ में 'बोधिसत्व' नाम से ही बुद्ध की प्रतिमायें बनीं क्योंकि कौशाम्बी, सारनाथ एवं श्रावस्ती जैसे बौद्ध केन्द्रों पर भी बुद्ध प्रतिमाएँ नयी चीज थीं। इसका संकेत इस बात से मिलता है कि भिक्षुबल एवं भिक्षुणी बुद्धमित्रा ने इन मूर्तियों पर यह लिखवाना आवश्यक समझा कि ये बोधिसत्व प्रतिमाएँ हैं। अवान्तर में बौद्ध धर्म में मूर्ति पूजा की स्वीकृति हो जानें पर इस प्रकार लिखवाना आवश्यक नहीं रह गया।[26]

महायान सम्प्रदाय में 'बोधिसत्व' की अवधारणा का विशाल फलक है। करूणा की भित्ति पर स्थापित बोधिसत्व भावी बुद्ध का वह रूप है जो तृष्णा में लिप्त विकल संसार के कल्याणार्थ ही अस्तित्वमान हुआ। ध्यानार्ह है कि बौद्ध मूर्ति लेखों के अन्त में प्रायः यह कामना की गयी है कि यह सभी प्राणियों के हित सुख का हेतु बने (*सर्वसत्वनं हितासुखार्त्थं*)[27] तथा सभी दुःखों का परिहार करे।[28] कोसम बौद्ध मूर्ति लेख से ज्ञात होता है कि बोधिसत्व की प्रतिमा को त्रिपिटकाचार्या भिक्षुणी बुद्धमित्रा ने स्थापित करवाया था। जबकि सारनाथ की बोधिसत्व प्रतिमा एवं छत्र–यष्टि की स्थापना एवं दान त्रिपिटकाचार्य भिक्षुबल ने माता–पिता, चारो परिषदों, उपाध्याय, अन्तेवासियों, विहार साथियों, आचार्या बुद्ध मित्रा, क्षत्रप वनस्स्पर एवं खर पल्लान के साथ किया। यहाँ संघीय अनुशासन पर ठोस प्रकाश मिलता है। इसी प्रकार सहेत–महेत (श्रावस्ती) बौद्ध मूर्ति लेख से विदित है कि भिक्षुबल ने बोधिसत्व की प्रतिमा एवं छत्र–यष्टि का दान किया। इन्हें भिक्षु पुष्पबुद्धि का विहार साथी कहा गया है। इस मूर्ति को प्रकाश में लाने का श्रेय कनिंघम महोदय को है। यह सम्प्रति इण्डियन म्यूजियम, कलकत्ता में संग्रहीत है। इन सभी अभिलेखों की लिपि कुषाण ब्राह्मी है तथा भाषा संस्कृत से प्रभावित प्राकृत है।

इस मूर्ति लेख (सहेत–महेत) को ब्लाख ने *एपिग्राफिया इण्डिका* के आठवें अंक (पृष्ठ 180) में सम्पादित किया तथा छत्र दण्ड लेख को इसी के 9वें अंक (पृ0 291) में प्रकाशित किया। सहेत–महेत बौद्ध मूर्ति लेख[29] से ज्ञात होता है कि श्रावस्ती भी मथुरा, कश्मीर के समान सर्वास्तिवादियों का एक महत्वपूर्ण केन्द्र था। इन आभिलेखिक साक्ष्यों से कनिष्क का शासन श्रावस्ती वाराणसी से लेकर बनारस एवं प्रयाग के दक्षिणवर्ती भू–भाग तक प्रमाणित होता है।

कुषाणों के पश्चात् इस क्षेत्र पर गुप्तों की सत्ता स्थापित हुई। यहाँ से समुद्रगुप्त (प्रयाग प्रशस्ति), चन्द्रगुप्त द्वितीय (गढ़वा अभिलेख), कुमारगुप्त प्रथम (मानकुंवर पाषाण अभिलेख, करमदण्डा शिवलिङ्ग, गढ़वा से प्राप्त दो अभिलेख), स्कन्दगुप्त (भीतरी स्तम्भ अभिलेख, कहौम स्तम्भ अभिलेख), कुमार गुप्त द्वितीय (सारनाथ बौद्ध पाषाण मूर्ति लेख, भीतरी मुहर लेख) तथा बुधगुप्त (सारनाथ बौद्ध पाषाण मूर्ति लेख) के अभिलेख मिले हैं।[30] ये सभी अभिलेख संस्कृत भाषा में निबद्ध हैं, इन सभी अभिलेखों में रचना शैली एवं विषय वस्तु की दृष्टि से सर्वाधिक महत्वपूर्ण अभिलेख समुद्रगुप्त की' *प्रयाग प्रशस्ति*[31] है जो कौशाम्बी के महामात्रों को सम्बोधित सम्राट अशोक के 35 फीट ऊँचे स्तम्भ पर उत्कीर्ण है तथा सम्प्रति इलाहाबाद के किले में अवस्थित है। सर्वप्रथम 1834 ई0 में कैप्टन ट्रायर ने इस अभिलेख को शिलामुद्रण के साथ *जे0बी0ए0एस0*, भाग 3 में प्रकाशित किया, तत्पश्चात डब्ल्यू0एच0 मिल ने इसी पत्रिका में इसका प्रकाशन करवाया। अन्ततः 1888 ई0 में लीट ने इसे *कार्पस*, भाग 3 में शिलामुद्रण, पाठ, आंग्ल अनुवाद, टिप्पणी के साथ प्रकाशित किया।[32] गद्य–पद्य (चम्पू शैली) में निबद्ध यह प्रशस्ति राजा एवं प्रशस्ति प्रणेता (हरिषेण) के शौर्य एवं वैदुष्य का अद्भुत साक्ष्य है।

परिष्कृत संस्कृत भाषा· में विरचित यह भारत का पहला अभिलेख है, जो शस्त्र–शास्त्र, राजा–विद्वान, लक्ष्मी एवं सरस्वती के नैसर्गिक वैषम्य को तोड़ता हुआ दिखायी देता है। यहाँ यह कहना अतिशयोक्ति नहीं कि

जिन काव्य तत्त्वों (प्रसाद गुण, वैदर्भी रीति, शब्दोपचित्य, छन्दों का प्रयोग) का सन्निवेश हरिषेण ने अपनी विदग्ध रचना *प्रयाग प्रशस्ति* (जिसे वह *एतच्च काव्यं* कहता है) में किया है, वह परवर्ती काव्यशास्त्रियों के लिए पुष्ट आधार था। इस अभिलेख से प्रच्छन्न रीति से ज्ञात होता है कि हरिषेण शिव भक्त था। प्रशस्ति के 9वें श्लोक में हरिषेण अपने इष्टदेव को यह कहकर स्मरण करता है कि पशुपति की जटाजूट रूपी अन्तर्गुहा से शीघ्र मुक्त होकर निकली गंगा की जलधारा जिस प्रकार तीनों लोकों को पवित्र करती है, उसी प्रकार समुद्रगुप्त की कीर्ति का वितान त्रिविध रीति से विस्तृत हुआ,[33] प्रकृष्ट दान देने, शास्त्र की व्याख्या करने, एवं भुज विक्रम से। ऐसा प्रतीत होता है कि हरिषेण अपने आराध्य को स्मरण करने का बहाना ढूँढ़ रहा था क्योंकि इस श्लोक की यहाँ कोई आवश्यकता वर्ण्य–विषय अथवा चम्पू की पूर्णता के संदर्भ में नहीं थी। उल्लेख्य है कि गुप्त वंशी राजा परम–वैष्णव थे लेकिन उनके उच्चपदस्थ राजकर्मचारी (सान्धिविग्रहिक, सचिव) परमशैव थे, यथा वीरसेन,[34] पृथ्वीषेण[35] इत्यादि। इस क्षेत्र से प्राप्त अभिलेखों में इलाहाबाद के करछना तहसील के गढ़वा (अर्थात् किला) नामक स्थान से चन्द्रगुप्त द्वितीय के दो (वर्ष–88) तथा कुमारगुप्त प्रथम के काल के दो अभिलेख मिले हैं। ये अभिलेख सत्र (यज्ञ) हेतु दान (10 दीनार) देने तथा दान का खण्डन करने पर पंचमहापातकों का भागी होने का विवरण देते हैं। चन्द्रगुप्त द्वितीय के लिए *'परमभागवत'* उपाधि का प्रयोग इन अभिलेखों में हुआ है[36] तथा ये ब्राह्मणों एवं याज्ञिक धर्म के पुनरूत्थान के सूचक हैं। मातृ दास नामक व्यक्ति एवं पाटलिपुत्र के गृहस्थ की भार्या द्वारा पुण्यार्जन हेतु इस दीनार का दान सत्र हेतु किये जाने का उल्लेख सिद्ध करता है कि यज्ञ एवं दान के प्रति गृहस्थों की आस्था बढ़ रही थी। सत्र (यज्ञ) की सूचना प्रदान करने वाले गढ़वा अभिलेखों से ऐसा प्रतीत होता है कि प्रयाग का समीपवर्ती क्षेत्र भी यज्ञ भूमि के रूप में प्रतिष्ठित हो गया था। प्रयाग का शाब्दिक अर्थ होता है वह भूमि जहाँ प्रकृष्ट यज्ञ सम्पन्न हुए हों। कुमार गुप्त प्रथम के शासनकाल (वर्ष 109 = 428 ई0) का मानकुंवर पाषाण प्रतिमा लेख[37] इलाहाबाद के करछना तहसील के अरइल परगने से 9 मील दक्षिण–पश्चिम की दूरी पर स्थित मानकुंवर ग्राम से प्राप्त है। यह प्रतिमा सर्वप्रथम इन्द्र जी महोदय को मिली थी जिसे कनिंघम ने 1880 ई0 में *ए0एस0आई0* भाग 10 में प्रकाशित किया। मूर्ति की पीठिका पर दो पंक्तियों में लेख उत्कीर्ण है, जिनके बीच में धर्मचक्र, लघु मानव एवं सिंह मूर्तियां बनी हैं। यह एक बौद्ध अभिलेख है। इस लेख से ज्ञात होता है कि भिक्षु–बुद्धमित्र ने इस प्रतिमा की स्थापना महाराज श्री कुमार गुप्त के शासन काल में करवायी थी, जिसका उद्देश्य सभी दुःखों का निराकरण *(सर्व दुक्ख – प्रहानार्थम्)* बताया गया है।

पूर्वी उत्तर प्रदेश से प्राप्त गुप्तों के अभिलेखों में कुमार गुप्त प्रथम के काल का तिथि युक्त (वर्ष 117-436 ई0) करमदण्डा पाषाण लिङ्ग अभिलेख[38] कई दृष्टियों से महत्त्वपूर्ण है, यथा, गुप्तों के मंत्री परिवार के चार पीढ़ियों की सूचना इस अभिलेख से मिलती है (छान्दोग्याचार्य कुमारव्य भट्ट, विष्णुपालित भट्ट, कुमारामात्य, मन्त्री शिखरस्वामी तथा कुमारामात्य, मंत्री जो बाद में महाबलाधिकृत के पद पर प्रतिष्ठित हुए पृथ्वीषेण)। चन्द्रगुप्त द्वितीय के उदयगिरि[39] गुहालेख में वीर सेन अपने को *'अन्वय प्राप्त सचिव'* कहता है, जिसकी पुष्टि इस लिङ्ग अभिलेख से भी होती है। इस अभिलेख में कुमार गुप्त के मंत्री कुमारामात्य पृथ्वीषेण द्वारा 'पृथ्वीश्वर' नाम से विख्यात् भगवान महादेव की धार्मिक कार्यों द्वारा सेवा के लिए भगवान शैलेश्वर स्वामी के पादमूल में अयोध्या के विभिन्न गोत्र, चरण, तप, स्वाध्याय करने वाले, सूत्र भाष्य एवं प्रवचन में निष्णात् ब्राह्मणों को दान देने का विवरण है। इसमें 'देवद्रोणी' का उल्लेख है, जो देवमूर्तियों के जुलूस एवं 'देवमन्दिर की सम्पत्ति के अधिकारी' की सूचना देता है। इस क्षेत्र से प्राप्त गुप्त शासकों के अभिलेखों में स्कन्दगुप्त के दो अभिलेख अत्यन्त महत्वपूर्ण हैं। प्रथम गाजीपुर जिले के सैदपुर तहसील से प्राप्त भीतरी स्तम्भ लेख[40] तथा द्वितीय, देवरिया जिले के सलेमपुर तहसील का कहौम (वर्तमान नाम कहॉव) स्तम्भ लेख (वर्ष 141)। भीतरी अभिलेख से बर्बर हूणों पर स्कन्दगुप्त की अप्रतिम विजय एवं पिता की कीर्ति, पुण्यवृद्धि के लिए विष्णु की प्रतिमा स्थापना की सूचना मिलती है। इस अभिलेख में

कहा गया है कि शार्ङ्गिण (विष्णु) की मूर्ति एवं उस ग्राम को भी जहाँ प्रतिमा स्थापित की गयी थी, स्कन्दगुप्त ने दान दिया था। पिता की पुण्य वृद्धि के लिए मतिमान स्कन्द गुप्त ने इस पुनीत कार्य का सम्पादन किया, ऐसा कथन दो स्थलों पर है लेकिन कहीं भी माता के नाम का उल्लेख न करना प्रश्न खड़ा करता है कि यह उपेक्षा स्कन्दगुप्त ने क्यों की ? स्कन्दगुप्त के कहौम अभिलेख[41] (वर्ष 141) से विदित है कि 461 ई0 तक आते–आते स्कन्दगुप्त अपने सभी शत्रुओं पर विजय प्राप्त कर चुका था क्योंकि उसके शासन वर्ष 141 = 461 को 'शान्ति का वर्ष' बताया गया है। यह लेख देवरिया के दक्षिण में जैन धर्म के बढ़ते प्रभाव को परिलक्षित करता है। इस अभिलेख से ज्ञात होता है कि इसका प्राचीन नाम 'ककुभ' था (*ख्यातेऽस्मिन्ग्रामरत्ने ककुभ इति जैन साधु संसर्ग पूते*) तथा यह ग्राम जैन साधुओं के संसर्ग से पवित्र था। इस पाषाण स्तम्भ पर जैन तीर्थंङ्करों की पाँच नग्न मूर्तियाँ तक्षित हैं। भगवान लाल इन्द्रजी ने इन मूर्तियों का समीकरण पाँच लोक तीर्थङ्करों की मूर्तियों से किया है। इनमें एक मूर्ति जैन धर्म के नवें तीर्थंकर पुष्पदन्त की होगी जो कहौम से थोड़ी ही दूरी पर स्थित काकंदी में पैदा हुए थे।[42] इस अभिलेख में भट्टिसोम नामक व्यक्ति को 'महात्मा' तथा प्रशस्तगुणों वाला कहा गया है, इनका पुत्र मतिमान, व्याघ्र नाम वाला रूद्रसोम हुआ जिसका पुत्र भद्र था जिसे ब्राह्मणों, गुरूओं एवं यतियों में अनुरक्त बताया गया है। इस मद्र ने ही संसार की नश्वरता का विचार कर, पुण्य संग्रह हेतु तीर्थङ्करों की प्रतिमाएं एवं सुन्दर शैल स्तम्भ भूमि में स्थापित करवाया।

इस अभिलेख की चर्चा सर्वप्रथम फ्रांसिस बुखनन ने 1816 ई0 में अपनी पुस्तक 'बंगाल प्रेसीडेंसी' की आख्या में की थी। इसी आधार पर माण्टगुमुरी ने 1836 ई0 में *'इस्टर्न इण्डिया'* पुस्तक लिखी जिसके दूसरे भाग में यह अभिलेख शिला मुद्रण सहित छपा। कुमार गुप्त द्वितीय के काल का सारनाथ बुद्ध प्रतिमा लेख (गु0सं0 154)[43] तथा बुद्धगुप्त के शासन काल (गु0सं0 157) का सारनाथ से प्राप्त बुद्ध प्रतिमा लेख[44] से विदित होता है कि इन शासकों के शासन काल में बौद्ध धर्म को फलीभूत होने का अनुकूल अवसर मिला। कुमार गुप्त द्वितीय कालीन सारनाथ बौद्ध प्रतिमा हाग्रीव्ज को सारनाथ से मिली थी। इस प्रतिमालेख में कहा गया है कि भक्ति से नम्र मन वाले मति अभय मित्र द्वारा 'शास्ता' की प्रतिमा का निर्माण पूजा हेतु करवाया गया। प्रतिमा स्थापना का उद्देश्य माता–पिता, गुरु, पूर्वज तथा सज्जनों को मुक्ति देना बताया गया है।

बुध गुप्त कालीन सारनाथ बुद्ध प्रतिमा–लेख[45] (गुप्त संवत् 157=476 ई0) भी हार्ग्रीब्ज को 1914–15 में मिला था। लेख प्रतिमा की चरण चौकी पर उत्कीर्ण है जो शाक्य भिक्षु अभय मित्र द्वारा प्रतिष्ठित बतायी गयी है। इस प्रतिमा को चित्र लक्षण (विन्यास) के अनुरूप निर्मित, दिव्य प्रतिमा कहा गया है, जो कला की दृष्टि से महत्त्वपूर्ण है।

प्रायः इसी काल में कुशीनगर से 18 किमी0 पूर्व फाजिलनगर में 'वेद–विद्या के अध्ययन' का एक महत्वपूर्ण केन्द्र स्थापित हुआ था जिसकी पुष्टि यहाँ से प्राप्त दो मुद्रा–छापों द्वारा होती है जिनमें से एक पर अंकित है *'श्रेष्ठिग्रामाग्रहारस्य'*[46] । यहीं से प्राप्त एक अन्य मुद्रा–छाप पर गुप्त ब्राह्मी में लेख अंकित है : *'ग्रेषूदक चातुर्विद्यस्य'*। यह लेख भी वेद–विद्या के इस क्षेत्र में अध्ययन की पुष्टि का आधार है। (द्र0 चित्र सं0 3)। अनुदान में प्राप्त अग्रहार' एक प्रकार का विद्या केन्द्र होता था जहाँ विद्वान ब्राह्मण अपने शिष्यों के साथ निवास करते थे, अध्ययन–अध्यापन एवं यज्ञादि कृत्य सम्पन्न करते थे। फाजिलनगर के समीप स्थित वर्तमान सठियाँव नामक स्थान गुप्त युग में श्रेष्ठिग्राम कहलाता था।

गुप्तोत्तर काल में पूर्वी उत्तर प्रदेश पर मौखरियों एवं वर्द्धनों की सत्ता स्थापित हुई। मौखरि शासक अवन्ति वर्मा का सोहनाग मुहर लेख[47] देवरिया जिले के सलेमपुर तहसील के सोहनाग नामक स्थान से प्राप्त है। इस अभिलेख में मौखरि वंश के प्रथम शासक हरिवर्मा से लेकर अवन्ति वर्मा तक की वंशावली माता–पिता के नाम के साथ उल्लिखित है। इस अभिलेख में हरिवर्मा को 'वर्णाश्रम व्यवस्था' की स्थापना के लिए उद्यत, चक्रधारी विष्णु

के समान प्रजा के कष्ट को दूर करने वाला कहा गया है। मौखरि शासक शैव थे, इसकी पुष्टि उनके अन्य अभिलेखों[48] तथा हर्षचरित से होती है। प्रस्तुत मुहर में भी अवन्तिवर्मा के लिए शैवोपाधि 'परम माहेश्वर' का प्रयोग किया गया है।[49] जिस स्थान से यह मुहर प्राप्त है वह शिव भक्त परशुराम की तपःस्थली के रूप में विख्यात है। इस अंचल के जौनपुर नामक स्थान से ईश्वर वर्मा का एक अभिलेख[50] प्राप्त है, जो खण्डित है तथापि ऐतिहासिक महत्व की कतिपय घटनायें इसमें सुरक्षित हैं। इस प्रस्तर लेख में कहा गया है कि क्रूर जनों के आगमन से उत्पन्न उपद्रव को ईश्वर वर्मा ने शान्त किया एवं लोक का कल्याण किया। इन्हें शत्रु नरेशों के लिए सिंह स्वरूप बताया गया है। यहाँ बर्बर जनों से तात्पर्य हूणों से ही है। हूणों का भारत में आगमन एवं उपस्थिति भारतीय सांस्कृतिक अवमूल्यन का कारण बनी, जिसे रोकने की प्रच्छन्न अभिव्यक्ति मौखरि एवं वर्धन शासकों की उपाधियों में हुई है, यथा, इन्हें वर्णाश्रम व्यवस्था के लिए उद्यत तथा कलियुग के अनाचार को दूर करने वाला बताया गया है।[51] हरिवर्मा के समान बॉसखेड़ा[52] एवं मधुबन ताम्र पत्रों[53] में प्रभाकर वर्धन को *'वर्ण्णाश्रम व्यवस्थापन प्रवृत्तिचक्र एक चक्रस्थ इव प्रजानामार्तिहरः'* कहा गया है जिसका आशय है, वर्णाश्रम की स्थापना में लगा हुआ, सूर्य (एक चक्ररथ) के समान प्रजा के कष्ट को दूर करने वाला।

स्पष्ट है कि भारतीय सामाजिक व्यवस्था का मूलाधार वर्णाश्रम को ही सर्वाधिक आघात इन विदेशी जनों के आगमन से लगा था, जिसे पुनर्प्रतिष्ठापित करना इस काल की प्रमुख उपलब्धियों में परिगणित हो गया। उल्लेख्य है कि गुप्त कालीन शासकों की महान सामरिक–सांस्कृतिक उपलब्धियों में कहीं भी वर्णाश्रम का उल्लेख नहीं है। वर्धन शासक हर्ष का मधुबन ताम्रपत्र[54] (सम्वत् 25 = 631 ई0) आजमगढ़ जिले के सगरी तहसील के नाथुपुर परगने के मधुबन नामक स्थान से प्राप्त है। यह लेख एक ही ताम्रपत्र पर उत्कीर्ण है तथा कई दृष्टियों से महत्वपूर्ण है। इसमें कूट शासन के माध्यम से 'सोमकुण्डका' नामक ग्राम (अग्रहार) का भोग करने वाले ब्राह्मण वामरथ्य से इस ग्राम को छीनकर सावर्णि गोत्र के सामवेदी (छान्दोग्यशाखा) ब्रह्मचारी भट्टवातस्वामी एवं विष्णुवृद्ध गोत्र के ऋग्वेदी (बहबृच शाखा) ब्रह्मचारी शिवदेवस्वामी को (दान धर्म के नियमों का अनुपालन करते हुए) दान में देने का उल्लेख है। बाँसखेड़ा ताम्रपत्र में भी छान्दोग्य एवं बहवृच शाखा के ब्रह्मचारी ब्राह्मणों को ही दान देने का उल्लेख है। ऐसा प्रतीत होता है कि वामरथ्य में दानगृहीता की पात्रता नहीं थी। निस्संदेह, वैदिक वाङ्मय के अध्ययन में इन दो शाखाओं की प्रतिष्ठा अधिक थी क्योंकि अन्य ताम्रपत्रों एवं मुहरों से भी इसकी पुष्टि होती है। उल्लेखनीय है कि जिस 'सोमकुण्डका' ग्राम को 'अग्रहार' के रूप में दान देने का उल्लेख मधुबन ताम्रपत्र में हुआ है उसे श्रावस्ती भुक्ति एवं कुण्डधानी विषय के अन्तर्गत बताया गया है। 'सोमकुण्डका' की पहचान अभी सुनिश्चित नहीं है लेकिन ओम प्रकाश लाल श्रीवास्तव[55] द्वारा 'सोहगौरा' से की गयी इसकी पहचान विचारणीय अवश्य है। इसमें संदेह नहीं कि 'सोहगौरा' बाँसगाँव (अर्थात् गोरखपुर) श्रावस्ती भुक्ति में आते थे, तथा नवपाषाण काल से अद्यावधि यह ग्राम अपनी पूरी सांस्कृतिक चेतना के साथ विद्यमान है। यहाँ के शाण्डिल्य ब्राह्मण अपनी अलग पहचान रखते हैं। उल्लेखनीय है कि शाण्डिल्य ब्राह्मणों का वेद 'सामवेद' है। सोमकुण्डका नामक ग्राम भी सामवेदी एवं ऋग्वेदी ब्राह्मणों को ही दिये गये थे।

हर्षोत्तर काल में पूर्वी उत्तर प्रदेश पर मलयकेतु, कलचुरि, सावर्णि एवं गाहडवाल राजवंशों की सत्ता स्थापित हुई। इनके अभिलेख वाराणसी, गोरखपुर, कुशीनगर, भाटपाररानी (देवरिया), लार (देवरिया), श्रावस्ती, सारनाथ, जौनपुर (मछलीशहर), गाजीपुर से प्राप्त हैं। इनमें से अधिकांश ताम्रपत्र हैं, जो भूमि अनुदान के प्रसंग में निर्गत हैं।

गोरखपुर के धुरियापार परगने के 'कहला' नामक स्थान से कलचुरि शासक सोढ़देव का अभिलेख प्राप्त है, जिसकी तिथि विक्रम संवत् 1135 = 1077 ई0 है। वी0वी0 मिराशी ने इसे *कार्पस* भाग 4, (पार्ट 2, पृ0 389) में प्रकाशित किया। इस अभिलेख की 32वीं पंक्ति में *'सरूवार'* शब्द का प्रयोग है जो सरयूपार का अपभ्रंश हैं।

इस ताम्रपत्र में[56] बांग्ला देश के 'कुलन्च' नामक ग्राम से आये हुए ब्राह्मणों के इसी क्षेत्र में बसने का उल्लेख है। कुलन्च शाण्डिल्य गोत्र के ब्राह्मणों के वास्तव्य के रूप में विख्यात् था। इसी प्रकार कर्णदेव के वाराणसी अभिलेख[57] में उल्लिखित है कि काशी प्रांत में स्थित 'सुस्री' नामक ग्राम विश्वरूप नामक ब्राह्मण को दान में दिया गया था जो वैशाली का रहने वाला था। इसे त्रिप्रवर कौशिक गोत्रोत्पन्न आमह का प्रपौत्र, वामन का पौत्र एवं नारायण का पुत्र कहा गया है। सहेत–महेत अभिलेख को गाहडवाल शासक गोविन्द चन्द्र ने अपने पिता मदनपाल के नाम पर निर्गत किया था। गोंडा–बहराइच की सीमा पर स्थित इस स्थान का तादात्म्य क्रमशः जेतवन और श्रावस्ती से किया गया है। यह अभिलेख विक्रम संवत् 1186 तद्नुसार 1128 ई0 में उत्कीर्ण हुआ। इसका प्रकाशन *एपिग्राफिआ इण्डिका* के भाग XI में हुआ जिसका सम्पादन दयाराम साहनी ने किया है। यह अभिलेख आर्थिक एवं सांस्कृतिक इतिहास की दृष्टि से महत्वपूर्ण है। इसमें कुछ करों का उल्लेख है– 'भाग–भोगकर', 'प्रवणिकर' एवं 'तुरूष्क दण्ड कर' (यह कर इस्लामी आक्रमण के समय संगृहीत कर था अथवा इस्लाम – मतानुयायियों पर लगाया गया कर था)। अभिलेख की 19वीं पंक्ति में महापंडित शाक्यरक्षित को उत्कल देशीय 'सौगत' (बौद्ध) 'परिव्राजक' कहा गया है एवं 20वीं पंक्ति से ज्ञात होता है कि शाक्यरक्षित ने जेतवन महाविहार को अपना वास्तव्य (स्थायी निवास स्थल) बना लिया *(श्रीमज्जेतवन महाविहार वास्तव्य)* था। ध्यातव्य है कि सामन्त युग की प्रमुख विशेषताओं में क्षेत्रीयता के वर्चस्व को प्रमुख माना गया है, जबकि यह अभिलेख भारत के एक छोर को दूसरे छोर से निर्वाध विनिर्गमन एवं वास्तव्य के द्वारा जोड़ने का साक्ष्य प्रस्तुत करता है। महाजनपद काल में कोसल की राजधानी श्रावस्ती (सावत्थि) जो कभी राम की गाथाओं से अनुगुंजित थी, किस प्रकार बौद्ध धर्म का केन्द्र बनी जिससे सुदूरवर्ती क्षेत्र में रहने वाले इस भूमि की ओर आकृष्ट हुए, यह अपने में एक महत्वपूर्ण तथ्य है। यह अभिलेख सांस्कृतिक समन्वय को उजागर करता है।

गगहा अभिलेख भी इस क्षेत्र के राजनैतिक महत्व को दर्शाता है। यह *एपिग्राफिया इण्डिका* के भाग XIII में प्रकाशित है तथा एल0डी0 बार्नेट ने इसका सम्पादन किया है। इसकी तिथि विक्रम संवत् 1199–1143 ई0 है। यह गोरखपुर से 21 मील दक्षिण–पश्चिम गगहा नामक स्थान से मिला है। यह अभिलेख भी गोविन्द चन्द्र गाहडवाल का है। इस अभिलेख से ज्ञात होता है कि गोविन्द चन्द्र के आदेश से महाराज पुत्र राजपाल देव ने 'हठौता पत्तला' में वत्स गोत्रीय तीन ब्राह्मण बन्धुओं – देवराम, भूपति, और श्रीधर को भूमिदान दिया। इस अभिलेख में *''बॉगर भूमि''* एवं *''कच्छ भूमि''* का भी उल्लेख है, जो इस क्षेत्र की भूमि की प्रमुख विशेषता है। उत्तर प्रदेश के देवरिया जिले के 'लार' नामक स्थान से भी गोविन्द चन्द्र गाहडवाल का एक अभिलेख प्राप्त है, जिसकी तिथि विक्रम संवत् 1202–1146 ई0 है। यह *एपिग्राफिया इण्डिका* भाग VII में प्रकाशित है। इसे कीलहार्न ने सम्पादित किया है। इस अभिलेख से ज्ञात होता है कि विजय–अभियान पर निकले गोविन्द चन्द्र के द्वारा (मुद्दगिरि में) गंगा स्नान के पश्चात् 'पांदल पत्तला' का पोतचवण नामक ग्राम दान में दिया गया। इस ग्राम को सरूवार (सरयूपार) स्थित बताया गया है (*सरूवारे दुधालि सम्बद्ध गोविशालके पांदल पत्तलायाम्*) । सहेत–महेत में उल्लिखित तीन राजकरों का उल्लेख इस अभिलेख की 26वीं पंक्ति में हुआ है। इसी क्रम में गोविन्द चन्द्र का 'दोनबुजुर्ग' अभिलेख भी अत्यन्त महत्वपूर्ण है। यह अभिलेख विक्रम संवत् 1176–1119–20 ई0 में उट्टंकित हुआ और *एपिग्राफिया इण्डिका* के XXVIII भाग में प्रकाशित है। दयाराम साहनी ने इसका सम्पादन किया है। 'दोनबुजुर्ग' मैरवा रेलवे स्टेशन के समीप स्थित 'दोन बुजुर्ग' नामक स्थान से मिला है। अभिलेख से ज्ञात होता है कि गाहडवाल शासक ने 'अलाप जनपद' में 'बड़ग्राम' (बड़गों) नामक ग्राम को एक ब्राह्मण को दान में दिया जिसका नाम 'तुलतायिच शर्मा' था। यह वत्सगोत्रीय तथा 'द्रोणायनसद' का रहने वाला था। द्रोणायनसद अत्यन्त महत्वपूर्ण नाम प्रतीत होता। वैदिक काल से ही 'सद' नामान्त स्थानों के नाम मिलते हैं यथा– नृसद, वनसद, गर्तसद, परिषद इत्यादि। गोरखपुर के धुरियापार परगने में स्थित 'पाली' नामक स्थान से भी अभिलेख मिला है

जिसमें 'पाली' तथा 'ओण्वल' नामक स्थानों का वर्णन है। ये स्थान घाघरा नदी के उत्तर गोरखपुर के धुरियापार में स्थित आधुनिक 'पाली' तथा 'उनवल' नामक स्थानों के द्योतक हैं। इस अभिलेख की तिथि विक्रम संवत् 1171–1114 ई0 है। विक्रम संवत् 1167–1111 ई0 के गोरखपुर जिले से प्राप्त कीर्ति पाल नामक व्यक्ति को *'दरदगण्डकी'* (घाघरा और बड़ी गण्डक के बीच का) का शासक कहा गया है।

उल्लेखनीय है कि सावर्णि शासक विक्रमपाल, कीर्तिपाल को भाटपार ताम्रलेख 1167 = 1111 ई0[58] में *'सौम्य सिन्धु', 'उत्तर समुद्र'* एवं *दरदगण्डकी* का शासक कहा गया है।[59]

पूर्वी उत्तर प्रदेश से प्राप्त लगभग 55 प्रमुख अभिलेखों से ज्ञात होता है कि आभिलेखिकी का सूत्रपात इसी क्षेत्र से हुआ, जिसका प्रमाण पिपरहवा एवं सोहगौरा ताम्रपत्र लेख हैं। भारत के सभी अभिलेखों में भाषा, वर्ण्य–विषय, लेखन–शैली, काव्य विन्यास की दृष्टि से उत्कृष्ट प्रयाग–प्रशस्ति का प्रणयन भी इसी क्षेत्र में हुआ, तथा अभिलेख प्रणेताओं के वैदुष्य की यह परम्परा प्रवाहमान रही यथा गाहडवाल रानी कुमारदेवी के सारनाथ अभिलेख में श्रीकुन्द नाम से विख्यात प्रशस्ति प्रणेता को साहित्य–शिरोमणि एवं कवि कहा गया है।[60] यह कवि सुन्दर वर्ण योजना में निष्णात् बताया गया है : अर्थात् ये अभिलेख शासन एवं शास्त्र के सुन्दर संगम थे। यहाँ से प्राप्त प्रारम्भिक पुराभिलेखों की भाषा प्राकृत है वहीं परवर्ती अभिलेख (गुप्त एवं गुप्तोत्तर) संस्कृत भाषा में निबद्ध हैं, जो लोक भाषा को स्थानापन्न कर आभिजात्य जनों की भाषाई वर्चस्व के साक्षी हैं। अभिलेखों की विषय–वस्तु का सर्वेक्षण करने पर ज्ञात होता है कि प्राङ्–मौर्य युग से लेकर कुषाण काल तक के अधिकांश अभिलेखों का प्रतिपाद्य बुद्ध एवं बौद्धधर्म था, निःसन्देह ये साक्ष्य बौद्ध धर्म से अभिभूत राजाओं, भिक्षु–भिक्षुणियों, भक्तों की श्रद्धा के अभिलिखित दस्तावेज हैं। ध्यातव्य है कि शुंग एवं गुप्तों के अभिलेख वैदिक यज्ञानुष्ठान के प्रति राजा एवं गृहस्थों के झुकाव को परिलक्षित करते हैं; साथ ही इनमें वैष्णव–शैव धर्म के अद्भुत समन्वय की अनुगूँज सुनाई देती है। इस काल के अभिलेखों से 'अग्रहार' (वेद–विद्या के अध्ययन केन्द्र) की स्थापना, विद्वान ब्राह्मणों का सम्मान तथा बौद्ध एवं जैन धर्मों के प्रति उदारता का उदाहरण भी प्राप्त होता है। गुप्त एवं गुप्तोत्तर (मौखरि–पुष्यभूति) अभिलेख बाह्य आक्रमण, सामाजिक विश्रृंखलन, कलियुग के अनाचार, वर्णाश्रम की स्थापना के लिए राजाओं की चिन्ता, संसार की असारता, लक्ष्मी की चंचलता और इन पर विजय पाने के लिए श्रेष्ठ वेदपाठी ब्रह्मचारी ब्राह्मणों को भूमिदान देने पर बल देते हुए दिखायी देते हैं जिसका उद्देश्य नैतिक पतन को रोकना था। ध्यातव्य है कि सामाजिक विश्रृंखलन को रोकने का सशक्त माध्यम शिक्षण–संस्थाएं ही होती हैं। पूर्व मध्यकालीन अभिलेखों – ताम्रपत्रों से ज्ञात होता है कि मलयकेतु, सावर्णि एवं गाहडवाल शासक वैष्णव थे जबकि कलचुरि शैव थे। इनके ताम्रपत्रों पर विष्णु के वराह अवतार एवं कमलपुष्प पर आसीन विष्णु का अंकन मिलता है लेकिन इनमें से अधिकांश के लिए 'परम माहेश्वर' की शैवोपाधि का प्रयोग हुआ है। ध्यातव्य है कि गाहडवालों के अभिलेखों से हरि एवं हर के समन्वय की सूचना मिलती है। इस काल की विशेषताओं में एक प्रमुख विशेषता ब्राह्मणों को भूमिदान देना एवं सुदूरवर्ती क्षेत्र (उत्कल, बंगाल, वैशाली इत्यादि) से उन्हें लाकर इस क्षेत्र में बसाना था। दूसरी विशेषता इनकी वे उपाधियां हैं जो इस क्षेत्र की भौगोलिक पहचान को एक नया आयाम प्रदान करती हैं, यथा *सौम्य सिन्धु, उत्तर समुद्र, दरदगण्डकी* एवं *सरयूपार जीवितम्*। ये उपाधियाँ राजाओं के शासन क्षेत्रों की सीमाएँ यहाँ की प्रमुख नदियों द्वारा निर्धारित करने की पुष्टि करती हैं। इन आभिलेखिक साक्ष्यों के आलोक में यह कहा जा सकता है कि आरम्भ से ही पूर्वी उत्तर प्रदेश नव–स्फूर्त सामाजिक–सांस्कृतिक चेतना तथा वैचारिक एवं धार्मिक समन्वय का पक्षधर रहा है।

सन्दर्भ

1. मिराशी, वी0वी0, *कार्पस,* भाग IV, (पार्ट 2) पृ0 389, एफ0 कीलहार्न, *(एपिग्राफिया इण्डिका),* भाग 7, पृ0 93.

2. पिपरहवा, सोहगौरा, भट्टप्रोलू, बड़ली एवं महास्थान, पाण्डेय, राजबली, *हिस्टॉरिकल ऐण्ड लिटरेरी इन्स्क्रीप्शन्स,* भाग 1, वाराणसी, 1962, पृ0 1.2.2.
3. श्रीवास्तव, के0एम0, *एक्सवेशन ऐट पिपरहवा एण्ड गनवरिया,* 1996, ए0एस0आई0, गवर्नमेण्ट ऑफ इण्डिया, 335, नई दिल्ली।
4. *तत्रैव*
5. *हिस्टॉरिकल ऐण्ड लिटरेरी इन्स्क्रीप्शन्स,* भाग–1, वाराणसी, 1962, पृ0 1.
6. *महापरिनिब्बान सुत्त,* 285; *भगवा अम्हाकं अति सेट्ठो। मयम्पि अरहाम भगवतो सरीरानं भागं। मयम्पि भगवतो सरीरानं थूपन्च महन्च करिस्मामा, ति।*
7. पाण्डेय, राजबली, *हिस्टॉरिकल ऐण्ड लिटरेरी इन्स्क्रिप्शन्स,* पृ0 1.
8. *तत्रैव,* पृ0 2.
9. गोयल, श्रीराम, *प्राचीन भारतीय अभिलेख संग्रह, भाग–1, जयपुर, 1982.*
10. *ऋग्वेद,* 2.32.6–8, 10.184.2.
11. *निरूक्त* XI , 31, वर्मा, सिद्धेश्वर, *एटिमोलॉजी ऑफ यास्क,* होशियारपुर, 1953, पृ0 148
12. *अथर्ववेद–* 2, 32, 6–8 (10, 184.2.)
13. लघु स्तम्भ लेख (संघ भेद) सारनाथ संस्करण, पृ0 113, लघु स्तम्भ लेख संघ भेद, प्रयाग संस्करण, पृ0 116, रुम्मिनदेई लघु स्तम्भ लेख पृ0 117, निगालीसागर लघु स्तम्भ लेख, पृ0 122, रानी का प्रयाग लघु स्तम्भ लेख, पृ0 120, अहरौरा (मिर्जापुर) लघु शिलालेख, पृ0 83, द्र0 गोयल, श्रीराम, *प्राचीन भारतीय अभिलेख संग्रह,* भाग 1, जयपुर, 1982.
14. पाण्डेय, राजबली, *अशोक के अभिलेख,* वाराणसी, संवत् 2022, पृ0 7.
15. सर्वप्रथम यह अभिलेख 11 नवम्बर 1961 में *लीडर,* दैनिक समाचार पत्र में प्रकाशित हुआ। तत्रैव, पृ0 7.
16. विनय में बताया गया है कि किस प्रकार के अपराध से संघ में भेद होता है – *भण्डन, कलह, विग्रह, विवाद, संघ भेद, संघराजि, संघवत्थानम्* इत्यादि, द्र0 राधाकुमुद मुकर्जी, *अशोक,* पृ0 196.
17. व्यूहलर, *इण्डियन एण्टीक्वेरी,* भाग 19, पृ0 122.
18. व्यूहलर, *एपिग्राफिया इण्डिका* भाग V, पृ0 169.
19. *तत्रैव*
20. *प्राचीन भारतीय अभिलेख संग्रह,* भाग 1, पृ0 222.
    चोदस वसाभिसितेन बुधस कोनाकमनस थुबे दुतियं बढिते।
    वीसतिवसाभिसितेन च अतन आगाच महीयिते शिला थमं च उसपापिते।
21. पाण्डेय, राजबली, *हिस्टॉरिकल एण्ड लिटरेरी इन्स्क्रिप्शन्स,* पृ0 44.
22. सरकार, डी0सी0, *सेलेक्ट इन्स्क्रिप्शन्स,* भाग–1, पृ0 94
23. कोसम (कौशाम्बी) – बौद्धमूर्ति लेख, (वर्ष 2 = 80 ई0), सरकार डी0सी0, *सेलेक्ट इन्स्क्रिप्शन्स,* भाग–1, 135–36, गोयल श्रीराम, तत्रैव, पृ0 235, फोगल, *एपिग्राफिया इण्डिका,* भाग 8, पृ0 173.
24. सारनाथ बौद्धमूर्ति लेख (वर्ष 3 = 81 ई0) *तत्रैव,* पृ0 136 – 38, *तत्रैव,* पृ0 237.
25. सहेत–महेत बौद्ध–मूर्ति लेख, सरकार, तत्रैव पृ0 144
26. *तत्रैव*
27. प्राचीन भारतीय अभिलेख संग्रह भाग–1, पृ0 237 (सारनाथ बौद्धमूर्ति लेख); *सर्वसत्वनं हित – सुखय भवतु,* कनिष्क का सुई – विहार ताम्रलेख, *तत्रैव,* पृ0 243.
28. *तत्रैव, सभ्यसं बुद्धस्य स्मतस्य देवस्य पयति सर्व्व–दुक्ख प्रहानार्थ* ।। प्रथम कनिष्क मथुरा बौद्ध मूर्ति लेख, पृ0 244.
29. द्र0 अभिलेखों की सूची (संख्या 1)

30. लीट, *कार्पस,* भाग–3, पृ0
31. *तत्रैव,* पृ0 6.
32. *तत्रैव,* पृ0 195, नं0 1, प्लेट 1.
33. *तत्रैव,* उदयगिरिगुहालेख।
34. करमदण्डा शिवलिंग अभिलेख, कनिंघम, *ए0एस0आई0* 3, पृ0 55.
35. गोयल, श्रीराम, *गुप्त कालीन अभिलेख,* पृ0 110–111.
36. *तत्रैव,* पृ0 147.
37. कनिंघम, *ए0एस0आई0,* 3, पृ0 55; गोयल, श्रीराम, *गुप्तकालीन अभिलेख,* 162–165.
38. लीट, *कार्पस,* भाग 3, पृ0 52.
39. *तत्रैव,* पृ0 65.
40. *हिस्टारिकल ऐण्ड लिटरेरी इन्स्क्रिप्शन्स,* भाग 1, पृ0
41. *आई0एच0क्यू0,* 28, पृ0 298–300.
42. गोयल, श्रीराम, *गुप्तकालीन अभिलेख,* पृ0 269.
43. *तत्रैव,* पृ0 274.
44. *तत्रैव,* पृ0 274–276.
    देवपुत्तवतो दिव्यां चित्र विन्यास–चित्रितां।
    यदस्ति पुण्यं प्रतिमां कारयित्वा ममास्तु तत्।।
45. दी0द0उ0गोरखपुर विश्वविद्यालय के प्राचीन इतिहास, पुरातत्त्व एवं संस्कृति विभाग के संग्रहालय में संरक्षित है।
46. थपल्याल, के0के0, *इन्स्क्रिप्शन्स ऑफ दि मौखरीज़, लेटर गुप्ताज़, पुष्यभूतिज एण्ड यशोवर्मा ऑव कन्नौज,* नई दिल्ली, 1985, पृ0 150.
47. गोयल, श्रीराम, *मौखरि–पुष्यभूति एवं चालुक्ययुगीन अभिलेख,* मेरठ, 1987.
48. थपल्याल के0के0, *तत्रैव, 'परममाहेश्वरो महाराजाधिराज श्री अवन्ति वर्मा मौखरि।'*
49. लीट, *कार्पस* भाग–3, पृ0 228, *नृपतिरीश्वर वर्मा . . . . . कृपानुराग शमितक्क्रुरागमोपद्द्रदैर लोकानन्दकरैर्गुणैर्गुणवतां कोनाम . . . . .।*
50. *तत्रैव*
51. गोयल, *मौखरि–पुष्यभूति एवं चालुक्य युगीन अभिलेख,* पृ0 86.
52. *तत्रैव,* पृ0 98.
53. *तत्रैव*
54. सोहगौरा में महाकवि बाण एवं श्रीहर्ष की भेंट।
55. ओमप्रकाश लाल श्रीवास्तव, पूर्व रजिस्ट्रीकरण अधिकारी
56. मिराशी, वी0वी0, *कार्पस,* भाग 4 (पार्ट 2), पृ0 389.
57. कीलहार्न, *एपि0इं0,* भाग 2, पृ0 297–310.
58. एफ0 कीलहार्न, *एपि0इं0,* भाग 7, पृ0 93.
59. *पूर्वा,* सम्पादित, प्रेमसागर चतुर्वेदी, 2009, विपुला दुबे, पूर्वी उत्तर प्रदेश की भौगोलिक एवं धार्मिक पहचान के पुरातात्विक संदर्भ, पृ0 25–28.
60. *साहित्योज्वलरत्नरोहण गिरिर्योह्यष्ट भाषा कविः।*
    ख्यातो वङ्गमहीभजः प्रणयभूः श्रीकुन्दनामाकृती
    तस्या सुन्दरवर्णगुम्फरचनारम्यां प्रशस्तिं व्यधात् ।। 25।।
    एषा प्रशस्तिरुत्कीर्णा वामनेन तु शिल्पिना।
    राजावर्त्तस्य सापल्यन्दधाने प्रस्तरोत्तमे।। 26।।
    – हिस्टारिकल एण्ड लिटरेरी इन्स्क्रिप्शन्स, पृष्ठ 183.

List of Inscriptions from Eastern Uttar Pradesh

Pre-Mauryan Inscriptions

S.No.	Name of Inscription	District	Reference
1.	Piprahwa Buddhist Vase Inscription	Siddharth Nagar	Buhler, J.R.A.S. 1898, p. 387, D.C. Sircar, S.I, I, p. 84, R.B. Pandey, Historical & Literary Inscriptions, p. 1.
2.	Sohagaura Copper Plate Inscription p. 2.	Gorakhpur	H. & L. I, p. 02, K.P. Jaysawal, Ep. Ind. XXII,
Mauryan-Inscriptions			
3.	Minor Pillar Edict : Saranath	Saranath	Hultzsch, C.I.I. I, p. 161, H & L. I, p. 37.
4.	Minor Pillar Edict : Kaushambi	Allahabad	Buhler, Ind. Ant. XIX. p. 122; H. 2, L. 9. p. 38.
5.	Minor Pillar Edict : Queen's,	Kaushambi	Buhler, Ind. Ant. XIX, p. 122, Hultscz, C.I.I., I, p. 158.
6.	Minor Pillar Edict : Rummindei	Nepal	Buhler, Ep. Ind. Vth. p. 169.
7.	Minor Pillar Edict : Nigalisagar	Nepal	Buhler, Ep. Ind., Vth. p. 1.
8.	Minor Rock Edict : Aharaura	Mirzapur	Shri Ram Goyal, Prachina Bhartiya Abhilekha Sangraha, Vol. I, p. 83.
Śuṅga-Inscriptions			
9.	Ayodhya Stone Ins. of Dhanadeva	Ayodhya (Faizabad)	D.R. Sahani, Ep. Ind. XX, p. 57, R.B. Pandey Historical & Literary Inscriptions, I, p. 44.
10.	Two Cave Inscriptions of Udaka (Year 10)	Pabhosa (Allahabad)	S.R. Goyal, Prachina Bhartiya Abhilekha Sangrah. I, p. 169.
Kushāṇa Inscriptions			
11.	Kosam Buddhist Image Ins. of Kanishka I, (Year 2).	Kaushambi (Allahabad)	D.C. Sircar, Select Inscriptions I, p. 135-36.
12.	Sarnath Buddhist image Ins. of Kanishka I	Sarnath (Varanasi)	Vogel, Epigraphia Indica, VIII, p. 173.
13.	Sahet-Mahet Buddhist Image Ins. of Kanishka I.	Śrāvastī (Gonda - Baharaich Border)	Sircar, S.I, Vol. I, p. 145, Ep. Ind., IX.
14.	Sahet-Mahet Chhatra - Yasti Ins. of Kaniṣka I	Śrāvastī	Sircar, S.I, Vol. I, p. 144.

Later Kuṣhāṇa - Inscriptions

15.	Kosam Stone Inscription of Bhdra Magh (Year 86)	Kaushambi (Allahabad)	Sircar, S.I, Vol. I, p. 163.
16.	Kosam image (Shiva - Parvati) inscription of Bhima Varma	Kaushambi (Allahabad)	Fleet, Corpus Inscriptionum Indicarum III, p. 266-271.

Gupta - Inscriptions

17.	Allahabad Pillar Ins. of Samudragupta	Kaushambi (Allahabad)	J.F. Fleet, C.I.I., III, p. 6, Sircar, S.I., Vol.I.,261
18.	Gadhawa Stone Inscription of Chandragupta II, (The year 88)	Allahabad (Karchhana Tahsil)	Fleet, C.I.I., III, No. 7, p. 36.
19.	Karamdanda Stone liṅga inscription of the reign of Kumāragupta I (G.E. 117= 436A.D.)	Ayodhya (Faizabad)	Sten Konow, Ep. Ind., X. p. 71, Raj Bali Pandey, Historical and Literary insc. I, p. 82.
20.	Mankuwar Stone image inscription of Kumāragupta, I, (The year 129)	Allahabad (Karchhana)	Cunningham, A.S.I, X, p. 7.
21.	Gadhawa Stone Inscription of Kumargupta I.	Allahabad	Fleet, C.I.I., III, No. 8; p. 39. Cunningham, A.S.I, III, p. 55.
22.	Gadhawa Stone inscription of Kumāragupta I, (Year 98 = 417A.D.)	Allahabad	Cunningham, A.S.I, X, p. 9, Fleet, Corpus, III, 9, p. 40.
23.	Bhitari Stone Pillar Inscription of Skandagupta	Ghazipur (Near Saidpur)	Fleet, C.I.I. III, No. 13, p. 52.
24.	Kahaum Stone Pillar Inscription of Skandagupta	Deoria	Fleet, C.I.I., III, p. 65, Ind. Ant. Vol. X, p. 125, R.B. Pandey, H. and L. Inscriptions, p. 92.
25.	Sarnath Buddhist image inscription of Kumāragupta II (G.F. 154=473 A.D.)	Sarnath	Sircar, S.I., Vol. I., p. 320.
26.	Saranath Buddhist image inscription of Budhagupta (G.E. 157 = 436 and 476 A.D.)	Sarnath	Sircar, S.I., Vol. I., p. 323.
27.	Bhitari seal of Kumāragupta II or III.	Ghazipur	Sircar, S.I., Vol. I, p. 321.
28.	Kosam stone Image Inscription of the Maharaja Bhimavarman (The year 139)	Kaushambi (Allahabad)	Fleet, Corpus, I.I.,. III, No. 65; p. 266.
29.	Deoria Stone Image Inscription,	Allahabad (Karchhana Sub-Division)	Fleet, C.I.I., Vol. III, No. 68; p. 271.
30.	Kasia Stone Image Inscription	Kushinagar	Fleet, Corpus Inscriptionum Indicarum, Vol. III, No. 69; p. 272-73.
31.	Sarnath Stone Inscription	Sarnath (Varanasi)	Fleet, C.I.I, Vol. III, No. 75, p. 281.
32.	Sarnath Stone Inscription of Prakaṭāditya	Sarnath	Fleet, C.I.I., Vol. III, No. 79; p. 284-85.

No.	Inscription	Place	Reference
Maukhari - Inscriptions			
33.	Jaunpur Inscription of Ishvaravarman	Jaunpur	Fleet, C.I.I., Vol. III, No. 51, p. 228.
34.	Sohanaga Seal Inscription of Avantivarman	Deoria (Salempur Tahsil)	K.K. Thaplyal, Inscriptions of the Maukharis, later Guptas Pushyabhutis and Yashovarma of Kanauj, New Delhi, 1985, p. 150.
35.	Iliya Inscription of Manorath Varmadeva	Varanasi (Chakia Tahsil)	Sircar, Ep. Ind. 34, p. 246-47.
Varadhan - Inscriptions			
36.	Madhuban Copper-Plate Inscription of Harṣha (year 25=631 A.D.)	Azamgarh	Buhler, Ep. Ind., I., p. 72, Sircar, Select Inscriptions, Vol. II, 1983, p. 224-225.
The Malayketu Inscriptions			
37.	Copper Plate Inscription of Jayaditya II	Gorakhpur	F. Kielhorn, Ep. Ind. Vol. XXI, p. 169,-171.
38.	Gurhma Copper-Plate Inscription of Jayaditya II (V.S. 927=870 A.D.)	Gorakhpur	Journal of the royal Asiatic Society of Bengal, Vol. 69, Part I, p. 76, 88; D.C. Sircar, The Gandak Valley in early Medieval Period, Bharti, 1963-64, Vol. VII, Part I.
The Kalachuri Inscriptions from Eastern U.P.			
39.	Kasia Inscription	Kushinagar	V.V. Mirashi, Corpus Inscription Indicarum, Vol. IV, Part II, p. 375.
40.	Varanasi Copper-Plate Inscription of Karnadeva	Varanasi	Kielhorn, Ep. Ind., Vol. II, p. 297-310.
41.	Kahala (Dhuriapar) Copper-plate Inscription of Soḍhadeva	Gorakhpur	Mirashi, Corpus, Vol. IV, (Part-2) p. 389.
The Savarni Inscriptions			
42.	Lucknow Museum Copper-plate Inscription of Kīrtipāla (V.S. 1167-1111 A.D.)	Deoria (Bhatapar Rani)	F. Kielhorn, Ep. Indica, Vol. VII, p. 93.

The Gahadavala Inscriptions

43.	Chandravati Copper-Plate Inscription of Chandradeva (year V.S. 1150-1092 AD)		Sircar, S.I, Vol. II, p. 273.
44.	Banaras Copper-Plate Grant of Govinda Chandra (V.S. 1162-1105 A.D.)	Varanasi	Arthervenis, Ep. Ind., Vol. II, p. 359-61.
45.	Pali Copper-Plate Inscription of Govind Chandra (V.S. 1171=1114 A.D.)	Gorakhpur	Ep. Ind. Vol. Vth, p. 114.
46.	Dona Bujurga Copper-Plate Inscription of Govinda Chandra (V.S. 1176 = 1019)	Mairava (Bihar)	D.R. Sahani, Ep. Ind. Vol. XXVIII.
47.	Pali Copper-Plate Inscription of Ralhana Devi and Govinda Chandra	Gorakhpur	F. Kielhorn, Ep. Ind. Vol. V., p. 113.
48.	Kamauli Copper-Plate Inscription of Govind Chandra (Vikram) (Year 1182 = 1125 A.D.)	Varanasi	Sircar, S.I., Vol. II, p. 283.
49.	Lar Copper-Plate Inscription of Govind Chandra (V.S. 1202=1146 A.D.)	Deoria (Salempur Tahsil)	Kielhorn, Ep. Ind. Vol. VII.
50.	Sahet-Mahet Copper-Plate Inscription of Govinda Chandra (V.S. 1186=1129 A.D.)	Sravasti	Sircar, S.I., Vol. II, p. 288, D.R. Sahani, Ep. Ind. Vol. XI.
51.	Saranath Inscription of Kumārdevī (C. 1114-55 A.D.)	Sarnath	Sten Konow, Ep. Ind. IX, p. 319-328; Sircar, S.I., Vol. II., p. 293.
52.	Gagaha Copper - Platc Inscription of Rājyapāladeva (V.S. 1199=1143 A.D.)	Gorakhpur	L.D. Barnet, Ep. Ind., Vol. XIII., p. 113-114.
53.	Unaval Copper-Plate Inscription of Rājyapāladeva, (V.S. 1201 = 1144 A.D.)	Gorakhpur	Bharati, Bulletin of the College of Indology, Vol. IX, Part 2, p. 174.
54.	Copper-Plate Inscription of Harisha Chandra (V.S. 1253=1196 A.D.)	Jaunpur	Ep. Ind., Vol. XX, p. 93-100.

Seals and Sealings

55.	Bhitari Seal of Kumārgupata II or III	Ghazipur District U.P. (Near Saidpur)	Sircar, S.I., Vol. I, p. 321; Fleet, Ind. Ant. XIX. 1890, p. 225.
56.	Fazilnagar sealing (02) of Gupta Period	Kushinagar	Kept in the Museum of Ancient History, Archaeology and Culture Deptt. D.D.U. Gorakhpur University.
57.	Sealing of the Atharvanika Charana	Rajghat (Varanasi)	The Journal of the Numismatic Society of India, Vol. XXVI, (1964), Part II, p. 214.

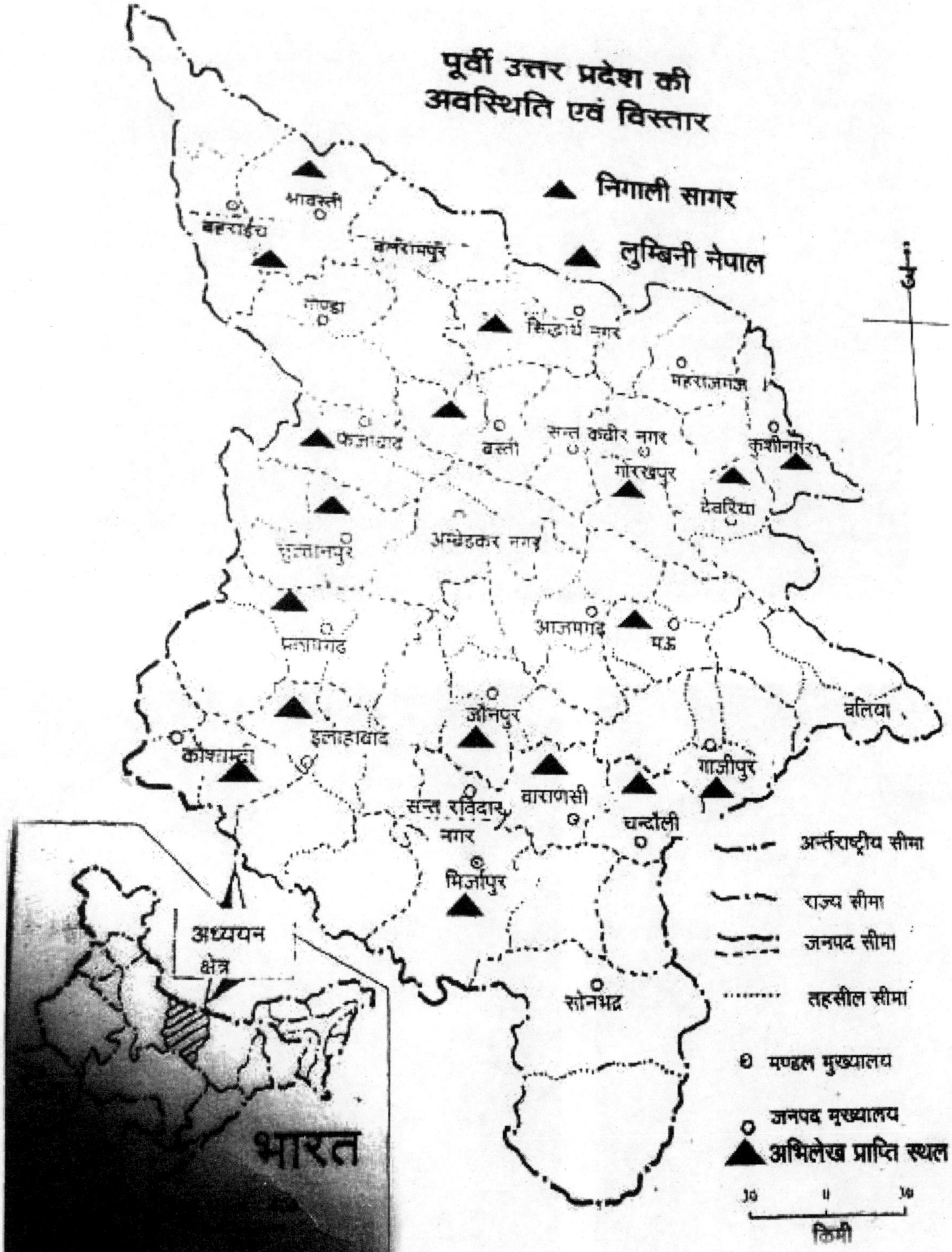

चित्र संख्या 1 – डॉ0 प्रभुनाथ तिवारी के शोध–प्रबन्ध से साभार

चित्र संख्या 2 – सोहगौरा ताम्रपत्र–लेख

चित्र संख्या 3 – फाजिलनगर के टीले से मृण्मुद्रा–छाप प्राचीन इतिहास विभाग, दी0द0उ0गो0वि0वि0 के संग्रहालय से साभार

चित्र संख्या 4 – फाजिलनगर के टीले से प्राप्त मृण्मुद्रा–छाप

20

मध्य गंगा के मैदान में मध्य पाषाण कालीन अस्थि-उपकरण

सरिता कुमारी

भारत में मानव सभ्यता के विकास में गंगा घाटी का विशिष्ट स्थान रहा है। आदिकाल से अपनी विस्तृत अजस्त्र धारा में अनेक संस्कृतियों के विकास व पतन की कहानी समेटे हुए गंगा आज भी भारत की जीवन दायनी शक्ति के रूप में लोक विश्रुत है। विन्ध्य क्षेत्र की पर्वत कन्दराओं से मानव ने जब पहली बार गंगा के मध्यवर्ती मैदान में कदम रखा तो उसे सहज रूप से पहाड़ों की दुरूह जिन्दगी से अवश्य ही राहत मिली होगी। फलतः मानव ने गंगा के विस्तृत समतल मैदान को अपना स्थायी आवास बना लिया।

इलाहाबाद विश्वविद्यालय के प्राचीन इतिहास, संस्कृति एवं पुरातत्व विभाग ने मध्य गंगा घाटी में 1969–70 से लेकर 1986–87 के बीच जो अन्वेषण और उत्खनन किये हैं, उनसे मध्य गंगा घाटी की मध्य पाषाण संस्कृति पर उल्लेखनीय प्रकाश पड़ा है। इन अन्वेषणों के फलस्वरूप मध्य पाषाण के 196 पुरास्थलों के विषय में जानकारी प्राप्त हुई है।[1] मध्य गंगा घाटी के प्रतापगढ़ जिले में स्थित सराय नहर राय, महदहा एवं दमदमा, इलाहाबाद के विछिया, जौनपुर के लोहिना नगोली तथा पुरा गंभीर शाह आदि मध्य पाषाण काल के प्रमुख स्थल है।[2] मध्य गंगा घाटी के प्रतापगढ़ में स्थित सराय नहर राय, महदहा एवं दमदमा का उत्खनन हुआ है। इन उत्खननों के परिणामस्वरूप मध्य गंगा घाटी के मध्य पाषाण के विषय में नवीन सूचनाएँ प्राप्त हुई हैं। लघु पाषाण उपकरण, बलुआ पत्थर और क्वार्टजाइट के बने सिल लोढ़े, पशुओं के सींग पर बने उपकरण एवं आभूषण, वन्य पशुओं की हड्डियाँ एवं मानव कंकाल की अस्थियाँ तीनों उत्खनित पुरास्थल से प्राप्त हुए हैं। मिट्टी के बर्तनों के अवशेष किसी भी पुरास्थल से नहीं मिले हैं।[3]

मध्य पाषाण काल मानव संस्कृति के क्षेत्र में क्रान्तिकारी युग की स्थिति को निरंतर बनाये हुए है। मध्य पाषाण काल एक ऐसे युग की स्थिति को जीवन्त करता है जो पूर्व पाषाण काल को नव पाषाणकाल से जोड़ने में महत्त्वपूर्ण भूमिका का निर्वाह करता है। भारत के संदर्भ में मध्य पाषाण काल एक सुसम्पन्न लघु पाषाण

उपकरणों की तकनीक का द्योतक है, जिसके साक्ष्य इस संदर्भ में विभिन्न क्षेत्रों से प्राप्त हुये हैं। तीनों ही पुरास्थल से इस संस्कृति के विभिन्न पक्षों पर प्रकाश पड़ा है।[4]

गंगा के मैदान में उपकरण निर्माण हेतु पत्थर सहज उपलब्ध नहीं थे। सम्भवतः इसलिए यहाँ के लघु उपकरण विन्ध्य क्षेत्र की तुलना में छोटे हैं, और कम संख्या में प्राप्त होते हैं। इस कमी को पूरा करने के लिए गंगा के मैदान में मध्य पाषाणिक मानव ने उपकरणों के निर्माण के लिए अस्थि का प्रयोग किया।[5] सरायनहर राय के उत्खनन से प्राप्त हड्डी के बने उपकरणों में स्क्रेपर और चाकू का विशेषतः उल्लेख किया जा सकता है। इनके अतिरिक्त पशुओं की सामान्य नुकीली हड्डियों से खोदने का काम किया जाता था।

महदहा के उत्खनन में बहुत अधिक संख्या में हड्डी के उपकरण उपलब्ध हुए हैं। इनमें हड्डी से निर्मित 45 उपकरणों में वाणाग्र, नोक ब्लेड, चाकू, छेनी, स्क्रेपर, आरी आदि सम्मिलित हैं।[6] इनके अतिरिक्त हड्डी से निर्मित कुछ अन्य वस्तुएँ भी उपलब्ध हुई हैं, लेकिन उनके प्रयोग के बारे में निश्चित ज्ञान नहीं है। वाणाग्रों का निर्माण अधिकांशतः खड़ी कटी हुई पशुओं की लम्बी हड्डियों अथवा सीगों पर किया गया है, जिन्हें चारों तरफ से रगड़ कर चिकना और नुकीला बनाया गया है। महदहा के उत्खनन ने भारतवर्ष में इस तरह के हड्डी के वाणाग्रो का प्राचीनतम प्रमाण प्रस्तुत किया है। इनकी नोक का निर्माण वाणाग्र की तरफ ही किया जाता था। उनका निर्माण अधिकांशतः हिरणों की छोटी सींगों पर किया गया है। यहाँ पर कुछ अर्धनिर्मित और निर्माण की विभिन्न अवस्थाओं में विद्यमान हड्डी के कुछ अन्य उपकरण मिले हैं जो इस तथ्य के संकेतक हैं कि उनका निर्माण यहीं पर किया जाता था।

महदहा के उत्खनन से हड्डी के बने 26 आभूषण प्राप्त हुए हैं, जिनमें से 19 पूर्ण निर्मित और 7 अर्धनिर्मित हैं। इनका निर्माण मृग श्रृंगों से किया गया है। इन आभूषणों में कान का कुण्डल और गले का हार सम्मिलित हैं। 11 छोटी मुद्रिकाओं वाला एक हार एक समाधि के मानव कंकाल के गले से प्राप्त हुआ था। यहाँ की तीन समाधियों में कुण्डल अथवा हार के प्रमाण प्राप्त हुए हैं। मानव द्वारा आभूषण के प्रयोग का यह प्राचीनतम प्रमाण माना जाता है। काटने के निशान से युक्त मृग श्रृगों से आभूषणों के निर्माण पद्धति पर प्रकाश पड़ता है।

महदहा से उपलब्ध पशुओं के अस्थि अवशेषों का विश्लेषण करते समय पी.पी. जोगलेकर को हड्डी से बने कुछ और उपकरण व आभूषण प्राप्त हुए हैं, जिनमें 83 उपकरण और एक अर्धनिर्मित मनका सम्मिलित है। जोगलेकर के अनुसार अस्थि उपकरण के निर्माण के लिए अधिकांशतः चीतल और सांभर की हड्डियों का प्रयोग किया गया है। इसके अतिरिक्त गाय, बैल, नीलगाय, चौसिंहा हिरन आदि की हड्डियाँ भी उपकरण निर्माण में प्रयुक्त की गयी हैं।[7]

दमदमा के उत्खनन में भी इस तरह के उपकरणों और आभूषणों के प्रमाण प्राप्त हुए हैं। यहाँ के उत्खनन से 13 हड्डी की बनी वस्तुएँ प्राप्त हुई, जिनमें छोटे व बड़े आकार के वाणाग्र, मनके और लटकन, चूड़ी और अलंकृत वस्तुएँ सम्मिलित हैं। हड्डी के बने वाणाग्र प्रायः गोले अथवा अण्डाकार अनुभाग के हैं, जिनका एक किनारा अधिक चिकना और नुकीला बनाया गया है। पशुओं की नुकीली हड्डियों और श्रृगों के नुकीले भाग को भी उपकरण के रूप में प्रयुक्त किया गया है। इन पर प्रयोग का स्पष्ट प्रमाण मिलता है। हड्डी की अधिकांश वस्तुओं का निर्माण जली अथवा अधजली हड्डियों से किया गया है। यहाँ के उत्खनन में समाधियों से हड्डी से बने आभूषण प्राप्त हुए हैं, जिनमें से कुछ का निर्माण हाथी दाँत पर किया गया है।[8]

मध्य पाषाण युगीन विभिन्न उपकरणों में लघु पाषाण उपकरण, हड्डी के उपकरण और क्वार्टजाइट तथा बलुआ पत्थर के बने सिल लोढ़े, हथौड़े, हाथगोले आदि सम्मिलित हैं।

संदर्भ

1. वर्मा, आर.के. 1986, *दि मेसोलिथिक एज इन मिर्जापुर,* इलाहाबाद, परम ज्योति प्रकाशन।
– शर्मा, जी.आर., वी.डी. मिश्र, डी. मंडल, बी.बी. मिश्र और जे.एन. पाल, *विगनिंग्स ऑफ एग्रिकल्चर* अविनाश प्रकाशन, इलाहाबाद।

2. मिश्र, वी.एन., 2002, *मेसोलिथिक कल्चर इन इण्डियाँ,* मेसोलिथिक इण्डिया, पृष्ठ 10–11

3. *पूर्वोक्त*।

4. शर्मा, जी.आर., 1973, 'मेसोलिथिक लेक कल्चर्स इन दि गंगा वैली', *प्रोसीडिंगस् ऑफ दि प्री–हिस्टॉरिक सोसाइटी,* वाल्यूम 39, पृ. 129–130
– शर्मा, जी.आर., 1975, 'सीजनल माइग्रेसन एण्ड मेसोलिथिक लेक कल्चर्स इन दि गंगा वैली', *के.सी. चट्टोपाध्याय मेमोरियल वाल्यूम,* पृष्ठ–1–20

5. शर्मा, जी.आर., वी.डी. मिश्र, डी. मंडल, बी.बी. मिश्र और जे.एन. पाल, 1980, *विगनिंग्स ऑफ एग्रिकल्चर,* अविनाश प्रकाशन, इलाहाबाद।

6. गुप्ता, एम.सी., 2000, *मेसोलिथिक बोन ऑब्जेक्टस् ऑफ दि मिडिल गंगेटिक प्लेन*।
– मिश्र, वी.डी., जे.एन. पाल द्वारा सम्पादित *मेसोलिथिक इण्डिया,* इलाहाबाद, पृष्ठ 306–312

7. जोगलेकर, पी.पी., वी.डी. मिश्र और जे.एन. पाल, 2003, फाइनल रिमेन्स फ्राम मेसोलिथिक महदहा, पी.पी. जोगलेकर, वी.डी. मिश्र, जे.एन. पाल और एम.सी. गुप्ता द्वारा लिखित *मेसोलिथिक महदहा : दि फाइनल रिमेन्स,* इलाहाबाद, पृष्ठ 54–60

8. शर्मा, जी.आर., वी.डी. मिश्र, जे.एन. पाल, 1980 *इंक्सकैवेसन्स एट महदहा,* इलाहाबाद
– वर्मा, आर.के., वी.डी. मिश्र, जे.एन. पाण्डेय, जे.एन. पाल, 1985, ए प्रिलीमिनरी रिपोर्ट आन दि इक्सकैवेसन्स एट दमदमा (1982–1984), *मैन एण्ड इनवायरमेन्ट,* अंक–9, पृष्ठ 45–65
– पाल, जे.एन. 2002, मेसोलिथिक गंगेटिक प्लेन, वी.डी. मिश्र व जे.एन. पाल द्वारा सम्पादित, *मेसोलिथिक इंडिया,* इलाहाबाद। पृष्ठ 289–305

21

पूर्वी उत्तर प्रदेश में पर्यावरण पुरातत्त्व के क्षेत्र में शोध की संभावनायें

पुष्पलता सिंह

भौगोलिक क्षेत्रफल के आधार पर पूर्वी उत्तर प्रदेश (24°16' - 27°40'N; 81°20' - 84°14'E) मध्य गंगा के 43% भाग में विस्तृत है जो बौद्ध साहित्य में वर्णित *मज्झिम देश* का एक भाग है। अद्यतन पुरातात्त्विक शोधों से यह स्पष्ट है कि यह क्षेत्र अपनी पारिस्थितिकी के कारण प्रागैतिहासिक काल से ही मनुष्य के आकर्षण का केन्द्र था। इस क्षेत्र की अनुकूल जलवायु, उपजाऊ भूमि, खाद्य सामग्री की उपलब्धता ने प्राचीन काल से मनुष्य को आकर्षित किया है। इसीलिये सुब्बाराव[1] ने अपने भौगोलिक एवं पुरातात्त्विक विभाजन में इस क्षेत्र को आकर्षण का केन्द्र *(एरियाज ऑफ एट्रैक्शन)* या नाभिकीय क्षेत्र *(न्यूक्लियर रीजन)* के अन्तर्गत सम्मिलित किया है।

पुरातात्त्विक सर्वेक्षण एवं उत्त्खनन के आधार पर इस क्षेत्र के पुरातात्त्विक सांस्कृतिक अनुक्रम की प्राचीनता अनुपुरापाषाण काल से मुस्लिम काल तक प्रतिष्ठापित होती है। इस क्षेत्र के उत्त्खनित पुरास्थलों में कौशाम्बी (25°20'N, 81°23'E) जिला कौशाम्बी; झूँसी (25°26'10"N, 81°54'30"E) जिला इलाहाबाद; सरायनाहरराय (25°48'N, 81°50'E), महदहा (25°29'2"N, 81°11'30"E), दमदमा (26°10'N, 82°20'36"E) जिला प्रतापगढ़, अयोध्या (26°48'N, 82°14'E) जिला फैजाबाद; श्रावस्ती (27°32'N, 82°2'E) जिला श्रावस्ती; लहुरादेवा (26°16'N, 82°57'E), कोपिया (26°51'N, 83°50'E) जिला सन्तकबीर नगर; सिसवनिया (26°45'N, 82°46'E), पिपरहवा (27°26'N, 83°7'E) जिला बस्ती; इमलीडीह खुर्द (26°30'30"N, 83°12'15"E); धुरियापार (26°25'25"N, 83°14'30"E), सोहगौरा (26°28'N, 83°47'E) जिला गोरखपुर; चरदा (27°56'45" N, 81°36'40"E), पीर पितनीशरीफ–त्रिलोकपुर (27°50'30"N, 81°36'40"E) जिला बहराइच; हरिहरपुर (25°36'23"N, 81°58'20"E) जिला जौनपुर; अकथा (25°22'N, 83°01'E), राजघाट (25°4'N, 83°1'E) जिला वाराणसी; भितरी (25°18'N,

83°12'E) जिला गाजीपुर; वैना (26°10'N, 83°15'E), भूनाडीह (25°19'10"N, 84°5'11"E), खैराडीह (26°10'N, 83°51'30" E) जिला बलिया; अगियाबीर (25°13'52"N, 82°38'41" E) जिला मिर्जापुर आदि है।

पुरापर्यावरण एक अन्तर्विषयी विषय है जिसके पुनर्निर्माण में भूगर्भविज्ञान, मृदाविज्ञान, पुरावनस्पति विज्ञान एवं पुराजीव विज्ञान का महत्त्वपूर्ण योगदान है। पूर्वी उत्तर–प्रदेश में पुरापर्यावरण के संदर्भ में हाल में बीरबल साहनी पुरावनस्पति संस्थान, उ.प्र., पुरातत्त्व राज्य निदेशालय, भूगर्भविज्ञान विभाग, लखनऊ विश्वविद्यालय, लखनऊ के द्वारा किये गये अध्ययन–अनुसंधानों से कुछ महत्त्वपूर्ण नवीन तथ्य प्रकाश में आये हैं।

पूर्वी उत्तर प्रदेश में भूदृश्य अध्ययन *(लैण्डस्केप स्टडी)* एवं प्राचीन अधिवास–प्रतिरूपों *(सेटिलमेंट पैटर्न)* के परस्पर संबन्धों पर शोध की नयी संभावनायें हैं क्योंकि इस क्षेत्र में हुये विवर्तनिक हलचलों ने भूदृश्य निर्माण को अत्यधिक प्रभावित किया एवं इस भूदृश्य निर्माण ने अधिवास प्रकिया को प्रभावित किया। प्रातिनूतनकाल के अन्त एवं अतिनूतन काल के प्रारंभ में विवर्तनिक हलचलों के कारण गंगा एवं उसकी सहायक नदियों ने अनेकों बार अपनी धाराओं को परिवर्तित किया था जिसके फलस्वरूप इस क्षेत्र में अनेक गोखुर झीलों का निर्माण हुआ। ये गोखुर झीलें रेखीय झीलों के रूप में उपलब्ध हैं। शुष्क जलवायु के कारण ये झीलें और छोटे–छोटे आकार में संकुचित हो गयी । इन झीलों के अवसादों से प्राप्त परागकणों के अध्ययन से यह संकेत मिलता है कि आज से लगभग 10,500 से 5000 वर्ष पूर्व के मध्य इस क्षेत्र में भारी वर्षा होने के कारण इन झीलों का निर्माण एवं विस्तार हुआ था। इन झीलों में उपलब्ध पानी, जलीय जीव–जन्तु एवं इन के किनारों पर उगी हुई जंगली वनस्पतियों की खाद्य सामग्री के रूप में सहज उपलब्धता ने प्राचीन मानव को इस क्षेत्र में सन्निवेश हेतु आकर्षित किया होगा जिसकी पुष्टि इन झीलों के किनारे अवस्थित अनुपुरापाषाणकालीन एवं मध्यपुरापाषाणकालीन पुरास्थलों से होती है।

अतिनूतनकाल या नूतनतम *(होलोसीन)* काल के प्रारंभ में यहाँ पर मानव अधिवास के सन्निवेश में तीव्रता आई थी जिसका संकेत इस क्षेत्र से प्राप्त 183 मध्यपाषाणिक स्थलों से मिलता है। इनमें 177 मध्यपाषाणिक स्थल प्रतापगढ़ एवं 7 इलाहाबाद जिले में अवस्थित हैं। 177 मध्यपाषाणिक पुरास्थलों में 167 पुरास्थल प्रतापगढ़ जिले में गोखुर झील के किनारे स्थित हैं जिनमें 155 पुरास्थल अज्यामितिक मध्यपाषाणिक चरण तथा 12 ज्यामितिक मध्य पाषाणिक चरण से सम्बद्ध हैं। इलाहाबाद जिले में अवस्थित 7 मध्यपाषाणिक स्थलों में 05 मध्यपाषाणिक स्थल गोखुर झील के किनारे अवस्थित हैं।[2] साधारणतया ये स्थल आकार में छोटे हैं जो लगभग 4.5 वर्गमीटर से 5 वर्गमीटर के क्षेत्र में विस्तृत हैं। किन्तु, इनमें कुछ बड़े स्थल भी हैं जैसे सरायनहरराय (1800 वर्गमीटर), महदहा (8000 वर्गमीटर) एवं दमदमा (8750 वर्गमीटर)। सरायनहरराय, महदहा एवं दमदमा उत्त्खनित मध्यपाषाणिक पुरास्थल हैं जो मध्यपूर्वी उ.प्र. के प्रतापगढ़ जिले में स्थित हैं। प्रतापगढ़ जिले में एक मध्यपाषाणिक पुरास्थल की दूसरे मध्यपाषाणिक पुरास्थल के मध्य की दूरी 5 से 10 किलोमीटर है जिसका कारण प्रतापगढ़ जिले में इन गोखुर झीलों का एक दूसरे के अत्यन्त समीप होना है किन्तु इलाहाबाद में इन पुरास्थलों के मध्य की दूरी अधिक है।

इस प्रारंभिक मध्यपाषाण काल से सम्बद्ध मानव द्वारा जिन सूक्ष्मपाषाण उपकरणों का प्रयोग किया जाता था वे अनुपुरापाषाणकालीन उपकरणों की तुलना में आकार में छोटे एवं बेलनघाटी के मध्यपाषाणकालीन उपकरणों के समान हैं। इन सूक्ष्मपाषाण उपकरणों के निर्माण में ग्रे चर्ट का प्रयोग किया गया है। किन्तु बेलनघाटी की तुलना में गंगा के क्षेत्र में प्रयोग किये जाने वाले सूक्ष्मपाषाण उपकरणों का आकार छोटा है एवं वे संख्या में भी कम हैं। इसका कारण इस क्षेत्र में उपकरण निर्माण हेतु पाषाण का अनुपलब्ध होना है। गंगा के इस क्षेत्र में निवास करने वाले मध्य पाषाणिक लोगों ने सूक्ष्मपाषाण उपकरणों के निर्माण हेतु बेलनघाटी के ग्रे चर्ट एवं जानवरों की

हड्डियों एवं सींगों का प्रचुर मात्रा में प्रयोग किया है। इन उपकरणों में वाणाग्र, ब्लेड, नुकीले उपकरण, चाकू आदि सम्मिलित हैं। यहाँ यह उल्लेखनीय है कि बेलन क्षेत्र में हड्डी पर बने सूक्ष्मपाषाणकालीन उपकरणों की संख्या कम है।

अद्यतन हुये पुरातात्त्विक सर्वेक्षण से दक्षिण मध्य गंगा क्षेत्र से नवपाषाणकाल से सम्बद्ध किसी भी पुरास्थल का प्रमाण नहीं मिला है। संभवतः इसका कारण पाषाण की अनुपलब्धता या नदियों की धारा में परिवर्तन अथवा जलोढ़ भूमि के कृषि कार्य हेतु प्रयोग किये जाने के कारण विनष्ट हो जाना रहा होगा। यद्यपि इलाहाबाद जिले में गोरमा, बेलन, तुन्दारी, सेवती नदियों के किनारे से कुछ नवपाषाणकालीन स्थल प्रकाश में आये हैं किन्तु गंगा नदी के किनारे से मात्र दो नवपाषाणकालीन पुरास्थल चोखाना (25°14'30"N; 82°8'E) एवं छाकुन्था गोरा (25°16'N; 82°10'E) प्राप्त हुये हैं। पुनः सोलह ताम्र–पाषाण काल से सम्बन्धित पुरास्थल प्रतापगढ़ एवं इक्कीस पुरास्थल इलाहाबाद जिले में नदियों के किनारे अवस्थित मिले हैं। इलाहाबाद जिले में स्थित ये ताम्र–पाषाणिक पुरास्थल बेलन, गोरमा, तुन्दारी, सेवती, टोंस आदि नदियों के किनारे स्थित हैं।[3]

पुरापर्यावरण की संरचना में पुरावनस्पतियों के अध्ययन का भी महत्त्वपूर्ण स्थान है। पुरावनस्पतियों के दो भाग हैं – वृहत पुरावनस्पतियों के अवशेष एवं सूक्ष्म पुरावनस्पतियों के अवशेष। सूक्ष्म पुरावनस्पतियों के अवशेषों के अन्तर्गत झीलों के अवसादों से प्राप्त परागकणों का अध्ययन पुराजलवायु की पुनर्संरचना में अत्यन्त सहायक है। पूर्वी एवं मध्य उ.प्र. में स्थित महत्त्वपूर्ण झीलों में लहुरादेवा (सन्त कबीरनगर), सनईताल(राय बरेली), बसहा झील (उन्नाव), मीसाताल एवं कथुवा ताल (लखनऊ) प्रमुख हैं जिनके अवसादों से प्राप्त परागकणों का अध्ययन कर यह स्थापित करने का प्रयास किया गया कि चतुर्थांश (क्वाटर्नरी) काल में किस प्रकार जलवायु परिवर्तन हुआ एवं उन जलवायु परिवर्तनों ने किस प्रकार तत्कालीन वनस्पतियों एवं मानव अधिवास को प्रभावित किया था।[4]

बीरबल साहनी पुरावनस्पति संस्थान के एम.एस. चौहान, अनिल कुमार पोखरिया तथा लखनऊ विश्वविद्यालय के भूवैज्ञानिक आई.वी. सिंह ने लहुरादेवा झील का जो कार्बन तिथियुक्त अधोलिखित पर्यावरणीय पार्श्वमानचित्र निर्मित किया है उससे अतिनूतनकाल में पूर्वी उ.प्र. के सम्बन्ध में नवीन पुरापर्यावरणीय प्रतिमान स्थापित हुए हैं जो इस क्षेत्र की पूर्ववर्ती सभी अवधारणाओं पर प्रश्न चिह्न लगाते हुये शोध को एक नयी दिशा प्रदान करते हैं –

लहुरादेवा झील की तिथियुक्त मृदा संरचना

सतह से गहराई	*कार्बन तिथि*	*असंशोधित तिथि*	*मृदा*
0.50 – 0.60	1040 ± 100 बी0पी0	950 बी0पी0	पादप जड़युक्त
0.75 – 1	1810 ± 100 बी0पी0	1714 बी0पी0	काली गीली मिट्टी
1.25 – 1.30	2180 ± 90 बी0पी0	2188 बी0पी0	काली गीली मिट्टी
2.30 – 2.40	7010 ± 170 बी0पी0	7822 बी0पी0	के साथ मिट्टी या कीचड़ + मिट्टी
2.50 – 2.60	8710 ± 90 बी0पी0	9720 बी0पी0	कार्बनिक गीली
2.70 – 2.80	9210 ± 170 बी0पी0	1025 बी0पी0	काली मिट्टी या कीचड़ + कार्बनिक मिट्टी

इसी प्रकार लहुरादेवा झील के अवसादों से प्राप्त परागकणों के आधार पर एक पराग आरेख निर्मित किया गया जिसे कालक्रम एवं वनस्पतियों के आधार पर क्रमशः पाँच विभिन्न परागक्षेत्रों I, II, III, IV एवं V में विभाजित किया गया। इसका समय कार्बन तिथि के आधार पर आज से लगभग 10,600 – 1300 वर्ष पूर्व निर्धारित किया गया है जो निम्न है–[5]

लहुरादेवा झील का तिथियुक्त परागकण पर्यावरणीय पार्श्व आरेख

परागकण क्षेत्र	कालक्रम	पर्यावरण	पादप पारिस्थितकी
लहुरादेवा–V	वर्तमान से 1350 वर्ष पूर्व	मानसून वर्षा में कमी	जलीय पौधों की कमी, वृक्षों की अभिवृद्धि और झील अपने पूर्ववर्ती आकार से संकुचित हो गयी + कृषि का प्रमाण देखा गया।
लहुरादेवा–IV	1350–4060 वर्ष पूर्व	मानक मानसून वर्षा जो लहुरादेवा–III से कम और लहुरादेवा–V से ज्यादा थी।	घने जंगल क्षेत्र की अभिवृद्धि + कृषि का प्रसार + पूर्ववर्ती झील दलदल के रूप में परिवर्तित होती गयी।
लहुरादेवा–III	4060 – 6400 वर्ष पूर्व	मानसून वर्षा में अभिवृद्धि	जलीय पौधों में अभिवृद्धि + कृषि प्रसार में अभिवृद्धि + जंगलों का प्रसार
लहुरादेवा–II	6400 – 9250 वर्ष पूर्व	लहुरादेवा I की तुलना में पर्यावरण में सुधार + मानसून वर्षा में अभिवृद्धि	जलीय पौधों में अभिवृद्धि + झील का प्रसार क्षेत्र विस्तृत हुआ।
लहुरादेवा–I	9250 – 10600 वर्ष पूर्व	ठंडा पर्यावरण और मानसून वर्षा में कमी	घास के मैदान और झीलों के किनारे पौधों का आविर्भाव

पूर्वी उत्तर प्रदेश में जिस समय प्रातिनूतन काल का अन्त और अतिनूतन काल का आविर्भाव हुआ था उस समय इस क्षेत्र का पर्यावरण ठंडा था और वर्षा बहुत कम होती थी। इस प्रकार की परिस्थिति वर्तमान से 9,250 वर्ष पूर्व तक बनी हुयी थी। इस समय तक मध्य गंगा का क्षेत्र भी प्रौढ़ नहीं हो सका था जिसकी पुष्टि उसके वर्तमान तल के नीचे के भूगर्भीय अध्ययन से होती है। साथ ही जिन गोखुर झीलों का उल्लेख पूर्वी उत्तर प्रदेश के संदर्भ में किया गया है, वे भी अपने निर्माण के शैशवकाल में ही थी। परन्तु इस काल खण्ड (10600 – 9250 वर्ष पूर्व) में इन नव निर्मित झीलों के किनारे मानवीय अधिवास की प्रकिया आरम्भ हो चुकी थी। यह निष्कर्ष मानवीय पुरावशेष के आधार पर नहीं अपितु इस क्षेत्र के परागकण विश्लेषण के आधार पर पुरावनस्पतिशास्त्रियों

ने स्थापित किया है। यद्यपि सरायनहरराय में इस कालखण्ड के तत्काल बाद हमें कार्बन तिथि युक्त मध्यपाषाण संस्कृति के अवशेष दिखायी पड़ने लगते हैं, लहुरादेवा के प्रथम काल खण्ड, जिसका समय आज से लगभग 10425 से 9720 वर्ष पूर्व है, उस समय तलछट अवसाद के जमाव की गति 2.8 मिली मीटर प्रति 100 वर्ष थी। इस प्रकार तलछट अवसाद के जमाव की अपरिवर्तित गति से स्पष्ट है कि लहुरादेवा के प्रथम कालखण्ड के अन्दर पर्यावरण में कोई ज्यादा परिवर्तन नहीं हुआ, अपितु वह एक समान अर्थात् कम वर्षा एवं शीतयुक्त था। इस कालखण्ड में सर्वाधिक वनस्पति के रूप में घास (60-80%) के मैदान थे। 26.5% सादे जलीय शैवालों से यह स्पष्ट है कि इस समय धीरे धीरे झीलों का आविर्भाव प्रारम्भ हो चुका था जिसके चारो तरफ घास का मैदान था। राजस्थान में इसी कालखण्ड (आज से 10,000 वर्ष पूर्व) का जो पराग पार्श्व नक्शा हमें साम्भर, डिडवाना, लुनकरनसार और पुष्कर झील से प्राप्त होता है उससे स्पष्ट होता है कि इस समय वहाँ का पर्यावरण शुष्क था जिसके फलस्वरूप राजस्थान में रेत के टीलों का निर्माण हुआ।

लहुरादेवा के द्वितीय कालखण्ड (9250 से 6400 वर्ष पूर्व) में पूर्ववर्ती काल की तुलना में मानसूनी वर्षा ज्यादा हुयी थी जिसके फलस्वरूप झील का निर्माण हुआ। इस कालखण्ड में तलछट अवसाद के जमाव की गति 1 मिली मीटर प्रति सौ वर्ष थी। तलछट अवसाद की गति में कमी स्वतः पूर्ववर्ती कालखण्ड से ज्यादा वर्षा की द्योतक है। इस समय छिटपुट बड़े पौधों का प्रमाण मिलता है परन्तु उनकी प्रचुरता नहीं थी। अपितु इसके विपरीत 61-70% सादे जलीय पौधों का प्रमाण दिखायी पड़ता है। सादे जलीय शैवालों की आवृत्ति 54% तक दिखायी पड़ती है जबकि फर्न प्रजाति के पौधों में 3.5 से 6 प्रतिशत तक लगातार अभिवृद्धि दिखायी पड़ती है। अतः इससे यह निष्कर्ष निकाला गया कि इस समय झील का निर्माण अधिक वर्षा के कारण हुआ। सम्भवतः यह वह समय रहा होगा जब पूर्वी उत्तर प्रदेश में गंगा और अन्य नदियों के अन्दर जल की अभिवृद्धि हुयी होगी और यह सम्पूर्ण क्षेत्र अत्यधिक वर्षायुक्त क्षेत्र के रूप में परिवर्तित हो चुका था। इसके विपरीत राजस्थान के इस कालखण्ड में लहुरादेवा के प्रथम कालखण्ड के समान घास के मैदान का विकास हुआ। इस क्षेत्र में औसत वर्षा 100–250 मिली मीटर होती थी जो निश्चय ही पूर्वी उत्तर प्रदेश की तुलना में कम थी।

लहुरादेवा के तृतीय कालखण्ड (6400–4060 वर्ष पूर्व) में द्वितीय कालखण्ड की तुलना में मानसूनी वर्षा ज्यादा हुयी जिसके कारण जलीय पौधों में अभिवृद्धि हुयी। इस समय तलछट अवसाद की जमाव की गति 1.7 मिली मीटर प्रति सौ वर्ष थी जो पहले से 0.7 मिली मीटर प्रति सौ वर्ष ज्यादा थी जिससे स्पष्ट है कि इस काल में पूर्ववर्ती काल की तुलना में वर्षा ज्यादा हुयी थी। पूर्ववर्ती काल की तुलना में इस काल में जलीय पौधों में 57% बढ़ोत्तरी हुयी जब कि फर्न प्रजाति की वनस्पतियों में पहले से कमी हुयी (2-3% फर्न दिखायी पड़ता है)। इस समय झीलों का आकार पहले से ज्यादा विस्तृत हो गया जिससे स्पष्ट है कि पूर्वी उत्तर प्रदेश की गंगा और उसकी सहायक नदियों के जलस्तर में अभिवृद्धि हुयी होगी। सिंघाड़े का प्रमाण स्वतः झील के पानी में वृद्धि का परिचायक है। इसी के साथ ही अन्न के दानों से सम्बद्ध परागकणों में वृद्धि से कृषि में विस्तार का संकेत मिलता है। इसी कालखण्ड में इस क्षेत्र में चावल की खेती का प्रसार हुआ जब कि राजस्थान में इस समय जलवायु समवर्षा युक्त थी, अर्थात् न तो सूखा था और न ही बाढ़ जैसी स्थिति थी। इस काल में पूर्वी उत्तर प्रदेश में कृषि का प्रसार हआ जिसकी पुष्टि लहुरादेवा और कोलडिहवा से प्राप्त अन्न के साक्ष्यों से होती है।

उपरोक्त वर्णित लहुरादेवा झील का वर्तमान धरातल से 2.8 मीटर गहराई तक तिथियुक्त परागकण विश्लेषण किया गया है। उससे स्पष्ट है कि लहुरादेवा के चतुर्थ कालखण्ड (वर्तमान से 4060 से 1350 वर्ष पूर्व) में वर्षा राजस्थान के पूर्ववर्ती काल में समान न तो ज्यादा होती थी और न ही कम, परन्तु अपने तृतीय कालखण्ड (6400 – 4060 वर्ष पूर्व) से इस कालखण्ड में वर्षा कम हुयी। इस कालखण्ड में तलछट अवसाद के जमाव की गति 7 मिली मीटर प्रति वर्ष थी जो पूर्ववर्ती कालखण्डों की तुलना में 700% ज्यादा थी। इससे स्पष्ट है कि इस

समय पहले की तुलना में वर्षा कम हुयी थी और झीलों का आकार पहले से छोटा होने लगा था। सेशलिया पादप के प्रतिशत में पहले की तुलना में ज्यादा वृद्धि हुयी जिससे स्पष्ट है कि इस काल में खेती का विस्तार ज्यादा हुआ। इस समय झील प्रायः दलदली रूप में परिवर्तित हो गयी थी। इसी कालखण्ड में राजस्थान में हड़प्पीय संस्कृति का विकास और पतन हुआ था। लहुरादेवा में इस कालखण्ड में 3–12% पाइन के परागकण मिलते हैं जो वास्तव में हिमालय क्षेत्र के थे। इससे स्पष्ट है कि हिमालय के क्षेत्र में फैले ये परागकण उत्तर–दक्षिण और उत्तर–दक्षिण–पूर्वी दिशा में तेज चलने वाली हवाओं के कारण इस क्षेत्र में प्रसारित हुए।

लहुरादेवा के पंचम कालखण्ड (वर्तमान से 1350 वर्ष पूर्व) में मानसून वर्षा में कमी हुयी जिसके कारण वृक्षों में कमी और कृषि में विस्तार हुआ था। अतः इस काल में जंगलों का अभाव देखा गया। पुरावनस्पति विज्ञानियों का यह निष्कर्ष पूर्ववर्ती उस अवधारणा को खण्डित करता है जिसके अनुसार गंगा का यह क्षेत्र बौद्ध काल में घने जंगलों से आच्छादित था और जिसे काटकर कृषि–योग्य भूमि पाने के लिये लौह उपकरणों की आवश्यकता थी।

पुरावनस्पतियों के अध्ययन के समान ही पुरापर्यावरण के पुनर्निर्माण में पुराजीव विज्ञान का भी महत्त्वपूर्ण योगदान है। पूर्वी उत्तर–प्रदेश के विभिन्न पुरास्थलों के विभिन्न सांस्कृतिक कालों के जमावों से प्राप्त पशुओं के जीवाश्मों के अध्ययन के आधार पर तत्कालीन पुराजलवायु के पुनर्निर्माण एवं जीविका निर्वाह के साधन पर भी प्रकाश पड़ता है। किन्तु, पूर्वी उत्तर प्रदेश के कुछ ही पुरास्थलों, जैसे नरहन[6], पीरवितनीशरीफ–त्रिलोकपुर[7], चरदा[8] एवं दमदमा आदि से ही प्राप्त पशुओं के जीवाश्मों का अध्ययन किया गया है। इन स्थलों से प्राप्त पशुओं की जली हुयी हड्डियों एवं कटे के निशान से इस तथ्य की पुष्टि होती है कि इन पशुओं का प्रयोग खाद्य सामग्री के रूप में किया जाता था। पुरापर्यावरण के अध्ययन की दृष्टि से इंस दिशा में एक महत्त्वपूर्ण विश्लेषण किया गया जिसमें चरदा (पूर्वी उत्तर प्रदेश) तथा दादूपुर एवं कल्ली पच्छिम (पश्चिमी उत्तर प्रदेश) से प्राप्त पशुओं *(बॉस इण्डिकस)* के दांतों के इनेमल के आक्सीजन आइसोटोप्स के आधार पर यह निष्कर्ष निकाला गया कि प्रारंभिक ऐतिहासिक काल में पश्चिमी उत्तर प्रदेश की तुलना में पूर्वी उत्तर प्रदेश के क्षेत्र में बारिश अधिक होती थी।[9] अतः यदि उपरोक्त स्थलों के समान ही पूर्वी उ.प्र. के अन्य पुरास्थलों के विभिन्न सांस्कृतिक कालों के जमावों से प्राप्त जीवाश्मों का अध्ययन इस विधि से किया जाय तो निश्चित रूप से पूर्वी उत्तर प्रदेश के पुरापर्यावरण के संदर्भ में महत्त्वपूर्ण परिणाम आने की संभावना है।

पुरापर्यावरण के पुनर्निर्माण में मृदा विज्ञान के विश्लेषण की भी महती भूमिका होती है। विभिन्न पुरास्थलों के सांस्कृतिक जमावों के अध्ययन के आधार पर प्राचीन काल में पूर्वी उत्तर प्रदेश में जलवायु आर्द्र थी अथवा शुष्क? इस पर प्रकाश डाला जा सकता है क्योंकि मृदा का निर्माण प्रत्यक्ष रूप से समकालीन जलवायु से जुड़ा होता है। मृदा के विश्लेषण से यह भी ज्ञात किया जा सकता है कि प्राचीन काल में क्षेत्र विशेष की मृदा अम्लीय थी अथवा क्षारीय? साथ ही अम्लीय तथा क्षारीय मृदा किस प्रकार के अन्न उत्पादन में सहायक रही होगी? इस प्रकार के विश्लेषण से न केवल क्षेत्र विशेष के विभिन्न कालों के खाद्य उत्पादन पर वरन् बारिश के प्रतिरूपों पर भी महत्त्वपूर्ण प्रकाश पड़ेगा। उदाहरणस्वरूप, हम पूर्वी उत्तर प्रदेश में ही स्थित लहुरादेवा पुरास्थल को लें जिसका विस्तार लगभग 10 हेक्टेयर है एवं जहाँ से नवपाषाण काल से लेकर प्रारंभिक ऐतिहासिक काल तक के सांस्कृतिक अनुक्रम का प्रमाण मिला है।[10] इसके प्रथम काल के उपकाल 'अ' के जमाव से जो लगभग 80 सेमी0 मात्र है, चिकनी मृदा के साथ बालू एवं कंकड़ के टुकड़े सम्मिलित मिले हैं जब कि प्रथम काल के ही उपकाल 'ब' का जमाव लगभग 50 सेमी0 मोटा है तथा इसमें पीले रंग की मृदा–सिल्ट का जमाव है। इन दोनों उपकालों के जमावों से यह इंगित होता है कि लहुरादेवा के प्रथम उपकाल 'अ' के समय की जलवायु उपकाल 'ब' की तुलना में अवश्य भिन्न रही होगी एवं जलवायु की इस भिन्नता ने अवश्य ही तत्कालीन कृषि के प्रतिरूपों को प्रभावित किया होगा।

यहाँ यह उल्लेखनीय है कि लहुरादेवा के प्रथम 'अ' उपकाल (सातवीं सहस्राब्दि के मध्य से – चौथी सहस्राब्दि के अन्त तक) एवं उपकाल 'ब' (तीसरी सहस्राब्दि से – दूसरी सहस्राब्दी तक) के अन्न उत्पादन में भी भिन्नता दिखायी पड़ती है। प्रथम 'अ' उपकाल में चावल की उत्पादित एवं वन्य दोनों प्रकार की प्रजातियाँ मिलती हैं जब कि प्रथम 'ब' उपकाल में अन्न के रूप में चावल के साथ जौ की खेती का भी प्रमाण मिलता है। यद्यपि पुरावनस्पतिशास्त्रियों के अनुसार पूर्वी उत्तर प्रदेश के इन क्षेत्रों के लोगों का जौ एवं गेहूँ से परिचय हड़प्पा संस्कृति के लोगों के सम्पर्क में आने के पश्चात् ही हुआ था।

उपरोक्त साक्ष्यों के आलोक में हम इस निष्कर्ष पर पहुँचते हैं कि पूर्वी उत्तर प्रदेश का क्षेत्र न केवल पुरातात्त्विक दृष्टि से वरन् पुरापर्यावरणीय अध्ययन की दृष्टि से भी अत्यन्त महत्त्वपूर्ण है। अतः पूर्वी उत्तर प्रदेश में पर्यावरण पुरातत्त्व के क्षेत्र में शोध की अनेक प्रबल संभावनायें विद्यमान हैं।

सन्दर्भ

1. सुब्बाराव, बी0 (1958), *द पर्सनाल्टी ऑफ इण्डिया,* बड़ौदा ।
2. शर्मा, जी0 आर0, वी0 डी0 मिश्र, डी0 मण्डल, बी0 बी0 मिश्रा एवं जे0 एन0 पाल (1980), *बिगनिंग ऑफ एग्रीकल्चर,* इलाहाबाद, पृ0 33, 123।
3. अन्सारी, शाहिदा (2005), एथनोआर्कियोलॉजी ऑफ प्रीहिस्टारिक सेटेलमेंट पैटर्न ऑफ साउथ–सेन्ट्रल गंगा वैली, *इण्डियन सोसायटी फॉर प्रीहिस्टारिक एण्ड क्वार्टनरी स्टडीज,* पुणे, पृ0 115।
4. सिंह, इन्द्रबीर (2005), 'क्वार्टनरी पैलियोइनवायरमेंट्स ऑफ दि गंगा प्लेन एण्ड एन्थ्रोपोलनिक एक्टिविटी', *मैन एण्ड इन्वायरन्मेन्ट,* XXX (I), पृ0 17–19।
5. चौहान, एम0 एस0, अनिल के0 पोखरिया एवं आई0 बी0 सिंह (2009), 'पॉलन रेकार्ड ऑफ होलोसीन वेजीटेशन, क्लाइमेट चेंज एण्ड ह्यूमन हैबिटेशन फ्राम लहुरादेवा लेक, सन्त कबीर नगर, डिस्ट्रिक्ट उत्तर प्रदेश, इण्डिया,' *मैन एण्ड इन्वायरमेन्ट,* XXXIV, No. 1, पृ0 92–95।
6. सिंह, पी0 (1994), *एक्सकेवेशन्स एट नरहन* (1984–89), वाराणसी, पृ0 247–254।
7. तिवारी, डी0 पी0 (2006), *एक्सकेवेशन्स एट पीरवितनीशरीफ त्रिलोकपुर,* लखनऊ, पृ0 142–176।
8. तिवारी, डी0 पी0 (2002), *एक्सकेवेशन्स एट चरदा,* लखनऊ, पृ0 139–163।
9. शर्मा, एस0, एम0 जोआशिमिक्शी, एच0 जे0 तौबरोल, आई0 बी0 सिंह, डी0 पी0 तिवारी एण्ड आर0 तिवारी (2004 बी), 'आक्सीजन आइसोटोप्स आफ बोवाइड टीथ ऐज आर्काइव्स ऑफ पैलियोक्लाइमेट वैरियेशन्स इन आर्कियोलॉजिकल डिपाजिट्स आफ दि गंगा प्लेन,' *इण्डिया क्वार्टनरी रिसर्च* 62, पृ0 19–28।
10. तिवारी, राकेश, आर0 के0 श्रीवास्तव, के0 के0 सिंह, के0 एस0 सारस्वत एण्ड आई0 बी0 सिंह (2002–2003), 'प्रिलिमनरी रिपोर्ट ऑफ एक्सकेवेशन एट लहुरादेवा, डिस्ट्रिक्ट सन्त कबीर नगर, यू0 पी0, 2001–2002,: वाइडर आर्कियालाजिकल इम्प्लिकेशन्स,' *प्राग्धारा,* नं0 13, पृ0 37–58।
    तिवारी, राकेश, आर0 के0 श्रीवास्तव, के0 के0 सिंह, के0 एस0 सारस्वत (2005–06), "फरदर एक्सकेवेशन्स एट लहुरादेवा, डिस्ट्रिक्ट सन्त कबीर नगर (यू0 पी0) : प्रिलिमनरी आब्जरवेशन्स," *पुरातत्त्व,* नं0 36, पृ0 68–75।

22

उत्तरी कृष्ण मार्जित पात्र का उद्भव एवं विस्तार

(दक्षिण एशिया में बौद्ध धर्म के प्रसार के आलोक में)

रवीन्द्र कुमार

भारत में उत्तरी कृष्ण मार्जित मृद्भाण्ड (एन.बी.पी.डब्ल्यू.) की खोज का इतिहास अब सौ वर्ष पुराना है, फिर भी इस परंपरा के पात्रों से संबंधित कुछ तथ्यों में अभी भी अस्पष्टता है। मार्शल ने जब 1911–12 में इलाहाबाद के भीटा नामक पुरास्थल के प्राक् मौर्य युगीन स्तर से श्याम वर्णी मृद्भाण्डों की खोज की तो सर्वप्रथम उनके जहन में काले ग्रीक पात्रों का ख्याल आया, जिनका संभवतः यहाँ आयात हुआ हो अथवा उसी प्रकार के पात्र स्थानीय कुम्हारों द्वारा बनाए गए हों। बाद में जब वैसे ही पात्र उन्हें भीर टीले से मिले तब इस परंपरा के पात्रों को लगभग 500 ई.पू. से सम्बद्ध किया गया।

घोष एवं पाणीग्रही (1964 : 37–55) द्वारा वर्ष 1940–44 में अहिच्छत्र के उत्खनन के पश्चात कृष्ण देव एवं व्हीलर (1964 : 55–58) ने 1946 में इस पात्र परंपरा के 18 पुरास्थलों की एक सूची प्रकाशित की जो सभी मध्य गंगा घाटी में अवस्थित थे। बी.बी. लाल ने बाद में एक अन्य सूची प्रकाशित कर उसमें ऐसे 25 नवीन पुरास्थलों का समावेश किया (1945–55 : 143–46)। इस विशिष्ट प्रकृति के पात्रों ने शोधार्थियों एवं विभिन्न अकादमिक संस्थानों में विशेष रूचि पैदा की जिसके परिणामस्वरूप अधिकाधिक संख्या में संबंधित पुरास्थल प्रकाश में आए। बाद में निगम (1961 : 45–46) ने 110 पुरास्थलों की सूची प्रकाशित की। इसी प्रकार अग्रवाल एवं अन्य ने (1971–72 : 76–83) उत्तरी कृष्ण मार्जित पुरास्थलों की संदर्भ–ग्रंथ सूची प्रस्तुत की। टी.एन. रॉय (1986 : 13) ने अपने शोध प्रबंध के माध्यम से 415 पुरास्थलों की सूचना उपलब्ध कराई जहाँ से इस परंपरा के पात्र मिले थे। प्रकाशित साक्ष्यों के आधार पर मिश्रा (1989 : 91, एफ.एन. 15) ने ऐसे ही 568 पुरास्थलों का उल्लेख किया है, साथ ही 80 उन पुरास्थलों का विवरण प्रस्तुत किया जहाँ उत्खनन से उत्तरी कृष्ण मार्जित परंपरा के पात्र मिले थे।

अपनी इस अभूतपूर्व महत्ता के कारण गंगा घाटी एवं अन्य क्षेत्रों में अवस्थित इस संस्कृति से संबंधित पुरास्थलों का व्यापक स्तर पर उत्खनन हुआ। इनमें से उत्तर प्रदेश में विद्यमान महत्त्वपूर्ण पुरास्थल हैं – श्रावस्ती, हस्तिनापुर, कौशाम्बी, राजघाट, भीटा, झूंसी, श्रृंगवेरपुर, खैराडीह, नरहन, मसोन, भारद्वाज आश्रम, पिपरहवा, सिसवनिया, अयोध्या इत्यादि। इसी प्रकार बिहार के महत्त्वपूर्ण उत्खनित स्थलों में सोनपुर, चिरांद, मांझी, ताराडीह, चम्पा, कुमरहार, वैशाली, चेंचर, मनेर, कटरागंज, ओरियम इत्यादि का नाम लिया जा सकता है। इसके अतिरिक्त उत्तर प्रदेश एवं बिहार से बाहर भी इस परंपरा के अनेकों पुरास्थल अवस्थित हैं एवं भारत में अब तक लगभग 100 ऐसे पुरास्थलों का उत्खनन हो चुका है।

भारतीय पात्रों के वैज्ञानिक विश्लेषण का इतिहास लगभग 70 वर्ष पुराना है। हमीद, प्लेंडरलिथ, सनाउल्लाह आदि वे विद्वान हैं जिन्होंने भारतीय पात्रों विशेषकर चित्रित धूसर मृद्भाण्डों (पी.जी.डब्लू.), उत्तरी कृष्ण मार्जित मृद्भाण्डों आदि के वैज्ञानिक विश्लेषण की प्रक्रिया का आरंभ किया। सनाउल्लाह (1946 : 58) ने यह मत व्यक्त किया कि पात्रों के विशिष्ट रंग का कारण आंवे का अनाक्सिकृत अवस्था में होना है। साथ ही, वे लुकास के इस कथन से असहमत थे कि केवल कार्बन के जमाव से काले रंग के पात्र बने जबकि वास्तविकता यह है कि आंवे में निश्चित–रूप से फेरस सिलिकेट का भी निर्माण हुआ। स्वतंत्र भारत में विभिन्न विद्वानों यथा हेगड़े (1962 : 159–61; 1966 : 62; 1975 : 187–90; 1978 : 141–55), भारद्वाज (1969 : 188–92), गोगटे एवं अन्य (1982 : 72–78), कृष्णन (1986), रॉय (1987), राय (1987 : 47–49), लेखक स्वयं (1989–1990 : 41–69; 1997 : 197–219), कृष्णन एवं शाह (2005 : 135–156) आदि ने प्राचीन भारतीय मृद्भाण्डों विशेषकर एन.बी.पी. पात्रों के संरचनात्मक विश्लेषण को समझने में अपना योगदान दिया है। आरंभिक चरण के विद्वानों के अध्ययन का मुख्य लक्ष्य पात्रों का रासायनिक विश्लेषण एवं प्रारंभिक सूक्ष्मदर्शी अध्ययन था जिससे संरचना संबंधी आंकड़े उपलब्ध हुए थे। पर, ऐसे आंकड़े व्याख्यात्मक दृष्टिकोण के आधार पर खरे नहीं थे एवं उनके माध्यम से आधारभूत समस्या जैसे किसी पात्र परंपरा के उद्भव, विकास अथवा उसके अवसान का आकलन संभव नहीं था। बाद में जैसे–जैसे पुरातत्वशास्त्रियों का रुझान पात्रों के वैज्ञानिक अनुसंधान की ओर बढ़ता गया, अनेक तकनीकी अध्ययन पात्रों के सामाजिक–सांस्कृतिक आयाम को समझने का आधार बने। इन अध्ययनों का केन्द्रबिन्दु पात्र निर्माण प्रक्रिया को समझना एवं विभिन्न परंपरा के पात्रों के उद्भव एवं विकास में तकनीक के योगदान का आकलन करना था।

दूसरी ओर परंपरागत शैली के पुरातत्वशास्त्रियों ने पात्रों के स्तरीकरण, भौतिक स्वरूप, आकार एवं प्रकार आदि के आधार पर उत्तरी कृष्ण मार्जित पात्रों के उद्भव के बारे में विभिन्न मत व्यक्त किए हैं। घोष (1950 : 71–72) ने राजगीर के उत्खनन के आधार पर यह पाया कि यहाँ के द्वितीय काल में कृष्ण लोहित पात्र (बी.आर. डब्ल्यू.) एवं उत्तरी कृष्ण मार्जित पात्र परंपरा में समान आकार प्रकार के थाली एवं कटोरे मिलते हैं। उनके अनुसार दोनों परंपरा के पात्रों में समान आकार–प्रकार की सह–उपस्थिति एक गणनीय विशेषता है जो उनके समान उद्भव एवं प्रयोजन की ओर इंगित करती है, सिवाय इसके कि बी.आर.डब्ल्यू. पात्रों में वह चमकदार सतह नहीं होती है (शरण 2006 : 23)। प्रचलित आकार जैसे तश्तरियाँ, कटोरे आदि सामान्यतया उत्तरी कृष्ण मार्जित एवं बी.आर.डब्ल्यू. दोनों ही पात्र परंपरा से मिलते हैं। चूंकि बी.आर.डब्ल्यू. प्राक् उत्तरी कृष्ण मार्जित स्तर से भी प्राप्त होती है इसलिए घोष का मानना है कि बी.आर.डब्ल्यू0 परंपरा के पात्रों में विकास के कारण ही उत्तरी कृष्ण मार्जित परंपरा के पात्रों का उद्भव हुआ।

अहिच्छत्र (1940–44), हस्तिनापुर (1950), कौशाम्बी (1951) एवं रोपड़ (1954–55) आदि पुरास्थलों के उत्खनन से कुछ विद्वानों ने, इस आधार पर कि पी.जी.डब्ल्यू. का अस्तित्व एन.बी.पी. स्तर से पहले भी था, यह मत व्यक्त किया है कि उत्तरी कृष्ण मार्जित का उद्भव पी.जी.डब्ल्यू. से हुआ। एन.आर. बनर्जी ने 1963–64 में जब अहिच्छत्र का पुनः उत्खनन किया तब उन्हें द्वितीय काल में एन.बी.पी. पात्रों की सह–उपस्थिति उसके पूर्ववर्ती

एवं परवर्ती कालों से भी मिली। भारत–नेपाल के तराई वाले क्षेत्रों में भी ऐसे पुरास्थल (श्रावस्ती, तिलौराकोट आदि) हैं जहाँ से उत्तरी कृष्ण मार्जित, चित्रित धूसर एवं कृष्ण लेपित पात्रों की सह–उपस्थिति दिखाई पड़ती है। गोगटे एवं अन्य (1982 : 72–76) विद्वानों ने फेरस/फेरिक अनुपात के तुलनात्मक अध्ययन एवं उत्तरी कृष्ण मार्जित पात्र तथा कृष्ण लेपित पात्रों में तत्वीय कार्बन की उपस्थिति के आधार पर यह व्यक्त किया कि उत्तरी कृष्ण मार्जित पात्र परंपरा, चित्रित धूसर पात्रों से पृथक पात्र परंपरा नहीं है, सिवाय इसके कि उत्तरी कृष्ण मार्जित पात्रों की सतह पर काला चमकीला लेप चढ़ा होता है। उपरोक्त उदाहरणों के आधार पर कुछ विद्वानों में यह सहमति बनी कि उत्तरी कृष्ण मार्जित पात्रों का उद्भव चित्रित धूसर पात्र परंपरा से हुआ।

मध्य गंगा घाटी में कृष्ण लेपित मृद्भाण्ड (बी.एस.डब्ल्यू.) की सह–उपस्थिति कृष्ण लोहित पात्रों एवं उत्तरी कृष्ण मार्जित पात्रों के साथ दिखाई पड़ती है। चम्पा, चिरांद, ओरिय, सोनपुर आदि पुरास्थलों पर हुए प्रारंभिक उत्खननों से यह पता चलता है कि यहाँ उत्तरी कृष्ण मार्जित पात्रों का प्रतिशत बी.एस.डब्ल्यू. पात्रों की अपेक्षा बहुत अधिक है जिससे विद्वानों में यह विचार फलीभूत हुआ कि बी.एस.डब्ल्यू. को उत्तरी कृष्ण मार्जित पात्रों के उद्भव का आधार नहीं माना जा सकता। परंतु, सिन्हा (1971–72 : 38) ने चित्रित धूसर पात्रों एवं उत्तरी कृष्ण मार्जित पात्रों का तुलनात्मक अध्ययन करते हुए यह विचार व्यक्त किया कि चित्रित धूसर पात्रों के साथ कृष्ण लेपित पात्र भी मिलते हैं जो तकनीकी आधार पर उत्तरी कृष्ण मार्जित पात्रों से अलग नहीं हैं। नरहन में हुए उत्खनन (सिंह 1994 : 19) में उत्तरी कृष्ण मार्जित पात्र स्तर से पहले कृष्ण लेपित पात्रों का पृथक स्तर मिला। ऐसे ही प्रमाणों के आधार पर विद्वानों को यह कहने का अवसर मिला कि कृष्ण लेपित पात्र परंपरा वह थी जिसके उत्थान की परिणति थी उत्तरी कृष्ण मार्जित पात्रों का उद्भव। उपरोक्त विवरण से यह स्पष्ट होता है कि उत्तरी कृष्ण मार्जित पात्रों के उद्भव के बारे में कम से कम चार मत प्रचलित (स्वीकार्य) हैं –

1. उत्तरी कृष्ण मार्जित पात्रों के उद्भव एवं विकास की प्रेरणा चित्रित धूसर पात्रों से मिलना।
2. उत्तरी कृष्ण मार्जित पात्रों का उद्भव मध्य गंगा घाटी में होना तथा पश्चिमी गंगा दोआब क्षेत्र में चित्रित धूसर पात्रों के साथ इसकी सह–उपस्थिति।
3. उत्तरी कृष्ण मार्जित पात्रों के उद्भव एवं विकास की प्रेरणा कृष्ण लोहित पात्रों से मिलना।
4. उत्तरी कृष्ण मार्जित पात्रों के उद्भव एवं विकास की प्रेरणा कृष्ण लेपित पात्रों से मिलना।

कृष्ण लेपित पात्रों एवं उत्तरी कृष्ण मार्जित पात्रों के ऐसे कई प्रकार हैं जो दोनों ही पात्र परंपराओं में मिलते हैं जैसे convex sided dishes with incurved rim and convex base, straight sided corrugated bowls, straight sided dishes with a carination at the meeting point of sides आदि। लेखक (1989–1990 : 67; 1997 : 218) द्वारा उत्तरी कृष्ण मार्जित पात्रों एवं उससे संबद्ध पात्रों, विशेष रूप से कृष्ण लेपित पात्रों पर किए गए शैलविधा संबंधी परीक्षण से यह तथ्य उजागर हुआ कि दोनों पात्र परंपराओं के बीच सजातीय संबद्धता थी। कृष्ण लेपित पात्रों के स्तरों की स्थिति, उत्तरी कृष्ण मार्जित पात्र प्रकार से उसकी समानता एवं दोनों पात्रों के शैलवैज्ञानिक परीक्षण से यह प्रमाणित होता है कि उत्तरी कृष्ण मार्जित परंपरा के पात्रों का विकास कृष्ण लेपित परंपरा के पात्रों से हुआ होगा।

विभिन्न विद्वानों द्वारा उत्तरी कृष्ण मार्जित पात्रों के गुणात्मक एवं द्रव्यात्मक विश्लेषण से यह निष्कर्ष प्राप्त होता है कि इस पात्र परंपरा का उद्भव मध्य गंगा घाटी में हुआ। इस विचारधारा के समर्थन में विद्वानों के बीच जिस प्रमुख बिंदु पर सहमति बनी, वह थी मध्य गंगा घाटी के अधिकतर पुरास्थलों से मिले एन.बी.पी. पात्र अथवा 'डीलक्स वेयर' जो इस श्रेणी के दूरस्थ पुरास्थलों की तुलना में बहुधा उच्च कोटि के थे एवं उनकी संख्या भी अधिक थी। उदाहरणार्थ, तक्षशिला के भीर एवं सिरकप, नासिक, अमरावती, अनुराधापुर (श्रीलंका), तिलौराकोट

एवं लुम्बिनी (नेपाल), वारी–इ–बटेश्वर एवं महास्थान (बांग्लादेश) इत्यादि ऐसे कुछ दूरस्थ पुरास्थल हैं जहाँ से एन.बी.पी. पात्र नगण्य संख्या में मिले हैं।

अनेक विद्वान यह अनुभव करते हैं कि दूरस्थ स्थानों पर एन.बी.पी. पात्रों के प्रसार का कारण बौद्ध धर्म या व्यापार था। सहाय का कथन है कि 'संभवतः इन पात्रों के प्रसार में बौद्ध भिक्षुओं, व्यापारियों, राजकुमारों एवं राजाओं का योगदान था क्योंकि ये पात्र प्रायः बौद्ध पुरास्थलों से मिलते हैं। इस कारण मुख्य रूप से इनका प्रसार बौद्ध भिक्षुओं द्वारा हुआ होगा (1969 : 151)। उनका यह भी मानना था कि चारों दिशाओं में इनका प्रसार गंगा घाटी, विशेषरूप से मगध होने के कारण ऐसा प्रतीत होता है कि इन पात्रों का उद्भव बिहार में हुआ, उत्तर प्रदेश में वे प्रचलित हुए एवं यहाँ से इनका प्रसार देश के अन्य क्षेत्रों में हुआ (वही : 153)। कृष्णदेव ने हालांकि यह सुझाया कि प्रारंभिक चरण में इन पात्रों का प्रसार व्यापारिक गतिविधियों के कारण हुआ परंतु बाद के चरणों में इसके प्रसार में बौद्ध धर्म ने महत्त्वपूर्ण भूमिका निभाई (वही : 153)। वर्तमान में इस परंपरा के पात्रों का विस्तार पाकिस्तान के स्वात घाटी में स्थित उदयग्राम से बांग्लादेश के वारी–इ–बटेश्वर तक; कश्मीर घाटी के सैमथन से तमिलनाडु के कोरकई एवं समुद्रपार श्रीलंका के अनुराधापुर तक मिलता है। इस व्यापक प्रसार को कुछ विद्वानों ने बौद्ध धर्म, मौर्य साम्राज्यवाद एवं व्यापार पथ आदि से जोड़ा है। किन्तु, बौद्ध धर्म अथवा मौर्य साम्राज्य को पूर्णतः कृष्ण मार्जित पात्रों के प्रसार का कारण नहीं माना जा सकता क्योंकि ऐसे पुरास्थलों के साक्ष्य हैं जिनका काल निश्चित रूप से प्राक् 500 ई.पू. अथवा प्राक् मौर्ययुगीन है। प्रारंभिक चरण के उत्खननों में नोह (685 ± 105 ई.पू.), मथुरा (730 ± 150 ई.पू. एवं 660 ± 100 ई.पू.) एवं झूसी (680 ± 90 ई.पू.) आदि कुछ ऐसे उदाहरण हैं जहाँ से इस पात्र परंपरा की प्राक् बुद्ध/प्राक् मौर्य तिथियां प्राप्त हुई हैं। श्रीलंका से प्राप्त एन.बी.पी. पात्रों को लगभग 400 ई.पू. अर्थात प्राक् मौर्य युगीन माना गया है (देरियानियागला 2004:8)। यद्यपि उत्खननकर्ता निश्चित रूप से यह कहने में असमर्थ हैं कि श्रीलंका में इस परंपरा के पात्र बौद्ध धर्म या व्यापार अथवा दोनों के माध्यम से पहुँचे तथापि उनका यह मानना है कि संभवतः अशोक के काल में बौद्ध धर्म के व्यापक प्रचलन से पहले ही यहाँ के वासियों को बौद्ध धर्म का ज्ञान हो गया था।

इस सन्दर्भ में बौद्ध साहित्य का इस आशय से परीक्षण करना समीचीन होगा कि क्या उत्तरी कृष्ण मार्जित पात्रों का उपयोग बौद्ध भिक्षुओं के द्वारा किया गया था। *विनयपिटक* में वर्णित तथ्यों से इस बात की पुष्टि होती है कि बुद्ध के आदेशानुसार बौद्ध भिक्षुओं को केवल दो प्रकार के पात्र यथा मृदापात्र अथवा लौह पात्र उपयोग करने की आज्ञा थी। अन्य प्रकार के पात्रों का उपयोग उनके लिए सर्वथा वर्जित था। *विनयपिटक* के अनुसार (अंग्रेजी में)

> ...Now at that time the group of six monks used various kinds of bowls, made of gold, made of silver.People .... spread it about, saying:
> "Like householders who enjoy pleasures of the senses". They told this matter to the Lord. He said: "Monks, a bowl made of gold should not be used, a bowl made of silver...made of pearls....beryl....crystal... tin....lead....copper should not be used. I allow you, monks. two (kinds of bowls: an iron bowl, a clay bowl) (*Vin.* iii: 243; iv : 123, 243)

मृदापात्र के गुण आदि की व्याख्या करते हुए इस साहित्य में (हॉर्नर 1992 : 292) वर्णित है (अंग्रेजी में):

> ... the pretext of a bowl means : ....like a copper bowl it is well turned, of beautiful hide, glossy, of black colour (lit. bee-coloured), it is called a clay bowl...

उपरोक्त विवरण पुरातत्वशास्त्रियों को यह सोचने के लिए विवश करते हैं कि *विनयपिटक* में वर्णित मिट्‌टी के पात्र संभवतः उत्तरी कृष्ण मार्जित पात्र हों। पर, साथ ही, उनका यह भी मानना है कि ये एक विशेष पात्र थे जिन्हें 'डीलक्स वेयर' का दर्जा दिया गया है। इनका उपयोग निश्चित रूप से समाज के उच्च वर्ग के लोग करते थे। चूंकि इस परंपरा के पात्रों में सामान्यतया कटोरे और थालियाँ ही मिलती हैं अतः ऐसा प्रतीत होता है कि इनका प्रयोग दैनिक कार्यों के लिए न होकर विशेष अवसरों पर कार्यविशेष के लिए होता रहा होगा। इनकी अपेक्षा अन्य श्रेणी के पात्रों, जैसे, कृष्ण लेपित पात्र, धूसर पात्र, लोहित पात्र आदि का उपयोग दैनिक कार्यों में होता रहा होगा (रॉय 1988 : 183)। यदि उच्च वर्ग के लोगों द्वारा इन पात्रों के उपयोग की बात को सत्य माना जाए तो एम. एस. पाण्डे (1969 : 154) के कथन में भी बल है कि बौद्ध भिक्षुओं के लिए विलासितापूर्ण पात्रों का उपयोग वर्जित था। इस स्थिति में दक्षिण एशिया के बड़े हिस्से में इन पात्रों के विस्तार को बौद्ध भिक्षुओं के साथ जोड़ना कहाँ तक उचित होगा?

इसी प्रकार टूटे एन.बी.पी. पात्रों के तांबे के तार से जोड़े गए टुकड़े विभिन्न पुरास्थलों यथा रोपड़, बैराट, उज्जैन, कुमरहार, सोनपुर, खैराडीह, जाफरडीह आदि से मिलते हैं, जिनमें इन पात्रों को तांबे की कील अथवा तार से जोड़ने के साक्ष्य मिले हैं। इन साक्ष्यों से यह सहज कल्पनीय है कि ये पात्र इतने मूल्यवान थे कि लोगों ने इनका उपयोग इन्हें जोड़कर भी किया। साक्ष्यों के आधार पर यह निश्चित रूप से नहीं कहा जा सकता कि सीमित संख्या के कारण केवल दूरस्थ स्थानों पर ही टूटे पात्र जोड़कर उपयोग में लाए गये थे क्योंकि ऐसे पात्रों के साक्ष्य कुमरहार (पाटलिपुत्र) से भी मिले हैं। वर्तमान के संदर्भ में यदि देखा जाये तो समाज के धनाढ्‌य अथवा उच्च वर्ग के लोग टूटे मूल्यवान पात्रों का उपयोग उन्हें जोड़कर करना पसंद नहीं करेंगे, अपितु उन पात्रों का त्याग कर उनके स्थान पर वे नवीन पात्रों का उपयोग करेंगे। विकल्प के रूप में यह भी संभव है कि टूटे हुए बहुमूल्य पात्र गृहकार्य में हाथ बंटाने वाले कर्मचारियों को दे दिए गए हों, जिन्हें वे अत्यंत आनन्द के साथ ग्रहणकर, जोड़कर उनका उपयोग करते रहे हों। कृष्णदेव जी भी इस विचार से सहमत थे जब मैंने उनसे जोड़े हुए टूटे एन.बी.पी. पात्रों के विषय में दिल्ली विरासत अनुसंधान एवं प्रबंधन संस्थान में चर्चा की थी। क्या बौद्ध भिक्षु भी टूटे एन.बी.पी. पात्रों की भिक्षा लेकर उन्हें जोड़कर उपयोग में लाते थे? यह शोध का विषय है।

बौद्ध साहित्य (जैसे, *विनयपिटक*) भिक्षुओं द्वारा टूटे मृदा पात्रों को जोड़कर उनके उपयोग की विस्तृत व्याख्या करता है। इसके अनुसार बौद्ध भिक्षुओं द्वारा नए मृदापात्र (भिक्षापात्र) का उपयोग, जो पाँच से कम स्थानों पर टूटा एवं जुड़ा हो, सर्वथा वर्जित था। यहाँ तक कि पाँच से कम स्थानों पर टूटे एवं जुड़े पात्रों के बदले नए पात्र का प्रयोग अपराध था और इस अपराध की सजा में भिक्षु से नया पात्र छीनकर उसे भिक्षु समूह को दे दिया जाता था। *बुक ऑफ डिसिप्लिन* (हॉर्नर : 121) के अनुसार वह पात्र जो पाँच से कम स्थानों पर जोड़ा गया हो टूटा पात्र कहलाता ही नहीं था।

उपरोक्त तथ्यों को संज्ञान में लेते हुए एन.बी.पी. पात्रों को बौद्ध भिक्षुओं से सम्बद्ध करना तर्कसंगत नहीं होगा क्योंकि इन पात्रों का उद्‌भव एवं विकास बुद्ध की तिथि से बहुत पहले हो चुका था। साथ ही, समाज में टूटे पात्रों, विशेष कर एन.बी.पी. पात्रों को जोड़कर उपयोग में लाने की प्रक्रिया समान रूप से दिखलाई पड़ती है। ऐसे पात्र विभिन्न पुरास्थलों के आवासीय स्तरों से मिलते हैं, जिन्हें बौद्ध धर्म से जोड़कर नहीं देखा जा सकता।

एन.बी.पी. पात्रों के विस्तार को मौर्य साम्राज्य के विस्तार के साथ सम्बद्ध करने की चेष्टा अनेक विद्वानों ने की है। व्हीलर (1959 : 31) ने चारसादा एवं उदयग्राम से मिले साक्ष्य के आधार पर यह कहा था कि इन पात्रों का इस क्षेत्र में मिलना मौर्य साम्राज्य का ही परिणाम है। इसी प्रकार थापर (1955 : 13) ने अनुभव किया कि दूरस्थ क्षेत्रों में एन.बी.पी. पात्रों का पहुँचना 'संभवतः' योजनाबद्ध मौर्य साम्राज्य के विस्तार का ही परिणाम है।'

शरण (2006 : 24) इन पात्रों को प्राक् मौर्य युगीन एवं इनका केन्द्र मगध को मानते हुए इस बात पर बल देते हैं कि इनका भली–भाँति विस्तार व्यापारिक सम्बन्धों से हुआ। हालांकि, सिन्हा ने (1969 : 174–84) ऐसे वक्तव्यों का पहले ही खंडन करते हुए दृढ़ता से यह कहा था कि मध्य गंगा घाटी में इन पात्रों का प्रचलन मौर्य साम्राज्य के विस्तार से पहले हो चुका था। यदि इन पात्रों का वितरण एवं विस्तार मौर्य साम्राज्य के विस्तार से जुड़ा होता तो कुमरहार (प्राचीन पाटलिपुत्र) से इन पात्रों का अत्यधिक सीमित संख्या में मिलना समझ से परे है (मिश्रा 1989 : 97)। साथ ही, प्राक् मौर्य युगीन नगर राजगीर से अत्यधिक मात्रा में इन पात्रों का मिलना भी मौर्य साम्राज्य के साथ एन.बी.पी. पात्रों का सम्बन्ध उजागर नहीं करता।

इसी प्रकार ऐसा कहना भी उचित नहीं प्रतीत होता कि मुख्य क्षेत्र से दूरस्थ क्षेत्रों में एन.बी.पी. पात्रों का पहुँचना मौर्य काल में बौद्ध धर्म की लोकप्रियता एवं उसके विस्तार के आलोक में संभव हुआ। पुरतात्विक साक्ष्य इसके विपरीत जाते हैं। अंतिम चरण के एन.बी.पी. पात्र, जिन्हें संभवतः मौर्य काल से जोड़ा जा सकता है, हर दृष्टि से अवनति दर्शाते हैं चाहे उनकी मिट्टी की गुणवत्ता हो, पात्र प्रकार हों, सतही चमक हो अथवा उन्हें पकाने की विधि हो। इन पात्रों की बनावट में गुणवत्ता का अभाव इनके मोटे कोर, निम्न कोटि की निस्तेज सतह आदि से परिलक्षित होता है।

आरंभिक एवं अंतिम चरण के एन.बी.पी. पात्रों के आकार–प्रकार एवं गुणवत्ता में स्पष्ट भेद दिखाई पड़ता है। तुलनात्मक अध्ययन से यह उजागर होता है कि आरंभिक चरण की अपेक्षा अंतिम चरण में कटोरे एवं थालियाँ कम संख्या में बनती थीं जबकि नाद एवं घड़ों का उत्पादन बढ़ गया था। पात्र प्रकार के आलोक में भी यह अनुभव किया गया है कि प्रारंभिक चरण में इनकी संख्या अधिक थी। एन.बी.पी. पात्रों की जो विशिष्ट पहचान थी, जैसे उनकी धातु तुल्य खनक, चमक आदि, वह संस्कृति के अंतिम चरण में दिखलाई नहीं पड़ती, जब पात्र तकनीकी दृष्टि से निम्न कोटि के हो गये थे। इन पात्रों की लोकप्रियता को बौद्ध धर्म अथवा मौर्य साम्राज्य के विस्तार के साथ जोड़ने के पहले उपरोक्त पुरातात्विक साक्ष्यों का संज्ञान लेना आवश्यक है।

कार्बन 14 तिथियों के आलोचनापूर्ण मूल्यांकन से ज्ञात होता है कि वे सर्वथा आदर्श एवं सापेक्ष तिथियाँ नहीं होती हैं। उदाहरण के लिए दूरस्थ क्षेत्रों से मिली एन.बी.पी. पात्र स्तर की तिथियाँ अपेक्षाकृत पहले की हैं (जैसे मथुरा, नोह आदि)। वहीं केन्द्रीय क्षेत्र से मिली तिथि अपेक्षाकृत बाद की है (जैसे कुमरहार)। इस संदर्भ में के.के. सिन्हा का मानना है कि एकल संस्कृति वाले पुरास्थलों जैसे हड़प्पा, लोथल, कालीबंगन आदि से प्राप्त कार्बन 14 तिथियाँ अधिक विश्वसनीय होती हैं, परंतु गंगा घाटी में जहाँ बहुधा बहु संस्कृतियों वाले पुरास्थल हैं इनकी विश्वसनीयता संभव नहीं है। स्तरों के विशिष्ट जमाव में, स्तरीकरण में अंशमात्र की भिन्नता बड़ा अंतर दिखा सकती है। उनके अनुसार 'पूर्वी उत्तर प्रदेश एवं बिहार में एन.बी.पी. पात्रों से संबंधित एक भी पृथक पुरास्थल नहीं हैं। यहाँ पुरास्थलों पर सामान्यतया पूर्ववर्ती एवं परवर्ती काल के अवशेष साथ–साथ एक स्थान पर मिलते हैं। बहु–सांस्कृतिक पुरास्थलों के उत्खनन की प्रायः अपनी एक सीमा होती है (सिन्हा 1969 : 154)। हालांकि यह प्रश्न अब भी अनुत्तरित रह जाता है कि कैसे बहु–सांस्कृतिक पुरास्थलों का स्तरविन्यास वैज्ञानिक कार्बन 14 तिथि को प्रभावित करता है।

उत्खनन के समय पारंपरिक दृष्टि से आवासीय स्तरों का मूल्यांकन कर उनका तिथि निर्धारण सर्वथा आदर्शमय नहीं होता। इस संदर्भ में उत्खनन कर्ताओं द्वारा उत्खनन में एकरूपता का अभाव होता है। सामान्यतया यह देखा गया है कि बहु–सांस्कृतिक जमाव वाले पुरास्थलों के उत्खनन में जैसे–जैसे हम निचले स्तरों का उत्खनन करते जाते हैं, उत्खनन क्षेत्र सीमित होता जाता है। प्रकाश सिन्हा (2001 : 904) के अनुसार, पारंपरिक दृष्टि से हुए उत्खनन में पुरातात्विक स्तरों का आदर्शपूर्ण निर्धारण करने के लिए कुछ आंकड़े जैसे उत्खनन क्षेत्र, खंतियों का आकार एवं उनकी प्रकृति एवं उत्खनित प्रति इकाई के घनत्व आदि का आकलन आवश्यक होता है।

उनके अनुसार, यदि एन.बी.पी. पात्रों वाले पुरास्थलों का उसके केन्द्रीय अथवा दूरस्थ स्थानों पर वितरण के आलोक में घनत्वीय आंकलन हो सके तो उनके तिथि निर्धारण में आसानी हो सकती है।

बौद्ध साहित्य, जैसे, *विनयपिटक* एवं विभिन्न जातकों में उल्लिखित विवरणों के अनुसार जनसामान्य के साथ ही बोधिसत्व का पात्रों से संबंध समाज में मृद्भाण्डों की महत्ता को प्रमाणित करता है। जातकों में प्रायः बुद्ध के बनारस (वाराणसी) में कुम्हारों अथवा व्यापारियों के घर जन्म लेने की कथा वर्णित है। *पन्हक जातक* (1973 : 11) के अनुसार एक समय काशी देश के बनारस शहर में ब्रह्मदत्त के राज्य में व्यापारी के घर जन्मे बोधिसत्व प्रायः मूल्यवान पात्रों से भरी 500 गाड़ियाँ लेकर व्यापार के उद्देश्य से पूर्व से पश्चिम की ओर यात्रा करते थे। *कच्छप जातक* (वही : 55) से हमें पता चलता है कि काशी के कुम्हार के घर में जन्में बोधिसत्व बड़ा फावड़ा लेकर मिट्टी एकत्र करने के लिए महान नदी के किनारे जाते थे। *कूटवनिक जातक* (वही : 293) के अनुसार व्यापारी के घर जन्में बोधिसत्व अन्य व्यापारियों के साथ भागीदारी में मूल्यवान पात्रों के 500 डिब्बों के साथ व्यापार के लिए जाते हैं। *कुम्भकार जातक* के अनुसार बोधिसत्व का जन्म काशी के कुम्हार परिवार में होता है। बड़े होने पर वे अपने परिवार की जीविका मृद्भाण्डों के हस्तशिल्प से चलाते थे (कॉवेल 1990 : 228)।

ऐसा कोई साक्ष्य नहीं है जिससे यह कहा जा सके कि कुछ कुम्हार केवल भिक्षुओं के लिए ही पात्र बनाते थे; वरन वे संपूर्ण समाज के साथ ही बौद्ध भिक्षुओं के लिए भी पात्र बनाते थे ऐसा बौद्ध साहित्य (हॉर्नर 1992 : 118) से प्रमाणित होता है। उपरोक्त के अनुसार (अंग्रेजी में):

> ... monks were invited by a certain potter who said "If these monks need a bowl, I (can supply them) with a bowl [*yasam ayyanam pattena attha aham pattena ti pacitiya*]"... they asked for large bowl for those who had small bowls...small bowls for those who had large bowls. Thus, that potter making many bowls for monks, could not make other goods for sale and he could not keep himself going... Then the Lord addressed the monks and said 'Monks a bowl is not to be asked for...'

मार्शल (1915 : 80–81) ऐसे पहले पुरातत्वशास्त्री थे जिन्होंने भीटा में हुए उत्खनन के आधार पर चमकीले काले पात्रों को (वर्तमान में एन.बी.पी. पात्र) 8वीं सदी ई.पू. का माना था। यद्यपि कौड्रिंगटन (1928 : 101) ने यहाँ अवैज्ञानिक तरीके से हुए उत्खनन पर अपनी प्रतिक्रिया व्यक्त करते हुए इन पात्रों को इतने पहले की तिथि से जोड़ना अव्यावहारिक माना। स्वतंत्रता प्राप्ति के बाद पिछली सदी में शोधार्थियों, विद्वानों, अकादमिक संस्थाओं, भारतीय पुरातत्व सर्वेक्षण, राज्यों के पुरातत्व विभाग आदि द्वारा किए गये कार्यों के फलस्वरूप एन.बी.पी. पात्र संस्कृति का काल निर्धारण छठी शती ई. पू. से 50 ई. पू. के बीच किया गया था (शर्मा, आर.एस. 1983 : 92)। परंतु, वर्तमान शताब्दी के प्रथम दशक में हुए शोधो से पूर्व के शोधों की प्रवृत्ति में बदलाव दिखायी पड़ता है। नवीन कार्बन 14 तिथियाँ अब एन.बी.पी. पात्रों का आरंभ दूसरी सहस्त्राब्दि के अंतिम चतुरांश की ओर इंगित करती हैं। उपरोक्त साक्ष्यों ने मध्य गंगा घाटी में भौतिक संस्कृति एवं सांस्कृतिक कालक्रम के पुनः निर्धारण का अवसर प्रदान किया है (सिंह 2007 : 1–2; शरण 2006 : 28)। हाल में नालन्दा जिले में स्थित जाफरडीह नामक पुरास्थल से एन.बी.पी. पात्रों के 10.61 मीटर मोटे जमाव से कई महत्त्वपूर्ण कार्बन 14 तिथियाँ प्राप्त हुई हैं। इन तिथियों (1259 ई.पू., 1562 ई.पू., 1002 ई.पू., 857 ई.पू.) का आकलन करते हुए उत्खननकर्ता का मानना है कि इस पुरास्थल पर एन.बी.पी. पात्रों का उदभव कम से कम 1200 ई0पू0 में तो हो ही गया था; साथ ही, उनका यह भी सुझाव है कि नवीन साक्ष्यों के आलोक में आस–पास के दूसरे ऐसे पुरास्थलों के भी पुनर्मूल्यांकन की आवश्यकता है। चारदा में हुए हाल के उत्खनन से एन.बीपी. पात्रों के स्तर से 764 ई.पू. की तिथि प्राप्त हुई (तिवारी 2002 : 47)। बहुचर्चित

अयोध्या उत्खनन (माझी एवं मणि 2003 : 271) की रिपोर्ट दृढ़ता पूर्वक यह दर्शाती है कि 'प्राकृतिक मिट्टी के ऊपर प्राचीनतम स्तर एन.बी.पी. पात्र काल का प्रतिनिधित्व करता है एवं इस प्राचीनतम अवशेष को तेरहवीं शती ई.पू. से संबद्ध किया जा सकता है'। यहाँ के एन.बी.पी. पात्र (प्रथम काल) स्तर से दो महत्त्वपूर्ण कार्बन 14 तिथियाँ (910 ± 100 ई.पू. एवं 880 ± 100 ई.पू.) प्राप्त हुई हैं। *बीरबल साहनी इन्स्टीट्यूट ऑफ़ पैलियोबॉटनी* द्वारा परीक्षित पुरा–वानस्पतिक नमूनों का आकलन एवं विश्लेषण करते हुए बी.बी. लाल (2008 : 36) का भी मानना है कि अयोध्या में एन.बी.पी. पात्र संस्कृति का काल 1000 ई.पू. से बहुत पहले का हो सकता है। इस प्रकार यह स्पष्ट है कि मध्य गंगा घाटी के पश्चिमी हिस्से से लेकर नालंदा जिले तक (शरण, 2008 : 59–73) इन पात्रों के संपूर्ण हृदय क्षेत्र, यथा पूर्वी उत्तर प्रदेश एवं बिहार से, आरंभिक तिथियाँ मिलती हैं (कुमार 2010 : 363)। इस संदर्भ में विदुला जायसवाल का यह अभिमत है कि एन.बी.पी. मृद्भाण्ड संस्कृति का उद्भव विशेष रूप से रामनगर में, (जिसका हाल में उन्होंने उत्खनन किया है) प्रथम सहस्त्राब्दि ई.पू. के प्रथम चरण में हो सकता है (व्यक्तिगत सूचना)।

कुछ पुरातत्वशास्त्रियों का मानना है कि एन.बी.पी. पात्रों का अपने मूल स्थल से दूरस्थ क्षेत्रों में वितरण उसके भौतिक स्वरूप में नही हुआ। यह उन पात्रों के निर्माण की केवल तकनीकी ही थी जो विभिन्न स्थानों तक पहुँची। इसी कारण हृदय क्षेत्र से मिले इन पात्रों की अपेक्षा दूरस्थ स्थानों के पात्रों की गुणवत्ता निम्न स्तर की है। टी.एन. राय (1986 : 183) के अनुसार 'उत्तरी कृष्ण मार्जित पात्रों में हमें उच्चतम तकनीकी कुशलता दिखाई पड़ती है जो कुम्हारों के ज्ञान, दिमाग व परिश्रम की परिणति थी। वास्तव में मिट्टी के पात्रों पर चमक पैदा करने की तकनीक अथवा विशिष्ट समीकरण या लेप तैयार करने के नुस्खे का – जो अभेद्य, दाग रहित, स्वस्थ एवं अत्यधिक चमकदार पात्रों के निर्माण के लिये उत्तरदायी था – बहुत बड़े भाग में विस्तार हुआ न कि स्वयं पात्रों का। उनकी मान्यता है कि इसी कारण मध्य गंगा घाटी के अनेकों केन्द्र के अतिरिक्त इसके बाहर भी इन पात्रों का निर्माण साथ–साथ हुआ। के.के. सिन्हा के अनुसार (1969 : 181), वास्तव में पात्रों के सतही गुण में विविधता के कारण इस अनुमान को बल मिलता है कि मध्य गंगा घाटी के बाहर संभवतः इन पात्रों की अनुकृति तैयार की जा रही थी (वही : 182)।

परन्तु साहित्यिक साक्ष्यों में उल्लिखित पात्रों के लम्बी दूरी के व्यापार के आलोक में पुराविदों का यह कथन कि 'एक स्थान से दूसरे स्थान पर इन पात्रों का भौतिक विस्थापन नहीं हुआ' सही नहीं प्रतीत होता। ऊपर यह उल्लेख किया गया है कि व्यापारियों के घर जन्में बोधिसत्व 500 मूल्यवान बर्तनों से भरी गाड़ियाँ लेकर व्यापार हेतु पूर्व से पश्चिम की यात्रा करते थे। इस जानकारी से स्पष्ट होता है कि बुद्ध के काल में निर्मित पात्रों का व्यापार दूर क्षेत्रों एवं बड़े भागों में होता था। इससे लगता है कि पात्रों के निर्माण में निहित तकनीकी ज्ञान को सतर्कतापूर्वक सुरक्षित रखा जाता था और तभी इन पात्रों का व्यापार प्रचलित भी था। इस संदर्भ में पूर्वी उत्तर प्रदेश के सिद्धार्थनगर जिले में कुछ कुम्हारों पर किया गया हमारा सर्वेक्षण महत्त्वपूर्ण है। यहाँ गाँवों के कुम्हारों को, कुछ मायने में ही सही, उत्तरी कृष्ण मार्जित पात्रों वाली चमक पैदा करने की तकनीक का ज्ञान है। उनसे जाँच पड़ताल करने पर यह ज्ञात हुआ कि काले पात्र बनाने की तकनीक को वह अपनी पुत्रियों से भी गुप्त रखते हैं जिससे विवाह के उपरांत पुत्री द्वारा भी दूसरे परिवारों तक यह तकनीक या ज्ञान न पहुँच सके। फलस्वरूप, पिपरहवा के समीप स्थित बर्डपुर में कुम्हारों द्वारा काले पात्र बनाने की कला विलुप्त होती जा रही है। परंतु सिद्धार्थनगर जिले के ही बांसी तहसील में स्थित भरमा गांव के कुम्हारों में ऐसी परंपरा दिखाई नहीं पड़ती। यहां के कुम्हार अन्य पात्रों के साथ–साथ काले पात्र भी बनाते हैं। उन्होंने अपनी इस कला का ज्ञान हमसे भी बांटा एवं पूरी प्रक्रिया हमारे सामने प्रस्तुत की। यद्यपि उनके अनुसार, इस परिश्रम को अधिक प्रोत्साहन न मिलने के कारण नई पीढ़ी के कुम्हारों में इस परंपरा के पात्र बनाने की रुचि समाप्त हो रही है।

दूरस्थ क्षेत्रों में स्थानीय मिट्टी से बने निम्न कोटि के उत्तरी कृष्ण मार्जित पात्रों की उपस्थिति के आलोक में हृदय क्षेत्र से उनका भौतिक स्थानान्तरण न्यायोचित प्रतीत नहीं होता है। ऐसा मध्य गंगा घाटी में विद्यमान उच्च कोटि की जलोढ़ मिट्टी की उपस्थिति से हो सकता है जिसकी इन पात्रों के निर्माण में महत्त्वपूर्ण भूमिका थी। एक कुम्हार के लिए उच्च कोटि की मिट्टी महत्त्वपूर्ण भूमिका रखती है। इस संदर्भ में वाराणसी में कुम्हारों के यहाँ जन्मे बोधिसत्व का उदाहरण खास है जो महान नदी के किनारे फावड़ा लेकर मिट्टी एकत्र करने जाया करते थे। लेखक द्वारा (1988–1990 : 68, 1997 : 211) मध्य गंगा घाटी में दो विभिन्न क्षेत्रों में अवस्थित पुरास्थलों से प्राप्त उत्तरी कृष्ण मार्जित पात्र एवं अन्य सम्बद्ध पात्रों के शैल वैज्ञानिक अध्ययन में भी इसी संदर्भ में रोचक तथ्य उजागर हुये हैं। दोनों स्थानों पर इन पात्रों के नमूनों में भिन्न सूक्ष्म–संरचना दिखाई पड़ी। नृतत्वशास्त्रीय सर्वेक्षण से समर्थित इस अध्ययन से यह ज्ञात होता है कि दोनों ही स्थानों पर उत्तरी कृष्ण मार्जित पात्रों के निर्माण में अलग–अलग मिट्टी का उपयोग हुआ था।

विभिन्न पुरास्थलों से प्राप्त उत्तरी कृष्ण मार्जित पात्र एवं अन्य सम्बद्ध पात्रों की सूक्ष्म–संरचना पर आधारित शैल वैज्ञानिक अध्ययन से भी पात्रों के निर्माण के सच को समझा जा सकता है। इस संदर्भ में महत्त्वपूर्ण पुरास्थलों, विशेष रूप से भारत से बाहर के पुरास्थल, जैसे वारी–इ–बटेश्वर एवं महास्थान (बांग्लादेश), तक्षशिला एवं उदयग्राम (पाकिस्तान), तिलौराकोट एवं लुम्बिनी (नेपाल), अनुराधापुर (श्रीलंका) आदि से प्राप्त पात्रों के नमूनों का उद्देश्यपूर्वक अनुसंधान आवश्यक है। इसी प्रकार भारत में भी विभिन्न पुरास्थलों जैसे तामलुक (ताम्रलिप्ति), अमरावती, कोरकई, चंद्रकेतुगढ़, शिशुपालगढ़, राजगीर, वैशाली, राजघाट, सैमथन वडनगर, जाफरडीह आदि से मिले पात्रों के नमूनों का महीन काट एवं शैल वैज्ञानिक अध्ययन तर्कसंगत होगा जिससे उनके दूरस्थ स्थानों पर वितरण की संभावना को तकनीकी अथवा व्यापार के आलोक में समझा जा सके। यहाँ यह बतलाना उचित होगा कि पात्रों के शैल वैज्ञानिक अध्ययन से उनका संविन्यास अभिलक्षण मालूम कर एवं स्थान विशेष की मिट्टी का परीक्षण कर उसके स्त्रोत का पता लगाया जा सकता है बशर्ते अनुसंधान क्षेत्र का भूविज्ञान ज्ञात हो।

उत्तरी कृष्ण मार्जित पात्रों के उपरोक्त विवेचन के फलस्वरूप कुछ महत्त्वपूर्ण विवादों, जैसे इनका उद्भव, विकास एवं वितरण आदि से संबंधित प्रश्न उपजते हैं। जहाँ तक इसके बौद्ध धर्म अथवा मौर्यकालीन साम्राज्यिक विस्तार से संबंध की बात है टी.पी. वर्मा (व्यक्तिगत सूचना) के अनुसार 'पुरातात्विक एवं साहित्यिक स्त्रोतों के आलेक में इनके पुनर्मूल्यांकन की आवश्यकता नहीं है।' उनके विचार से देश व काल के परिप्रेक्ष्य में मिले साक्ष्य हमें उत्तरी कृष्ण मार्जित पात्रों को बौद्ध धर्म अथवा मौर्य साम्राज्य से सम्बद्ध करने की अनुमति नहीं देते हैं। इन पात्रों का भौगोलिक विस्तार अशोक के साम्राज्य से कहीं अधिक विस्तारित है एवं इनका कालक्रम लगभग एक सहस्त्राब्दि पहले का है। बुद्ध का जन्म भी इस 'डीलक्स वेयर' के काफी बाद में हुआ एवं स्वयं उनके द्वारा उन्नत किस्म के पात्रों का उपयोग वर्जित किया गया था। हाँ, यह अवश्य संभावित है कि इन पात्रों का मूल स्थान प्राचीन कोशल अथवा मगध में रहा हो। इस संदर्भ में एक महती आवश्यकता इस बात की है कि हम उत्तरी कृष्ण मार्जित पात्र संस्कृति एवं उससे सम्बद्ध उन लोगों की पहचान करें जिन्होंने इस संस्कृति का प्रसार इस महाद्वीप से लेकर श्रीलंका तक किया।

सन्दर्भ

1. अग्रवाल, आर.सी., शंकर नाथ एवं एस.पी. गुप्ता, 1971–72, 'बिबलियोग्राफी ऑफ दि एन.बी.पी.डब्लू.', *पुरातत्त्व, बुलेटिन ऑफ दि इण्डियन आर्कियोलाजिकल सोसाइटी, सं. 5 (प्रासीडिंग्स ऑफ दि सेमिनार ऑन ओ.सी.पी. एण्ड एन.बी.पी.डब्लू., ऐपेण्डिक्स I*, संपा. एस.पी. गुप्ता), नई दिल्ली, पृ. 76–83

2. कॉवेल, ई.बी., 1973, *दि जातक,* भा. 1, पृ. 11; भा. 5, पृ. 228
3. कुमार, रवीन्द्र, 1989–1990, 'प्राचीन मृद्भाण्डों का महीन–काट एवं शैल वैज्ञानिक अध्ययन : सेनुआर एवं इमलीडीह खुर्द से प्राप्त भाण्ड–खण्डों के परिप्रेक्ष्य में, भगवन्त सहाय (संपा.) *दी जनरल ऑफ दि बिहार पुराविद् परिषद (लाला आदित्य नारायण कमेमोरेशन वॉल्यूम),* खण्ड 13–14, पटना, पृ. 41–69
4. कुमार रवीन्द्र, 1997, 'पैट्रोग्राफिक स्टडी ऑफ एन्शिएन्ट सिरेमिक्सः ए केस स्टडी ऑफ सैम्पुल्स फ्रॉम इमलीडीह एण्ड सेनुआर', पी.सी. पन्त एवं विदुला जायसवाल (संपा.), *एन्शिएन्ट सिरेमिक्सः हिस्टोरिकल इन्क्वायरीस एण्ड साइन्टिफिक एप्रोचेस,* अगम कला प्रकाशन, दिल्ली, पृ. 197–219
5. कुमार रवीन्द्र, 2010, 'रिसर्चेस इन दि मिडिल गोमती बेसिन, स्कोप, फॉर फर्दर इन्वेस्टिगेशन्स', त्रिपाठी, वी (संपा.), *आर्कियोलॉजी ऑफ गंगा बेसिन : पैराडाइम शिफ्ट,* वॉ0 2, शारदा पब्लिशिंग हाउस, दिल्ली, पृ. 359–365
6. कृष्णन, के. 1986, *'केमिकल एण्ड पैट्रोलॉजिकल स्टडीज इन एन्शिएन्ट पॉटरी,,* पी.एच.डी. थीसिस (अनपब्लिश्ड), एमएस. यूनिवर्सिटी ऑफ बड़ौदा, वड़ोदरा।
7. कृष्णन, के. एण्ड काजल शाह, 2005, 'बियॉन्ड वेयर्स एण्ड शेप्स गेनिंग ए पेट्रोग्राफिक पर्सपैक्टिव ऑन एन्शिएन्ट इण्डियन पॉटरी', ए.के. विश्वास (संपा.), *साइन्स इन आर्कियोलॉजी एण्ड आर्कियोमैटेरियल्स,* डी.के. प्रिन्टवर्ल्ड, नई दिल्ली, पृ. 135–156
8. गोगटे, वी.डी. एवं अन्य, 1982, 'क्लासीफिकेशन ऑफ पॉटरी टाइप्स बाई फेरस / फेरिक रेशियो एण्ड एलीमेन्टल कार्बन इन पॉटरी' *बुलेटिन ऑफ दि डेकन कॉलेज पो. ग्रे. एण्ड रिसर्च इंस्टीट्यूट,* वॉ. 41, पुणे, पृ. 72–76
9. घोष ए., 1950, 'राजगीर', *एन्शिएन्ट इण्डिया, बुलेटिन ऑफ दि आर्कियोलॉजिकल सर्वे ऑफ इण्डिया,* सं. 7, न्यू दिल्ली, पृ. 71–72
10. घोष ए. एण्ड के.सी. पाणिग्रही, 1946, 'दि पॉटरी ऑफ अहिच्छत्र, डिस्ट्रिक्ट बरेली, यू.पी.', *एन्शिएन्ट एण्डिया, बुलेटिन ऑफ दि आर्कियोलॉजिकल सर्वे ऑफ इण्डिया,* सं. 1. न्यू दिल्ली, पृ. 37–55
11. जायसवाल, विदुला 2006–2007, 'रिपोर्ट III रामनगर एक्सकवेशनः 2007', *बुलेटिन सं. 10, ज्ञानप्रवाह, सेन्टर फॉर कल्चरल स्टडीज एण्ड रिसर्च,* वाराणसी, पृ. 237–240
12. तिवारी, डी.पी., 2002, *'एक्सवेशन एट चारदा',* तरुण प्रकाशन, लखनऊ
13. थापड़, बी.के., 1955, 'प्रकाश 1955–ए चालकोलिथिक साइट इन तापी वैली', *एन्शिएन्ट इण्डिया, बुलेटिन ऑफ दि आर्कियोलॉजिकल सर्वे ऑफ इण्डिया,* सं. 20–21, न्यू दिल्ली, पृ. 13 एण्ड 71–75
14. देरनियागल, एस. यू., 2004 'प्रीहिस्टॉरिक बेसिस फॉर दि राइज ऑफ सिविलाइजेशन इन श्रीलंका एण्ड सदर्न इण्डिया', *पेपर इन सैकण्ड वेसक कमेमोरेशन लेक्चर एट दि म्यूजियम थियेटर,* चेन्नई, पृ. 1–8
15. देव, कृष्ण, 1969, डिस्कशन ऑन सच्चिदानन्द सहाय'स पेपर, 'ओरिजिन एण्ड स्प्रेड ऑफ दि नॉर्दर्न ब्लैक पॉलिश्ड वेयर', बी.पी. सिन्हा, (संपा.), *पॉटरीज इन एन्शिएन्ट इण्डिया,* ए.आई.एस.सी. एण्ड आर्कियोलॉजी डिपार्टमेन्ट, पटना, पृ. 153
16. देव कृष्ण एवं सर आरईएम व्हीलर, 1946, 'नॉर्दर्न ब्लैक पॉलिश्ड वेयर', *एन्शिएन्ट एण्डिया, बुलेटिन ऑफ दि आर्कियोलॉजिकल सर्वे ऑफ इण्डिया,* सं. 1. अपेंडिक्स ए, न्यू दिल्ली, पृ. 55–58
17. निगम, जे.एस., 1961, 'नॉर्दर्न ब्लैक पॉलिश्ड वेयर', मार्ग सं. 3, वॉ IV, बॉम्बे
18. पाण्डेय, एम.एस. 1969, डिस्कशन ऑन सच्चिदानन्द सहाय'स पेपर, 'ओरिजिन एण्ड स्प्रेड ऑफ दि नॉर्दर्न ब्लैक पॉलिश्ड वेयर', बी.पी. सिन्हा, (संपा.), *पॉटरीज इन एन्शिएन्ट इण्डिया,* ए.आई.एस.सी. एण्ड आर्कियोलॉजी डिपार्टमेन्ट, पटना, पृ. 154
19. भारद्वाज, एच.सी., 1969, 'सम टेक्निकल ऑबजर्वेशन्स ऑन एन.बी.पी. स्लिप', बी.पी. सिन्हा, (संपा.) *पॉटरीज इन एन्शिएन्ट एण्डिया,* ए.आई.एस.सी. एण्ड आर्कियोलॉजी डिपार्टमेन्ट, पटना, पृ. 188–92
20. माझी, हरी एण्ड बी.आर मणी, 2003, 'अयोध्या : 2002–03 एक्सकैवेशन्स एट दि डिस्प्यूटेड साइट', *रिपोर्ट सबमिटेड*

टू दि स्पेशल फुल बेन्च, लखनऊ ऑफ दि ऑनरेबुल हाईकोर्ट, इलाहाबाद, वॉ. I (टेक्स्ट),, आर्कियोलॉजिकल सर्वे ऑफ इण्डिया, जनपथ, नई दिल्ली।

21. मार्शल, जे., 1915, *एनुअल रिपोर्ट ऑफ दि आर्कियोलॉजिकल सर्वे ऑफ इण्डिया 1911–12,* कलकत्ता, पृ. 80–81
22. मिश्रा, ए.के. 1988, *दि इण्डियन ब्लैक वेयर, (फर्स्ट मिलेनियम बी.सी.),* प्रतिभा प्रकाशन, नई दिल्ली
23. राय, सुभाष, 1987, 'ए फ्रेश स्टडी ऑफ एनबीपी वेयर ग्लेज', ए.एम. शास्त्री एवं अन्य (संपा.), *वाजपेयः एसे ऑन इण्डियन आर्ट एण्ड कल्चर, (प्रो. के.डी. बाजपेयी फेलिसिटेशन वॉयूम),* अगम कला प्रकाशन, दिल्ली, पृ. 47–49
24. रॉय, टी.एन. 1986, *ए स्टडी ऑफ नॉर्दर्न ब्लैक पॉलिश्ड वेयर एन आयरन एज कल्चर ऑफ इण्डिया,* रामानन्द विद्याभवन, नई दिल्ली
25. लाल, बी.बी., 1954–55, 'एस्कवेशन ऐट हस्तिनापुर एण्ड अदर एक्सप्लोरेशन्स इन सतलुज बेसिन (1950–52)', *एन्शिएन्ट इण्डिया, बुलटिन ऑफ दि आर्कियोलॉजिकल सर्वे ऑफ इण्डिया,* सं. 10–11, नई दिल्ली, पृ. 143–46
26. लाल, बी.बी., 1954–55, 'एस्कवेशन ऐट हस्तिनापुर एण्ड अदर एक्सप्लोरेशन्स इन सतलुज बेसिन (1950–52)', *एन्शिएन्ट इण्डिया, बुलेटिन ऑफ दि आर्कियोलॉजिकल सर्वे ऑफ इण्डिया,* सं. 10–11, नई दिल्ली, पृ. 143–46
27. लाल, बी.बी., 2008, *राम'स हिस्टॉरिसिटी, मंदिर एण्ड सेतु : एवीडेन्स ऑफ लिटरेचर, आर्कियोलॉजी एण्ड अदर साइन्सेज,* आर्यन बुक्स इंटरनेशनल, नई दिल्ली
28. व्हीलर, सर आरइएम, 1959, *'अर्ली इण्डिया एण्ड पाकिस्तान',* थेम्स एण्ड हडसन, लंडन, पृ. 26–33
29. सनाउल्लाह, एम., 1946, 'रिपोर्ट ऑफ दि आर्कियोलॉजिकल केमिस्ट', *एन्शिएन्ट इण्डिया, बुलेटिन ऑफ दि आर्कियोलॉजिकल सर्वे ऑफ इण्डिया,* सं. 1, नई दिल्ली, पृ. 58
30. सहाय सच्चिदानन्द, 1969, 'ओरिजिन एण्ड स्प्रेड ऑफ दि नॉर्दर्न ब्लैक पॉलिश्ड वेयर', बी.पी. सिन्हा, (संपा.), *पॉटरीज इन एन्शिएन्ट इण्डिया,* ए.आई.एस.सी. एण्ड आर्कियोलाजी डिपार्टमेन्ट, पटना, पृ. 145–153
31. सिन्हा के.के., 'दि एनबीपी वेयर–फ्रेश हाइपोथिसिस इन दि लाइट ऑफ श्रावस्ती एविडेन्स', बी.पी. सिन्हा (संपा.) *पॉटरीज इन एन्शिएन्ट इण्डिया,* ए.आई.एस.सी. एण्ड आर्कियोलॉजी डिपार्टमेन्ट, पटना, पृ. 174–182
32. सिन्हा के.के., 1971–72, 'सेशन ऑन एनबीपी.', एस.सी. गुप्ता (संपा.), *पुरातत्व, जनरल ऑफ दि इण्डियन आर्कियोलॉजिकल सोसायटी,* सं. 5, दिल्ली, पृ. 38
33. सिन्हा प्रकाश, 2001, 'बुद्धिस्ट साइट्स ऑफ दि एज ऑफ बुद्ध : आर्कियोलॉजिकल एविडेन्स ऑन डेटिंग एण्ड अर्बनाइजेशन', जी.सी. पाण्डे (संपा.), लाइफ थॉट एण्ड कल्चर इन इण्डिया (फ्रॉम सी. 600 बी.सी. टू ए.डी. 300), वॉ. 1, पार्ट 2, पृ. 890–911
34. सिंह ए.के., 2007, 'इमलीडीह खुर्द, डिस्ट्रिक्ट गोरखपुरः रीएसेससमेन्ट ऑफ द मैटेरियल कल्चर एण्ड क्रोनोलॉजी' *पेपर सबमिटेड इन दि फोर्टीफर्स्ट एनुअल कांफ्रेन्स ऑफ दि इणडियन आर्कियोलॉजिकल सोसायटी,* रायपुर, पृ. 1–2
35. सिंह पुरुषोत्तम, 1994, *एस्कवेशन्स एट नरहन (1984–89),* बी.आर. पब्लिशिंग कॉरपोरेशन, दिल्ली
36. शर्मा, आर.एस., 1983, *मैटीरियल कल्चर एण्ड सोशल फार्मेशन इन एन्शिएन्ट इण्डिया,*, मैकमिलन इण्डिया, नई दिल्ली।
37. शरण, एस.सी., 2006, 'दि नॉर्दर्न ब्लैक पॉलिश्ड वेयर–ओरिजिन, डेवलप्मेन्ट, हिस्टारिसिटी, डेटिंग एण्ड दि एथनिक रिलेशनशिप इन दी मिडिल गंगा प्लेन', बी.आर. मणि एण्ड एस.सी. शरण (संपा.), *पुराभारती स्टडीज इन अरली हिस्टारिकल आर्कियोलॉजी एण्ड बुद्धिज्म (कमोमोरेशन वाल्यूम इन रेस्पेक्ट ऑफ प्रो. बी.पी. सिन्हा),* वॉ. I, शारदा पब्लिशिंग हाउस, दिल्ली, पृ. 18–31
38. शरण, एस.सी., एवं अन्य, 2008, 'एस्कवेशन्स एट जाफरडीह एण्ड इट्स आइडेन्टीफिकेशन विथ कुलिक', के.एन. दीक्षित (संपा.), *पुरातत्व, जनरल ऑफ दि इण्डियन आर्कियोलॉजिकल सोसायटी,* सं. 38, नई दिल्ली, पृ. 59–73
39. हार्नर, आई.बी. 1982, (पु.मु.) *'द बुक ऑफ डिसिप्लिन (विनयपिटक)', वॉ. IV (महावग्ग), वॉ. V (चुल्लवग्ग),* दि पालीटेक्स्ट सोसाइटी, ऑक्सफोर्ड

40. हेगड़े, के.टी.एम., 1962, 'टेक्निकल स्टडीज इन नॉर्दर्न ब्लैक पॉलिश्ड वेयर' *जनरल ऑफ दि एम.एस. यूनिवर्सिटी ऑफ बड़ौदा,* 11(1), वड़ोदरा, पृ. 159–61

41. हेगड़े, के.टी.एम., 1966, 'इलैक्ट्रॉन माइक्रोप्रोब स्टडी ऑन दि नॉर्दर्न ब्लैक पॉलिश्ड (एनबीपी) वेयर ऑफ इण्डिया' *करेन्ट साइन्स,* सं. 24, पृ. 623

42. हेगड़े, के.टी.एम., 1975, 'दि पेन्टेड ग्रे वेयर ऑफ इण्डिया;, *ऐन्टीक्विटी,* पृ. 187–90

43. हेगड़े, के.टी.एम., 1978, 'एनालिसिस ऑफ एन्शिएन्ट डीलक्स वेयर्स' *आर्कियोफिजिका, 10, प्रोसीडिंग्स ऑफ दि एटीन्थ इंटरनेशनल सिम्पोजियम ऑन आर्कियोमेट्री,* बॉन, पृ. 141–55

23

भीटा में शैव धर्म के पुरातात्त्विक अवशेष

सुषमा श्रीवास्तव

ईसा पूर्व छठी शताब्दी में मध्य देश के प्रमुख जनपदों में वत्स जनपद का उल्लेख है। इस जनपद का बारा नामक ग्राम 25° 15" अक्षांश उत्तर तथा 81° 43" देशान्तर पूर्व में इलाहाबाद एवं बाँदा के राजमार्ग पर स्थित है[1]। इसी ग्राम में यमुना के दाहिने किनारे पर तीन बड़े–बड़े टीले हैं। यही स्थल भीटा नाम से जाना जाता है जिसकी पुष्टि यहाँ से प्राप्त एक मुहर से होती है जिस पर *'बीतभयपत्तन'* अंकित था[2]। कनिंघम ने इसकी पहचान उस प्राचीन *बीतभयपत्तन* स्थान से की है जिसके संबंध में जैन ग्रंथ *'वीरचरित्र'* में उल्लेख मिलता है तथा उसमें यह भी वर्णित है कि महावीर के समय यह स्थल समृद्धशाली था। उल्लेखनीय है कि भीटा यमुना के तट पर स्थित था अतः व्यापारिक पत्तन हेतु इसकी स्थिति अनुकूल थी। अतः मुहर पर अंकित स्थल का समीकरण जैन ग्रंथ में वर्णित *बीतभयपत्तन* से किया गया एवं इसका नाम *बीथा* (*भीटा*) रखा गया[3]। इस स्थल के नामकरण के संबंध में यहीं से प्राप्त दो अन्य मुहरें भी बहुत महत्त्वपूर्ण है जिन पर क्रमशः *'सहजाति निगमस'*[4] तथा *विच्छिग्राम'*[5] अंकित है। इतिहासकारों ने *विनयपिटक*[6] तथा *अंगुत्तरनिकाय*[7] तथा अन्य बौद्ध ग्रंथों के आधार पर इस वर्तमान भीटा स्थल को 'सहजाति' कहा है। किन्तु वास्तव में सहजाति शब्द स्थानवाची नहीं है। 'सहजाति' का तात्पर्य समान जातीय शिल्पियों एवं व्यापारियों के संघ से है।[8] इसके संबंध में कोश ग्रंथों में भी उल्लेख है जिसमें समान जातियों (सहजातियों) के संघ को श्रेणी कहा गया है[9]। इसके नामकरण के संबंध में *'विच्छिग्राम'* अंकित एक अन्य मुहर भी महत्त्वपूर्ण है। जॉन मार्शल ने *विच्छिग्राम* की पहचान भीटा से की है[10]। अधिकांश इतिहासकार इसके संबंध में मौन हैं। लेकिन *'विच्छि'* शब्द भीटा के संदर्भ में महत्त्वपूर्ण है। उल्लेखनीय है कि *'विच्छिय'* शब्द प्राकृत भाषा का है जिसका तात्पर्य नष्ट होना या विरल होना है[11]। भीटा का क्षेत्र लगभग 300 ई.पू. से 600 ई. के मध्य समृद्ध नगरीय केन्द्र था किन्तु सातवीं शती में इसका नगरीय स्वरूप समाप्तप्राय हो गया और यह एक विरल ग्राम के रूप में परिवर्तित हो गया। अतः *विच्छि* शब्द भीटा के लिए ही प्रयुक्त हुआ प्रतीत होता है। यद्यपि

600 ई. के बाद भीटा की आर्थिक गतविधियाँ सीमित हो गयीं, किन्तु पूर्वमध्यकाल में भी भीटा विभिन्न राजवंशों की प्रशासनिक इकाई के रूप में महत्त्वपूर्ण रहा।

उल्लेखनीय है कि छठी शताब्दी ई.पू. में वत्स के राजा उदयन की राजधानी कौशाम्बी का विस्तार भीटा क्षेत्र तक था। प्रारंभ में वत्स चेदि देश का अंग था और भीटा स्थल उत्तर से दक्षिण तथा पूर्व से पश्चिम जाने वाले मार्ग के मध्य में स्थित था। अतः स्पष्ट है कि भीटा अपनी उपयुक्त भौगोलिक स्थिति के कारण ही विभिन्न राजवंशों की आर्थिक एवं धार्मिक गतिविधियों का केन्द्र बना। यह क्षेत्र क्रमशः मौर्य, शुंग, कुषाण, मघ, गुप्त, चन्देल, गाहडवाल एवं कलचुरि राजवंशों के प्रशासकीय एवं आर्थिक जीवन का केन्द्र बना फलस्वरूप भीटा में धामिक गतिविधियों की पूर्व पीठिका तैयार हुई।

प्रस्तुत शोधपत्र भीटा में शैव धर्म की परंपरा से संबंधित है। अतः इसके अन्तर्गत उसी से संबंधित पुरातात्त्विक अवशेषों का अध्ययन किया गया है। इस संदर्भ में उल्लेखनीय है कि उत्तर भारत के जो स्थल छठी शती तक बौद्ध धर्म से संबंधित थे कालान्तर में वे अधिकांशतः पौराणिक धर्म के केन्द्र बन गए। भीटा से प्राप्त मुहरों, मूर्तियों, मन्दिरों एवं विभिन्न राजवंशों के शासकों के अभिलेखों के आधार पर यह कहा जा सकता है कि भीटा भी शैव धर्म के एक केन्द्र के रूप में विकसित हो चुका था। मार्शल को इस स्थल के उत्खनन से लगभग 210 मुहरें एवं मुद्रांकन प्राप्त हुए हैं जो लगभग 120 प्रकार के हैं। इनके अतिरिक्त बहुसंख्यक मात्रा में मूर्तियाँ, आभूषण एवं मनकें भी प्राप्त हुए हैं।[12] सुवीरा जायसवाल ने यहाँ से प्राप्त मुहरों का वर्गीकरण किया है। उनके अनुसार 120 मुहरों में से 25 मुहरें शैव धर्म से, 21 मुहरें वैष्णव धर्म, 6 मुहरें सौर्य मत तथा शेष अन्य विषयों से संबंधित है।[13] शैव धर्म से संबंधित मुहरों पर शिव प्रतीकों के अंकन के साथ अभिलेख भी हैं जैसे, *कालेश्वर प्रीयताम्* (सं. 14), *कालंजर भट्टार्कस्य* (सं. 15), *भद्रेश्वर* (सं. 16), *महेश्वर* (सं. 17), आदि अभिलेख अंकित मुहरें हैं।[14] इसके अतिरिक्त शैव धर्म से संबंधित अन्य मुहरों पर *नन्दि पद* (सं. 37 एवं 77), *नन्दि* (सं. 7 एवं 1) तथा शेष अन्य मुहरों (सं. 25, 26, 27, 28 तथा 86) पर शैव प्रतीकों का अंकन है।[15] यहाँ भीटा से प्राप्त विभिन्न मुहरों का विश्लेषण करना समीचीन होगा। *कालेश्वर प्रीयताम* अंकित मुहर पर शैव धर्म का प्रतीक त्रिशूल का अंकन है। उल्लेखनीय है कि *स्कन्दपुराण* में कालेश्वर एक शिवलिंग का नाम है। अतः यह मुहर शैव धर्म से ही संबंधित है। संभवतः इसका निर्माण भीटा के किसी शिव मन्दिर में पूजार्थ किया गया होगा।[16] उल्लेखनीय है कि कुषाणकालीन मथुरा की मूर्तियों पर भी *'प्रीयतम'* एवं *'प्रीयताम्'* अभिलेख का अंकन है।[17] अतः इस तथ्य की पुष्टि होती है कि व्रतानुष्ठित (मनौती) हेतु प्रतीकयुक्त मुहरों का निर्माण किया जाता था।

भीटा से प्राप्त शैव धर्म से संबंधित एक अन्य मुहर पर *कालंजर भट्टार्कस्य* अंकित है जिसका तात्पर्य है कालंजर का स्वामी। इस मुहर पर अंकित शिवलिंग के नीचे पहाड़ी का अंकन है। ऐसा प्रतीत होता है कि यह मुहर कालंजर क्षेत्र से प्रेषित की गयी होगी,[18] क्योंकि ईसा की 7वीं–8वीं शती में कालंजर शैव धर्म का प्रमुख केन्द्र था। इसके अतिरिक्त भीटा से ही गुप्तकालीन *'क(ा) ल(ा)(ञ)'* जर अंकित एक मुहर प्राप्त हुई है।[19] ऐसा प्रतीत होता है कि चौथी–पाँचवीं शती में कालंजर शैव धर्म के एक प्रमुख केन्द्र के रूप में विकसित हो चुका था। भीटा से प्राप्त *भद्रेश्वर* एवं *महेश्वर* अंकित मुद्राएँ तो स्पष्टतः शैव धर्म से संबंधित हैं। *भद्रेश्वर* शिव का ही एक अन्य अभिधान है जिसका उल्लेख *वामन पुराण* में है।[20]

भीटा से प्राप्त तांबे की मुद्रिका (अंगूठी) भी महत्त्वपूर्ण है जिसके अण्डाकार भाग में नन्दि का अंकन है तथा चौथी–पाँचवी शती की ब्राह्मी लिपि में *'रुद्रा–चा–र्या'* शब्द का अंकन है। इस नाम से स्पष्ट है कि यह किसी शैव आचार्य की मुद्रा रही होगी, जिसकी पुष्टि मुहर पर नन्दि के अंकन से भी होती है।[21]

भीटा से प्राप्त शैव धर्म से संबंधित पुरातात्त्विक साक्ष्यों के आधार पर इस स्थल से शैव धर्म की प्राचीनता की भी जानकारी होती है। उल्लेखनीय है कि सैन्धव सभ्यता के विभिन्न स्थलों से प्राप्त लिंग, योनि तथा मुहरों

पर पशुपति रुद्र के अंकन से संबंधित साक्ष्यों के आधार पर कहा जा सकता है कि शैव धर्म के अस्तित्व के प्रमाण सैन्धव काल तक जाते हैं। प्राचीनतम साहित्यिक कृति *ऋग्वेद* से भी इस धर्म के प्रचलन के प्रमाण मिलते हैं। भीटा से इस पूर्व प्रचलित धर्म के बहुसंख्यक पुरातात्त्विक अवशेष प्राप्त हुए हैं जिन की प्राचीनता लगभग प्रथम शती ईसा पूर्व तक जाती है। उल्लेखनीय है कि यहाँ से प्राप्त विभिन्न मुहरों एवं मुद्रांकनों का काल लगभग 400 ईसा पूर्व से 9वीं–10वीं शती है। इन मुहरों के अतिरिक्त जो शिवलिंग प्राप्त हुए हैं, उनके आधार पर भीटा में शैव धर्म की प्राचीनता प्रथम शती ईसा पूर्व में निर्धारित की जा सकती है। गोपीनाथ राव ने अपने ग्रंथ *एलीमेन्टस ऑफ हिन्दू आइकोनोग्रेफी* में निर्दिष्ट किया है कि मनुष्य निर्मित अद्यतन सबसे प्राचीन मुखलिंग भीटा से प्राप्त हुआ है जो लखनऊ म्यूजियम में है।[22] दक्षिण भारत में मद्रास के गुडिमल्लम् नामक स्थान से भी एक मुख लिंग प्राप्त हुआ है जिसको गोपीनाथ भीटा के बाद के काल का मानते हैं। भीटा के शिवलिंग में अभिलेख अंकित है – *खजहुति पुतनं लिंगो पतिठापितो वासेठि–पुतेन नागसिरिना पियताम् देवता,* जिसका अर्थ है कि खजहुति के पुत्रों में वासेठि के पुत्र नागसिरि के द्वारा देवताओं को प्रसन्न करने के लिए लिंग की स्थापना की गई। इस अभिलेख के आधार पर कहा जा सकता है कि इस शिवलिंग को उपासना हेतु प्रतिष्ठापित किया गया था। इस लेख की लिपि के आधार पर आर.डी. बनर्जी ने इसका काल प्रथम शताब्दी ई.पू. निर्धारित किया है।[23] इस महत्त्वपूर्ण मूर्ति एवं आभिलेखिक साक्ष्य के आधार पर कहा जा सकता है कि उत्तर भारत में ही नहीं अपितु सम्पूर्ण भारत में शैव धर्म की उपासना के प्राचीनतम प्रमाण भीटा से प्राप्त होते हैं।

भीटा का मुखलिंग द्विभुजी है जिसमें शिव का दाहिना हाथ अभयमुद्रा में प्रदर्शित है और बाएँ हाथ में घट का अंकन किया गया है। यद्यपि मुख का कुछ भाग खण्डित हो गया है किन्तु केश, कुण्डल एवं ग्रैवेयक का अंकन स्पष्ट दिखाई देता है। इस विग्रह के चारों ओर चार मुख भी बने हुए हैं जिन्हें आवक्ष तक उकेरा गया है। आर. डी. बनर्जी ने भीटा के मुखलिंग के संबंध में विस्तृत जानकारी प्रदान की है।[24] उन्होंने मुखलिंग के पंचमुख को क्रमशः ईशान, तत्पुरूष, अघोर, वामदेव तथा सद्योजात से समीकृत किया है। मुखलिंग की एक मूर्ति के केश एवं केयूर उसके स्त्री मुख होने का संकेत देते हैं। एक विग्रह मुण्डित है। विग्रह के शेष दो मुखों में से एक में भालपट्ट और दूसरे में उष्णीष उत्कीर्ण है। मुण्डित एवं उष्णीष वाले मुख सौम्य प्रतीत होते हैं। भालपट्ट वाली मूर्ति में दाढ़ी–मूछों का अंकन है; साथ ही, बाहर निकले हुए दांत स्पष्ट हैं। *महाभारत* में शिव के इन चार मुखों की व्याख्या प्राप्त होती है। इसके अनुसार, शिव पूर्व मुख से इन्द्रपद का शासन करते हैं, पश्चिम मुख सौम्य है, दक्षिण मुख संहार हेतु है और उत्तर मुख उमा से वार्तालाप के लिए है। इससे स्पष्ट है कि प्रयाग के परिक्षेत्र कौशाम्बी, भीटा इत्यादि स्थलों पर शिवलिंग एवं शैव प्रतिमा के अंकन महाभारत में वर्णित शैव प्रतिमा विधान के अनुरूप होने लगे थे।[25]

भीटा से ही एक अन्य विशिष्ट प्रतिमा प्राप्त हुई है जो सर्वतोभद्र पद्धति में निर्मित है। यह सम्प्रति लखनऊ संग्रहालय में है। उल्लेखनीय है कि इस प्रतिमा के एक ओर मुकुट है, द्विभुजधारी प्रतिमा के एक हाथ में कलश है। कलशधारी प्रतिमा के पीछे भाग में द्विभुज आकृति का अंकन है। इस मूर्ति के ऊपर के भाग में मानव मुख व नीचे के भाग में वराह एवं शिव बने हैं। इस मूर्ति का दाहिना हाथ अभय मुद्रा में है, बाएं हाथ में संभवतः कोई वस्तु रही होगी जो भग्न स्थिति में है। दोनों ही द्विभुजी प्रतिमाएँ यक्ष प्रतिमाओं के अनुरूप ही निर्मित की गयी है।[26] प्रश्न यह उठता है कि इस मूर्ति का समीकरण किस देवता के साथ किया जाए जिसमें कलश, सिंह एवं वराह तीनों की संगति के साक्ष्य मिलते हों। सामान्यतः तो शिव को घट धारण किए हुए नहीं दिखाया गया है। किन्तु कतिपय साक्ष्यों के आधार पर इस मूर्ति को शिव से समीकृत किया जा सकता है। जैसे, कनिष्क की मुद्राओं पर अंकित चतुर्भुजी शिव के हाथ में घट अंकित है।[27] उज्जयिनी की मुद्राओं पर भी कमण्डलधारी त्रिशीर्ष शिव का अंकन है।[28] उल्लेखनीय है कि शिव की एक उपाधि *कलशेश्वर* भी थी जिसकी पुष्टि शिव अंकित एक मृण्मुहर

से होती है जिस पर सातवीं शती की लिपि में *श्री कलशेश्वर* उत्कीर्ण है।[29] शिव की *कलशेश्वर* नामक उपाधि की पुष्टि *लिंगपुराण* से भी होती है जिसमें शिव के कलश से उत्पन्न होने का प्रसंग सन्दर्भित है।[30] भीटा से प्राप्त उक्त विशिष्ट प्रतिमा में सिंह व वराह के अंकन का शिव के साथ संयोजन का प्रश्न भी विचारणीय है। इस संदर्भ में उल्लेखनीय है कि भीटा के अतिरिक्त अन्य स्थलों जैसे, मथुरा के माट स्थल से शिव की प्रतिमा सिंह के साथ अंकित की गयी है।[31] *महाभारत* में एक स्थल पर शिव को *सिंहग* और *सिंहवाहन* कहा गया है।[32]

कानपुर के मूसानगर से प्राप्त एक वेदिका में शिव की द्विभुजी प्रतिमा के एक हाथ में घट है एवं दूसरा हाथ अभयमुद्रा में है। इसमें शिव के दायीं तरफ सिंह का अंकन है।[33] शिव की प्रतिमा के साथ सिंह के अंकन के अतिरिक्त वराह की प्रतिमा का अंकन भी विचारणीय है। इस संदर्भ में पुनः *महाभारत* का संदर्भ उल्लेखनीय है जिसमें शिव का एक अभिधान *वराह* भी है।[34] कूर्मपुराण में भी शिव को *वराह श्रृंगधारी* के रूप में अभिहित किया गया है।[35]

अतः भीटा से प्राप्त शिव अभिधान अंकित मुहरें, मुखलिंग एवं सर्वतोभद्र मूर्ति यह स्पष्ट प्रमाणित करते हैं कि प्रथम शती ईसा पूर्व में यह शैव धर्म का केन्द्र बन चुका था।

उल्लेखनीय है कि भीटा में राज्य स्थापित करने वाले राजवंशों में मुख्यतः कुषाण, मघ एवं कलचुरि शासक शैव मतावलम्बी थे। कुषाणवंशी शासक कनिष्क, हुविष्क एवं वासुदेव के सिक्के व साँचें भी भीटा से प्राप्त हुये हैं। यद्यपि हुविष्क बौद्ध था किन्तु कनिष्क की तरह उसके सिक्कों पर भारतीय एवं इरानी–रोमन देवताओं का भी अंकन है। वासुदेव तो शैव मतावलम्बी था। उक्त शासकों के शैव धर्म से संबंधित चिन्हांकित सिक्के प्राप्त हुए हैं। उनके काल में भी भीटा में शैव धर्म का प्रभाव अवश्य रहा होगा। कुषाणों के पश्चात भीटा में मघ वंश का राज्य स्थापित हुआ। मघों का शासन प्रारंभ में बान्धवगढ़, रीवा (बघेलखण्ड) क्षेत्र में था। द्वितीय शती ईसवी में भद्रमध ने कौशाम्बी एवं उसके समीपवर्ती क्षेत्र को कुषाणों से विजित किया था। यहाँ से शक संवत 81 (159 ई.) का एक लेख प्राप्त हुआ है।[36] वह शैव मतावलम्बी था। मघ शासक वासिष्ठीपुत्र की भी भीटा से मुहर प्राप्त हुई है[37]। भीटा के ही गींज नामक स्थान से शक संवत 52 (130 ई.) की एक मुहर प्राप्त हुई है। महाराज भीमवर्मन के कौशाम्बी से 2 अभिलेख मिले हैं जो शक संवत् 130 एवं 139 क्रमशः 208 एवं 217 ई. के हैं[38] तथा उसके शैव धर्मावलम्बी होने का प्रमाण प्रस्तुत करते हैं। कौशाम्बी से मघ शासक भीमवर्मन के काल की एक शिव–पार्वती की संयुक्त मूर्ति प्राप्त हुई है जिस पर अभिलेख भी अंकित है। शिवमघ (महाराजा गौतमी पुत्र शिवमघ) की एक मुहर से ज्ञात होता है कि उसने भीटा में शासन किया। उल्लेखनीय है कि मघ शासक शैव मतावलम्बी थे। अतः इनके काल में भी भीटा में शैव धर्म को प्रश्रय मिला था। इस प्रकार ईसा की तृतीय शती में भी यहाँ पर शैव धर्म की परंपरा अनवरत बनी रही। भीटा से लगभग तृतीय शती की गौतमीपुत्र विन्ध्यसेन की एक मुहर प्राप्त हुई है। उसके संबंध में अन्य किसी साक्ष्य से जानकारी नहीं मिलती किन्तु इसमें उसके संबंध में यह कहा गया है कि उसने अपना राज्य माहेश्वर एवं महासेन से प्राप्त किया है। यह कथन लाक्षणिक है जिसका तात्पर्य है कि शिव के अनुग्रह से उसको यह राज्य मिला था। उसकी पताका में नन्दी का अंकन भी था। इससे भी यह पुष्ट होता है कि भीटा का उक्त शासक भी शैव मतावलम्बी रहा होगा।[39]

मघों के पश्चात् गुप्तों के काल में भीटा से वैष्णव एवं शैव धर्म से संबंधित प्रमाण मिलते हैं। किन्तु गुप्तों के पश्चात् भीटा में शैव धर्म की प्रधानता हो गयी एवं यह शैव धर्म का मुख्य केन्द्र बन गया। लगभग 700 ई. से 1200 ई. के मध्य यहाँ पर शैव धर्म से संबंधित साक्ष्य अपेक्षाकृत अधिक हैं। इस अवधि में शैव धर्म से संबंधित कुछ नवीन तथ्य प्रकाश में आने लगते हैं। इस संदर्भ में *कालंजर भट्टार्कस्य* अंकित मुहर एवं भीटा की शैव गुफा एवं गींज तथा छिड़ी के शैव मन्दिरों का उल्लेख प्रासंगिक है। इसी संदर्भ में भीटा के राजनीतिक एवं प्रशासनिक परिदृश्य की जानकारी भी आवश्यक है। उल्लेखनीय है कि लगभग नवीं शती में *'डाहलमण्डल'* (रीवा, सतना,

दमोह, जबलपुर) में कलचुरियों का राज्य स्थापित हुआ। इनकी राजधानी त्रिपुरी (जबलपुर) थी। ये कलचुरि माहिष्मती के कलचुरियों के उत्तराधिकारी थे। इनके काल में यमुना के पार वत्स जनपद तक कलचुरि–सत्ता का विस्तार हुआ था। ये शैव मतावलम्बी थे। इन्होंने लगभग 750–775 ई. में बन्धोगढ़ में मन्दिर निर्माण की परंपरा प्रारंभ की।

कनिंघम[40] तथा बूह्लर[41] के अनुसार *डाहलमण्डल* ही प्राचीन चेदि जनपद था। *स्कन्दपुराण*[42] में वर्णित है कि डाहलमण्डल ही चेदि का नाम है जो प्राचीन काल से बुन्देलखण्ड का भाग था।[43] इसी बुन्देलखण्ड क्षेत्र के बाँदा क्षेत्र में कालंजर (कालिंजर) था।[44] उल्लेखनीय है कि कालिंजर पर कलचुरियों एवं चन्देलों दोनों ने राज्य किया। किन्तु कालंजर का क्षेत्र प्रारंभ में कलचुरियों के अधीन था जो डाहलमण्डल का एक भाग था (कालान्तर में उसे चन्देल शासक धंग ने 950–1002 जीता था)।

शैव धर्म से संबंधित भीटा से प्राप्त *कालंजर भट्टार्कस्य* नामक मुहर दो दृष्टि से महत्त्वपूर्ण है। प्रथम तो यह भीटा पर कलचुरियों के अधिकार की द्योतक है। दूसरा, भट्टारक एक उपाधि थी जो शैव मठाधीश के एक वर्ग के लिए प्रयुक्त होती थी।[45] कालंजर क्षेत्र में तथा डाहलमण्डल में शैव मठ के निर्माण की परंपरा कलचुरियों के शासन काल में प्रारंभ हो गयी थी। इस वंश के शासकों में युवराज देव प्रथम केयूरवर्ष (915–945 ई.) जो शिव का अनन्य उपासक था, मत्तमयूर के धर्मगुरू प्रभवशिव को अपने राज्य में आमंत्रित किया एवं उनके लिए शैव मठ बनवाया। उसने रीवा से 12 मील पूर्व गुर्गी में शिव मन्दिर बनवाया।[46] युवराज देव के पुत्र लक्ष्मणराज द्वितीय ने अपने पिता की परंपरा को जारी रखा एवं उसने भी मत्तमयूर गुरू हृदयशिव को वैद्यनाथ का मठ दान दिया तथा उसने अपने शिष्य अघोर शिव को दान दिया।[47] अतः ऐसा प्रतीत होता है कि कलचुरियों द्वारा मठ निर्माण की परंपरा का विस्तार भीटा क्षेत्र तक हो गया था जिसकी पुष्टि भीटा की शैव गुफा से होती है। भीटा की शैव गुफा की बाहरी दीवार पर शिव के विभिन्न स्वरूपों की सात मूर्तियाँ उत्कीर्ण हैं। उनमें से एक मूर्ति शिव के भैरव रूद्र रूप से संबंधित प्रतीत होती है। इसके गले में मुण्डमाला है; यह रौद्र मुद्रा में है तथा दाँत निकले हुए हैं। संभवतः यह गुफा कलचुरियों द्वारा शैव मतावलम्बियों को आवास हेतु दी गयी थी। अनुमानतः इसमें शैव तान्त्रिकों का आवास रहा होगा।[48]

इसके अतिरिक्त भीटा में गींज की पहाड़ी पर शिव का मन्दिर स्थित है जो भग्नावस्था में है। यह मन्दिर शैव तान्त्रिक परंपरा का प्रतीत होता है। वर्तमान में मन्दिर खण्डित अवस्था में है। मन्दिर के ललाट बिम्ब पर शिव–पार्वती की मूर्तियाँ उत्कीर्ण हैं जिससे प्रतीत होता है कि यह शिव का मन्दिर था। मन्दिर के खंडित अवशेष मन्दिर परिसर में ही बिखरे हुए हैं। इस मन्दिर का वैशिष्ट्य यह है कि इसका गर्भ गृह अधिष्ठान के समानान्तर न होकर नीचे की ओर है जहाँ सोपानों के माध्यम से पहुँचा जाता है। यह वास्तु–वैशिष्ट्य तान्त्रिक शैव मन्दिर की परंपरा का द्योतक है।

भीटा के समीप ही छिड़ी नामक ग्राम में एक विशाल मन्दिर के अवशेष मिले है जो गींज के मन्दिर की अपेक्षा विशाल एवं कुछ सुरक्षित अवस्था में है। यह भी शैव धर्म से संबंधित है। इस मन्दिर का गर्भ गृह भी अधिष्ठान के ऊपर न बनाकर नीचे की ओर बनाया गया है जिसमें सोपानों से पहुँचा जा सकता है।

भीटा में निर्मित उक्त शैव मन्दिरों का निर्माण भी संभवतः कलचुरियों के काल में ही हुआ था। यद्यपि मन्दिरों से कोई अभिलेख प्राप्त नहीं है किन्तु 10वीं–11वीं शती में कलचुरि शासक गांगेयदेव (1015–1041 ई.) ने गंगा–यमुना के दोआब में अपना आधिपत्य स्थापित किया था तथा प्रयाग को अपनी दूसरी राजधानी बनाया था। उसने मेरू प्रकार के मन्दिरों के निर्माण की परंपरा प्रारंभ की थी। उल्लेखनीय है कि उसके पुत्र कर्ण (1041–1073 ई.) ने प्रयाग में कर्णतीर्थ नामक घाट बनवाया था जिसकी पहचान अभी तक नहीं की जा सकी है। किन्तु, ऐसा प्रतीत होता है कि प्रयाग पर कलचुरियों के दीर्घकालीन शासन के दौरान भीटा क्षेत्र में गींज एवं छिड़ी

के मन्दिरों का निर्माण कराया गया। इन मन्दिरों की निर्माण–शैली पर तांत्रिक परंपरा का स्पष्ट प्रभाव दिखाई देता है जिसके अंतर्गत मन्दिरों का गर्भगृह अधिष्ठान के धरातल पर न होकर नीचे बनाया गया है। कलचुरियों के चन्द्रेह (सीधी जिला, म.प्र., 950 ई.)[50] एवं बान्धोगढ़ के मन्दिर गींज एवं छिड़ी के मन्दिरों की परंपरा के समान हैं। इसके अतिरिक्त भीटा में स्थित नाग की प्रतिमा जो मनुष्याकृति में है, प्राप्त हुई है। तांत्रिक परंपरा में नाग प्रतिमा का निर्माण शैव तान्त्रिक स्थलों की सुरक्षा हेतु किये जाने का विधान है। अतः ऐसा प्रतीत होता है कि कलचुरियों के मत्तमयूर के सम्प्रदाय का प्रभाव भीटा पर भी था। निःसन्देह यह तान्त्रिक परंपरा से संबंधित था, जिसका प्रभाव प्रयाग के शैव धर्म पर अधावधि दिखाई पड़ता है।

उपरोक्त विवरण के आधार पर यह स्पष्टतः कहा जा सकता है कि भीटा का पुरास्थल लगभग द्वितीय शती ईसा पूर्व से 9वीं–10वीं शती ईसवी तक शैव धर्म का एक प्रमुख केन्द्र था। यहाँ के प्रारम्भिक अवशेषों में मुखलिंग निर्माण परंपरा में महाभारत में वर्णित सन्दर्भों एवं परवर्ती अवशेषों में शैव तांत्रिक–धारा का स्पष्ट प्रभाव दिखाई देता है।

सन्दर्भ

1. *उत्तर प्रदेश जिला गजेटियर,* इलाहाबाद, 1985, पृ. 229
2. *नेविल डिस्ट्रिक्ट गजेटियर,* इलाहाबाद, 1911, पृ. 235, द्रष्टव्य, शालिग्राम श्रीवास्तव, प्रयाग–प्रदीप, इलाहाबाद, 1937, पृ. 289
3. *उत्तर प्रदेश जिला गजेटियर,* पृ. 19
4. *आर्कियोलॉजिकल सर्वे ऑफ इण्डिया एनुअल रिपोर्ट* (ए.एस.आई.ए.रि.), 1911–12, 37–47, प्लेट XVII सं. 1
5. पूर्वोक्त, पृ. 289
6. *विनयपिटक* 3.2, द्रष्टव्य मोतीचन्द्र, *सार्थवाह,* पटना, 1966, पृ. 16
7. *अंगुत्तर निकाय,* 5.9.3
8. सुषमा श्रीवास्तव, 'भीटा से प्राप्त सहजाति निगमस तथा विच्छिग्राम अंकित मृण्मुद्राओं का पुनर्मूल्यांकन', *द सोर्सेज फार द ऐंन्शियेन्ट हिस्ट्री ऑफ इलाहाबाद, लिटरेचर एण्ड आर्कियोलॉजी,* प्रोसीडिंग्स ऑफ नेशनल सेमिनार, सम्पादक, नसरीन बेगम, इलाहाबाद, 2004, पृ. 30–35.
9. अमरकोष II.10.5; मोनियर–मोनियर विलियम्स, *ए संस्कृत इंग्लिश डिक्शनरी,* पृ. 1193.
10. *ए.एस.आई., ए.रि.,* 1911–12, पृ. 38
11. *प्राकृत टैक्स्ट सिरीज,* जि, VII प्राकृत टैक्टस सोसाईटी, वाराणसी, 1963, पृ. 776
12. *ए.एस.आई., ए.रि.,* 1911–12, पृ.
13. सुवीरा जायसवाल, *वैष्णव धर्म का उद्भव और विकास,* नई दिल्ली, 1996, पृ. 194
14. *ए.एस.आई., ए.रि.,* 1911–12, पृ. 46–47
15. *पूर्वोक्त,* पृ. 47
16. *ए.एस.आई., ए.रि.,* 1911–12, सं. 14, पृ. 49
17. *एपिग्रेफिया इण्डिका,* Vol-1, पृ. 386; IX पृ. 240, वोगेल *केटलॉग आफ मथुरा म्यूजियम,* C–13
18. *ए.एस.आई., ए.रि.,* 1911–12, पृ. 49
19. *ए.एस.आई., ए.रि.,* 1911–12, पृ. 49
20. *वामन पुराण,* अध्याय 46, उद्धृत, *ए.एस.आई., ए.रि.,* 1911–12, पृ. 49
21. *ए.एस.आई., ए.रि.,* 1911–12, पृ. 48

22. टी.ए. गोपीनाथ राव, *एलीमेन्ट्स ऑफ हिन्दू आइकोनोग्राफी,* जिल्द II, भाग I, द्वितीय संस्करण, दिल्ली, 1993, पृ. 63
23. *पूर्वोक्त,* पृ. 64
24. टी.ए. गोपीनाथ राव, *पूर्वोक्त,* पृ. 64
25. वी.सी. शुक्ला, *भारतीय कला, नए संदर्भ नए विमर्श,* इलाहाबाद, 2008, पृ. 5
26. एन.पी. जोशी, *प्राचीन भारतीय मूर्ति विज्ञान,* बिहार, 1977, पृ. 25–26
27. रोजेन फील्ड, जे.एम. *द डॉयनेस्टिक आर्ट ऑफ द कुषाणाज,* कैलिफोर्निया, 1967, पृ. 92
28. जे.एन. बनर्जी, *डेवलपमेन्ट ऑफ हिन्दू आइकोनोग्राफी,* कलकत्ता, 1956, पृ. 117
29. भारत कलाभवन, काशी हिन्दू वि.वि., वाराणसी में संग्रहीत है द्रष्टव्य, के.के. थपल्याल, *स्टडीज इन ऐंश्येण्ट इण्डियन सील्स,* लखनऊ, 1972, पृ. 139
30. द्रष्टव्य, वी.सी. शुक्ला, *पूर्वोक्त,* पृ. 11
31. अग्रवाल, वी.एस. केटलॉग ऑफ मथुरा म्यूजियम, *जनरल ऑफ यू.पी. हिस्टोरिकल सोसाईटी,* वाल्यू. 22 पृ. 127
32. महाभारत, अनुशासन पर्व, अध्याय 17, श्लोक III, सिंहनाद : सिंह द्रेंष्ट; सिंहग; सिंहवानः
33. एन.पी. जोशी, *पूर्वोक्त,* पृ. 35
34. *महाभारत,* अनुशासन पर्व, अध्याय 17, श्लोक 138 *वरो वराहो वरदो वरेण्यः सुमहास्वनः*
35. आर.सी. मजूमदार, *द एज ऑफ इम्पीरियल यूनिटी,* भाग 2, सातवाँ संस्करण, मुम्बई, 2001, पृ. 177
36. आरसी. मजूमदार, *द एज ऑफ इम्पीरियल यूनिटी,* भाग 2, सातवाँ संस्करण, मुम्बई, 2001, पृ. 177
37. *पूर्वोक्त,* पृ. 177
38. *सेलेक्ट इन्सिक्रिप्शन्स,* पृ. 365; *एपिग्राफिया इण्डिका,* XVIII, पृ. 159 से आगे, XXIII, पृ. 445; XXIV, पृ. 146–48
39. आर.सी. मजूमदार, *पूर्वोक्त,* पृ. 177, संदर्भ संख्या II
40. *ए.एस.आई.ए.रि.,* IX, 106
41. *विक्रमांकचरित,* XVIII, 95
42. *स्कन्दपुराण,* रेंवा खण्ड, अध्याय 56
43. एन.एल. डे, *द जियोग्राफिकल डिक्शनरी ऑफ ऐन्शियन्ट एण्ड मेडिवल इण्डिया,* तृतीय संस्करण, दिल्ली, 1927, पृ. 84
44. एन.एल. डे, *पूर्वोक्त,* पृ. 84
45. मोनियर–मोनियर विलियम्स, *ए संस्कृत इंग्लिश डिक्शनरी,* पृ. 745
46. कृष्ण देव, *टेम्पल्स ऑफ इण्डिया,* जिल्द I, नई दिल्ली, 1995, पृ. 153
47. *पूर्वोक्त,* पृ. 154
48. लेखक डॉ. सुषमा श्रीवास्तव ने भीटा के समस्त स्थलों का सर्वेक्षण किया है तथा *'इलाहाबाद के प्राचीन मन्दिरों का सर्वेक्षण'* नामक लघु परियोजना में इसका विस्तार से उल्लेख किया है।
49. *पूर्वोक्त,* जिल्द I, पृ. 155
50. कृष्ण देव, *पूर्वोक्त,* जिल्द II, प्लेट 197, 198.

24

पाँचोंसिद्ध का पुरातत्त्व

पीयूषकान्त शर्मा

पुरातन कोशल जनपद के दक्षिणी उपान्त पर स्थित प्रतापगढ़ जनपद पाषाण काल से ही मानव के संरक्षण का केन्द्र रहा है। यहाँ से प्राप्त उच्च पुरापाषाणिक एवं मध्य पाषाणिक अवशेष गंगा जमुना के इस मैदानी भाग में पल्लवित सर्वप्राचीन संस्कृति के प्रमाण प्रस्तुत करते हैं।[1] तत्पश्चात ताम्र पाषाणिक, आरंभिक ऐतिहासिक, मध्यकालीन संस्कृतियों के अविच्छिन्न क्रम के प्रमाण मृदभाण्डों, उपकरणों सहित विविध पुरावशेषों के रूप में प्राप्त हुए हैं। यहाँ के अजगरा[2] पण्डवासी, हण्डौर, महदहा, बारडीह, पाँचोंसिद्ध आदि अनेक पुरास्थलों को परंपरा के आधार पर महाभारत काल से सम्बन्धित किया जाता है और राम वनगमन मार्ग भी यहीं से गुजरता है।[3]

पाँचोंसिद्ध (अक्षांश 25° 53' 50" उत्तर, देशान्तर 81° 55' 35" पूर्व) नामक पुरास्थल प्रतापगढ़ जिला मुख्यालय से 5 किमी. दूर दक्षिण–पश्चिम में प्रतापगढ़–लखनऊ राजमार्ग पर सई–सकरनी संगम पर स्थित है। राजस्व अभिलेखों में यह पुरास्थल बनवीरपुर काँछ के नाम से दर्ज है।

लगभग 5 हेक्टेयर में फैले इस पुरास्थल की ऊँचाई लगभग 10 मीटर है। यह दक्षिण से आने वाली पौराणिक नदी सई (स्यन्दिका) एवं दक्षिण पूर्व से प्रवाहित सकरनी के संगम पर स्थित है। इस स्थान का चयन अत्यन्त सूझ–बूझ के साथ किया गया प्रतीत होता है। नदी यहाँ के वासियों को पेयजल के साथ–साथ निकटवर्ती क्षेत्रों की सिंचाई के लिये जल भी उपलब्ध कराती रही होगी। यह जलमार्ग का कार्य भी करती रही होगी क्योंकि सई तट पर देवघाट, भोजपुर, महमतपुर, चौहरजन, बेलखरनाथ आदि अनेक पुरास्थल स्थित हैं जिनमें अवश्य ही पारस्परिक सम्बन्ध रहे होंगे।

इस पुरास्थल की योजना अभेद्य जल दुर्ग जैसी प्रतीत होती है। पश्चिम की ओर सई नदी एवं दक्षिण की ओर सकरनी नदी इसे प्राकृतिक सुरक्षा उपलब्ध कराती हैं। जबकि पूर्व एवं उत्तर दिशा में कृत्रिम रूप से परिखा उत्खनित कर पुरास्थल को सुरक्षित किया गया है। इससे इस पुरास्थल के महत्त्वपूर्ण होने का भान होता

है। इस तरह की परिखा योजना प्रारंभिक ऐतिहासिक कालीन कौशाम्बी, राजघाट, चम्पा, श्रावस्ती, वैशाली, पाटलिपुत्र, मथुरा, उज्जैन, एरण आदि अन्य पुरास्थलों से भी प्राप्त होती है।[4] यह परिखा उत्तर दिशा में अधिकांशतः पूरित हो गयी है, किन्तु इसके चिन्ह स्पष्ट रूप से देखे जा सकते हैं।

परिखा के अतिरिक्त इस सन्निवेश की सुरक्षा हेतु चतुर्दिक प्राचीर की व्यवस्था भी की गयी थी। पश्चिम की ओर यह प्राचीर विशेष रूप से सुदृढ़ दिखाई पड़ता है। संभवतः यह इस ओर सई नदी की अवस्थिति के कारण था जो कि वर्षा के दिनों प्रलयंकरी रूप धारण कर लेती रही होगी।

टीले पर सन्निवेश के दक्षिणी—पश्चिमी कोने पर प्राचीर के बराबर ऊँचाई का लगभग 50 मीटर लम्बाई का एक बंध निर्मित मिलता है। यह बंध आगे बढ़कर संगम के नजदीक तक जाता है। यह बंध संभवतः सुरक्षा कर्मियों द्वारा दक्षिणी भाग पर नजर रखने के लिए प्रयुक्त किया जाता रहा होगा। कदाचित् संगम दर्शन के लिये भी इस बंध को प्रयुक्त किया गया होगा। आज भी इस बंध से संगम का दृश्य अत्यंत सुंदर दिखाई देता है। आजकल टीले की ऊपरी सतह पर कृषि की जाती है। टीले पर दो ऊँचे उभरे भाग विद्यमान हैं। ये दोनों भाग मूल जमाव के अंग नहीं प्रतीत होते। इनमें से एक जो दक्षिण पश्चिम में है कृषि के लिये खेतों की जुताई करते समय प्रतिवर्ष निकले ईंटों के टुकड़ों के अंबार से निर्मित हुआ है। निकटवर्ती ग्रामवासी गृह निर्माण के लिये गिट्टी की आवश्यकता की पूर्ति इसी से करते हैं। साथ ही, टीले से निकली ईंटों से बनी कई दीवारों; विशेषकर पशुशालाओं को देखा जा सकता है। द्वितीय, ऊँचा भाग यहाँ पर मिट्टी का जमाव किये जाने से बना है। इस पर कुछ वर्ष पूर्व एक साधु द्वारा कुटी का निर्माण किया गया था।

इस पुरास्थल से संबंधित कई स्थानीय परम्परायें प्रचलित हैं। प्रथम परंपरा के अंतर्गत इस स्थल को सोमवंशी राजा लखनसेन के गढ़ के रूप में माना जाता है जिसकी माँ यहाँ पर झूँसी (प्रतिष्ठानपुर) से आयी थी। कहा जाता है कि प्रतिष्ठानपुर के राजा वीरसेन की ऋषि शाप से मृत्यु के बाद अपने वंशजों की रक्षा के लिये सोमवंशी रानी झूँसी को छोड़कर पाँचों सिद्ध में आकर रहने लगी। यहाँ पर लखनसेन का जन्म 1246 ई. में हुआ जिसने बड़े होकर निकटवर्ती क्षेत्रों में अवस्थित भर शासकों एवं रैकवार क्षत्रियों को हराकर अपने राज्य का विस्तार किया।[5]

द्वितीय परंपरा के अनुसार यह स्थल महाभारतकालीन पाँच राजकुमारों से जुड़ा है, जिनके नाम वीरबाहु, सुबाहु, भद्रबाहु, अलर्क एवं काशिराज पुत्र हैं। इन पाँचों के यहाँ सिद्ध होने से यह स्थल पाँचों सिद्ध के नाम से विख्यात हुआ। अलर्क के नाम पर इस क्षेत्र को अलर्कपुर (अरउर) के नाम से भी जाना जाता है। इस पुरास्थल पर अवस्थित लाखौरी ईंटों से बने मंदिर के मुख्य द्वार के बायें भाग में नागरी में लेख अंकित है जिसमें इन पाँचों राजकुमारों के नामों का उल्लेख है।[6]

वर्तमान मंदिर के गर्भगृह में मुख्य प्रतिमा के स्थान पर मंदिर के भार को संभालने के लिये स्तंभों के ऊपर लगी भारवाही की प्रतिमा स्थापित है। इसी तरह की भारवाही की प्रतिमा प्रतापगढ़ नगर में स्थित प्राचीन पंचमुखी मंदिर में भी स्थापित है। इस मंदिर से मिले अभिलेखानुसार इसे 1449 वि.सं. में निर्मित माना जाता है।[7] दोनों ही मंदिरों के नाम में पंच एवं पाँचों की समानता के साथ मूर्तियों एवं वास्तु की भी समता है।

एक अन्य परंपरानुसार माना जाता है कि अज्ञातवास के समय एक रात्रि के लिये पाण्डवों ने इस स्थल पर वास किया था।

इस पुरास्थल पर कई प्रस्तर खण्ड पड़े हुए हैं। ये किसी संरचना, संभवतः मंदिर की द्वारशाखा, चौखट, सीढ़ियों आदि के अंग रहे होंगे। इनमें से एक की पूजा स्थानीय लोग लोटवा बाबा के नाम से करते हैं। संभवतः यहाँ पर वर्तमान मंदिर की संरचना के पूर्व भी भव्य मंदिर की संरचना रही होगी।

पुरास्थल पर मिलने वाले मद्भाण्डों में कृष्ण–लेपित मृदभाण्ड, लाल–लेपित मृदभाण्ड, लाल मृदभाण्ड और कांचित मृदभाण्ड प्रमुख हैं। मुख्य पात्र प्रकारों में स्प्रिंकलर, बॉटलनेक जॉर, कटोरे, घड़े, हांडी, लोटा इत्यादि प्रमुख हैं। लाल लेपित मृदभाण्डों में अनेक पतली गढ़न के पात्रों पर सुन्दर लेपन मिलता है। कांचित मृदभाण्ड अत्यन्त सुंदर प्रकृति के हैं जिन पर बहुधा हरे और नीले रंग में ज्यामितीय चित्रण मिलते हैं। ये चित्रण प्रायः अंदर की ओर किये गये हैं। पात्र प्रकारों में मुख्य प्लेट एवं कटोरे हैं। एक विशेष प्रकार का कांचित पात्र खण्ड मिला है, जो बना तो मिट्टी का है किन्तु ऊपर से एक सतह कांचित पालिश की लगायी गयी है। बाहर से देखने पर यह कांचित पात्रों की तरह ही दिखाई पड़ता है। यह पात्र खण्ड इस पुरास्थल पर मृदभाण्ड के ऊपर कांचित प्रलेप लगाने का अभिनव प्रयोग प्रदर्शित करता है।

पात्र खण्डो के अतिरिक्त प्राप्त अन्य पुरावशेषों में चूड़ियाँ, सिल–लोढ़े, मृण्मूर्ति खण्ड आदि प्रमुख हैं।

इस प्रकार प्राप्त पुरावशेषों एवं परंपराओं के आधार पर इस पुरास्थल को कुषाण काल से लेकर मध्य काल तक आवासित माना जा सकता है। परंपरा, इस स्थल को महाभारत से भी संबंधित मानती है। किन्तु अजगरा, हंडौर आदि महाभारत काल से जुड़े जनपद के अन्य पुरास्थलों से भी महाभारत में वर्णित स्थलों; हस्तिनापुर, मथुरा, अहिच्छत्र, इन्द्रप्रस्थ, पानीपत आदि की भांति चित्रित घूसरपात्र सर्वेक्षण में नहीं प्राप्त हुए हैं। साथ ही, अजगरा एवं हंडौर से मिलने वाले उत्तरी कृष्ण मार्जित (एन.बी.पी.) पात्र भी यहाँ से नहीं मिले हैं। संभवतः भविष्य में होने वाले अध्ययनों एवं अनुसंधानों से इस समस्या का समाधान संभव हो सकेगा।

सन्दर्भ

1. पाल, जे.एन., 1984, इपिपैलियोलिथिक साइट्स, इन प्रतापगढ़ डिस्ट्रिक्ट, उ.प्र., *मैन एण्ड इनवायरमेंट,* अंक–8, पृ. 28–38
2. शुक्ल, विमलचन्द, 1986, *पुरानुसंधान,* इलाहाबाद, पृ. 24–32
3. पाल, रामनरेश, 2005, *प्रतापगढ़ का पुरातत्त्व,* इलाहाबाद, पृत्र 31
4. शर्मा, पीयूष कान्त, 2008, प्राचीन भारतीय नगर वास्तु का प्रमुख अंग–परिखा, यू.पी. हिस्ट्री कांग्रेस के इलाहाबाद में आयोजित 19वें अधिवेशन में पढ़ा गया शोध पत्र।
5. सिंह, अमरपाल, 1991, *प्रतापगढ़ के क्षत्रियों का संक्षिप्त इतिहास,* प्रतापगढ़, पृ. 34
6. सिंह, अमरपाल, *वही,* पृ. 35
7. शलभ, अनिल सिंह, 2005, *प्रतापगढ़–एक परिचय,* इलाहाबाद, पृ. 57

25

गोन्डे-गोबरी की प्रतिमाएँ

बृजभानु सिंह

उत्तर प्रदेश का प्रतापगढ़ पुरातात्त्विक दृष्टि से अत्यंत महत्त्वपूर्ण है। इस जनपद का संपूर्ण भाग प्राचीनकाल में कोशल के अधीन था। मध्यपाषाण काल से लेकर ऐतिहासिक काल के विभिन्न युगों की संस्कृतियाँ यहाँ बिखरी पड़ी हैं। दुर्भाग्यवशात् अभी तक इस जनपद के पुरास्थलों एवं पुरावशेषों का व्यवस्थित अध्ययन नहीं हो सका है; आकस्मिक उपलब्धि के रूप में मात्र कुछ सामग्री ही प्रकाशित की जा सकी है। यत्किंचित प्रकाशित सामग्री में से एक गोन्डे–गोबरी भी है जो प्रतापगढ़ शहर मुख्यालय से लगभग सात किलोमीटर दूर प्रतापगढ़–सुल्तानपुर मार्ग पर स्थित है। इस स्थल का अति संक्षिप्त विवरण फ्यूहरर ने प्रकाशित किया था, जिसके अनुसार इस स्थल पर गुप्तकालीन प्रस्तरमूर्तियाँ विद्यमान थीं।[1] लेखक ने अपने सहयोगियों के साथ इस स्थल का सर्वेक्षण कर अनेक महत्त्वपूर्ण प्रतिमाओं को देखा जो न केवल शिल्प अपितु प्रतिमा विज्ञान की दृष्टि से भी नवीन तथ्यों को उद्घाटित करती हैं। प्रस्तुत लेख में इनमें से कुछ महत्त्वपूर्ण प्रतिमाओं का विवरण प्रस्तुत करने का प्रयास किया गया है –

सूर्य प्रतिमा का शीर्षफलक

यहाँ से सूर्य प्रतिमा का वृत्ताकार शीर्षफलक उपलब्ध हुआ है जो बालुकाश्म निर्मित है। दशदल कमल से अलंकृत इसके प्रभामंडल की बाह्य पट्टिका पत्रावली अलंकरण युक्त है। प्रभामण्डल पूर्णतया वृत्ताकार है। शिल्पशास्त्रों में भी सूर्य के वृत्ताकार प्रभामण्डल बनाने का उल्लेख है। प्रभामण्डल के दाहिनी ओर मकरमुख से निकलते हुए कमल पर उषा का अंकन किया गया है, जिसकी पीठ पर तूणीर बंधा है और वह शरसंधान करती हुई प्रदर्शित है। बाँयी ओर भी मकरमुख निःसृत पद्म पर प्रत्यूषा का अंकन है जो शरसंधान हेतु तूणीर से शर निकाल रही

है। वृत्ताकार फलक के आकार से यह अनुमान किया जा सकता है कि प्रतिमा कम से कम चार फुट ऊँची अवश्य रही होगी।

रेवन्त प्रतिमा

शिल्प की दृष्टि से कलाकार के तक्षण नैपुण्य एवं अप्रतिम मेधा का परिचायक रेवन्त का यहाँ पर रखा हुआ एक प्रस्तर फलक है जिसका परिमाप 133 सेमी. x 64 सेमी. है। बालुकाश्म निर्मित इस प्रस्तर फलक पर रेवन्त की मृगया का दृश्य है। दृश्य में रेवन्त मध्य में अश्व पर आसीन प्रदर्शित किये गये हैं, जिसका शीर्ष भाग खंडित हो चुका है। रेवन्त के शीर्ष के ऊपर छत्र भी निर्मित किया गया था। रेवन्त के अश्व के समीप एक पुरुष आकृति निर्मित है जो संभवतः छत्र धारण किये थी। उसके पीछे ताका लिए हुए एक पुरुष का अंकन है और फलक के दाहिने उपान्त के मध्य में कने पर मृतक पशु लिए हुए पुरुष की आकृति अंकित है। रेवन्त के आगे एक व्यक्ति उन्हें सुरापूरित चषक प्रदान करते हुए प्रदर्शित है तथा अन्य व्यक्ति कन्धे पर लकुट के सहारे खाद्यसामग्री को पाटली में लिए हुए प्रदर्शित किया गया है। उसके आगे अश्व पर सवार अन्य योद्धा है जो पीछे दृष्टि घुमाकर रेवन्त को देख रहा है। सबसे आगे कोई वाद्य यन्त्र मुख से बजाते हुए व्यक्ति का अंकन है। अश्वों के पैरों के बीच में कुत्तों का अंकन है जो मृगया में सहायक होते थे। फलक के दाहिनी ओर ऊर्ध्व उपान्त में आसीन मुद्रा में चतुर्भुजी आकृति का अंकन है जिसके एक हाथ में खड्ग जैसी कोई वस्तु तथा दूसरे हाथ में चषक जैसी कोई वस्तु है। ऊर्ध्व वामहस्त में भी किसी वस्तु को अंकित किया गया है जो स्पष्ट नहीं है, परन्तु वाम अधःहस्त बायें जानु पर प्रदर्शित है। यह प्रतिमा सुखासन मुद्रा में है। इसके बाँयी ओर नवग्रहों का अंकन है। सूर्य के दोनों हाथ ऊपर की ओर उठे हैं जिनमें कमल प्रदर्शित है। सोम, मंगल, बुध, बृहस्पति, शुक्र एवं शनि त्रिभंग मुद्रा में खड़े प्रदर्शित किये गये हैं। इनका बांया हाथ कट्यावलम्बित है तथा पात्र पकड़े हुए है एवं दाहिना हाथ अभयमुद्रा में है। राहु आसीन मुद्रा में है तथा सर्पाकृति अधोभाग युक्त केतु दायें हाथ से पात्र पकड़े तथा स्थानक रूप में प्रदर्शित है। फलक के शीर्ष वाम उपान्त में सप्त मातृकाओं का अंकन है जिनके एक ओर एक गण तथा दूसरी ओर चतुर्भुजी गणेश अंकित हैं। फलक की पाद पीठिका पर भी कतिपय दृश्यों का अंकन था जो पूर्णतया नष्ट हो चुका है।

रेवन्त सूर्य के पुत्र रूप में मान्य हैं जो सुरेणु या संज्ञा नामक सूर्य की पत्नी से उत्पन्न हुए थे।[2] यह उल्लेखनीय है कि वैदिक साहित्य और *महाभारत* में सूर्य और उनकी पत्नी संज्ञा से उत्पन्न यम, यमी, मनु और अश्विनीकुमारद्वय का ही उल्लेख प्राप्त होता है। रेवन्त का उल्लेख अपेक्षाकृत परवर्त्ती ग्रन्थों यथा *विष्णुपुराण, मार्कण्डेयपुराण* तथा *भविष्यपुराण* में प्राप्त होता है। *कलिका पुराण*[3] में रेवन्त की उपासना का विस्तृत विवरण अंकित है। प्रारंभ में इतिहासकारों की यह धारणा थी कि रेवन्त की उपासना केवल पूर्वी भारत में ही प्रचलित थी परंतु यह धारणा उचित नही प्रतीत होती। गुजरात क्षेत्र में रेवन्त की उपासना का प्रमाण श्रृंगारदेव का वंठली ताम्रलेख है जिसमें रेवन्त की स्तुति की गयी है।[5] रेवन्त की प्रतिमाएं बंगाल[5], बिहार[6], उत्तर प्रदेश[7] तथा राजस्थान[8] से प्राप्त हुई हैं यद्यपि उनकी संख्या प्राचीन भारत की शिल्प संपदा को देखते हुये अत्यल्प ही है। रेवन्त की प्रतिमा निर्माण से संबंधित शास्त्रीय लक्षण भी साहित्यिक साक्ष्यों में प्रायः अनुपलब्ध हैं। *विष्णुधर्मोत्तरपुराण*[9] में मात्र यह उल्लेख प्राप्त होता है कि रेवन्त को सूर्य की भाँति चित्रित करना चाहिए। *मार्कण्डेयपुराण*[10] में रेवन्त को खड्गी, धन्वी, तन्त्रृधृक, अश्वारूढ़ तथा बाण–तूणीर समन्वित इत्यादि विशेषणों से अभिहित किया गया है। इससे स्पष्ट है कि रेवन्त की जो प्रतिमाएं प्राप्त हुई हैं उनके लक्षण *मार्कण्डेय पुराण* की रचना के समय तक निर्धारित हो चुके थे।

विवेच्य प्रतिमा में कलाकार ने कतिपय मौलिक उद्भावनाएँ प्रस्तुत की हैं जो अन्य रेवन्त प्रतिमाओं में या तो अनुपलब्ध है या दूसरे रूप में प्राप्त होती हैं। सामान्यतया सप्तमातृकाओं यथा माहेश्वरी, वैष्णवी, ब्रह्माणी, कौमारी, ऐन्द्री, वाराही तथा चामुण्डा का अंकन उनके विशिष्ट वाहन वृष, गरुड़, हंस, मयूर, हाथी, वराह या महिष तथा शव के साथ किया जाता था अथवा उनके विविध आयुधों के साथ किया जाता था। प्रस्तुत फलक में सभी मातृकाओं को द्विभुजी रूप में तथा नृत्य मुद्रा में प्रदर्शित किया गया है। पुरुष आकृति के पश्चात् क्रमशः ब्रह्माणी, माहेश्वरी, कौमारी, वैष्णवी, वाराही, ऐन्द्री एवं चामुण्डा तत्पश्चात् नृत्य गणेश का अंकन है। नवग्रहों में द्विभुजी सूर्य के दोनों हाथ ऊपर उत्थित प्रदर्शित किये गये हैं। सोम, मंगल, बुध, बृहस्पति, शुक्र और शनि एक ही प्रकार से द्विभुजी तथा एकहस्त कट्यावलम्बित अंकित किए गए हैं एवं सर्पाकृति अधोभाग युक्त केतु खड़े हुए अंकित हैं। नवग्रह अंकन प्राचीन काल में अधिसंख्य प्राप्त हुए हैं। उन्हें आसीन एवं स्थानक दोनों रूपों में प्रदर्शित किया गया है। सोम, मंगल, बुध, बृहस्पति के अंकन में किञ्चित वैभिन्न न होने के कारण उनकी आकृतियाँ समरूप हैं और अभिज्ञान का आधार गतानुगतिक ही है। सामान्यतया रेवन्त का अंकन आखेट के लिए प्रस्थान अथवा आखेट करने के पश्चात् प्रत्यावर्तन के रूप में प्राप्त होता है। इसमें शिकार के पश्चात् लौटते हुए मार्ग में रूककर मद्यपान करते हुए उन्हें प्रदर्शित किया गया है। परन्तु, अश्व की ग्रीवा तथा उस पर सवार योद्धा की ग्रीवा पीछे की ओर मुड़ी हुई है। सामान्यतया रेवन्त के फलक पर बांयी ओर शीर्ष भाग में सूर्य का अंकन किया जाता था परंतु प्रस्तुत प्रतिमा में सूर्य के स्थान पर चतुर्भुजी किसी अन्य देवता का अंकन है जो किसी पशु पर आसीन है परंतु हाथों में जिन वस्तुओं को धारण किये है, वे स्पष्ट नहीं है।

रेवन्त के फलक गुप्तकाल में ही प्राप्त होने लगते हैं परन्तु उनके आखेट दृश्य का विस्तारित अंकन सातवीं शती ईसवीं के पश्चात विशेष रूप से लोकप्रिय होने लगा।[11] विवेच्य फलक भी सातवीं–आठवीं शती ईसवी के मध्य रखा जा सकता है।

रावणानुग्रह–उमामाहेश्वर फलक

यह फलक भी बालुकाश्म पर निर्मित है। 107 सेमी. x 52 सेमी. के इस फलक पर उमामाहेश्वर का अत्यन्त अभिराम अंकन किया गया था। यदि यह प्रस्तर फलक अखण्डित रहा होता तो अद्भुत तक्षणनैपुण्य का निदर्शन होता। इसमें द्विभुजी शिव का अंकन है जो एक हाथ में अपेक्षाकृत दीर्घ त्रिशूल धारण किये हैं तथा दाहिने हाथ से पार्वती को सांत्वना प्रदान कर रहे हैं। शिव का दाहिना पाद पीठिका पर स्थित है तथा बाँया पैर जानु भाग से किंचित मुड़ा हुआ है। वे सुखासन मुद्रा में बैठे हैं। शिव पार्वती की ओर देख रहे हैं तथा पार्वती शिव को निहार रही हैं। दुर्भाग्यवशात् शिव और पार्वती दोनों का शीर्ष भाग खंडित है। पार्वती का बाँया पैर आधार पीठिका पर अवलम्बित है तथा दाहिना पैर जानु से मुड़ा हुआ बायें पैर पर टिका है। उमा माहेश्वर प्रतिमाओं में पार्वती के पैरों की यह मुद्रा अपेक्षाकृत कम प्राप्त होती है। पार्वती का दाहिना हाथ शिव की ग्रीवा को आवेष्टित करते हुए उनके दाहिने स्कन्ध पर है। आधारासन में शिव के पैर के समीप वृष का अंकन है तथा पार्वती के पैर के पास सिंह की आकृति प्रदर्शित की गयी है। रावण को दोनों हाथों से कैलाश को ऊपर उठाते हुए प्रदर्शित किया गया है। शिव के शीर्ष के समीप दाहिनी ओर कट्यावलम्बित तथा त्रिभंग मुद्रा में बाये हाथ में चामर धारिणी स्त्री का अंकन है। ऐसी ही आकृति पार्वती के शीर्ष भाग में बांयी ओर उपान्त पर प्रदर्शित है। सामान्यतया चामरधारिणी परिचारिकाओं का अंकन नीचे किया जाता था। शिव के समीप दाहिनी ओर एक हाथ में खट्वांग तथा दूसरे हाथ में मद्य चषक जैसी वस्तु को धारण किये हुए पुरुष का अंकन है। यह आकृति भैरव की हो सकती है। पार्वती के समीप बांयी ओर उपान्त पर वीणाधारी पुरुष का अंकन है। फलक के शीर्ष पर दाहिनी ओर पद्मासन मुद्रा में ब्रह्मा का अंकन

है तथा बांयी ओर उपान्त पर मानवाकृति गरुड़ पर बैठे चतुर्भुजी विष्णु का अंकन है। मध्य में मालाधारी विद्याधर उड़ते हुए प्रदर्शित है। उमामाहेश्वर तथा रावणानुग्रह–उमामाहेश्वर की प्रतिमाएं गुप्तकाल से प्राप्त होने लगती हैं।[12] परंतु मूर्तियों की प्रचुरता पूर्वमध्यकाल में ही देखने को मिलती है। सामान्यतया ऐवी प्रतिमाओं में पार्वती को शिव के वाम उरु पर आसीन प्रदर्शित किया जाता था परंतु प्रस्तुत फलक में पार्वती की यह मुद्रा नहीं प्राप्त होती, साथ ही साथ शिव के वाम हस्त को पार्वती के कुच का स्पर्श करते हुए भी नहीं प्रदर्शित किया गया है। कालिदास[13] ने शिव–पार्वती के इस रूप का अत्यंत मनोहारी वर्णन किया है। शिव ने पार्वती के ग्रीवा को आवेष्टित करते हुए अपने हाथ के अग्र भाग अर्थात हथेलियों को पार्वती के कुच पर रखा है और पार्वती की ओर ऐसे देख रहे हैं मानो मुँह से नहीं अपितु नेत्रों से उमामुख का पान कर रहे हों –

तस्याः स कण्ठे पिहितास्तनाग्रन्यधत्त मुक्ताफलहारवल्लीम्।
या प्राप मेरुर्द्वितस्य मूर्ध्नि स्थितस्य गांगौघ युगस्य लक्ष्मीम्।।
घूर्णमाननयनं स्खलत्क्थं स्वेन्विन्दुमदकारणस्मितम्।
आननेन न तु तावदीश्वर चक्षुषा चिरमुमामुखं पपौ।।

मत्स्यपुराण[14] में उमामाहेश्वर की चतुर्भुजी अथवा द्विभुजी प्रतिमा के निर्माण के सन्दर्भ में जटाभार युक्त शीर्ष पर चन्द्रमा, लोचनत्रय युक्त तथा एक हाथ उमा के स्कन्ध पर, दक्षिण हाथ में शूल तथा बायें हाथ से पार्वती के कुच का आलिंगन करते हुए एवं शिव के पार्श्व में हाथों से शिव का उपगूढ़ करती हुई पार्वती का चित्रण करने का विधान है –

चतुर्बाहुं द्विबाहुं वा जटाभारेन्दुभूषितम्।
लोचनत्रयसंयुक्तमुमैकस्कन्धपाणिनम्।।
दक्षिणेनोल्वणं शूलं वामं कुचभरं करम्।
वामे तु संस्थिता देवी तस्यौरौ बाहुगूहिता।।

हेमाद्रि[15] ने शिव के अष्टभुजी रूप तथा पार्वती के हाथ में दर्पण चित्रित किये जाने का विधान प्रस्तुत किया है।

प्रस्तुत प्रतिमा कई दृष्टियों से महत्त्वपूर्ण एवं विवेच्य है। सामान्यतया त्रिशूल का अंकन शिव के दाहिने हाथ में किया जाता था, परंतु इस प्रतिमा में त्रिशूल का अंकन वामहस्तधृत हुआ है। इसमें शिव और पार्वती के तरुण विलास के स्थान पर उस भाव को प्रधानता दी गयी है जिसके अनुसार रावण के द्वारा कैलाश को उठाने का प्रयास करने पर पार्वती भयभीत हो गयी थी और शिव उन्हें सांत्वना प्रदान कर रहे थे। शिव का वाम पाद जो आधारासन पर टिका है उसका केवल अग्र भाग ही कैलाश पर्वत को स्पर्श कर रहा है। शिव ने पैर के अग्र भाग से ही कैलाश पर्वत को दबा दिया था जिससे रावण कैलाश पर्वत उठाने में असमर्थ रहा। इसी भाव की प्रमुखता के कारण शिव के द्वारा कुचस्पर्श का अंकन नहीं किया गया है जो प्रायः सभी उमामाहेश्वर प्रतिमाओं में प्राप्त होता है। नन्दी और सिंह दोनों सहमे हुए प्रदर्शित किये गये हैं। प्रस्तुत फलक में कलाकार ने कथानक यद्यपि रावण द्वारा कैलाश उठाने के प्रसंग से ग्रहण किया है परंतु शिव और पार्वती दोनों को प्रस्तर आधारासन अर्थात् चौकी पर आसीन प्रदर्शित किया गया है जो चतुर्पाद पर टिका था। सम्मुख के दो पाद स्पष्ट एवं सुष्ठु रूप से दिखाई पड़ते हैं। इस फलक में शिव और पार्वती दोनों की आकृति लम्बोन्नत (**elongated**) रूप से प्रदर्शित की गयी है। आभूषणों में बाहुबन्ध एवं वलय को छोड़कर अन्य का अंकन नहीं प्राप्त होता। इसमें प्रतिहार काल

के अंतिम चरण तथा परवर्ती चन्देल और कलचुरि कालीन कृत्रिमता एवं अलंकरण–बोझिलता नहीं प्राप्त होती। अतः इस फलक का काल छठीं से आठवीं शती ईसवी के मध्य रखा जा सकता है।

नृत्य गणेश

इस स्थल से नृत्य गणेश की अत्यन्त मनोहारी प्रतिमा प्राप्त हुई है। दशभुजी इस प्रतिमा के अधिकांश हाथ यद्यपि खंडित हो चुके हैं परंतु प्रतिमा प्रथमदृष्ट्या ही प्रभावोत्पादक एवं सुष्ठु शिल्प का प्रमाण उपस्थित करती है। शारीरिक अवयवों का ओजपरक प्रदर्शन इस प्रतिमा का वैशिष्ट्य है। अधिकांश हस्त खंडित होने के कारण उनमें धारण की गयी वस्तुओं का पूर्णतया अभिज्ञान संभव नहीं है। परशु, डमरू तथा सर्प स्पष्ट हैं। एक हस्त नृत्यकट्यावलम्बित है। उनके वामपार्श्व में पैरों के समीप वाहन मूषक आश्चर्य मुद्रा में देखते हुए चित्रित है। गणेश की उपासना अत्यंत प्राचीन है। गणेशोपासना का मूल यक्षों और नागों की उपासना में कतिपय विद्वानों[16] ने स्वीकार किया है। रामकृष्ण गोपाल भंडारकर[17] ने गणपति का सम्बन्ध विनायकों से जोड़ा है। कालान्तर में विनायक गणेश की उपाधि के रूप में प्रतिष्ठित हो गयी। गणेश की प्राचीनतम मूर्तियाँ लाल चित्तिदार प्रस्तर पर निर्मित की गयीं थीं जिनका समय तृतीय–चतुर्थ शती ईसवी स्वीकार किया गया है। ये मूर्तियाँ द्विभुजी हैं। प्रारंभिक गणेश प्रतिमाएँ प्रायः खड़ी या आसीन मुद्रा में प्राप्त होती हैं। मोदकपात्र, परशु, मूली, सर्पयज्ञोपवीत, बीजपूरक प्रारंभिक गणेश प्रतिमाओं में प्रायः द्रष्टव्य हैं। काबुल से प्राप्त[18] दो गणेश प्रतिमाओं में व्याघ्राम्बर स्पष्टतः प्रदर्शित हैं। दोनो प्रतिमाएं गुप्त कालीन हैं। नृत्यगणेश, महागणपति, उच्छिष्टगणपति इत्यादि रूपों का विकास गुप्तकाल के पश्चात् हुआ।[19] *अपराजितपृच्छा, अंशुमदभेदागम, उत्तरकालिकागम, विष्णुधर्मोत्तर, रूपमण्डन* आदि में गणेश के चतुर्भुजी रूप का ही विधान प्राप्त होता है।[20] परंतु कला में अष्टभुजी, दशभुजी तथा द्वादशभुजी प्रतिमाएं भी अत्यंत लोकप्रिय रहीं। *मत्स्यपुराण* में दशभुजी नृत्य भैरव का उल्लेख प्राप्त होता है।[22] परंतु विनायक के रूप में गणेश के चतुर्भुजीरूप का ही अंकन प्राप्त होता है।[23] इसी पुराण में यह भी उल्लेख मिलता है[24] कि दशभुजी प्रतिमाओं की स्थापना नगर में, चतुर्भुजी का खर्वट में तथा ग्राम अथवा वन में द्विबाहु प्रतिमाओं की स्थापना करनी चाहिए। इससे स्पष्ट है कि दशभुजी गणेश की प्रतिमाएं जन सामान्य में प्रतिष्ठित होने के पंश्चात् भी अत्यधिक संकुल स्थानों पर स्थापित की गयी।

स्थानक विष्णु प्रतिमाएं

इस स्थल से स्थानक मुद्रा में प्राप्त विष्णु की चतुर्भुजी प्रतिमा अनेक दृष्टियों से विचारणीय है। करण्ड मुकुटधारी इस प्रतिमा में आजानुप्रसारित वनमाला स्पष्ट रूप से प्रदर्शित है। प्रतिमा के दक्षिण ऊर्ध्व हस्त में गदा का अंकन है। अधः दक्षिण हस्त वरद मुद्रा में है। पैर के पास दाहिनी ओर दो परिचारक स्थानक तथा एक आसीन मुद्रा में है। वाम ऊर्ध्व हस्त भग्न हो चुका है तथा वाम अधोहस्त में बीजपूरक या फल का अंकन है। नीचे परिचारिका तथा चमरधारिणी प्रदर्शित है। विष्णु के वाम भाग में स्कन्ध के उपान्त पर वराह पर आसीन वराहमुखी वाराही का अंकन है। वह ललितासन मुद्रा में है तथा अपने वामहस्त में गदा जैसी किसी वस्तु को धारण किये हैं। सामान्यतया चतुर्भुजी विष्णु की प्रतिमाओं में शंख, चक्र, गदा, पद्म का अंकन प्राप्त होता है। कभी–कभी एक हाथ अभय या वरद मुद्रा में भी प्रदर्शित किया जाता था।[25] चतुर्भुजी विष्णु की प्राचीनतम प्रतिमा मल्हार[26] (म.प्र.) से प्राप्त हुई है जिसे उस पर उल्लिखित लेख के आधार पर द्वितीय शती ई.पू. का स्वीकार किया गया है। कुषाण काल में चतुर्भुजी विष्णु की प्रतिमाएं अनेक स्थलों से प्राप्त हुई हैं। कुषाण काल तक विष्णु की वनमाला अपेक्षाकृत लघु

रूप में प्रदर्शित की जाती थी, परंतु गुप्तकाल में वह आजानुप्रसारित बनने लगी।[27] यह परंपरा कालान्तर में अत्यधिक लोकप्रिय हुई। कुषाण काल से ही विष्णु के हाथ में फल प्रदर्शित करने की भी परंपरा प्रयाग परिक्षेत्र में[26] प्रारंभ हुई। सामान्यतया यह दाहिने हाथ में प्रदर्शित किया जाता था, परंतु विवेच्य प्रतिमा में यह वामहस्त में प्रदर्शित है। प्रतिमा के विवेचन से स्पष्ट है कि गुप्तकाल में प्रारंभ होने वाली परंपराओं का इसमें पूर्णतया निर्वहन हुआ है। अतः इसे गुप्तरोत्तरकाल में रखना ही समीचीन होगा। विष्णु के वाम स्कन्ध के पास वाहन पर आरूढ़ वाराही की प्रतिमा उल्लेख्य है। सामान्यतया अन्य मातृकाओं के साथ वाराही का अंकन नहीं प्राप्त होता। विष्णु के दाहिने स्कन्ध के पास वाराह का भी अंकन हुआ है, जिसके दोनों हाथ जानु पर रखे हैं। मानवमुखी यह वराह वीर रस की सृष्टि करता हुआ प्रतीत होता है। शिल्पशास्त्रों में वाराही मातृका को महिषारूढ़ा अंकित करने का विधान प्राप्त होता है,[29] परंतु विवेच्य प्रतिमा में उसे वराहासीन प्रदर्शित किया गया है।[30] वाराही तथा अन्य मातृकाओं को *अपराजितपृच्छा* में[31] चतुर्भुजी रूप में निर्मित करने का निर्देश है। *विष्णुधर्मोत्तर*[32] के अनुसार उन्हें छह भुजाओं से युक्त प्रदर्शित करना चाहिए। *अपराजितपृच्छा*[33] में अक्षसूत्र, घंटा, कमण्डलु तथा खड्ग को वाराही के हाथों में अंकित करने का उल्लेख है। *मत्स्यपुराण* में[34] गदा और चक्र धारण करने का उल्लेख प्राप्त होता है। यह उल्लेखनीय है कि स्वतंत्र रूप से मातृकाओं की प्रतिमा निर्मित करने में उन्हें चतुर्भुजी रूप में अंकित करने का विधान है परंतु सप्तमातृकाओं का एक साथ द्विभुजी रूप में अंकन अनेक स्थलों से प्राप्त है।

विष्णु की एक अन्य स्थानक प्रतिमा लगभग 125 सेमी. 75 समी. परिमाप की इस स्थल पर रखी हुई है। प्रतिमा का शीर्ष भाग, प्रभामण्डल, खंडित तथा अस्पष्ट है। प्रतिमा के दाहिने ऊर्ध्वहस्त में लम्बी गदा का अंकन है तथा दक्षिण अधःहस्त वरद मुद्रा में प्रदर्शित है। वाम ऊर्ध्वहस्त चक्र धारण किये हुए है तथा वाम अधः हस्त में फल प्रदर्शित किया गया है। सामान्यतया विष्णु के दाहिने हाथ में खुली हथेली पर प्रदर्शित होने वाले फल को इस प्रतिमा के वाम हस्त में अंगुष्ठ उंगलियों के द्वारा पकड़े हुए प्रदर्शित किया गया है। दोनों ओर पैर के समीप परिचारिकाओं का अंकन है तथा ऊपर विद्याधर प्रदर्शित हैं। अन्य अंकन अधिक स्पष्ट नहीं हैं।

गणेश और सिंहवाहिनी अंकनयुक्त फलक

एक अन्य फलक जो किसी विशिष्ट एवं विशाल शैव प्रतिमा का उपान्त भाग रहा होगा, अत्यन्त विशिष्ट है। दो भागों में विभाजित इस फलक के निम्न भाग में आसीन गणेश निर्मित है। प्रतिमा अष्टभुजी है। ऊपर के दोनों हाथों में सर्प को प्रदर्शित किया गया है। दक्षिण हस्त में एक में माला तथा एक हाथ को घुटने पर रखे हुए अंकित किया गया है। अन्य का अंकन स्पष्ट नहीं है। वामहस्त में से एक में मोदक पात्र, एक दन्त तथा एक में घंटी का अंकन है तथा एक हाथ घुटने पर प्रदर्शित है जिसकी मुष्टिका बंधी हुई है। ऊपर माला लिए विद्याधर अंकित है तथा अन्य परिचारिका का अंकन है। *शारदा तिलक* तथा *मेरुतन्त्र* में गणेश के दस स्वरूपों का उल्लेख हुआ है जिसमें से हेरम्ब गणेश को अष्टहस्त, विघ्नराज, लक्ष्मीगणपति, शक्ति गणेश, क्षितिप्रसादन गणेश, वक्रतुण्ड, पीतगणेश तथा उच्छिष्ठ गणपति को चतुर्भुज तथा महागणपति को द्वादश भुज एवं विरंचित गणपति को दशहस्त प्रकल्पित किया गया है।[35]

फलक के ऊपरी भाग में स्थानक मुद्रा में एक देवी की आकृति प्रदर्शित है जिसके पैर के दोनों ओर आसीन सिंह का अंकन किया गया है। दोनों ओर दो परिचारिकाओं को भी प्रदर्शित किया गया है। प्रतिमा के शीर्ष भाग के दोनों उपांत पर दो मालाधारी विद्याधर उड़ते हुए अंकित हैं। प्रतिमा चतुर्भुजी है। ऊर्ध्व दक्षिण हस्त में त्रिशूल प्रदर्शित है तथा अधः दक्षिणहस्त नीचे की ओर लम्बित तथा अभय मुद्रा में प्रदर्शित है। वाम ऊर्ध्वहस्त में घंटी तथा वाम अधः हस्त में कमण्डल अंकित है। यह प्रतिमा कई दृष्टियों से विचारणीय है। पैरों के पास सिंह

का अंकन होने के कारण इसे सिंहवाहिनी की संज्ञा प्रदान की जा सकती है। प्रारंभ में यह धारणा व्यक्त की गयी थी[36] कि सिंहवाहिनी की प्रतिमाओं का अंकन गुप्तकाल से पहले स्वीकार करना अधिक तर्कसंगत नहीं प्रतीत होता परंतु नवीन अनुसंधानों के आलोक में यह मत उचित नहीं प्रतीत होता। राजस्थान के नगर या कर्कोटनगर से प्राप्त प्रथम शती ई. के एक मृत्फलक पर[37] चतुर्भुजी महिषमर्दिनी का अंकन प्राप्त होता है जिसके दाहिने हाथ में त्रिशूल है। देवी के वाहन सिंह का भी अंकन प्राप्त होता है। कुषाण काल में सिंह वाहिनी दुर्गा की प्रतिमाएँ अधिकाधिक लोकप्रिय हो चुकी थी। सिंहासीन तथा पैरों के समीप सिंह की आकृति युक्त दोनों रूपों में देवी की प्रतिमाओं का अंकन किया जाने लगा था। मथुरा से मिली चतुर्भुज प्रतिमाओं में त्रिशूलधृत, खड्गधृत तथा अभय मुद्रा एवं कटिविन्यस्त अवस्था में हाथों का प्रदर्शन किया गया है। शंखान ढेरी से चतुर्भुज दुर्गा की एक प्रतिमा प्राप्त है[39] जिसके दो हाथ ऊपर की ओर उठे हैं तथा दो हाथ नीचे की ओर लम्बित है। निम्न दक्षिणहस्त में कमण्डलु प्रदर्शित है। कुषाण काल के बाद दुर्गा के द्विभुजी और चतुर्भुजी रूप के अतिरिक्त षड्भुजी, अष्टभुजी, द्वादशभुजी, अष्टादशभुजी इत्यादि रूपों का भी चित्रण किया जाने लगा। *अपराजितपृच्छा*[40] में दुर्गा के नौ रूपों यथा महालक्ष्मी, नन्दा, क्षेमकरी, शिवदूती, महाचन्डा, भ्रामरी, शिवमंडला, रेवती तथा हरसिद्धि का उल्लेख मिलता है। इनमें से केवल शिवदूती और हरसिद्धि के हाथों में कमण्डलु का विधान किया गया है परंतु इनके द्वारा त्रिशूल और घंटा धारण करने का विधान प्राप्त नहीं होता। महाचन्डा के हाथ में त्रिशूल और घंटा धारण करने का उल्लेख है परंतु कमण्डलु नहीं।[41] प्रस्तुत प्रतिमा में त्रिशूल, घण्टा और कमण्डलु एक साथ प्रदर्शित किये गये हैं। इस दृष्टि से यह प्रतिमा विशेषतः उल्लेखनीय है।

इसके अतिरिक्त इस स्थल से भग्न सूर्यमूर्ति का प्रस्तरफलक प्राप्त हुआ है जिसमें दण्डी, पिंगल, चामरधारिणी स्पष्ट हैं। सूर्य का पाद भाग भी सुरक्षित है, शेष खंडित है। मन्दिर वास्तु के अनेक भग्न अवशेष भी पड़े हैं। मरकमुख प्रणाल विशेष उल्लेखनीय है। यहां से लगभग पांच फीट लम्बा एक सिरदल प्राप्त है जिसके मध्य में चतुर्भुजी विष्णु योगासन मुद्रा में आसीन हैं। उनके ऊपर के दोनों हाथों में शंख और गदा जैसी वस्तु है। नीचे के दोनों हाथों की हथेली एक दूसरे पर रखी हुई है। ललाटविम्ब के रूप में विष्णु के अंकन से यह स्पष्ट है कि सातवीं–आठवीं शती में यहाँ पर कोई विष्णु मंदिर रहा होगा। सिरदल बकुलमाला अलंकरण से युक्त है।

गोन्डे–गोबरी के इस संक्षिप्त विवरण से स्पष्ट है कि यह स्थल धार्मिक दृष्टि से अत्यंत महत्त्वपूर्ण था तथा सभी पौराणिक धर्मों की सह प्रतिष्ठा इस स्थल पर थी। यदि गोन्डे–गोबरी के चतुर्दिक समीपवर्ती ग्रामों का व्यापक सर्वेक्षण किया जाए तो और अधिक कलाकृतियाँ प्रकाश में आ सकती हैं।

सन्दर्भ

1. प्रतापगढ़ के मध्य पाषाणिक स्थलों में सरायनहरराय, महदहा और दमदमा का उत्खनन प्राचीन इतिहास, संस्कृति एवं पुरातत्त्व विभाग इलाहाबाद विश्वविद्यालय द्वारा किया जा चुका है। द्रष्टव्य, गोवर्द्धनाय शर्मा का लेख–'सीजनल माइग्रेशन एण्ड मेसोलिथिक लेक कल्चर्स आव दि गंगा वैली', *पं. क्षेत्रेश चन्द्र चट्टपोध्याय मेमोरियल वाल्यूम,* प्रयाग 1975, पृ. 1–20 तथा 'एक्सकेवेशन एट महदहा', प्रयाग 1980 एवं श्री विद्याधर मिश्र का लेख 'एक्सकेवेशन एट दमदमा', संग्रहालय पुरातत्व पत्रिका भाग–41–42, पृ. 59–64।
2. भगवंत सहाय – *आइकोनोग्राफी आव सम इम्पार्टेन्ट माइनर हिन्दू एण्ड बुद्धिस्ट डिटीज,* पृ. 89
3. पूर्वोक्त – पृ. 89 तथा जे.एन. बनर्जी, *डेवलपमेन्ट आव हिन्दू आइकोनोग्राफी* पृ. 442
4. वी.सी. श्रीवास्तव, *सन वर्शिप इन एन्शिएन्ट इन्डिया,* पृ. 388
5. जे.एन. बनर्जी पूर्वोक्त, पृ. 442–443.

6. ब्लाख, *सप्लीमेन्ट्री कैटलाग ऑव दि आर्कियोलॉजिकल कलेकशन इन दि इंडियन म्यूजियम एट कलकत्ता*–पृ. 85, संख्या 3621, 37751, 3777 द्वारा उद्धृत भगवन्त, सहाय, *पूर्वोक्त,* पृ. 91–93
7. बी.एन.शर्मा 'रेवन्त इन लिटरेचर एण्ड आर्ट'–*पुराण* अंक 13 भाग 2 पु. 139–143 तथा प्रमोदचन्द्र–*स्टोन स्कल्पचर्स इन दि इलाहाबाद म्यूजियम* पृ. 108 तथा 113 फलक 92–260 तथा फलक 98–278
8. बी.एन.शर्मा, *वही,* पृ. 143
9. *विष्णुधर्मोत्तरपुराण,* काण्ड 3 अध्याय 70 श्लोक 4
10. *मार्कण्डेय पुराण* – अध्याय 78 श्लोक 22
11. जे.एन. बनर्जी, *वही,* पृ. 442
12. आर्कियोलॉजिकल म्यूजियम मथुरा, संख्या 35.2577 द्वारा उद्धृत नीलकंठ पुरुषोत्तम जोशी–*मथुरा स्कल्पचर्स,* फलक 83
13. *कुमारसंभव* 8.8
14. *मत्स्यपुराण* (मोर संस्करण) अध्याय 259 श्लोक 11–14
15. द्विजेन्द्रनाथ शुक्ल, *भारतीय प्रतिमाविज्ञान,* पृ. 256 पर उद्धृत
16. जे.एन. बनर्जी, *वही,* पृ. 256
17. नीलकंठ पुरुषोत्तम जोशी–*प्राचीन भारतीय मूर्ति विज्ञान* पृ. 169 गणेश की उपासना परंपरा के मूल में क्रियाशील एवं सहायक तत्वों की विवेचना अनेक विद्वानों द्वारा की गयी है जिनके सार–संक्षेप हेतु द्रष्टव्य–वी.सी. श्रीवास्तव का विद्वत्तापूर्ण लेख–हिस्टीरियोग्राफी ऑव गणेश. कल्ट, *पं. क्षेत्रेशचन्द्र चट्टपोध्याय वाल्यूम,* प्रयाग 1975 पृ. 136–157
18. आर.सी. अग्रवाल – ऊर्ध्वरेतस गणेश फ्राम अफगानिस्तान, *ईस्ट एण्ड वेस्ट,* जिल्द 18 मार्च–जून 1968, पृ. 166–68
19. *विष्णुधर्मोत्तरपुराण,* काण्ड 3, अध्याय 71 श्लोक 11–13 में भी व्याघ्रचर्माम्बरधर तथा सर्पयज्ञोपवीती गणेश का उल्लेख हुआ है, द्रष्टव्य नीलकंठ पुरुषोत्तम जोशी–वही पृ. 171
20. जे.एन. बनर्जी, *वही,* पृ. 358
21. *पूर्वोक्त,* पृ. 358–359 तथा लालमणि दूबे–*अपराजितपृच्छा–ए क्रिटिकल स्टडी,* पृ. 215–216
22. *मत्स्यपुराण,* अध्याय 258 श्लोक 11–12, पूर्वोक्त–अध्याय 259 श्लोक 52–54
विनायकं प्रवक्ष्यामि गजवक्त्रं त्रिलोचनम्।
लम्बोदरं शूर्पकर्णं व्यालयज्ञोपवीतिनम्।
ध्वस्तकर्णं बृहत्तुण्डमेक दंष्ट्रं पृथूदरम्।
स्वदन्तं दक्षिणकरेउत्पलञ्चापरे तथा।।
मोदकं परशुं चैवं वामतः परिकल्पयेत।
बृहत्वात् क्षिप्तवदनं पीन स्कन्धांघ्रिप्राणिनाम्।।
युक्तं तु ऋद्धिबुद्धिभ्यामधस्तान्मूषिकान्वितम्।
23. *पूर्वोक्त*
24. *स्थापयेत् स्वेष्टनगरे भुजान्द्वादश कारयेत। चतुर्भुजः खर्वटे स्याद्वने ग्रामे द्विबाहुकः। मत्स्यपुराण* अ0 259, श्लोक 47
25. नीलकंठ पुरुषोत्तम जोशी–*प्राचीन भारतीय प्रतिमा विज्ञान,* पृ. 74–95 तथा लालमणि दूबे–*तत्रैव,* पृ. 309
26. कृष्णदत्त वाजपेयी–*कल्चरल हिस्ट्री आव इण्डिया* भाग–1 (मध्य प्रदेश) पृ. 94 तथा मल्हार, पृ. 27
27. कुषाण कालीन विष्णु प्रतिमाओं हेतु द्रष्टव्य नीलकंठ पुरुषोत्तम जोशी, *तत्रैव,* पृ. 74–80
28. जोशी–*वही* पृ. 84 तथा *स्टोन स्कल्पचर्स इन दि इलाहाबाद म्यूजियम,* चित्र फलक 50–120 चित्रफलक 62.196, चित्रफलक 80.231 प्रयाग के समीप कुटारी से प्राप्त हरिहर के उत्कीर्णन में विष्णु के वाम हस्त में फल का अंकन प्राप्त होता है और उसके नीचे चक्र पुरुष का अंकन है – द्रष्टव्य – *वही* चित्रफलक 68.203। साहित्य में विष्णु के द्वारा फल धारण करने का संदर्भ विश्रुत नहीं है। *पद्मपुराण* में *'शक्तिचित्र फलोदग्रं शंखचक्रगदाधरम्'* के रूप

में चित्र या विचित्रफलक का उल्लेख प्राप्त होता है द्रष्टव्य–*पद्मपुराण,* सृष्टिखंड, अ0 43, श्लोक 139 तथा *मत्स्यपुराण,* अध्याय 171, श्लोक 25 में भी यही कथन प्राप्त होता है।

29. *मत्स्यपुराण,* अध्याय 260 श्लोक 30–31
वाराहीञ्च प्रवक्ष्यामि महिषोपरि संस्थिताम्।
वराहसदृशी देवी शिरश्चामरधारिणी
गदाचक्रधरा तद्वद्दानवेन्द्रविनाशिनी।
देवी भागवत पुराण में भी 'वराह महिषासना' का उल्लेख प्राप्त होता है।
30. वराह पर आसीन प्रतिमाएं अन्य स्थानों से भी प्राप्त हुई है; द्रष्टव्य आर.सी. अग्रवाल, मोर स्कल्पचर्स फ्राम अमझरा, राजस्थान, आर्ट्स एशियाटेक जिल्द 12 19 65 पृ. 175 तथा नीलकंठ पुरुषोत्तम जोशी – प्राचीन भारतीय *प्रतिमा विज्ञान,* पृ. 175
31. *अपराजित पृच्छा* 223, 15–21
32. *विष्णुधर्मोत्तरपुराण,* अध्याय 119, 28–58
33. *अपराजितपृच्छा* 223, 16
34. *मत्स्यपुराण*–अध्याय 260, श्लोक 31
35. द्विजेन्द्रनाथ शुक्ल – *पूर्वोक्त,* पृ. 486–487
36. भगवन्त सहाय – *पूर्वोक्त,* पृ. 183
37. *ललितकला* 1–2, 1855–56, पृ. 72–74
38. आनन्द केंटिश कुमार स्वामी, *कैटलॉग आफ इन्डियन कलेक्शन्स* भाग 1 तथा 2 फलक 3 संख्या 21.1709 पृ. 46 द्वारा उद्धृत नीलकंठ पुरुषोत्तम जोशी–पूर्वोक्त, पृ. 146
39. *एन्शिएन्ट पाकिस्तान* (बुलेटिन आव दि डिपार्टमेन्ट आव आर्क्योलाजी यूनिवर्सिटी आव पेशावर) भाग 21, 965–66, पृ. 39, फलक 21)
40. *अपराजितपृच्छा* में गोआसना गौरी के बारहरूपों को वर्णित किया गया है, जिनमें उमा, पार्वती, गौरी, ललिता, कृष्णा, रम्भा, सवितृ, श्रीखंडा के हाथ में कमण्डलु प्रदर्शित करने का विधान उल्लिखित है परन्तु सभी रूप गोआसना ही है। द्रष्टव्य – *अपराजितपृच्छा,* 222, 5–19
41. *पूर्वोक्त*

26

काशी के मृण्पुरावशेषों में लोक कलायें

सुरेन्द्र कुमार यादव

काशी प्राचीन काल से ही सांस्कृतिक चेतना, धार्मिक समन्वय एवं कला की दृष्टि से समृद्ध रहा है। इस क्षेत्र में परम्परागत धर्म एवं कला से इतर लोक जीवन से संबंधित कलाओं का प्रमाण भी सामानान्तर रुप से मिलता है, जिसकी अक्षुण्ण परम्परा किसी न किसी रूप में आज भी ग्रामीण अंचलों में स्थापत्य, मूर्ति शिल्प, मृद्भाण्ड़ों एवं मृण्मूर्तियों आदि रूपों में विद्यमान है। काशी के उत्खनित एवं सर्वेक्षित पुरावशेषों में विविध प्रकार की कलाकृतियाँ प्राप्त हुयी हैं, जिनमें मृण की बनी हुयी कलाकृतियाँ भी महत्वपूर्ण हैं। इन मृण कलाकृतियों में लोक कला, लोक जीवन एवं लोक धर्म की झलक दिखाई पड़ती है। ये कलाकृतियाँ जहाँ एक ओर अर्द्धविकसित समाज अथवा ग्रामीण परिवेश में व्याप्त सामाजिक एवं धार्मिक अवस्था का ज्ञान कराती हैं, वहीं दूसरी ओर समाज में प्रचलित विभिन्न प्रकार की प्रथाओं, रीति–रिवाज़, त्यौहार, पूजा–पाठ, देवी–देवताओं तथा कला आदि में छिपे हुये उपयोगी तथ्यों को सांस्कृतिक–ऐतिहासिक सूत्रों से जोड़कर इस अंचल की संस्कृति का अभिज्ञान कराती हैं।

प्रस्तुत शोध पत्र काशी के मृण्पुरावषेशों में लोक कला के अध्ययन पर आधारित है। इसमें इस क्षेत्र के उत्खनित पुरास्थलों राजघाट, सरायमोहाना, अकथा एवं रामनगर (ओरियाघाट) के साथ ही सर्वेक्षित पुरास्थलों से प्राप्त मृण्पुरावषेशों का अध्ययन किया गया है। इन मृण्पुरावषेशों में विविध प्रकार की कलाकृतियाँ, यथा मृद्भाण्ड, खिलौने, दैनन्दिन सामग्रियाँ एवं धार्मिक मूर्तियाँ प्रमुख हैं, जिनके आधार पर तत्कालीन समाज में प्रचलित धर्म, संस्कृति एवं लोक कला पर गहनता से विचार–विमर्श क़रने के साथ ही आज के परिवेश में इनके प्रचलन एवं महत्त्व पर प्रकाश डाला गया है।

काशी में प्राचीन काल से ही लोगों ने अपनी लौकिक एवं धार्मिक भावनाओं को व्यक्त करने के लिये जिन विविध माध्यमों को चुना, उनमें मृण की बनी कलाकृतियाँ सबसे प्राचीन हैं एवं मानव की सरलतम कलात्मक अभिव्यक्ति की सूचक हैं। *कुम्भकार जातक*[1] एवं *घटिकारसुत्त*[2] में वाराणसी के आस–पास कुम्भकारों की बस्तियों का उल्लेख है, जो मृण से बने खिलौने बनाने में निपुण थे। बाद के ग्रन्थों विषेशतः *उक्तिव्यक्तिप्रकरण* में भी

वाराणसी के संदर्भ में मृण्मूर्तियों का वर्णन मिलता है। इस क्षेत्र के सर्वेक्षित एवं उत्खनित पुरास्थलों से प्राप्त मृण्मूर्तियों के आधार पर यह कहा जा सकता है कि मृण कला के इतिहास में यहाँ के लोगों ने अपना विशिष्ट स्थान बना लिया था। काशी में उत्खनन एवं सर्वेक्षण से उपलब्ध मृण्पुरावषेशों को उनकी विषय–वस्तु के आधार पर विभक्त कर लोक कला का अध्ययन किया जा सकता है।

मृद्भाण्ड़ों में लोक कला

काशी की समृद्धि में सर्वाधिक महत्त्वपूर्ण भूमिका व्यावसायिक एवं औद्योगिक शिल्प की रही है। साहित्यिक साक्ष्यों में काशी के संदर्भ में विविध प्रकार के शिल्प उद्योगों यथा वस्त्रोद्योग, काशिकचन्दन, हस्तिदन्त, बड्ढ़की उद्योग (बढ़ईगीरी), स्वर्णकारी, लौहकर्म आदि के साथ ही मृद्भाण्ड उद्योग के विषय में अनेकविध विवरण प्राप्त होते हैं। इस क्षेत्र में उत्खनित पुरास्थलों राजघाट, सरायमोहाना, कमौली, अकथा, अनेई एवं ओरियाघाट आदि के साथ ही सर्वेक्षित पुरास्थलों से प्रभूत मात्रा में मृद्भाण्ड प्राप्त हुये हैं। काशी में मानव के स्थायी निवास के साथ ही मृद्भाण्ड़ों का प्रचलन मिलने लगता है। ये पात्र दैनिक जीवन में उपयोग की आवश्यकतानुसार ही बनाये जाते थे। सामान्य जन के अतिरिक्त कुछ विशिष्ट उपयोग के निमित्त भी इनका निर्माण हुआ। इनमें तत्कालीन समाज के लोक जीवन की झाँकी दिखती है।

काशी के ग्रामीण परिवेश वाले दो पुरास्थलों अनेई[4] एवं अकथा[5] के प्रथम काल से छिद्रित पात्र (Perforated Pottery) के प्रमाण मिले हैं। वर्तमान में वाराणसी एवं उससे सटे हुये विभिन्न जिलों में झिझिया नाम की एक प्रथा देखने को मिलती है, जिसे अश्विन के नवरात्र के अवसर पर महिलाएं भाई की उम्र – वृद्धि तथा रक्षा हेतु मनाती हैं। इसके लिये महिलायें मिट्टी की छिद्रित हाँडी लेती हैं। प्रत्येक औरत अलग–अलग हाँडी लेती है। रात्रि में उसके अन्दर जलता हुआ दीपक रखकर इसे सिरपर रखती है तथा समूह बनाकर गाँव में नाचते–गाते हुये चलती है। किसी–किसी गाँव में एक हाँडी के ऊपर क्रमशः छोटे आकार की कई हाँडियाँ रखी जाती हैं तथा सबसे ऊपर की हाँडी पर जलता हुआ दीपक रखा जाता है। महिलाएँ भाई की उम्र वृद्धि हेतु गीत गाती हैं। उसी से डायन (गाँव के जादू –टोना करने वाली औरतों) को गाली देती हैं। इसमें औरते इस लिये गाती हैं कि कोई छिद्र की गिनती न कर सके। ऐसी मान्यता है कि यदि कोई गिनती कर लेती है तो उसके भाई के लिये अशुभ हो जायेगा। यह प्रक्रिया पूरे नवरात्रि तक चलती है और अन्तिम रात्रि को मिट्टी की हाँडी को तोडकर नदी एवं तालाब में प्रवाहित कर दिया जाता है।

काशी की दूसरी पात्र परम्पराओं से संबंधित लोक कला का वर्णन सामा – चकवा खेल से संबंधित है। यह दीपावली की रात्रि से प्रारम्भ होकर कार्तिक पूर्णिमा तक चलता है। इसमें मृण की बनी हुयी देवी के दोनो कन्धों पर अथवां हाथों में घुण्डीदार ढक्कन की तरह छोटा सा चकवा (दीपिका) लिये हुये दिखाया जाता है तथा पैरो को एक गोल आधार से संयुक्त किया जाता है। कभी – कभी एक गोल आधार पर दो चार मूर्तियाँ भी बनायी जाती हैं। इस प्रकार की प्रतिमा को सामा कहते है। राजघाट के उत्खनन से दो खण्डित मातृदेवी की प्रतिमा बेलनाकार पीठिका पर आसीन हैं। इसकी बाँयी भुजा पर शिशु एवं हाथ में दीपिका है। दाहिना हाथ खण्डित है पर उसमें भी इसी प्रकार का अंकन होने की संभावना है (छाया चित्र 1)।

काशी में लोक परम्परा से संबंधित एक अन्य पात्र अर्चना कुण्ड या मनौती कूप (Votive Tank) है। इस प्रकार के पात्र राजघाट के अतिरिक्त इस क्षेत्र में सर्वेक्षण से भी प्राप्त हुये हैं। इन पात्रों को लोक कला एवं लोक धर्म से संबंधित किया जा सकता है। ये अनेक आकार – प्रकार के हैं। सामान्यतया थालीनुमा पात्र के किनारे छोटे– छोटे दिये बने होते हैं। कभी–कभी इन पात्रों के किनारों पर पशु–पक्षियों की आकृतियों, सर्पों की भद्दी आकृतियाँ एवं सीढ़ियों[9] (छाया चित्र 2, 3) के साथ ही ढ़ोलकी लिये हुये बौने मानव के अंकन भी मिलते हैं[10]।

आज भी वाराणसी में जन्माष्टमी से दो दिन पहले ललही छठ के त्योहार में इस प्रकार की आकृतियाँ बनायी जाती हैं। ये पात्र दूसरी शताब्दी ईसापूर्व से लेकर कुषाण काल तक मिलते हैं।

काशी के पुरास्थलों से प्राप्त मृद्भाण्डों पर अनेकानेक प्रकार के चित्रण एवं अलंकरण मिलते हैं। राजघाट के उत्खनन से विविध प्रकार के टोटीदार पात्र मिले हैं, जो ग्रामीण जीवन के अभिन्न अंग रहे हैं। इनमें टोटी का मुख विभिन्न पशु पक्षियों की आकृतियों का है (छाया चित्र 4, 5)। साथ ही, इन पात्रों पर विभिन्न प्रकार के अलंकरण मिलते हैं, जिनमें विविध पशु, पीपल एवं कमल के साथ ही ज्यामितीय आकृतियाँ प्रमुख हैं (छाया चित्र 6)। ये अलंकरण आज भी काशी के ग्रामीण अंचलो में पात्रों के साथ ही घरों की दीवालों, कोहबरों, धार्मिक उपयोग की वस्तुओं एवं वस्त्रों आदि पर देखने को मिलते हैं। इसी प्रकार पुरास्थलों से छोटे, बडे एवं मध्यम आकार के कटोरे बड़ी संख्या में विभिन्न काल खण्डों से मिले हैं। खान–पान के अतिरिक्त ये पात्र धार्मिक प्रयोजनों में भी प्रयोग में लाये जाते रहे होगे। आज भी काशी में अन्नकूट के अवसर पर छोटे आकार के पात्रों को भडेहर के रुप में धार्मिक प्रयोजन के लिये प्रयुक्त किया जाता है। इस प्रकार हम कह सकते है कि इन पात्रों से काशी के प्राचीन कालीन लोक जीवन की स्पष्ट अभिव्यक्ति मिलती है, जिसकी निरन्तरता आज भी जनमानस में बनी हुयी है।

मृण खिलौनों में लोक कला

काशी में इसकी प्राचीनता लगभग तीन हजार वर्षों तक जाती है, क्योंकि राजघाट के प्रथम काल से ही विभिन्न प्रकार के खिलौने जिनमें, मृण्मण्डल, गेंद, मूर्तियाँ एवं मनके आदि प्रमुख हैं मिलने प्रारंभ हो जाते हैं। काशी में उत्खनन एवं सर्वेक्षण से प्राप्त खिलौनों का संक्षिप्त विवरण निम्नलिखित हैः

मृण्मण्डल

काशी के लगभग प्रत्येक पुरास्थल से मृण्मण्डल (Terracotta Disc, Pottery Disc or Hop Scotch) का प्रमाण मिला है(छाया चित्र 7, 8)। इन मृण्मण्डलों का प्रयोग संख्या गिनने, पिड्डू , पिट्टू (Pittu Game) एवं चम्भा नामक खेल खेलने के लिये किया जाता है। आज भी काशी के ग्रामीण अंचलों में इस प्रकार के खेल देखने को मिलते है, जिनमें एक चौकोर लाइन खीच कर उसे असमान भागों में विभाजित कर संख्या का अंकन किया जाता है। तत्पश्चात् उसमें मृण्मण्डल को फेका जाता है और वर्ग में एक पैर से प्रवेश कर मृण्मण्डल को उठाया जाता है। वहीं पिट्टू नामक खेल के प्रयोग में पात्र के टुकडें को काटकर गोल आकृति का बनाया जाता है। इसमें कुछ मृण्मण्डल को एक के ऊपर एक रख कर गेंद से गिराने और पुनः रखने का खेल खेला जाता है। इसे गाँवों में गेंदतड़ी के नाम से जाना जाता है (छाया चित्र 9, 10)।

गेंद एवं गोली

काशी के विभिन्न पुरास्थलों से मृण्मय छोटी एवं बड़ी आकार वाली गेंदो एवं गोलियों का प्रमाण मिला है, जो विभिन्न खेलों के प्रयोग में लायी जाती रही होगी। संभवतः इसका प्रयोग बच्चे कंचे खेलने के लिये, गुलेल चलाने के लिये, मछली पकडने के लिये, गिनती सीखने के लिये एवं खेतों में चिड़ियाँ उड़ाने आदि कार्यों के लिये करते रहे होंगे। आज भी गाँवों में इन्ही सब खेलों में मृण्मय गेंदों का प्रयोग मिलता है। राजघाट से लगभग 1200 की संख्या में गेंदे प्राप्त हुयी हैं।(छाया चित्र 11) अकथा एवं अनेई के अतिरिक्त विभिन्न सर्वेक्षित पुरास्थलों से भी विभिन्न आकार की गेंदे प्राप्त हुयी हैं।

खिलौना गाड़ी

खिलौना गाड़ी प्राचीन काल से ही बच्चों के खेलने का प्रिय साधन रहा है। सैन्धव सभ्यता से ही इसके प्रमाण मिलने लगते हैं। काशी में राजघाट एवं सरायमोहाना से खिलौना गाड़ी के प्रमाण मिले हैं। राजघाट के पंचम काल[13] से तीन तथा सरायमोहाना[14] के द्वितीय एवं तृतीय काल से एक–एक खिलौना गाड़ी का प्रमाण मिला है (छाया चित्र 12, 13)। इसके साथ ही राजघाट, सरायमोहाना, अकथा एवं अनेई से सादे एवं अलंकृत पहियों का प्रमाण मिला है। ओरियाघाट से नाव का खिलौना भी प्राप्त हुआ है[15] (छाया चित्र 14)। इन खिलौना गाड़ियों से खेल के अतिरिक्त तत्कालीन समाज में लोगो द्वारा प्रयोग में किये जाने वाले यातायात के साधनों का भी अनुमान लगाया जा सकता है। आज भी काशी के ग्रामीण क्षेत्रों में बच्चों के खेलने के लिये खिलौना गाड़ी तो मिलता ही है, साथ ही साथ यातायात एवं सामान ढोने के लिये बैलगाड़ी एवं नाव का प्रयोग भी दिखाई है, जो काशी के ग्रामीण जीवन में परिवहन के अभिन्न अंग हैं।

फिरंगी या फिरकी

फिरकी बच्चों के खेलने का एक अन्य मनोरंजक साधन है। राजघाट के उत्खनन में प्रथम काल के उपचरण 'ब' से फिरकी का प्रमाण मिला है, जो धूसर रंग के पात्र को गोल आकार देकर एवं उसमें दो छिद्र करके बनाया गया है[16] (छाया चित्र 15, 16)। इस प्रकार की फिरकी को खेलने के लिये उसमें डोरी डालकर हाथ से नचाया जाता है। इसका प्रचलन आज भी काशी के गाँवों में देखने को मिलता है, जिसमें मृण, धातु एवं लकड़ी की फिरकी विशेष रुप से बने मिलते हैं।

शतरंज/पासा

इस प्रकार का खेल बच्चों के मानसिक स्तर को दर्शाता है। राजघाट एवं सरायमोहाना के उत्खनन से शतरंज के पासों के प्रमाण मिले हैं। राजघाट के द्वितीय, तृतीय, चतुर्थ एवं पंचम काल से शतरंज के पासे मिले हैं[17] (छाया चित्र 17)। ग्रामीण स्तर पर मिट्टी के बने पासे को जमीन पर लकीर खींचकर शतरंज की बिसात बनाकर आज भी खेला जाता है।

झुनझुना

छोटे बच्चों के लिये झुनझुना नामक खिलौना का प्रचलन प्राचीन काल से ही मिलता है। यह एक लोकप्रिय एवं सर्वप्रचलित खिलौना है, जो सभी घरो में समान रुप से पाया जाता है। राजघाट के द्वितीय एवं तृतीय काल से इसके प्रमाण मिले हैं। इसके दो प्रकार महत्वपूर्ण हैं। प्रथम झुनझुना अनार की आकृति का तथा द्वितीय चिड़िया के आकार का बना हुआ है। दोनो ही झुनझुने छिद्रयुक्त व अन्दर से खोखले आकार के हैं, जिनमें कंकड़ आदि डालकर बजाने योग्य बनाया गया है (छाया चित्र 18)। सरायमोहाना से शंकु के आकार का झुनझुना प्राप्त हुआ है[19] (छाया चित्र 19)। काशी में छोटे बच्चों को खेलने के लिये आज भी झुनझुने का प्रचलन है, यद्यपि इसके आकार एवं प्रयोग सामग्री में समायान्तर के अनुसार परिवर्तन देखने को मिलता है। यह परिवर्तन इसके निर्माण में मिट्टी के अतिरिक्त काष्ठ, धातु एवं प्लास्टिक के उपयोग के रुप में दिखाई पड़ता है।

पशु–पक्षी

लोक कला में खिलौनो के अन्तर्गत पशु–पक्षी वाली आकृतियाँ छोटे बच्चों को सबसे अधिक आकृष्ट करती हैं। इनका प्रचलन सर्वत्र एवं सर्वकाल खण्ड में देखने को मिलता है। राजघाट एवं सरायमोहाना के अतिरिक्त काशी में सर्वेक्षण से विभिन्न पशु–पक्षियों के खिलौने प्राप्त हुये हैं। राजघाट के तृतीय, चतुर्थ एवं पंचम काल से बन्दर के खिलौनो वाली आकृतियाँ प्राप्त हुयी हैं (छाया चित्र 20)। वहीं सरायमोहाना से हाथी, घोड़ा, गाय, बैल, कुत्ता, भेड़ा एवं चिड़ियाँ आदि की आकृति वाले खिलौने मिले है[21] (छाया चित्र 21, 22)। सर्वेक्षण से भी विभिन्न पशु–पक्षियों की आकृतियों वाली मृण्मूर्तियाँ प्राप्त हुयी हैं। काशी में आज भी पशु–पक्षियों की आकृतियों वाले खिलौनों का प्रचलन जनमानस में व्यापक रुप से प्रााप्त है।

गृह उपयोगी एवं प्रसाधनिक पुरावशेषों में लोक कला

मुण्मय पुरावशेषों में लोक कला का एक अन्य सशक्त माध्यम गृह उपयोगी एवं प्रसाधनिक सामग्रियों में दिखता है। दैनिक जीवन में प्रयुक्त होने वाली सामग्रियों में मृणमय कला का अंकन बहुधा 'भातुकली–भातुकली' अर्थात 'घर–घर खेल' के लिये प्रयुक्त किये जाने वाले खिलौनों में दिखायी पड़ता है। इसमें तवा, चूल्हा, लोढ़ा, पीढ़ा, छोटे आकार के पात्र एवं घण्टी–घण्टुला आदि प्रमुख है। इसके अतिरिक्त कुछ मृण्मय सामग्रियों का प्रयोग दिन–प्रतिदिन के उपयोग वाली सामग्रियों हेतु किया गया है। राजघाट में हाथ से बने हुये पीढ़े का प्रमाण मिला है, जिनमें चार पावे लगे हैं[22] (छाया चित्र 23)। राजघाट के तृतीयकाल से ही बच्चों को दूध पिलाने वाली सुतुही नामक पात्र **(Feeder)** का प्रमाण मिला है[23] (छाया चित्र 24)। यह चाक से निर्मित चौरस एवं तस्तरी नुमा है, जिसे सूखने से पूर्व ही दोनो तरफ से मोड़ कर कुछ लम्बे आकार का बनाया गया है। इसके अतिरिक्त राजघाट एवं सरायमोहाना से विभिन्न आकार के लोढ़े[24] (छाया चित्र 25) एवं झाँवे[25] **(Skin rubber)** (छाया चित्र 26) मिले हैं।

मृण के बने प्रसाधनिक पुरावशेषों में विविध आकार–प्रकार वाले मनकों, ताबीजों, लटकनों, गुरियों एवं चूड़ियों आदि का उल्लेख किया जा सकता है। राजघाट के सभी कालखण्डों से 1522 की संख्या में मनको के प्रमाण मिले हैं, जो काशी में मनके की लोकप्रियता को दर्शाता है। राजघाट से विभिन्न आकार वाले सुपाड़ीनुमा, पीपेनुमा, गोलाकार, घटनुमा, आमलकनुमा, नलिकाकार आदि आकार वाले मनके मिले हैं[26] (छाया चित्र संख्या 27)। इसके अतिरिक्त विभिन्न आकार – प्रकार वाले लटकन के प्रमाण मिले हैं, जिनमें पशु, कछुए, मछली एवं शंख की आकृति के साथ ही आयताकार ताबीज के अंकन हैं[27] (छाया चित्र 28) । ये मनके, लटकन एवं ताबीज लोगो के जीवन में अलंकरण के अभिन्न अंग रहे होंगे। ताबीज का प्रचलन निश्चित रुप से रक्षा कवच के रूप में रहा होगा। आज भी काशी में मिट्टी के बने हुये आभूषणों का प्रचलन जनमानस में सामान्य रुप से देखा जा सकता है। ताबीज का प्रचलन तो जन्तर–मन्तर के रुप में काशी के ग्रामीण जीवन का अभिन्न अंग बना हुआ है, जो लोककला एवं लोक जीवन के बहुत करीब है।

मृण्मूर्तियों में लोक कला

काशी की लोक संस्कृति की स्पष्ट छाप मृण्मूर्तियों में दिखायी पड़ती है। मृण्मय मूर्तियाँ सामान्य जन के अधिक निकट रही है। इनमें लोगो के लौकिक जीवन की अभिव्यक्ति के साथ ही उनकी धार्मिक भावनाओं का निर्दशन सम्यक्रूपेण द्रष्टव्य है। काशी में धार्मिक रुप से सर्वप्रथम मातृदेवी की मृण्मूर्तियाँ बनी, जिनमें निरन्तर विकास होता रहा। इसके अतिरिक्त नाग, नैगमेश, कुबेर, शिवलिंग एवं गणेश आदि की मृण्मूर्तियाँ काशी के विभिन्न पुरास्थलों से प्राप्त हुयी हैं। ये सभी मृण्मूर्तियाँ लोक जीवन से अभिन्नतः संबंधित रही हैं।

मातृदेवी

काशी में मातृदेवी की मृण्मूर्तियाँ आद्यैतिहासिक काल से ही मिलने लगती हैं। प्रारम्भ में हस्तनिर्मित मूर्तियाँ बनी, जो संख्या में अधिक मिलने के कारण धार्मिक महत्व को दर्शाती हैं। यद्यपि इन मूर्तियों को कोई भी नाम देना कठिन है, लेकिन लोकप्रियता एवं प्राचीन परम्परा की व्यापकता के आधार पर इन्हें महीमाता के नाम से उल्लिखित किया गया है। मातृदेवी की इन मृण्मूर्तियों में निरन्तर विकास होता रहा और कालान्तर में ये विभिन्न देवियों के रुप में प्रचलित हुयी। राजघाट से विभिन्न आकार – प्रकार वाली मातृदेवी की मृण्मूर्तियाँ प्राप्त हुयी हैं (छाया चित्र 29)। काशी में आज भी मातृदेवी की मृण्मूर्तियों का प्रचलन है, जो लोक जीवन का अभिन्न अंग है।

नैगमेश

काशी में उत्खनन एवं सर्वेक्षण से नैगमेश की प्रतिमाएँ मिली हैं। मृत्तिका कला में इनसे संबंधित मृण्मूर्तियों में एक विशिष्ट लक्षण दिखाई पड़ता है। इनमें मुख बकरे के आकार का (अजमुख) तथा धड़ पुरुष अथवा स्त्री का होता है। अजमुख के आधार पर इस प्रकार की मृण्मूर्तियों का संबंध हरिणेगमेशी के साथ स्थापित किया जाता है, जो जैन देवता नैगमेश के रुप में प्रतिष्ठित है। *कौमारभृत्यतन्त्र* में नैगमेश को बच्चों का संरक्षक कहा गया है[28]। मूलतः संतान प्राप्ति हेतु इस देवता की पूजा की जाती थी[29]। राजघाट से नैगमेश की मूर्तियाँ प्रथम शती ईसवी से सातवीं–आठवीं शती के स्तरों से प्राप्त हुयी हैं[30]।

वाराणसी में कुरुँ नामक पुरास्थल से नैगमेश की पुरुष एवं स्त्री रूपों वाली मृण्मूर्तियाँ प्राप्त हुयी हैं। नैगमेश से संबंधित पुरुष मृण्मूर्तियों की संख्या तीन है, जिन्हें घुटने मोड़ कर बैठे हुये दिखलाया गया है। मृण्मूर्तियों का चेहरा चिपटा है। मुख का अंकन लकीर द्वारा तथा आँखों को दर्शाने के लिये अलग से गोल मिट्टी लगाकर उसमें छिद्र किया गया है। मुख कोरदार तथा दोनो हाथ सामने की ओर हैं। स्त्री नैगमेश मूर्तियाँ आठ की संख्या में प्राप्त हुयी हैं। इनके बकरी जैसे मुख को दिखलाने के लिये आगे की ओर थोड़ा सा चिपटा कर लकीर खीच दिया गया है। मस्तक के पीछे की ओर हल्का–सा उभार है। कान को दिखलाने के लिये अलग से मिट्टी का लोआ लेकर चिपकाया गया है तथा कुछ मूर्तियों में हल्का सा छिद्र किया गया है। स्तन दिखलाने के लिये अलग से मिट्टी न लगाकर हाथ से ही गोला कर बनाया गया है। गले में माला का अंकन किया गया है, जिसके लिये अलग से मिट्टी लगाकर उसमें छिद्र किया गया है। कुछ मूर्तियों में पैर को दिखलाने के लिये निचला हिस्सा संयुक्त कर लकीर खीच दिया गया है। किन्तु कुछ मूर्तियों में पैर न दिखला कर पेंदी समतल बनाई गई है (छाया चित्र 30)।

यक्ष प्रतिमा

काशी में यक्ष पूजा की परम्परा प्राचीन काल से ही लोक देवता के रुप में मान्य रही है। वर्तमान में इन्हें बीर अथवा बरम या ब्रह्म देवता के रुप में जाना जाता है। काशी क्षेत्र के हीरापट्टी नामक पुरास्थल से कुबेर की मृण प्रतिमा प्राप्त हुयी है। प्रस्तुत प्रतिमा 25 × 25 सेमी. आकार की है, जिसमें कुबेर का सिर गायब है तथा वे सुखासन मुद्रा में बैठे हैं। उनके दोनों हाथों में पात्र है, दाहिने हाथ में चषक तथा बाये हाथ में छोटा घरिया है, जिसको ऊपर से गोल–गोल पिण्डों से भरा दिखाया गया है। संभवत ये पिण्ड मुद्रा के परिचायक हैं। कुबेर का पेट निकला हुआ है तथा शरीर पर कहीं भी अलंकरण नहीं किया गया है (छाया चित्र 31)। इसी प्रकार की एक प्रतिमा मोहाली से प्राप्त हुयी है, जिसकी तिथि तीसरी–चौथी शती की जाती है। सम्प्रति यह राष्ट्रीय संग्रहालय मथुरा में है, और

बलुएँ पत्थर की बनी है[31]। राजघाट से बनी मृद्भाण्ड के हत्थे पर यक्ष की प्रतिमा प्राप्त हुयी है (छाया चित्र 32)। काशी में यक्षों के साथ ही नाग पूजा का भी प्रचलन रहा है। भगवान बुद्ध ने वाराणसी में नाग एरकपत्त को उपदेश दिया था[32]। यहाँ के प्रसिद्ध नागकुआँ स्थल जिसे करकोटक तीर्थ के नाम से भी जाना जाता है, पर श्रावण मास में आज भी नागपंचमी का त्योहार मनाया जाता है। राजघाट से नाग की अनेक मृण्मूर्तियाँ प्राप्त हुयी हैं (छाया चित्र 33)।

इसके अतिरिक्त राजघाट एवं सरायमोहाना से गणेश, शिव, शिवलिंग, विष्णु महिषासुरमर्दिनी दुर्गा तथा नागों की मृण्मूर्तियाँ प्राप्त हुयी हैं (छाया चित्र 34)। साथ ही राजघाट से लौकिक जीवन से संबंधित मृण्मूर्तियाँ भी प्राप्त हुयी है, जिनमें मिथुन, दम्पति, बच्चो को खेलाते हुयी स्त्री (छाया चित्र 35) एवं ढोलक बजाते हुये पुरुष की मूर्तियाँ प्रमुख हैं[33] (छाया चित्र 36)।

निष्कर्ष

उपरोक्त सन्दर्भों से सुस्पष्ट है कि काशी मे प्राचीन काल से ही मृण कला लोक कला का सशक्त माध्यम रही है। लोगो ने अपनी भावनाओं एवं विचारों की अभिव्यक्ति के लिये इसे अपना प्रथम माध्यम बनाया। काशी में यह कला परिवार के बडे बुजुर्गो द्वारा परम्परागत रुप से पीढी दर पीढ़ी हस्तानान्तरित होती रही और बिना किसी शिक्षण संस्थान के एक प्रमुख शिल्प उद्योग के रुप में लगातार फलती –फूलती रही। काशी के दैनिक जीवन के खान–पान में मृद्भाण्ड़ों का महत्वपूर्ण योगदान रहा है। इसके अतिरिक्त कुछ विशिष्ट पात्रों को धार्मिक प्रयोजनो के निमित्त निर्मित किया गया। इन पात्रों पर किये गये अलंकरण कलात्मकता के साथ ही धार्मिक महत्व को भी दर्शाते हैं, जो लोक जीवन के बहुत करीब हैं। काशी प्रारम्भ से ही धार्मिक नगरी के रुप में प्रतिष्ठित थी, जिसके कारण यहाँ कोई न कोई पर्व, त्योहार अथवा उत्सव का आयोजन होता रहा। इन आयोजनों ने इस मृण कला को बहुत अधिक प्रोत्साहित किया। मेलों में विविध प्रकार के खिलौनों को बिक्री के लिये बनाया एवं बेचा जाता था। यह परम्परा आज भी काशी में देखने को मिलती है। मृण् कला काशी के लोक धर्म को बखूबी रेखांकित करती है। इनमें मातृदेवी एवं नैगमेश से संबंधित प्रतिमाएँ स्थानीय स्तर पर लोगों की धार्मिक प्रवृत्ति एवं अभिरुचि को इंगित करती हैं। मातृदेवी की मूर्तियों में निरन्तर विकास के लक्षण दृष्टिगोचर होते हैं, जो क्षेत्र के लोगों की इनके प्रति अक्षुण्ण निष्ठा के परिचायक हैं। वहीं नैगमेश की प्रतिमाएँ विकसित एवं अर्द्धविकसित धर्म के मध्य कड़ी के रूप में हैं, इनकी उपासना बच्चों के संरक्षण व संतान प्राप्ति हेतु की जाती थी। कुबेर एवं यक्ष से संबंधित प्रतिमाएँ लोक परम्परा एवं लोक जीवन को आत्मसात् करती हुयी दिखायी पड़ती हैं। कुबेर से संबंधित प्रतिमायें समकालीन आर्थिक विकास अथवा इस क्षेत्र की समृद्धि के रुप में भी देखी जा सकती हैं। इनके अतिरिक्त नाग, शिव, गणेश, कार्तिकेय, विष्णु एवं महिषासुरमर्दिनी दुर्गा आदि की मृण्मूर्तियाँ प्राप्त हुयी हैं जो इस क्षेत्र के लोगों की मान्यताओं एवं कला–बोध के साथ ही काशी के ग्रामीण अंचल में व्याप्त धार्मिक–सामाजिक अवस्था की सूचक हैं। खिलौनों के रुप में प्राप्त विविध प्रकार की पशु–पक्षियों की मूर्तियाँ तत्कालीन समाज में इनकी आवश्यकता एवं महत्त्व को रेखांकित करती हैं। राजघाट से हाथी, बैल एवं गाय की अनेक मृण्मूर्तियाँ प्राप्त हुयी हैं। काशी में हस्तिदन्त उद्योग[34] एवं हस्तिमंगलोत्सव[35] की परम्परा विद्यमान थी। गाय–बैल आज की तरह तत्कालीन समाज में कृषि एवं पशुपालन से संबंधित थे। राजघाट से प्राप्त प्रथम शताब्दी ईसा पूर्व की एक मुहर पर "गवायक श्रेणी" का उल्लेख है, जो दुग्ध व्यवसाय करने वाले ग्वालों की श्रेणी से संबंधित हैं[36]। बच्चों के खेलने के विविध प्रकार के उपकरणों यथा मृण्मण्डल, फिरकी, गेंद, शतरंज के पासे आदि मनोरंजन के अतिरिक्त लोगों के शारीरिक एवं बौद्धिक स्तर को दर्शाते हैं। राजघाट एवं सरायमोहाना से प्राप्त खिलौना गाड़ी एवं उड़ियाघाट से प्राप्त नाव सामान्यजन के प्रतिदिन के आवागमन एवं यातायात के साधन की ओर इंगित करते हैं। दैनन्दिन जीवन में प्रयोग

में आने वाली सामग्रियों में पीढ़ा, लोढ़ा, सुतही एवं झावाँ आदि से तत्कालीन समाज में प्रयुक्त होने वाली वस्तुओं को अनुमानित किया जा सकता है। काशी के लोक जीवन में आमोद–प्रमोद एवं मनोरंजन के साधनों को वादक प्रतिमाओं से अनुमानित कर सकते हैं जो यह निदर्शित करती है कि यहाँ के लोगो के जीवन में संगीत का कितना अधिक महत्व था। विभिन्न प्रकार की चूडियाँ, कर्णाभूषण, मनके, लटकन एवं ताबीज लोगों में साज–सज्जा एवं जादू–टोना की उस प्रवृत्ति के सूचक हैं जिसका सातत्य आज भी लोक–जीवन में बहुविध परिलक्षित है।

संक्षेप में यह कहा जा सकता है कि ये मृण्पुरावशेष काशी के बहु–आयामी लोक जीवन की सहज अभिव्यक्ति के साथ लोक कला की समृद्धि को प्रभावी रीति से रेखांकित करते हैं।

संदर्भ

1. कौसल्यायन, भदन्त आनन्द (अनुवाद), *जातक*, हिन्दी साहित्य सम्मेलन, प्रयाग, संवत् 2008, भाग–4, संख्या 408
2. वापट, पी0 वी0 व जगदीश कश्यप (सम्पादक), *मज्झिमनिकाय*, पालि (सुत्तपिटक), नालन्दा देवनागरी पालि सिरीज, पालि प्रकाशन बोर्ड बिहार, 1958, भाग–2, 31, पृ0 280
3. जिनविजय मुनि (सम्पादक), *उक्तिव्यक्तिप्रकरण* (दामोदर विरचित), सिन्धी जैन ग्रन्थमाला, ग्रन्थांक नं0 39, सिन्धी जैन शास्त्र शिक्षापीठ भारतीय विद्याभवन, बम्बई, 1953, 37/24, 44/20
4. यादव, सुरेन्द्र कुमार, *वारुणेय क्षेत्र का पुरातात्विक इतिहास*, शारदा पब्लिशिंग हाउस, दिल्ली, 2010. पृ0 133, चित्र संख्या 2
5. जायसवाल, विदुला, *एंशियन्ट वाराणसी, एन आर्कियोलॉजिकल पर्सपेक्टिव* (एक्सकवेशन ऐट अकथा), आर्यन बुक इंटरनेशनल नई दिल्ली, 2009 पृ0 75, चित्र संख्या 21: 112, 115
6. सिन्हा, ए0 के0, मध्य गंगा घाटी क्षेत्र की लोक संस्कृतिः एक पुरातात्विक अवलोकन, *विचार*, अर्द्धवार्षिक सांदर्भिक शोध पत्रिका, जयनारायण स्नातकोत्तर महाविद्यालय, लखनऊ, पृ0 12–18, अंक–2, 2008
7. सिन्हा, ए0 के0, पूर्वोक्त, पृ0 12.–18, अंक–2, 2008
8. नारायण, ए0 के0 एवं पी0 के0 अग्रवाल, *एक्सकवेशन ऐट राजघाट*, (टेराकोटा ह्यूमन फिगिरिंग्स) चतुर्थ भाग (A-B), बी0 एच0 यू0, वाराणसी, 1978, पृ0 75 प्लेट VII/1-2
9. नारायण, ए0 के0 एवं पी0 के0 अग्रवाल, *एक्सकवेशन ऐट राजघाट*, (टेराकोटा ह्यूमन फिगिरिंग्स) चतुर्थ भाग ;(A-B), बी0 एच0 यू0, वाराणसी, 1978 पृ0 79 – 80 प्लेट XIII/1, XIV/1-4
10. जायसवाल, विदुला, *कुषाण क्ले आर्ट ऑफ गंगा प्लेन*, अगम कला प्रकाशन, दिल्ली, 1991. पृ0 45–46
11. चन्द्र मोती, *काशी का इतिहास*, विश्वविद्यालय प्रकाशन, वाराणसी, 1985 (द्वितीय संस्करण) पृ0 78
12. नारायण, ए0 के0 एवं पुरुषोत्तम सिंह, *एक्सकवेशन ऐट राजघाट*, (स्माल फाइंडस), तृतीय भाग, बी0 एच0 यू0, वाराणसी ,1977 पृ0 65 प्लेट XVII-A
13. नारायण, ए0 के0 एवं पुरुषोत्तम सिंह, *एक्सकवेशन ऐट राजघाट* (स्माल फाइंडस), तृतीय भाग, बी0 एच0 यू0, वाराणसी 1977, पृ0 61 प्लेट XIII
14. सिंह, बीरेन्द्र प्रताप एवं अशोक कुमार सिंह, *एक्सकवेशन ऐट सरायमोहाना* (1967–68) *भारती*–27, 2002–03, बुलेटिन ऑफ दि डिपार्टमेन्ट ऑफ ए0 आई0 एच0 सी0 ऐण्ड आर्कियोलॉजी, बी0 एच0 यू0, वाराणसी, पृ0 101, प्लेट XXIX-A, XXIX-B
15. जायसवाल, विदुला, *आदिकाशी से वाराणसी तक*, आर्यन बुक्स इन्टरनेषनल, नई दिल्ली, 2011, पृ0 138 चित्र 55
16. नारायण, ए0 के0 एवं पुरुषोत्तम सिंह, *एक्सकवेशन ऐट राजघाट* (स्माल फाइंडस), तृतीय भाग, बी0 एच0 यू0, वाराणसी, 1977 पृ0 59 प्लेट X/6.
17. नारायण, ए0 के0 एवं पुरुषोत्तम सिंह, *एक्सकवेशन ऐट राजघाट* (स्माल फाइंडस), तृतीय भाग,, बी0 एच0 यू0, वाराणसी 1977 पृ0 64 प्लेट XVI/7-12

18. नारायण, ए0 के0 एवं पुरुषोत्तम सिंह, *एक्सकवेशन ऐट राजघाट* (स्माल फाइंडस), तृतीय भाग, बी0 एच0 यू0, वाराणसी, 1977 पृ0 68 प्लेट XVIIB/1-2
19. सिंह, बीरेन्द्र प्रताप एवं सिंह, अशोक कुमार, एक्सकवेशन ऐट सरायमोहाना (1967–68) *भारती*–27, 2002–03, बुलेटिन ऑफ दि डिपार्टमेन्ट ऑफ ए0 आई0 एच0 सी0 ऐण्ड आर्कियोलॉजी, बी0 एच0 यू0, वाराणसी, पृ0 108, प्लेट XXXIII B/3
20. नारायण, ए0 के0 एवं पी0 के0 अग्रवाल, *एक्सकवेशन ऐट राजघाट,* चतुर्थ भाग (A-B),, बी0 एच0 यू0, वाराणसी, 1978 पृ0 146, 149 एवं प्लेट LXIX एवं LXX
21. सिंह, बीरेन्द्र प्रताप एवं सिंह, अशोक कुमार, एक्सकवेशन ऐट सरायमोहाना (1967–68) *भारती*–27, 2002–03, बुलेटिन ऑफ दि डिपार्टमेन्ट ऑफ ए0 आई0 एच0 सी0 ऐण्ड आर्कियोलॉजी, बी0 एच0 यू0, वाराणसी, पृ0 88, प्लेट XXIV A, XXIVB, XXV
22. नारायण, ए0 के0 एवं पुरुषोत्तम सिंह, *एक्सकवेशन ऐट राजघाट* (स्माल फाइंडस), तृतीय भाग, बी0 एच0 यू0, वाराणसी, 1977 पृ0 60, प्लेट XI A
23. नारायण, ए0 के0 एवं पुरुषोत्तम सिंह, *एक्सकवेशन ऐट राजघाट* (स्माल फाइंडस), तृतीय भाग, बी0 एच0 यू0, वाराणसी, 1977 पृ0 60, प्लेट XI B
24. नारायण, ए0 के0 एवं पुरुषोत्तम सिंह, *एक्सकवेशन ऐट राजघाट* (स्माल फाइंडस), तृतीय भाग, बी0 एच0 यू0, वाराणसी, 1977 पृ0 65, प्लेट XVIII
25. नारायण, ए0 के0 एवं पुरुषोत्तम सिंह, *एक्सकवेशन ऐट राजघाट* (स्माल फाइंडस), तृतीय भाग, बी0 एच0 यू0, वाराणसी, 1977 पृ0 69, प्लेट XX
26. नारायण, ए0 के0 एवं पुरुषोत्तम सिंह, *एक्सकवेशन ऐट राजघाट* (स्माल फाइंडस), तृतीय भाग, बी0 एच0 यू0, वाराणसी, 1977 पृ0 48, प्लेट VI
27. नारायण, ए0 के0 एवं पुरुषोत्तम सिंह, *एक्सकवेशन ऐट राजघाट* (स्माल फाइंडस), तृतीय भाग, बी0 एच0 यू0, वाराणसी, 1977 पृ0 51–52, प्लेट VII
28. देव, अत्रि (अनुवादक) *सुश्रुत संहिता* (धन्वंतरि विरचित), मोतीलाल बनारसीदास, दिल्ली, 1975, *कौमार भृत्य तन्त्र* XXXVI-9
29. अग्रवाल, वासुदेव शरण, दि टेराकोटा फिगरिन्स ऑफ अहिच्छत्रा, *एंशियेण्ट इण्डिया,* नं0–4, पृ0 119
30. नारायण, ए0 के0 एवं पी0 के0 अग्रवाल, *एक्सकवेशन ऐट राजघाट,* चतुर्थ भाग (A), बी0 एच0 यू0, वाराणसी 1978 पृ0 85
31. खण्डेलवाल, कार्ल (सम्पादक) *द गोल्डेन एज गुप्ता आर्ट एण्ड इम्पायर : प्रोतबंगस् इन इन्फ्लूयेंस,* मार्क पब्लिकेशन 1991, नम्बर 46.3232, पृ0 8
32. ई डब्लू0 बरलिंगम, *धम्मपदठ्ठकथा* (अंग्रेजी अनुवाद), पालिटेक्स सोसायटी, लुजाक ऐण्ड कम्पनी लिमिटेड, लन्दन, 1969, 3 / 230
33. सिंह, रामचन्द्र, *राजघाट की मृण्मूर्तियाँ,* उत्तर प्रदेश राज्य पुरातत्व विभाग, लखनऊ, 1978, पृ0 29 चित्र 35–40
34. कौसल्यायन, भदन्त आनन्द (अनुवाद), *जातक,* हिन्दी साहित्य सम्मेलन, प्रयाग, संवत् 2013, भाग–1, संख्या 72, *सीलवनाराज जातक*

    –– कौसल्यायन, भदन्त आनन्द (अनुवाद), *जातक,* हिन्दी साहित्य सम्मेलन, प्रयाग, संवत् 2011, भाग–5, संख्या 514 छद्दन्त जातक
35. कौसल्यायन, भदन्त आनन्द (अनुवाद), जातक, हिन्दी साहित्य सम्मेलन, प्रयाग, संवत् 2014, भाग–2, संख्या 163 *सुसीम जातक*
36. अग्रवाल, वासुदेव शरण, *क्ले सीलिंग्स फ्राम राजघाट, जे0 एन0 एस0 आई0,* XXIII पृ0 410–411

छाया चित्र 1 : शिशु एवं दीपिका लिये हुये मातृ देवी की प्रतिमा

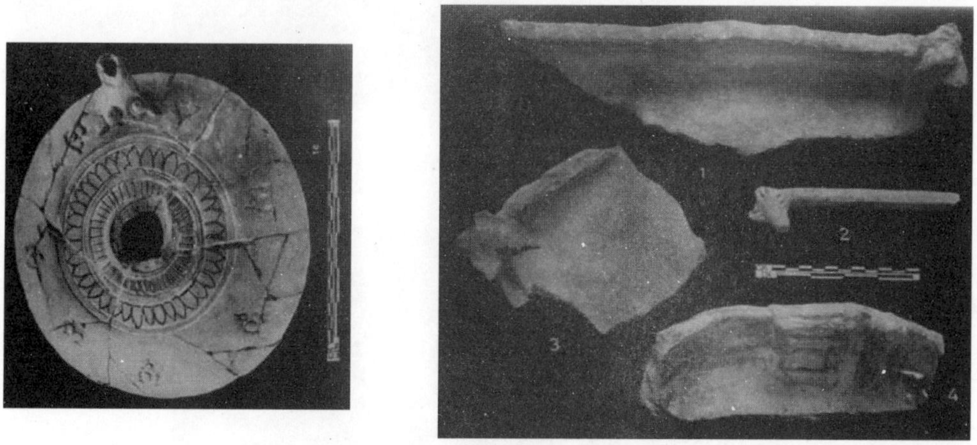

छाया चित्र 2, 3 : अर्चनाकुण्ड

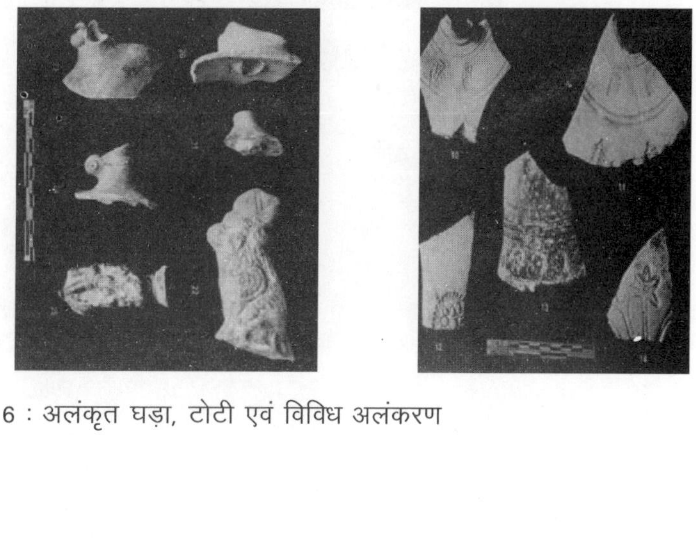

छाया चित्र 4, 5, 6 : अलंकृत घड़ा, टोटी एवं विविध अलंकरण

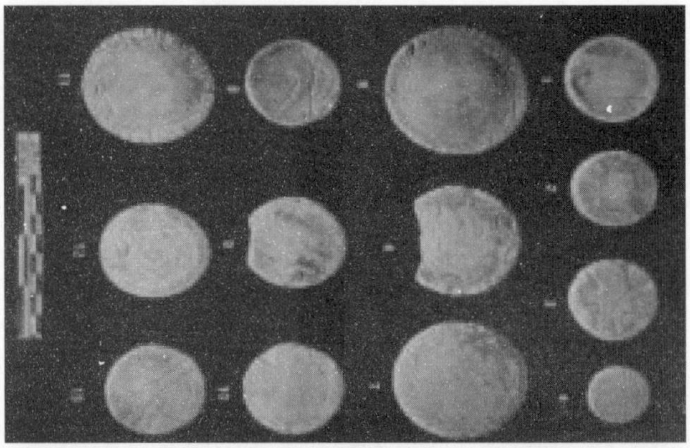

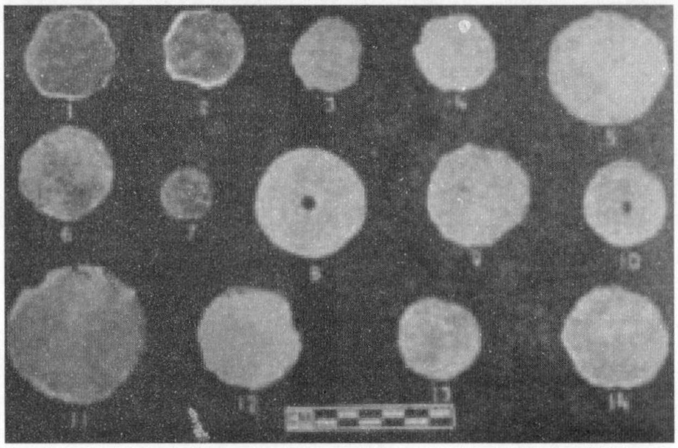

छाया चित्र 7, 8 : मृण्मण्डल

छाया चित्र 9, 10 पिट्टू (Pittu Game)

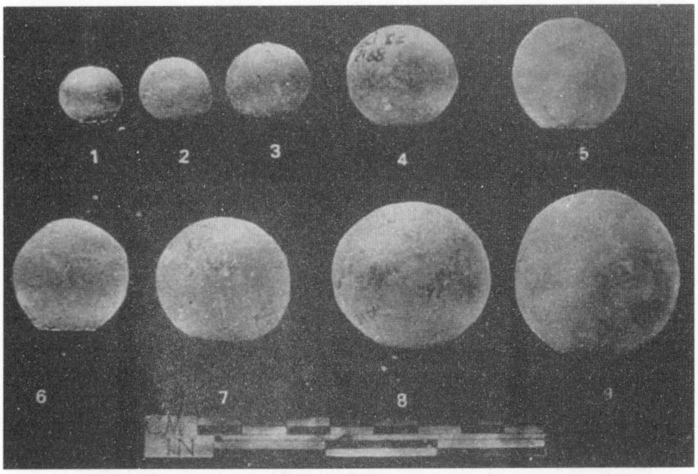

छाया चित्र 11 : गेंद

छाया चित्र 12 : गाड़ी का ढाँचा व पहिया

छाया चित्र 13, 14 खिलौना गाड़ी एवं नाव

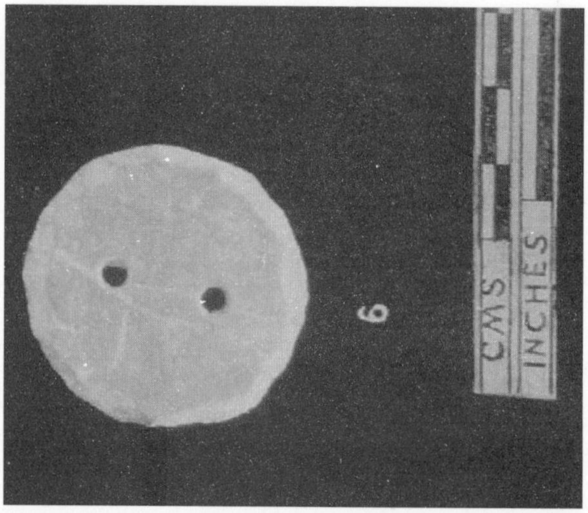

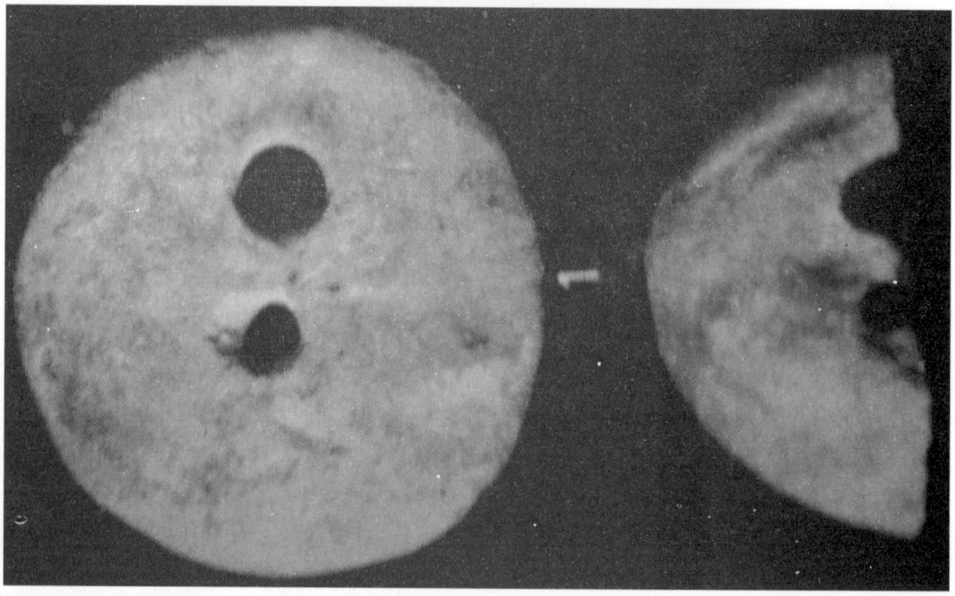

छाया चित्र 15, 16 : फिरकी

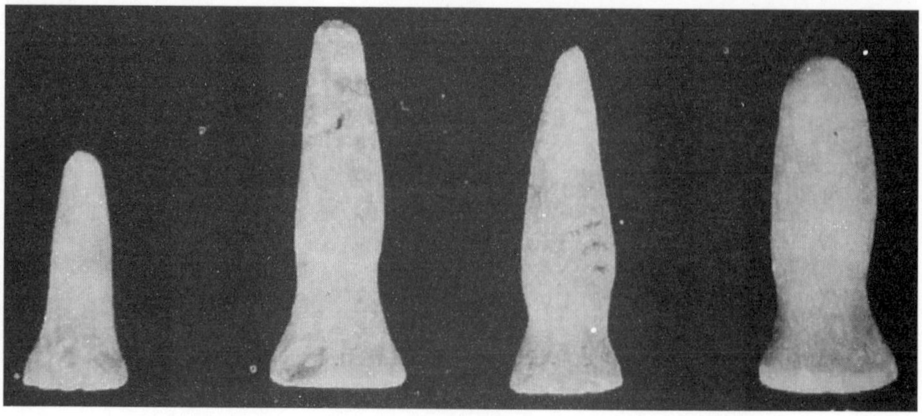

छाया चित्र 17 : शतरंज के पासे

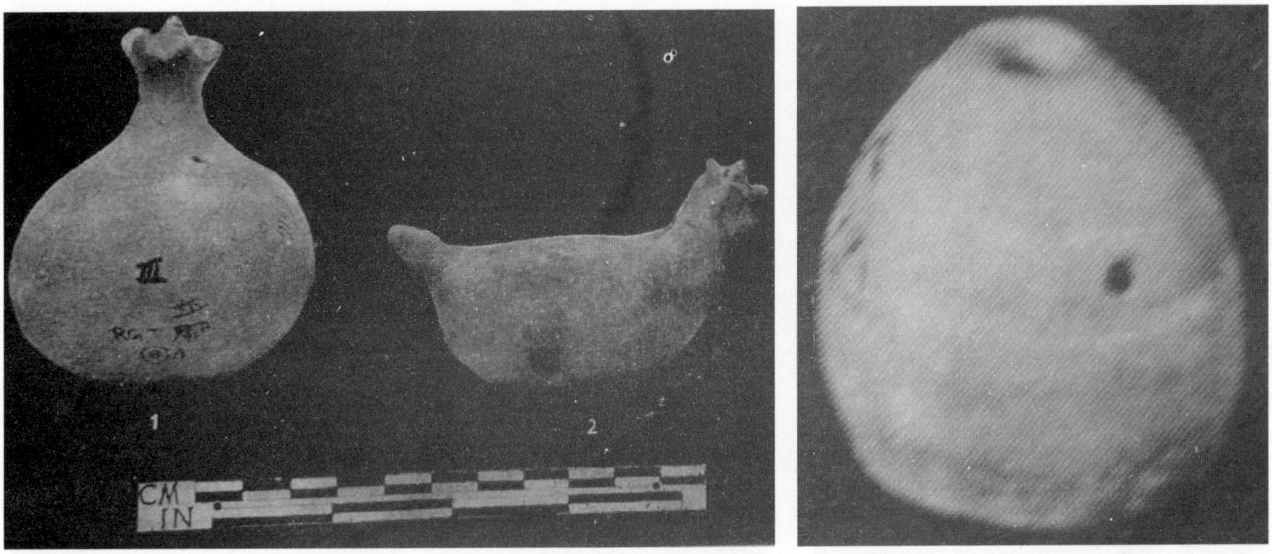

छाया चित्र 18,19 : झुनझुना

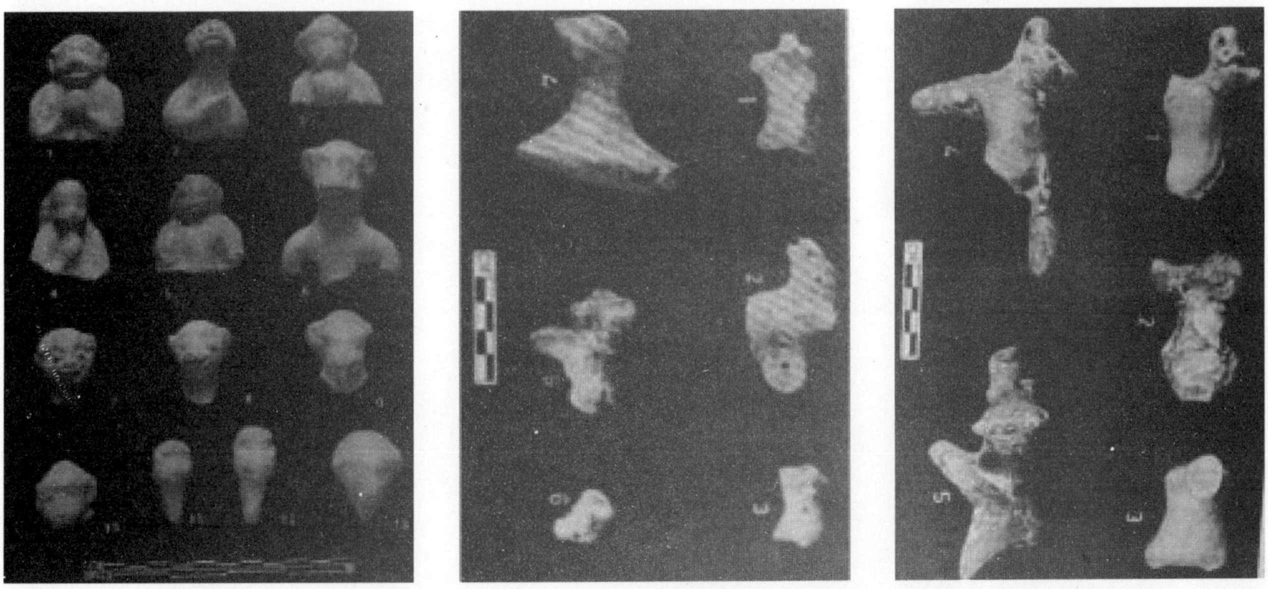

छाया चित्र 20, 21, 22 : बन्दर, पक्षी, गाय, कुत्ता एवं हाथी

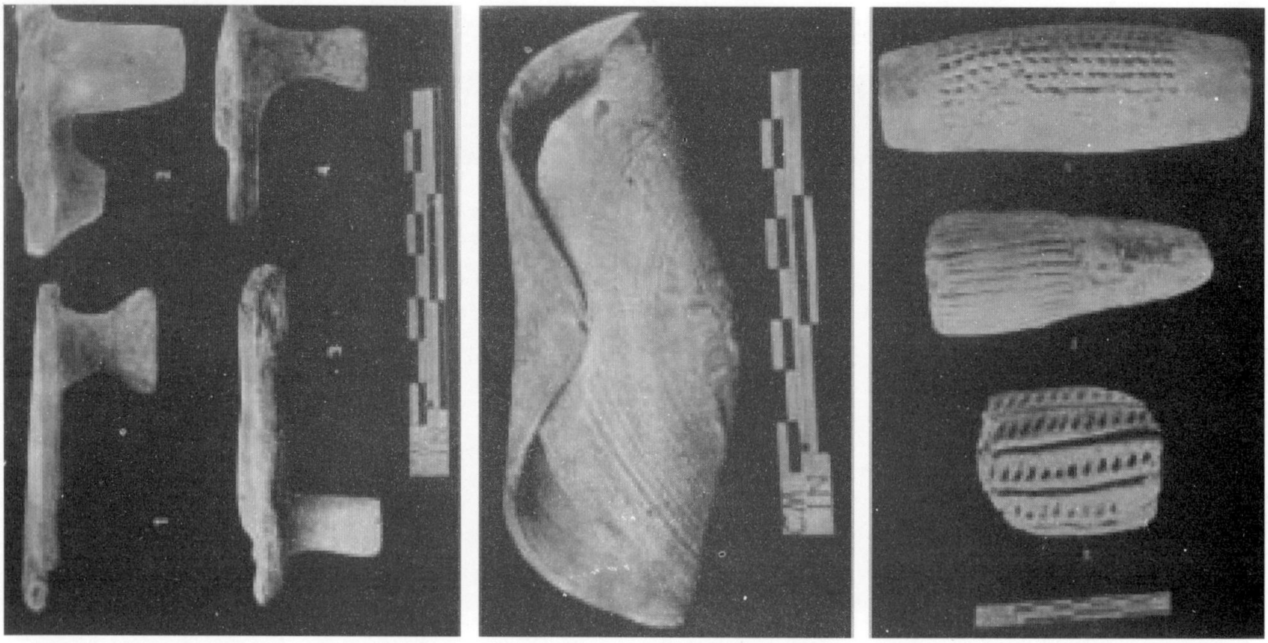

छाया चित्र संख्या 23, 24, 25 : पीढ़ा, सुतुही एवं लोढ़ा

छाया चित्र 26 : झाँवा

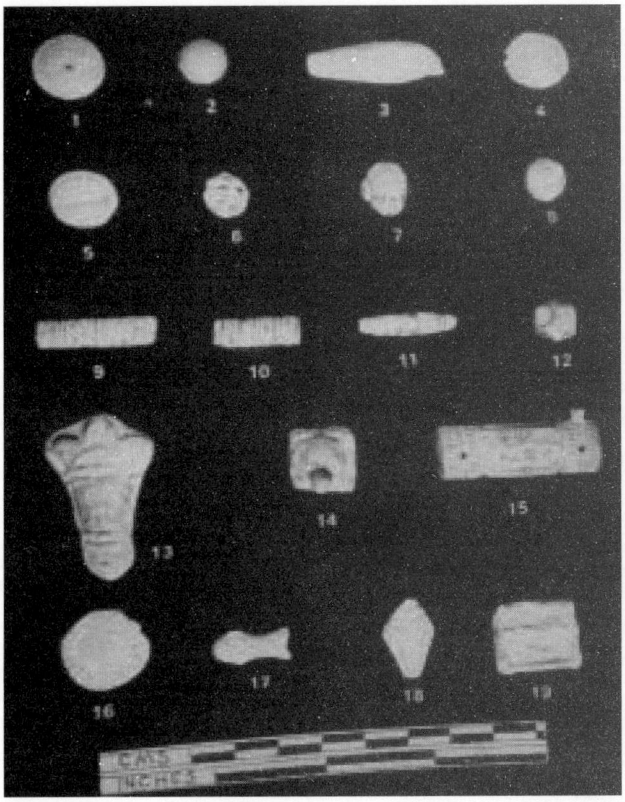

छाया चित्र 27 : मनके

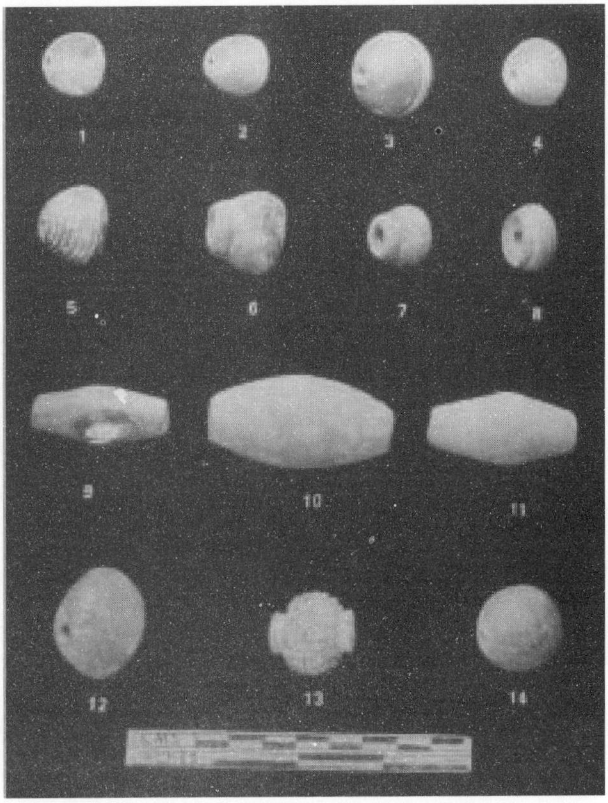

छाया चित्र 28 : मनके

छाया चित्र 29 : मातृदेवी

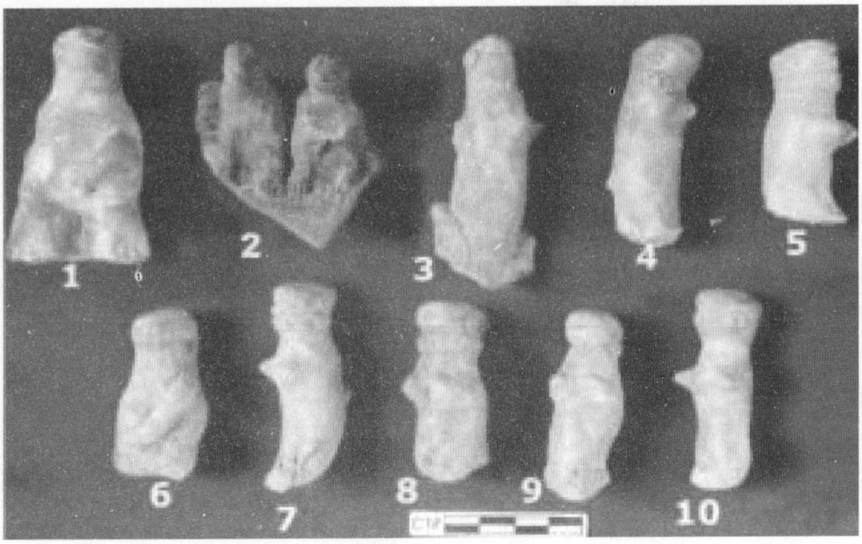

छाया चित्र 30 : नैगमेश

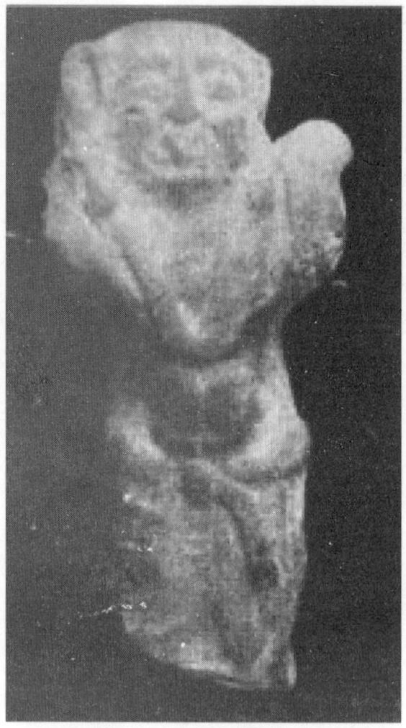

छाया चित्र 31, 32 33 : कुबेर, यक्ष एवं नाग

छाया चित्र 34, 35, 36 : गणेश, महिषासुरमर्दिनी, विष्णु, माता व शिशु एवं वादक

27

इलाहाबाद मण्डल की ताम्रपाषाणिक संस्कृति

प्रज्ञा मिश्रा

मानव संस्कृति के विकास में ताम्रपाषाणिक स्तर एक विशिष्ट युग की सूचना देता है। यह वह युग था, जब मनुष्य ने सर्वप्रथम प्रस्तर के उपकरणों के साथ–साथ ताँबे के उपकरणों का प्रयोग करना प्रारम्भ किया। इसी युग ने सर्वप्रथम नगरों का अभ्युदय देखा। दजला–फरात की घाटी, नील की उपत्यका, यूनान में क्रीट तथा भारतीय उपमहाद्वीप में मानव इतिहास में प्रथम नगरीकरण के जो साक्ष्य मिलते हैं वे सब ताम्रपाषाणिक स्तर से ही जुड़े हैं। इस युग से मनुष्य ने कृषि, व्यापार–वाणिज्य आदि क्षेत्रों में जो उपलब्धियाँ अर्जित की, उसने एक ऐसी व्यवस्था को जन्म दिया, जिसमें 'अधिशेष' की प्रबल सम्भावनाएं थीं।

भारतीय उपमहाद्वीप में ताम्रपाषाणिक संस्कृति के संदर्भ में जो सूचनाएं प्राप्त होती हैं, उनके आधार पर इन संस्कृतियों को कई वर्गों में विभाजित किया जाता है[1]। प्रारम्भ में प्राक् हड़प्पा ग्रामीण संस्कृतियों के दर्शन होते हैं, जो ताँबे का प्रयोग तो कर रही थी लेकिन उनसे जुड़े लोगों के जीवन में कोई क्रांतिकारी परिवर्तन नहीं आया था। ऐसी संस्कृतियों के दर्शन पाकिस्तान के बलूचिस्तान के मेहरगढ़ तथा अन्य स्थलों पर दिखाई पड़ते हैं। नाल[2], क्वेटा[3], झोब[4] संस्कृतियों को भी इसी श्रेणी में रखा जा सकता है। विकास के दूसरे चरण का निर्धारण वे संस्कृतियाँ करती हैं तो कालक्रम की दृष्टि से प्रौढ़ हड़प्पा संस्कृति के पहले की हैं लेकिन उनमें ऐसे तत्त्व भी दिखाई पड़ते हैं, जिन्हें हड़प्पा संस्कृति के बीजमंत्र के रूप में देखा जा सकता है, जैसे मिट्टी के बर्तनों पर पीपल के पत्ते का अंकन, मिट्टी की बनी हस्तमुष्ठिकाएं आदि। रहमानढेरी[5] के उत्खनन से इस धरातल से मिट्टी के बर्तनों पर खींचे गये ऐसे चिन्ह भी दिखाई पड़े, जिन्हें हड़प्पा संस्कृति की लिपि का पूर्व रूप समझा जाता है।

इस संस्कृति में कतिपय स्थलों में बस्ती के चारों ओर घेरेबंदी के भी प्रमाण मिलते हैं। इस चरण का विस्तार पहले चरण (प्राक्–हड़प्पा) की तुलना में बड़े भू–भाग पर दिखाई पड़ता है। पाकिस्तान के बलूचिस्तान, पंजाब और सिंध में इस प्रारम्भिक हड़प्पा संस्कृति के साक्ष्य तो मिलते ही हैं। भारत में राजस्थान, हरियाणा और

गुजरात से भी इस चरण के साक्ष्य उपलब्ध हुए हैं। संदर्भित स्थलों में मेहरगढ़, आमरी[6], कोटदीजी[7], राखीगढ़ी[9], बेरहना[10] तथा धौलावीरा[11] का उल्लेख किया जा सकता है। हड़प्पा संस्कृति स्वयं में ताम्रपाषाणिक ही है और यही स्थिति परवर्ती हड़प्पा संस्कृति की भी है। हड़प्पा संस्कृति के जीवनकाल में ही अथवा उसके विघटन के बाद भारत के विभिन्न क्षेत्रों में क्षेत्रीय ताम्रपाषाणिक संस्कृतियों के साक्ष्य मिलने लगते हैं। इस संदर्भ में राजस्थान में आहाड़ संस्कृति[12], मध्य प्रदेश के मालवा क्षेत्र में कायथा[13] और मालवा संस्कृतियाँ[14] तथा पश्चिमी महाराष्ट्र में नासिक–जोर्वे[15] संस्कृति उल्लेखनीय हैं।

ऊपरी गंगा घाटी में परवर्ती तथा गैरिक भाण्डीय और ताम्र निधियाँ[16] इस क्षेत्र की ताम्र–पाषाणिक संस्कृतियों के स्वरूप को उद्घाटित करती हैं तो मध्य गंगा घाटी में हाल के उत्खननों ने ताम्रपाषाणिक संस्कृति का अपेक्षाकृत व्यवस्थित रूप प्रस्तुत किया है। प्रमुख उत्खात स्थलों में इलाहाबाद में झूँसी[17], हेतापट्टी[18], श्रृंगवेरपुर[19], कौशाम्बी में कौशाम्बी[20], मिर्जापुर में अगियावीर[21], वाराणसी में रामनगर[22], राजघाट[23], अक्था[24], गाजीपुर में मसोनडीह[25], बलिया में खैराडीह[26], भूनाडीह[27] तथा वैना[28], गोरखपुर में सोहगौरा[29], नरहन[30], इमलीडीह[31] तथा सन्तकबीर नगर में लहुरादेवा[32] के नाम उल्लेखनीय हैं। विभिन्न स्थलों से प्राप्त तिथियों के आलोक में मध्यगंगा घाटी की ताम्रपाषाणिक संस्कृति को 1800 ई0पू0 से लेकर 700 ई0पू0 तक रखा जाता है[33]।

इलाहाबाद मण्डल में इलाहाबाद, कौशाम्बी, फतेहपुर और प्रतापगढ़ जनपद समाहित हैं। इनमें से भूतात्त्विक संरचना की दृष्टि से इलाहाबाद में कोराँव, बारा, करछना, मेजा के कुछ हिस्सों एवं कौशाम्बी में जमुना के तट पर स्थित पभोसा को छोड़कर मण्डल का शेष भाग मैदानी है जिसका निर्माण गंगा व उसकी सहायक नदियों ने किया है। कुछ समय पहले तक यह समझा जाता था कि इस क्षेत्र में मानव इतिहास का प्रारम्भ छठीं शताब्दी ई0पू0 से पहले नहीं हुआ होगा। लेकिन विगत् पाँच दशकों में प्राचीन इतिहास, संस्कृति एवं पुरातत्त्व विभाग, इलाहाबाद विश्वविद्यालय के निर्देशन में इलाहाबाद के दक्षिणी क्षेत्र में सघन पुरातात्त्विक अन्वेषणों के फलस्वरूप इस क्षेत्र में न केवल प्रातिनूतन कालीन जमाव प्रकाश में आए अपितु निम्न पुरापाषाणकाल से लेकर नवपाषाण काल तक मानव संस्कृति के विकास की अविरल कहानी के भी साक्ष्य मिले हैं। इतना ही नहीं, विभिन्न भूतात्त्विक जमावों से जीवाश्म भी बड़ी संख्या में उपलब्ध हुए हैं। प्राप्त साक्ष्यों से यह पता चलता है कि उच्च पुरापाषाणकाल के परवर्ती चरण में मनुष्य ने गंगा घाटी में प्रवेश किया। इस अनुपुरापाषाण काल से सम्बन्धित कई स्थल इलाहाबाद एवं प्रतापगढ़ जिलों में प्रकाश में आए हैं। मध्यपाषाण काल में स्थलों की संख्या में भारी वृद्धि दिखाई देती है। वह अब तक 200 से अधिक पहुँच गई है। ये मध्यपाषाणिक स्थल कौशाम्बी, इलाहाबाद तथा प्रतापगढ़ सभी जिलों में फैले दिखाई पड़ते हैं। प्रतापगढ़ जिले में स्थित सरायनाहरराय[34], महदहा[35] तथा दाँरीकला दमदमा[36] के उत्खननों से न केवल मध्यपाषाणिक शवाधान, अपितु जानवरों की हड्डियाँ भी बड़ी संख्या में उपलब्ध हुई हैं। पत्थर के उपकरणों के साथ–साथ हड्डी के बने उपकरण भी प्राप्त हुए हैं। निश्चय ही पुरातात्त्विक दृष्टि से यह एक बहुत बड़ी उपलब्धि समझी जाती है।

प्रस्तुत शोध पत्र में इलाहाबाद मण्डल की ताम्रपाषाणिक संस्कृति की रूपरेखा प्रस्तुत करने का प्रयास किया गया है। इस संदर्भ में यह उल्लेखनीय है कि इलाहाबाद, कौशाम्बी व प्रतापगढ़ में ऐसे अनेक स्थल प्रकाश में आए हैं, जिनसे प्राप्त होने वाले पुरावशेषों के आधार पर उन्हें ताम्रपाषाणिक कहा जा सकता है। कौशाम्बी जनपद में कौशाम्बी के अतिरिक्त कड़ाधाम[37] तथा महगाँव[38] के पुरास्थल इस कोटि में आते हैं तो इलाहाबाद में बेलनघाटी और गंगा के मैदान में ऐसे स्थलों की संख्या दो दर्जन से अधिक दिखाई पड़ती है। प्रतापगढ़ में भी ऐसे स्थलों की संख्या 30 के लगभग है[39]। लेकिन जिन स्थलों पर उत्खनन का कार्य हुआ है, उनकी संख्या सीमित ही है। इस संदर्भ में बेलन घाटी में कोल्डिहवा[40] व खजुरी[41] तथा गंगा के मैदान में झूँसी, हेतापट्टी और श्रृंगवेरपुर का नाम उल्लेखनीय है। कौशाम्बी में लम्बे समय तक उत्खनन का कार्य हुआ है। वहाँ की रक्षाभित्ति के पास

उत्खनन से कुछ ऐसे साक्ष्य मिले हैं जिन्हें भी ताम्रपाषाणिक युग से सम्बन्धित किया जा सकता है।

सभी उत्खात स्थल नदियों के किनारे दिखाई पड़ते हैं। कौशाम्बी जमुना के तट पर है तो झूँसी, हेतापट्टी व श्रृंगवेरपुर गंगा के तट पर, कोल्डिहवा व खजुरी बेलन नदी के बायें व दायें किनारों पर स्थित हैं। इन उत्खात स्थलों से जो मिट्टी के बर्तन प्राप्त हुए हैं उन्हें लाल, कृष्णलेपित, कृष्णलोहित आदि उपवर्गों में विभाजित किया गया है। बर्तन चाक पर बन रहे थे। यद्यपि हाथ के बने बर्तन भी कभी–कभी मिल जाते हैं। पहाड़ी इलाके में (कोल्डिहवा व खजुरी) बर्तन बनाने में प्रयुक्त मिट्टी अच्छी तरह गूंथी नहीं दिखाई पड़ती। लेकिन झूँसी, हेतापट्टी, श्रृंगवेरपुर के पात्र अपेक्षाकृत अच्छी तरह गूंथी मिट्टी के बने हैं। मैदानी स्थलों के पात्र पहाड़ी क्षेत्रों की तुलना में अच्छी तरह पके दिखाई पड़ते हैं। प्रमुख पात्र–प्रकारों में तरह–तरह के कटोरे, थालियाँ, तसले, हाँड़ी, अनाज रखने के लिए प्रयुक्त होने वाले बड़े बर्तन, नाद, मटके आदि उल्लेखनीय हैं। यदा–कदा कुछ पात्रों पर चित्रण के साक्ष्य भी उपलब्ध हो जाते हैं। इस संदर्भ में कोल्डिहवा विशेष रूप से उल्लेखनीय है। चित्रण के अतिरिक्त पात्रों पर अलंकरण की अन्य विधाएं भी दृष्टिगत होती हैं। इसमें आसंजन तथा बर्तन की सतह पर किसी नोंकदार उपकरण से कुछ अलंकरण बना देना आदि हैं। पात्रों की विविधता को देखकर यह आसानी से समझा जा सकता है कि इनका प्रयोग तरह–तरह के कार्यों में किया जाता था। खाने–पीने में प्रयुक्त होने वाले पात्रों के अतिरिक्त संग्रहण आदि में भी उनके प्रयोग का संकेत मिलता है। तत्कालीन कुम्भकार ने अपने पेशे में दक्षता प्राप्त कर ली थी और वह न केवल पात्रों का निर्माण कर रहा था अपितु उपयोगिता के साथ–साथ इन पात्रों के माध्यम से वह अपने सौन्दर्यबोध को भी मुखरित कर रहा था।

ताँबें, हड्डी तथा पत्थर के बने उपकरण उत्खात स्थलों से प्राप्त होते हैं। ताँबे के उपकरणों की संख्या अत्यंत सीमित दिखाई पड़ती है। हड्डी के बने उपकरणों में बाणाग्र विशेष रूप से उल्लेखनीय हैं। ये निर्माण के विभिन्न चरणों का भी संकेत करते हैं जिनसे यह पता चलता है कि इनका निर्माण संदर्भित स्थलों पर ही किया जाता रहा होगा। कोल्डिहवा, खजुरी, झूँसी, हेतापट्टी और श्रृंगवेरपुर से लघुपाषाणोकरण भी मिले हैं। कोल्डिहवा और खजुरी चूँकि विन्ध्य क्षेत्र में स्थित हैं इसलिए इन स्थलों से प्राप्त होने वाले लघुपाषाणोपकरणों की संख्या अधिक दिखाई पड़ती है। प्राप्त उपकरणों में तरह तरह के फलक, नोंक, बाणाग्र, खुरचनी, अर्द्धचन्द्र, त्रिभुज, समलम्ब चतुर्भुज आदि उल्लेखनीय हैं। इन उपकरणों के साथ–साथ क्रोड, फलक आदि भी बड़ी संख्या में मिलते हैं। इनका निर्माण चल्सेडिनी, चर्ट, कार्नेलियन, अगेट, क्वार्ट्ज जैसे उपरत्नों पर किया गया है। ये उपकरण संदर्भित स्थलों पर ही बनाये जाते थे। इन उपकरणों के अतिरिक्त पत्थर के सिल–बट्टे, गोफन (Sling ball) आदि भी उत्खात स्थलों से मिलते हैं। कुछ आभूषणों की भी प्राप्ति होती है। इनमें मनकें, चूड़ियाँ आदि विशेष रूप से उल्लेखनीय हैं। मनके प्रायः उपरत्नों पर ही बने दिखाई पड़ते हैं। लेकिन कभी–कभी वे मिट्टी, हड्डी व ताँबे आदि के भी मिल जाते हैं।

प्राप्त साक्ष्यों से यह पता चलता है कि लोग कृषिकर्मी थे। चावल, जौ, गेहूँ के साथ–साथ मूंग, मसूर, तिल, अलसी, मटर आदि के साक्ष्य उपलब्ध हुए हैं। पालतू पशुओं में गाय, भैंस, भेड़, बकरी, कुत्ते व सुअर का उल्लेख किया जा सकता है, तो जंगली पशुओं में तरह–तरह के हिरन व जंगली सुअर आदि का। उत्खात स्थलों से चिड़ियों तथा जलचरों (मछली, कछुआ आदि) की भी हड्डियाँ उपलब्ध हुई हैं। प्राप्त साक्ष्यों से यह संकेत मिलता है कि तत्कालीन लोगों के भोज्य पदार्थ में मांस की अहम भूमिका थी।

उत्खात स्थलों में से किसी से भी पत्थर की प्रतिमाएं नहीं प्राप्त हुई हैं। लेकिन कोल्डिहवा से मिट्टी की मातृदेवी की प्रतिमा प्राप्त हुई है। इस संदर्भ में यह उल्लेखनीय है कि विन्ध्य क्षेत्र में मातृदेवी की उपासना के संकेत उच्च पुरापाषाण काल से मिलने लगते हैं। बेलन घाटी में लोंहदा नाले के पास हड्डी की बनी मातृदेवी की प्रतिमा 24,000 ई0पू0 के धरातल से प्राप्त हुई है[42] तो सोन घाटी में बघोर–प्रथम से भी अनुपुरापाषाण काल

में मातृदेवी की पूजा के संकेत मिलने लगते हैं[43]।

आवास के संदर्भ में भी सूचनाएँ मिलती हैं। नरकुल और बांस की खपाचियों से बनी झोपड़ियों के संकेत मिलते हैं जिन पर अन्दर व बाहर दोनों तरफ से गीली मिट्टी से लेपन किया जाता था। इनके किनारे स्तम्भगर्त के साक्ष्य भी मिलते हैं। ये झोपड़ियाँ आकार–प्रकार में गोल या अण्डाकार दिखाई पड़ती हैं। कोल्डिहवा से मिट्टी के बने आवास के बारे में सूचना मिलती है। इनके साथ ही साथ हमें फर्श के भी प्रमाण मिलते हैं, जिनके निर्माण में मिट्टी और मोरम को कूटे जाने के साक्ष्य मिलते हैं। इस धरातल से चूल्हे भी मिलने लगते हैं। मकान की छत के बारे में साक्ष्य नहीं मिलते लेकिन नृतत्वशास्त्रीय सूचनाओं के आधार पर यह अनुमान लगाया जाता है कि झोपड़ियों की छत नुकीली रही होगी, जबकि मिट्टी के बने मकान की छत ढलुआ। कौशाम्बी को छोड़कर किसी भी स्थल से इस युग में ईंट के प्रयोग की सूचना नहीं मिलती और न ही खपरैल के प्रयोग की।

इलाहाबाद मण्डल की ताम्रपाषाणिक संस्कृति के तिथि निर्धारण में पुरातात्त्विक जमावों के अतिरिक्त मिट्टी के बर्तन, लघुपाषाणोपकरण आदि के साथ–साथ कतिपय उत्खात स्थलों से प्राप्त रेडियो कार्बन तिथियों का भी सहारा लिया जाता है। इस तिथि निर्धारण में गंगा घाटी के कतिपय अन्य स्थलों से प्राप्त तिथियाँ भी सहायक सिद्ध होती हैं। कोल्डिहवा[44] से इस धरातल से दो तिथियाँ प्राप्त हुई है जो 1450 ± 120 ई0पू0 तथा 1035 ± 155 ई0पू0 की है। श्रृंगवेरपुर[45] से प्राप्त होने वाली तिथि 850 ई0पू0 की है। झूँसी[46] से प्राप्त होने वाली तिथि 1340 ± 90 ई0पू0 की है। इस संदर्भ में यह उल्लेखनीय है कि सोहगौरा[47] के संदर्भित धरातल से दो तिथियाँ – 1235 ± 130 ई0पू0 तथा 1335 ± 110 ई0पू0 प्राप्त हुई हैं। नरहन[48] से भी दो तिथियाँ प्राप्त हुई हैं जो 1123 ± 110 ई0पू0 तथा 1133 ± 110 ई0पू0 की हैं। खैराडीह[49] से तीन तिथियाँ प्रकाश में आयी हैं जो 1120 ± 90 ई0पू0, 1030 ± 160 ई0पू0 तथा 940 ± 150 ई0पू0 है। चिराँद[50] से पाँच तिथियाँ उपलब्ध हुई हैं जो 720 ± 105 ई0पू0, 1050 ± 85 ई0पू0, 1540 ± 90 ई0पू0, 1585 ± 100 ई0पू0, 1655 ± 100 ई0पू0 की हैं। सेनुवार[51] के नवपाषाणिक/ताम्रपाषाणिक संधि स्थल से चार तिथियाँ प्राप्त हुई हैं जो 1770 ± 120 ई0पू0, 1660 ± 120 ई0पू0, 1500 ± 110 ई0पू0 तथा 1400 ± 110 ई0पू0 की हैं। लहुरादेवा[52] से प्राप्त तिथि 2000 ई0पू0 के आसपास की दिखाई देती है। इस तरह प्राप्त साक्ष्यों के आलोक में इलाहाबाद मण्डल की ताम्रपाषाणिक संस्कृति को 1500 ई0पू0 से 700 ई0पू0 के बीच रखा जा सकता है। इस संदर्भ में यह उल्लेखनीय है कि इस क्षेत्र में 1100 ई0पू0 के आसपास लोगों को लोहे की जानकारी हो गयी थी। इस आधार पर ताम्रपाषाणिक संस्कृति को दो चरणों में रखने की आवश्यकता प्रतीत होती है। प्रथम चरण 1500 ई0पू0 से लेकर 1100 ई0पू0 का होगा जो शुद्ध रूप से ताम्रपाषाणिक है तो परवर्ती चरण 1100 ई0पू0 से लेकर 700 ई0पू0 के अन्तर्गत रखा जा सकता है। इस उपचरण में प्रथम उपचरण के सारे अवयव विद्यमान दिखाई पड़ते हैं, परिवर्तन केवल इतना ही दिखाई देता है कि अब लोगों को लोहे की जानकारी हो गयी थी।

इलाहाबाद मण्डल की ताम्रपाषाणिक संस्कृति के उद्‌भव के लिए हमें विन्ध्य क्षेत्र की ओर दृष्टिपात करना होगा, क्योंकि उस क्षेत्र में निम्न पुरापाषाणकाल से लेकर नवपाषाण काल तक संस्कृतियों में सातत्य दिखाई पड़ता है। कोल्डिहवा के उत्खनन से इस बात के संकेत मिलते हैं कि यहाँ की ताम्रपाषाणिक संस्कृति नवपाषाणिक संस्कृति से उद्‌भूत हुई होगी। इस संदर्भ में यह उल्लेखनीय है कि यदि हम नवपाषाणिक और ताम्रपाषाणिक संस्कृतियों के लक्षणों पर दृष्टिपात करे तो हमें यह जानकारी मिलती है कि इन दोनों संस्कृतियों में आवास निर्माण एक ही तरह का दिखाई पड़ता हैं। दोनों संस्कृतियों में पशु पालन और कृषि के साक्ष्य भी लगभग एक जैसे हैं। साथ ही, पशुपालन और कृषि पर आग्रह के साथ हमें इस बात के भी प्रमाण मिलते हैं कि लोग अब भी जंगली जानवरों का शिकार करते थे तथा मछली, कछुए जैसे जलीय जन्तु उनके आहार के प्रमुख अंग थे। इतना ही नहीं, चिड़ियों के शिकार की भी सूचना मिलती है। हड्डी के बने बाणाग्र दोनों संस्कृतियों में दिखते हैं। यही

स्थिति लघुपाषाणोपकरणों की भी है। ताम्रपाषाणिक पात्र परम्परा मे मिट्टी के बर्तनों पर गाढ़ा लेपन, बर्तनों के चमकाने का प्रयास, उनके निचले हिस्से को कभी–कभी खुरदुरा बनाना तथा अलंकरण में आसंजन्न विधि का प्रयोग आदि ऐसे आयाम हैं, जिनके मूल स्वरूप नवपाषाणिक पात्र–परम्परा में देखे जा सकते हैं, तो दूसरी तरफ नवपाषाणिक संस्कृति के कतिपय पात्र प्रकार हमें ताम्रपाषाणिक संस्कृति में मिल जाते हैं। इसी तरह कृष्ण–लोहित पात्र परम्परा, डोरीदार पात्र–परम्परा, रूक्ष पात्र परम्परा, चमकीली काली पात्र परम्परा, भी दोनों संस्कृतियों में समान रूप से दिखाई पड़ती है। इन साक्ष्यों से स्पष्ट हो जाता है कि इलाहाबाद मण्डल की ताम्रपाषाणिक संस्कृति के उद्भव के सम्यक् अवबोध के लिए नवपाषाणिक संस्कृति की ओर दृष्टिपात करना आवश्यक हो जाता है।

इलाहाबाद मण्डल की ताम्रपाषाणिक संस्कृति ने भावी संस्कृति के लिए मार्ग प्रशस्त किया। इस संदर्भ में यह उल्लेखनीय है कि झूँसी में प्राक् एन0बी0पी0 धरातल का संस्कृतिक जमाव 4.35 मीटर मोटा दिखाई पड़ता है। इसे दो भागों में विभक्त किया गया है – प्रारम्भिक चरण 2.75 मीटर तथा परवर्ती चरण 1.60 मीटर मोटा है। इस मोटे जमाव ने यह रूप ग्रहण करने मे कई शताब्दियाँ देखी होंगी। प्राप्त साक्ष्यों से यह पता चलता है कि यहाँ पर 1100 ई0पू0 के आस–पास लोग निश्चय ही लोहे से परिचित हो गये थे। झूँसी, श्रृंगवेरपुर, हेतापट्टी आदि के उत्खननों से यह संकेत मिलता है कि ताम्रपाषाणिक संस्कृति के परवर्ती चरण तथा उत्तरी काली ओपदार (एन0बी0पी0) भाण्डीय संस्कृति के बीच समय का अन्तराल नहीं दिखाई पड़ता। शताब्दियाँ–दर–शताब्दियाँ बीतती गयीं, लेकिन इनके साथ ही साथ मानव विकास की कहानी भी आगे बढ़ती गयी। छठीं शती ई0पू0 में झूँसी, श्रृंगवेरपुर, कौशाम्बी नगर के रूप में दिखाई पड़ते हैं। इस संदर्भ में यह उल्लेखनीय है कि प्रारम्भिक बौद्ध साहित्य और पुरातात्त्विक साक्ष्यों में इस बात के साक्ष्य मिलते हैं कि छठीं शती ई0पू0 में मध्य गंगाघाटी में नगरीकरण का युग था। उपरोक्त स्थलों के अतिरिक्त वाराणसी, वैशाली, राजगृह, चम्पा, श्रावस्ती आदि उस युग के प्रमुख नगर थे। भारतीय पुरातत्त्व के संदर्भ में इस नगरीकरण की प्रक्रिया को 'द्वितीय नगरीकरण' के रूप में जाना जाता है। कहने की आवश्यकता नहीं कि ताम्रपाषाणिक संस्कृति ने वह आधार प्रस्तुत किया, जिस पर सातवीं/छठीं शती ई0पू0 के द्वितीय नगरीकरण का राजप्रासाद खड़ा किया जा सका। इस संदर्भ में यह उल्लेखनीय है कि भारत में दो अलग–अलग क्षेत्रों में दो विभिन्न युगों में नगरीकरण के दर्शन होते है। पश्चिमोत्तर भारत में नगरीकरण का जो स्वरूप दिखाई पड़ता है, उसके मूल में ताम्रपाषाणिक संस्कृति है, लेकिन गंगाघाटी का नगरीकरण लौहयुग से सम्बन्धित दिखाई पड़ता है।

संक्षेप में, इलाहाबाद के उत्खात पुरातात्त्विक साक्ष्यों के आलोक में यह कहा जा सकता है :

1. मध्य गंगाघाटी के अन्य अंचलों की तरह इलाहाबाद मण्डल में भी ताम्रपाषाणिक संस्कृति के अवशेष प्राप्त हुए हैं।
2. झूँसी से प्राप्त रेडियो कार्बन तिथि के अनुसार इस क्षेत्र में ताम्रपाषाणिक संस्कृति की प्राचीनतम सीमा रेखा फिलहाल 15वीं शताब्दी ई0पू0 में खींची जा सकती है।
3. प्राप्त साक्ष्यों से यह संकेत मिलता है कि इलाहाबाद मण्डल की ताम्रपाषाणिक संस्कृति के बीजमंत्र विन्ध्यक्षेत्र की ताम्रपाषाणिक संस्कृति में छिपे दिखाई पड़ते हैं। इस संदर्भ में इलाहाबाद के कोरांव सम्भाग में स्थित कोल्डिहवा के साक्ष्य विशेष रूप से उल्लेखनीय हैं।
4. इलाहाबाद मण्डल की ताम्र पाषाणिक संस्कृति के दो उपचरण दिखाई पड़ते हैं। प्रारम्भिक उपचरण में लोहे के उपकरण नहीं मिलते; इसकी तिथि 1500 ई0पू0 – 1100 ई0पू0 प्राप्त रेडियोकार्बन तिथियों के आलोक में निर्धारित की जा सकती है। जबकि द्वितीय चरण 11वीं शताब्दी ई0पू0 से 7वीं शताब्दी ई0पू0 के मध्य का दिखाई पड़ता है। इस कालखण्ड में लोहे के उपकरणों का प्रयोग सीमित दायरे में प्रारम्भ हो चुका था। लेकिन संस्कृति के अन्य पक्ष पहले जैसे ही चलते दिखाई पड़ते हैं। इतना अवश्य है कि

इस धरातल से प्राप्त होने वाली पात्र परम्पराओं मे पहले की तुलना में अधिक निखार दिखाई पड़ता है।

5. जैसा कि पहले स्पष्ट किया जा चुका है कि इलाहाबाद मण्डल में ताम्रपाषाणिक संस्कृति नवपाषाणिक और प्रारम्भिक ऐतिहासिक संस्कृतियों के बीच एक संक्रमणकालीन अवस्था की द्योतक है। एक तरफ इस संस्कृति के विभिन्न अवयव नवपाषाणिक संस्कृति में दिखाई पड़ते हैं तो दूसरी तरफ इस संस्कृति ने प्रारम्भिक ऐतिहासिक संस्कृति के लिए मार्ग प्रशस्त किया। झूँसी और हेतापट्टी के उत्खननों से नवपाषाणकाल से लेकर प्रारम्भिक ऐतिहासिक युग तक संस्कृतियों के विकास का अविरल प्रवाह दिखाई पड़ता है। अतः मध्य गंगाघाटी की छठी शती ई0पू0 की नागर संस्कृति के स्वरूप को समझने के लिए इस क्षेत्र की ताम्रपाषाणिक संस्कृति के स्वरूप को समझना अपरिहार्य हो जाता है।

References

1. Agrawal, D.P. 1971. *The Copper Bronze Age in India.* Munshiram Manoharlal, Delhi, pp. 12-44; Agrawal, D.P. 1984. *The Archaeology of India.* Select book Service Syndicate, New Delhi, pp. 90-192; Asthana, Shashi 1985. *Pre-Harappan Cultures of India and the Borderlands.* Books and Books, New Delhi; Agrawal D.P. and J.S. Kharakwal, 2003, *Bronze and Iron ages in South Asia,* Aryan Books International, New Delhi, pp. 22-119; D.K. Chakrabarti 2006. *The Oxford Companion to Indian Archaeology*: Oxford University Press, pp. 115-135; Jarrige, Jean, Francois Jarrige, Richard, H. Meadow and Genzaque Quivron (1995) Ed. *Mehrgarh, Field Reports* 1974-1985 Karanhi Government of Sindh; Misra, V.D. 2007. Food Production and Sattlements-Transition from Neolithic to the Chalcolithic: *A Golden Chain of Civilization : Indic, Iranic, Semitic and Hellenic* up to 600 BC. Vol. I Part 4, (Ed. G.C. Pande) Project of History of Indian Service, Philosophy and culture, 36 Tuglakabad, Institutional area, New Delhi, pp. 132-149.
2. Sankalia, H.D. 1974. *The Prehistory and Protohistory of India and Pakistan,* Deccan College Post Graduate and Research Intitute, Pune, pp. 318-320.
3. Chakravarti, D.K. 1999. *India, an Archaeological History,* Oxford University press, Oxford, pp. 126-128.
4. Chakravarti, .D.K. 1999. *op. cit.* pp. 126-128.
5. Durrani, F.A. 1981. Indus Civilization : Evidence west of Indus, *Indus Civilzation, New perspective* (ed. A.H. Dani), pp. 133-137; see also Shashi Asthana 1985., *Pre Harappan Cultures of India and the Borderlands,* pp. 94-97.
6. Majumdar, N.G. 1934. Exploration in Sind, *Memoir of Archaeological Survey of India,* No. 48; Wheeler Mortimar (Sir) 1968. *The Indus Civilization,* Cambridge University Press, Cambridge, pp. 18-20.
7. Khan, F.A. 1965. Excavation at Kot-Dizi, *Pakistan Archaeology,* No. 2, pp. 11-86; F.A. Khan 1981. Kot-Dizi Culture- its greatness, *Indus Civilization, New Perspective* (Ed. A.H. Dani), pp. 15-24.
8. Lal, B.B. et.al., 2003, The Exacavations at Kalibangan the *Early Harappans,* p. 51.
9. Nath, A. 1998. Rakhigarhi, A Harappan Metropolis in the Saraswati- Drishadvati Divide, *Puratattva* No. 28, pp. 39-45; Nath, A. 1999. Further Excavtion at Rakhigarhi, *Purātattava* No. 29, pp. 46-49.
10. Rao, L.S. Nandani V. Sahu, U.S. Shastry, Pravesh Sahu and Samir Diwan 2006. Bhirrana Exacavations 2005-2006, *Puratattva* No. 36, pp. 45-49.
11. Bisht, R.S. 1991, Dholavira, New Horizon of the Indus Civilization, *Purātattva*-20, pp. 71-82.
12. Sankalia, H.D., S.B. Deo and Z.D. Ansari 1969, *Exacavations at Ahar* (Tambavati) 1962; See also V.N. Mishra 1967, *Pre and Protohistory of the Berach Basin, South Rajasthan;* also M.K. Dhavalikar 1997, *Indian Protohistory;* D.P. Agrawal and J.S. Kharakwal 2006. *Bronze and Iron Ages in South Asia;* H.D. Sankalia 1974. *Prehistory and Protohistory of India and Pakistan.*
13. Wakankar, V.S. 1967. Kayatha Excavations, *Journal of Vikram University;* Dhavalikar, M.K. 1970, Kaytha : A New Chalcolithic Culture of India 7(2) pp. 85-93; Dhavalikar, M.K. 1979. Early Farming Cultures of Central India, *Eassays in Indian Protohistory* (ed.) D.P. Agrawal and D.K.

Chakravarti, pp. 299-345; M.K. Dhavalikar 1997, *Indian Protohistory*; D.P. Agrawal and J.S. Kharakwal 2003, *Bronze and Iron Ages in South Asia*, pp. 153-55.

14. Sankalia, H.D., S.B. Deo and Z.D. Ansari 1958. *Exacavations at Maheswar and Navdatoli*; Sankalia, H.D. et al. (1971) *Chalocolithic Navdatoli*; Sankalia, H.D. (1974), *Prehitory and Protohistory of India and Pakistan*; M.K. Dhavalikar (1997), *Indian Protohistory*; D.P. Agrawal and J.S. Kharakwal (2003), *Bronze and Iron Ages in South Asia.*
15. Agrawal D.P. and J.S. Kharakwal 2003. *Op. cit.* pp. 167-170.
16. Agrawal D.P. and J.S. Kharakwal 2003. *Op.cit.* p. 211.
17. Misra, V.D., B.B. Misra, J.N. Pandey and J.N. Pal 1996, A preliminary report on the excavations at Jhushi, *Prāgdhārā* No. 6, pp. 63-66; Misra V.D., J.N. Pal and M.C. Gupta 1999, Further excavations at Jhusi, Allahabad, *Prāgdhārā* No. 9, pp. 43-49;
    Misra, V.D. J.N. Pal and M.C. Gupta 2000. Further Excavations at Jhusi, *Prāgdhārā* No. 10, pp. 23-30.
18. Pal, J.N. and M.C. Gupta 2005. Excavations at Hetapatti (Allahabad District) : Some Prelimnary observations, *Journal of Interdisciplinary Studies in History and Archaeology*, Vol. 2. No. 2 pp. 325-330.
19. Lal, B.B. and K.N. Dikshit 1997. *Śṛiṅgaverpura : A key site for the Protohistory and Early History of the Central Ganga Valley*, pp. 103-307; Indian Prehistory 1980 (ed. V.D. Misra and J.N. Pal).
20. Sharma, G.R. 1960. *Excavations at Kaushambi Defences and Śyenacifi* : Department of Ancient History, Culture and Archaeology, University of Allahabad; Sharma, G.R. 1969. Excavations at Kaushambi. *Memoir of Archaeological Survey of India*, No. 74.
21. Singh, P. and Ashok Singh, 1999, Agiabir : A Preliminary report, *Purātattva* No. 29, Singh, P. and A.K. Singh 2000. Excavations at Agiabir, District Mirazapur (U.P.), *Prāgdhārā*-10, pp. 31-55.
22. Jaysawal, Vidula and Manoj Kumar 2006. Excavations at Ram Nagar, Discovery of a supporting settlement of Anceint Varanasi, *Purātattva* No 36 : pp. 85-92.
23. Narain, A.K. and Purushottam Singh 1977. *Excavations at Rajghat*, Part-2, Banaras Hindu University, Varanasi.
24. Jaiswal, Vidula 2002. Aktha : A Satellite Settlement at Sarnath, Varanasi (Report of Excavations conducted in 2002), *Bhāratī* Vol. 26, Bulletin of the Department of Ancient Indian History and Archaeology, Banaras Hindu University, Varanasi, pp. 61-80.
25. *Indian Archaeology* — A Review, 1963-64, pp. 57-58.
26. Singh, B.P. 1989. Khairadih- A Chalcolithic Settlement, *Puratattva*-18, pp. 28-34.
27. Singh, P. and A.K. Singh, 1997-98. Trial Excavation at Bhunadih, District Ballia (U.P.), *Prāgdhārā* 8, pp. 12-29.
28. Singh, P. and A.K. Singh, 1995-96. Trial Excavations at Waina, District Ballia (U.P.), *Prāgdhārā* 6, pp. 41.-61.
29. *I.A.R.* 1974-75, pp. 46-47; Chaturvedi, S.N. 1985, Advances of Vindhyan Neolithic and Chalcolithic cultures to the Himalayan Tarai : Excavations and Explorations in the Saryupar Ragion of Uttar Pradesh, *Man and Environment* IX, pp. 12ff.
30. Singh, P. 1994. *Excavatiosn at Narhan* (1984-89), Banaras Hindu University, Varanasi and B.R. Publishing corporation, New Delhi.
31. Singh, P. 1992-93. Archaeological Excavation at Imlidih-Khurd, *Prāgdhārā* 4, pp. 44-48; Singh, P. A.K. Singh, and Indrajeet Singh 1992. Excavations at Imlidih Khurd, *Purātattva* 22, pp. 120-122.
32. Tewari, Rakesh, R.K.Srivastava and K.K. Singh, Excavations at Lahuradeva, Sant Kabir Nagar, *Purātattva* 32, pp. 54-62; Tewari, Rakesh, R.K. Srivastava, K.K. Singh, K.S. Saraswat and I.B. Singh 2003, Prelimiary Report of the Excavations at Lahuradeva, District Sant Kabir Nagar, U.P. 2001-2002; Wider Archaeological Implications, *Prāgdhārā* 13, pp. 37-68
33. Misra, V.D. and M.C. Gupta 2006. Pre-N.B.P. Cultures of the Middle Ganga Valley : Some observations, *Prāgdhārā* No. 16, pp. 29.

34. Sharma, G.R. 1973. Mesolithic Lake Culture in the Ganga Valley, *Proceedings of Prehistoric Society* XXX, pp. 129-46; see also Sharma, G.R. 1975. Seasonal Migrations and Mesolithic Lake Culture of the Ganga Valley, *K.C. Chattopadhyaya Memorial Volume,* Department of Ancient History, Culture and Archaeology, University of Allahabad, pp. 1-20.
35. Sharma, G.R., V.D. Misra and J.N. Pal 1980. Excavations at Mahadaha, Department of Ancient History, Culture and Archaeology, University of Allahabad, Allahabad; *Indian Archaeology- A Review* (in the following pages obbreviated as I.A.R.) 1977-78, pp. 58-59; *I.A.R.* 1978-79, pp. 59-60; Kennedy, K.A.R., John R. Lukacs, Robert F. Pastor, Thomas L. Johnston, Nancy, C. Lovell, J.N. Pal, Brian E. Hemphill and Chrstopher B. Burrow 1992. *Human Skeletal Remains from Mahadaha : A Gangetic Mesolithic site, South Asia,* occasional papers and thesis No. 11, Ithaca, Cornel University, for the fauna of the site see Joglekar, P.P., V.D. Misra, J.N. Pal and M.C. Gupta 2003. *Mesolithic Mahadaha: The Faunal Remains,* Department of Ancient History, Culture and Archaelogy, University of Allahabad, Allahabad.
36. *I.A.R.* 1982-93, pp. 99-100; *I.A.R.* 1983-84, PP. 90-92; *I.A.R.* 1985-86, PP. 83-84; *I.A.R.* 1986-87, PP. 83-84; Misra, V.D. 1988. Excavations at Damdama (Warikalan), Pratapgarh U.P., *Bulletin of Museums and Archaeology in U.P.* (ed. S.D. Trivedi), No. 41-42, Lucknow, pp. 59-63; Varma, R.K., V.D. Misra, J.N. Pandey and J.N. Pal 1985. A Preliminary report on the Excavations at Damdama (1982-85), *Man and Environment* IX, pp. 45-65.
37. Site was recently explored by V.D. Misra, J.N. Pal and M.C. Gupta : A Pre-N.B.P. Sattlement is indicated at the site.
38. Site was recently explored by V.D. Misra, J.N. Pal and M.C. Gupta, A Pre-N.B.P. Sattlement is indicated at the site.
39. Misra, V.D. 1990. *Protohistoric Investigations in Pratapgarh District, U.P.* pp. 196-200. Adaptation and other Essays (ed. N.C. Ghosh, Subrata Chakrabarti), *Research Publications,* Visva-Bharti, Santiniketan; Pal, Ram Naresh, 2005. *Pratapgarh Janpada Ka Puratattva,* pp. 1993-1994, Swabha Prakashan, Allahabad.
40. Misra, V.D. 1977. *Excavations at Koldihwa, Some Aspects of Indian Archaeology,* pp. 107-119, Prabhat Prakashan, Allahabad; Misra, B.B. 2006. Koldihwa- A key sile for the Neolthic and chaleolithic Cultures of the Vindhyas - Art Archeaology and cultural History of India (*U.N. Roy Felicitaition Vol.* Part I) (ed.) C.P. Sinha, B.R. Publishing corporation, Delhi, pp. 143-181.
41. *Indian Archaeology — A Review,* 1985-86, pp. 75-76.
42. Misra, V.D. 1977, *op. cit.* pp. 49.
43. Kenoyer, J.M. et.al. 1983, An Upper Palaeolithic Shrine in India, *Antiquity* 57, pp. 88-94.
44. Possehl, G.L. and Paul C. Rissman, 1992. *Chronology in the Old World Archaeology,* IIIrd Edition, R.W. Ehrich (ed.), Vol. I (India). Table-4, p. 461.
45. Agrawal, D.P. and J.S. Kharakwal, 2003. *Bronze and Iron Ages In South Asia,* p. 235, Aryan Books International, New Delhi.
46. Misra, V.D., J.N. Pal and M.C. Gupta, 1999-2000, Further Excavations at Jhusi 1998-99, *Prāgdhārā* 10, pp. 28 (Table-1).
47. Possehl, G.L. and Paul, C. Rissman 1992. *op.cit.* p. 463, University of Chicago Press, Chicago London.
48. Singh, P. 1994. *op. cit.* p. 32.
49. Singh, B.P. 1989. Khairadih- A Chalcolithic Settlement, *Purātattva*-18, p. 33.
50. Agrawal, D.P. 1984. *Archaeology of India,* New Delhi, p. 279.
51. Singh, B.P. 1990, Early Farming Communities of Kaimur Foot Hills, *Purātattva* 19, p.18.
52. Tewari Rakesh, et.al, 2004, Excavations at Lahuradeva, Sant Kabir Nagar. *Purātattva* 32, pp. 54-32.

28

पूर्वी उत्तर प्रदेश की पूर्व मध्ययुगीन वैष्णव मूर्तियाँ

सीमा श्रीवास्तव

प्राचीन भारतीय भूगोल की दृष्टि से पूर्वी उत्तर प्रदेश की सीमा का विस्तार श्रावस्ती से सदानीरा के पूर्वी भाग तक जहाँ से बिहार की सीमा प्रारंभ होती है, उत्तर में हिमवन्त के चरण प्रान्तर से जहाँ शिवालिक की सीढ़िया प्रारंभ होती हैं, से दक्षिण की ओर मध्य गंगाघाटी में स्यन्दिका तक था। प्रस्तुत शोध–पत्र में पूर्वी उत्तर प्रदेश के अंतर्गत कुशीनगर, देवरिया, गोरखपुर, महराजगंज, बस्ती, सिद्धार्थनगर, गोण्डा एवं बहराइच आदि जनपदों के अतिरिक्त भाषिक ऐक्य के आधार पर आजमगढ़, बलिया, गाजीपुर एवं वाराणसी को भी स्वीकार किया गया है जिसे वर्तमान में 'पूर्वांचल तथा भोजपुरी क्षेत्र' कहा जाता है। इस अध्ययन में राप्ती से गण्डक तक के क्षेत्रों की पूर्व मध्यकालीन वैष्णव मूर्तियों को ही विशेष रूप से चुना गया है।

पूर्वमध्यकालीन कला के अंतर्गत निर्मित मूर्तियों में सौंदर्य और कलात्मकता में ह्रास स्पष्ट रूप से परिलक्षित होता है। धार्मिक जीवन में निरन्तर बढ़ रही प्रतिस्पर्धा एवं जटिलताओं के कारण इस युग में पौराणिक धर्म के शैव, वैष्णव, शाक्त आदि के साथ ही बौद्ध और जैन धर्म से सम्बद्ध विविध देवी–देवताओं, बोधिसत्वों और तीर्थंकरों आदि की मूर्तियां निर्मित होने लगी थीं। इन मूर्तियों का प्रमुख वैशिष्ट्य शास्त्रीयग्रंथों के आधार पर इनका निर्माण करना था। यथा–विष्णु की मूर्तियों के निर्माण में उनकी भुजाओं की संख्या और उनमें धारण आयुधों का निर्धारण शास्त्रीय परंपरानुसार किया गया। परिणामस्वरूप मूर्तिकार द्वारा अपने विवेक एवं कल्पना के स्थान पर शास्त्रीय विधान को अधिक महत्त्व दिया जाने लगा। ये मूर्तियां यद्यपि कला की दृष्टि से अच्छी नहीं हैं तथापि इस काल में भी ऐसी वैष्णव मूर्तियों का निर्माण हुआ जो मूर्तिकला की उत्कृष्ट उदाहरण हैं। इन मूर्तियों में पौराणिक धर्म का स्पष्टतः प्रभाव दिखाई देता है। मूर्तियों के निर्माण हेतु पुराणों में उल्लिखित आख्यानों को कलाकार ने विशेष रूप से ध्यान में रखा है।

संदर्भित मूर्तियों के विश्लेषणात्मक अध्ययन से जो तथ्य मुख्यतः सामने आता है, वह है उनकी क्षेत्रीयता या स्थानीयता। प्रायः हर क्षेत्र की मूर्तियों का अपना एक निजत्व या अपनापन है। इसके अतिरिक्त इन मूर्तियों

में अलंकरण–प्रविधि पर अधिक बल दिया गया है, फलस्वरूप जहाँ मूर्तियाँ भव्य और आकर्षक हो गई हैं, वहीं दूसरी ओर इस प्रक्रिया में पूर्ववर्ती मूर्तियों की सहजता और स्वाभाविकता क्रमशः समाप्त होती दिखाई पड़ती है। इस युग की मूर्तियों में न केवल अलंकरणों और आभूषणों में वृद्धि हुई, अपितु मुखमुद्रा एवं भावभंगिमा भी आकर्षक एवं तीखी हो गयी हैं तथा संपूर्ण परिकर को विभिन्न आकृतियों से पूरी तरह भर दिया गया है। वस्तुतः इन मूर्तियों के निर्माण में अब हृदय के स्थान पर बुद्धि और विवेक का अधिक प्रयोग किया गया है। परिणामस्वरूप तकनीकी रूप से ये मूर्तियाँ श्रेष्ठ और सुंदर होती गई हैं। इन मूर्तियों में आभूषण एवं केश–विन्यास विशेषतः द्रष्टव्य हैं। मूर्तियों में प्रयुक्त देवादि के नवीन स्वरूपों की कल्पना की गई और उनके करों की संख्या, उसमें धारित आयुधों, वाहनों तथा परिकर की पार्षद आकृतियों की संख्या में वृद्धि की गई, परिणामतः कलाकार इनमें बँधकर रह गया और मूर्तियों की सहजता क्रमशः कम होती गयी।

इस युग में अधिकांश मूर्तियों के निर्माण में पीले, भूरे, काले रंग के मुलायम बेसाल्ट प्रस्तर का प्रयोग किया गया है। प्रस्तर की इस विशेषता के ही कारण मूर्तियों में लक्षण एवं वस्त्राभूषण को अत्यधिक सूक्ष्मता के साथ उकेरने की प्रवृत्ति दिखायी देती है। इन मूर्तियों में पूर्ण रूप से प्रतिमाशास्त्रीय विवरणों का प्रयोग किया गया, यथा–विष्णु मूर्तियों में पार्षदों के साथ ही दोनों पार्श्व में वीणाधारिणी सरस्वती और चामरधारिणी लक्ष्मी का अंकन मिलता है। मूर्तियों में इनको शंख, चक्र, गदा, पद्मधारी चतुर्भुजी स्थानक रूप में चित्रित किया गया है। देव मूर्तियों के निर्माण का उद्देश्य धार्मिक होता था, इसी कारण शास्त्रीय विधानों के अनुरूप उनका उत्कीर्णन आवश्यक था। विभिन्न सम्प्रदायों में देवकुल में वृद्धि के फलस्वरूप नवीन देवी–देवताओं के करों की संख्या, आयुध, परिकर सहायक आकृतियों के विवेचन से मूर्तियाँ प्रतिमा शास्त्रीय दृष्टि से क्लिष्ट होती गयी जिनके निर्माण में विष्णु धर्मोत्तर पुराण, साधनमाला, रूपमण्डन, मत्स्यपुराण आदि शास्त्रीय ग्रन्थों के निर्देशों का पालन किया गया। यद्यपि शास्त्रकारों द्वारा निर्मित मूर्तियों में लक्षणों का पालन अनिवार्य होने से मूर्तिकार की निजी कल्पना तथा अनुभव की स्वतंत्रता समाप्त हो गयी, फिर भी शिल्पी द्वारा शास्त्रीय मर्यादा में रहते हुए एकरसता के निस्तारण हेतु स्थान–स्थान पर अपनी रचनात्मक प्रतिभा को अभिव्यक्त करने की पूरी चेष्टा की गई है।

संदर्भित प्रायः सभी मूर्तियाँ कोरकर बनायी गई हैं या पाषाण शिला पर उत्कीर्ण फलक शिल्प की परम्परा में बनी हैं। पीठिका और ऊपर के फलक भाग को क्रमशः विस्तार देते हुए अत्यधिक अलंकृत रूप में बनाया गया है। इन पर देवताओं के वाहन एवं उपासकों तथा पार्श्वों में सहायक देवों आदि की आकृतियाँ उकेरी गयी हैं। इस प्रकार पूरा फलक आसन, पृष्ठभाग एवं प्रभावशाली मुख्य देवादि आकृति के साथ एकीकृत होकर सुंदर ढंग से अभिव्यक्त हुआ है। ये मूर्तियाँ अत्यधिक अलंकृत और कभी–कभी अलंकरणें से बोझिल तथा समरूप बनने लगी, जिनमें विभिन्न अलंकरणों एवं आयुधों को भी इस सीमा तक अलंकृत रूप में दिखाया गया है कि उनका मूल स्वरूप ही उसमें विलुप्त सा हो गया है। यद्यपि मूर्तिकला की परंपरा पूर्व से ही अत्यन्त समृद्ध थी किन्तु मूर्ति निर्माण की दृष्टि से यह उत्कर्ष का काल रहा है। रूप की दृष्टि से सम्बन्धित सभी तत्व इस काल की मूर्तिकला के विकास की पराकाष्ठा के द्योतक हैं।

यद्यपि पूर्व मध्यकाल में यह क्षेत्र मुख्यतः सम्प्रदायों से सम्बद्ध रहा है किन्तु यहाँ से प्राप्त कतिपय विशिष्ट एवं विलक्षण वैष्णव प्रतिमाओं की प्राप्ति यह द्योतित करती है कि इस क्षेत्र में वैष्णव सम्प्रदाय भी पल्लवित एवं पुष्पित हो रहा था। इस तथ्य की पुष्टि विवेच्य क्षेत्र की वैष्णव प्रतिमाओं के विभिन्न स्वरूपों की प्राप्ति से होती है। इस काल तक अनेक स्वतंत्र प्रतिमालाक्षणिक ग्रंथों की रचना हो जाने के कारण इनके आधार पर विविध रूपों का निर्माण शिल्पी द्वारा किया जाने लगा। ऐसा प्रतीत होता है कि तत्कालीन युग में इस क्षेत्र में विष्णु की उपासना चतुर्दिक व्याप्त थी, इसी से प्रेरित होकर तत्कालीन शिल्पी ने विष्णु की दशावतार एवं विश्वरूप सहित विविध मूर्तियों के माध्यम से जनमानस की धार्मिक भावनाओं को प्रदर्शित किया। विवेच्य क्षेत्र से प्राप्त विष्णु की कतिपय

दुर्लभ मूर्तियों का विवरण निम्नवत् है –

देवरिया जनपद के अन्तर्गत खुखुन्दु से 96 x 48 सेमी. की बलुआ प्रस्तर की 12वीं शताब्दी ई. की विष्णु की एक दशावतार प्रतिमा प्राप्त हुई है जो एक फलक पर उत्कीर्ण है। इसमें चतुर्भुजी विष्णु का सामान्य दक्षिण कर वरद मुद्रा में है जिसमें चक्र का अंकन है तथा उपरि दक्षिण कर खण्डित है। वाम सामान्य कर में शंख एवं उपरि वामकर में सनालपद्म का अंकन है।

समभंग स्थानक मुद्रा में प्रदर्शित देवता को किरीट, कुण्डल, हार, यज्ञोपवीत, वनमाला, मेखला, केयूर तथा नूपुर धारण किये चित्रित किया गया है। वामपार्श्व में त्रिभंग वीणावादिनी सरस्वती तथा दक्षिण पार्श्व में लक्ष्मी का अंकन है। ये दोनों देवियाँ कुण्डल, हार, यज्ञोपवीत, केयूर, मेखला, नूपुर तथा मुकुट धारण किये हैं। साधारण प्रभामण्डल से युक्त देव के साथ लक्ष्मी देवी के पार्श्व में शंख पुरुष तथा सरस्वती के पार्श्व में चक्र पुरुष का अंकन है। इनका वामकर कट्यावलम्बित है तथा वे दक्षिणकर में क्रमशः शंख और चक्र धारण किये हैं। देव को पद्मपीठिका पर स्थानक मुद्रा में चित्रित किया गया है। देव के वाम चरण के नीचे (अलंकृत पीठिका के) पार्श्व में नमस्कार मुद्रा में पुरुष आकृति में गरुड़ अंकित है। पीठिका के दक्षिण ओर अञ्जलिमुद्रा में एक सेवक तथा सेविका का अंकन है। विष्णुदेव के दक्षिण पार्श्व में नीचे से ऊपर पशुअवतारों का अंकन है जिनमें से मात्र मत्स्यावतार और कूर्मावतार ही चित्रित हैं। शेष फलक भाग खण्डित है। देव के वामपार्श्व में ऊपर से नीचे परशुराम, राम, बलराम, बुद्ध तथा कल्कि का चित्रण है। कल्कि के अतिरिक्त सभी मानवी अवतार स्थानक मुद्रा में प्रदर्शित हैं। सबसे ऊपर चित्रित परशुराम के दक्षिणकर में परशु है तथा वामकर कट्यावलम्बित है। परशुराम के नीचे राम का चित्रण धनुष–बाण लिये हुए किया गया है। तद्नन्तर बलराम को दक्षिण कर में मूसल लिये हुये और वामकर कटि पर अवस्थित दिखाया गया है। इसके पश्चात् अंकित बुद्ध अवतार का दक्षिण कर वरद मुद्रा में और वामकर वक्ष के सम्मुख प्रदर्शित है। मानवीय अवतारों के क्रम में सबसे नीचे कल्कि अवतार का अंकन है। इनको अश्वारूढ़ मुद्रा में दक्षिण कर में खड्ग तथा वाम कर में रास पकड़े हुए प्रदर्शित किया गया है। देवता के वाम स्कन्ध से नीचे तक प्रसरित पारदर्शक वस्त्र का ज्ञान उनकी चुन्नटों के माध्यम से होता है। अलंकृत प्रभामण्डल का वामभाग ही अवशिष्ट है।

उपर्युक्त मूर्ति से तुलनीय मूर्तियाँ एक भीटी तिवारी (पीपीगंज) गोरखपुर तथा दूसरी बलुआ (सिकरीगंज) गोरखपुर से प्राप्त हुई हैं। भीटी तिवारी की विष्णु की दशावतार मूर्ति 70 x 36 सेमी. के काले प्रस्तर पर निर्मित है। खुखुन्दु से प्राप्त मूर्ति के समान यह चतुर्भुजी है तथा स्थानक मुद्रा में विष्णु प्रदर्शित हैं, किन्तु इनका प्रभामण्डल अनलंकृत है जिसके शीर्ष भाग पर छत के समान निकला हुआ भाग है। उपरि दक्षिण कर में गदा, वाम सामान्य कर में पद्म तथा उपरि वामकर में चक्र का अंकन है। देवता के दोनों पार्श्वों में दशावतारों का अंकन है जिसके अन्तर्गत नीचे से ऊपर की ओर बुद्ध, नृसिंह, वामन, बलराम, कल्कि की आकृतियाँ निर्मित की गयी हैं। शेष खुखुन्दु विष्णु मूर्ति के ही समान हैं।

इसी के समतुल्य विष्णु की एक दशावतार मूर्ति बलुआ से प्राप्त हुयी है। यह 60 x 59 सेमी. की है ओर पीले बलुआ प्रस्तर में निर्मित है। यह 11वीं शती से सम्बन्धित है। सामान्य वामकर में देव को शंख लिये हुये प्रदर्शित किया गया है। ऊपर मध्य में सूर्यनारायण की आसनस्थ मूर्ति निर्मित है। किरीट के वाम पार्श्व में उमा महेश्वर और दक्षिण पार्श्व में आसन मुद्रा में ब्रह्मा और ब्रह्माणी का अंकन किया गया है। भुजाओं के दोनों पार्श्व में व्याल बनाये गये हैं। दक्षिण पार्श्ववर्ती व्याल के नीचे बुद्ध और परशुराम उसके ऊपरी भाग पर नृवराह तथा उसके भी ऊपर मत्स्य का अंकन है जिसके पीछे चार पुरुष आकृतियां बनायी गयी हैं। इन आकृतियों की पहचान चार वेदों से की जाती है। दाहिने गन्धर्व के पीछे वामन और वाम गंधर्व के पीछे बलराम अंकित हैं। बलराम के पार्श्व में कूर्मावतार का अंकन, उसके नीचे क्रमशः नृसिंह और धनुर्धारी राम हैं। तदनन्तर नीचे की ओर बढ़ते हुए

वामवर्ती व्याल के नीचे अश्वारूढ़ कल्कि है। पीठिका पर पैरों के नीचे कमल का चित्रण किया गया है। शेष चित्रण खुखुन्दु और बलुआ मूर्ति के समान है।

दशावतार मूर्तियों के साथ ही विष्णु की विश्वरूप प्रतिमा की प्राप्ति, इस क्षेत्र में वैष्णव उपासना की विविधता को द्योतित करती है। इस प्रकार की अनेक प्राप्त मूर्तियों में से दो विशिष्ट मूर्तियाँ उल्लेखनीय हैं। तमकुही के निकट शिवसरया ग्राम, जनपद, कुशीनगर से 235 x 130 सेमी. की प्रस्तर की विश्वरूप प्रतिमा प्राप्त हुई है जिसमें देवता को स्थानक समभंग मुद्रा में दसभुजी तथा दोहरे कमलपीठ पर प्रदर्शित किया गया है। विश्वरूप के वामकर में ऊपर से क्रमशः वज्र, चक्र, धनुष है तथा एक कमलनाल पर स्थित है। दक्षिण दूसरे कर में पताका अथवा दण्ड तीसरे में शंख तथा एक में पद्म है; शेष भुजायें खण्डित हैं। इसमें प्रधान मुख पुरुष (नर) का, दक्षिण मुख नृसिंह का तथा वाम पार्श्व का मुख वराह का है। देव के दोनों पार्श्व में दशावतारों का अंकन है। वाम पार्श्व में वीणावादिनी सरस्वती तथा दक्षिण पार्श्व में पद्मधारिणी लक्ष्मी का अंकन है। त्रिभंग मुद्रा में समस्त वस्त्राभूषणों से अलंकृत, लक्ष्मी के पार्श्व में उनके आयुध गदा तथा सरस्वती के पार्श्व में चक्र पुरुष का अंकन है। फलक में सबसे ऊपर सप्तर्षियों का अंकन है और उसके नीचे नवग्रहों का प्रदर्शन है। चतुर्दिक सनक, सनन्दन, सनत्कुमार और सनातन ऋषि कुमारों के साथ ही संपूर्ण प्रभावली में अनेक मानव तथा पशु अंकित किये गए हैं। ऐसा प्रतीत होता है कि संपूर्ण विश्व को फलक में स्थित विष्णु रूप में समाहित कर लिया गया है। संभवतः इसीलिए इनका यह रूप विश्वरूप कहलाता है। शेष अंकन विष्णु की सामान्य मूर्ति के समान हैं।

एक अन्य दुर्लभ विश्वरूप मूर्ति सपही चन्द्रोटा ग्राम, पड़रौना, जनपद कुशीनगर से प्राप्त हुयी है। पाषाण–निर्मित यह मूर्ति 215 x 108 सेमी. परिमाप की है जिसमें त्रिभंग मुद्रा में स्थानक विश्वरूप को समस्त वस्त्राभूषण से अलंकृत निर्मित किया गया है। दसभुजी देवता के वामकर में एक सम्मुख वास्तविक कर कट्यावलम्बित है। उसके बाद के करों में क्रमशः चक्र, धनुष, अंकुश का अंकन है। इनके दक्षिण वास्तविक कर में दण्ड–पाश अन्य दो करों में शंख और खड्ग हैं तथा अन्य भुजाये खंडित हैं। सम्मुख पुरुष मुख के अतिरिक्त नृसिंह और वराह मुख का अंकन हैं तथा संपूर्ण अलंकृत फलक पर चतुर्दिक पशु, मानव आकृतियाँ अंकित हैं। शेष चित्रण शिवसरया मूर्ति के समान हैं।

इस परिक्षेत्र से विष्णु की सामान्य मूर्तियाँ रूद्रपुर, देवरिया तथा राजकीय उद्यान, गोरखपुर से प्राप्त हुई हैं। बेसाल्ट प्रस्तर पर निर्मित ये मूर्तियाँ 12वीं शताब्दी ईसवी की हैं। इनमें रूद्रपुर, देवरिया की विष्णु मूर्ति 134. 5 x 63.5 सेमी. की है। चतुर्भुजी विष्णु के दक्षिण सामान्य कर में चक्र, उपरि दक्षिण कर में दण्ड, वाम सामान्य कर में शंख तथा उपरि वाम कर में नालयुक्त पद्म अंकित हैं। इनके वाम पार्श्व में वीणावादिनी सरस्वती एवं दक्षिण पार्श्व में पद्मधारिणी लक्ष्मी का त्रिभंग मुद्रा में समस्त वस्त्राभूषणों से अलंकृत अंकन है। लक्ष्मी के पार्श्व में शंखपुरुष तथा सरस्वती के पार्श्व में चक्रपुरुष का अंकन है। गरुड़ का अंकन पूर्ववत् हुआ है।

गोरखपुर से प्राप्त विष्णु की प्रस्तर मूर्ति 350 x 145 सेमी. की है। यह दोहरे पद्म पर स्थानक मुद्रा में प्रदर्शित है। देवता के ऊपरी दक्षिण भुजा में गदा है। अन्य भुजायें खण्डित हैं। समस्त अलंकरणों एवं विद्याधरों से युक्त प्रतिमा के मध्य के पार्श्वों में हरितव्यालों का अंकन है जिनके मुख से पद्म नलिकायें निकलती हुई दर्शायी गयी हैं। स्तम्भों के बाहर दोनों पार्श्वों में सिंहव्याल का अंकन है। देव के दक्षिण पार्श्व में चामरधारिणी देवी तथा वामपार्श्व में त्रिभंग पद्मपुरुष अंकित किये गए हैं। पीठिका का निचला भाग, पद्मलता, पुष्प व नलिकाओं से अलंकृत किया गया है।

उपर्युक्त समस्त मूर्तियों में अनेक समानतायें स्पष्टतः दृष्टिगत होती हैं। समस्त मूर्तियाँ समभंग–स्थानक मुद्रा में शंख, चक्र, गदा, पद्म, दण्ड आदि के साथ चित्रित हैं। इनके एक दक्षिण कर को कभी–कभी वरद मुद्रा में प्रदर्शित किया गया है। ये सभी अलंकृत मूर्तियाँ अपने समस्त पार्षद देवी–देवताओं से युक्त हैं जो इनके

विकसित रूप एवं तत्कालीन समाज में वैष्णव धर्म की लोकप्रियता को द्योतित करते हैं। ये मूर्तियाँ प्राचीनतम् प्रतिमालाक्षणिक ग्रंथ *वृहत्संहिता*[1], *मत्स्यपुराण*[2], *अग्निपुराण*[3], *विष्णु पुराण*[4] के आधार पर निर्मित की गई प्रतीत होती हैं। इस काल में विष्णु के आयुधों को प्राकृतिक एवं मानवीय दोनों रूपों में बनाया गया है।

प्राप्त मूर्तियों के तुलनात्मक अध्ययन से विदित होता है कि पालकालीन मूर्तियों के समान यहाँ भी देवता के दोनों पार्श्वों से कमलनाल निकल रहे हैं जिनके सिरों पर पद्म का अंकन है और दोनों प्राकृतिक भुजायें उन पर स्थित हैं। इन मूर्तियों में अंकित पद्म पीठिका पर सारनाथ शैली का प्रभाव दृष्टिगोचर होता है[5]। बलुआ की प्रतिमा अपने विशिष्ट लक्षणों के कारण महत्त्वपूर्ण है। इस मूर्ति में देवता के किरीट के ऊपर सूर्य–नारायण का अंकन इसकी एक विशेषता है। इसमें किरीट के वामपार्श्व में उमामहेश्वर और दक्षिण में ब्रह्मा–ब्रह्माणी के अंकन मध्यप्रदेश में 11–12वीं शताब्दी में प्रचलित परंपरा के समान हैं।[6] स्पष्टतः शिल्पी ने शिल्पशास्त्रीय ग्रन्थों के नियमों का पालन करते हुए इन मूर्तियों को निर्मित किया। लगभग सभी मूर्तियां काले चमकदार प्रस्तर पर निर्मित हैं। ध्यातव्य है कि *विष्णुधर्मोत्तरपुराण* कालीमिर्च के समान काले प्रस्तर को उत्तमशिला बताता है।[7] बलुआ प्रस्तर को शिल्पी द्वारा प्रयुक्त करने का एक प्रमुख कारण यह था कि यह सर्वाधिक मुलायम प्रस्तर होने के कारण कला को प्रदर्शित करने का एक सशक्त माध्यम रहा है।

मूर्तियों में विष्णु को उत्तरीय तथा अधोवस्त्र पहने दिखाया गया है। अधोवस्त्र के माध्यम से इनके कटि प्रदेश को ढका गया है। यह वस्त्र देवता के घुटनों तक और कभी पैरों से कुछ ऊपर तक रहता है।[8] विष्णु को मौलि (सिर पर पहनने वाला आभूषण) धारण किये हुए दिखाया गया है। यह सिर पर किरीट धारण किये हुये हैं। वैष्णव पुराणों में विष्णु को 'किरीटिन' कहा गया है।[9] शिल्प शास्त्रीय ग्रंथ *मानसार* में कहा गया है कि विष्णु के योग्य किरीट मुकुट ही होता है।[10] यह ऊपर को नुकीली ऊँची उठी हुई टोपी के रूप में होता है जो चारों ओर से अथवा मात्र सामने से बहुमूल्य मणियों से जड़ा होता है।[11] खुखुन्दु की विष्णु प्रतिमा में इसी प्रकार के मुकुट का अंकन किया गया है। मूर्तियों के वक्षस्थल पर धारण हार को कौस्तुभ मणि नाम दिया गया है।[12] विष्णु को श्रीवत्स लांछन से युक्त दिखाया गया है। *वृहत्संहिता* में विष्णु को श्रीवत्सांकित वक्षा[13] कहा गया है। इससे स्पष्ट है कि श्रीवत्स वक्ष स्थल पर ही चित्रित है। मूर्तियों में धारित नूपुर का उल्लेख *श्रीमद्भागवत*[14] भी करता है। विष्णु को कर्ण कुण्डल से सुशोभित प्रदर्शित किया गया है।[15] कटि में धारित मेखला के समान शास्त्रों में काञ्ची शब्द का प्रयोग हुआ है।[16] इसकी (काञ्ची) लटकती हुई लड़ियाँ विष्णु के श्रोणि प्रदेश को शोभित कर रही हैं।[17] इनकी भुजाओं के ऊर्ध्व भाग में धारित आभूषणों को केयूर,[18] भुजबन्द[19] तथा आगे कलाई में धारण किये गए आभूषण को कड़ा अर्थात् कङ्कण,[20] वलय[21] आदि शब्दों से सम्बोधित किया गया है।

इस अध्ययन के आधार पर इन मूर्तियों की कुछ प्रमुख विशेषताएं निम्नवत् हैं –

1. मूर्तिकला में मानव ही अभिव्यक्ति का प्रधान केन्द्र बिन्दु रहा है। देवी–देवताओं की लाक्षणिक अभिव्यक्तियाँ नारी और पुरुष के विभिन्न रूपों और मुद्राओं के माध्यम से प्रदर्शित हैं। इनके साथ ही सहायक या पार्श्ववर्ती देवी–देवताओं के रूप में भी मनुष्य रूप के ही दर्शन होते हैं। इसके अंकन में परिलक्षित विविधता, क्षेत्रीयता के समावेश को प्रदर्शित करती है।
2. आभूषणों की अधिकता, किंचित भारी और स्थिर शरीर रचना, पार्षद आकृतियों की बढ़ती हुयी संख्या इनका एक मुख्य वैशिष्ट्य है।
3. नारी शरीर के कतिपय अंग, यथा नितम्ब आदि के भराव के माध्यम से ऐन्द्रिक–भाव को व्यक्त किया गया है जिसके उदाहरण विवेचित क्षेत्र से प्राप्त मूर्तियों में दृष्टव्य हैं। इस समय नारी मूर्ति के निर्माण में, उसके लम्बे नेत्र, आकर्षक शुकनासिका, गोलमुखाकृति, भरे हुए कपोल, नीचे का ओष्ठ मोटा और ऊपर का पतला आदि को भलीभांति प्रदर्शित कर उसकी सौन्दर्य–वृद्धि–हेतु प्रयास किया गया है।

4. अलंकृत वस्त्राभूषण, आकृतियों (मूर्तियों) में पूर्णतः समाहित होकर उनके स्वाभाविक अंग प्रतीत होते हैं।
5. विवेच्य काल की अधिकांश मूर्तियाँ गाहड़वाल, पाल तथा परवर्ती प्रतिहार शैली के आधार पर निर्मित हुई हैं। इन मूर्तियों में शरीर रचना की दृष्टि से हल्की, संयत और पतली किन्तु कभी–कभी मांसल काया वाली आकृतियाँ प्रदर्शित हैं।
6. इस काल की मूर्तियों में कटि से पद तक के भाग के निर्माण में कलाकार ने विशेष ध्यान नहीं दिया है। फलतः यह भाग भारी–भरकम और बिना जोड़ों के संकेत के कड़ापन लिये हुए दिखाया गया है। कटि से ऊपर के भाग के निर्माण में कलाकार ने कुशलता का परिचय दिया है जो अत्यन्त सजीव है।
7. इस युग में संरचित शिल्प–शास्त्रीय ग्रन्थों के आधार पर विभिन्न देवताओं के अलग–अलग स्वरूपों की लाक्षणिक विशेषतायें निर्धारित की गई हैं।
8. ब्राह्मण धर्म के अन्तर्गत प्रतिमा निर्माण से सम्बन्धित लाक्षणिक ग्रंथों में *अपराजितपृच्छा, रूपमण्डन, समरांगणसूत्रधार, रूप प्रकाश, वास्तुविद्या, अंशुमद्भेदागम, सुप्रभेदागम, कामिकागम,* जैन प्रतिमा के लाक्षणिक ग्रंथों में *आचार दिनकर, निर्वाणकलिका, प्रतिष्ठासारद्धार* और बौद्ध शिल्पशास्त्रों में *साधनमाला* और *निष्पन्नयोगावली* विशेषतः उल्लेखनीय हैं। इनमें सम्बन्धित धर्मों के देवमूर्ति लक्षणों का विस्तार के साथ उल्लेख मिलता है। इस स्थिति में कलाकार द्वारा शिल्पांकन में स्वतंत्रता बाधित हुई और शास्त्रीय परंपरा के प्रति प्रतिबद्धता से मूर्तियों के निर्माण में यान्त्रिकता का भाव क्रमशः बढ़ता गया जिसमें लाक्षणिक सन्दर्भों की प्रधानता होती गयी।
9. मूर्तियों में एकरसता का समावेश होता गया और वे क्रमशः बोझिल होती चली गयी। उनकी लाक्षणिक विशेषताओं को एक नया तथा विस्तृत आयाम प्राप्त हुआ। विविध लक्षणों और लांछनों के साथ ही देव मूर्तियों की शरीर रचना में विभिन्न गणितीय अनुपात (अष्टताल, नवताल, दसताल) आदि भी निश्चित किये जाने लगे।
10. 12वीं शती ईसवी के मध्य तक मूर्तियों की सजीवता तथा जीवन्तता पूरी तरह समाप्त हो गयी। वे निर्जीव और शास्त्रीय विवरणों से बोझिल हो गयी। उनकी भव्यता तथा सौंदर्यात्मक भंगिमाओं में पूरी तरह यान्त्रिकता के दर्शन होने लगे।

इन विशेषताओं के विवेचन से स्पष्ट हो जाता है कि मूर्तियों में जो सर्वाधिक महत्त्वपूर्ण परिवर्तन हुआ उसके अंतर्गत काया निर्माण में मृदुता, सादगी, स्वाभाविकता, गतिशीलता का क्रमशः अभाव होता गया और उनका स्थान कड़ापन और भाव–भंगिमा तथा मुद्राओं में स्थिरता के भाव ने ले लिया। अब मूर्तियों में नतोदर शरीर–यष्टि बनने लगी। अतः मूर्तियों में तीखी रेखाओं और घुमावदार भंगिमाओं ने अपना स्थान सुरक्षित कर लिया जिनसे मूर्तियाँ आकर्षक होने के बाद भी कृत्रिम दिखने लगी। इस काल की पाल और प्रतिहार शैली की मूर्तियों में शरीर–रचना की मृदुता और स्वाभाविकता देखने को मिलती है। इस काल में चतुर्दिक सभी क्षेत्रों में सर्वाधिक संख्या में मंदिरों का निर्माण हुआ तथा उनके स्वाभाविक अंग के रूप में मूर्तियों का निर्माण कर उन्हें मन्दिरों में जड़ा गया। किन्तु, दसवीं शती ईसवी के बाद से यह स्वाभाविक अनुपात क्रमशः कम होता गया और मूर्तियों की अत्यधिक संख्या भीड़ का भाव व्यक्त करने लगी। इनमें क्षेत्रीयता का पुट स्पष्टतः परिलक्षित है। मूर्तियों में शारीरिक आकर्षण और तकनीकी श्रेष्ठता है, जिनमें शास्त्रीय लक्षणों में वृद्धि के कारण यान्त्रिकता और शैलीगत जीवन्तता एवं लयात्मकता के स्थान पर स्थिरता एवं भावशून्यता क्रमशः प्रभावी होती दिखाई देती है।

वस्तुतः 11वीं शताब्दी तक मूर्तिकलाकार अपने सतत् प्रयास में पूर्ण रूप से दक्ष हो गया था। उसने सांकेतिक भावों के माध्यम से ओज एवं तेज को व्यक्त किया। शरीर के विभिन्न अंग–विन्यास को पूर्ण संतुलित

एवं सौंदर्यपूर्ण बनाने का प्रयास शिल्पी द्वारा किया गया। मुख्य मूर्ति के अलंकरणार्थ विविध पार्श्व या गौण मूर्तियों का निर्माण किया गया है। शरीर का प्रत्येक अंग आभूषणों से अंलकृत है। शरीर में गति एवं लोच उत्पन्न करने का प्रयास किया गया है किन्तु उनसे कोई भाव व्यक्त नहीं होता। ये मूर्तियाँ भार से दबी हुई प्रतीत होती है फलस्वरूप स्वाभाविकता का विलोप परिलक्षित होता है। यद्यपि ये मूर्तियाँ सौंदर्य शास्त्र की दृष्टि से सुरूचिपूर्ण नहीं है किन्तु मूर्तिकार ने यदा–कदा ऐसी मनोरम मूर्तियों का सृजन किया है जिन्हें देखकर आश्चर्य होता है। वस्तुतः आर्थिक दृष्टि से कलाकार ने मंदिर को सुसम्पन्न बनाने के लिए भी इस प्रकार की मूर्तिशिल्प का सृजन किया होगा। यद्यपि क्षेत्रीय विशेषताओं का दर्शन गुप्त युग से ही होने लगता है किन्तु पूर्व मध्ययुग में यह विशेषता पूर्णतः स्पष्ट हो गई। अतः इस समय की मूर्तिकला पूर्णतः भारतीय परंपरा का प्रतिनिधित्व करती हुई तत्कालीन वैभव, सौंदर्य एवं विलासमय जीवन की परिचायिका है।

संदर्भ

1. *वृहत्सहिता* 58 / 31–35, 58 / 34, 58 / 32
2. *मत्स्य पुराण* 258 / 4–15
3. *अग्नि पुराण* 44 / 47–49
4. *विष्णु पुराण* 6 / 7 / 82, 1 / 9 / 67
5. अग्रवाल, वी.एस., प्लेट 5, चित्र सी.
6. अवस्थी, रामाश्रय, *खजुराहों की देव प्रतिमाएं,* चि.सं. 17, 30, 31, 32
7. *विष्णु धर्मोत्तर पुराण,* 90 / 21–22
8. *विष्णु धर्मोत्तर पुराण,* 5 / 7 / 23, *श्रीमद्‌भागवत पुराण,* 8 / 8 / 17
9. *विष्णु धर्मोत्तर पुराण,* 1 / 12 / 45, *वृहत्संहिता* 59 / 32, *श्रीमद्‌भागवत पुराण,* 8 / 18 / 2, 3 / 31 / 12
10. *मानसार,* 43 / 30
11. राव, गो.नाथ, *ऐ.हि.आई.,* वाल्यूम 2, भाग 1, पृ. 26
12. *श्रीमद्‌भागवत् पुराण,* 6 / 8 / 5
13. *वृहत्संहिता,* 58 / 32
14. *श्रीमद्‌भागवत् पुराण.* 3 / 28 / 15, 6 / 4 / 38
15. *अपराजितपृच्छा,* पृ. 236
16. *श्रीमद्‌भागवत पुराण,* 3 / 8 / 28
17. *श्रीमद्‌भागवत पुराण,* 3 / 28 / 16
18. *विष्णु पुराण,* 6 / 7 / 87
19. *विष्णु पुराण,* 1 / 12 / 41
20. *श्रीमद्‌भागवत् पुराण,* 8 / 9 / 7
21. *श्रीमद्‌भागवत् पुराण,* 3 / 15 / 40

29

वाराणसी में भित्ति चित्रांकन परंपरा

अनुपमा श्रीवास्तव

पूर्वी उत्तर प्रदेश में स्थित वाराणसी को विश्व की प्राचीनतम जीवन्त नगरी माना जाता है। वेदों और पुराणों में भी वाराणसी का उल्लेख आया है, जो इसकी प्राचीनता को सिद्ध करता है। इन उल्लेखों से प्रमाणित होता है कि प्रारंभ से ही, सांस्कृतिक मूल्यों से ओत–प्रोत यह आध्यात्मिक नगरी विभिन्न धार्मिक संप्रदायों की शरणस्थली रही है। इसका एक कारण संभवतः यह है कि प्राचीनकाल से ही भगवान शिव की यह नगरी पावन तीर्थस्थल के रूप में प्रसिद्ध है, इसलिए भारत के सभी प्रांतों के लोग यहाँ आकर बसते रहे, जिससे विभिन्न धर्मों के साथ–साथ विभिन्न कलाओं एवं संस्कृतियों का भी समन्वित रूप वाराणसी में देखने को मिलता है। शैव, शाक्त, वैष्णव, बौद्ध, जैन, इसाई एवं मुस्लिम आदि लगभग सभी संप्रदायों से जुड़े धार्मिक मूल्यों एवं धरोहरों को वाराणसी के इतिहास में खोजा जा सकता है। वाराणसी को काशी एवं बनारस के नाम से भी जाना जाता है।

प्रागैतिहासिक काल के शिलाचित्रों से यह प्रमाणित होता है कि भारत में चित्रकला की परंपरा अत्यंत प्राचीन काल से चली आ रही है। भारत के लगभग हर प्रांत में ऐसे शिलाचित्रों की उपस्थिति भारतीयों की कलाप्रियता की स्पष्ट परिचायक है। भारत में सबसे ज्यादा शैलचित्र मध्यप्रदेश में खोजे गए हैं। मध्य प्रदेश के बाद उत्तर प्रदेश में स्थित मिर्जापुर दूसरा सबसे बड़ा क्षेत्र है, जहाँ सबसे ज्यादा चित्रित शैलाश्रय मिले हैं। दूसरी बात, मिर्जापुर इसलिये भी ज्यादा महत्त्वपूर्ण है कि विश्व में सबसे पहले शैलचित्रकला की खोज यहीं की गई थी। वाराणसी से सटे हुए मिर्जापुर में (प्राचीन काल में काशी जनपद के अंतर्गत था) जब चित्रित शैलाश्रयों के साक्ष्य इतनी बड़ी संख्या में मिलते हैं तो निश्चय ही वाराणसी में भी प्रागैतिहासिक काल से ही चित्रकला परंपरा की जड़ें रही होंगी किन्तु उनके साक्ष्य हमें नहीं मिलते।

वाराणसी एवं उसके आसपास के क्षेत्रों में मृद्भाण्डों एवं मृण्मूर्तियों पर चित्रकारी की परंपरा को कम से कम छठी शती ई.पू. या इससे पहले का माना जा सकता है, जिसका प्रमाण राजघाट उत्खनन से मिले पात्रों एवं मृण्मूर्तियों से मिलता है। वाचस्पति गैरोला के अनुसार 'बौद्ध साहित्य *धम्मपद* (*अट्ठकहा* 2/69) में वाराणसी के

एक ब्राह्मण का उल्लेख हुआ है, जो चाक पर बर्तन बनाने में दक्ष था तथा बरगद की पत्तियों पर घोड़े, हाथी आदि पशुओं के चित्र बनाकर अपनी जीविका चलाता था'।[1] वाराणसी में आज भी चाक पर काम करने वाले (कुम्हार) लोग बर्तन बनाने के साथ–साथ लोगों के घरों की दीवारों पर शुभ शकुन सूचक चित्रों को बनाकर अपनी जीविका चलाते हैं, जो इस परंपरा की निरन्तरता का द्योतक है। पन्द्रहवीं शताब्दी के जैन *कल्प सूत्र* में काशी जनपद के जौनपुर क्षेत्र में कागज पर बने विभिन्न अंकनों का उल्लेख मिलता है। मोतीचन्द्र के अनुसार 'गाहड़वाल युग के लेखों से पता चलता है कि गाहड़वाल काल में वाराणसी में ग्रामीण अपने सादे घरों में सुन्दरता लाने के लिए द्वारों को सजाते थे (दुआर मांड), चौक पूरते थे (चौकु पुर) और उसकी दीवारों पर चित्र लिखते थे (चित्रु रच)'।[2]

हृदय नाराण मिश्र के अनुसार 'बनारस में चित्रों के प्रारंभिक साक्ष्य 18वीं शताब्दी के मध्य से ही मिलने आरंभ हो जाते हैं, जिसके प्रथम दो उदाहरण भारत कला भवन, काशी हिन्दू विश्वविद्यालय में हैं। इन चित्रों में पहला बनारस के नगरसेठ ग्वालदास साहू का चित्र है। दूसरा यहाँ के सूबेदार मीर रुस्तम अली का होली खेलते हुए चित्र है। ये दोनों चित्र दो अलग–अलग शैलियों में हैं। 19वीं शती के पहले से ही बनारस की अपनी एक शैली थी, जिसके ऊपर राजस्थानी शैली का प्रभाव था'।[3]

सामान्य तौर पर देखा जाए तो 18वीं शती में लगभग पूरे उत्तर भारत में राजस्थानी चित्रकला शैली में ही चित्र बनाए जा रहे थे। बाद में धीरे–धीरे मुगल चित्रकला शैली प्रभावी हुई तथा 19वीं शताब्दी में कम्पनी शैली का प्रभाव भी स्थानीय कला शैली पर पड़ा। इस तरह से हम देखते हैं कि वाराणसी की चित्रकला शैली पर राजस्थानी, मुगल और कम्पनी तीनों कला शैलियों का प्रभाव पड़ा, फलस्वरूप स्थानीय कला शैली समय के साथ लुप्त हो गई।

18वीं शती का अंत आते–आते ईस्ट इंडिया कंपनी ने भारत के काफी बड़े हिस्से पर अपना अधिकार जमा लिया था। अपनी कूटनीतियों के द्वारा उन्होंने कई राजा–महाराजाओं से उनके अधिकार छीन लिए थे और उन्हें निर्वासन की सजा देकर बनारस भेज दिया था। इस तरह से भारत के अलग–अलग हिस्सों से निर्वासित होकर आने वाले ये राजा–महाराजा अपने साथ विश्वस्त अनुचरों एवं प्रिय गुणीजनों को लेकर बनारस में ही बस गए। इनके अलावा महाराष्ट्र और राजस्थान के कई राजाओं ने इस नगरी के धार्मिक सम्मोहन से वशीभूत होकर यहाँ रहने के लिए अपनी हवेलियाँ बनवाई, जहाँ वे अपने परिवार के साथ आते–जाते रहते थे। इस तरह से धीरे–धीरे वाराणसी विद्वानों, कलाकारों एवं व्यवसायियों के आगमन से राजनीतिक, व्यापारिक एवं सांस्कृतिक क्रियाकलापों का एक महत्त्वपूर्ण केन्द्र बन गई। इसी क्रम में परवर्ती मुगल शैली में पारंगत चित्रकार लाल जी मसव्वर भी बनारस आए और उनके आगमन का यहाँ के चित्रकारों एवं स्थानीय चित्रकला शैली पर विशेष प्रभाव पड़ा। इसके पहले वाराणसी में राजस्थानी एवं स्थानीय कलाशैली में चित्र बनाए जा रहे थे। बाद में काशी नरेश महाराज उदित नारायण सिंह (1705–1835) के समय तक बनारस, कम्पनी शैली का एक प्रमुख केन्द्र बन चुका था।

इनके बाद महाराज ईश्वरी नारायण सिंह ने काशी की राजगद्दी संभाली, जो प्रकाण्ड विद्वान होने के साथ–साथ कला मर्मज्ञ भी थे। अन्य कलाओं के साथ उन्होंने अलग–अलग प्रान्तों से आए चित्रकारों को भी प्रश्रय दिया और स्वयं रुचि लेते हुए उनसे बहुत से चित्र भी बनवाए। महाराज ईश्वरी नारायण सिंह के काल के प्रसिद्ध चित्रकारों में से दल्लूलाल शबीहें बनाने में, चुन्नीलाल कागज पर चित्र बनाने में, मुन्नीलाल अबरख की चित्रकला में तथा मिश्रीलाल भित्तिचित्र बनाने में दक्ष थे। इस तरह के विभिन्न उल्लेखों से प्रमाणित होता है कि इस काल तक आते–आते वाराणसी में प्रचलित राजस्थानी, मुगल और कम्पनी इन तीनों कलाशैलियों में दक्ष कलाकारों को राज्याश्रय और प्रसिद्धि मिलने लगी थी। शास्त्रीय चित्रकला में दक्ष ये कलाकार अपने परिवार के सदस्यों के साथ–साथ अन्य इच्छुक लोगों को भी चित्रकारी सिखाने लगे थे।

नगर के प्रमुख मंदिरों, किलों तथा संपन्न परिवारों की हवेलियों की भित्तियों पर चित्र बनाने के लिए शास्त्रीय शैली में शिक्षित चित्रकारों की सेवा ली जाती थी। 40–50 वर्ष पहले तक वाराणसी की गलियों–मुहल्लों में सामान्यतया ऐसे भित्ति चित्रों के उत्कृष्ट उदाहरण देखने को मिल जाते थे। किन्तु अब बड़ी संख्या में ऐसे प्राचीन चित्र रख–रखाव के अभाव में या तो नष्ट हो गए हैं या नष्टप्राय हैं। वाराणसी में रहने वाली अधिकांश जनसंख्या तो शायद इन अमूल्य चित्रों की धरोहर से पूर्णतया अनभिज्ञ है। ये चित्र जिन पुरानी हवेलियों, मठों, मंदिरों तथा किलों में चित्रांकित हैं, वहाँ इन्हें रोज देखने वाले लोग संभवतः इनके सांस्कृतिक मूल्य से अपरिचित हैं। यही नहीं, इनके संरक्षण के लिए प्रयास करने की जगह अब प्रायः पुरानी हवेलियों को गिराकर नये मकान बनवाये जा रहे हैं।

कमल गिरि के अनुसार वाराणसी में भित्तिचित्रों के उल्लेखनीय उदाहरणों में '18वीं शती के अंत में चित्रित भोसलघाट स्थित लक्ष्मीनारायण मंदिर, रामनगर किले में स्थित काली मंदिर, पीताम्बर मंदिर, अमेठी राजा द्वारा बनवाया गया मणिकर्णिका घाट स्थित देवी मंदिर, ईश्वरगंगी स्थित महामाया मंदिर, जैतपुरा का बागेश्वरी देवी मंदिर, रामपुरा स्थित देवकीनन्दन की हवेली, अस्सी का शीतलदास मठ, जंगमबाड़ी स्थित जंगमबाड़ी मठ, राजा पटनीमल की बारादरी तथा ब्रह्माघाट स्थित आवासीय भवन प्रमुख हैं'।[4]

कालान्तर में चित्रकारों के कई घराने बन गए थे। इन्हीं घरानों में कुछ ऐसे भी चित्रकार थे जो ज्यादा कुशल नहीं थे अतः वे चित्रकला पारखियों की कृपादृष्टि से वंचित थे। ये कम कुशल चित्रकार जन साधारण के लिए, उनकी रुचि एवं आवश्कता के अनुरूप चित्र बनाते थे क्योंकि इस समय तक भित्तिचित्र बनवाने का प्रचलन आम हो गया था, फिर भी, साधाराण जनता अपने घरों तथा गलियों में स्थित छोटे–छोटे मंदिरों की भित्तियों पर चित्र बनाने के लिए बड़े एवं प्रसिद्ध चित्रकारों की सेवा नहीं ले पा रही थी। ऐसे में शास्त्रीय शैली में शिक्षित होने पर भी जो बहुत मंजे हुए कलाकार नहीं थे, उन्हें भी काम मिल जाता था। इस तरह से हम देखते हैं कि वाराणसी में एक ही काल में दो तरह के चित्र बनाए जा रहे थे। पहली श्रेणी में वे चित्र थे जो चित्रकला की शास्त्रीय शैली में प्रशिक्षित विज्ञ चित्रकारों द्वारा बनाए जा रहे थे एवं देवी–देवताओं तथा पौराणिक कथाओं से सम्बन्धित थे तथा दूसरी श्रेणी में वे चित्रकार थे जो लोकजनों की रुचि के अनुरूप लोक जीवन की दिनचर्या से जुड़े विषयों वाले चित्र बना रहे थे।

वाराणसी में नगरीय और ग्रामीण दोनों क्षेत्र आते हैं। अतः यहाँ की चित्रकला भी दो धाराओं में साथ–साथ आगे बढ़ी। इस प्रक्रिया में लोक (ग्रामीण) एवं नागर (शास्त्रीय) दोनों ही शैलियों ने एक दूसरे को प्रभावित किया। लोक चित्रकला के रूप में पूर्वी उत्तर प्रदेश के इस हिस्से में विभिन्न त्यौहारों तथा विवाह आदि अवसरों पर प्रायः देवी–देवताओं या फिर हाथ में तलवार लिए दरबान, दूध–दही या मछली लिए औरत या कलश के साथ केले का वृक्ष आदि के चित्र बनाए जाते हैं। विभिन्न विषयों वाले इन भित्तिचित्रों का एक अद्भुत संसार है जो आने–जाने वाले लोगों को ठिठक कर खड़ा होने के लिए विवश कर देता है। यही कारण है कि वर्तमान समय में वाराणसी में भित्तिचित्रकला की दो प्रमुख श्रेणियाँ दिखाई देती हैं (1) वे चित्र, जो विज्ञ चित्रकारों के द्वारा मंदिरों, किलों, हवेलियों और मठों में बनायी गयी कला के उत्कृष्ट उदाहरण हैं तथा (2) वे चित्र, जो जनसामान्य की रुचि के अनुरूप लोक चित्रकारों द्वारा बनाए गए। प्रथम श्रेणी के चित्र शास्त्रोक्त नियमों के अंतर्गत पक्के रंगों से बनाए जाने के कारण दीर्घजीवी रहे हैं, वहीं द्वितीय श्रेणी के चित्र नियमों की उपेक्षा एवं कच्चे रंगों से बनाए जाने के कारण धूप एवं वर्षा के प्रहार से शीघ्र ही नष्ट हो जाते हैं। कमल गिरि के अनुसार 'इनके माध्यम और शैली में भी अंतर दिखाई देता है। प्रथम वर्ग के चित्रों में जहाँ पारंपरिक या शास्त्रीय, उदाहरणार्थ राजस्थानी और कंपनी शैली का प्रभाव दिखाई देता है, वहीं दूसरे वर्ग के चित्र स्थानीय शैली और लोकजीवन से प्रभावित हैं। इनके विषय भी अलग हैं'।[5]

धार्मिक मूल्यों से ओत–प्रोत वाराणसी के भित्ति चित्रों की विषयवस्तु भी स्वाभाविक रूप से धर्म प्रधान ही रही हैं। हृदय नारायण मिश्र के अनुसार 'जैन और बौद्ध साहित्य के साक्ष्यों से ज्ञात होता है कि काशी में नागों और यक्षों की पूजा होती थी। मोतीचन्द्र के अनुसार संभवतः इन्हीं यक्षों में शिव की पूजा निहित है क्योंकि बौद्ध साहित्य में एक स्थल पर काशी के प्रधान यक्ष को 'महाकाल' कहा गया है और महाकाल शिव को भी कहते हैं। शिव पूजा के प्रसार से काशी में यक्षपूजा का ह्रास हुआ (*मत्स्य पुराण,* अध्याय 180)। ऐसा लगता है कि यक्षपूजा का शिव पूजा में अन्तर्भान हो गया।[6] काशी में जगह–जगह वीर–मंदिर भी स्थित हैं जैसे लहुरावीर, मुड़कट्ठा बाबा आदि जो संभवतः यक्षपूजा परंपरा में ही आते हैं। शिव की नगरी काशी में हर गली–मुहल्ले में शिवलिंग स्थापित मिल ही जाते हैं, जिनके पीछे लंबा इतिहास व कथा जुड़ी हुई है। शिव के साथ–साथ गणेश, राम, कृष्ण, हनुमान एवं विभिन्न देवियों के प्राचीन मंदिर भी हैं। जिस प्रकार किसी भी मंदिर में मुख्य रूप से प्रतिष्ठित देवी या देवता की मूर्ति के अलावा अन्य देवी–देवताओं की भी मूर्तियाँ स्थापित की जाती हैं उसी प्रकार से भित्ति पर अन्य देवी–देवता के चित्र भी अंकित किए जाते रहे हैं जैसे वाराणसी के संकटमोचन स्थित हनुमान मंदिर के प्रांगण में अन्य देवी–देवताओं के भी भित्तिचित्र उल्लेखनीय हैं।

वाराणसी नगर की भित्तियों पर ऐतिहासिक काल से लेकर वर्तमान काल तक जो भी चित्र बनाए गए हैं, उनमें परंपरा की अविच्छिन्न धारा स्पष्ट देखी जा सकती है। यहाँ अनेक ऐसे छोटे मंदिर हैं जिनकी भित्तियों पर अंकित चित्र प्रायः देखने को मिल ही जाते हैं। लेखिका ने ऐसे चित्रों को भी संकलित करने का प्रयास किया है। वर्तमान लोक चित्रकारों द्वारा बनाए जा रहे ये चित्र वाराणसी एवं आसपास के नगरों की मृतप्राय भित्तिचित्रकला के सुंदर उदाहरण हैं। इन चित्रकारों ने चित्रकला की विधिवत शास्त्रीय शिक्षा नहीं ली है वरन् घर के किसी बुजुर्ग या परिचित कलाकार से सीखकर, निरंतर अभ्यास से निपुणता प्राप्त की है। बहुत से मंदिर तो ऐसे हैं जहाँ मात्र भक्तगण ही जाते हैं, कलापारखी नहीं। ऐसे में इन कलाकारों को वह सराहना या प्रशंसा भी नहीं मिलती जिसके वे पात्र हैं। अतः इनके द्वारा बनाए गए कुछ चित्रों की एक झलक देखिए, उन्हें सराहिए एवं समाज में उनकी आवश्यकता पर विचार कीजिए। प्रस्तुत लेख ऐसे ही चित्रकारों को प्रोत्साहन देने का भी एक प्रयास है।

संदर्भ

1. वाचस्पति गैरोला, 1963, पृ. 93, *'भारतीय चित्रकला'*, मित्र प्रकाशन, इलाहाबाद।
2. मोतीचन्द्र, 1985, पृ. 147, *'काशी का इतिहास'*, विश्व विद्यालय प्रकाशन, वाराणसी।
3. हृदय नारायण मिश्र, 2002, पृ. 18, *'बनारस की चित्रकला'*, कला प्रकाशन, वाराणसी।
4. कमल गिरि, पृ. 22, *'काशी की लोककला'*, जिला सांस्कृतिक समिति, संस्कृति विभाग, उत्तर प्रदेश।
5. *पूर्वोक्त*, पृ. 21
6. हृदय नारायण मिश्र, *पूर्वोक्त*, पृ. 57

30

पूर्वी उत्तर प्रदेश की गाहडवालयुगीन अभिलेखीय पुरासंपदा

इन्दुधर मिश्र

पुराभिलेखिक पुरासंपदा की दृष्टि से उत्तर प्रदेश का पूर्वी क्षेत्र प्रागैतिहासिक काल से ही अत्यंत समृद्ध रहा है। एक विशिष्ट भू–सांस्कृतिक इकाई के रूप में गाहडवालयुगीन अभिलेखों में इसकी ख्याति 'सरयूपार' के रूप में है जो मूलतः सरयू और अचिरावती जैसी नदियों के द्वारा सिंचित भूभाग के लिए प्रयुक्त होता रहा है। प्राचीन काल में वैदिक, जैन, बौद्ध, आजीविक एवं अन्य संप्रदायों के धर्मोपदेशकों की प्रज्ञा भूमि होने का गौरव भी इसी क्षेत्र को प्राप्त हुआ है।

इस क्षेत्र की एक समृद्ध अभिलेखीय पुरसम्पदा 11–12 वीं शताब्दी ईसवी के गाहडवाल युग से सम्बद्ध है। यह सर्वविदित है कि गाहडवालों के शताधिक अभिलेख जो मूलतः दान देख हैं, इस क्षेत्र के तीर्थों से जारी किये गये हैं। इन अभिलेखों में 11–12वीं शताब्दी ईसवी के राजनीतिक, प्रशासनिक, सामाजिक, आर्थिक, धार्मिक तथा नैतिक जीवन के विविध पक्षों की प्रचुर सूचनाएँ संग्रहीत हैं। अतः प्रस्तुत शोध–पत्र में गाहडवालयुगीन अभिलेखों की पुरासम्पदा का विषयगत अध्ययन करने का प्रयास किया गया है।

इस क्षेत्र में गाहडवालों से सम्बन्धित सूचनाएँ मूलतः उनके संस्कृत भाषा एवं नागरी लिपि में निबद्ध तथा विक्रम सम्वत् 1171 से 1202 तक की विभिन्न तिथियों में उट्टंकित गोरखपुर तथा देवरिया जिलों से प्राप्त ताम्रलेखों से प्राप्त होती है। इन दोनों जिलो में गाहडवालों के सर्वाधिक अभिलेख प्राप्त हुए हैं जिनका मुख्य प्रतिपाद्य राजाओं और राजपुत्रों द्वारा दिये गये भूमिदान का अंकन ही है तथापि परोक्षतः इनके द्वारा सरयूपार के इतिहास, भूगोल एवं संस्कृति पर प्रचुर प्रकाश पड़ता है।

इस क्षेत्र से प्राप्त कलचुरि तथा गाहडवाल अभिलेखों में 'सरूवार' का उल्लेख इस बात का परिचायक है कि पूर्वमध्यकाल में सरूवार (सरयूपार) की पहचान एक पृथक भौगोलिक इकाई के रूप में स्थापित हो चुकी थी। 11वीं शती के पूर्वार्द्ध में मध्य और दक्षिण–पश्चिम भारत की विभिन्न राजनीतिक शक्तियों में कन्नौज तथा काशी पर अधिकार करने के लिए जो प्रतिस्पर्धा चल रही थी उसके परिणामस्वरूप उत्तर भारत में व्याप्त

राजनीतिक अस्थिरता का लाभ उठा लेना गाहड़वाल वंशीय राजपुरूषों के लिए बहुत दुष्कर नहीं था।[1] ऐसे में गाहड़वाल वंश के वास्तविक संस्थापक चन्द्रदेव ने कनौज और काशी में गाहड़वालों की स्वतंत्र सत्ता की स्थापना की।

गाहडवाल शासक चन्द्रदेव (1090–1103 ईसवी) के आभिलेखिक साक्ष्यों से विदित होता है कि काशी तथा अयोध्या सहित गंगा और सरयू के तटवर्ती प्रदेश (आधुनिक रूहेलखण्ड, अवध तथा पूर्वी उ. प्र.) उसके अधिकार क्षेत्र के अंतर्गत थे। इन्हीं को आधार बनाकर (1072–73 ईसवी में कलचुरि कर्ण की मृत्यु के अनन्तर) उसने अपने भुजबल से कान्यकुब्ज पर भी अधिकार कर लिये।[2] तुर्की आक्रमणों के कारण उत्तर भारत में व्याप्त अराजक तथा अरक्षित अवस्था का अंत कर उसने काशी (वाराणसी), कुशिक (कन्नौज), उत्तर कोशल (अवध) तथा इन्द्र स्थानीय (दिल्ली–इन्द्रप्रस्थ) के परिपार्श्ववर्ती प्रदेशों पर अधिकार कर लिया।[3] इन उपलब्धियों के लिए उसे अनेक राजाओं से संघर्ष करना (*क्रान्त द्विषन्मण्डलः*) पड़ा। कान्यकुब्ज अपने राजनीतिक महत्व के ही कारण गाहडवालों की राजधानी कहलाता था, उनकी वास्तविक (सांस्कृतिक) राजधानी वाराणसी थी।[4] 1093 ईसवी के चन्द्रावती अभिलेख में चन्द्रदेव द्वारा नरपति, गजपति, गिरिपति और त्रिशंकुपति पर विजय प्राप्त करने का उल्लेख है। इनमें नरपति और गजपति को इतिहासविदों ने कलचुरि राजाओं अथवा सामंतों की उपाधियों के रूप में स्वीकार किया है।[5] ऐसा प्रतीत होता है कि गिरिपति और त्रिशंकुपति की उपाधियों से सरयूपार के कलचुरियों तथा दरदगण्डकी देश के सावर्णिवंशियों की ओर इंगित किया गया है। अभिलेखों से ज्ञात होता है कि 11वीं शती के अंत तथा 12वीं शती के आरंभ में क्रमशः सरयूपार में कलचुरियों की एक शाखा तथा गण्डक घाटी में सावर्णिवंश का शासन था।

चन्द्रदेव के पश्चात् उसका पुत्र 'मदनपाल' (1103–13 ई.) गाहडवाल साम्राज्य का उत्तराधिकारी बना। इसके कुल प्राप्त पांच अभिलेखों में सम्भवतः पांचवा दानपत्र ही उसका निजी दान पत्र है।[6] इसके दुर्बल शासनकाल में सरयूपार ने पुनः स्थानीय स्वतंत्रता की लालिमा देखी और वहां सावर्णिवंशियों का अधिकार हो गया किन्तु पराक्रमी गाहडवाल नरेश गोविन्दचन्द्र ने सरयूपार पर विजय प्राप्त कर उसे अपने साम्राज्य का अंग बना लिया।

पूर्वांचल क्षेत्र में गाहडवाल सत्ता का चरमोत्कर्ष चन्द्रदेव के पौत्र एवं रानी राल्हणदेवी से उत्पन्न मदनपाल के पुत्र 'गोविन्दचन्द्र' (1113–54 ई.) के शासनकाल से प्रारंभ होता है। उसने अपने पैतृक साम्राज्य को स्थायी रखने में ही सफलता प्राप्त नहीं की वरन् अनेक दिशाओं में साम्राज्य का विस्तार भी किया। एक स्वतंत्र शासक के रूप में उसकी सैनिक तथा सांस्कृतिक उपलब्धियाँ इतनी विविध और महत्त्वपूर्ण थी कि कुछ ही समय में वह न केवल हर्ष और मिहिरभोज की तरह आर्यावर्त का राजशिरोमणि बन गया अपितु उसके कारण कन्नौज की भाग्यलक्ष्मी पुनः प्रतिष्ठित हो गयी। काशी और कन्नौज राजनय, विद्या और धर्म के प्रख्यात केन्द्र बन गये।

इस क्षेत्र के विभिन्न स्थानों से प्राप्त उसके 40 से अधिक अभिलेख तथा उसके महासांधिविग्रहिक लक्ष्मीधर की कृतियों से उसके सत्ता–विस्तार, संप्रभुता, सैनिक सफलता, राजनीतिक प्रभाव, साहित्यिक अभिरूचि और कलासम्पदा विषयक विपुल सूचनायें मिलती हैं। इन साक्ष्यों में पूर्वी उत्तर प्रदेश के बनारस, गोण्डा, गोरखपुर तथा देवरिया जिलों से प्राप्त अभिलेखों की संख्या अधिक है। केवल गोरखपुर तथा देवरिया जिलों से अभी तक उसके 7 अभिलेख प्राप्त हुए हैं।

विवेच्य क्षेत्र से गोविन्दचन्द्र के शासन काल का प्रथम तिथियुक्त अभिलेख पाली (गोरखपुर जिले में धुरियापार परगना) नामक गांव से प्राप्त हुआ है जो वि.सं. 1171 (1114 ईसवी) के भाद्रपद मास में जारी किया गया। इस अभिलेख में गोविन्दचन्द्र की प्रशंसा इस बात के लिए की गई है कि उसने 'नवराज्यगज' पर अधिकार कर लिया।[7] अभिलेख में इसकी पहचान निश्चित रूप से नहीं हो सकी है। इस ताम्रशासन में सरूवार के ओणवल पठक के अंतर्गत सिरसी पत्तला के पाली ग्राम में 30 हल भूमि के दान का अंकन है। चूंकि अभिलेख अपूर्ण है

अतः अन्य प्रासंगिक तथ्यों का ज्ञान नहीं हो पाता है।[8]

इस क्षेत्र से गोविन्दचन्द्र का दूसरा अभिलेख दोनबुजुर्ग से वि.सं. 1176 (1120 ईसवी) का प्राप्त हुआ है। इसमें कुल 36 पंक्तियां हैं जिनमें 19 प्रथम फलक पर तथा शेष 17 द्वितीय फलक पर उत्कीर्ण हैं। इस अभिलेख का प्रयोजन गोविन्दचन्द द्वारा वि.सं. 1176 के ज्येष्ठ मास के शुक्ल पक्ष की अष्टमी तिथि, दिन मंगलवार को, अलंविमहापुर के मन्दलिया ग्राम में स्थित अपने शिविर में निवास करते हुए, गंगा में स्नानोपरांत, द्रोणायणषड[9] के वत्सगोत्रीय ब्राह्मण टुल्टाइच शर्मा को अलाप पत्तला में स्थित बड़ग्राम के दान का अंकन करना है। बड़ग्राम की पहचान दयाराम साहनी[10] ने देवरिया जिले की सलेमपुर तहसील में स्थित बड़गो ग्राम से तथा दिवाकर प्रसाद तिवारी[11] ने पूर्वोत्तर रेलवे के बनकटा तथा मैरवा रेलवे स्टेशनों के बीच रेलमार्ग से दक्षिण स्थित बड़गांव नामक दो ग्रामों में से किसी एक के साथ स्थापित की है। इसी प्रकार द्रोणायणषड की पहचान दयाराम साहनी ने दोनबुजुर्ग (मैरवा रेलवे स्टेशन से लगभग 11 किमी. उत्तर, बिहार के सीवान जिले में स्थित) से की है।

गोरखपुर जिले से गाहडवालों का एक अन्य अभिलेख प्राप्त हुआ है। भारतीय पुरातत्त्व सर्वेक्षण विभाग की 1973 की एक रिपोर्ट में 'उत्तर प्रदेश' शीर्षकान्तर्गत इस ताम्रलेख का संक्षिप्त विवरण प्रकाशित किया गया है।[12] तद्नुसार यह संस्कृत भाषा में निबद्ध, नागरी लिपि में उत्कीर्ण, गोविन्दचन्द्र के शासनकाल की तिथि वि.स. 1176 (1120 ई.) से युक्त है। इस अभिलेख के उट्टंकन का प्रयोजन राजा द्वारा अपने शिविर (भ) 'दस' से वत्स गोत्र तथा वत्स, सावर्ण्ण, अंगिरस, दैवल, भार्ग्गव प्रवर के ब्राह्मण श्री धीरी शर्मा को सरूवार में स्थित चिमान सिवचलियापाटक के दान का अंकन करना है। इस अभिलेख और दोनबुजुर्ग अभिलेख की तिथि तथा दानग्रहीता ब्राह्मणों के गोत्र एक समान हैं।

इस क्षेत्र से प्राप्त, चौथा अभिलेख, गोविन्दचन्द्र एवं उसकी माता राल्हणदेवी का पाली अभिलेख (द्वितीय पाली अभिलेख वि.सं. 1189) है जो ठक्कुर विष्णु द्वारा लिखित एवं एफ. कीलहार्न[13] द्वारा सम्पादित किया गया है। यह ताम्रशासन 13.50 x 10" आकार के दो ताम्रफलकों के एक ओर उत्कीर्ण है। इनके साथ एक वर्तुलाकार मुहर भी मिली है जिसके ऊर्ध्वार्द्ध भाग में नागरी लिपि में 'श्रीमद्गोविन्दचन्द्रदेव' लेख अंकित है। लेख के ऊपर दक्षिणाभिमुखी गरूड़ाकृति तथा नीचे शंखाकृति है। परमभट्टारक महाराजाधिराज परमेश्वर गोविन्दचन्द्रदेव इसमें अंकित करता है कि वैशाख मास के शुक्ल पक्ष में अक्षय तृतीया के पर्व पर स्वप्नेश्वरघट्ट पर सती (नदी)[14] में स्नान कर, ओणवल पठक के गोयर पत्तला में स्थित गुदुवी ग्राम में 10 नालुक भूमि, मुद्गल गोत्र तथा इन्द्रादित्य के पुत्र ठक्कुर जयपाल शर्मा को उपहार स्वरूप देने के लिए उसने अपनी माता महाराज्ञी राल्हणदेवी को हस्तांतरित किया। दानग्रहीता के पक्ष में भाग भोगकर तथा प्रवनिकर का उल्लेख है। पंक्ति 34 में अभिलेख मात्र अंकों में तिथ्यांकित है।

राज्यपाल देव के गगहा (गोरखपुर) अभिलेख वि.स. 1199 (1143 ईसवी) को एस.सी.एल. कार्लाइल ने बांसगांव तहसील में, राप्ती नदी के पश्चिमी कांठे से प्राप्त किया था। इस अभिलेख की विषयवस्तु अन्य अभिलेखों जैसी ही है। इसमें यशोविग्रह, महीचन्द्र, चन्द्रदेव, मदनपाल और गोविन्दचन्द्र की प्रशंसा की गई है।

अभिलेख का मुख्य प्रयोजन परमभट्टारक महाराजाधिराज परमेश्वर परममाहेश्वर मदनपाल के पुत्र परमभट्टारक महाराजाधिराज परमेश्वर परममाहेश्वर गोविन्दचन्द्र के शासनकाल में उसके पुत्र एवं युवराज महाराजपुत्र श्रीमद्राज्यपालदेव द्वारा गुझडग्राम स्थित अपने शिविर में निवास के समय, पिता की सम्मति लेकर, त्रिवेणी में स्नान कर तथा वासुदेवादि की पूजा कर वत्सगोत्रीय, गर्ग, भार्गव, च्यवन, त्रिप्रवरीय यजुर्वेद शाखानुयायी ठक्कुर श्री महीधर के पौत्र, ठक्कुर श्री जसराम के पुत्र ठक्कुर श्री देवराम, ठक्कुर श्री भूपति तथा ठक्कुर श्री श्रीधर नामक तीन सहोदर भाइयों को, संवत् 1199 के फाल्गुन मास के शुक्ल पक्ष की एकादशी तिथि को हथौण्ड पत्तला में कुण्डग्राम के पश्चिम, बिछिया ताल के पूर्व बीच में स्थित काछ भूमि तथा गगहा के पूर्व ऊपरी बांगर भूमि के

दान का अंकन है। ये दोनों शब्द वर्तमान प्रचलित 'कछार' और 'बांगर' के पूर्वरूप हैं। तिथि के उल्लेख में शब्दों तथा अंकों का प्रयोग भी उल्लेखनीय है। यह लेखक कर्णिक वीवीक या बीबीक द्वारा लिखा गया।

उनवल से भी राज्यपालदेव का वि.सं. 1201 का एक ताम्रपट्टाभिलेख प्राप्त हुआ है। इसकी खोज 1965 में शिवाजी सिंह ने की थी और वी.एस. पाठक के सहयोग से सर्वप्रथम सम्पादित किया।[15] बांसगांव तहसील से प्राप्त यह अभिलेख सुरक्षित अवस्था में है जो राजा साहब श्री चूड़ामणि प्रताप नारायण सिंह के पास है। यह अभिलेख घोषित करता है कि वि.सं. 1201 के कार्तिक मास के शुक्ल पक्ष की चतुर्दशी, दिन बृहस्पतिवार को, राज्यपालपुर में गंगा स्नान कर विविध कर्मकाण्डों को विधिवत् पूर्ण करने के उपरांत, महाराजपुत्र राज्यपालदेव ने दोहरी पत्तला में स्थित मलवली नाम ग्राम को वाड़ा पाठक सहित, दामोदर शर्मा नामक ब्राह्मण को दान में दिया। इस ताम्रशासन का लेखक चक्रस्वामी का पुत्र था। वह छांदोग्य शाखानुयायी भारद्वाज गोत्रीय ठक्कुर श्री वीवीक है। यह करणिक वीवीक राज्यपालदेव के दो अन्य अभिलेखों गगहा ताम्रलेख (वि. 1199) तथा भदैनी ताम्रशासन (वि. 1203) द्वारा सुविदित है।

इसी क्षेत्र से वि.सं. 1202 का गोविन्दचन्द्र का लार (देवरिया जिला) दानशासन प्राप्त हुआ है जिसमें यह उल्लेख है कि अपने शिविर मुद्‌गगिरि में निवास करते समय, गंगा में स्नानोपरांत वर्ष 1202, वैशाख सुदि 3, दिन सोमवार को राजा ने ठक्कुर उद्धरण के पौत्र ठक्कुर माधव के पुत्र, चारों वेदों में निष्णात, काश्यप गोत्रीय तथा काश्यप, आवत्सार और नैध्रुव–विप्रवरीय ब्राह्मण ठक्कुर श्रीधर को सरूवार में दुधालि से सम्बद्ध गोविसालक मे पान्दल पत्तला के अंतर्गत स्थित पोटाचवड नाम ग्राम का दान किया। इस अभिलेख की विशेषता यह है कि इसमें दान की तिथि शब्दांकों में की गई है। इसके लेखक करणिक ठक्कुर सेल्हण हैं। एफ. कीलहार्न ने इसे संपादित किया है।[16]

गोविन्दचन्द्र का कमौली (बनारस) से प्राप्त वि.सं. 1176 के अभिलेखानुसार गोविन्दचन्द्र ने वाराणसी में गंगा स्नानोपरांत सरू (गा?)र में एक गांव का दान महापुरोहित जागू शर्मा को किया था। इसका लेखक ठक्कुर गागूक है।[17]

गोविन्दचन्द्र का एक अभिलेख सहेत–महेत (वि.सं. 1186) से भी मिला है, जिसमें किसी 'गाधिपुराधिराज्य'[18] का उल्लेख है किन्तु स्पष्टतः इसकी पहचान नहीं हो सकी है। रमाशंकर त्रिपाठी[19] के अनुसार उपर्युक्त राज्य कन्नौज ही था जिसके राजा को 'गाधिपुराधिप' कहा गया है।

गाहडवाल शक्ति के इस क्षेत्र में विस्तार से सम्बन्धित एक अभिलेख गोरखपुर से लगभग 35 किमी. उत्तर–पश्चिम में पीपीगंज के निकट प्राप्त हुआ है। इसकी तिथि वि. सं. 1179 है। यह गोविन्दचन्द्र गाहडवाल का अभिलेख है जिसमें वत्स गोत्रीय धीरीशर्मा को दिये गये ग्रामदान का उल्लेख किया गया है। इस ग्राम और दानग्रहीता का उल्लेख अभिलेख की 12वीं पंक्ति में है और यहां स्पष्ट रूप से यह कहा गया है कि यह क्षेत्र सरवार में स्थित था। उल्लेखनीय है कि सरवार या सरूवार का उल्लेख कलचुरि अभिलेख में भी मिलता है। ऐसा प्रतीत होता है कि गाहडवाल शासकों ने कलचुरियों से सत्ता छीन ली थी। गोविन्दचन्द्र गाहडवाल ने इस क्षेत्र में वि.सं. 1171 के बाद ही अपना शासन स्थापित किया होगा क्योंकि कलचुरि शासक, कहला ताम्रलेख के अनुसार वि.सं. 1135 अर्थात् 1077 ई. तक इस क्षेत्र में स्थित थे। कलचुरियों की सत्ता की समाप्ति और गाहडवाल सत्ता की स्थापना के बीच 37 वर्षों का अंतराल दिखाई देता है।

इन 37 वर्षों के राजनीतिक इतिहास पर प्रकाश वि.सं. 1167 के एक अभिलेख से पड़ता है जो परमभट्टारक महाराजाधिराज परमेश्वर परममाहेश्वर श्री कीर्तिपाल देव का है। देवरिया जनपद के भाटपार से प्राप्त इस अभिलेखानुसार उसने दो ग्राम 'दरदगंडकी' देश में अनुदान में दिये थे। रोमा नियोगी[20] के अनुसार दरत का अर्थ है पर्वत तथा गण्डकी निश्चय ही आधुनिक गंडक का द्योतन करता है। इस प्रकार इस अभिलेख से

प्रमाणित हो जाता है कि कीर्तिपाल का साम्राज्य आधुनिक देवरिया से हिमालय की तराई तक फैला हुआ था। यद्यपि अभिलेख यह सूचित नहीं करता कि कीर्तिपाल किस वंश का शासक था किंतु निश्चय ही 1111 ईसवी में वह इस क्षेत्र का शासक था। 1114 ईसवी में गोविन्दचन्द्र गाहडवाल गोरखपुर के पाली क्षेत्र में एक भूखंड दान कर रहा है और 1119 ईसवी में वह भाटपार जो कीर्तिपाल के उपर्युक्त अभिलेख का प्राप्ति स्थल है, के सन्निकट मैरवा में एक ग्राम का दान करते हुए प्रदर्शित है।

उपर्युक्त आभिलेखिक प्रमाणों से यह प्रबल संभावना प्रकट होती है कि, गोविन्दचन्द्र गाहडवाल ने कीर्तिपाल से यह क्षेत्र प्राप्त किया। इसकी सम्पुष्टि पाली, दोनबुजुर्ग के अतिरिक्त उपर्युक्त अप्रकाशित पीपीगंज से प्राप्त गोविन्दचन्द्र गाहडवाल के अभिलेख से भी होती है। इस अभिलेख से एक अन्य संभावना भी प्रकट होती है कि पाली, गगहा, लार, दोनबुजुर्ग आदि के अभिलेख, जहां गोविन्दचन्द्र गाहडवाल की उस विजय के साक्षी हैं जो सरयूपार के पूर्वी और दक्षिणी क्षेत्रों में की गयी थी, वहीं पीपीगंज का अभिलेख गाहडवाल शासक के पश्चिम और उत्तर के क्षेत्रों की विजयों का सूचक है। इससे सहज अनुमान लगाया जा सकता है कि इस शासक के काल में गाहडवालों का राजनीतिक वर्चस्व नेपाल की तराई तक फैल चुका था।

गोविन्दचन्द्र की रानी कुमारदेवी के सारनाथ से प्राप्त एक तिथि विहीन अभिलेख में कहा गया है कि गोविन्दचन्द्र दुष्ट तुरुष्क वीर से वाराणसी की रक्षा के लिए हर (शंकर) द्वारा नियुक्त मानो हरि (विष्णु) का अवतार था।[21] पाठक[22] के अनुसार यह उल्लेख उसके युवराजत्व काल में तुर्कों के विरूद्ध लड़े गये युद्धों का संकेतक है, क्योंकि मसूद तृतीय के बाद कन्नौज, वाराणसी अथवा गाहडवाल क्षेत्रों के किसी स्थान पर तुर्कों के किसी आक्रमण की सूचना हमें नहीं प्राप्त होती है।

गाहडवालों के कतिपय अन्य पुरातात्त्विक साक्ष्यों की प्राप्ति से भी पूर्वांचल पर उनका प्रभाव स्पष्ट होता है। प्राचीन कोशल क्षेत्र से गोविन्दचन्द्र के सिक्कों की एक बड़ी निधि प्राप्त हुई है। आधुनिक बहराइच जिले के 'नानपारा' नामक स्थान से 1887 ईसवी में एक मुद्रानिधि भी प्राप्ति हुई थी, जिसमें 800 सोने के सिक्के बताये जाते हैं। इन सिक्कों में सोने की मात्रा कम है एवं अन्य सहयोगी धातुओं की मात्रा अधिक है।

उपर्युक्त विवेचन से स्पष्ट होता है कि विवेच्य क्षेत्र का अधिकांश भाग 12वीं शती ईसवी के अंतिम चरण तक गाहडवाल शासकों के अधीन रहा तथा इन राजाओं के काल में विवेचित स्थलों का विशेष महत्त्व था। कालान्तर में गाहडवाल राजा जयचन्द्र के समय मुहम्मद गोरी के सफल आक्रमण के फलस्वरूप गाहडवाल साम्राज्य की नींव हिल गयी और उसने सम्भवतः बनारस तक लूटपाट की। परंतु जौनपुर जिले में मछलीशहर तहसील से जयचन्द्र के पुत्र हरिश्चन्द्र का वि.सं. 1255 का एक दान पत्राभिलेख[23] मिला है जिसमें उसके लिए स्वतंत्रता–बोधक उपाधियों का प्रयोग किया गया है। इसकी स्वतंत्र राजनीतिक स्थिति का समर्थन 1197 ईसवी के राणक श्री विजयकर्ण के मिर्जापुर जिले के बेलखरा स्तंभ अभिलेख[24] से भी होता है। इस लेख से इतना तो स्पष्ट हो ही जाता है कि मिर्जापुर–वाराणसी–जौनपुर के क्षेत्रों में हरिश्चन्द्र पूर्णरूप से 1197–98 ईसवी तक अधिकार सम्पन्न था किंतु उस तिथि के बाद उसकी अथवा कन्नौज–काशी के गाहडवाल राज्य के अन्य किसी भी प्रतिनिधि की कोई जानकारी नहीं है।

संदर्भ

1. पाठक, विशुद्धानन्द, *उत्तर भारत का राजनीतिक इतिहास,* पृ. 347
2. *तत्रैव,* पृ. 348
3. *तत्रैव,* पृ. 348–49, उद्धृत – *एपिग्राफिया इण्डिका,* जिल्द 18, पृ. 16

4. राय, एच. सी., *डायनेस्टिक हिस्ट्री ऑफ नार्दर्न इण्डिया,* वाल्यूम–1, पृ. 507
5. पाठक, विशुद्धानन्द, *उत्तर भारत का राजनीतिक इतिहास,* पृ. 349, पाद टि. – 2
6. *जर्नल ऑफ उत्तर प्रदेश हिस्टारिकल सोसायटी,* भाग 14, पृ. 66 और आगे
7. *जे.बी.ओ.आर.एस.,* जि. 19, भाग 1, 2 पृ. 233–38
8. नियोगी, रोमा, *गाहडवाल डायनेस्टी,* परिशिष्ट–बी. एपिग्राफिक नोट्स 9 पृ. 247
9. साहनी, दयाराम, *एपिग्राफिया इण्डिका* जि. 18, (1925–26), पृ. 219 एवं अनु.
10. *इण्डियन आर्कियोलोजी,* 1965–66, पृ. 68
11. *गोरखपुर परिक्षेत्र का इतिहास,* प्रथम संस्करण : 2004, पृ. 243
12. *इण्डियन आर्कियोलॉजी,* 1965–66, ए रिव्यू (सं. ए. घोष), पृ. 68
13. *एपिग्राफिया इण्डिका,* जि. 5, पृ. 113–15
14. रोमा नियोगी ने सती नदी को गंगा माना है। द्रष्टव्य, *पूर्वोक्त,* परिशिष्ट।
15. सिंह, शिवाजी, 'ए न्यू कापरप्लेट इन्सक्रिप्सन आव द गाहड़वाल महाराजपुत्र राज्यपालदेव डेटेड वी.एस. 1201, *बुलेटिन आव द कालेज आव इण्डोलाजी,* बी.एच.यू. 1965–66, अंक 9, भाग 2, पृ. 174 एवं अनु.।
16. एफ. कीलहार्न, *'लार प्लेट्स आव गोविन्द चन्द्र आव कन्नौज',* *एपिग्राफिया इण्डिका,* जि. 7, पृ. 98–100
17. *डायनेस्टिक हिस्ट्र का नार्दर्न इण्डिया,,* भाग 1, पृ. 517–18, *ऐपिग्राफिया इण्डिका,,* जिल्द 4, पृ. 109 एवं आगे–कीलहार्न द्वारा संपादित। तिथि संदिग्ध है।
18. *श्रीमद गाधि पुराधि (ज्यं) मसमं.......*। *ऐपिग्राफिया इण्डिका,,* भाग 11, पृ. 24–25
19. त्रिपाठी, रमाशंकर, *हिस्ट्री ऑफ कन्नौज,* पृ. 301
20. नियोगी रोमा, *हिस्ट्री ऑफ गाहड़वाल डायनेस्टी,* पृ. 122
21. *एपिग्राफिया इण्डिका,* भाग 1, पृ. 324, श्लोक 16
22. पाठक, विशुद्धानन्द, *उत्तर भारत का राजनीतिक इतिहास,* पृ. 353
23. *ऐपिग्राफिया इण्डिका,,* भाग 10, पृ. 93–100
24. *जर्नल ऑफ एशियाटिक सोसायटी ऑफ बंगाल,* 1911, पृ. 763–65

31

पूर्वी उत्तर प्रदेश के जैन पुरास्थल एवं पुराभिलेख

दयामणि कुशवाहा

पूर्वी उत्तर प्रदेश आर्य एवं श्रमण संस्कृतियों की समन्वय स्थली के रूप में ख्यात है। उन्मेषशालिनी भारतीय संस्कृति के मार्ग में आये गत्यावरोधों को दूर करने में इस क्षेत्र ने सदैव से ही अग्रणी भूमिका का निर्वहन किया है। ये अवरोध चाहे इस भारत भूमि की उपज रहें हो या विदेशियों द्वारा थोपे गये हों, उन्हें विदीर्ण करने की क्रान्तिकारी पहल इसी क्षेत्र द्वारा की गयी जिसे छठी शती ई.पू. मे महावीर स्वामी व गौतम बुद्ध के रूप में, मध्य युग में गोरख एवं कबीर के रूप में तथा आधुनिक युग में मंगल पाण्डेय, राम प्रसाद बिस्मिल सदृश क्रान्तिकारियों के रूप में देखा जा सकता है।

किसी राष्ट्र की स्मृतियाँ ही उसका इतिहास है और इतिहास उन स्मृतियों से संबंधित लिखित दस्तावेजों और वस्तुओं से पुष्टि प्राप्त करता है। प्राचीन भारतीय इतिहास को पुष्टि प्रदान करने वाले लिखित दस्तावेज की प्रामाणिकता पुरावस्तुओं पर ही अधिक निर्भर करती है। अतः इतिहास की रचना में पुरावस्तुओं की महत्ता और अधिक बढ़ जाती है।

छठी शती ई.पू. में भारत वर्ष के धार्मिक जीवन मूल्यों में आयी गिरावट का प्रभाव इसके सामाजिक, आर्थिक व राजनीतिक जीवन पर भी पड़ा जिससे भारतीय संस्कृति की उदात्तता पर प्रश्न चिन्ह जैसी स्थिति उत्पन्न हो गयी। ऐसी दशा में इसी क्षेत्र से महावीर एवं महात्मा बुद्ध जैसे महापुरूषों ने धार्मिक क्रान्ति का बिगुल बजाया और राष्ट्र के धार्मिक जीवन को शुचिता और सदाचार से समन्वित कर दिया। सौभाग्य से इन दोनों महापुरूषों ने पूर्वी–उत्तर–प्रदेश की इस पावन धरा की गोद में अपनी अंतिम जीवन यात्रा भी की।

महावीर ने संसार–चक्र एवं दुःखों से मानवमात्र की मुक्ति हेतु आत्म–संयम और इन्द्रिय–निग्रह पर अपेक्षाकृत अधिक बल दिया। वे स्वयं इन्द्रियों के रागद्वेषादि विकारों पर विजय प्राप्त करने के कारण 'जिन' व उनके अनुयायी 'जैन' कहलाए।

"राग–द्वेषादि दोषान् कर्मशत्रून् जयतीति जिनः
तस्यानुयायिनो जैनाः।"

अर्थात् जिसने रागद्वेषादि कर्म शत्रुओं पर विजय प्राप्त कर ली हो, वह 'जिन' है और उसके अनुयायी 'जैन' हैं।[1]

जैन धर्म के अनुयायियों ने कालान्तर में महावीर के अतिरिक्त उनके पूर्ववर्ती 23 अन्य 'जिनों' के अस्तित्व को स्वीकृति प्रदान कर इनकी संख्या 24 कर दी। इन 'जिनों' को जैन परंपरा में 'तीर्थंकर' भी कहा जाता है। जैन धर्मानुयायियों ने इन सभी तीर्थंकरों या जिनों की उपासना हेतु मन्दिरों और मूर्तियों का निर्माण प्रारंभ कर दिया जिनके अवशेष अद्यावधि पुरातात्त्विक सर्वेक्षणों एवं उत्खननों में प्राप्त हो रहे हैं। इस प्रकार के अवशेषों से पूर्वी–उत्तर–प्रदेश भी खाली नहीं है। इस क्षेत्र के अनेक पुरास्थलों जैसे रूद्रपुर, पावा, काकन्दी, कहांव आदि से इस धर्म से सम्बन्धित अनेक पुरावस्तुएँ प्राप्त हुई हैं जिनका संक्षिप्त परिचय अग्रलिखित पंक्तियों में द्रष्टव्य है।

रूद्रपुर

यह पूर्वी–उत्तर प्रदेश के देवरिया जनपद के अन्तर्गत एक तहसील मुख्यालय है जो जिला मुख्यालय से लगभग 25 किमी. दक्षिण में स्थित है। प्राचीन काल में इसे 'नामीकाशी' के नाम से जाना जाता था किन्तु 1605 ईसवी में श्रीनेत्रवंशीय शासक रूद्रसेन द्वारा यहाँ के प्राचीन दुर्ग के स्थान पर एक नवीन दुर्ग के निर्माण के बाद इस स्थान को रूद्रपुर कहा जाने लगा।[2] यहाँ से प्राप्त ध्वंसावशेषों का एक टीला पुरातात्त्विक अन्वेषणों की एक महत्त्वपूर्ण उपलब्धि है जिससे मौर्यकाल से लेकर 12वीं शती तक के पुरावशेष प्राप्त हो चुके हैं। इन पुरावशेषों में ब्राह्मण व जैन धर्म से सम्बन्धित प्रतिमाएं सम्मिलित हैं। जैन धर्म से सम्बन्धित प्रतिमाओं में महावीर स्वामी की प्रतिमा विशेष उल्लेखनीय है।[3] रूद्रपुर कस्बे के पश्चिम में स्थित टीले से कार्लायल महोदय को एक खण्डित जैन प्रतिमा प्राप्त हुई थी जिसकी पादपीठ पर कुटिल लिपि में संवत् 1161 का एक लेख उत्कीर्ण है।[4] यहाँ से प्राप्त पुरावस्तुओं को देखते हुए 1991–92 में भारतीय पुरातत्त्व सर्वेक्षण विभाग के तत्कालीन निदेशक पी.सी. जोशी ने इस क्षेत्र के सर्वेक्षण के दौरान इस स्थल को संभावनाओं से भरापूरा स्थल कहा था।[5] यहाँ से प्राप्त विभिन्न धर्मों से संबंधित प्रतिमाएं इस स्थल में व्याप्त धार्मिक सहिष्णुता की द्योतक हैं।

खुखुन्दु

यह पूर्वी–उत्तर प्रदेश के देवरिया जनपद के अन्तर्गत देवरिया–भटनी रेलमार्ग के नूनखार रेलवे स्टेशन से 3 कि.मी. दक्षिण में स्थित है। यह प्राचीनकाल में किष्किन्धापुर या काकन्दी नगर के नाम से जाना जाता था।[6] श्वेताम्बर मान्यतानुसार यहाँ पर नौवे जैन तीर्थंकर पुष्पदन्त (सुविधिनाथ प्रभु) का जन्म, दीक्षा, केवल ज्ञान व कल्याणक (जैन तीर्थंकरों के जीवन से सम्बन्धित महत्त्वपूर्ण घटनाएँ) सम्पन्न हुए थे।[7] साथ ही यहाँ पर अनेकबार महावीर स्वामी का समवशरण भी आया था[8] तथा जैन मुनि अभय घोष ने यहीं पर निर्वाण प्राप्त किया था।[9]

कनिंघम महोदय ने यह संभावना व्यक्त की है कि यह वही ग्राम हो सकता है जिसको ह्वेनसांग ने अपने यात्रा वृत्तान्त में कसया से बनारस मार्ग पर कसया से 200 ली. (30 मील) दक्षिण–पश्चिम में स्थित बताया है।[10] यहाँ पर 1.5 कि.मी. की परिधि में 30 टीले हैं जिन पर मंदिरों व स्तूपों के ध्वंशवशेष, खण्डित दीवालें, अलंकृत ईंटें व ब्राह्मण तथा जैन धर्म से संबंधित अनेक प्रतिमाएँ प्राप्त हुई हैं। कनिंघम ने यहाँ से प्राप्त प्रभूत पुरावशेषों की तुलना नालन्दा के पुरावशेषों से की है और यह मत व्यक्त किया है कि यहाँ से अधिक पुरावशेष नालन्दा के

अतिरिक्त अन्य किसी पुरास्थल से प्राप्त नहीं हुये हैं।[11]

यहाँ से प्राप्त प्रमुख जैन–पुरावशेषों में आदिनाथ, शान्तिनाथ, पार्श्वनाथ व महावीर की असंख्य प्रतिमाएँ सम्मिलित हैं। यहाँ के स्थानीय लोग महावीर की प्रतिमा को 'जगवीर' या 'युगवीर' कहते हैं।[12] यहाँ की मूर्तिकला के अन्य सुंदर नमूनों में विरल आभूषण युक्त आसन मुद्रा में दो नग्न प्रतिमाएँ प्रमुख हैं जिनको फ्यूहरर ने वर्द्धमान महावीर स्वामी के माता–पिता, त्रिशला एवं सिद्धार्थ के साथ समीकृत किया है।[13] यहाँ से प्राप्त नेमिनाथ की एक प्रतिमा को गुप्तकाल की कृति स्वीकार किया गया है।[14]

रामपूजन पाण्डेय ने साहित्यिक साक्ष्यों के आधार पर इसे रघुवंशीय नरेश ककुस्थ की राजधानी बताया है। जैन ग्रन्थ *'सत्यार्थ यज्ञ'* में इसे पुष्पदन्त के पिता इक्ष्वाकुवंशीय राजा सुग्रीव की राजधानी बताया गया है, जो मूल रूप से काकन्द ऋषि की निवास स्थली थी।[15] प्राचीन काल में यह भी श्रावस्ती, कौशाम्बी, व कपिलवस्तु की ही भांति एक प्रमुख नगरी थी।

जैन ग्रन्थ *'तीर्थ दर्शन'* में बिहार राज्य के मुंगेर जिलान्तर्गत् काकन्दी तीर्थ को पुष्पदन्त की जन्मस्थली माना गया है। जहाँ पर अर्वाचीन निर्मित एक जिनालय में पार्श्वनाथ की एक प्राचीन चरण पादुका के अतिरिक्त अन्य कोई पुरावशेष प्रकाश में नहीं आया हैं। किन्तु देवरिया जनपद के अंतर्गत खुखुन्दू से प्राप्त प्रमुख पुरावशेष व साहित्यिक साक्ष्य इसे ही पुष्पदन्त की जन्मस्थली सिद्ध करते प्रतीत होते हैं।

कहौम (कुकुभ ग्राम)

यह भी देवरिया जनपद के अन्तर्गत ही खुखुन्दू से 16 किमी. दक्षिण पूर्व में स्थित है। यह जैन धर्म से संबंधित पुरास्थल है। यहाँ पर नवें जैन तीर्थंकर भगवान पुष्पदन्त ने धर्मचक्र प्रर्वतन किया था। यहाँ पर पुष्पदन्त प्रभु व महावीर स्वामी के अनेक समवशरण भी आये।[17] इस गाँव के उत्तर–पूर्व में एक सुविस्तृत टीले पर अनेक पुरावस्तुएँ प्राप्त हुई हैं जिनमें एक अभिलेख, कूप, ध्वस्त जिनालय तथा जलाशय हैं। पुराविदों ने यहाँ के ध्वस्त जिनालय के बोधगया के विशाल मन्दिर की शैली पर निर्मित होने की संभावना व्यक्त की है जिसमें तीर्थंकर मूर्तियाँ स्थापित की गयी थी।[18] अभिलेख से ज्ञात होता है कि गुप्त युग में यह जैन धर्म का एक प्रमुख केन्द्र था। इस समय भी यहाँ के अधिकांश निवासियों का निरामिश होना, उन पर जैन धर्म के अहिंसात्मक उपदेशों का प्रभाव प्रकट करता है। अभिलेख में इस ग्राम का नाम ककुभग्राम दिया हुआ है।

कहौम अभिलेख

कहौम ग्राम में स्थित इस अभिलेख की खोज फ्रांसिस बुकानन ने 1806–1816 के मध्य की थी जिसको 1838 ईसवी में माण्टगोमरी मार्टिन ने अपनी पुस्तक *Eastern India* में प्रकाशित किया तथा जेम्स प्रिंसेस ने इसे अंग्रेजी अनुवाद सहित प्रकाशित किया। बाद में 1871 व 1883 ईसवी में क्रमशः कनिंघम व भगवान लाल इन्द्रजी ने भी अपने–अपने पाठ प्रकाशित किये।[19]

यह स्तंभ 24'3" ऊँचा गहरे धूसर रंग के एकाश्म से निर्मित है।[20] इसके वर्गाकार आधार पर पार्श्वनाथ की तथा शीर्ष पर चारों दिशाओं में आदिनाथ, शान्तिनाथ, नेमिनाथ, व महावीर की प्रतिमाएँ अंकित हैं।[21] यह स्तंभ वर्गाकार, वर्तुलाकार, बहुकोणीय आदि विभिन्न ज्यामितीय आकार में तराशा गया है।[22] इसके मध्य भाग में गुप्तयुगीन ब्राह्मी लिपि व संस्कृत भाषा में 12 पंक्तियों का एक लेख उत्कीर्ण है[23] जिसका उद्देश्य स्कन्दगुप्त के शासन काल, गुप्त संवत 141 (460 ईसवी) में मद्र नामक ब्राह्मण द्वारा पुण्यार्जन हेतु 5 तीर्थंकर प्रतिमाओं के

दान का उल्लेख करना है। इसमें सोमिल तक उसकी वंशावली दी गयी है।[24]

1. सिद्धाम (1)
   यस्योपस्थान भूमिर्नृपति–शत–शिरःपात–वातावधूता
2. गुप्तानां वन्शजस्य प्रविसृत–सशसस्तस्य सर्वोत्तमर्द्धेः (।)
3. राज्ये शक्रोपमस्य क्षितिप–शत–पतेःस्कन्दगुप्तस्य शान्ते
4. वर्षे त्रिन्शद्देशैकोत्तरक–शततमें ज्येष्ठ–मासि प्रपन्नें (1)
5. ख्याते(S) स्मिन्ग्राम–रत्ने ककुभ इति जनैस्साधु–संसर्ग–पूते (।)
6. पुत्तो यस्सोमिलस्य प्रचुर–गुण–निधेर्भट्टिसोमो महा(त्मा) (।)
7. तत्सूनू रूद्रसोमः पृथुल–मति–यशाव्याघ्र इत्यन्य–संज्ञो।
8. मद्रस्तस्यात्मजो(S) भूद्द्विज–गुरू–यतिषु प्रायशः प्रीतिमान्यः (2)
9. पुण्य–स्कन्धं स चक्क्रे जगदिदमखिलं संसरद्वीक्ष्य भीतो
10. श्रेयोर्त्थं भूत–भूत्यै पथि नियमवतामर्हतामादिकर्त्तृन् (।)
11. पंचेन्द्रां स्थापयित्वा धरणिधरमयान्सन्निखातस्ततोऽयम्
12. शैल–स्तंभः सुचारूगिरविर–शिक्षरग्रोपमः कीर्ति कर्त्ता (3)

सठियांव (पावा)

वर्तमान् पूर्वी–उत्तर प्रदेश के कुशीनगर जिले में स्थित सठियांव गांव की पहचान प्राचीन काल के पावा के रूप में की गई है।[25] के.एल. सरवागी महोदय ने इसे ही महावीर स्वामी की निर्वाण स्थली माना है।[26] छठी शती ई. पू. में यह एक प्रमुख नगर था। *उत्तर–पुराण* से ज्ञात होता है कि धन–धान्य से संपन्न मल्लों की राजधानी पावानगरी में कार्तिक कृष्ण चतुर्दशी की रात्रि में महावीर स्वामी ने मोक्ष पद प्राप्त किया।[27] इस समय यहाँ पर कई टीले हैं। इनके चारों ओर खंडहर दिखाई देते हैं जिनमें एक भग्न स्तूप व कई अन्य पुरावशेष प्राप्त हुए हैं। इनमें जैन पुरावस्तुओं की प्राप्ति की भी संभावना व्यक्त की जा रही है।[28] यहाँ से प्राप्त अभिलिखित मुहरों से इस गाँव का गुप्तकालीन अग्रहार होना सिद्ध होता है।[29]

कुछ समय पूर्व तक महावीर की निर्वाण स्थली पावा की पहचान के प्रश्न पर विद्वानों में मतभेद था, किन्तु अब अधिकांश विद्वान संठियांव गांव के पावा के साथ समीकरण से सहमत हो चुके हैं।[30] इसके पक्ष में यहाँ पर स्थित एक सरोवर व तालाब का पाया जाना, शाल वृक्ष का पाया जाना, पावा (संठियाव) व कुशीनगर के मध्य धागी नदी (ककुत्था नदी) का प्रवाहित होना, भगवान बुद्ध के निर्वाण स्थली से इसकी निकटता व इसका मल्ल गणराज्य के क्षेत्र में स्थित होना आदि तथ्य हैं।[31]

निष्कर्षतः हम कह सकते हैं कि जैन धर्म की केन्द्र भूमि पूर्वी उत्तर प्रदेश में भले ही मथुरा व देवगढ़ जैसे पुरास्थल विद्यमान नहीं हैं तथापि यहाँ पर जैन पुरावशेष पर्याप्त मात्रा में विद्यमान हैं और यह क्षेत्र जैन पुरावस्तुओं की प्राप्ति की दृष्टि से संभावनाओं से भरा हुआ है।

संदर्भ

1. मुनि, राजेन्द्र – *जैन धर्म,* उदयपुर, राज., वि–सं. 2038, पृ. 19
2. *जनपद – देवरिया – अतीत से वर्तमान तक* – सूचना एवं संपर्क विभाग, देवरिया 2003–2004 पृ. 81
3. भारतीय पुरातत्व सर्वेक्षण विभाग की वार्षिक रिपोर्ट – 1906–7, पृ. 195–196
4. तिवारी, दिवाकर प्रसाद – *गोरखपुर परिक्षेत्र का इतिहास,* प्राच्य अध्ययन मंडल देवरिया, 2004, पृ. 32।
5. *पूर्वोक्त*।
6. *तिल्लोयपण्णति* – 4/534 – जीवराज ग्रंथमाला, शोलापुर।
7. प्रसाद, शिव – *जैन तीर्थों का ऐतिहासिक अध्ययन,* पार्श्वनाथ विद्याश्रम शोध संस्थान वाराणसी–1991, पृ. 14।
8. जैन, भागचन्द्र जैन – *जैन संस्कृति कोष, कला, एवं धर्म,* शोध संस्थान वाराणसी 2002, पृ. 479
9. *पूर्वोक्त*।
10. तिवारी, दिवाकर प्रसाद, *पूर्वोक्त* पृ. 33।
11. *पूर्वोक्त*।
12. जैन, भागचन्द्र, *पूर्वोक्त*।
13. तिवारी, दिवाकर प्रसाद, *पूर्वोक्त*।
14. जैन, भागचन्द्र, *पूर्वोक्त*।
15. तिवारी, दिवाकर प्रसाद, *पूर्वोक्त*।
16. *तीर्थ दर्शन* – पृ. 52।
17. जैन, भागचन्द्र, *पूर्वोक्त*।
18. तिवारी, दिवाकर प्रसाद, *पूर्वोक्त*।
19. गुप्ता, पी.एल., *प्राचीन भारत के प्रमुख अभिलेख,* भाग–2, वाराणसी, संवत् 2039, पृ. 146।
20. तिवारी, दिवाकर प्रसाद, *पूर्वोक्त*।
21. गुप्ता, पी.एल., *पूर्वोक्त*।
22. तिवारी, दिवाकर प्रसाद, *पूर्वोक्त*, पृ. 34।
23. गुप्ता, पी.एल., *पूर्वोक्त*, पृ. 146।
24. जैन, हीरालाल, सम्पा., *जैन शिलालेख संग्रह,* नागपुर, भाग–2, 1952, पृ. 59।
25. त्रिपाठी, कृष्णानन्द – *सिद्ध पावा क्षेत्र,* गोरखपुर – 1993, पृ. 95।
26. सरावगी, के.एल. – *पावासमीक्षा* – सारण, बिहार 1972, पृ. 95।
27. जैन, बाबू कामता प्रसाद – *संक्षिप्त जैन इतिहास* – भाग–1, कपाड़िया भवन, सूरत–1932, पृ. 226।
28. जैन, भागचन्द्र – *पूर्वोक्त*, पृ. 116।
29. *पूर्वांचल की पुरासम्पदा* – राज्य पुरातत्व विभाग, पत्रक लखनऊ 1979।
30. जैन तीर्थ–दर्शन, *पूर्वोक्त*, पृ. 39।

32

पूर्वी उत्तर प्रदेश के चन्दौली जनपद में सुदूर संवेदन एवं भौगोलिक सूचना प्रणाली का उपयोग करके पुरातत्त्व डाटाबेस का सृजन

संघर्ष राव

सारांश

उत्तर प्रदेश पुरातत्त्व निदेशालय ने चन्दौली जिले का अन्वेषण कार्य वर्ष 1999–2000 में किया था। यह कार्य पूर्व में प्राचीन इतिहास एवं पुरातत्त्व विभाग, इलाहाबाद विश्वविद्यालय व प्राचीन भारतीय इतिहास, बनारस हिन्दू विश्वविद्यालय एवं भारतीय पुरातत्त्व सर्वेक्षण के कार्यो को आगे बढाते हुए किया गया है जिसमें पुरातत्त्व की दृष्टि से कुल 24 महत्वपूर्ण क्षेत्रों की जानकारी प्रकाशित हुई है। इन्ही क्षेत्रों के आधार पर पुरातत्त्व अन्वेषण का डाटाबेस तैयार किया गया है जिसमें प्रमुख सड़कों, नदी–तालाबों, रेल लाइन, कस्बों आदि को भौगोलिक सूचना प्रणाली के माध्यम से चित्रण किया गया है। तत्पश्चात् विभिन्न प्रकार के विश्लेषण किये गये हैं व उपग्रहीय सुदूर संवदेन आंकड़ों का उपयोग कर उच्चकोटि के मानचित्र बनाये गये हैं।

भूमिका

अत्यन्त कम समय और लागत में शीघ्रता से धरातलीय धटनाओं की सूचनाओं को क्षेत्रीय विस्तार के साथ पुनरावृतिक रूप मिलने के कारण पिछले कुछ दशकों में सुदूर संवेदन एवं भौगोलिक सूचना प्रणाली के उपयोगों का अध्ययन–क्षेत्र विस्तृत हुआ है। उपग्रहीय सुदूर संवेदन एवं भौगोलिक सूचना प्रणाली दोनों ही कम्प्यूटर पर

आधारित सफलतम तकनीक हैं जो भू–आकृतियों, भूमि उपयोग, भू–आच्छादन एवं धरातलीय कालिक परिवर्तनों के विश्लेषण, मानचित्रण तथा प्रस्तुतीकरण में विशेष भूमिका निभाती हैं। इसी क्रम में, प्रस्तुत शोध पत्र उत्तर प्रदेश पुरातत्त्व विभाग के वर्ष 1999–2000 में चन्दौली जनपद के अन्वेषण कार्य, *प्राग्धारा* अंक–10, में प्रकाशित 24 पुरास्थलों की जानकारी को सुदूर संवेदन डाटा का समावेश कर तैयार किया गया है।

पूर्वी उत्तर प्रदेश में कई पुरातात्त्विक महत्व के टीले व क्षेत्र अवस्थित हैं जिन पर गंगा घाटी की सभ्यता के परिप्रेक्ष्य में समय–समय पर विद्वानों द्वारा शोध कार्य किया गया है। इस शोध पत्र के माध्यम से पुरातत्त्व विज्ञान में सुदूर संवेदन तथा भौगोलिक सूचना प्रणाली की उपयोगिता सिद्ध करने का प्रयास किया गया है। चन्दौली जनपद वाराणसी से अलग हुआ जनपद है जो कि पूर्व में उत्तर प्रदेश की सीमा बिहार राज्य से बनाता है। कर्मनासा नदी उत्तर प्रदेश व बिहार की सीमा निर्धारित करती है व पुरातत्त्व की दृष्टि से अति महत्वपूर्ण है। चन्दौली जनपद गंगा नदी के दक्षिणवर्ती क्षेत्रों से प्राप्त पुरातत्त्व निधियों का प्रतिनिधित्व करता है जिनके अन्तर्गत पाषाण युग से ही साक्ष्य मिलने प्रारम्भ हो जाते हैं।

अध्ययन क्षेत्र

चन्दौली जनपद का क्षेत्रफल लगभग 2536.71 वर्ग किलोमीटर हैं जिसका देशांतरीय विस्तार 83°01′ पूर्व से 83°33′ पूर्व तथा अंक्षासीय विस्तार 24°43′ उत्तर से 25°32′ उत्तर के मध्य है जो कि भारतीय सर्वेक्षण संस्थान की शीट संख्या 63 O/2, 63O/3, 63O/4, 63O/6, 63O/7, 63O/8, 63O/11, 63P/1, 63P/2, 63P/5, 63P/6 के अन्तर्गत आता है। पूर्व में स्थित कर्मनासा नदी उत्तर प्रदेश व बिहार के मध्य सीमा विभाजित करती है। जनपद में तीन तहसील (चकिया, चन्दौली व सकलडीहा) एवं पॉच विकासखण्ड (चकिया, चन्दौली, नौगढ़, सकलडीहा, साहबगंज) हैं। जनपद चन्दौली लगभग 1800 गावों को समाहित करता है।

सुदूर संवेदन

वास्तवित संपर्क या बिना छुये किसी वस्तु के बारे में भौतिक आंकड़े एकत्र करना सुदूर संवेदन कहलाता है। कई वैज्ञानिकों द्वारा सुदूर संवेदन शब्द का उपयोग वृहत दूरी से सुदूर लक्ष्यों (पृथ्वी, चन्द्रमा, वायुमण्डल, अन्य उपग्रह, स्टेलर धटनाओं इत्यादि) के अध्ययन के लिये किया गया है। यद्यपि सुदूर संवेदन विशुद्ध रूप से परिभाषित नहीं है तथापि व्हाइट के अनुसार इसके अन्तर्गत उन सभी विधियों को सम्मिलित किया जाता है जो कुछ दूरी से पृथ्वी के घरातल की तस्वीरों या विद्युत–चुम्बकीय अभिलेखों के कई रूपों को प्राप्त कर, आँकडों को परिष्कृत एवं संशोधित करती हैं। विस्तृत अर्थो में सुदूर संवदेन का सम्बन्ध विद्युत–चुम्बकीय विकिरण का संसूचन तथा अभिलेखन से होता है जिसे किसी धरातलीय परिदृश्य के लक्ष्य–क्षेत्रों से संवेदक यंत्रों द्वारा प्राप्त किया जाता है। यह विकिरण लक्ष्य–क्षेत्र के अलग–अलग घटकों से सीधे उत्पन्न या घटकों से प्राप्त सौर्यक ऊर्जा का या स्वयं संवेदक से लक्ष्य क्षेत्र को संचारित ऊर्जा का परावर्तन हो सकता है।

भौगोलिक सूचना प्रणाली

भौगोलिक सूचना प्रणाली पृथ्वी के धरातल के संदर्भ में ऑकड़ों का अधिग्रहण, संग्रह, निरीक्षण, परिचालन, विश्लेषण तथा प्रदर्शन करने वाली कम्प्यूटर आधारित प्रणाली है। यहाँ आँकड़ा आधार धरातलीय आकृतियों,

क्रियाओं या घटनाओं का अवलोकन होता है। इन्हें स्थान विशेष पर बिन्दु, रेखा तथा क्षेत्रीय आकृति से दर्शाया जाता है। भौगोलिक सूचना प्रणाली का उपयोग इन बिन्दुओं, रेखाओं तथा क्षेत्रीय आकृतियों के बारे में सूचनाओं की पुनर्प्राप्ति, पूंछताछ तथा प्रसारण एवं परिचालन के लिए होता है जिसे किसी धरातलीय परिदृश्य के लक्ष्य–क्षेत्रों से संवेदक यंत्रों द्वारा प्राप्त किया जाता है। धरातलीय आंकड़ों को एक से अधिक वर्गो में वर्गीकृत किया जाता है। प्रत्येक वर्ग एक परत का कार्य करता है, प्रत्येक परत या तो बिन्दु या तो रेखा या बहुभुज आकृति के रूप में प्रदर्शित की जाती है।

विधि तंत्र

भारतीय सर्वेक्षण संस्थान के नक्शों तथा उपग्रहीय सुदूर संवदेन लैडसेट व एस0आर0टी0एम0 डाटा का प्रयोग करके निम्नलिखित सट्टश परतों का सृजन किया गयाः

- पुरास्थल – बिन्दु
- समुद्र तल से ऊंचाई – बिन्दु
- कस्बे – बिन्दु
- रेलमार्ग – रेखा
- प्रमुख सड़क मार्ग – रेखा
- नदी, नाले – रेखा
- झील, तालाब – क्षेत्रीय आकृतियां

तत्पश्चात् पुरातत्त्व आंकड़ों (सारणी–1, 2), सुदूर संवेदन डाटा के आंकड़ों व धरातलीय सर्वेक्षणों पर आधारित आंकड़ों का परतों के माध्यम से प्रतिस्थापन कर सभी सूचनाओं का संश्लेषण एवं समाकलन किया गया (सारणी–3, 4, 5, 6) तथा मानचित्र बनाये गये।

परिणाम एवं निष्कर्ष

भौगोलिक सूचना प्रणाली का उपयोग कर पुरास्थलों की समुद्र तल से ऊँचाई ज्ञात की गई (सारणी–5) जिनके आधार पर 18 पुरास्थल 77 से 90 मी. की ऊँचाई पर है। 2 पुरास्थल 90 से 250 मीटर की ऊँचाई पर शेष 4 पुरास्थल 250 से 335 मीटर की ऊँचाई पर पाये गये। भूमि उपयोग की दृष्टि से ये 4 पुरास्थल वन क्षेत्र में आते हैं (सारणी–6); शेष 20 पुरास्थलों में से 17 पुरास्थल कृषि भूमि पर हैं, 2 बाढ़ क्षेत्र में व एक आवासीय क्षेत्र में स्थित है। 13 पुरास्थल चन्द्रप्रभा नदीं के जल संग्रहण क्षेत्र में, 9 कर्मनासा व 3 गुरवल नदी के जल संग्रहण क्षेत्र में स्थित हैं (सारणी–5)। 24 पुरास्थलों में से कुल 5 पुरास्थल ऊपरी विन्ध्य कैमूर समूह के पठार व उनके गिरिपाद मैदान में स्थित हैं (सारणी–6)। अन्य सभी नदी कण से बने क्षेत्र में स्थित हैं, भू–आकृति अध्ययन से ज्ञात हुआ है कि 5 पुरास्थल विच्छेदित ऊपरी पठार पर स्थित हैं, 3 पुरास्थल उनके गिरिपाद पर व 13 पुरास्थल जलोढ मैदान में स्थित हैं। 01 पुरास्थल पुराविंसर्प के समीप व 2 बाढ़ क्षेत्र में स्थित हैं (सारणी–6)।

उपसंहार

सुदूर संवेदन व भौगोलिक सूचना प्रणाली द्वारा किया गया यह शोध मात्र 24 पुरास्थलों पर आधारित है किन्तु इसका विस्तार अन्य पुरास्थलों को समाहित कर किया जा सकता हैं। इसके द्वारा सृजित डाटाबेस आसानी से उपयोग में लाया जा सकता है क्योंकि इसमें ऑकड़ों के एकीकरण को संचालित करने का विस्तृत प्रावधान होता है। कोई भी संगठन या संस्था सूचनाओं का विस्तृत आधार तैयार कर किसी उचित निष्कर्ष पर पहुंचने में सफल हो सकती है। अगर हम पृथक सूचनाओं को इस तकनीक के माध्यम से संग्रहीत करें तथा असंख्य लेखों, पाण्डुलिपियों एवं पुरातात्त्विक साक्ष्यों को उपयोगकर्ता की सुविधा अनुसार अल्पावधि में मानचित्र के रूप में दर्शायें तो इतिहास के प्रतिरूपण में भौगोलिक सूचना प्रणाली का महत्वपूर्ण योगदान हो सकता है।

सारणी–1

पुरास्थल का नाम	समय/काल	पुरावशेष
नौगढ कोट	उत्तरी कृष्ण मार्जित पात्र परम्परा, मध्य काल	कृष्ण लेपित पात्र, धूसर पात्र, लाल पात्र, उत्तरी कृष्ण मार्जित पात्र, कृष्ण लोहित पात्र, तस्तरी, सुराही
सेमर/साधोपुर	मध्य पाषाण काल से पहले	मानव एवं पशु मृण मूर्तियां, ज्यामितिक एवं वानस्पतिक अलंकरण
देवदारी झरना	मध्य पाषाण काल	मानव एवं पशु, मृण मूर्तियां, नृत्य की मुद्रा में, औजार
गुरूत्वा मोड सीता स्वोरख पहाड़	मध्य पाषाण काल	पाषाण शिला, पाषाण संरचना, लाल पात्र
पुराना डीह	18वीं सहस्त्राब्दि	पाषाण शिला, पाषाण संरचना, लाल पात्र
प्रभुनरायण–हिरामनपुर		तस्तरी, कटोरे
बेन	10वीं से 13वीं सहस्त्राब्दि	कृष्ण लेपित पात्र, धूसर पात्र, खण्डित शिव लिंग, विष्णु प्रतिमा
भिकमपुर	मध्य काल	किला, परिखा
पछवनला	गुप्त काल के पश्चात्	उत्तरी कृष्ण मार्जित पात्र, कृष्ण लोहित पात्र, लाल पात्र
बाराडीह	300 साल पुराना	लाल पात्र
टकिया	शुंग काल	कृष्ण लेपित पात्र, उत्तरी कृष्ण मार्जित पात्र, कृष्ण लोहित पात्र
सिकन्दरपुर	मध्य काल	कृष्ण लेपित पात्र, उत्तरी कृष्ण मार्जित पात्र, कृष्ण लोहित पात्र, राजपूत काल के ईट के टुकड़े
बन्दा डीह	गुप्त काल के पश्चात्	उत्तरी कृष्ण मार्जित पात्र, कृष्ण लोहित पात्र
लथौरा	उत्तरी कृष्ण मार्जित पात्र परम्परा, मध्य काल	कृष्ण मार्जित पात्र, धूसर पात्र, उत्तरी कृष्ण मार्जित पात्र
उत्रौन्ट	मध्य काल	उत्तरी कृष्ण मार्जित पात्र, कृष्ण लोहित पात्र एवं अन्य मृद भाणड
भौरसर	मध्य काल	कृष्ण मार्जित पात्र, धूसर पात्र, उत्तरी कृष्ण मार्जित पात्र
परसयी कालान	गुप्त काल के पश्चात्	मध्य काल से सम्बन्धित कृष्ण लीला स्तम्भ
चनहेटा		उत्तरी कृष्ण मार्जित पात्र, कृष्ण लोहित पात्र, धूसर पात्र, लाल पात्र
खुरहुन्जा		कृष्ण लोहित पात्र, लाल पात्र, लाल के लेपित पात्र
निन्दौर	प्रागैतिहासिक	कृष्ण लोहित पात्र, धूसर पात्र, लाल पात्र, कृष्ण लोहित पात्र, कटोरे, तस्तरी, ईट
केरा ड़ीह	गुप्त काल के पश्चात् एवं मध्य काल	लाल पात्र
रामपुर	गुप्त काल के पश्चात्	पकी ईट एवं लाल पात्र
जसुरी	नवीन	कृष्ण लोहित पात्र, लाल पात्र, नवीन समय के छोटे मन्दिर

सारणी–2

पुरास्थल का नाम	क्षेत्रफल अनुपात	क्षेत्रफल	समीप नदी नालें
नौगढ कोट		उपलब्ध नहीं	कर्मनासा नदी के बाये किनारे पर
सेमर/साधोपुर		उपलब्ध नहीं	
देवदारी झरना		उपलब्ध नहीं	
गुरूत्वा मोड सीता स्वोरख पहाड़		उपलब्ध नहीं	
पुराना डीह		उपलब्ध नहीं	
प्रभुनरायण–हिरामनपुर	200x300x3	60000.00	
बेन	80x80x5	6400.00	
भिकमपुर		उपलब्ध नहीं	चन्द्रप्रभा नदी के बाये किनारे पर
पछवनला		उपलब्ध नहीं	
बाराडीह			
टकिया	150x100x100	10000–15000	कर्मनासा नदी के दाये किनारे पर
सिकन्दरपुर	300x300	90000.00	चन्द्रप्रभा नदी के बाये किनारे पर
बन्दा डीह	80x80 x5	4000.00	चन्दौती नदी का दाया किनारा
लथौरा	50x50	2500.00	चन्दौती नदी का दाया किनारा
उतरौन्ट		50.00	चन्दौती नदी का बाया किनारा
भौरसर	100x100	10000.00	कर्मनासा नदी के किनारे पर
परसयी कालान	70x100	7000.00	कर्मनासा नदी के दाये किनारे पर
चनहेटा		उपलब्ध नहीं	मरई नदी के बाये किनारे पर
खुरहुन्जा		उपलब्ध नहीं	मरई नदी के बाये किनारे पर
निन्दौर	750x750x20	562500.00	
केरा डीह	500x500	250000,00	कर्मनासा नदी के बाये किनारे पर
रामपुर	300x300	90000.00	
जसुरी		उपलब्ध नहीं	
माटीगांव		उपलब्ध नहीं	

सारणी–3

पुरास्थल का नाम	टोपोशीट संख्या	स्थिति	विकास खण्ड	तहसील
नौगढ कोट	63/P/1	चकिया	नौगढ़	चकिया
सेमर/साधोपुर	63/P/5	चकिया	नौगढ़	चकिया
देवदारी झरना	63/P/5	चकिया	नौगढ़	चकिया
गुरूत्वा मोड सीता स्वोरख पाहाड	63/P/1	चकिया	नौगढ़	चकिया
पुराना डीह	63/P/1	पुराना डीह	चकिया	चकिया
प्रभुनरायण–हिरामनपुर	63/0/4	मुजफ्फरपुर	चकिया	चकिया
बेन	63/0/8	बेन	शाहाबगंज	चकिया
भिकमपुर	63/0/4	भिकमपुर	चकिया	चकिया
पछवनला	63/0/4	पछवनिया	चकिया	चकिया
बाराडीह	63/0/8	मदरा	शाहाबगंज	चकिया
टकिया	63/0/8	टकिया महरौर	शाहाबगंज	चकिया
सिकन्दरपुर	63/0/4	सिकन्दरपुर	चकिया	चकिया
बन्दा डीह	63/0/4	टिकारी	चकिया	चकिया
लथौरा	63/0/4	लथौरा	चकिया	चकिया
उतरौन्ट	63/0/4	भभुवर	चकिया	चकिया
भौरसर	63/0/8	भौरसर	शाहाबगंज	चकिया
परसयी कालान	63/0/8	परसयी कला	चन्दौली	चन्दौली
चनहेटा	63/0/4	चन्हौटा	चन्दौली	चन्दौली
खुरहुन्जा	63/0/4	खुरूहुजा	चन्दौली	चन्दौली
निन्दौर	63/0/8	प्रतापपुर	चन्दौली	चन्दौली
केरा डीह	63/0/4	माधोपुर	चन्दौली	चन्दौली
रामपुर	63/0/8	चन्दौली	चन्दौली	चन्दौली
जसुरी	63/0/7	जसौरी	चन्दौली	चन्दौली
माटीगांव	63/0/3	फरसन्द मोहनपुर	सकलडीहा	सकलडीहा

सारणी–4

पुरास्थल का नाम	टोपोशीट संख्या	नजदीकी शहर	रेल लाइन से दूरी	प्रमुख मार्ग से दूरी	नदी से दूरी	समीपवर्ती नदी का नाम	समीपवर्ती नदी तालाब
नौगढ़ कोट	63/P/1	नौगढ़	44825.8	346.152	31.7421		1894.579766
सेमर/साधोपुर	63/P/5	नौगढ़	43524.1	496.566	340.328	गुरवल नाला	544.8104722
देवदारी झरना	63/P/5	नौगढ़	42157.4	404.017	295.752	करमनासा नदी	193.7139877
गुरूत्वा मोड सीता स्वोरख पहाड़	63/P/1	नौगढ़	36025.8	70.2678	23.8146		125.8189717
पुराना ड़ीह	63/P/1	चकिया	28441.7	730.945	16.0995	चन्द्रप्रभा नदी	96.66910719
प्रभुनारायण–हिरामनपुर	63/O/4	चकिया	26663.1	335.261	35.0578		132.933887
बेन	63/O/8	चकिया	21963.6	258.074	1148.39		249.4145053
भिकमपुर	63/O/4	चकिया	21175.1	93.9549	1763.99		483.8623168
पछवनला	63/O/4	चकिया	19941.1	73.885	1294.58		1541.737084
बाराडीह	63/O/8	चकिया	19094.6	68.8922	481.977		859.7827183
टकिया	63/O/8	चकिया	19450.9	65.694	27.9261	करमनासा नदी	226.0043748
सिकन्दरपुर	63/O/4	चकिया	20052.6	91.4077	598.83	चन्द्रप्रभा नदी	399.07279232
बन्दा डीह	63/O/4	चकिया	17889.9	297.1	2845.32		530.2824175
लथौरा	63/O/4	चकिया	18133.6	317.897	1299.07		916.2557257
उत्रौन्ट	63/O/4	बबूरी	14950.4	192.079	260.287		1464.647387
भौरसर	63/O/8	बबूरी	13470.5	198.893	53.972	करमनासा नदी	72.12553185
परसयी कालान	63/O/8	बबूरी	10786.4	140.099	148.859	करमनासा नदी	209.9859113
चनहेटा	63/O/4	बबूरी	6550.03	639.171	23.4596	गरई नदी	281.0763941
खुरहुन्जा	63/O/4	बबूरी	6008.84	223.544	265.088	गरई नदी	90.63507353
निन्दौर	63/O/8	चन्दौली	3583.84	63.4387	2415.9	गरई नदी	1280.11799
केरा डीह	63/O/4	चन्दौली	2223.33	92.8206	758.556	गरई नदी	329.0974382
रामपुर	63/O/8	चन्दौली	1589.59	99.6486	1954.51	गरई नदी	233.1311788
जसुरी	63/O/7	चन्दौली	942.393	282.638	2336.04	गरई नदी	501.2297547
माटीगांव	63/O/3	मजगाँव	1674.14	149.98	5414.69		192.6883108

सारणी–5

पुरास्थल का नाम	समुद्र तल से ऊचांई (मी.)	बेसिन	जल संग्रहण क्षेत्र
नौगढ कोट	280	निचली गंगा	चन्द्रप्रभा
सेमर/साधोपुर	335	निचली गंगा	गुरवट
देवदारी झरना	254	निचली गंगा	गुरवट
गुरूत्वा मोड सीता स्वोरख पाहाड	251	निचली गंगा	चन्द्रप्रभा
पुराना डीह	110	निचली गंगा	चन्द्रप्रभा
प्रभुनरायण–हिरामनपुर	101	निचली गंगा	चन्द्रप्रभा
बेन	84	निचली गंगा	कर्मनासा
भिकमपुर	86	निचली गंगा	चन्द्रप्रभा
पछवनला	89	निचली गंगा	चन्द्रप्रभा
बाराडीह	81	निचली गंगा	
टकिया	85	निचली गंगा	कर्मनासा
सिकन्दरपुर	85	निचली गंगा	चन्द्रप्रभा
बन्दा डीह	84	निचली गंगा	चन्द्रप्रभा
लथौरा	84	निचली गंगा	चन्द्रप्रभा
उत्रौन्ट	82	निचली गंगा	चन्द्रप्रभा
भौरसर	86	निचली गंगा	कर्मनासा
परसयी कालान	81	निचली गंगा	कर्मनासा
चनहेटा	77	निचली गंगा	चन्द्रप्रभा
खुरहुन्जा	77	निचली गंगा	चन्द्रप्रभा
निन्दौर	77	निचली गंगा	
केरा डीह	79	निचली गंगा	चन्द्रप्रभा
रामपुर	78	निचली गंगा	
जसुरी	77	निचली गंगा	
माटीगांव	82	निचली गंगा	

सारणी–6

पुरास्थल का नाम	भूमि उपयोग/भू आच्छादन	शैल समूह	शैल प्रकार	भू–आकृति
नौगढ कोट	वन	ऊपरी विन्धयावन (कैमूर समूह)	परती बालू, पत्थर	विच्छेदित ऊपरी पठार
सेमर/साधोपुर	वन	ऊपरी विन्धयावन (कैमूर समूह)	परती बालू, पत्थर	विच्छेदित ऊपरी पठार
देवदारी झरना	वन	ऊपरी विन्धयावन (कैमूर समूह)	परती बालू, पत्थर	विच्छेदित ऊपरी पठार
गुरूत्वा मोड सीता स्वोरख पाहाड	वन	ऊपरी विन्धयावन (कैमूर समूह)	परती बालू, पत्थर	विच्छेदित ऊपरी पठार
पुराना डीह	पुरा बाढ का मैदान	ऊपरी विन्धयावन (कैमूर समूह)	परती बालू, पत्थर	ऊपरी पूरा नदी मैदान
प्रभुनरायण–हिरामनपुर	कृषि भूमि	ऊपरी विन्धयावन (कैमूर समूह)	परती बालू, पत्थर	उथली गिरी पाद मैदान
बेन	कृषि भूमि	असंगठित कण क्षेत्र	मृतिका बहुल बालू	उथली गिरी पाद मैदान
भिकमपुर	कृषि भूमि	असंगठित कण क्षेत्र	बालू, बहुल मृतिका	गहरा गिरी पाद मैदान
पछवनला	कृषि भूमि	असंगठित कण क्षेत्र	रिहायशी क्षेत्र	रिहायशी क्षेत्र
बाराडीह	कृषि भूमि	असंगठित कण क्षेत्र	मृतिका बहुल बालू	ऊपरी पूरा नदी मैदान
टकिया	कृषि भूमि	असंगठित कण क्षेत्र	बालू, बहुल मृतिका	ऊपरी पूरा नदी मैदान
सिकन्दरपुर	कृषि भूमि	असंगठित कण क्षेत्र	बालू, बहुल मृतिका	ऊपरी पूरा नदी मैदान
बन्दा डीह	कृषि भूमि	असंगठित कण क्षेत्र	बालू, बहुल मृतिका	ऊपरी पूरा नदी मैदान
लथौरा	कृषि भूमि	असंगठित कण क्षेत्र	बालू, बहुल मृतिका	ऊपरी पूरा नदी मैदान
उत्तरौन्ट	कृषि भूमि	असंगठित कण क्षेत्र	बालू, बहुल मृतिका	ऊपरी पूरा नदी मैदान
भौरसर	कृषि भूमि	असंगठित कण क्षेत्र	बालू, बहुल मृतिका	ऊपरी पूरा नदी मैदान
परसयी कालान	कृषि भूमि	असंगठित कण क्षेत्र	बालू, बहुल मृतिका	ऊपरी पूरा नदी मैदान
चनहेटा	कृषि भूमि	असंगठित कण क्षेत्र	मृतिका बहुल बालू	ऊपरी पूरा नदी मैदान
खुरहुन्जा	कृषि भूमि	असंगठित कण क्षेत्र	मृतिका बहुल बालू	ऊपरी पूरा नदी मैदान
निन्दौर	कृषि भूमि	असंगठित कण क्षेत्र	मृतिका बहुल बालू	ऊपरी पूरा नदी मैदान
केरा डिह	कृषि भूमि	असंगठित कण क्षेत्र	मृतिका बहुल बालू	ऊपरी पूरा नदी मैदान
रामपुर	कृषि भूमि	असंगठित कण क्षेत्र	मृतिका बहुल बालू	ऊपरी पूरा नदी मैदान
जसुरी	कृषि भूमि	असंगठित कण क्षेत्र	मृतिका बहुल बालू	ऊपरी पूरा नदी मैदान
माटीगांव	कृषि भूमि	असंगठित कण क्षेत्र	मृतिका बहुल बालू	पूरा विसर्प

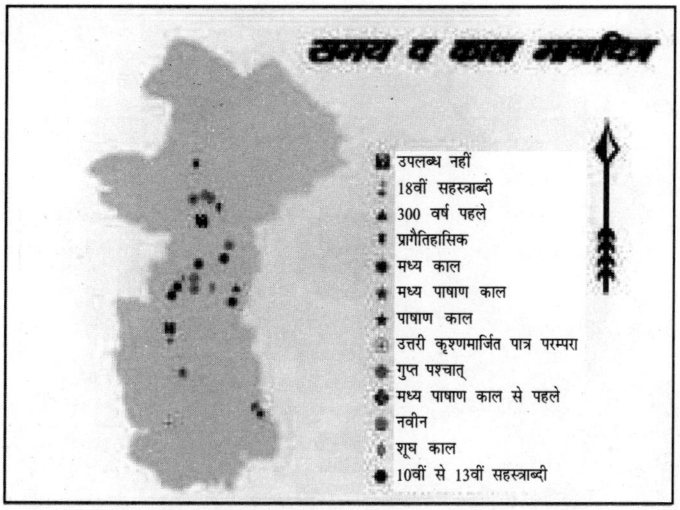
उपलब्ध नहीं
18वीं सहस्त्राब्दी
300 वर्ष पहले
प्रागैतिहासिक
मध्य काल
मध्य पाषाण काल
पाषाण काल
उत्तरी कृश्णमार्जित पात्र परम्परा
गुप्त पश्चात्
मध्य पाषाण काल से पहले
नवीन
शूघ काल
10वीं से 13वीं सहस्त्राब्दी

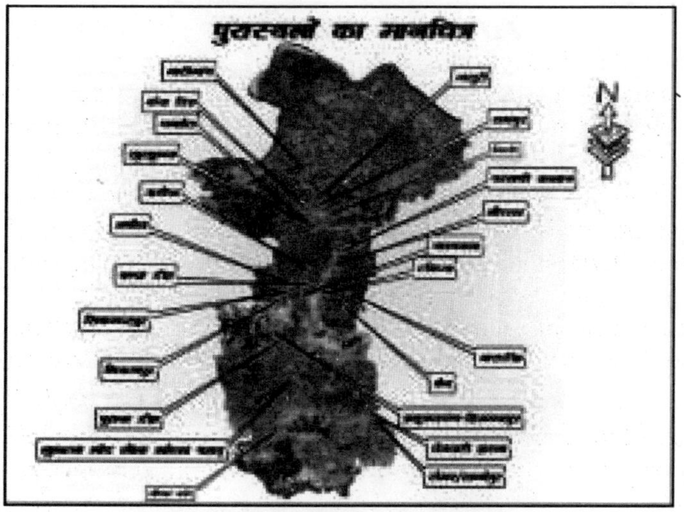
पुरास्थलों का मानचित्र

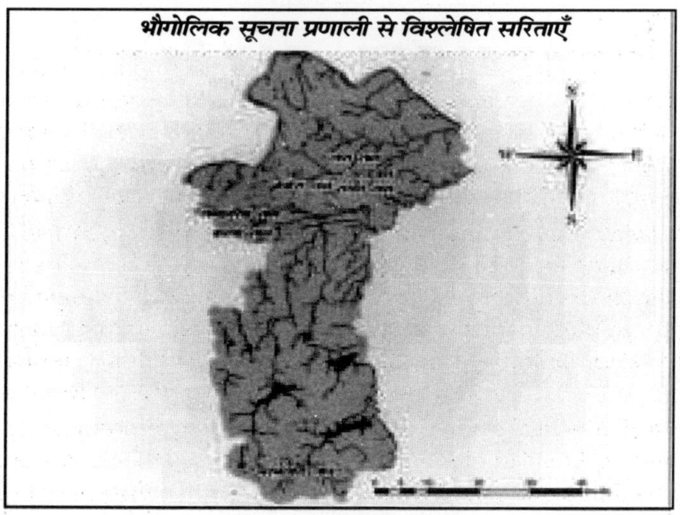
भौगोलिक सूचना प्रणाली से विश्लेषित सरिताएँ

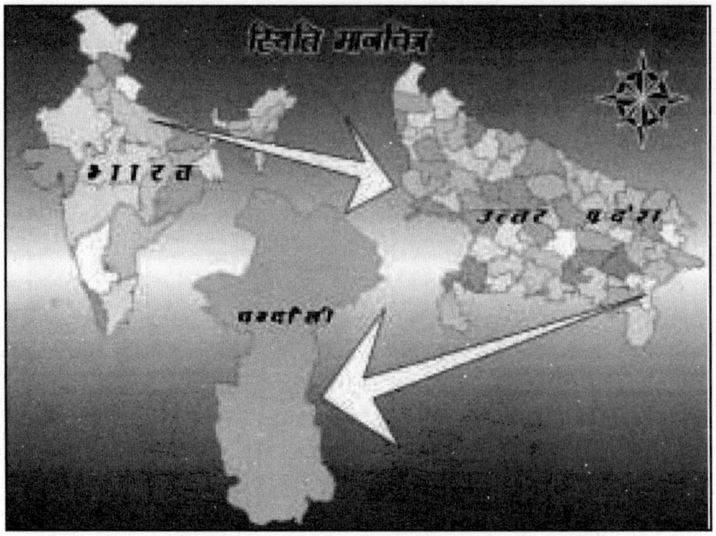
स्थिति मानचित्र
भारत
उत्तर प्रदेश
चन्दौली

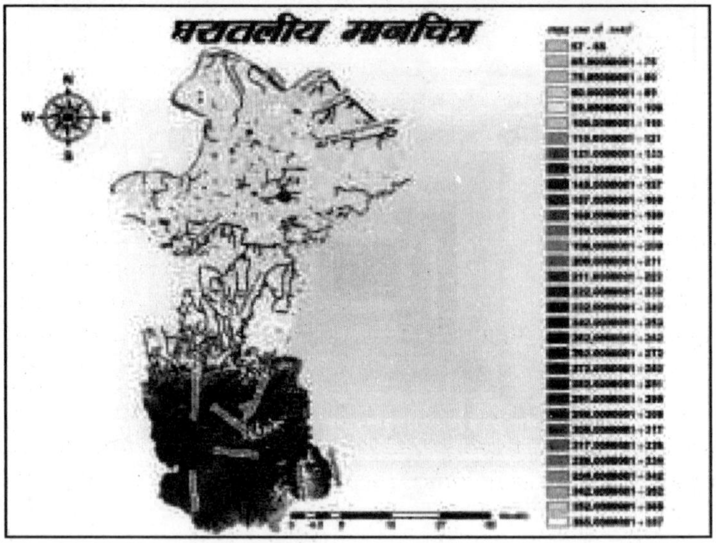
धरातलीय मानचित्र
N
W
E
S

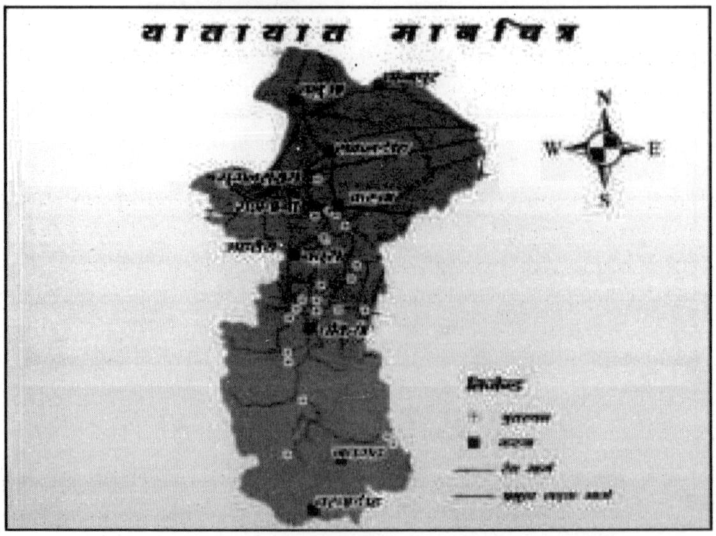
यातायात मानचित्र
N
W
E
S